CHINA'S ELITE POLITICS
Political Transition and Power Balancing

Series on Contemporary China (ISSN: 1793-0847)

Series Editors: Joseph Fewsmith *(Boston University)*
Zheng Yongnian *(East Asian Institute, National University of Singapore)*

Published*

Vol. 23 Social Cohesion in Greater China: Challenges for Social Policy and Governance
edited by Ka Ho Mok & Yeun-Wen Ku

Vol. 24 China's Reform in Global Perspective
edited by John Wong & Zhiyue Bo

Vol. 25 The Transition Study of Postsocialist China: An Ethnographic Study of a Model Community
by Wing-Chung Ho

Vol. 26 Looking North, Looking South: China, Taiwan, and the South Pacific
edited by Anne-Marie Brady

Vol. 27 China's Industrial Development in the 21st Century
edited by Mu Yang & Hong Yu

Vol. 28 Cross-Taiwan Straits Relations Since 1979: Policy Adjustment and Institutional Change Across the Straits
edited by Kevin G. Cai

Vol. 29 The Transformation of Political Communication in China: From Propaganda to Hegemony
by Xiaoling Zhang

Vol. 30 The Great Urbanization of China
edited by Ding Lu

Vol. 31 Social Structure of Contemporary China
edited by Xueyi Lu

Vol. 32 EastAsia: Developments and Challenges
edited by Yongnian Zheng & Liang Fook Lye

Vol. 33 China and East Asia: After the Wall Street Crisis
edited by Peng Er Lam, Yaqing Qin & Mu Yang

Vol. 34 The World Turned Upside Down:
The Complex Partnership between China and Latin America
by Alfredo Toro Hardy

Vol. 35 Township Governance and Institutionalization in China
by Shukai Zhao

*To view the complete list of the published volumes in the series, please visit:
http://www.worldscientific.com/series/scc

Series on Contemporary China – Vol. 8

CHINA'S ELITE POLITICS

Political Transition and Power Balancing

Bo Zhiyue

East Asian Institute, National University of Singapore, Singapore

NEW JERSEY · LONDON · SINGAPORE · BEIJING · SHANGHAI · HONG KONG · TAIPEI · CHENNAI

Published by

World Scientific Publishing Co. Pte. Ltd.
5 Toh Tuck Link, Singapore 596224
USA office: 27 Warren Street, Suite 401-402, Hackensack, NJ 07601
UK office: 57 Shelton Street, Covent Garden, London WC2H 9HE

Library of Congress Cataloging-in-Publication Data
Bo, Zhiyue.
  China's elite politics : political transition and power balancing / Bo Zhiyue.
    p. cm. -- (Series on contemporary China ; v. 8)
  Includes bibliographical references and index.
  ISBN-13 978-981-270-041-4 -- ISBN-10 981-270-041-2
  1. Elite (Social sciences)--China. 2. Balance of power. 3. China--Politics and government--1949–

JQ1510 .Z46247 2007
320.951--dc22
                                                                    2006051891

British Library Cataloguing-in-Publication Data
A catalogue record for this book is available from the British Library.

First published 2007
Reprinted 2014 (paperback edition only)
ISBN 978-981-4603-72-0 (pbk)

Copyright © 2007 by World Scientific Publishing Co. Pte. Ltd.

All rights reserved. This book, or parts thereof, may not be reproduced in any form or by any means, electronic or mechanical, including photocopying, recording or any information storage and retrieval system now known or to be invented, without written permission from the Publisher.

For photocopying of material in this volume, please pay a copying fee through the Copyright Clearance Center, Inc., 222 Rosewood Drive, Danvers, MA 01923, USA. In this case permission to photocopy is not required from the publisher.

Typeset by Stallion Press
Email: enquiries@stallionpress.com

Printed in Singapore

To My Parents

Contents

List of Tables and Figures   ix
Acknowledgments   xiii

Introduction: Toward a Power Balancing Model on
         Elite Politics in China   1

Part I: Political Transition and Power Balance

1. Power Transfer from Jiang Zemin to
   Hu Jintao at the Sixteenth Party Congress   17
2. The Sixteenth Central Committee:
   Technocrats in Command?   55
3. Balance of Formal Power   109
4. Balance of Factional Power   139

Part II: Dynamics of Factional Politics

5. Politics of SARS   203
6. Ideological Institutionalization and Politics of Development   255

7. Jiang Zemin's Complete Retirement   297
8. Hu Jintao's Power Consolidation   349
Conclusion: Institutionalization and Political Transition   427

Index   435

List of Tables and Figures

List of Tables

Table 1.1	Average Age of Central Advisory Committee Members (1982)	20
Table 1.2	Average Age of Politburo Retirees (1985)	20
Table 1.3	Average Age of Politburo Members (1982–2002)	21
Table 1.4	Age Structure of the Fifteenth Politburo (2002)	22
Table 1.5	Directors of the COD (10/1949-10/2002)	33
Table 1.6	Directors of the CPD (10/1949-10/2002)	35
Table 2.1	State Leaders and their Status in the Politburo (1954–2003)	59
Table 2.2	Standing Committee of the Presidium of the Sixteenth National Congress of the CCP (2002)	75
Table 2.3	Composition of the Presidium of the Sixteenth National Congress of the CCP (2002)	78
Table 2.4	The Sixteenth Politburo (2002)	79
Table 2.5	Educational Levels of Sixteenth and Fifteenth Central Committee Members (2002 and 1997)	81
Table 2.6	Part-Time Educational Experiences of Sixteenth Central Committee Members (2002)	82

Table 2.7	Study Abroad Experience Among Sixteenth and Fifteenth Central Committee Members	84
Table 2.8	Countries of Foreign Learning Experience Among Sixteenth and Fifteenth Central Committee Members	85
Table 2.9	Average Ages of Sixteenth and Fifteenth Central Committee Members (2002 and 1997)	89
Table 2.10	Work Experience of Sixteenth Central Committee Members (2002)	92
Table 2.11	Party Standing of Sixteenth Central Committee Members (2002)	93
Table 2.12	Distribution of Home Provinces of Sixteenth and Fifteenth Central Committee Members	94
Table 2.13	Females in the Sixteenth and Fifteenth Central Committees (2002 and 1997)	96
Table 2.14	Distribution of Nationalities Among Sixteenth Central Committee Members	97
Table 2.15	Graduates of Natural Sciences and Engineering in the Sixteenth Central Committee (2002)	101
Table 2.16	Majors of Part-Time Students in the Sixteenth Central Committee (2002)	102
Table 2.17	Career Patterns of Sixteenth Central Committee Members (2002)	104
Table 2.18	Technocrats in the Central Committees of the Chinese Communist Party (1982–2002)	105
Table 2.19	The Sixteenth Central Committee Members with Provincial Experience (2002)	107
Table 3.1	The Sixteenth Central Committee by Category	111
Table 3.2	Elite Provincial Units in China (1969–2002)	113
Table 3.3	Provincial CC Representation (1969–2002)	117
Table 3.4	Central Party-Institution Central Committee Representation (2002)	122
Table 3.5	Central Government Central Committee Representation (2002)	125
Table 3.6	Military Central Committee Representation (2002)	129

Table 4.1	Members of the Shanghai Gang in the Sixteenth Central Committee (2002)	142
Table 4.2	Group Cohesion Matrix of Shanghai Party Leaders in the Sixteenth Central Committee	149
Table 4.3	Group Cohesion Matrix of Shanghai Government Leaders in the Sixteenth Central Committee	150
Table 4.4	Princelings in the Sixteenth Central Committee (2002)	152
Table 4.5	Qinghua Graduates in the Sixteenth Central Committee (2002)	176
Table 4.6	Group Cohesion Matrix of Qinghua Graduates in the Sixteenth Central Committee	177
Table 4.7	CCYL Cadres in the Sixteenth Central Committee (2002)	184
Table 4.8	Group Cohesion Matrix of Former CCYL Leaders in the Sixteenth Central Committee	191
Table 5.1	Votes of Members of the State Central Military Commission (March 15, 2003)	210
Table 5.2	Votes of CNPPCC Leaders (March 13, 2003)	212
Table 5.3	Votes of State Leaders (March 15, 2003)	214
Table 5.4	SARS Cases in China by May 30, 2003	239
Table 7.1	The Fifteenth Central Committee (1997–2002)	299
Table 7.2	New Generals of the PLA (June 2004)	313
Table 8.1	China's Provincial Party Secretaries (July 2006)	379
Table 8.2	Mobility of Former CYL Cadres Since the Sixteenth Party Congress	381
Table 8.3	China's Governors (July 2006)	386
Table 8.4	Promotions (and Transfers) of CYL Cadres Since the Sixteenth Party Congress	390
Table 8.5	Former Princeling Generals	399
Table 8.6	Current Princeling Generals in the PLA	410

List of Figures

Figure 3.1	Balance of Institutional Power in China (2002)	136
Figure 4.1	Work Ties of Shanghai Party Leaders in the Sixteenth Central Committee	148
Figure 4.2	Work Ties of Shanghai Government Leaders in the Sixteenth Central Committee	151
Figure 4.3	School Ties of Qinghua Graduates in the Sixteenth Central Committee	179
Figure 4.4	Personal Ties of Former CCYL Cadres in the Sixteenth Central Committee	193
Figure 4.5	Balance of Power Among Factional Groups in China	198
Figure 4.6	Group Cohesion Indexes of Factional Groups in China	198

Acknowledgments

Interestingly, my scholarly activities in the past five years have paralleled the development of China's elite politics. As the Chinese top leadership was preparing for the Sixteenth National Congress of the Chinese Communist Party (CCP) in the summer of 2001, I unexpectedly received an invitation from David M. Finkelstein and Maryanne Kivlehan of the CNA Corporation to prepare a paper for a conference on the upcoming Sixteenth National Party Congress. The paper, "The Provinces: Training Ground for National Leaders or a Power in Their Own Right?," later became a contributing chapter in a book edited by David M. Finkelstein and Maryanne Kivlehan, *China's Leadership in the Twenty-First Century: The Rise of the Fourth Generation* (Armonk, NY: M.E. Sharpe, 2003). A presentation at a press conference of the book launch on the eve of the Sixteenth Congress of the CCP on November 7, 2002, and subsequent interviews by Reuters correspondents from Beijing before and after the Congress forced me to pay close attention to what was going on at the Congress and to interpret its related news as an "expert."

Immediately after the new central committee was elected on November 14, 2002, I went to Harvard to deliver a talk on governing China in the 21st century. Soon after a new Politburo, a new Secretariat, and a new Central Military Commission were elected the following day, I found myself talking to one of the best scholars on elite politics in China, Professor Joseph Fewsmith of Boston University. Our conversation thereafter became long email exchanges, and email exchanges became academic exchanges with published articles. I subsequently benefited tremendously from my interactions with my colleagues at the East Asian Institute (EAI) of the National University of Singapore, my colleagues from Tarleton State University, where I served as the inaugural holder of the Joe and Theresa Long Endowed Chair in Social Science, and my colleagues from the Chinese University of Hong Kong, where I served as visiting professor. I have also learned a great deal from participants at workshops and seminars at Harvard, Columbia, the National University of Singapore, the University of Hong Kong, the Chinese University of Hong Kong, Northwestern University, Tarleton State University, Western Carolina University at Cullowhee, and the University of Chicago, where I made presentations on China's elite politics in the past two years.

I would like to thank Joseph Fewsmith for his stimulating questions, Professor Wang Gungwu and Professor John Wong of the East Asian Institute of the National University of Singapore for having invited me to visit the EAI twice in the past two years and for having taught me many things by their commendable examples and tireless instructions. I would also like to thank the East Asian Institute of the National University of Singapore, Tarleton State University, the Chinese University of Hong Kong, and St. John Fisher College for their financial and academic support for my ongoing research projects. My thanks also go to Professor Zheng Yongnian of the University of Nottingham for introducing me to World Scientific Publishing, to one anonymous reviewer for his/her pertinent comments and suggestions, and to Ms. Chean Chian Cheong and Ms. Sandhya of World Scientific Publishing for their assistance throughout the entire process of this book project.

Finally, I dedicate this book to my parents, Bo Tingxiang and Zhang Shaoqing, for their nurturing over the years.

I am grateful to the publishers for permitting me to reprint the following articles with revisions:

Introduction, "Toward a Power Balancing Perspective on Elite Politics in China," Chapter 1, "Power Transfer from Jiang Zemin to Hu Jintao at the Sixteenth Party Congress," and Chapter 5, "Politics of SARS," were partly originally published in *Issues & Studies*, Vol. 41, No. 1 (March 2005); parts of Chapter 2, "The Sixteenth Central Committee: Technocrats in Command?," were originally published in *Asian Profile*, Vol. 32, No. 6 (December 2004); Chapter 3, "Balance of Formal Power," and Chapter 4 "Balance of Factional Power," were partly originally published in *Journal of Contemporary China*, Vol. 13, No. 39 (May 2004); Chapter 6, "Ideological Institutionalization and Politics of Development," combined parts of my original articles published in *Journal of Chinese Political Science*, Vol. 9, No. 2 (Fall 2004) and in *Journal of Social Sciences*, Vol. 12, No. 2 (December 2004); parts of Chapter 8, "Hu Jintao's Power Consolidation," were originally published in *Issues & Studies*, Vol. 42, No. 1 (March 2006).

Introduction: Toward a Power Balancing Model on Elite Politics in China

The purpose of this study is twofold. It aims to provide a new theoretical framework for understanding Chinese elite politics and then to apply the theoretical framework to the analyses of elite politics in reality. A new theoretical framework in the subfield of Chinese elite politics, as late Tang Tsou observed, is long overdue.[1] Efforts have been made to understand the sinews of the Chinese political system,[2] but no systematic theories have been produced as a result. The most dominant model so far is that of "winner-takes-all" that postulates a recurrent pattern of elite power struggles in which the winner of all emerges at the expense of his/her political rivals.

This study attempts to introduce an alternative model — power balancing model. Based on a recognition that the existing studies of Chinese elite politics have not yet gone beyond unit-level analyses,[3] this new model aims at looking at political actors and their interactions in a broader institutional framework. This new model differs not only from the model of "winner-takes-all" but also from other

---

[1] Tang Tsou, "Chinese politics at the top: factionalism or informal politics? Balance-of-power politics or a game to win all," in Jonathan Unger (ed), *The Nature of Chinese Politics: From Mao to Jiang* (Armonk, NY: M.E. Sharpe, 2002), pp. 98–159.

[2] The most significant contribution in this regard is Avery Goldstein, *From Bandwagon to Balance-Of-Power Politics: Structural Constraints and Politics in China, 1949–1978* (Stanford: Stanford University Press, 1991). A major collective effort is Jonathan Unger (ed), *The Nature of Chinese Politics*.

[3] Avery Goldstein labeled unit-level approaches as "reductionalist methodology." For his criticisms of these approaches, see his book, *From Bandwagon to Balance-Of-Power Politics: Structural Constraints and Politics in China, 1949–1978* (Stanford: Stanford University Press, 1991), p. 4.

models of Chinese politics such as bandwagon politics and balance-of-power politics.

WINNER-TAKES-ALL MODEL

The conventional model for explaining Chinese elite politics is winner-takes-all. According to Tang Tsou, the most persistent feature of elite politics in China is that "at irregular intervals the struggle for power among the Chinese elite, involving either supreme political power or power one level below that, always involves one side winning all and/or the other side losing all."[4] He insisted that this is a feature not only of elite CCP politics but of Chinese politics throughout the 20th century. He urged scholars of China studies to consider it the central feature of Chinese politics. He used examples from the history of Chinese politics to illustrate its significance. As he stated,

> Total victory and total defeat, as distinguished from elite pluralism or day-to-day struggles for power or over policy, frequently signifies important turning points in Party history. Mao's ultimate total victory over Wang Ming in 1938 at the 6th Plenum of the 6th Central Committee meant Mao's policy of "both struggle and unity" with Chiang Kai-shek triumphed over Wang Ming's policy of following a more conciliatory line toward the Kuomintang. Mao's destruction of Liu Shaoqi heralded a partial disintegration of the Party system. The arrest of the Gang of Four marked the end of a ten-year period of chaos started by the Cultural Revolution. The total triumph of Deng and the elimination of Hua Guofeng's "faction" as an effective political force signified the beginning of a new era of economic reform and growth.[5]

The critical point of the theory is that Chinese elite politics is a zero-sum game because "supreme political power is considered one

---

[4] Tsou, "Chinese politics at the top," in *The Nature of Chinese Politics*, p. 100.
[5] *Ibid.*, p. 129.

and indivisible."⁶ A political leader either has the absolute power or has none; there is nothing in between. From the perspective of this theory, the most important thing one would expect is the recurrent pattern of total victory and total defeat. Once one identifies such an event in Chinese politics, one is able to infer with almost certainty that there is the winner of all and the loser of all.

Although this model of "winner-takes-all" is logical and consistent with the facts of elite politics during the Maoist era, it is not yet a full-fledged theory of elite politics and is less applicable to post-Mao eras. The model is logical because a political struggle for power has to be all or nothing if power is absolute and indivisible. The cases of Mao versus Wang Ming, Mao versus Peng Dehuai, Mao versus Liu Shaoqi, and Mao versus Lin Biao are indeed power struggles of increasingly life-or-death nature. Yet the model does not explain what causes the indivisibility of power in China. Is it because of authoritarian personalities of certain political leaders? Or is it because of factional competition or the political structure in China?

BANDWAGON POLITICS MODEL

Based on systems theory, Avery Goldstein developed two models on Chinese politics: bandwagon politics and balance-of-power politics.⁷ Political outcomes, according to Goldstein, are essentially determined by the structure of the political system. A bandwagon polity is hierarchically structured, with little functional differentiation, and a skewed distribution of capabilities. It is hierarchically structured because the authority of position and the authority of expertise are well established. In this structure, a subordinate obeys the commands of a superior either because of the latter's official status or because of the latter's expertise. In addition, superiors also have at their disposal negative and positive sanctions. In the bandwagon polity, there is very little functional differentiation since "the locus of political choice is essentially the same regardless of the task

---

⁶ *Ibid.*, p. 129.
⁷ Goldstein, *From Bandwagon to Balance-Of-Power politics: Structural Constraints and Politics in China, 1949–1978* (Stanford: Stanford University Press, 1991).

addressed."[8] The distribution of capabilities in such a polity is highly skewed in favor of superiors. In such a polity, the typical behavior is getting along, producing a bandwagon effect.

Specifically developed for the analysis of the Chinese politics of 1949–1966, the bandwagon politics model lacks theoretical comprehensiveness. For instance, even though it is basically accurate to describe the Chinese polity in the pre-Cultural Revolution period as one with little functional differentiation, there is no analytical reason why a bandwagon polity as a theoretical model has to be limited to only one variant. It is conceivable that a hierarchically-structured polity could also have functional differentiation. Moreover, because of its historical specification, the bandwagon politics model cannot be used to explain Chinese politics in general.

BALANCE-OF-POWER POLITICS MODEL

To explain the Chinese politics of the Cultural Revolution (1966–1978),[9] Goldstein developed a different theoretical model: balance-of-power politics. In contrast to the hierarchically organized bandwagon polity, the balance-of-power polity is anarchically arranged. In this polity, the extent of functional differentiation is also minimal, but capabilities are more dispersed among political actors. In such a polity, political survival becomes "a problem of ever-present concern,"[10] and the typical behavior is balancing.

The balance-of-power politics model is less intuitive and less convincing. Why would anyone choose to back the weaker instead of the stronger? Why would anyone join the loser instead of the winner? Goldstein's argument is that since political actors have to ensure their survival in a condition of anarchy, they would have to balance.[11] But how could they ensure their survival if they decide

---

[8] *Ibid.*, p. 64.
[9] Goldstein uses 1978 as the end year, but the Cultural Revolution usually is considered ended in 1976.
[10] Goldstein, *From Bandwagon to Balance-of-Power Politics: Structural Constraints and Politics in China* (Stanford: Stanford University Press,1991), p. 164.
[11] *Ibid.*, p. 185.

to go against the winner? Wouldn't their chances of survival in a condition of anarchy be better if they chose to get along?

Admittedly, as Goldstein presented it, the structure of the Chinese political system was fundamentally transformed at the beginning of the Cultural Revolution from one of hierarchy to one of anarchy.[12] As political leaders at various levels were purged *en masse,* their authority was seriously undermined. The hierarchy of political power was destroyed, and anarchy ensued.

Nonetheless, it is not accurate to describe the political behavior during the Cultural Revolution as balancing. On the contrary, the nature of the political behavior during the Cultural Revolution hardly changed: Political actors continued to bandwagon under drastically different circumstances. Red guards and revolutionary rebels, for instance, attacked former authority figures as capitalist roaders, not as a balancing act in a condition of anarchy but in response to Chairman Mao's call. On the surface, political actors acted differently before and during the Cultural Revolution. But in essence, their behavior is the same: bangwagoning. They went along with their superiors in the pre-Cultural Revolution period because their superiors were powerful; they went along with Chairman Mao during the Cultural Revolution because Chairman Mao was the most powerful. The different appearances are results of different structures. In short, Goldstein is accurate about the structural changes but not accurate about the nature of political behavior.

Again, as a model developed for a specific historical period, the balance-of-power politics model cannot be used to explain political patterns of other historical periods.[13]

POWER BALANCING MODEL

Built upon some elements of the above two models, the power balancing model postulates a fundamentally different conception of

---

[12] *Ibid.*, pp. 137–159.
[13] Goldstein was well aware of these limitations. See *ibid.*, pp. 255–258.

Chinese elite politics of the 21st century. It argues that Chinese elite politics of the 21st century is fundamentally different from that of earlier eras because of political institutionalization. Political institutionalization refers to a dual process in which the authority of position is restored at the expense of the authority of political correctness, and the authority of expertise is restored at the expense of the authority of "redness."[14] A hierarchical system emerges when subordinates accept the duty to obey superiors simply because of their higher positions. A system of functional differentiation also emerges when different offices are specialized and officeholders are respected because of either their mastery of a body of knowledge or demonstrated technical competence.[15]

Political institutionalization results in a political structure in which formal institutions play more important roles than informal networks do. The structure of the Chinese political system consists of both formal and informal substructures,[16] both of which are hierarchically organized.[17] The formal substructure, because of its clearly articulated superordinate–subordinate relationships, may be represented by a pyramid with the core at the top; the informal substructure, because of its irregular connections, may be represented by a spider web with the core at the center.[18] In the era of Mao Zedong,

---

[14] "Authority of position," as defined by Goldstein, is "rooted in the values of subordinates and sanctions at the disposal of superiors" and is "largely independent of the personal ability of the incumbent." See his book, *From bandwagon to balance-of-power politics*, p. 58.

[15] *Ibid*. For a recent analysis of the functional differentiation in post-Deng China, see Andrew J. Nathan, "China's changing of the guard: authoritarian resilience," *Journal of Democracy*, Vol. 14, No. 1 (January 2003), pp. 1–13.

[16] The discussion on the political structure is based on Tsou, "Chinese politics at the top," p. 131.

[17] For a different understanding, see Xiaowei Zang, "Institutionalization and elite behavior in reform China," *Issues & Studies*, Vol. 41, No. 1 (March 2005), pp. 204–217. In this article, Zang equated informal politics to hierarchy and formal politics to functional differentiation.

[18] Tang Tsou used different terms for these cores. For the core of the formal substructure, he called it "a leader at the top"; for the core of the informal network, he called it the "core." Tsou, "Chinese politics at the top," p. 131.

the core of the formal substructure corresponded to the core of the informal network, because Mao was the embodiment of both. Yet, the informal network played a significantly more important role in politics than did the formal substructure. Mao was able to alter the formal substructure almost at will. The dominance of the informal substructure continued in the era of Deng Xiaoping when Deng was the core of the informal network but not the core of the formal substructure of the political system. Deng was able to wield power over the formal substructure from any position he held. In the era of Jiang Zemin, the formal substructure began to play a more important role than did the informal networks. The fundamental change occurred in 1992 when Deng Xiaoping decided to withdraw from politics completely, and the Central Advisory Commission, the shadow Politburo, was abolished. Consequently, although informal networks still played some accessory roles, formal institutions became dominant in Chinese politics.

As a result of political institutionalization, the nature of elite politics in China has been fundamentally altered. First, the passing of the highest political office from one political leader to another can be politically meaningful because of the authority of position. Second, institutional loyalty can be separated from personal loyalty and may supersede personal loyalty. Third, instead of the winner of all (or the loser of all) in a game to win all, the political game could have multiple winners. Finally, a power balance among political actors could be obtained because of functional differentiation.

POWER BALANCING MODEL AND ITS COMPETING MODELS

The power balancing model is different from the conventional model of the winner-takes-all in two areas. First, instead of envisioning a zero-sum game as in the model of the winner-takes-all, the power balancing model allows the possibility of a nonzero-sum political game. According to the winner-takes-all model, the political game is zero-sum, because political power is indivisible, whereas, according to the power balancing model, the political game can be nonzero-sum because political power can be divisible due to functional differentiation. In a functionally differentiated system, power is no longer absolute and indivisible, and power space — the domain where power can be exercised — has been expanded. The second difference between the model of power balancing and the model of the winner-takes-all game is that instead of a recurrent pattern of total victory and total defeat, as predicted by the model of the winner-takes-all game, the model of power balancing entertains the possibility of multiple winners in terms of political outcomes.

This model of power balancing also differs fundamentally from Avery Goldstein's two theoretical models. The model of power balancing is different from the balance-of-power model because the latter is based on the assumption that the political structure is anarchic while the former explicitly assumes that the political structure is hierarchically organized. The model of power balancing is different from the bandwagon politics model because there is no functional differentiation in the latter, while functional differentiation is a key feature of the former. Most fundamentally, Goldstein's models are too historically specific to be useful for an analysis of post-Mao eras. Since 1978 when a hierarchically ordered polity was reestablished, as Goldstein has admitted regarding the balance-of-power model, "the necessary structural conditions for the relevance of balance-of-power theory, used to explain recurrent patterns of political behavior and outcomes between 1966 and 1978, no longer obtained."[19]

These three competing theoretical models — especially the model of the winner-takes-all game — have tremendous explanatory power for the political dynamics of China's elite politics of the earlier eras. The power balancing model is likely to offer a better alternative perspective on elite politics in the 21st century, because it has taken into account a fundamental structural change of the 1990s — political institutionalization. As a result of political institutionalization, the authority of position has been restored, the formal substructure has become more dominant, institutional loyalty has mostly superseded personal loyalty, and functional differentiation has been substantial.

---

[19] Goldstein, *From Bandwagon to Balance-of-Power politics: Structural Constraints and Politics in China, 1949–1978* (Stanford: Stanford University Press, 1991) p. 255.

CHAPTER OUTLINE

The rest of the book is divided into two parts. Part I deals with the political transition at the Sixteenth Party Congress and the power balance as a result of the Congress. Chapter 1 introduces the rules of exits for political elites in China and the issue of Jiang Zemin's retirement and explains the power transfer from Jiang Zemin to Hu Jintao at the Sixteenth Party Congress in terms of the power balancing model. Contrary to the conventional claim that power transfer did not occur at the Sixteenth Party Congress, this chapter argues that due to political institutionalization, power transfer did take place at the Congress. The chapter further argues that the contradiction between Jiang and Hu in the aftermath of the Sixteenth Party Congress was essentially a contradiction between a two-front arrangement and generational succession.

Chapter 2 presents a systematic evaluation of the Sixteenth Central Committee in terms of political entry, demographic characteristics, and technocracy. It introduces formal and informal rules on political entry, especially for Politburo candidates; analyzes the selection process for central committee and Politburo members; describes the Sixteenth Central Committee in terms of their demographic characteristics; and evaluates the thesis of technocracy in the early 21st century with the Sixteenth Central Committee members as a sample of China's political elites. It challenges the conventional wisdom on technocracy and provides an alternative explanation of the dominance of generalists such as political elites with local governance experiences.

Chapter 3 evaluates the balance of power among formal institutions. There are three major formal institutions in China: provincial units, central institutions, and the military. Business people in China are beginning to emerge as a political group in the 21st century, and thus it is important to examine their political power as well. In order to make comparison possible, a power index was assigned to each member of the Sixteenth Central Committee according to his/her status in the central committee, and the resultant power indices were used to illustrate the power balance among the four formal institutions.

Chapter 4 assesses the balance of power among factional groups, the group cohesion of factional groups, and factional overlap. There are four major factional groups in Chinese politics: the Shanghai Gang, the Princelings, the Qinghua Clique, and the Chinese Communist Youth League (CCYL) Group. The power indices of each group are aggregated, and the balance of factional power is depicted in a chart. Using corporate ties as the basis, this chapter also produces a group cohesion index for each factional group and compares the group cohesiveness of these factional groups. Finally, this chapter unravels the myth of factional exclusion. Studies of political factions in China tended to assume that somehow these factional groups were mutually exclusive. The reality is, as this study demonstrates, that there are overlaps among these factional groups with various degrees.

Part II deals with dynamics of factional politics. Chapter 5 discusses politics of severe acute respiratory symptom (SARS) epidemic. The Shanghai Gang under the leadership of Jiang Zemin competed for power at the National People's Congress meeting in March 2003 and made substantial gains. Yet, when the SARS epidemic hit Beijing the Shanghai Gang members were the first to flee. Jiang Zemin, newly "reelected" chairman of the Central Military Commission of the People's Republic of China (PRC), disappeared from the scene, so did Huang Ju, Politburo Standing Committee member and executive vice premier. Zhang Wenkang, minister of health at that time and one of Jiang's men, lied to the world about the extent of the epidemic in China at a press conference on April 3, 2003. To deal with this national crisis, Hu Jintao and Wen Jiabao took effective measures and brought the situation under control. They removed Zhang Wenkang as health minister and Meng Xuenong as mayor of Beijing and mobilized the Chinese people in a campaign against the SARS epidemic. In the process, Hu and Wen also exposed a corruption case in Shanghai involving Zhou Zhengyi, the richest man of the metropolis, which had implications for some of the Shanghai Gang members such as Chen Liangyu, Huang Ju, and even Jiang Zemin himself. Yet the case was not thoroughly investigated because of the Shanghai Gang's strong resistance, and Zhou was sentenced for only three years.

Chapter 6 focuses on ideological institutionalization and factional politics over economic policies. Ideological institutionalization resulted from political institutionalization. Once in power as the Party boss, Hu Jintao began to introduce his own ideological guidelines. He introduced a series of new ideas such as "new three people's principles," "two imperatives," and "building the Party in the public interest and governing the country for the people" within a month of his ascendancy as general secretary of the Party. He also took the opportunity of a routine speech on July 1 and elaborated his own ideas in the name of studying the "Three Represents" and deprived Jiang of the right to interpret this ideology on behalf of the Party, because Jiang was no longer general secretary of the Party. Most importantly, Hu introduced a new ideology of his own — the scientific concept of development — and had it endorsed by the Sixteenth Central Committee of the CCP at its Third Plenum in October 2003 as the CCP's guideline. Based on the scientific concept of development, Premier Wen Jiabao introduced a new initiative on economic policies in early 2004. Alarmed by the statistics of the first quarter of 2004, Wen called for effective measures to ward off threatening inflation. The Shanghai Gang members such as Huang Ju and Chen Liangyu, however, challenged Wen's assessment of the economic situation in China. With Hu Jintao's support, central leaders all jumped the bandwagon of cooling the economy and local leaders demonstrated their compliance with the central policies. In the end, Hu-Wen declared a political victory.

Chapter 7 analyzes Jiang Zemin's complete retirement. Jiang was reluctant to give up his last post of Central Military Commission chairmanship. Instead of planning a complete retirement, he was actually staging a comeback in early 2004. He walked in front of Hu Jintao at the annual National People's Congress meeting, promoted 15 officers, including his bodyguard to the rank of general, and played up the Taiwan issue during his meeting with Condoleezza Rice, the US president's national security adviser. With the approaching of Deng Xiaoping's centennial birthday, however, Jiang was increasingly under pressure to retire from the Central Military Commission. Jiang wrote a letter of resignation on September 1, 2004, and the central committee accepted his resignation half a month later. Once Jiang lost his position, his "military thought" immediately lost its luster. The main content of military political indoctrination between June 2003 and September 2004, "Jiang Zemin's thinking on national defense and army building," became an empty slogan in September 2004 when Hu Jintao took over as the commander-in-chief of the military. Starting in December 2005, few military leaders mentioned Jiang's empty slogan. A special column on Jiang Zemin's military thought in the *PLA Daily* was discontinued in January 2006, and the People's Liberation Army moved on without Jiang and his "military thought."

Chapter 8 discusses Hu Jintao's power consolidation. In addition to ideological gains, Hu Jintao further consolidated his power in policies, in the military, and in the personnel changes. As soon as he took over as chairman of the state Central Military Commission in March 2005, Hu Jintao introduced a new policy toward Taiwan. Coupled with an anti-session law adopted by the National People's Congress in the same month, this policy proved to be very effective. By altering the nature of cross-strait relations from one of reunification versus independence to one of war versus peace, Hu Jintao raised the stake of cross-strait game. Consequently, opposition parties in Taiwan such as the Guomindang, the People First Party, and the New Party all sent delegations to visit Beijing to ease the tension between the two sides of the Taiwan Strait. Hu thus regained initiatives in the cross-strait relations. Hu Jintao began to increase his power in the military through Politburo study sessions and introduced his own military thought in March 2005. Known as "three provides and one play," Hu's military thought was quickly accepted by the PLA leaders and was subsequently being promoted among the officers and men of the military in China. As a result of the generational changes, the Shanghai Gang furthered its decline following the retirement of Jiang Zemin. Jiang's son, Jiang Mianheng, was sent back to Shanghai from Beijing; Zhao Qizheng, the mastermind of a notorious biography of Jiang Zemin, was retired; and Huang Ju, Jiang's confidant, became terminally ill. On the other hand, the CCYL Group was on the rise with numerous promotions in provinces as well as in Beijing. In the meantime, the

Princeling generals were also emerging as an important part of military elites in China. Some of them have overcome the first barrier of deputy positions and will overcome the second barrier of the central committee.

Finally, the conclusion provides some reflections on studies of China's elite politics in the early 21st century. It summarizes the main theoretical themes of the power balancing model and illustrates the usefulness of the model with the major historical developments of elite politics since the Sixteenth National Party Congress in 2002.

Part I
Political Transition and Power Balance

Chapter 1

Power Transfer from Jiang Zemin to Hu Jintao at the Sixteenth Party Congress

This chapter seeks to understand the power transfer from Jiang Zemin to Hu Jintao at the Sixteenth Party Congress through the power balancing perspective, in contrast to the model of the winner-take-all game. It will introduce the issue of Jiang Zemin's retirement in terms of rules on political exit, explain Jiang Zemin's trick before the Sixteenth Party Congress, illustrate the power balancing model with the power transfer at the Sixteenth Party Congress, and analyze the underlying patterns of political succession from a historical perspective.

RULES ON POLITICAL EXIT AND JIANG ZEMIN'S RETIREMENT

A key personnel issue before the Sixteenth Party Congress was whether Jiang Zemin should step down from all of his positions. Jiang held three most important posts in China before September 2002. He was president of the People's Republic of China (PRC), general secretary of the Chinese Communist Party (CCP), and chairman of the Central Military Commission (CMC).[1]

---

[1] This last position is in fact two: one in the Party and one in the central government. This is because there are two CMCs: One is the CMC of the CCP and one is the CMC of the PRC.

Jiang Zemin should step down as the president of the PRC in accordance with constitutional stipulations. According to the Constitution of the PRC (1982), the president should serve no more than two consecutive terms (Article 79).[2] Jiang's second term would come to an end in 2003. Short of constitutional amendments, Jiang would be ineligible for the post in 2003. Jiang Zemin was the second political leader in the history of the PRC who completed two consecutive terms as the head of state. Mao Zedong was the first to have served as the head of state for two consecutive terms. He served as the chairman of the Central People's Government from 1949 to 1954 and later as the president of the PRC from 1954 to 1959. Liu Shaoqi succeeded Mao in 1959 and was elected to a second term in 1965. But Liu was soon purged in 1968 and passed away in 1969. After a 13-year gap (1969–1982), the post was reinstated in 1982. Li Xiannian (1983–1988) and Yang Shangkun (1988–1993) both served one term in this post. Jiang replaced Yang in 1993 as president and was reelected in 1998.

Constitutional stipulations for the post of chairman of the Standing Committee of the National People's Congress (NPC) and premier are the same as those for president. That is, no one should serve more than two consecutive terms in these posts. From this perspective, both Li Peng and Zhu Rongji could stay for another term.[3] Li Peng was elected as chairman of the Standing Committee

---

[2] "Zhongguo Gongchandang Zhangcheng" ("The Constitution of the CCP" 1982), *Shiyijie Sanzhong Quanhui Yilai Dang de Lici Quanguo Daibiao Dahui Zhongyang Quanhui Zhongyaowenjian Xuanbian* (*Selections of important documents of the Plenums and Party congresses since the Third Plenum of the Eleventh Central Committee*) (Beijing: Zhongyang Wenxian Chubanshe, 1998), Vol. 1, pp. 284–312.

[3] It is not accurate to say that Li and Zhu would have served for two terms by 2003, as Susan Shirk alleged. For her report on this issue, see Susan L. Shirk, "The delayed institutionalization of leadership politics," in Hung-mao Tien and Yun-han Chu (eds), *China under Jiang Zemin* (Boulder, CO: Lynne Rienner Publishers, 2000), p. 305, where she wrote that "At the 2003 National People's Congress Jiang, Li and Zhu, having served for two terms in their government posts (as President, NPC Chair and Premier, respectively) should also hand these positions over to younger leaders."

of the NPC in March 1998, and he was finishing his first term in 2003. In the history of the PRC, Zhu De was an exception. He served in the post for three terms (1959–1976) until his death in 1976. Others served only one term (Ye Jianying, 1978–1983; Peng Zhen, 1983–1988; Wan Li, 1988–1993; and Qiao Shi, 1993–1998). Since that was Li Peng's first term, he could continue to serve in the post for another term until 2008, without amending Article 66 of the Constitution. The same is true of Zhu Rongji, premier in 2002. According to Article 87 of the Constitution (1982), the premier could serve no more than two consecutive terms. Zhu was elected premier in 1998 and could work for another five years in the post. However, he would have to be nominated by the president (Item 5, Article 62). Since Jiang Zemin would retire as president, Zhu would not depend on his nomination. Jiang's replacement, Hu Jintao, would have to decide whether Zhu would be an ideal candidate. Although both Li and Zhu would be 80 years old at the end of their second term in 2008, that would not be an issue because the Constitution does not specify the maximum age for any posts in the government. In sum, according to the Constitution, Jiang should certainly leave his post in 2003; Li Peng could stay on; and Zhu Rongji would have to be nominated for a second term.

Jiang Zemin should step down as general secretary of the Party in accordance with some established informal rules. Although there were very few formal rules on the exit from the top institutions in the CCP, a few informal rules on how to manage the political changes at the Politburo level had been gradually established due to the political institutionalization since 1979.[4] The first informal rule concerns the age limit of a political leader. During the period of Mao, political leaders in China had lifelong tenure until their death, unless they were purged for political reasons. When Deng Xiaoping started a retirement system for veteran leaders in the early 1980s, he did not specify the retirement age for top leaders. The standing

---

[4] Formal rules refer to written rules. Informal rules refer to unwritten rules. For a systematic treatment of informal rules and their relations to formal rules, see Lowell Dittmer, Haruhiro Fukui, and Peter N.S. Lee (eds), *Informal politics in East Asia* (New York: Cambridge University Press, 2000).

Table 1.1 Average Age of CAC Members (1982)

	Obs	Mean	Std. Dev.	Min	Max
Chairman and vice chairmen	5	78.80	4.60	74	86
Standing members	24	76.00	4.12	67	86

Source: Shen Xueming and Zheng Jianying (eds), *Zhonggong Diyijie zhi Dishiwujie Zhongyangweiyuan* (*The central committee members of the Chinese Communist Party from the First through the Fifteenth Central Committee*) (Beijing: Zhongyang Wenxian Chubanshe, 2001).

Table 1.2 Average Age of Politburo Retirees (1985)

	Obs	Mean	Std. Dev.	Min	Max
Politburo retirees	10	77.90	7.09	67	88

Source: Shen Xueming and Zheng Jianying (eds), *Zhonggong Diyijie zhi Dishiwujie Zhongyangweiyuan* (*The central committee members of the Chinese Communist Party from the First through the Fifteenth Central Committee*) (Beijing: Zhongyang Wenxian Chubanshe, 2001).

members of the Central Advisory Commission (CAC) in 1982 were 76 years old on average, with the youngest (Chen Xilian) at 67 and the oldest (Li Weihan) at 86 (Table 1.1). The leaders of the CAC (the chairman and vice chairmen) were older, at 79 on average. In 1985 when a group of Politburo members voluntarily retired, the average age of the retirees was 78, with the youngest (Zhang Tingfa) at 67 and the oldest (Ye Jianying) at 88 (Table 1.2).

As a result of Deng Xiaoping's efforts, the average age of Politburo members was sharply reduced in the late 1980s and early 1990s (Table 1.3). In 1982, for instance, the average age of all Politburo members (28) was 71, with the oldest (Ye Jianying) at 85. The average age of the standing members in that year was 76. In 1987, the average age of all Politburo members (18) was reduced to 64, with the oldest (Yang Shangkun) at 80. In 1992, the average age was further reduced to 62, with the oldest (Liu Huaqing) at 76.

Table 1.3 Average Age of Politburo Members (1982–2002)

Politburo Members	1982	1987	1992	1997	2002
Alternate	64.7	58.0	58.5	58.5	63.5
Full*	70.8	64.8	61.8	62.4	67.2
Standing	76.0	63.6	63.7	65.4	70.4
Total	71.0	64.1	62.1	63.0	67.9

Notes: *This is calculated without standing members.
Source: Shen Xueming and Zheng Jianying (eds), *Zhonggong Diyijie zhi Dishiwujie Zhongyangweiyuan* (*The central committee members of the Chinese Communist Party from the First through the Fifteenth Central Committee*) (Beijing: Zhongyang Wenxian Chubanshe, 2001).

In 1997 when a consensus was reached that no one in the Politburo except for Jiang Zemin could be older than 70,[5] the average age of all Politburo members (24) increased slightly to 63. Before the Sixteenth Party Congress in 2002, the average age of all Politburo members (23) was 68 years, and the average age of the standing members was over 70.

After two decades of rejuvenation, it was difficult to justify the age of 75 or older for the beginning of a new five-year term in any posts in the Party, even for the post of general secretary. It was more difficult to make another exception for Jiang Zemin this time. One of the difficulties lies in the age structure of the Politburo (Table 1.4). The Fifteenth Politburo was composed of old people. Over 60 percent of them were above 65 years old and about 44 percent (10 people)[6] above 70 years. Moreover, five out of seven (71 percent) standing members were 70 years older.[7]

---

[5] Richard Baum, "Jiang takes command: the Fifteenth National Party Congress and beyond," in *China under Jiang Zemin*, p. 24.

[6] They were Jiang Zemin (76), Li Peng (74), Zhu Rongji (74), Qian Qichen (74), Zhang Wannian (74), Tian Jiyun (73), Ding Guan'gen (73), Chi Haotian (73), Jiang Chunyun (72), and Wei Jianxing (71).

[7] They were Jiang Zemin, Li Peng, Zhu Rongji, Wei Jianxing, and Li Lanqing.

Table 1.4 Age Structure of the Fifteenth Politburo (2002)

Age Groups	Freq.	Percent	Cum.
58–60	3	13.04	13.04
61–65	6	26.09	39.13
66–70	4	17.39	56.52
71–76	10	43.48	100.00
Total	23	100.00	

Source: Shen Xueming and Zheng Jianying (eds), *Zhonggong Diyijie zhi Dishiwujie Zhongyangweiyuan* (*The central committee members of the Chinese Communist Party from the First through the Fifteenth Central Committee*) (Beijing: Zhongyang Wenxian Chubanshe, 2001).

If Jiang were to stay in the Politburo, at least nine others could argue for their stay in the Politburo as well.

The second informal rule is the term limit. In the Constitution of the CCP, there is no explicit term limit for any post in the Party. *The Regulation on Selecting and Appointing Leading Cadres of the Party and Government* (2002) stipulates that a leading cadre in a local party committee or government should be rotated after 10 years of service in the same post (Item 2, Article 52).[8] Although 10 years happens to be the number of years for two terms at certain levels, this stipulation is not meant to specify the maximum number of terms one may serve. However, the limitation of most government posts to two consecutive terms in the Constitution of the PRC (1982) has

---

[8] Zhonggong Zhongyang Zuzhibu Ganbuyiju (ed), *Dangzheng Lingdao Ganbu Xuanba Renyong Gongzuo Tiaoli Wenda* (*Questions and Answers on the Regulation on Selecting and Appointing Leading Cadres of the Party and Government*) (Beijing: Dangjian Duwu Chubanshe, 2002), p. 19. For an English translation of the temporary regulation of 1995 and relevant documents, see Zhiyue Bo, "Selection and appointment of leading cadres in post-Deng China," *Chinese Law and Government*, Vol. 32, No. 1 (1999).

some indirect impact on the thinking of the number of consecutive terms one may serve in Party posts. From this perspective, Jiang Zemin should step down from his post as general secretary regardless of his age, because he would have served more than two consecutive terms.

The third rule is not a rule that directly governs the exit from the Politburo; it is a rule as a consequence of the exit from the Politburo. It is a rule that governs the exit from government posts. The rule is that both NPC chairman and premier should be Politburo members. In the history of the PRC, NPC chairmen have been Politburo members. Ye Jianying, NPC chairman from 1978 to 1983, was a standing member of the Politburo. His successor, Peng Zhen (1983–1988), was a full member; Peng's successor, Wan Li (1988–1993), was also a full member of the Politburo. Qiao Shi upgraded the post of NPC chairman to the Politburo Standing Committee level in 1993, and his successor, Li Peng (1998–2003), maintained the status. Premiers have also been Politburo members. Hua Guofeng became chairman of the Party a few months after being appointed to acting premier in 1976. It was the first time in the history of the PRC that the premier was also Party chairman. This situation lasted for about four years until September 1980, when Zhao Ziyang took over as premier. Zhao was a standing member of the Politburo at that time. For a brief period between January 1987 and April 1988, Zhao was both the premier and general secretary of the Party. When Li Peng succeeded Zhao as premier in 1988, he was a standing member of the Politburo. Zhu Rongji was also a standing member when he succeeded Li Peng in 1998.

Neither Li Peng nor Zhu Rongji had to retire according to the two-term limit rule in the government, but they both had to retire from the Politburo according to the age limit. If they were to retire from the Politburo, then they would have to retire from their government posts according to the rule of Politburo membership. At the age of 74 in 2002, they were both too old to stay in the Politburo. Without being a Politburo member, they could not continue to serve in their government posts. In other words, a more important informal constraint on their eligibility to stay on for the second term is not age requirement *per se* but the membership in the Politburo. Although there are no stipulations either in the Constitution of the PRC or in the Constitution of the CCP that require a state leader to be a Politburo member at the same time, the past practices indicate that a state leader has to be a Politburo member. If one is not eligible for a membership in the Politburo, he is unlikely to be a candidate for a leading post in the government. In other words, although Li Peng and Zhu Rongji did not have to retire in accordance with the Constitution, they would have to as the rule of Politburo membership requirement.

Jiang Zemin should also step down as the chairman of the CMC in accordance with political institutionalization and generation change. Jiang Zemin had three predecessors as CMC chairman of the Party: Mao Zedong was CMC chairman from October 1949 to September 1976, Hua Guofeng was in the position from October 1976 to June 1981, and Deng Xiaoping served in the position from June 1981 to November 1989. The two rules mentioned above — the age limit and the term limit — were not in favor of Jiang Zemin's stay as CMC chairman. He was too old and was CMC chairman for too long (more than two terms) to justify for his continuation in the post. The Constitution of the CCP originally stipulated in 1982 that the CMC chairman has to be a standing member of the Politburo (Article 23 of the 1982 CCP Constitution),[9] but the stipulation was dropped in 1987 for the sake of retaining Deng Xiaoping's service.[10] Starting with Jiang Zemin, however, the requirement actually became that the office holder of the CMC chairmanship has to be general secretary of the Party. Jiang would not be eligible for the post if he were to step down as general secretary of the Party. Moreover, Jiang's stay is not justified in terms of generation change. Jiang is the core of the third generation leadership, and he should step down along with his colleagues in the third generation leadership.

---

[9] "Zhongguo Gongchandang Zhangcheng" ("The Constitution of the CCP" 1982), *Shiyijie Sanzhong Quanhui Yilai Dang de Lici Quanguo Daibiao Dahui Zhongyang Quanhui Zhongyaowenjian Xuanbian* (*Selections of Important Documents of the Plenums and Party Congresses Since the Third Plenum of the Eleventh Central Committee*) (Beijing: Zhongyang Wenxian Chubanshe, 1998), Vol. 1, p. 299.
[10] *Ibid.*, p. 498.

Jiang reportedly expressed his desire to retire from all of these positions: He would step down as general secretary of the Party and chairman of the CMC of the Party at the Sixteenth Party Congress in 2002 and step down as president of the PRC and chairman of the CMC of the PRC at the first meeting of the Tenth NPC in March 2003.[11] And his request had been accepted by the Party. As Jiang revealed in his letter of resignation dated September 1, 2004:

> In the interest of the long-term peace and stability of the party and state, and for the sake of achieving the institutionalization, standardization, and proceduralization of the succession of new high-ranking party and state leaders to the old, I informed the Center of my desire to retire from my leadership positions in the Central Committee and to step down from the Central Committee before the Sixteenth National Congress of the CCP. The Center accepted my request at the time.[12]

It seems that the first informal rule of age 70 was well observed at the Sixteenth Party Congress. In spite of numerous speculations on the contrary, Jiang retired from the post of general secretary. Four other Politburo standing members at the age of 70 or older (Li Peng, Zhu Rongji, Wei Jianxing, and Li Lanqing) also retired. Moreover, six additional Politburo members at the age of 70 or older (Zhang Wannian, Qian Qichen, Tian Jiyun, Chi Haotian, Ding Guan'gen, and Jiang Chunyun) stepped down. It is not clear whether or not the second informal rule of term limit played any role in the leadership transition. The rule of two-term limit does not really apply to Politburo members, because a membership in the Politburo is a status instead of a post. The only post this rule is applicable to is that of general secretary. However, Jiang retired

---

[11] Zong Hairen, *Disidai* (*China's New Leaders: The Fourth Generation*) (New York: Mirror Books, 2002), p. 524. This report has been partially confirmed by Jiang Zemin himself in his resignation letter of September 1, 2004.

[12] Jiang Zemin, "Jiang Zemin tongzhi qingqiu ciqu zhonggong zhongyang junshiweiyuanhui zhuxi zhiwu de xin" (Resignation letter, September 1, 2004), *Renmin ribao*, September 19, 2004, http://www.people.com.cn/GB/shizheng/1026/279 3951.html.

more because of his age than because of his tenure. Yet since he retired after two consecutive terms, this may set a precedent for future leaders.[13]

The rule of generation change seems to have been the reason for the retirement of two relatively "young" Politburo members. Li Tieying was "only" 66 years old in 2002, but he served as a state councilor for two consecutive terms between 1988 and 1998 and as a Politburo member since 1987. He belongs to the third generation leadership in China. Li Ruihuan's case was similar, but with another layer of politics to it. Li Ruihuan (68 years old in 2002) entered the Politburo in November 1987, along with Jiang Zemin, and entered the Standing Committee of the Politburo in June 1989, along with Jiang Zemin. Although he is a member of the third generation leadership in China, one could make a case that he also belongs to the fourth generation as his age was not above 70 years and thus should stay. According to Zong Hairen, Li Ruihuan was listed as a candidate of the Sixteenth Politburo Standing Committee until October 17, 2002. At a meeting of the Fifteenth Politburo Standing Committee on that day, Jiang Zemin asked Li Ruihuan to withdraw his candidacy from the Sixteenth Politburo Standing Committee. Jiang's argument was that Li belonged to the same generation as he did and that it would be good for Hu Jintao if Li could retire along with Jiang.[14] That obviously was a calculated political move. Li reportedly was irritated by Jiang's ploy and criticized Jiang. Li then told the Fifteenth Politburo Standing Committee that he would not want to enter the Sixteenth Central Committee. Apparently, Li, a long-term political rival to Jiang, was outmaneuvered and pushed out by Jiang.[15]

---

[13] Hu Jintao, for instance, will be 69 years old in November 2012 because he was born in December 1942. However, it is very likely that he would retire after two consecutive terms, if a new rule of two-term limit is to be established.

[14] Zong Hairen, *Aimei de Quanli Jiaojie* (*Ambiguous Transition*) (New York: Mirror Books, 2003), pp. 40–45.

[15] According to Willy Wo-Lap Lam, Jiang introduced a new rule to shove aside Li Ruihuan. This new rule is "*qishang baxia*" (seven, go up; eight, come down), meaning that Li should leave the Politburo because he was 68 years old. See Lam's article, "Party bosses slog it out in Beijing," *China Brief* 3, Issue 2 (January 28, 2003),

The biggest surprise, nonetheless, was the fact that Jiang Zemin stayed on as chairman of the CMC of the Sixteenth Central Committee of the CCP without being a central committee member. In the *People's Daily* of November 16, 2002, Jiang Zemin's photo appeared to the left of General Secretary Hu Jintao's photo,[16] and Jiang's resume was posted above Hu's resume.[17] That was a signal that Jiang would not only stay on as CMC chairman of the CCP but he would continue to be more important than the new general secretary, Hu Jintao. By accepting the position of CMC chairman in the new central committee, Jiang Zemin ostensibly ignored the rule of term limit, violated the rule of generation change, and breached the rule on the combination of general secretary with CMC chairman.

JIANG ZEMIN'S TRICK: INSTALLING LOYALISTS BEFORE THE CONGRESS

Apparently, there was some maneuvering regarding Jiang Zemin's retirement. He had made a gesture for complete retirement before the Sixteenth Party Congress so that his political rival, Li Ruihuan, would retire from the Politburo. In the meantime, by "giving up" all of his positions, he would also gain more power over the personnel arrangement of the next Politburo. Before the opening of the Sixteenth Party Congress, for instance, it had already been decided that three of Jiang Zemin's protégés would enter the Sixteenth Politburo Standing Committee and another three of his protégés would enter the Politburo. On October 23, 2002, half a month before the opening of the Sixteenth Party Congress, it was announced in the *People's Daily* that the Party center decided to transfer Jia Qinglin and Huang Ju to the center, replace Jia and Huang by Liu Qi and Chen Liangyu as party secretary of Beijing and party secretary of Shanghai, respectively, and replace He Guoqiang

---

http://china.jamestown.org/pubs/view/cwe_003_002_004.htm. However, Li Tieying also came down from the Politburo at the age of 66.
[16] *Renmin ribao*, November 16, 2002, p. 1.
[17] *Renmin ribao*, November 16, 2002, p. 2.

by Huang Zhendong as party secretary of Chongqing.[18] Two days later, it was announced in the *People's Daily* that the Party center decided to replace Zeng Qinghong by He Guoqiang as the director of the Central Organization Department (COD) and replace Ding Guan'gen by Liu Yunshan as the director of the Central Propaganda Department (CPD).[19]

Jia Qinglin is a personal friend of Jiang Zemin. Jia and Jiang both worked in the First Ministry of Machine-Building in the 1960s, but they probably were not acquainted then. Their careers converged in 1971 when Jia returned to the First Ministry of Machine-Building as a staff in the Policy Research Department of the General Office.[20] Jiang was vice director of the Foreign Affairs Bureau of the same ministry at that time.[21] Later, Jiang was promoted to director of the Foreign Affairs Bureau, and Jia was appointed as the head of the Product Management Bureau of the same ministry. They began to work closely in 1978 when Jia was promoted to general manager of the China National Machinery and Equipment Import and Export Corporation under the dual leadership of the First Ministry of Machine-Building and the Ministry of Foreign Economic Relations and Trade. When Jiang was made vice-chairman of the State Foreign Investment Management Commission and the State Import/Export Management Commission in 1980, Jia and Jiang worked even closer.

After Jiang Zemin became general secretary of the Party in June 1989, he was in a position to promote his old friend.[22] He made Jia acting governor of Fujian in November 1990 and party secretary of Fujian in December 1993. In October 1996, in an effort to destroy the Beijing Gang under the leadership of Chen Xitong (former

---

[18] *Renmin ribao*, October 23, 2002, p. 1.
[19] *Renmin ribao*, October 25, 2002, p. 1. See also http://past.people.com.cn/GB/shizheng/252/9823/9824/20021024/850186.html.
[20] For Jia Qinglin's bio, see http://news.xinhuanet.com/ziliao/2002-01/16/content_240595.htm.
[21] For a chronology of Jiang Zemin's life, see Robert Lawrence Kuhn, *The man who changed China: the life and legacy of Jiang Zemin* (New York: Crown Publishers, 2004), pp. 581–584.
[22] See Zong Hairen, *Disidai*, pp. 471–475.

Politburo member and party secretary of Beijing), Jiang transferred Jia to Beijing as the acting mayor. One year later, Jia became party secretary of Beijing and entered the Politburo. When a corruption scandal in Fujian involving Jia Qinglin's wife, Lin Youfang, and possibly Jia himself broke out in 1999, Jiang took extraordinary measures to protect Jia.[23] He paid a special visit to Beijing on January 24, 2000 and openly supported Jia Qinglin.[24] Now Jiang transferred Jia to the Party center half a month before the opening of the Sixteenth Party Congress, sending the signal that Jia would enter the Politburo Standing Committee soon. In retrospect, this signal was reflected in the wording of the announcement. In the announcement, Jia was said to be transferred to the Party center and he would "no longer concurrently assume the positions of member, standing member, and secretary of the Beijing Municipal Party Committee."[25] Jia did not have any position in the "center."[26] His only position was party secretary of Beijing. As such, he was also member and standing member of the Beijing Municipal Party Committee as well as member of the Politburo. Without the position of party secretary of Beijing, Jia in fact was jobless. Yet Jia was not being demoted. He was being promoted to the center. Since Jia was already a Politburo member, his promotion would be into the Standing Committee of the next Politburo.

The same is true of Huang Ju. Huang is Jiang's protégé from Shanghai and thus a typical member of the Shanghai Gang. A native of Zhejiang, Huang worked in Shanghai for almost four decades. In June 1985, both Huang and Jiang became deputy party secretaries of Shanghai. Jiang ranked number one, and Huang ranked number four.[27] A month later, Jiang was appointed as the mayor of Shanghai.

---

[23] For details, see Joseph Fewsmith, *China since Tiananmen* (New York: Cambridge University Press, 2001), pp. 224–226.
[24] *Renmin ribao*, January 25, 2000, p. 1.
[25] *Renmin ribao*, October 23, 2002, p. 1.
[26] The Chinese term *zhongyang* (center) refers vaguely to the central apparatus of the CCP. It could mean the Central Committee of the CCP or the Politburo of the CCP or even the Politburo Standing Committee of the CCP.
[27] *Dangdai Zhongguo de Shanghai* (*Shanghai of Contemporary China*) (Beijing: Dangdai Zhongguo Chubanshe, 1993), Vol. 2, p. 649.

Huang became Jia's associate in October 1986 when he was made a vice mayor of Shanghai.[28] Huang reportedly was very loyal to Jiang, and Jiang twice tried in vain to transfer Huang to Beijing.[29] Huang entered the Fourteenth Central Committee in 1992 as the mayor and deputy secretary of Shanghai and entered the Fourteenth Politburo two years later as party secretary of Shanghai. His promotion to the Standing Committee of the Sixteenth Politburo would definitely add Jiang's weight in the Chinese politics of the subsequent five years.

Zeng Qinghong has been well known as Jiang's protégé and chief advisor.[30] A native of Jiangxi, Zeng was born in Anhui on August 29, 1939.[31] His father, Zeng Shan, and his mother, Deng Liujin, were both veteran revolutionaries. Zeng Shan later became the first vice mayor of Shanghai (May 1949 to December 1949),[32] minister of Commerce (August 1952 to November 1956), and minister of Internal Affairs (November 1960 to September 1967).[33] Because of his father's connections in Beijing and Shanghai, Zeng Qinghong was appointed as a deputy director of the Organization Department of the Shanghai Municipal Party Committee in July 1984 and was promoted to director of the Department four months later.[34] In the Shanghai leadership reshuffle in June 1985, Zeng entered the Standing Committee of the Shanghai Municipal Party Committee. His boss at that time was Rui Xinwen, party secretary of Shanghai. With Rui's recommendation, Zeng became deputy secretary of Shanghai

---

[28] *Ibid.*, p. 659.

[29] See Zong Hairen, *Disidai*, p. 271 and 477.

[30] For Zeng Qinghong's official bio, see http://news.xinhuanet.com/ziliao/2002-01/16/content_240615.htm.

[31] Ting Wang, *Zeng Qinghong and the Strong Men of the Sunset Race* (2nd edition) (Hong Kong: Celebrities Press, 2001), p. 136. The official record of Zeng's birth is July 1939, but that is the date in Chinese lunar calendar.

[32] *Dangdai Zhongguo de Shanghai*, p. 652.

[33] The Ministry of Internal Affairs became dysfunctional in September 1967 when Zeng Shan was being publicly criticized. Ting Wang, *Zeng Qinghong*, p. 119.

[34] For details, see Gao Xin, *Lingdao Zhongguo de Xinrenwu: Zhonggong Shiliujie Zhengzhiju Changwei (China's Top Leaders: Bios of China's Politburo Members)* (Carle Place, NY: Mirror Books, 2003), Vol. 1, pp. 234–235; Ting Wang, *Zeng Qinghong*, pp. 152–157.

in October 1986. Zeng began to work under Jiang Zemin in Shanghai in November 1987 when Jiang succeeded Rui as party secretary of Shanghai. There were altogether four deputy secretaries under Jiang at that time: Yang Di, Huang Ju, Wu Bangguo, and Zeng Qinghong.[35] Zeng earned Jiang's trust and respect in the subsequent 20 months. When Jiang Zemin was made the general secretary of the CCP in June 1989, he took Zeng to Beijing.[36] Zeng was appointed as deputy director of the General Office (July 1989 to March 1993). He was later promoted to director of the General Office (March 1993 to March 1999) and director of the COD of the CCP (March 1999 to October 2002). Zeng became a member of the Fifteenth Central Committee of the CCP, an alternate member of the Fifteenth Politburo, and a member of the Fifteenth Secretariat in September 1997.

Because of Zeng's extraordinary contributions to Jiang's power consolidation, Jiang reportedly twice tried to promote Zeng to a full membership in the Politburo.[37] But this time, Jiang would want Zeng to get a seat not only in the Politburo but also in its Standing Committee.

Liu Qi, Jia Qinglin's replacement as party secretary of Beijing, and Chen Liangyu, Huang Ju's replacement as party secretary of Shanghai, are both Jiang Zemin's men and both were likely to enter the Sixteenth Politburo because of their positions. Liu Qi is from the same province as Jiang. Liu's hometown is Wujin, Jiangsu,[38] and Jiang's hometown is Yangzhou, Jiangsu. Both cities are located in the southern part of Jiangsu (*sunan*). After graduation from the Beijing Institute of Iron and Steel Engineering in 1968, Liu went to Wuhan and worked in the Wuhan Iron and Steel Company for the

---

[35] *Dangdai Zhongguo de Shanghai*, p. 659.
[36] According to Ting Wang, Jiang also took Hua Jinmin, Jiang's secretary, to Beijing. But Hua did not go to Beijing until 1996. See Ting Wang, *Zeng Qinghong*, p. 171.
[37] See Murray Scot Tanner, "Hu Jintao's succession: prospects and challenges," in David M. Finkelstein and Maryanne Kivlehan (eds), *China's Leadership in the 21st Century: The Rise of the Fourth Generation* (Armonk, NY: M.E. Sharpe, 2003), p. 49.
[38] For Liu Qi's bio, see http://news.xinhuanet.com/ziliao/2002–02/21/content_284282.htm.

subsequent 25 years.[39] He was made minister of Metallurgy in 1993, but his ministry was abolished in the restructuring of the State Council in 1998. Liu was transferred to Beijing as a deputy secretary of Beijing in March 1998 and became concurrent vice mayor of Beijing one month later. He was promoted to mayor of Beijing in February 1999. Since Beijing is an elite provincial unit with the Politburo rank, Liu's promotion to party secretary of Beijing would secure him a seat in the next Politburo.

Chen Liangyu is in the same situation.[40] Technically, Chen is not Jiang's protégé. Chen did not have direct work relations with Jiang. When Jiang was mayor and party secretary of Shanghai in the late 1980s, Chen at first was in the Retired Cadre Bureau of the Shanghai Municipal Party Committee as deputy director and director and then worked in the Huangpu District as deputy party secretary and concurrently head. Yet Chen is Jiang's protégé by association, because Chen is Huang Ju's protégé. Chen worked with Huang Ju for a decade in Shanghai and is Huang's confidant. Chen became the acting mayor of Shanghai in December 2001 and party secretary of Shanghai 10 months later. With the title of party secretary of Shanghai, Chen had secured a place in the Sixteenth Politburo.

Finally, He Guoqiang, Zeng's replacement as director of the COD, and Liu Yunshan, Ding Guan'gen's replacement as director of the CPD, would also likely enter the Sixteenth Politburo. Historically, directors of the COD were mostly central committee members but a few of them were Politburo members and secretariat members (Table 1.5). Chen Yeping and Zhang Quanjing were two exceptions to the central committee membership. Chen Yeping was

---

[39] A story goes that Liu Qi and Jiang Zemin became acquainted in Wuhan while Jiang worked in Wuhan as director of the Wuhan Power Engineering Research Institute. But their encounter must have been very brief if the story is true because Liu went to Wuhan in June 1968 and Jiang left Wuhan for Hunan in 1968. See Gao Xin, *Lingdao Zhongguo de Xinrenwu: Zhonggong Shiliujie Zhengzhiju Weiyuan* (*China's Top Leaders: Bios of China's Politburo Members*) (Carle Place, NY: Mirror Books, 2003), Vol. 2, p. 472.

[40] For Chen Liangyu's bio, see http://news.xinhuanet.com/ziliao/2002-02/22/content_285938.htm.

Table 1.5 Directors of the COD (October 1949–October 2002)

Name	Period	Birth	CC	Politburo	Secretariat
Peng Zhen	October 1949–April 1953	1902	Full	Full	N/A
Rao Shushi	April 1953–April 1954	1903	Full	No	N/A
Deng Xiaoping	April 1954–November 1956	1904	Full	Standing	Full
An Ziwen	November 1956–August 1966	1909	Full	No	No
Guo Yufeng	June 1975–December 1977	1919	Full	No	N/A
Hu Yaobang	December 1977–December 1978	1915	Full	No	N/A
Song Renqiong	December 1978–February 1983	1909	Full	Full	No
Chen Yeping	February 1983–April 1984	1915	No	No	No
Qiao Shi	April 1984–July 1985	1924	Full	No	Alternate
Wei Jianxing	July 1985–May 1987	1931	Full	No	No
Song Ping	May 1987–December 1989	1917	Full	Standing	No
Lu Feng	December 1989–December 1994	1927	Full	No	No
Zhang Quanjing	December 1994–March 1999	1931	No	No	No
Zeng Qinghong	March 1999–October 2002	1939	Full	Alternate	Full
He Guoqiang	October 2002	1946			

Source: Updated from Ting Wang, *Zeng Qinghong and the Strong Men of the Sunset Race* (Hong Kong: Celebrities Press, 2001), Table 28-7, p. 189.

a veteran communist. He joined the CCP in 1933 and became a deputy director of the COD in 1960. He was already 68 years old in 1983 when he was promoted to director of the COD.[41] He had been elected into the CAC the previous year. He was obviously a transitional figure and served in the position for only a year. Zhang Quanjing was in a similar situation. He was promoted to director of the COD in December 1994 and got too old in September 1997 (66 years) to enter the central committee.

Since 1978, three directors have been Politburo members. Song Renqiong started off as a central committee member and became a Politburo member almost four years later, shortly before his retirement from the directorship. Song Ping entered the Politburo half a

---

[41] For his bio, see http://auction2.guaweb.com/auction_db/artist_info.cfm?artist_code=53983.

year after he became the director and was promoted to the Politburo Standing Committee half a year before his retirement. Zeng Qinghong seems to have been the one who sets a precedent for He Guoqiang to follow. Zeng had already been an alternate member of the Politburo and a member of the Secretariat when he took the position of the COD director in March 1999. Being Zeng's successor, He Guoqiang would likely enter the Politburo and the Secretariat. Again, He Guoqiang is Jiang Zemin's protégé by association: He is Zeng's protégé.

Liu Yunshan, Ding Guan'gen's replacement as director of the CPD, was also likely to enter the Politburo and the Secretariat, because Ding had been a Politburo member and a Secretariat member (Table 1.6). But Liu is not Jiang's protégé. Liu once served as deputy secretary of the Communist Youth League (CYL) in Inner Mongolia between July 1982 and February 1984 and was a member of the CYL Central Committee under the leadership of Wang Zhaoguo and Hu Jintao.[42] He is thus considered a member of the CYL Group.

In sum, half a month before the opening of the Sixteenth Party Congress, Jiang manipulated to secure seats for three of his protégés (Jia Qinglin, Huang Ju, and Zeng Qinghong) in the Sixteenth Politburo Standing Committee and for another three of his associates (Liu Qi, Chen Liangyu, and He Guoqiang) in the Sixteenth Politburo. Jia, Huang, and Zeng were freed from responsibilities of their previous jobs and would concentrate on competing for power and fighting for Jiang during this critical period. That was a blatant violation of the CCP Constitution, because, according to Article 21 of the CCP Constitution, members of the Sixteenth Politburo and its Standing Committee were supposed to be elected by the Sixteenth Central Committee, which, according to Article 19 of the same Constitution, was supposed to be elected by deputies to the Sixteenth National Party Congress.[43]

---

[42] For Liu Yunshan's official bio, see http://news.xinhuanet.com/ziliao/2002–10/24/content_607117.htm.

[43] "Zhongguo Gongchandang Zhangcheng" ("The Constitution of the CCP" 1982), *Shiyijie Sanzhong Quanhui Yilai Dang de Lici Quanguo Daibiao Dahui Zhongyang*

Table 1.6 Directors of the CPD (October 1949–October 2002)

Name	Period	Birth	CC	Politburo	Secretariat
Lu Dingyi	October 1949–September 1952	1906	Full	No	N/A
Xi Zhongxun	September 1952–July 1954	1913	Alternate	No	N/A
Lu Dingyi	July 1954–May 1966	1906	Full	Alternate	Full
Tao Zhu	May 1966–January 1967	1908	Full	Standing	Full
Zhang Pinghua	October 1977–December 1978	1907	Full	No	N/A
Hu Yaobang	December 1978–February 1980	1915	Full	Full	N/A
Wang Renzhong	February 1980–April 1982	1917	Full	No	Full
Deng Liqun	April 1982–July 1985	1915	Full	No	Full
Zhu Houze	July 1985–January 1987	1931	Full	No	No
Wang Renzhi	January 1987–December 1992	1933	Full	No	No
Ding Guan'gen	December 1992–October 2002	1929	Full	Full	Full
Liu Yunshan	October 2002	1947			

Source: Author's database.

POWER TRANSFER AT THE SIXTEENTH PARTY CONGRESS

The political succession that took place at the Sixteenth National Congress of the CCP in November 2002 is both fascinating and intriguing. The congress is fascinating because it went smoothly, peacefully, and predictably;[44] compared to previous attempts at

---

Quanhui Zhongyaowenjian Xuanbian (*Selections of Important Documents of the Plenums and Party Congresses Since the Third Plenum of the Eleventh Central Committee*) (Beijing: Zhongyang Wenxian Chubanshe, 1998), Vol. 1, p. 298.

[44] For the most systematic attempt to predict what would happen at the Sixteenth Party Congress and beyond, see David M. Finkelstein and Maryanne Kivlehan (eds), *China's Leadership in the 21st Century: The Rise of the Fourth Generation*. Many predictions in the volume had been made in November 2001 and turned out to be very accurate. Based on new information available in October 2002, some of the authors of the volume such as Joseph Fewsmith, Cheng Li, and Zhiyue Bo made more accurate predictions in the media immediately before the opening of the Sixteenth Party Congress. Many websites also made quite accurate predictions. According to Gao Xin, www.duoweinews.com accurately predicted not only the composition of Sixteenth Politburo Standing Committee but also its lineup. See Gao Xin, *Lingdao Zhongguo de Xinrenwu*, Vol. 1, p. 265.

political succession, this was the first time in the history of the PRC that the CCP experienced an institutionalized transfer of the highest political office in China. Yet the congress is also intriguing because scholars of Chinese politics have arrived at drastically different conclusions about what transpired at the Sixteenth Congress and their implications for elite politics in China. Some scholars declared that political succession did not occur at the Sixteenth Party Congress,[45] whereas others suggested that political succession did take place on institutionalized terms, though the rule of man may still play a major role in elite politics.[46]

More fundamentally, these different assessments of the outcome of the Sixteenth Party Congress reflected, consciously or subconsciously, different theoretical perspectives on Chinese politics. An "either/or" assessment may suggest the nature of a zero-sum game in which a winner is likely to be the winner of all (and conversely, a loser is likely to be the loser of all). More objectively, the outcome may be viewed in terms of the balancing of political powers among key players. Moreover, a systems approach may go beyond the unit-level analyses and consider the constraints of the political institutionalization on the behavior of individual players.[47]

---

[45] Joseph Fewsmith, "The Sixteenth National Party Congress: the succession that didn't happen," *China Quarterly*, No. 173 (March 2003), pp. 1–16. Implicitly, this view is also shared by Lowell Dittmer, who saw Jiang Zemin as a victor of the CCP's Sixteenth National Congress when "Jiang's own political power has reached unprecedented heights." See Lowell Dittmer, "The 16th Party Congress as a Chinese developmental process," *China Quarterly*, No. 176 (December 2003), pp. 903–926. Noticably, Joseph Fewsmith modified his view slightly after Jiang Zemin's retirement from the CMC in September 2004. See Joseph Fewsmith, "Political succession: changing guards and changing rules," in Tun-jen Cheng, Jacques deLisle, and Deborah Brown (eds), *China under Hu Jintao: Opportunities, Dangers, and Dilemmas* (Singapore: World Scientific Publishing, 2006), pp. 27–46.
[46] Andrew J. Nathan, "China's changing of the guard: authoritarian resilience," *Journal of Democracy*, Vol. 14, No. 1 (January 2003), pp. 6–17; and Zheng Yongnian and Lye Liang Fook, "Elite politics and the fourth generation of Chinese leadership," *Journal of Chinese Political Science*, Vol. 8, Nos. 1 & 2 (Fall 2003), pp. 65–86.
[47] See the introduction for a detailed discussion of this point.

Applying the model of the winner-takes-all game to the analysis of the Sixteenth Party Congress, Joseph Fewsmith reached a conclusion that the political succession did not occur at the Sixteenth National Party Congress.[48] Jiang Zemin presented a political report that endorsed his major themes, incorporated his theory of the "Three Represents"[49] in a newly revised CCP Constitution, packed the Politburo and its Standing Committee with his allies, and retained his position as head of the Party's CMC. Hu Jintao, on the other hand, was reduced to applauding Jiang's accomplishments, even though he was named general secretary; Hu would have to wait for at least another five years to assume real power. In a word, Jiang was the winner of all, and Hu was the loser of all.

Although the facts presented above are mostly accurate, the assessment is debatable. First, the role of Jiang Zemin in Chinese politics is overstated. There is a tendency among China scholars to exaggerate Jiang's role in Chinese politics because of his unexpected political longevity.[50] That Jiang did not end up like Hu Yaobang or Zhao Ziyang may be attributed, to some extent, to his political skills, but there could be a number of other reasons as well. Among them, Deng Xiaoping's support was critical.[51] Some claim that Jiang asserted his control over the People's Liberation Army (PLA) by removing Yang Shangkun, president of the PRC and

---

[48] Fewsmith, "The Sixteenth National Party Congress."
[49] That is, the CCP has always represented the most advanced productive forces, the most advanced culture, and the fundamental interests of the broad masses of the Chinese people. According to Zong Hairen, it was Li Peng who suggested using the expression of the "important thought of the Three Represents" instead of "Jiang Zemin's important thought of the Three Represents" in the CCP Constitution. See his book, *Aimei de Quanli Jiaohuan*, p. 48.
[50] They underestimated his staying power earlier and now are overestimating his influence to avoid being wrong again. The problem is that they paid too much attention to personal factors but not enough attention to institutional factors.
[51] Without Deng's support, Jiang would not have survived. Deng threatened to remove Jiang during his tour of the south China in 1992. For a report, see "Xiaoping Nanxun 'Shouxi Jiedaiguan' Chen Kaizhi shui Nanxun" ("Chen Kaizhi recalls Deng Xiaoping's southern tour"), *Xinkuai bao*, April 27, 2004, http://www.people.com.cn/GB/14677/22097/2459739.html.

executive vice-chairman of the CMC, and his half brother, Yang Baibing, secretary-general of the CMC, from the military commission.[52] This view is not accurate. The fact that Jiang had more control over the PLA after the Yang brothers had been removed does not mean Jiang removed the Yang brothers in order to control the PLA. More likely is that Deng was the one who decided to dismiss the Yang brothers to help Jiang gain control over the PLA.[53] Without Deng Xiaoping, Jiang could have been toppled by the Yang brothers.

Formal institutions were also an important factor. Jiang had power not because he was a charismatic leader.[54] His power did not come from his revolutionary credentials either, simply because he had very few of them. Instead, his power was institution based. He was powerful because he was general secretary of the Party, chairman of the CMC, and president of the PRC. His official power was supplemented by his informal network within the Shanghai Gang.[55]

In terms of the outcome of the Sixteenth Party Congress, Jiang was a winner but not the winner of all. As the first general secretary of the CCP in the past two decades who exited from office without being disgraced, Jiang in this sense was a winner. Otherwise, it is not clear how his stepping down from the highest office in the Party

---

[52] Hung-mao Tian and Yun-han Chu (eds), *China under Jiang Zemin*, p. 1.

[53] According to Liu Huaqing, it was Deng Xiaoping who decided the make-up of the new CMC in October 1992. In his letter of October 6, 1992, Deng not only made specific suggestions for the new CMC but also asked the military professionals — instead of Jiang Zemin — to select their successors. See Liu Huaqing, *Liu Huaqing Huiyilu* (Autobiograhy of Liu Huaqing) (Beijing: Jiefangjun Chubanshe, 2004), p. 630.

[54] On the contrary, as his biographer, Bruce Gilley, has portrayed him, Jiang in fact was charisma challenged. See Bruce Gilley, "Jiang Zemin: on the right side of history?" *Current History* (September 1999), pp. 249–253; and *Tiger on the Brink: Jiang Zemin and China's New Elite* (Berkeley and Los Angeles, CA: University of California Press, 1998).

[55] For a systematic discussion of factional groups including the Shanghai Gang in the Sixteenth Central Committee, see Zhiyue Bo, "The Sixteenth Central Committee of the Chinese Communist Party: formal institutions and factional groups," *Journal of Contemporary China*, Vol. 13, No. 39 (May 2004), pp. 223–256.

makes him a winner, especially given the evidence that he was seriously contemplating continuing in office.[56] Moreover, the general understanding among China watchers is that Jiang did not choose his successor. Deng Xiaoping was the one who chose the core of the fourth generation leadership in 1992, while helping the core of the third generation leadership to consolidate power. Furthermore, Jiang does not deserve kudos for such an unprecedented transition because it was not something of his own making.[57] Deng Xiaoping deserves more credit in this regard, despite having long left the stage. The real credit, nevertheless, should be given to political institutionalization.[58]

Second, it is not accurate to portray Hu Jintao as the loser of all. Hu was not simply named general secretary but he — rather than Jiang — was elected general secretary. Since there is only one office of general secretary, Hu in this case should be regarded as the winner of all and Jiang the loser of all. The fact that Jiang read the political report did not make him a winner, nor did it make Hu a loser. Although seldom having read the political report to a national Party congress, Mao was beyond the doubt the man of real power. By competing with Hu over such symbolic matters, Jiang in fact revealed his weaknesses. On this point, Hu was rather gracious and generous.

The question is whether or not the passing of the office of general secretary from Jiang to Hu represents a meaningful power

---

[56] Fewsmith, "The Sixteenth National Party Congress," p. 1.

[57] As Zheng Yongnian and Lye Liang Fook correctly observed, the transition occurred under Jiang's watch, though Jiang did not necessarily seek to achieve such an outcome. See Zheng and Fook, "Elite politics and the fourth generation of Chinese leadership," p. 65.

[58] As explained in the introduction to this book, Goldstein criticized China scholars for attempting to reduce political phenomena in China to the unit-level variables. Individual actors may make a difference in some cases, but the structure plays even more important roles in Chinese politics. This is why some China scholars and watchers could not comprehend Chinese politics until they discover (or invent) personal reasons. For them, if it was not Jiang, it must be Hu. For Goldstein's critique, see his book, *From Bandwagon to Balance-Of-Power Politics*, especially, pp. 3–6.

transfer. My own estimate is that the office is institutionalized to a large extent and the officeholder does have significant power not only in name but also in reality. As the incumbent general secretary, Hu clearly has an institutional advantage over Jiang.

However, it is not accurate to say that Hu was the absolute winner and Jiang was the absolute loser as a result of the Sixteenth Party Congress. As general secretary of the Party, Hu clearly has power in party affairs. As chairman of the CMC, Jiang continues to exert influence on military affairs. Jiang would be unable to interfere with party affairs without Hu's clear endorsement. Hu would likely continue to respect Jiang's authority in military affairs. The net result, therefore, is a power balance between the two due to the division of labor. In other words, because of functional differentiation, the game is no longer a zero-sum one.

From this perspective, we may argue that Jiang's gains in ideological terms were not necessarily Hu's losses. There is no evidence that Hu Jintao objected to the "Three Represents" theory. On the contrary, he was the earliest supporter and the most frequent advocate of the "Three Represents" among Standing Committee members of the Fifteenth Politburo. He first declared his support for the "Three Represents" publicly on April 18, 2000 during his visit to Inner Mongolia.[59] He reiterated his endorsement on five other occasions between April 18 and June 20, 2000.[60] The next most frequent speaker of the "Three Represents" among Standing Committee members of the Fifteenth Politburo was Wei Jianxing, who voiced his endorsement three times, while the rest of the Standing Committee members announced their support only once during the same period. As the most enthusiastic supporter of the theory, Hu was also a winner in ideological terms when the "Three Represents" was written into CCP Constitution. If Liu Ji's statement

---

[59] *Renminwang* (People's Daily online), April 19, 2000, http://www.people.com.cn/GB/paper464/426/42014.html.
[60] This is based on a search using "*sange daibian*" in Chinese as the key word in *Renminwang* between February 1 and June 20, 2000. The total entries generated were 143.

about Hu as a major participant in the creation of the "Three Represents" theory is true,[61] then Hu should even more firmly be viewed as a winner.

Moreover, it is not entirely accurate to portray Jiang as an all-mighty politician who — against Hu's objections — single-handedly packed the Sixteenth Politburo and its Standing Committee with his personal allies. First, these members all have their own credentials as candidates for the Politburo and its Standing Committee. All nine members of the Sixteenth Politburo Standing Committee had been members of the Fifteenth Politburo: one had been a Standing Committee member, seven had been full members, and one had been an alternate member. The Standing Committee member was elected general secretary. The seven full members were the only full members that had stayed on, and they were uniformly promoted. The alternate member was Zeng Qinghong, Jiang's right-hand man. He experienced a two-level promotion from an alternate to a Standing Committee member of the Politburo. Even his promotion, however, cannot be entirely attributed to Jiang. Zeng had been known for his own talents, and — in addition to his status as an alternate member of the Politburo — had occupied other important positions such as director of the General Office of the Central Committee, member of the Secretariat, and director of the Organization Department of the Central Committee. It was rumored that Zeng's promotion had been a result of Hu's efforts instead of Jiang's.

Second, Hu is not necessarily Jiang's enemy. The general consensus is that although Hu was not Jiang's choice as a successor,

---

[61] Liu Ji, director of the Research Center on China's National Conditions, is a protégé of Jiang Zemin. He observed in an interview in November 2003 that the new collective leadership under General Secretary Hu Jintao has long participated in the core work of the central leadership and was directly involved in creating Deng Xiaoping Theory and the important thought of the "Three Represents." See *Renminwang*, November 20, 2003, http://www.people.com.cn/GB/shizheng/1026/2201412.html. For a detailed discussion of Liu Ji's relations with Jiang Zemin, see Joseph Fewsmith, *China since Tiananmen*, pp. 183–189.

Jiang gradually accepted Hu as his legitimate and qualified successor. Jiang in fact helped to promote Hu to important positions in both the Party and the government.[62] By the same token, Jiang's allies are not necessarily Hu's enemies. There is no clear evidence that Hu had had any serious problems with any members of the Sixteenth Politburo and its Standing Committee — whether they were Jiang's allies or not.

Finally, it is not entirely correct to assume that Jiang promoted his allies simply because they were his cronies. Nor is it accurate to predict that Jiang would be able to maintain the same authority over them after his exit from the post of general secretary. One critical conceptual distinction should be made between institutional and personal loyalty. Jiang very likely promoted some of his allies to the Politburo because of their personal loyalty. Yet equally likely is that these ambitious politicians expressed their personal loyalty to Jiang not as a person but as general secretary. If this were the case, then the same people would not very likely continue to express their personal loyalty to Jiang to the same extent after he was retired from the position, especially at the expense of jeopardizing their relationship with their new boss. Deng Xiaoping the citizen could count on President Yang Shangkun's personal loyalty in 1992, but Jiang Zemin is no Deng Xiaoping. Few in China were sincerely impressed by either Jiang's abilities or his virtues as a state leader.

TWO-FRONT ARRANGEMENT VERSUS GENERATIONAL SUCCESSION

On the surface, Jiang's stay after having retired from the Politburo resembles Deng's stay after 1987, but the actual power arrangement was fundamentally different in Jiang's case. To understand the fundamental change, it is useful to take a look at the power structure under Mao and Deng.

---

[62] For a detailed discussion, see Murray Scot Tanner, "Hu Jintao's succession: prospects and challenges," pp. 45–65.

Mao Zedong started a two-front arrangement in the 1950s.[63] According to Frederick C. Teiwes, as early as in 1952, Mao talked with Liu Shaoqi about his idea of dividing the leadership into "two fronts" — a "first front" that would be responsible for daily work and a "second front" where the Chairman would ponder larger problems. The issue was subsequently raised at a Politburo meeting in August–September 1952.[64] But more likely is that Mao was convinced of the need for the two fronts in the aftermath of Stalin's death in 1953.[65] The two-front arrangement was officially introduced at the Eighth Party Congress in 1956 when a post of honorary chairman was created for Mao in case he decided to retire to the second front in the Party. The arrangement was further disclosed in January 1958 when Mao drafted a document on work methods, "Sixty Articles on Work Methods (Draft)." Article 60 stated:

---

[63] For detailed studies of the two-front arrangement, see Jing Huang, *Factionalism in Chinese Communist Politics* (New York: Cambridge University Press, 2000), pp. 205–266; Chien-min Chao and Wen-shuen Tsai, "Mao Zedong Shiqi 'Erxian Fengong' de Yuanzuo jiqi dui Juece Guocheng de Yihan" ("The 'two-front arrangement' under Mao and its implications for decision-making processes") *Mainland China Studies*, Vol. 48, No. 2 (June 2005), pp. 1–30; and Chien-min Chao and Wen-shuen Tsai, "Zhonggong Jingying Zhengzhi de 'Jiegou-Xingdongzhe' Muoshi" ("Elite politics in the People's Republic of China: a 'structure-agent' model") *Mainland China Studies*, Vol. 49, No. 1 (March 2006), pp. 1–26.

[64] Frederick C. Teiwes, *Politics at Mao's Court: Gao Gang and Party Factionalism in the Early 1950s* (Armonk, New York: M. E. Sharpe, 1990), pp. 32, 116, 117.

[65] Roderick MacFarquhar, *The Origins of the Cultural Revolution: Contradictions among the People 1956–1957*, (New York: Columbia University Press, 1974), Vol. 1, pp. 152–156. According to Deng Xiaoping, Mao introduced the proposal at the end of 1953. See Deng Xiaoping, "Dui Qicao 'Guanyu Jianguo Yilai Dang de Ruogan Lishi Wenti de Jueyi' de Yijian" ("Suggestions on drafting 'the resolution on some historical issues of the Party since the founding of the People's Republic of China'"), *Deng Xiaoping Wenxue (Selected Works of Deng Xiaoping)* (Beijing: Renmin Chubanshe, 1987), Vol. 2, p. 293. But in the same paragraph, Deng also pointed out that Gao Gang became more active after Mao's introduction of the proposal. According to Mao's biography, Gao became very active during June–August 1953 when the National Financial and Economic Conference was held in Beijing. In other words, Mao probably mentioned his idea before June 1953. For Gao's activities, see Peng Xianzhi and Jin Chongji, *Mao Zedong Zhuan (1949–1976) (Biography of Mao Zedong (1949–1976))* (Beijing: Zhongyang Wenxian Chubanshe, 2003), Vol. 1, pp. 276–284.

It is necessary to make before September of this year a preliminary exchange of views on the question of my giving up the chairmanship of the People's Republic of China. Airing of views and debates should be organized first among cadres at all levels and later among factories and cooperatives to solicit the views of the cadres and the masses and to obtain the consent of the majority. This is because by relinquishing the office of chairman of the Republic and serving exclusively as chairman of the Party Central Committee, I can save a lot of time to do things which I am required by the Party to carry out. It is also more suitable for my state of health. If in the course of debate the masses should feel antagonistic to and disapprove of this suggestion, it should be explained to them that if the country is in a state of emergency in the future, provided the Party so decides, I still can take up the duties of state leadership. Now that we are in time of peace, it is more advantageous for me to relinquish the duties of one of the chairmanships. This request has been endorsed by the Political Bureau of the Central Committee and many comrades of the Central Committee and local administrations, and is regarded as a good idea.[66]

With the approval of the Sixth Plenum of the Seventh Central Committee on December 10, 1958, Mao formally stepped down as chairman of the PRC in April 1959 and theoretically retired to the second front.[67]

---

[66] Mao Zedong, "Gongzuo Fangfa Liushitiao (cao an)" ("Sixty articles on work methods (draft)") (January 1958), *Jianguo Yilai Mao Zedong Wengao* (*Collections of Mao Zedong since 1949*) (Beijing: Zhongyang Wenxian Chubanshe, 1992), Vol. 7, pp. 45–65. For English translation, see MacFarquhar, *The Origins of the Cultural Revolution*, Vol. 1, p. 154. See also Mao Zedong, "Dui tongyi Mao Zedong Buzuo Xiajie Guojia Zhuxi Houxuanren de Juedinggao de Piyu he Xiugai" ("Comments and corrections on the decision of agreeing that Mao Zedong would not be a candidate for the next term as the head of state") (December 8, 9, 1958), *Jianguo Yilai Mao Zedong Wengao*, Vol. 7, pp. 633–635.

[67] It is wrong to state that Mao retreated to the second front in April 1959 to take responsibilities for the failure of the Great Leap Forward. See Wen-Shuen Tsai, "An analysis of the 'factional politics approach in the CCP: the origin of the great leap

The two-front arrangement was a succession model in which the preeminent leader gradually gives up his positions and power and the potential successor takes up more and more responsibilities. In such a model, the preeminent leader does not retire completely and the potential successor is not assured of the eventual succession. When Lord Montgomery of Britain asked Mao in 1960 who would be his successor, Mao replied: "Very clearly, Liu Shaoqi is the one. He is the first vice chairman of our Party. It will be him after my death."[68] But eight years later, Liu was expelled from the Party once and for all and was dismissed from all of his posts within and outside the Party; he died a miserable death soon thereafter. Lin Biao was designated as Mao's successor, and his designation was written into the CCP's Constitution at the Ninth Party Congress in 1969. Two years later, however, Lin Biao the successor died in a plane crash in Outer Mongolia. The failure of the two-front arrangement as a succession model is essentially due to its inherent instability. The preeminent leader retires partially but retains the ultimate power. He can dismiss the potential successor almost at will.

Deng Xiaoping adopted the same model of succession with significant modifications.[69] As Mao, Deng also served as the preeminent leader in the second front with the ultimate power, and he could also dismiss the leaders of the first front almost at will. However, there are a number of significant differences between Mao's two-front arrangement and Deng's. First, Deng did not occupy the most

---

forward as an example" (in Chinese), *Mainland China Studies*, Vol. 48, No. 1 (March 2005), pp. 85–104. Tsai used a footnote (no. 13 on p. 88) to indicate the source of this opinion. But the source material does not contain such a statement. See Parris H. Chang, *Power and Policy in China* (2nd and Enlarged Edition) (University Park and London: The Pennsylvania State University Press, 1978), p. 190.
[68] See Peng Xianzhi and Jin Chongji, *Mao Zedong Zhuan (1949–1976)* (Biography of Mao Zedong (1949–1976)), (Beijing: Zhongyang Wenxian Chubanshe, 2003), Vol. 2, p. 1173. After that, Montgomery pursued, "Will it be Zhou Enlai after Liu Shaoqi?" Mao replied, "It will be none of my business after Liu Shaoqi."
[69] For a different assessment, see Joseph Fewsmith, *Elite Politics in Contemporary China* (Armonk, NY: M. E. Sharpe, 1990), especially Introduction.

important position of the Party — the position of Party chairman or general secretary. Second, the second front did not consist of only one man, i.e., Deng, but a group of veteran leaders. Moreover, the second front was more institutionalized, and most of these second-front veteran leaders were members of a newly created CAC.[70] Third, elite conflicts under Deng were much more rational, and their resolution was much more civilized. After his dismissal as general secretary, Hu Yaobang remained a Politburo member until his death in April 1989. Zhao Ziyang was removed from the office of general secretary in June 1989 but not publicly criticized and humiliated.

Finally and most importantly, Deng decided to abandon the two-front arrangement in favor of a new model of succession — generational succession. On the one hand, Deng dismantled the second front. In the aftermath of the Tiananmen Incident of 1989, Deng decided to give up his last official post — chairman of the CMC. Deng also abolished the CAC in 1992.

On the other hand, Deng put forth a new theory on political succession with two components. First, he introduced a model of generational succession. He reinterpreted the succession history of the CCP in generational terms and laid out generational changes for future leaders. He said,

> The first stable and mature collective of leaders of the Chinese Communist Party was formed by Mao Zedong, Liu Shaoqi, Zhou Enlai, and Zhu De. All previous ones had been unstable and immature. From Chen Duxiu to the Zunyi Conference, not a single leading group was truly mature. For one period of time, a worker was dragged into the post of general secretary because, it was argued, it was necessary to stress the leadership of the working class. In the history of the Party, Mao, Liu, Zhou, and Zhu formed the first generation of truly mature leadership.

---

[70] For a similar view, see Frederick C. Teiwes, "The politics of succession: previous patterns and a new process," in John Wong and Zheng Yongnian (eds), *China's Post-Jiang Leadership Succession: Problems and Perspectives* (Singapore: Singapore University Press and World Scientific Publishing, 2002), p. 39.

During the early period of their tenure, that generation of leaders was good, but during the later period the Cultural Revolution caused a catastrophe. Hua Guofeng was merely an interim leader and cannot be counted as representing a generation. He had no ideas of his own but the "two whatevers." We are of the second generation, now being replaced by the third.[71]

According to Deng, Mao Zedong, Liu Shaoqi, Zhou Enlai, and Zhu De were the first generation leaders; his generation was the second; and now it was being replaced by the third generation. Obviously, the third generation leadership would also be replaced by the fourth generation, which in turn would be replaced by the fifth generation, so on and so forth.

The second component of this generational succession model is the structure of each generation leadership. As Deng explained,

> The Communist Party should establish its third generation of collective leadership. Historically, our Party never had a mature central leadership before the Zunyi Conference. Chen Duxiu, Qu Qiubai, Xiang Zhongfa, Li Lisan, and Wang Ming all failed to form a capable central leadership. It was only after the Zunyi Conference that the collective leadership of the Party began to take shape. That leadership was composed of Comrades Mao Zedong, Liu Shaoqi, Zhou Enlai, Zhu De, and Ren Bishi. After Comrade Bishi passed away, Comrade Chen Yun was added to the leadership. At the Eighth National Congress of the Party, the Central Committee established a Standing Committee composed of Mao, Liu, Zhou, Zhu, Chen, and Deng. Later on, Lin Biao was added to the Standing Committee. This collective leadership lasted until the Cultural Revolution.

---

[71] Deng Xiaoping, "Zucheng yige shixing gaige de youxiwang de lingdao jiti" ("We must form a promising collective leadership that will carry out reform" (May 31, 1989)), *Deng Xiaoping Wenxuan (Selected Works of Deng Xiaoping)* (Beijing: Renmin Chubanshe, 1993), Vol. 3, pp. 296–301.

In the long history before the Cultural Revolution, no matter what mistakes our Party made and no matter how the composition of the leadership changed, it always remained a collective leadership with Comrade Mao Zedong as the core. That was the first generation of collective leadership.

At the Third Plenary Session of its Eleventh Central Committee, the Party established a new collective leadership — the second generation. Actually, it can be said that in this leadership I am in the key position. Ever since the establishment of this collective leadership, I have been arranging for my successor. Neither of the successors I chose retained their post for long, but at the time, given their experience in struggle, their achievements in work and their political and ideological level, they were the best choices I could make. Besides, people change.

A collective leadership must have a core; without a core, no leadership can be strong enough. The core of our first generation of collective leadership was Chairman Mao. Because of that core, the Cultural Revolution did not bring the Party down. Actually, I am the core of the second generation. Because of this core, even though we changed two of our leaders, the Party's exercise of leadership was not affected but always remained stable. The third generation of collective leadership must have a core too; all you comrades present here should be keenly aware of that necessity and act accordingly. You should make an effort to maintain the core — Comrade Jiang Zemin, as you have agreed. From the very first day it starts to work, the new Standing Committee should make a point of establishing and maintaining this collective leadership and its core.[72]

According to Deng, each generation leadership should be a collective leadership, and each collective leadership should have a core. Mao Zedong was the core of the first generation collective

---

[72] *Ibid.*

leadership. Deng Xiaoping was the core of the second generation collective leadership. And Jiang Zemin would be the core of the third generation collective leadership. Deng not only selected the core of the third generation leadership in 1989 but also designated the core of the fourth generation leadership in 1992.

Now with Jiang's stay as CMC chairman, the issue became a contradiction between the two-front arrangement and the generational succession model. Hu Jintao replaced Jiang Zemin in accordance with Deng Xiaoping's model of generational succession: Hu represents the fourth generation leadership and Jiang the third. The political transition from Jiang to Hu was a generational succession in which the fourth generation replaced the third. In the meantime, Hu as the core of the fourth generation leadership replaced Jiang as the core of the third generation leadership. Jiang Zemin, on the other hand, attempted to reintroduce the two-front arrangement in which he would be the leader at the second front and Hu would be the leader of the first front. In this arrangement, Jiang would delegate everyday work to Hu while retaining the ultimate power, including the power of letting Hu go.

Jiang's stay caused two problems for the fourth generation leadership. First, it disrupted the generational transition from the third to the fourth. It is well known that Jiang Zemin was the core of the third generation leadership in China. Hu's leadership has been often referred to as a new generation of collective leadership (*xinyidai lingdaojiti*). Logically, a new generation after the third generation must be the fourth generation. With only one exception,[73] however, none of the scholars and news media sources in Mainland China used the term of the fourth generation leadership in China either before or after the Sixteenth Party Congress. Clearly, this omission

---

[73] Hu Angang, a researcher of the Chinese Academy of Social Sciences and a professor of Qinghua University is the only one who ever mentioned the concept of the fourth generation of leadership in China in *Renminwang*. He used the concept in an interview on November 8, 2002. See Zhang Xiantang, "Hu Angang: Zhongguo dui Renlei Zuo Jiaodagongxian de Shidai Lailingle" ("Hu Angang: The times for China to make a greater contribution to the mankind have come"), *Renminwang*, http://www.people.com.cn/GB/jinji/36/20021108/861721.html.

has something to do with Jiang Zemin's presence in the new leadership. There might even be an internal policy, prohibiting the use of the term "fourth generation" in the media. Otherwise, it would be difficult to justify Jiang's continued presence in the central leadership. As a leader of the third generation, Jiang was no longer eligible for any position in the fourth generation leadership.

The second problem Jiang's stay caused was disruption of further generational changes from the fourth to the fifth generation. Jiang reportedly vetoed the idea of installing candidates for the core of the fifth generation in the Sixteenth Politburo Standing Committee after the fashion of the Fourteenth Party Congress in 1992 when Hu Jintao was made a member of the Fourteenth Politburo Standing Committee. In a seemingly very confusing way, he presented his veto as an exchange for his complete retirement.[74] In retrospect, it is clear that Jiang was not ready to move out of politics and was definitely not eager to see the coming of the fifth generation.

What Jiang intended to do was to follow Deng Xiaoping's example of 1987 and go back to the two-front arrangement in which Jiang would be the source of the ultimate power from his position of CMC chairmanship. There were rumors immediately after the Sixteenth Party Congress that Hu Jintao promised to "seek instruction and listen to the views" of Jiang Zemin in his acceptance speech.[75] Although Hu might have made similar remarks out of modesty, Hu probably made no promise to consult Jiang. Even less likely is that "the Party congress made a secret resolution to consult Jiang, as it did in 1987 when it promised to consult a retiring Deng."[76] There is no evidence that Hu ever officially consulted Jiang on anything of significance since the Sixteenth Party Congress.

---

[74] Zong Hairen, *Disidai*, pp. 24–26.

[75] Fewsmith, "The Sixteenth National Party Congress," p. 14, where he quoted it from Erik Eckholm, "China's new leader promises not to sever tether to Jiang," *The New York Times*, November 21, 2002, A1. Lowell Dittmer also indicated in his article that Hu Jintao promised "in (leaked) internal leadership briefings that Jiang would preview all 'important' Politburo decisions," but did not provide his sources of information. See Dittmer, "The 16th Party Congress as a Chinese developmental process," p. 915.

[76] Fewsmith, "The Sixteenth National Party Congress," p. 14.

What the advocates of the winner-takes-all game including Jiang himself have failed to appreciate is the impact of political institutionalization on the power structure of Chinese politics. When Deng retired from the Politburo while retaining the post of CMC chairmanship in 1987, the Chinese political system was not institutionalized. Although Deng was commander-in-chief, he worked more as the Party boss. He was retained not as a military professional whose concern was only about military affairs. Instead, Deng was retained as a political leader who would provide guidance on major political issues. In other words, Deng was a military leader in name but a political leader in essence.

Due to political institutionalization, the power structure has been significantly altered. Military leaders can no longer interfere with political affairs. In this more institutionalized context, Jiang's position is quite awkward. He might have intended to stay on as a political leader as Deng had done earlier, but he actually stayed on as a military leader because of his post. The irony is that Jiang stayed on as a military leader without any substantial military experiences. It should be recalled that Jiang was installed as CMC chairman in the first place not because of his military qualifications but because of his position as general secretary of the Party. As Deng Xiaoping explained in November 1989, "Comrade Jiang Zemin is well qualified to be the Chairman of the Military Commission because he is well qualified to be General Secretary of the Party."[77] Once Jiang stepped down from the post of general secretary, he immediately lost any justifications for staying on as CMC chairman.

In other words, Deng Xiaoping stayed on as a military leader but worked as a political leader, whereas Jiang Zemin stayed on as a military leader and would have to work as a military leader. In a two-front arrangement, Deng had the ultimate power over military as well as political affairs. In an institutionalized context, Jiang had power over military affairs but not over political affairs.

---

[77] Deng Xiaoping, "Huijian Canjia Zhongyang Junwei Kuodahuiyi Quantitongzhi shi de Jianghua" ("Speech at the enlarged meeting of the CMC," November 12, 1989), *Deng Xiaoping Wenxuan* (*Selected Works of Deng Xiaoping*) (Beijing: Renmin Chubanshe, 1993), Vol. 3, p. 334.

CONCLUDING REMARKS

With Deng Xiaoping's push, China has established some rules on political exit. The two-term limit is stipulated in the Constitution of the PRC and serves as a major check on the power of state leaders. For this reason, Jiang Zemin had to step down as the president of China after having served for two consecutive terms. But there are not formal rules on political exit in the CCP Constitution. The age 70 for Politburo members and two-term limit for general secretary of the CCP were informal rules, which may or may not be strictly followed. Jiang Zemin stepped down as general secretary of the CCP more because of the age limit than because of the term limit.

Jiang maneuvered to install six of his protégés in the Sixteenth Politburo half a month before the opening of the Sixteenth Party Congress in a blatant violation of the CCP Constitution and managed to push out his main political rival, Li Ruihuan. Taking advantage of the loophole in the CCP Constitution that CMC chairman does not have to be a Politburo member, Jiang Zemin stayed on as CMC chairman without being a central committee member.

Nevertheless, power transfer did occur at the Sixteenth Party Congress. As the office of general secretary was transferred from Jiang Zemin to Hu Jintao, Hu instead of Jiang became the most powerful person in the Party. This is because of the political institutionalization in Chinese politics where the authority of position has been restored. Yet the power transfer was incomplete because of Jiang's stay as CMC chairman.

Contrary to the expectations of the winner-takes-all model, the political transition at the Sixteenth Party Congress produced neither the winner of all nor the loser of all. Consistent with the expectations of the power balancing model, the power transition was real and meaningful and created a power balance between Jiang and Hu.

The contradiction between Jiang and Hu was in essence a contradiction between two models of political succession: two-front arrangement versus generational succession. Historically, Mao Zedong started the tradition of a two-front arrangement in which Mao retreated to the second front, while others such as Liu Shaoqi,

Zhou Enlai, and Deng Xiaoping worked in the first front. The problem was that Mao wielded too much power including the power of dismissing his designated successors. Deng Xiaoping adopted Mao's two-front model with significant modifications. Instead of one man, Deng included a group of veteran leaders in the second front and institutionalized the second front with the creation of the CAC.

In the aftermath of the Tiananmen Incident, Deng decided to change the succession model from the two-front arrangement to generational succession. In this new model, there are different generation leaderships succeeding one after another, and each generation leadership has a core. According to this model, once a new generation leadership is in place and the older generation retires, the older generation should no longer intervene in the affairs of the new generation.

By having stayed on as CMC chairman of the new central committee of the fourth generation, Jiang Zemin was attempting to reintroduce the two-front arrangement in which he would be the one to call the shots. But the Chinese political system was much more institutionalized in 2002 than in 1987. Deng stayed on as CMC chairman in 1987 but actually served as the Party boss, whereas Jiang stayed on as CMC chairman in 2002 and would have to serve as CMC chairman.

Chapter 2

The Sixteenth Central Committee: Technocrats in Command?

This chapter will present and evaluate the Sixteenth Central Committee. It will introduce formal and informal rules on political entry, especially for Politburo candidates; analyze the selection process for central committee and Politburo members; describe the Sixteenth Central Committee in terms of their demographic characteristics; and evaluate the thesis of technocracy in the early 21st century with the Sixteenth Central Committee members as a sample of China's political elites.

RULES ON POLITICAL ENTRY

Formal Rules

There are some basic formal rules in the Constitution of the Chinese Communist Party (CCP) about the entry into the Politburo. First, a Politburo member has to be a central committee member. Failure to become a full central committee member has prevented a number of political aspirants from entering this vital political organ in the past. Deng Liqun (1915–), former head of the Central Propaganda Department and member of the Twelfth Secretariat, failed to enter the Politburo in 1987 because he was eliminated from the list of candidates for central committee members in the first round of balloting.¹ Xiao Yang (1929–1998),² former governor of Sichuan, also failed to enter the Politburo in 1992 because he was only an alternate member of the central committee. Xiao, a local leader with strong centralist tendencies,³ was extremely unpopular among the deputies to the Fourteenth National Congress of the CCP. Although he had been groomed for becoming a Politburo member, he received the least number of votes as an alternate member and thus was disqualified for a membership in the Politburo.⁴

The second formal rule is that members of the Politburo, members of the Standing Committee of the Politburo, and the general secretary have to be elected by a central committee plenum (Article 22).⁵ Obviously (but not explicitly stated), standing members of the Politburo have to be Politburo members. The third formal rule is that the general secretary has to be a standing member of the

---

[1] Richard Baum, *Burying Mao: Chinese Politics in the Age of Deng Xiaoping* (Princeton: Princeton University Press, 1994), p. 216. Lowell Dittmer must have mistaken Deng Liqun's membership in the Secretariat for a membership in the Politburo, as he stated, "Deng Liqun, a Twelfth CC Politburo member, was unexpectedly dropped from the Politburo because of his failure to be reelected to the CC at the Thirteenth Congress." See his chapter, "Sizing up China's new leadership: division of labor, political background, and policy orientation," in Hung-mao Tien and Yun-han Chu (eds), *China under Jiang Zemin*, p. 35. Deng was a Twelfth CC Secretariat member but not a Twelfth CC Politburo member.

[2] Although their English spellings are the same, we should not confuse this Xiao Yang with another one, whose Chinese character of the given name is different. This one worked in Chongqing and Sichuan in the 1980s and 1990s and passed away in 1998. Another Xiao Yang (1938–) is president of the Supreme People's Court. He is alive and well, currently a member of the Sixteenth Central Committee.

[3] He was referred as "a Sichuanese who spoke only Mandarin" by local people because he was paying too much attention to central decisions at the expenses of his locale. This phase comes from Lijian Hong, "Provincial leadership and its strategy toward the acquisition of foreign investment in Sichuan," in Peter T.Y. Cheung, Jae Ho Chung, and Zhimin Lin (eds), *Provincial Strategies of Economic Reform in Post-Mao China* (Armonk, N.Y.: M.E. Sharpe, 1998), p. 392.

[4] *Ibid.*, pp. 393, 394.

[5] *Ibid.*, p. 13.

Politburo.⁶ A case in point is Jiang Zemin. Jiang became a central committee member at the Twelfth National Congress of the CCP in 1982 and a Politburo member at the First Plenum of the Thirteenth Central Committee in 1987. During the Tiananmen Incident, he was only a full member of the Politburo. The standing members at the time were Zhao Ziyang (general secretary), Li Peng, Qiao Shi, Hu Qili, and Yao Yilin. Therefore, Jiang made it to the Politburo Standing Committee first before he was made general secretary in June 1989, though these two distinctive procedures occurred simultaneously.

Finally, there is only one formal rule for selecting a person as a candidate for the central committee in accordance with the Constitution of the CCP: He or she has to have a Party standing of at least five years (Article 21).⁷

Informal Rules

There are some informal rules about the entry into the Politburo. First, the head of state usually is a standing member of the Politburo with one exception. Mao Zedong, Liu Shaoqi, Li Xiannian, and Jiang Zemin were all standing members of the Politburo during their tenure. Yang Shangkun was the exception. He was only a full member of the Politburo when he was elected as the president of the People's Republic of China (PRC) in 1988.⁸

Second, vice presidents of the PRC do not have to be Politburo members.⁹ In some cases, they do not even have to be members of

---

⁶ *Ibid.*, pp. 13, 14.
⁷ "Zhongguo Gongchandang Zhangcheng (1992)" ("The Constitution of the Chinese Communist Party (1992)"), in *Zhongguo Gongchandang Dangnei Fagui Xuanbian, 1978–1996* (*Laws and Regulations of the Chinese Communist Party, 1978–1996*) (Beijing: Falü Chubanshe, 1996), p. 13.
⁸ For the list of former presidents of the PRC and their bios, see http://news.xinhuanet.com/ziliao/2002–01/23/content_249791.htm.
⁹ For a list of vice presidents of the PRC and their bios, see http://news.xinhuanet.com/ziliao/2002–01/23/content_249791.htm.

the CCP. In the beginning of the PRC (1949–1954), half of vice presidents were not CCP members (Song Qingling, Li Jishen, and Zhang Lan). Later, Song Qingling served another two consecutive terms as a vice president of the PRC (1959–1966) without being a CCP member. But Zhu De (1886–1976) was a standing member, and Dong Biwu (1886–1975) was a full member of the Politburo. Ulanhu (1906–1988) was a full member of the Politburo, but Wang Zhen (1908–1993) was not even a member of the central committee. Rong Yiren (1916–2005), however, was a "secret" CCP member. He joined the CCP in 1985, but his CCP membership was not revealed until his death in October 2005.[10] Hu Jintao, however, was a standing member of the Politburo.

Third, the premier should be a standing member of the Politburo. In the history of the PRC, this rule was held without exception (Table 2.1). Zhou Enlai, Hua Guofeng, Zhao Ziyang, Li Peng, and Zhu Rongji were all standing members of the Politburo during their tenure as the premier. Fourth, as mentioned in Chapter 1, the chairman of the National People's Congress Standing Committee has to be at least a full member of the Politburo and, since 1993, has to be assumed by a standing member of the Politburo. Peng Zhen and Wan Li were full members of the Politburo during their tenure, and Liu Shaoqi, Zhu De, Ye Jianying, Qiao Shi, and Li Peng were all standing members of the Politburo.[11]

Fifth, the chairman of the Chinese National People's Political Consultative Conference (CNPPCC) has to be a full member of the Politburo with some exceptions. Mao Zedong, Zhou Enlai, Deng Xiaoping, and Li Ruihuan were all standing members of the Politburo; Deng Yingchao was a full member of the Politburo for the first two years of her service; and Li Xiannian was neither a

---

[10] For a report, see Ji Honggen, "Huiyi Rong Yiren: Sixiang Zaorudang Xiaoshi Kanfengge Gangzheng Qiliangda" ("Rong Yiren: a CCP member in thought, a gentleman in details, and a character of strength and tolerance"), http://news.xinhuanet.com/politics/2006-06/13/content_4687017.htm.

[11] For the list of former chairmen of the National People's Congress Standing Committees and their bios, see http://news.xinhuanet.com/ziliao/2004-11/15/content_2221419.htm.

Table 2.1 State Leaders and their Status in the Politburo (1954–2003)

Name	Title	Tenure	The Politburo	From
Zhou Enlai	Premier	1954–1976	Standing Member	1945
Hua Guofeng	Premier	1976–1980	Standing Member	1976
Zhao Ziyang	Premier	1980–1988	Standing Member	1980
Li Peng	Premier	1988–1998	Standing Member	1987
Zhu Rongji	Premier	1998–2003	Standing Member	1992
Chen Yun	Vice Premier	1954–1966	Standing Member	1950
Chen Yun	Vice Premier	1979–1980	Standing Member	1978
Lin Biao	Vice Premier	1954–1966	Standing Member	1958
Peng Dehuai	Vice Premier	1954–1959	Member	1945
Deng Xiaoping	Vice Premier	1954–1966	Standing Member	1956
Deng Xiaoping	Vice Premier	1973–1976	Standing Member	1975
Deng Xiaoping	Vice Premier	1977–1980	Standing Member	1977
Deng Zihui	Vice Premier	1954–1965	Non-Member	
He Long	Vice Premier	1954–1966	Full Member	1956
Chen Yi	Vice Premier	1954–1966	Full Member	1956
Ulanhu	Vice Premier	1954–1966	Alternate Member	1956
Li Fuchun	Vice Premier	1954–1966	Standing Member	1966
Li Xiannian	Vice Premier	1954–1966	Full Member	1956
Li Xiannian	Vice Premier	1975–1980	Standing Member	1977
Nie Rongzhen	Vice Premier	1959–1966	Full Member	1966
Bo Yibo	Vice Premier	1959–1966	Alternate Member	1956
Bo Yibo	Vice Premier	1979–1982	Non-Member	
Tan Zhenlin	Vice Premier	1959–1966	Full Member	1958
Lu Dingyi	Vice Premier	1959–1966	Alternate Member	1956
Luo Ruiqing	Vice Premier	1959–1966	Non-Member	
Xi Zhongxun	Vice Premier	1959–1962	Non-Member	
Ke Qingshi	Vice Premier	1965–1965	Full Member	1958
Tao Zhu	Vice Premier	1965–1966	Standing Member	1966
Xie Fuzhi	Vice Premier	1965–1966	Alternate Member	1966
Zhang Chunqiao	Vice Premier	1975–1976	Standing Member	1973
Chen Xilian	Vice Premier	1975–1980	Full Member	1969
Ji Dengkui	Vice Premier	1975–1980	Full Member	1973
Hua Guofeng	Vice Premier	1975–1976	Standing Member	1976
Chen Yonggui	Vice Premier	1975–1980	Full Member	1973
Wu Guixian (female)	Vice Premier	1975–1982	Alternate Member	1973
Wang Zhen	Vice Premier	1975–1980	Full Member	1978
Yu Qiuli	Vice Premier	1975–1982	Full Member	1977
Gu Mu	Vice Premier	1975–1982	Non-Member	

(*Continued*)

Table 2.1 (*Continued*)

Name	Title	Tenure	The Politburo	From
Sun Jian	Vice Premier	1975–1978	Non-Member	
Xu Xianqian	Vice Premier	1978–1980	Full Member	1977
Geng Biao	Vice Premier	1978–1982	Full Member	1977
Fang Yi	Vice Premier	1978–1982	Full Member	1977
Kang Shi'en	Vice Premier	1978–1982	Non-Member	
Chen Muhua (female)	Vice Premier	1978–1982	Alternate Member	1977
Wang Renzhong	Vice Premier	1978–1980	Non-Member	
Yao Yilin	Vice Premier	1979–1993	Standing Member	1987
Ji Pengfei	Vice Premier	1979–1982	Non-Member	
Zhao Ziyang	Vice Premier	1980–1982	Standing Member	1980
Wan Li	Vice Premier	1980–1988	Full Member	1982
Yang Jingren	Vice Premier	1980–1982	Non-Member	
Zhang Aiping	Vice Premier	1980–1982	Non-Member	
Huang Hua	Vice Premier	1980–1982	Non-Member	
Li Peng	Vice Premier	1983–1988	Standing Member	1987
Tian Jiyun	Vice Premier	1983–1993	Full Member	1985
Qiao Shi	Vice Premier	1986–1988	Full Member	1985
Wu Xueqian	Vice Premier	1988–1993	Full Member	1985
Zhu Rongji	Vice Premier	1991–1998	Standing Member	1992
Zou Jiahua	Vice Premier	1993–1998	Full Member	1992
Qian Qichen	Vice Premier	1993–2003	Full Member	1992
Li Lanqing	Vice Premier	1993–2003	Standing Member	1997
Wu Bangguo	Vice Premier	1995–2003	Full Member	1992
Wen Jiabao	Vice Premier	1998–2003	Full Member	1997
Jiang Chunyun	Vice Premier	1995–1998	Full Member	1992
Yu Qiuli	State Councilor	1982–1983	Full Member	1977
Geng Biao	State Councilor	1982–1983	Non-Member	
Fang Yi	State Councilor	1982–1988	Full Member	1977
Gu Mu	State Councilor	1982–1988	Non-Member	
Kang Shi'en	State Councilor	1982–1988	Non-Member	
Chen Muhua (female)	State Councilor	1982–1988	Alternate Member	1977
Bo Yibo	State Councilor	1982–1983	Non-Member	
Ji Pengfei	State Councilor	1982–1988	Non-Member	
Huang Hua	State Councilor	1982–1983	Non-Member	
Zhang Jingfu	State Councilor	1982–1988	Non-Member	
Zhang Aiping	State Councilor	1982–1988	Non-Member	
Wu Xueqian	State Councilor	1983–1988	Non-Member	
Wang Bingqian	State Councilor	1983–1988	Non-Member	
Song Ping	State Councilor	1983–1988	Non-Member	

(*Continued*)

Table 2.1 (*Continued*)

Name	Title	Tenure	The Politburo	From
Song Jian	State Councilor	1986–1998	Non-Member	
Li Tieying	State Councilor	1988–1998	Full Member	1987
Qin Jiwei	State Councilor	1988–1993	Full Member	1987
Wang Fang	State Councilor	1988–1993	Non-Member	
Zou Jiahua	State Councilor	1988–1993	Non-Member	
Li Guixian	State Councilor	1988–1998	Non-Member	
Chen Xitong	State Councilor	1988–1993	Non-Member	
Chen Junsheng	State Councilor	1988–1998	Non-Member	
Chi Haotian	State Councilor	1993–2003	Full Member	1997
Ismail Amat	State Councilor	1993–2003	Non-Member	
Peng Peiyuan (female)	State Councilor	1993–1998	Non-Member	
Luo Gan	State Councilor	1993–2003	Full Member	1997
Wu Yi (female)	State Councilor	1998–2003	Alternate Member	1997
Wang Zhongyu	State Councilor	1998–2003	Non-Member	

Sources: *Zhongguo Gongchandang Zhizheng Sishinian* (*The forty years of the Chinese Communist Party*) (Beijing: Zhonggong Dangshi Ziliao Chubanshe, 1989), pp. 560–565; http://www.people.com.cn/item/lianghui/zlhb/rd/8jie/newfiles/a1160.html; http://www.people.com.cn/item/lianghui/zlhb/rd/9jie/newfiles/a1430.html; http://news.xinhuanet.com/ziliao/2004-10/19/content_2108720.htm; http://news.xinhuanet.com/ziliao/2004-10/19/content_2110171.htm.

member of the Politburo nor a member of the central committee of the CCP.[12] Since 1993, this office has been assumed by a standing member of the Politburo.

Sixth, since 1988, vice premiers have all been full members of the Politburo and the executive vice premier has been a standing member of the Politburo. Three vice premiers (Yao Yilin, Tian Jiyun, and Wu Xueqian) in 1988 were all full members of the Politburo; and Yao Yilin, the executive vice premier, was a standing member of the Politburo. Zhu Rongji (1928–) was only an alternate member of the Thirteenth Central Committee when he was appointed as a vice premier in April 1991, but he soon entered the Politburo as a standing member at the First Plenum of the Fourteenth Central Committee

---

[12] For the list of former CNPPCC chairmen and their bios, see http://news.xinhuanet.com/ziliao/2004-11/15/content_2221260.htm.

in October 1992. Therefore, four vice premiers (Zhu Rongji, Zou Jiahua, Qian Qichen, and Li Lanqing) in 1993 were all full members of the Politburo; Zhu Rongji, the executive vice premier, was a standing member of the Politburo. The same was true of the vice premiers of 1998 (Li Lanqing, Qian Qichen, Wu Bangguo, and Wen Jiabao): They were all full members of the Politburo with Li Lanqing (executive vice premier) as a standing member of the Politburo.[13]

Seventh, state councilors are generally not members of the Politburo, but a few of them did enter the Politburo. Yu Qiuli (1914–1999) and Fang Yi (1916–1997) were major exceptions, because they entered the Politburo as vice premiers instead of state councilors. Both were full members of the two consecutive Politburos (1977–1987). Yu was a vice premier from 1975 to 1982, and Fang was a vice premier from 1978 to 1982, but they were both reappointed as state councilors along with seven other former vice premiers in the reshuffles of May 1982. Similarly, Chen Muhua (1921–) had also served as a vice premier (1978–1982) before she was made a state councilor in May 1982. She was an alternate member of the Politburo from 1977 to 1987.

As mentioned in Chapter 1, Li Tieying (1936–) presented a unique case. He was a state councilor for two consecutive terms from 1988 to 1998 and was a full member of the Politburo for three consecutive terms from 1987 to 2002.[14] In retrospect, Li might have been groomed for a more important position. His experience in the central committee of the CCP parallels that of Hu Jintao. He entered the Twelfth Central Committee in September 1982 as an alternate member along with Hu Jintao and was promoted to a full membership in September 1985 along with Hu Jintao. He entered the Politburo five years earlier than Hu Jintao but became stagnated afterwards. He is the only state councilor who was a full Politburo member during his entire tenure. Luo Gan (1935–) also served as a state councilor for

---

[13] For a detailed description of Zhu Rongji's cabinet members, see Ning Xianghan and Wen Siyuan, *Zhu Rongji de Neige* (*Zhu Rongji's cabinet*) (Carle Place, NY: Mirror Books, 1998).

[14] For a detailed evaluation of Li Tieying, see Zong Hairen, *Disidai*, pp. 464–468.

two consecutive terms (1993–2003), but he did not enter the Politburo until 1997. Wu Yi (1938–) was only an alternate member of the Politburo during her tenure as a state councilor.

Qin Jiwei (1914–1997) and Chi Haotian (1929–) became full members of the Politburo not for their assignment as state councilors but as representatives of the Central Military Commission. Qin entered the Twelfth Politburo as an alternate member in September 1982 and became a full member of the Politburo in November 1987. He was subsequently made a member of the Central Military Commission of the PRC as well as a state councilor and defense minister in April 1988. Chi's story is slightly different. He took over as a state councilor and defense minister in March 1993, but did not enter the Politburo until 1997.[15]

Eighth, pursuant to the last point, there should usually be two Politburo members from the military. One person, as mentioned above, usually is concurrently a state councilor and defense minister; another, vice chairman of the Central Military Commission. This practice emerged in the late 1980s. In the Thirteenth Politburo, the two military members were Yang Shangkun and Qin Jiwei. In the Fourteenth Politburo, the two military members were Liu Huaqing and Yang Baibing. Interestingly, Liu Huaqing was made a standing member of the Politburo, whereas Yang Baibing was removed from the Central Military Commission. The two military members in the Fifteenth Politburo were Chi Haotian and Zhang Wannian.

Ninth, party secretaries of elite provincial units[16] are also likely to be members of the Politburo. However, not all elite provincial units are fixed in their elite status. Tianjin and Sichuan both had seats in the Politburo in 1987, but were later dropped. Shandong and Guangdong emerged in 1992, while Tibet got it and lost it in the same year. Party Secretary Li Changchun of Henan entered the

---

[15] Yang Baibing was inducted into the Politburo in 1992 probably as an exchange for his membership in the Central Military Commission.

[16] An elite provincial unit is one that has a seat in the Politburo. For a detailed discussion, see Zhiyue Bo, *Chinese Provincial Leaders: Economic Performance and Political Mobility Since 1949* (Armonk, N.Y.: M.E. Sharpe, 2002), pp. 24–27.

Politburo in 1997 for an assignment in Guangdong, while Party Secretary Xie Fei (a Politburo member) of Guangdong was getting ready to retire. Two centrally administered municipalities — Beijing and Shanghai — have basically maintained their elite status since 1987. All party secretaries of Beijing between 1987 and 2002 were Politburo members. Li Ximing (1926–), party secretary of Beijing since 1984, entered the Politburo at the First Plenum of the Thirteenth Central Committee in November 1987.[17] Chen Xitong (1930–) entered the Politburo in October 1992 before he was appointed as party secretary of Beijing in December 1992.[18] Wei Jianxing (1931–) was already a Politburo member when he replaced Chen Xitong in April 1995; his successor, Jia Qinglin (1940–), entered the Politburo in September 1997. Similarly, most party secretaries of Shanghai between 1987 and 2002 were full members of the Politburo, except for Zhu Rongji. Jiang Zemin, Wu Bangguo, and Huang Ju all became Politburo members, because they were the party secretaries of Shanghai.

Finally, as far as candidates for the central committee are concerned, an informal rule is that provincial party secretaries and governors as well as ministers should usually be full members of the central committee, but this rule has not always been strictly followed.[19]

---

[17] For his bio, see Shen Xueming and Zheng Jianying (eds), *Zhonggong Diyijie zhi Dishiwujie Zhongyangweiyuan* (*The Central Committee Members of the Chinese Communist Party from the First through the Fifteenth Central Committee*) (Beijing: Zhongyang Wenxian Chubanshe, 2001), pp. 347–348.

[18] For his bio, see Shen Xueming and Zheng Jianying, *Zhonggong Diyijie zhi Dishiwujie Zhongyangweiyuan*, p. 479.

[19] For a detailed analysis of the central-committee membership of the provincial party secretaries and governors between 1982 and 2001, see Zhiyue Bo, "The provinces: training ground for national leaders or a power in their own right?" in David M. Finkelstein and Maryanne Kivlehan (eds), *China's Leadership in the 21st Century: The Rise of the Fourth Generation*, (Armonk, NY: M. E. Sharpe, 2003), pp. 81–85.

Specific Rules for the Sixteenth Central Committee

At a meeting on the Sixteenth Party Congress in March 2001, the Fifteenth Politburo Standing Committee introduced guidelines for the composition of the Sixteenth Central Committee and specified qualifications for its members.[20] In addition to a very general ideological guideline, the Party center outlined the age structure of the new central committee: Those who age below 50 years should take at least one fifth of all central committee members.

As for candidates for a membership in the new central committee, they would have to possess the following qualifications.[21] First, they would have to "hold high the banner of Deng Xiaoping Theory and take the lead in implementing the important thought of 'Three Represents.'" This was an ideological qualification. Deng Xiaoping Theory is Deng Xiaoping's policy of economic reforms and opening to the outside world; this theory was enshrined into the CCP Constitution in 1997. No one including Jiang Zemin dared to remove this theory as this being an important ideological qualification for a new central committee member. But Jiang Zemin hastened to add his own theory of the "Three Represents" as another ideological criterion, quietly elevating himself to the same status as that of Deng Xiaoping. Yet the "Three Represents" was a political slogan void of any policy implications. Aspirant politicians simply needed to mouth this slogan in their political discourse.

Second, they ought to have consistently acted in unison with the Party Center with Jiang Zemin at the core. This was a political qualification that was especially significant for local leaders. Since the

---

[20] See He Ping and Liu Siyang, "Xinhuashe: Jianfuqi Jiwangkailai de Zhangyao Shiming — Dang de Xinyijian Zhongyang Weiyuanhui Danshengji" ("Xinhua News Agency: shoulder the solemn mission of succession — the story of the birth of a new central committee of the Chinese Communist Party"), *Renminwang*, November 15, 2002. http://www.peopledaily.com.cn/GB/shizheng/252/8956/9419/20021115/867200.html.

[21] The following description of these qualifications is based on He Ping and Liu Siyang, "Xinhuashe: Jianfuqi Jiwangkailai de Zhangyao Shiming." But the interpretations of these qualifications are mine.

early 1990s, Jiang Zemin had been rotating local leaders between the Center and provinces and among different provincial units in order to maintain central control over localities. Local leaders, especially provincial leaders, gradually lost their local identities because of constant reshuffling and became loyal agents of the Center.[22]

Third, they ought to have maintained a good thinking style, learning style, work style, leadership style, and lifestyle. This was about the personal character of a candidate. Fourth, they ought to have been open minded, pragmatic, responsible, innovative, and outstanding in performance. Finally, they ought to have established a correct view of power, of status, and of interests; to have closely related to the masses and served the people wholeheartedly; and to have been clean, virtuous, and to have enjoyed good reputation within and outside the Party. These three qualifications were all very important but difficult to determine. Whether a candidate possessed these qualifications has to be determined on an individual basis.

SELECTION PROCESS

Selecting Top Party Leaders

China's top leaders such as Politburo members are chosen through a two-stage process: selection and election. At the first stage candidates are selected according to the rules mentioned above. The group that makes the selection may be properly called the "selectorate." The "selectorate" in China, according to Susan L. Shirk, consists of fewer than 500 top party leaders including (i) the central committee, (ii) the Communist Party elders, (iii) the leaders of the PLA, and (iv) the preeminent leader.[23] However, neither the central

---

[22] For a detailed study of elite management in the Post-Deng era, see Zhiyue Bo, "The institutionalization of elite management in China," in Barry J. Naughton and Dali L. Yang (eds), *Holding China Together: Diversity and National Integration in the Post-Deng Era*, (New York: Cambridge University Press, 2004), pp. 70–100.

[23] Susan L. Shirk, *The Political Logic of Economic Reform in China* (Berkeley, CA: University of California Press, 1993), p. 81. It should be noted that Shirk's theory has yet to be empirically affirmed. For a critical analysis of her theory, see Dali Yang,

committee as a whole nor the leaders of the PLA are usually involved in the selection process.

In the eras of Mao Zedong and Deng Xiaoping, the preeminent leader usually had the final say in selecting a candidate for the office of Party chairman (or later general secretary). Yet, different preeminent leaders had different weights in deciding the fate of the candidate for the topmost office. Mao Zedong seems to have had the ultimate and unchallengeable authority in this regard. It was he who decided initially that Liu Shaoqi be his successor as Party chairman. But he later struck Liu down and propelled Lin Biao to the highest position next to his. After Lin died in a plane crash in 1971, Mao first favored Wang Hongwen and then turned to Deng Xiaoping and eventually chose Hua Guofeng.

In contrast, Deng Xiaoping was dominant in selecting a candidate for the post of general secretary but he also needed to consult with a number of other elderly veteran leaders. Deng selected Hu Yaobang as the top Party leader in 1980 but decided to fire him in 1987 because of his deviation from Deng's political line. Deng supported Zhao Ziyang as general secretary of the Party in 1987 but dismissed him two years later in the midst of the Tiananmen Incident.

During its 10 years of existence from 1982 to 1992, the Central Advisory Commission (CAC) played some limited roles in selecting the top Party leader. Although the CAC played a critical role in ousting Hu Yaobang and installing Zhao Ziyang in 1987,[24] its role was often a bit exaggerated. This is because China scholars tend to regard Deng Xiaoping, Chen Yun, and Li Xiannian as Party elders irrespective of their formal institutional affiliations. According to Richard Baum, for instance, Chen Yun was a member of the CAC in

---

"Governing China's transition to the market: institutional incentives, politicians' choices, and unintended outcomes," *World Politics*, Vol. 48, No. 3 (April 1996), pp. 424–452. For an empirical test of her hypothesis that does not support her theory, see Zhiyue Bo, *Chinese Provincial Leaders*, Chapter 2.

[24] Richard Baum, *Burying Mao: Chinese Politics in the Age of Deng Xiaoping* (Princeton, NJ: Princeton University Press, 1994), pp. 206–208.

January 1987. As he wrote, "Endorsed by key members of the CAC, including Chen Yun, Zhao's nomination was unanimously approved by the Politburo."[25] But Chen Yun was not a member of the CAC at the time of the enlarged Politburo meeting on January 16, 1987. He was a standing member of the Politburo and did not become a member of the CAC until November 1987 at the Thirteenth National Congress. Moreover, Deng Xiaoping was also a standing member of the Politburo at that time. In addition to Hu Yaobang, the rest of the Politburo standing members in January 1987 included Zhao Ziyang and Li Xiannian. In other words, out of the five standing members three (Deng Xiaoping, Chen Yun, and Li Xiannian) were veteran elders. Institutionally, these elders made the decision not on behalf of the CAC but on behalf of the Politburo Standing Committee.[26] According to a report from the *People's Daily*, the Standing Committee of the Politburo called for a party-life meeting between January 10 and 15, at which Hu Yaobang presented his resignation.[27] In view of this new evidence, the enlarged meeting of the Politburo on January 16, which was attended by 18 Politburo members and 17 leading members of the CAC,[28] was less significant than we used to believe it to be. Another well-known but often misconstrued example is the agreement between Deng Xiaoping and Chen Yun in 1987 that Yang Shangkun should continue in the Politburo after both of them retired. Again, both Deng and Chen were standing members instead of CAC members.

---

[25] *Ibid.*, p. 211.

[26] For a similar view, see Frederick C. Teiwes, "The paradoxical post-Mao transition: from obeying the leader to 'normal politics'" in Jonathan Unger (ed), *The Nature of Chinese Politics: From Mao to Jiang* (Armonk, N.Y.: M.E. Sharpe, 2002), pp. 81–85.

[27] See "Zhongguo Gongchandang Bashinian Dashiji: 1987" ("The chronology of the eighty years of the Chinese Communist Party: 1987"), *Renminwang*, http://news. Xinhuanet.com/ziliao/2004-10/15/content_2093969.htm. This episode is ostensibly missing from Baum's account.

[28] *Zhongguo Gongchandang Zhizheng Sishinian* (*The Forty Years of the Chinese Communist Party in Power*) (Beijing: Zhonggong Dangshi Ziliao Chubanshe, 1989), p. 551.

With the recommendations of Chen Yun and Li Xiannian,[29] Deng Xiaoping chose Jiang Zemin as Zhao Ziyang's replacement in May 1989. In this case, Deng, Chen, and Li acted as Party elders because none of them were members of the Politburo at that time. Deng, again as the preeminent leader and a Party elder, also selected Hu Jintao as Jiang Zemin's successor in 1992, even though he had no political office at that time.

Jiang Zemin was not a preeminent leader; he was simply the first among equals. He had to accept Deng Xiaoping's choice for his own replacement, although he might favor someone else.[30] It is reported that Jiang failed twice in 2000[31] and 2001[32] to promote his confidant, Zeng Qinghong, from an alternate to a full member of the Politburo.[33]

As for selecting the Politburo members, the selectorate might initially be a small group in charge of personnel changes at the next Party congress. The Gao-Rao Affair, for instance, was triggered by a draft list of Politburo members of the Eighth Central Committee proposed by An Ziwen, deputy director of the Central Organization

---

[29] For an account with "leaked" secret documents, see Zhang Liang, Andrew J. Nathan, and Perry Link, *The Tiananmen Papers: The Chinese Leadership's Decision to Use Force Against Their Own People — in Their Own Words* (New York: Public Affairs, 2001), pp. 297–317.

[30] Evidently, the "core" became weaker, as both Parris Chang and Frederick Teiwes noted. See Parris Chang, *Power and Policy in China* (3rd edition) (Dubuque, Iowa: Kendall/Hunt, 1991), pp. 243–270; Teiwes, "The paradoxical post-Mao transition," p. 96.

[31] Lowell Dittmer, "The changing form and dynamics of power politics," in *The Nature of Chinese Politics: from Mao to Jiang*, p. 237. He quoted from Willy Lam, "Not all the president's men," *South China Morning Post*, October 25, 2000.

[32] Susan L. Shirk, "The delayed institutionalization of leadership politics," in *The Nature of Chinese Politics: from Mao to Jiang*, p. 308.

[33] However, according to Zong Hairen, these were simply rumors and the fact is that Zeng's promotion to the full membership of the Politburo was never listed in the agenda of the Plenums of the Fifteenth Central Committee. See Zong Hairen, *Disidai*, pp. 313, 314.

Department at that time.[34] Zhou Enlai, Kang Sheng, and Huang Yongsheng were in charge of drafting a list of Politburo members for the Ninth Central Committee.[35]

Historically, some family members of top leaders were somehow also involved in the process. Ye Qun, Lin Biao's wife, for instance, reportedly took advantage of Lin's illness to endorse a draft list of Politburo members on behalf of Lin without his knowledge.[36] Occasionally, some former senior leaders could also play some role in the process. Bo Yibo, for instance, was reportedly instrumental in establishing the rule of age 70 for Politburo members with the exception of Jiang Zemin.[37]

But once an initial list was drafted, it would have to be endorsed by the preeminent leader and other standing members of the Politburo. Politburo standing members all have some influence on the composition of the next Politburo because the Standing Committee of the Politburo is the organ that discusses and deliberates the membership of the next Politburo. Finally, this list has to be approved by the Politburo.

Apparently, it was the Fifteenth Politburo Standing Committee that decided the composition of the Sixteenth Politburo, especially its standing committee and Jiang Zemin and Li Peng played a very important role. According to Zong Hairen, the Fifteenth Politburo Standing Committee made the critical decision with regard to the new Politburo Standing Committee on October 17, 2002, and Jiang Zemin and Li Peng conspired to remove Li Ruihuan and install Jia Qinglin and Huang Ju.[38] Before then, the candidates for the new

---

[34] See Frederick Teiwes, *Politics at Mao's Court: Gao Gang and Party Factionalism in the Early 1950s* (Armonk, NY: M.E. Sharpe, 1990), pp. 96–104.

[35] Frederick C. Teiwes and Warren Sun, *The Tragedy of Lin Biao* (Honolulu: University of Hawaii Press, 1996), p. 13.

[36] *Ibid.*, p. 13.

[37] Richard Baum, "Jiang takes command: the Fifteenth National Party Congress and beyond," in Hung-mao Tien ad Yun-han Chu (eds), *China under Jiang Zemin* (Boulder, CO: Lynne Rienner, 2000), pp. 24, 25.

[38] Zong Hairen, *Aimei de Quanli Jiaohuan* (*Ambiguous Transition*) (Carle Place, NY: Mirror Books, 2003), pp. 41–44.

Politburo Standing Committee had been seven people: Hu Jintao, Li Ruihuan, Wen Jiabao, Wu Bangguo, Zeng Qinghong, Luo Gan, and Li Changchun. What this meeting eventually decided was to replace Li Ruihuan with Wu Guangzheng, Jia Qinglin, and Huang Ju. Challenged by Jiang Zemin, Li Ruihuan indicated his desire not to enter the new Politburo. He then nominated Wu Guangzheng as a candidate for the new Politburo Standing Committee. After the Fifteenth Politburo Standing Committee agreed to Wu's candidacy, Li Peng introduced Jia Qinglin and Huang Ju as candidates for the new Politburo Standing Committee. Jiang Zemin immediately expressed his endorsement and passed the issue to Hu Jintao. With Hu's agreement, a final list of candidates for the new Politburo Standing Committee was decided. As mentioned in Chapter 1, Jiang Zemin sprang into action within a week. His private secretary, Jia Ting'an, reportedly telephoned Tian Congming, head of the Xinhua News Agency, in the afternoon of October 21, 2002 and asked Tian to make an announcement about personnel changes in which Jia Qinglin and Huang Ju were to be transferred to the Center.[39] The next day, October 22, 2002, when Jiang Zemin was departing for his final official visit to the United States,[40] the Xinhua News Agency released the news.[41] Clearly, Jiang wanted to prevent the Politburo from changing its mind on Jia and Huang as candidates for the new Politburo Standing Committee during his trip abroad.[42]

Because of Jiang Zemin's objections, Li Keqiang[43] and Xi Jinping[44] failed to be listed as candidates for the new Politburo. Li and Xi had been groomed as candidates for the Sixteenth Politburo Standing Committee since the spring of 2001. The small group in charge of personnel changes for the Sixteenth Central Committee

---

[39] Zong Hairen, *Aimei de Quanli Jiaohuan*, p. 46.
[40] See http://past.people.com.cn/GB/shizheng/252/2140/2840/20021022/848090.html.
[41] See http://past.people.com.cn/GB/shizheng/19/20021023/848844.html.
[42] Zong Hairen, *Aimei de Quanli Jiaohuan*, p. 46.
[43] For a detailed evaluation of Li Keqiang, see Zong Hairen, *Disidai*, pp. 421–463.
[44] For a detailed evaluation of Xi Jinping, see Zong Hairen, *Disidai*, pp. 389–420.

evaluated both of them and made a report to the Fifteenth Politburo Standing Committee. Its comments on Li Keqiang's performance as governor of Henan were very favorable.[45] Out of his selfish motivations, Jiang rejected Li and Xi at a meeting on October 9, 2002.[46] According to Jiang, there were no such things as the fourth generation leadership and the fifth generation leadership, and the Party center was not arranging a lineup for the fourth generation leadership, nor was it grooming a fifth generation leadership. Under the suggestion of Zeng Qinghong, the Party center decided to transfer Xi Jinping from Fujian to Zhejiang. Three days later, on October 12, 2002, Xi Jinping was removed as governor of Fujian and nominated as a candidate for the post of Zhejiang's governor.[47]

Jiang Zemin also reportedly blocked the promotion of Song Defu, party secretary of Fujian, into the Politburo. Song Defu (1946–) had been a strong candidate for a membership in the Sixteenth Politburo.[48] His seniority in the central committee of the CCP is comparable to that of a number of candidates for the Sixteenth Politburo Standing Committee. He entered the Twelfth Central Committee as an alternate member in September 1985 along with Wu Bangguo, Wu Guangzheng, Li Changchun, and Luo Gan, and had been a full member of the Thirteenth, Fourteenth, and Fifteenth Central Committees. In contrast, Huang Ju was only an alternate member of the Thirteenth Central Committee, and Jia Qinglin did not enter the central committee until 1992. According to Zong Hairen, Jiang objected Song Defu partly out of his consideration for the balance of different factional groups in the new Politburo: Since Hu Jintao, Wang Zhaoguo, and Liu Yunshan had already been made candidates for the new Politburo as representatives of the Chinese Communist Youth League (CCYL) Group, the CCYL Group would be overrepresented if Song Defu were to be added.[49]

---

[45] Zong Hairen, *Aimei de Quanli Jiaohuan*, p. 214.
[46] *Ibid.*, p. 71.
[47] See http://past.people.com.cn/GB/other4583/4595/5840/20021012/840764.html.
[48] For his bio, see http://news.xinhuanet.com/ziliao/2002-02/22/content_286747.htm.
[49] Zong Hairen, *Aimei de Quanli Jiaohuan*, p. 204.

Finally, contrary to the expectations of Shirk's theory, the central committee did not play any role in the selection process. Neither the Sixth Plenum (September 24–26, 2001) nor the Seventh Plenum (November 3–5, 2002) of the Fifteenth Central Committee mentioned anything about candidates for the new Politburo.[50]

Selecting Central Committee Members

Simultaneous to the process of selecting top Party leaders, candidates for the new central committee were also being selected. Formal selection process for the new central committee started in March 2001 when Jiang Zemin chaired a meeting of the Fifteenth Politburo Standing Committee and a meeting of the Fifteenth Politburo on the Sixteenth National Party Congress.[51] These meetings focused on personnel issues, laid out guiding lines and basic principles in these regards, and designated a task force in charge of the preparation for the Sixteenth Party Congress. The Party leadership decided that under the direct leadership of the Fifteenth Politburo Standing Committee, the task force would be responsible for recommending, screening, and nominating candidates for the Sixteenth Central Committee and the Sixteenth Central Disciplinary Inspection Commission. The task force was also made responsible for managing and directing the election of deputies to the Sixteenth National Party Congress. These meetings decided that the Sixteenth Party Congress would be held in the latter half of 2002 and that one of the most important agendas of the Congress would be to elect a new central committee and a new central disciplinary inspecting commission.

The Sixteenth Party Congress task force initially proposed 514 candidates for the central committee and 199 candidates for the central disciplinary inspection commission accordingly. Between May 2001 and March 2002, 51 screening teams were sent to 98 central

---

[50] See http://news.xinhuanet.com/ziliao/2003-01/20/content_697219.htm.
[51] See He Ping and Liu Siyang, "Xinhuashe: Jianfuqi Jiwangkailai de Zhangyao Shiming."

party and government institutions, 11 financial institutions, 23 key state enterprises, 31 provincial units, and all military regions as well as armed police forces. These teams conducted more than 19,200 interviews and collected numerous surveys. As a result, these teams recommended 462 candidates for the central committee and 179 candidates for the central disciplinary inspection commission.

The Fifteenth Politburo Standing Committee served as the selectorate throughout the entire process. It held 12 meetings during this period, listening to reports and issuing instructions. On October 31, 2002, the Fifteenth Politburo Standing Committee approved a list of candidates for the Sixteenth Central Committee and the Sixteenth Central Disciplinary Inspection Commission, and the same list was approved by the Politburo the following day.[52]

Again, the Fifteenth Central Committee probably did not play any role in the selection of these initial candidates. There is no mention of any discussion of the recommended list at its Seventh Plenum of November 3–5, 2002.

The Presidium of the Sixteenth National Congress

Once an initial list of candidates had been selected, the first stage — selection — was over; the second stage — election — began. In the election process, the Presidium of a Party congress usually plays a formal management role during the congress. Yet the CCP Constitution has no specification of the role and functions of the Presidium of a Party congress.

The Sixteenth Party Congress had 2,114 deputies and 40 guest deputies.[53] At its preparation meeting on November 7, 2002, the deputies approved by a show of hands a list of 24 members for a qualification review committee, a list of 236 members for a presidium, and Hu Jintao as secretary general.[54] In the same day, the presidium held its first meeting and approved a list of 32 members for the Standing Committee of the Presidium.

---

[52] *Ibid.*
[53] *Renmin ribao*, November 8, 2002, p. 1.
[54] *Renmin ribao*, November 8, 2002, p. 1.

Table 2.2 Standing Committee of the Presidium of the
Sixteenth National Congress of the CCP (2002)

	Number	Percent
Standing members of the Fifteenth Politburo	7	21.88
Full members of the Fifteenth Politburo	14	43.75
Alternate members of the Fifteenth Politburo	2	6.25
Second generation leaders	7	21.88
Others	2	6.25
Total	32	100.00

Source: Author's database.

The Standing Committee of the Presidium was composed of two groups of people: the Fifteenth Politburo members and veteran officials (Table 2.2). Among the 32 standing members, 23 were from the Fifteenth Politburo, representing 72 percent. Among the rest of the Standing Committee of the Presidium, one may find former senior leaders such as Bo Yibo, Song Ping, Song Renqiong, Wan Li, Qiao Shi, and Liu Huaqing. Apparently, the majority of the standing members were not candidates for the Sixteenth Central Committee. Thirteen out of 23 Fifteenth Politburo members retired, representing 57 percent. The remaining nine non-Fifteenth Politburo members were not candidates for the Sixteenth Central Committee. In other words, 69 percent of the members of the Standing Committee of the Presidium were people other than those who would have direct personal stakes in the election. In this sense, the Standing Committee of the Presidium was not a completely self-selecting one.

Moreover, the core of the Standing Committee of the Presidium, the Fifteenth Politburo Standing Committee, was mostly composed of people who would not be candidates for the Sixteenth Central Committee. Among the seven members of the Fifteenth Politburo Standing Committee, six (86 percent) would not be candidates for the Sixteenth Central Committee. In this sense, the core of the Standing Committee of the Presidium selected others instead of themselves.

The Sixteenth Party Congress began on November 8, 2002. Theoretically, that was the day when the Fifteenth Central

Committee and its Politburo came to an end and the Presidium of the Congress took over. But since the Fifteenth Politburo members were all members of the Standing Committee of the Presidium, it did not really matter much in practical terms.

The Presidium held three meetings during the congress of November 8–14, 2002. At its second meeting on November 10, 2002, Hu Jintao — on behalf of the Fifteenth Politburo — explained a list of candidates as full and alternate members in the Sixteenth Central Committee and a list of candidates for the Sixteenth Central Disciplinary Inspection Commission. The Presidium approved these lists and passed them onto deputies.[55] After deliberation, delegations conducted a preelection: 198 candidates out of 208 were elected as full members of the Sixteenth Central Committee; 158 candidates out of 167 were elected as alternate members of the Sixteenth Central Committee; 121 candidates out of 128 were elected as members of the Sixteenth Central Disciplinary Inspection Commission.[56]

At its third meeting on November 13, 2002, the Presidium approved the lists of preelected candidates by a show of hands.[57] Amazingly, these candidates were all elected intact by the Party Congress on November 14, 2002: No one was eliminated; no one was added; and nobody's status was changed. The Congress produced 198 full members and 158 alternate members of the Sixteenth Central Committee and 121 members of the Sixteenth Central Disciplinary Inspection Commission.[58]

In retrospect, the Presidium was a self-serving apparatus. Among the members of the Presidium, 136 (58 percent) were members of the Fifteenth Central Committee: 111 full members and 25 alternate members. However, 100 of them were reelected to the Sixteenth Central Committee, representing 74 percent of the

---

[55] He Ping and Liu Siyang, "Xinhuashe: Jianfuqi Jiwangkailai de Zhangyao Shiming." It should be noted that these were not reported in *Renmin ribao*. See *Renmin ribao*, November 11, 2002, p. 1.
[56] *Ibid.*
[57] *Renmin ribao*, November 14, 2002, p. 1.
[58] *Renmin ribao*, November 15, 2002, p. 1.

Fifteenth CC members of the Presidium. Among these 100 people, 97 entered the Sixteenth CC as full members and only three as alternate members. In other words, among the original full members, 76 out of 77 (99 percent) stayed on as full members; among the original alternate members, 21 out of 23 (91 percent) were promoted to full members. Only 34 full members and two alternate members[59] of the Fifteenth Central Committee who were members of the Presidium did not make it to the Sixteenth Central Committee. Clearly, at least 100 members of the Presidium were in fact selecting themselves for the Sixteenth Central Committee, representing 42 percent of all members of the Presidium.

Moreover, among these 100 members of the Presidium who were not members of the Fifteenth Central Committee, 49 (49 percent) were elected into the Sixteenth Central Committee. Among these new central committee members, 37 (76 percent) were full members and 12 (24 percent) were alternates. In other words, there were altogether 149 members of the Presidium who were selecting themselves, representing 63 percent of all members of the Presidium (Table 2.3). Clearly, this Presidium is not one that serves as a rubber stamp for a list of other candidates. The majority of the members were actually selecting themselves as candidates for the Sixteenth Central Committee. It was a self-serving presidium.

At its First Plenum on November 15, 2002, the Sixteenth Central Committee elected its Politburo and its Standing Committee, approved a Secretariat nominated by the Politburo Standing Committee of the Sixteenth Central Committee, decided a Central Military Commission, and approved the secretary, deputy secretaries, and standing members of the Sixteenth Central Disciplinary Inspection Commission elected by its First Plenum. After more than two years of preparation and negotiation, a new central committee was finally born.

---

[59] They are Chen Jiaer and Guo Shuyan. Both of them would be too old for a membership in the Sixteenth Central Committee. Chen was born in 1934 and was 68 years old in 2002; and Guo was born in 1935 and was 67 years old in 2002.

Table 2.3 Composition of the Presidium of the Sixteenth National Congress of the CCP (2002)

	Number	Percent
Sixteenth CC members		
Full members	134	
Alternate members	15	
Subtotal	149	63.1
Non-Sixteenth CC members		
Subtotal	87	36.9
Total	236	100.0

Source: Author's database.

Outcome

Evidently, the Fifteenth Politburo Standing Committee played a very important role in determining the lineup of the new Politburo, and Jiang Zemin's influence was more prominent than other standing members. The Sixteenth Politburo Standing Committee was expanded from seven to nine members (Table 2.4). They were Hu Jintao, Wu Bangguo, Wen Jiabao, Jia Qinglin, Zeng Qinghong, Huang Ju, Wu Guangzheng, Li Changchun, and Luo Gan. Three of them (Wu Bangguo, Zeng Qinghong, and Huang Ju) were Shanghai Gang members, and Jia Qinglin was Jiang's old friend. Therefore, at least four of nine were Jiang's men. Moreover, Jiang's political rival, Li Ruihuan, had been pushed out. Furthermore, Jiang also managed to have installed a few more of his cronies in the Politburo: Liu Qi, Zeng Peiyan, and Chen Liangyu. Finally, Li Keqiang, Xi Jinping, and Song Defu all failed to enter the Politburo. What is most amazing is that there were no "accidents": All these candidates including Jia Qinglin and Huang Ju who had been selected by a small group of top Party leaders before the Congress were elected intact.

The Presidium of the Sixteenth Party Congress was a self-serving apparatus. Sixty-three percent of its members were selecting themselves into the new central committee. The preelection between

Table 2.4 The Sixteenth Politburo (2002)

Name	Birth	Age	Home	Prior Position/ Membership
Standing members				
Hu Jintao	1942	60	Anhui	Fifteenth Politburo Standing Member
Wu Bangguo	1941	61	Anhui	Fifteenth Politburo Member
Wen Jiabao	1942	60	Tianjin	Fifteenth Politburo Member
Jia Qinglin	1940	62	Hebei	Fifteenth Politburo Member
Zeng Qinghong	1939	63	Jiangxi	Fifteenth Politburo Alternate Member
Huang Ju	1938	64	Zhejiang	Fifteenth Politburo Member
Wu Guanzheng	1938	64	Jiangxi	Fifteenth Politburo Member
Li Changchun	1944	58	Liaoning	Fifteenth Politburo Member
Luo Gan	1935	67	Shandong	Fifteenth Politburo Member
Politburo members				
Wang Lequan	1944	58	Shandong	Xinjiang Party Secretary
Wang Zhaoguo	1941	61	Hebei	CLD Director
Hui Liangyu (Hui)	1944	58	Jilin	Jiangsu Party Secretary
Liu Qi	1942	60	Jiangsu	Beijing Party Secretary
Liu Yunshan	1947	55	Shanxi	CPD Director
Wu Yi (female)	1938	64	Hubei	Fifteenth Politburo Alternate Member
Zhang Lichang	1939	63	Hebei	Tianjin Party Secretary
Zhang Dejiang	1946	56	Liaoning	Zhejiang Party Secretary
Chen Liangyu	1946	56	Zhejiang	Shanghai Party Secretary
Zhou Yongkang	1942	60	Jiangsu	Sichuan Party Secretary
Yu Zhengsheng	1945	57	Zhejiang	Hubei Party Secretary
He Guoqiang	1943	59	Hunan	COD Director
Guo Boxiong	1942	60	Shaanxi	CMC Member
Cao Gangchuan	1935	67	Henan	CMC Member
Zeng Peiyan	1938	64	Zhejiang	SDPC Director
Politburo alternate members				
Wang Gang	1942	60	Jilin	General Office Director

Acronyms: CMC: Central Military Commission; COD: Central Organization Department; CPD: Central Propaganda Department; CLD: Central Liaison Department; SDPC: State Development and Planning Commission.
Source: http://news.xinhuanet.com/ziliao/2004-06/22/content_1540150.htm.

November 10 and 13, 2002 was critical, because the final outcome of the formal election on November 14, 2002 was identical to the results of the preelection; yet it is not clear how these preelections were conducted.

CHARACTERISTICS OF THE SIXTEENTH CENTRAL COMMITTEE

Educational Backgrounds

Educational credentials have become a very important factor in political elite recruitment since the beginning of economic reforms in the late 1970s. Education has been one of the four requirements for a new contingent of leaders in the modernization drive, and a college diploma has been critical for one's political career.

The Sixteenth Central Committee (CC) members are highly educated. According to a report from the Xinhua News Agency, 98.6 percent of the Sixteenth CC members have at least a three-year college education, 6.2 percent higher than that of the Fifteenth CC and 15.2 percent higher than that of the Fourteenth CC.[60] Since we do not have complete information on all members, we cannot verify the accuracy of the percentage. But we can estimate the percentage with available information. Among 287 members with known educational backgrounds, 282 (98.26 percent) have at least a three-year college education. With a standard error of 0.008, the 95 percent confidence interval is between 96.7 percent and 99.8 percent. In other words, 98.6 may be an accurate number for the percentage of those with at least a three-year college education.

Moreover, in contrast to the Fifteenth CC where alternate members were more educated (94.7 percent with at least a three-year college education) than full members (91.7 percent), the full

---

[60] Wu Qingcai and Qi Bing, "Zhongxinshe: Xinshiji, Xinbaizi, Xintedian" ("The Xinhua News Agency: The new century, the new leadership, and the new characteristics"), *Renminwang*, November 15, 2002, http://www.peopledaily.com.cn/GB/shizheng/252/8956/9419/20021115/867131.html.

Table 2.5 Educational Levels of Sixteenth and Fifteenth Central Committee Members (2002 and 1999)

	Obs.	Mean	Std. Dev.	Min.	Max.	Std. Err.	(95% Conf. Interval)	
Sixteenth Central Committee								
Full members	175*	0.983	0.130	0	1	0.010	0.963	1.000
Alternate members	112**	0.982	0.133	0	1	0.013	0.957	1.010
Total	287	0.983	0.131	0	1	0.008	0.967	0.998
Fifteenth Central Committee								
Full members	193	0.917	0.276	0	1	n/a	n/a	n/a
Alternate members	151	0.947	0.225	0	1	n/a	n/a	n/a
Total	344	0.930	0.255	0	1	n/a	n/a	n/a

Notes: *23 *cases missing;* **46 *cases missing.*
Sources: Shen Xueming and Zheng Jianying (eds.), *Zhonggong Diyijie zhi Dishiwujie Zhongyangweiyuan* (*The central committee members of the Chinese Communist Party from the First through the Fifteenth Central Committee*) (Beijing: Zhongyang Wenxian Chubanshe, 2001); *People's Daily* online.

members of the Sixteenth CC were slightly more educated (98.3 percent versus 98.2 percent) (Table 2.5). The Sixteenth CC also has more members with graduate degrees than the Fifteenth CC does. In the Fifteenth CC, 43 out of 344 members had graduate degrees, representing 12.5 percent of the total. In the Sixteenth CC, 71 out of 287 people with information on education had graduate degrees, representing a quarter of the cases. The number of Ph.D. holders also increased from four in the Fifteenth CC to 12 in the Sixteenth CC.

Furthermore, many Sixteenth CC members obtained their degrees on the part-time basis. Du Qinglin, for instance, obtained a master's degree in management in 1996 from the School of Economic Management at Jilin University while he was a deputy secretary of Hainan Provincial Party Committee and chairman of the Hainan Provincial People's Congress. Among the Sixteenth CC members, 26 people obtained their degrees while holding offices

Table 2.6 Part-time Educational Experiences of Sixteenth Central Committee Members (2002)

Degree	Freq.	Percent	Cum.
Three-year college	5	19.23	19.23
Bachelor	3	11.54	30.77
Master	13	50.00	80.77
Ph.D.	5	19.23	100.00
Total	26	100.00	

Source: Same as in Table 2.4.

(Table 2.6). Five obtained a three-year college degree, three obtained a four-year college degree, 13 received a master's degree, and five got a doctoral degree.

Among the last, one may find Li Keqiang (party secretary of Henan),[61] Xi Jinping (party secretary of Zhejiang), Li Yuanchao (party secretary of Jiangsu), Zhou Xiaochuan (governor of the People's Bank of China), and Liu Yandong (director of the United Front Department of the Central Committee of the CCP). These five people's educational experiences are illustrative of the composition of the new leadership. Liu Yandong is the oldest of all. She went to Qinghua University in 1964 (before the Cultural Revolution) and graduated in 1970. She obtained her Ph.D. in political science from Jilin University probably in the 1990s. She represents those in the fourth generation leadership who went to college before the Cultural Revolution. Zhou Xiaochuan and Xi Jinping, on the other hand, are typical of those who went to college during the Cultural Revolution. Zhou graduated in 1975 from the Beijing Institute of Chemical Engineering. He obtained a doctoral degree in economic systems management from Qinghua University 10 years later. Xi went to Qinghua University in October 1974, the latter part of the Cultural Revolution, as a "worker-peasant-soldier" student. He later went back to his alma mater for a doctoral degree in law. Li Keqiang

---

[61] Li Keqiang is currently party secretary of Liaoning.

and Li Yuanchao, finally, are among those who went to college through rigorous college entrance exams in the era of economic reforms. Li Keqiang was admitted to the Law Department of Beijing University in 1978 and graduated in 1982. He later went back to his alma mater for both a master's and a doctoral degree in economics. Li Yuanchao was admitted to Fudan University in 1978, majoring in mathematics. He later obtained a master's degree in economic management from Beijing University in 1986 and a Ph.D. degree from the Central Party School in 1998. These leaders are young and ambitious. They are preparing themselves for the most important jobs in China.

The Sixteenth CC has fewer people with foreign study experience than the Fifteenth CC. Twenty people in the Sixteenth CC had foreign study experience, whereas 33 people in the Fifteenth CC studied abroad. All but one of the 20 people went to only one country. Bai Chunli, vice president of the Chinese Academy of Sciences, was a postdoctoral fellow at the California Institute of Technology between 1985 and 1987. He was a visiting professor in Northeast University in Japan in the early 1990s. In contrast, among the 33 people in the Fifteenth CC with foreign learning experience, 28 went to one country, four to two countries, and one to three countries. Zhou Guangzhao, former president of the Chinese Academy of Sciences, was a researcher in the Soviet Union in the 1950s. He became a visiting professor at the University of Virginia and the University of California in the 1980s. He was also a researcher at the Center for Nuclear Research in Western Europe. In terms of learning experience, the dominant pattern in the Sixteenth CC was serving as visiting scholars (40 percent), but the trend prevailing in the Fifteenth CC was to obtain a bachelor's degree (39 percent) (Table 2.7).

In terms of the distribution of countries where these members studied, Western countries in general and the United States in particular were the most popular among the Sixteenth CC members. Three-fourths went to Western countries, and 30 percent went to the United States. In contrast, the Soviet Union was the most popular country among the Fifteenth CC members. Forty-eight percent went there. This contrast reflects the difference of eras. Those who went

Table 2.7 Study Abroad Experience Among Sixteenth and Fifteenth Central Committee Members

Study Abroad Experience	Sixteenth Central Committee			Fifteenth Central Committee			
	Number of Countries			Number of Countries			
	One	Two	Total	One	Two	Three	Total
Visiting professor	0	0	0	1	0	1	2
Post-doctoral fellow	1	1	2	1	1	0	2
Training	2	0	2	5	0	0	5
Visiting scholar	8	0	8	5	2	0	7
BA	4	0	4	12	1	0	13
MA	0	0	0	1	0	0	1
Ph.D.	3	0	3	2	0	0	2
Work	1	0	1	1	0	0	1
Total	19	1	20	28	4	1	33

Source: Same as in Table 2.4.

to the Soviet Union did so in the 1950s, and those who went to the United States did so in the 1980s and 1990s (Table 2.8).

The emphasis on educational credentials has produced some unexpected consequences in recent years. In order to boost their educational qualifications, some cadres have developed several "innovative" ways. One way is to use the word "equivalent" to meet the requirement. Even though some cadres never went to any college, their educational level was considered "equivalent to" a three-year or a four-year college education. Another way is to substitute their training in Party ideology for academic credentials. Since a candidate for a new post is often sent to the party school for ideological training, many take the opportunity to enhance their educational credentials. A number of people have received graduate degrees from party schools. A third way is to get a degree on a part-time basis. This is the way many ambitious young politicians obtained their graduate degrees. The problem is that some cadres are too busy to attend classes on a regular basis and they often do not take exams themselves. Many of them send their secretaries to take

Table 2.8 Countries of Foreign Learning Experience Among Sixteenth and Fifteenth Central Committee Members

Countries	Sixteenth Central Committee		Fifteenth Central Committee	
	Freq.	Percent	Freq.	Percent
Western countries				
United States	6	30.00	4	12.12
Australia	1	5.00	1	3.03
Sweden	1	5.00	1	3.03
Western Germany	1	5.00	1	3.03
Norway	0	0.00	1	3.03
Japan	1	5.00	1	3.03
Great Britian	2	10.00	4	12.12
Belgium	1	5.00	0	0.00
Switzerland	1	5.00	0	0.00
Canada	1	5.00	0	0.00
Subtotal	15	75	13	39.39
Eastern countries				
Soviet Union	2	10.00	16	48.48
Eastern Germany	1	5.00	1	3.03
Czechoslovakia	0	0.00	1	3.03
Yugoslavia	1	5.00	1	3.03
North Korea	1	5.00	1	3.03
Subtotal	5	25.00	20	60.60
Total	20	100.00	33	99.99*

*The total does not add up to 100 due to rounding.
Source: Same as in Table 2.4.

exams on their behalf. Because of serious absenteeism among part-time students, especially government cadres and corporate leaders, two schools of Beijing University (the School of Economics and the Guanghua School of Management) decided to close down their part-time doctoral programs beginning in 2003.[62] As one Beijing University professor commented, "a good cadre cannot be a good

---

[62] Chen Lumin, "Zaizhi Boshi: 'Boxia Longzhong, Shouhuo Tiaozao'" (Part-time doctoral programs: Planting the seed of a dragon and getting the result of a flea"),

student; and a good student cannot be a good cadre."⁶³ This is because it is impossible to pay full attention to both study and work at the same time.

For those who did not even want to bother going through the hassles of enduring the entire process of educational training, moreover, they simply obtained their diploma through connections. Hu Changqing, former vice governor of Jiangxi, is a case in point. Hu was born in a remote village in Hunan. He joined the PLA in 1968 and became a Party member the following year. In 1979, he was demobilized from the army. In order to meet the requirement of a college education, he got a fake diploma from Beijing University through his connections.⁶⁴ As a party member with a college degree, Hu thus made himself a good candidate for higher positions. He was appointed an assistant governor of Jiangxi in 1995 and was elected as a vice governor in 1998. His case was exposed because of his involvement in economic crimes. He was sentenced to death and executed in March 2000.

Hu was not alone in this regard. According to an investigation conducted by the Organization Department of the Hohhot Municipal Party Committee between December 2002 and March 2003, 110 division-level cadres were found to have questionable diplomas. Some obtained a three-year college degree in only one year, and some received a degree from colleges and universities that did not exist.⁶⁵

Renminwang, January 7, 2003, http://www.people.com.cn/GB/guardian/30/20030107/902485.html. The author is suggesting that some of the diplomas were fake real ones. They were real because they were obtained through a real program in a real university; they were fake because the cadres did not really attend all the classes and/or take the exams themselves.
⁶³ *Ibid*.
⁶⁴ See "Cantong de Jiaoxun Shenke de Jingshi: Jiangxi Yuanfushengzhang Hu Changqing Shouhui ji Fuhuaduoluo Paoxi" ("Painful lessons and serious warnings: an analysis of the corruption case of former Vice-Governor Hu Changqing"), *Renminwang*, April 14, 2000, http://www.people.com.cn/GB/channel1/11/20000414/37269.html.
⁶⁵ "Hohehoute: 110 duoming chuji ganbu de wenping you wenti" ("Hohhot: more than 110 division-level cadres have questionable diplomas"), *Renminwang*, March 28, 2003, http://www.peopledaily.com.cn./GB/shizheng/19/20030328/957026.html.

Generally speaking, there are four kinds of diplomas that cadres have obtained. First, the diploma could be a "real real" one. It is the one a cadre obtained through actually attending the college. Second, it could be a "real fake" one. The cadre was registered in a real academic program, but someone else did the homework and took the exams. Third, it could be a "fake real" one. The college and the academic program were both real, but the cadre obtained the diploma through connections. Finally, it could be a "fake fake" one. There are in fact two subtypes of "fake fake" diplomas. A cadre may get a "fake fake" one from the black market, or get it from a college that does not exist. Hu Changqing, for instance, had a "fake fake" diploma. He commissioned an agent to obtain a "real fake" one from Beijing University, but the agent was rejected. The agent then bought him a fake diploma on the black market. In a sense, Hu Changqing was rather "innocent" because he did not know he was actually getting a "fake fake" diploma instead of a "real fake" one as he had initially requested.

In sum, the Sixteenth CC members are highly educated. In comparison to the Fifteenth CC, the Sixteenth CC has more educated full members, more members with graduate degrees including Ph.D. degrees, and fewer members with foreign learning experience. The Sixteenth CC members enhanced their educational credentials through part-time programs, especially graduate programs. Among those who did study abroad, there was a tendency to go to Western countries, in particular the United States, instead of the Soviet Union and other Eastern European countries. They often went abroad as visiting scholars instead of full-time students.

Age

Age is another important factor in determining one's prospect for upward mobility in China. Because of their measurability, age and educational credentials have been used as the hallmark of the institutionalization of leadership transitions in China. As a result of the decades-long campaign for rejuvenation, a new norm has emerged in selecting and appointing a candidate for a post: The candidate has to be young and the younger the better.

Several age limits were used in the past two decades to determine the fate of a political leader in China. Age 70, for instance, is the retirement age for Politburo members. Those who are at age 70 or older are no longer eligible for a membership in the Politburo. Age 65 is the retirement age for chief provincial/ministerial positions, and age 60 is the retirement age for deputy provincial/ministerial positions. Now, age 50 has become another important criterion. One of the mandates from the Fifteenth Politburo Standing Committee for the composition of the Sixteenth Central Committee was that those who aged 50 years or below in 2002 should constitute at least one-fifth of the total.[66]

There are, however, two ways to calculate the age: Use the year of birth or use the month of birth. There is a small difference between the two methods. According to the first method, the average age of 356 cases in the Sixteenth CC is 56.05 years (Table 2.9), 0.65 years older than the one (55.4) reported by the Xinhua News Agency.[67]

It is likely that those who were born in December reported their age according to the month of birth instead of the year of birth. Subtracting one year from those who were born in December, we got the average age of 55.9, still half a year older than the reported one (Table 2.9).

On the other hand, the same report seems to have underestimated the average age of the Fifteenth CC members. According to the report, the average age of the Fifteenth CC members was 55.9 years in 1997. Since we do have information on all members of the Fifteenth CC, we can easily verify the number against the data. According to the year of birth, the average age of the Fifteenth CC came to 56.5 years in 1997. Since the Fifteenth Party Congress was held in September 1997, those who were born in October, November, and December should be considered one year younger

---

[66] See He Ping and Liu Siyang, "Xinhuashe: Jianfuqi Jiwangkailai de Zhangyan Shiming."
[67] Wu Qingcai and Qi Bing, "Zhongxinshe: Xinshiji, Xinbaizi, Xintedian."

Table 2.9 Average Ages of Sixteenth and Fifteenth Central Committee Members (2002 and 1997)

	Obs.	Mean	Std. Dev.	Min.	Max.
Sixteenth Central Committee[a]					
Full members	198	58.63	4.14	41	67
Alternate members	158	52.82	4.87	39	64
Total	356	56.05	5.33	39	67
Sixteenth Central Committee[a]					
Full members	198	58.51	4.11	41	67
Alternate members	158	52.70	4.89	39	64
Total	356	55.93	5.32	39	67
Fifteenth Central Committee[a]					
Full members	193	58.91	4.83	42	76
Alternate members	151	52.58	4.83	40	62
Total	344	56.13	5.76	40	76

Notes: [a] Ages are calculated according to the year of birth.
Source: Same as in Table 2.4.

than they were according to the month of birth. The resultant average was 0.4 years lower than the one according to the year of birth, because there were 134 people who were born in these months (43 in October, 44 in November, and 47 in December). However, the average age was still a bit higher than the reported one. Our number is 56.1 (Table 2.9), while the reported one is 55.9. In other words, the reported average age exaggerated the youth of the Fifteenth CC by 0.2.[68]

The issue is not how much the report underestimated the average age of the Fifteenth CC. It is rather that the notion of being young has been blown out of proportion, and both candidates and the

---

[68] It should be indicated that 0.2 is the real difference between the reported average age and the real average age of the Fifteenth Central Committee. It is more significant than being "statistically significant" because we are here dealing with "population parameters" instead of "sample statistics." For an explanation of these two concepts, see David Knoke, George W. Bohrnstedt, and Alisa Potter Mee, *Statistics for Social Data Analysis* (Fourth Edition) (Itasca, IL: F. E. Peacock, 2002), pp. 69–74.

media tend to underreport the age. The point here is that the Sixteenth CC did not seem to be younger than the Fifteenth CC. The actual average age of the Fifteenth CC was 56.1 years, while the average age of the Sixteenth CC was 55.9 years, a mere difference of 0.2.

Nevertheless, the Sixteenth Politburo in 2002 was indeed younger than the Fifteenth Politburo in 1997. The Sixteenth Politburo as a whole was 60.5 years old in 2002, two-and-a-half years younger than the Fifteenth Politburo in 1997. The average age of the standing members of the Sixteenth Politburo was 62 years in 2002, two-and-a-half years younger than their counterparts in 1997. The full members of the Sixteenth Politburo (excluding standing members) were 59.6 years old on average, about three years younger than the full members of the Fifteenth Politburo (excluding standing members) in 1997. The only exception is the alternate member of the Sixteenth Politburo, who was slightly older than the average age of the alternate members of the Fifteenth Politburo (60 versus 58.5).

As in the case of educational credentials, some cadres have also abused this criterion. In order to meet the requirement of being young, some politically ambitious cadres have been quite creative for staying young or even getting younger. One technique is to report the age instead of the date of birth in a background check form. This way, one has control over how old one is according to the criterion for target positions. If a target position requires a candidate to be no older than 50 years, for instance, the potential candidate can then report an age of 48, even though he or she may actually be older than 50 years. In some cases, one could stay in that age for a number of years or even get younger as years go by.

Work Experience

According to the Xinhua News Agency report, the Sixteenth CC members all entered the workforce after the liberation (1949).[69]

---

[69] Wu Qingcai and Qi Bing, "Zhongxinshe: Xinshiji, Xinbaizi, Xintedian."

Among 342 people with known starting years of work, the earliest is 1952, three years after the liberation, and the latest is 1982, four years into the era of economic reforms. Ismail Amat, a Uygur, joined the revolutionary work in 1952, a few years after the CCP took over the Xinjiang Province. He joined the Party the following year. His political career is impeccable. He became a full member in the Tenth Central Committee elected in 1973 and has stayed in that status ever since. His seniority in the central committee is unmatched in the Sixteenth CC. He entered the central committee nine years earlier than Jiang Zemin did, the core of the third generation leadership in China. In the Fifteenth CC, only Hua Guofeng, Mao's designated successor, stayed in the central committee longer than he did. At the other extreme, Zhang Qingwei did not begin to work until 1982. Zhang, a national hero who, along with his colleagues in the Chinese Academy of Satellite Launching Technology, successfully launched numerous satellites for both Chinese and foreign clients, was elevated to a full member in the Sixteenth CC. He skipped the alternate membership.[70]

The range between the earliest and the latest is 30 years, a full generation apart. Although a significant number of Sixteenth CC members (138) joined the workforce during the Cultural Revolution, a large percentage of them started to work before the Cultural Revolution. Fifty-five percent entered the workforce between 1966 and 1976, and 43 percent began to work before 1966. Only two percent started working after 1976 (Table 2.10). If we follow Cheng Li's categorization of political generations in China where the third generation is the pre-Cultural Revolution generation and the fourth generation is the Cultural Revolution generation,[71] we may find that the

---

[70] That being selected as a member of the Central Committee is a reward for the scientific contribution of a scientist may sound strange for the ear of a Westerner, but it is quite "natural" in China. For an overview of scientific elite in China, see Cong Cao and Richard Suttmeier, "China's new scientific elite: distinguished young scientists, the research environment and hopes for Chinese science," *China Quarterly*, Vol. 168 (December 2001), pp. 960–984.

[71] Cheng Li, *China's Leaders: The New Generation* (New York: Rowman & Littlefield, 2001).

Table 2.10 Work Experience of Sixteenth Central Committee Members (2002)

Joining the Work Force	Freq.	Percent	Cum.
Before the Cultural Revolution (1952–1965)	130	38.01	38.01
During the Cultural Revolution (1966–1976)	201	58.77	96.78
In the era of economic reforms (1977–1982)	11	3.22	100.00
Total	242	100.00	

Source: Same as in Table 2.4.

Sixteenth CC members belong to the third and fourth generations in terms of work experience.

Party Standing

Similar to work experience, party standing is also very diverse. On the one hand, the most senior communist party member in the Sixteenth CC joined the Party in 1953 with a party standing of almost 50 years, while the most junior member became a party member in 1986, only 16 prior to the opening of the Sixteenth National Party Congress. The most senior communist party member is Ismail Amat. The most junior communist party member is Su Xintian, secretary of the Party General Branch of the Meiling Village in Fujian Province. It is not clear why Su was selected as a candidate for an alternate membership in the Sixteenth CC, but his presence in the central committee reminds us of such model peasants as Chen Yonggui and Li Shunda of the 1960s and 1970s. With a middle school education, Su began his career as a farmer in 1959 when he was 16 years old. He joined the Party in 1986 and became party secretary of the Meiling Village two years later. In the early 21st century, he was a rarity.

In terms of historical periods, 36 percent joined the Party before the Cultural Revolution, 47 percent joined the Party during the Cultural Revolution, and only 17 percent have joined the Party since 1977 (Table 2.11). In terms of individual years, 1965 and 1966 were the most prominent with 27 (10.38 percent) and 23 (8.85 percent)

Table 2.11 Party Standing of Sixteenth Central Committee Members (2002)

Joining the CCP	Freq.	Percent	Cum.
Before the Cultural Revolution (1953–1965)	92	35.77	35.77
During the Cultural Revolution (1966–1976)	123	47.31	83.08
In the Era of Economic Reforms (1977–1986)	44	16.92	100.00
Total	260	100.00	

Source: Same as in Table 2.4.

members joining the Party, respectively. Again, the presence of the third generation leaders is considerable, but the presence of the fourth generation leaders in the Sixteenth CC is significant.

Home Province[72]

The Sixteenth CC members are from all provincial units except Hong Kong and Macao. Jiangsu tops the list with 46 members (12.9 percent of the total), followed by Shandong with 42 members (11.8 percent). Others among the top 10 include Hebei (26 members), Zhejiang (24 members), Hunan (18 members), Liaoning (17 members), Anhui (16 members), Hubei (16 members), Henan (16 members), and Shaanxi (15 members). Among the least represented, one may find Qinghai (1), Taiwan (1), Hainan (1), Inner Mongolia (3), Ningxia (3), Tibet (3), Guangxi (4), Xinjiang (4), and Yunnan (4). Many of these are inland provincial units; five of them (Inner Mongolia, Ningxia, Tibet, Guangxi, and Xinjiang) are minority regions (Table 2.12).

In terms of regional distributions, the East Region is the most prominent with 143 members (40.2 percent). The Central Region is a

---

[72] Home province is *"jiguan"* in Chinese, usually the province where one's father was born. It is different from birthplace (*chushengdi*), the province where one was born. In an official document, home province is often reported. For instance, Jia Qinglin's home province is Hebei, but he was born in Shandong. Zeng Qinghong's home province is Jiangxi, but he was born in Anhui.

Table 2.12 Distribution of Home Provinces of Sixteenth and Fifteenth Central Committee Members

	Sixteenth Central Committee		Fifteenth Central Committee	
	Freq.	Percent	Freq.	Percent
North				
Beijing	10	2.81	6	1.74
Tianjin	7	1.97	9	2.62
Hebei	26	7.30	16	4.65
Shanxi	10	2.81	13	3.78
Inner Mongolia	3	0.84	2	0.58
Subtotal	56	15.73	46	13.37
Northeast				
Liaoning	17	4.78	25	7.27
Jilin	8	2.25	18	5.23
Heilongjiang	8	2.25	6	1.74
Subtotal	33	9.28	49	14.24
East				
Shanghai	9	2.53	6	1.74
Jiangsu	46	12.92	50	14.53
Zhejiang	24	6.74	22	6.40
Anhui	16	4.49	17	4.94
Fujian	5	1.40	7	2.03
Shandong	42	11.80	46	13.37
Taiwan	1	0.28	1	0.29
Subtotal	143	40.16	149	43.30
Central				
Jiangxi	9	2.53	10	2.91
Henan	16	4.49	12	3.49
Hubei	16	4.49	8	2.33
Hunan	18	5.06	18	5.23
Subtotal	59	16.57	48	13.96
South				
Guangdong	8	2.25	8	2.33
Guangxi	4	1.12	3	0.87
Hainan	1	0.28	1	0.29
Hong Kong	0	0.00	0	0.00
Macao	0	0.00	0	0.00
Subtotal	13	3.65	12	3.49

(*Continued*)

Table 2.12 (*Continued*)

	Sixteenth Central Committee		Fifteenth Central Committee	
	Freq.	Percent	Freq.	Percent
Southwest				
Sichuan	7	1.97	10	2.91
Chongqing	5	1.40	2	0.58
Guizhou	5	1.40	4	1.16
Yunnan	4	1.12	4	1.16
Tibet	3	0.84	3	0.87
Subtotal	24	6.73	23	6.68
Northwest				
Shaanxi	15	4.21	10	2.91
Gansu	5	1.40	1	0.29
Qinghai	1	0.28	1	0.29
Ningxia	3	0.84	1	0.29
Xinjiang	4	1.12	4	1.16
Subtotal	28	7.85	17	4.94
Total	356	100.00	344	99.98*

*The total is not 100 due to rounding.
Source: Same as in Table 2.4.

distant second with 59 members (16.6 percent). The South Region has the least representation with only 13 members (3.7 percent). Compared to the pattern in the Fifteenth CC, however, the East Region was less dominant in the Sixteenth CC, but the Central Region became a bit more prominent. The Northeast Region dropped from number two in the Fifteenth CC to number four in the Sixteenth CC because of the dramatic reduction of members from Liaoning and Jilin. Twenty-five Fifteenth CC members were from Liaoning and 18 from Jilin. But in the Sixteenth CC, only 17 and eight were from Liaoning and Jilin, respectively. In contrast, the Northwest Region witnessed a large increase both in absolute numbers and in percentages. There were 28 Sixteenth CC members from the Northwest Region, representing 7.9 percent instead of 4.9 percent previously.

Gender

Women were not very well represented in the Sixteenth Central Committee. Out of 356 members, only 27 were women, representing 7.58 percent. There is no female standing member of the Politburo; there is only one female (Wu Yi) out of 24 Politburo members. Nevertheless, the Sixteenth CC in general was a bit better than the Fifteenth CC, where 25 out of 344 were women, representing 7.27 percent. If we break down the Sixteenth CC into full and alternate members, we will see that women were less well represented as full members than they were as alternate members. Only five full members were women, taking 2.53 percent of all full members. Female alternate members (22 cases) took 13.92 percent of all alternate members. Compared to the Fifteenth CC, the female alternate membership increased, but the female full membership decreased (Table 2.13). As far as the Sixteenth CC is concerned, Chinese politics is still essentially a game of men.

Nationality

China is a country of 56 nationalities. Han is dominant with 91.9 percent, and 55 minorities make up 8.1 percent. From this perspective, minorities are in fact slightly overrepresented. There were

Table 2.13 Females in the Sixteenth and Fifteenth Central Committees (2002 and 1997)

	Freq.	Percent
Sixteenth Central Committee		
Full members	5	2.53
Alternate members	22	13.92
Total	27	7.58
Fifteenth Central Committee		
Full members	8	4.15
Alternate members	17	11.26
Total	25	7.27

Source: Same as in Table 2.4.

Table 2.14 Distribution of Nationalities Among Sixteenth Central Committee Members

Nationality	Freq.	Percent	Cum.
Han	322	90.45	90.45
Zhuang	2	0.56	91.01
Tibetan	5	1.40	92.42
Yi	1	0.28	92.70
Uighur	3	0.84	93.54
Tujia	2	0.56	94.10
Miao	2	0.56	94.66
Mongolian	2	0.56	95.22
Manchu	3	0.84	96.07
Hui	7	1.97	98.03
Yao	1	0.28	98.31
Kasak	1	0.28	98.60
Dai	1	0.28	98.88
Buyi	1	0.28	99.16
Korean	2	0.56	99.72
Li	1	0.28	100.00
Total	356	100.00	

Source: Same as in Table 2.4.

34 minority members in the Sixteenth CC, representing 9.55 percent of the total (Table 2.14). The distribution among minorities, however, is not even. Some minorities have much higher representation than others, and some minorities are not represented at all. Noticeably, Hui is best represented with a total of seven members (1.97 percent). Tibetan (five members), Uygur (three members), and Manchu (three members) followed.

Again, as in the case of female members, minority members were more likely to be alternate members than to be full members. Minority full members took only 8.17 percent of all full members, and minority alternate members took 12.66 percent of all alternate members.

Clearly, as described above, a typical member of the Sixteenth Central Committee is someone who is in the mid-fifties, a man, and a Han. His home province is more likely to be in the East Region, especially Jiangsu or Shandong, than any other regions, and he is likely to be well educated. He is likely to have joined the workforce either before or during the Cultural Revolution, and his party standing is about 32 years.

TECHNOCRATS IN COMMAND?

China's political elites, as Hong Yung Lee observed in 1991, experienced a fundamental change in the era of economic reforms. The revolutionary cadres, who were originally recruited largely from poor peasants with a low level of education, were gradually replaced by bureaucratic technocrats with a high level of education. The new leaders, according to Lee, "have their academic training mainly in engineering and production-related fields and their career backgrounds in specialist positions at functional organizations."[73] Do the Sixteenth Central Committee members still fit the profile of Lee's description as bureaucratic technocrats with academic training in engineering and career backgrounds in specialist positions? Or have they experienced another fundamental change as a result of the economic reforms? If so, what is the best characterization of the new leaders of China in the 21st century?

Technocrats: A Definition

To conduct a technocratic evaluation of the Sixteenth CC, we need to know what makes a technocrat in the first place. A technocrat, according to Cheng Li, is someone "who is concurrently specialized by training in a technical science, holds a professional occupation, and has a leadership position."[74] According to this definition, to qualify for being a technocrat, a person has to meet three basic requirements at the same time: academic training in a technical

---

[73] Hong Yung Lee, *From Revolutionary Cadres to Party Technocrats in Socialist China* (Berkeley and Los Angeles: University of California Press, 1991), pp. 387–388.
[74] Li, *China's Leaders*, p. 27.

science, a professional occupation, and a leadership position. In other words, meeting any of the requirements does not automatically make a person a technocrat. He or she has to meet all of them.

According to the definition, a college graduate is not necessarily a technocrat. Graduates of humanities are not technocrats; nor are graduates of economics and social sciences.[75] To make the definition more consistent with the conventional classification of college students in China, we classify college students into two categories: those who study social sciences and humanities (*wen ke*) and those who study natural sciences and engineering (*ligong ke*). According to this revised definition, only those who studied natural sciences and engineering are qualified for being technocrats; those who studied social sciences and humanities are not qualified for being technocrats. For instance, Hu Jintao, general secretary, studied hydroelectric power at Qinghua University and thus met the academic requirement for being a technocrat. Wang Gang, alternate member of the Politburo, was a student of philosophy at Jilin University and did not meet the academic requirement for being a technocrat. Therefore, although a highly educated leadership is likely to be technocratic, a technocratic leadership at least has to be filled with graduates of natural sciences and engineering.

For the career requirement, moreover, we may also want to use Lee's definition of career backgrounds in specialist positions at functional organizations. In other words, they have to have work experience as specialists in production-related fields.[76] The career experiences of political leaders are usually classified into (i) engineering, (ii) economic management, (iii) party affairs, (iv) government affairs, (v) military, (vi) CCYL work, or (vii) others. Those who have experience in engineering or economic management are considered specialists. It should be noted that those who obtain a degree in a natural science or engineering do not automatically become technocrats if they do not meet the career requirement. A good example is Jia Chunwang, procurator-general of the

---

[75] *Ibid.*, pp. 27, 28.

[76] Lee, *From Revolutionary Cadres to Party Technocrats in Socialist China*, p. 402.

Supreme People's Procuratorate. Jia is a graduate of Qinghua University with a degree in engineering physics. After his graduation, however, he embarked on a career in youth work. In the subsequent 20 years, he served as deputy head of the University Committee of the CCYL Central Committee, secretary of the CCYL Qinghua University Committee, and secretary of the CCYL Beijing Municipal Committee. Even though he has academic training in engineering physics, he is not a technocrat in terms of his career experience.

Third, a technocrat has to occupy a leadership position. For studies on national or provincial leaders, this variable is under control. Yet central committee members may or may not occupy a leadership position. In this regard, we will adopt Xiaowei Zang's suggestion that being a full central committee member makes one a political leader in China,[77] even though in reality an alternate-member governor may exert greater influence on Chinese politics than a full-member scientist. Since we are evaluating the nature of the central committee of the CCP, this definition is sufficient for our purposes.

Technocracy: An Evaluation

Academic requirement

A technocrat, according to the above definition, is someone with a college degree in a natural science or engineering. There is, however, a difference between a three-year college education (*dazhuan*) and a four-year college education (*benke*). In this study, we are going to use four-year college education as the minimum requirement because this is one of the basic requirements for leadership positions at many different levels. The full central committee members of the Sixteenth CC, as presented in Table 2.5, are highly educated with 98.3 percent of them having at least a three-year

---

[77] Xiaowei Zang, "The Fourteenth Central Committee of the CCP: technocracy or political technocracy?" *Asian Survey*, Vol. 33 (August 1993), pp. 787–803.

Table 2.15 Graduates of Natural Sciences and Engineering in the Sixteenth Central Committee (2002)

	Total Obs.	Valid Obs.	Freq.	Valid Percent
Politburo Standing Committee	9	9	9	100.00
Politburo	15	15	7	46.67
Secretariat	7	7	4	57.14
Full members	198	175	72	41.14
Alternate members	158	112	28	25.00
Total	356	287	100	34.84

Source: Same as in Table 2.4.

college education. Those with at least a four-year college education, however, are fewer at 78.8 percent.

As Table 2.15 indicates, those who met the academic requirement of a technocrat are in a descending order by rank. The Politburo Standing Committee is filled with graduates of natural sciences and engineering. All of the standing members studied natural sciences and engineering at college (100 percent). The majority of Secretariat members obtained a degree in natural sciences and engineering, taking 57 percent. Less than half of the Politburo members (excluding standing members) were educated in natural sciences and engineering (47 percent). Out of 175 full members with valid information on educational backgrounds, 72 (41 percent) had academic training in natural sciences and engineering. Finally, only a quarter (28 out of 112) of alternate members in the sample met the academic requirement.[78]

---

[78] It seems that Li Cheng and Lynn White calculated the percentages by dividing the total number of full and alternate central-committee members by the number of graduates of natural sciences and engineering. For instance, they found 57 specialists in the Thirteenth CC that represented 20 percent of the total. Unless they had the complete information on all members, the result of this method may not be accurate. Moreover, in this method, there is no differentiation between full and alternate members. See Li Cheng and Lynn White, "The Thirteenth Central Committee of the Chinese Communist Party: from mobilizers to managers," *Asian Survey*, Vol. 28 (April 1988), pp. 371–399.

It appears that those with degrees in natural sciences and engineering dominate the Sixteenth CC, if we look at the Politburo Standing Committee alone. But this should not lead to a conclusion that in the Sixteenth CC technocrats are in command for three reasons. First, at the level of full central committee members, only 41 percent had academic training in natural sciences and engineering. If we believe that full members are future Politburo members and alternate members are future full members, the trend seems to point to possible decline of those with degrees in natural sciences and engineering.

Second, as an indication of the decline of those with degrees in natural sciences and engineering, the Sixteenth CC members who obtained their degrees on a part-time basis had majors other than natural sciences and engineering. Among 26 people who received a degree on a part-time basis, 20 were full central committee members. None of them had a degree in natural sciences or engineering. Their majors are mostly in social sciences and economics, including ideology, economics, world economy, management, political science, and law. Forty percent of them (eight cases) received their training in ideology; 20 percent (four cases) obtained a degree in management; 15 percent (three cases) studied economics; and another 10 percent (two cases) studied law (Table 2.16).

Table 2.16 Majors of Part-Time Students in the Sixteenth Central Committee (2002)

Major	Freq.	Percent	Cum.
Ideology	8	40.00	40.00
Economics	3	15.00	55.00
Political Science	1	5.00	60.00
Management	4	20.00	80.00
Law	2	10.00	90.00
World Economy	1	5.00	95.00
Unknown	1	5.00	100.00
Total	20	100.00	

Source: Same as in Table 2.4.

The most illustrative of the decline of natural science and engineering majors among central committee members are those who obtained their doctoral degrees on a part-time basis. Four full members of the Sixteenth CC received their Ph.D. degrees on a part-time basis. They are Liu Yandong, Li Keqiang, Zhou Xiaochuan, and Xi Jinping. Three of them, Liu, Zhou, and Xi, had a college degree in engineering, but obtained a doctoral degree in a social science. Liu's college major was chemical engineering (at Qinghua University), but her area of study for Ph.D. was political science (at Jilin University). Zhou also studied chemical engineering at college (Beijing Institute of Chemical Engineering), but received a doctoral degree in economic management (from Qinghua University). Xi also went to Qinghua for a college degree in chemical engineering during the Cultural Revolution, but he later obtained a doctoral degree in law from the same university. Their college degrees may provide them with initial qualifications, but they later went back to school for more appropriate knowledge for their jobs.

Finally, even those with a degree in a natural science or engineering are not technocrats because academic training is one of the three requirements. In addition to the leadership requirement and academic requirement, one has to meet the career requirement to be considered a technocrat.

Career requirement

As defined earlier, a technocrat has to have a career background in specialist positions at functional organizations. In this regard, only those who have been mainly involved in engineering or economic management are candidates for being technocrats. As Table 2.17 indicates, not everyone who has academic training in natural sciences or engineering has a career background in engineering or economic management. Some were mainly engaged in party affairs; some worked for the government; some worked as CCYL cadres; and some worked in colleges, research institutions, and other organizations.

Table 2.17 Career Patterns of Sixteenth Central Committee Members (2002)

Career Patterns	Freq.	Percent	Cum.
Engineering	56	77.78	77.78
Economic management	1	1.39	79.17
Party affairs	2	2.78	81.94
Government affairs	4	5.56	87.50
Military	1	1.39	88.89
CCYL	2	2.78	91.67
Others	6	8.33	100.00
Total	72	100.01	

Source: Same as in Table 2.4.

Tian Chengping, currently minister of Labor and Social Security, had a degree in architecture from Qinghua University. But he served as a propaganda cadre in a chemical factory in Beijing after his graduation. He was a secretary of the CCYL Committee of the factory before he became a deputy secretary of the party committee of another factory under the same company. Bai Keming, party secretary of Hebei Province, studied in the Missile Engineering Department of the Harbin Institute of Military Engineering but spent a decade in the General Office of the State Education Commission between 1978 and 1988. These leaders are not technocrats in terms of their career patterns. Even Xu Kuangdi, former mayor of Shanghai, does not have a career background in engineering or economic management. He spent most of his early career in teaching. He was assistant professor in Shanghai Industrial College, assistant professor and lecturer in Shanghai Mechanics College, and associate professor in Shanghai Industrial University.

About 78 percent (56 cases) of the Sixteenth CC full members with academic training in natural sciences and engineering had career background in engineering. Another one percent (one case) had a career background in economic management. Altogether they make 79 percent of those with academic training in natural sciences and engineering. In terms of the total number of valid cases (175)

Table 2.18 Technocrats in the Central Committees of the Chinese Communist Party (1982–2002)

Central Committee Full Members	Total Obs.	Valid Obs.	Freq.	Valid Percent
Twelfth Central Committee (1982)	210	190	10	5.26*
Thirteenth Central Committee (1987)	175	133	44	33.08*
Fourteenth Central Committee (1992)	189	182	65	35.71*
Fifteenth Central Committee (1997)	193	193	98	50.78*
Sixteenth Central Committee (2002)	198	175	57	32.57

Note: *The percentages have been recalculated.
Sources: Hong Yung Lee, *From revolutionary cadres to party technocrats in socialist China*, Table 46, p. 268; Cheng Li, *China's leaders*, Table 2.3, p. 41; Xiaowei Zang, "The Fourteenth Central Committee of the CCP: technocracy or political technocracy?" Table 7, p. 800.

with information on educational backgrounds, however, they only represent 32.6 percent, less than one third. In other words, 57 full members of the Sixteenth CC can be identified as technocrats, because they met all three requirements of being a full member, having academic training in a natural science or engineering, and having a career background in specialist positions at functional organizations. And they constitute less than one third of the Sixteenth CC.

How does this figure compare with similar figures from the previous central committees of the CCP? Does it represent a significant increase over the previous central committees? From Table 2.18, we can see that technocratic representation in the Sixteenth CC is in fact the lowest among four central committees since 1987. It is not only significantly lower than that in the Fifteenth CC, but also lower than that in both the Thirteenth CC and the Fourteenth CC. If the Fifteenth CC represented "full-fledged technocratic leadership,"[79] then the Sixteenth CC witnessed a significant decline of technocratic

---

[79] Li Cheng and Lynn White, "The Fifteenth Central Committee of the Chinese Communist Party: full-fledged technocratic leadership with partial control by Jiang Zemin," *Asian Survey*, Vol. 38, No. 3 (March 1998), pp. 231–264.

leadership. Evidently, China's new leadership in the early 21st century is not technocracy, because most of them are not technocrats.

China's Political Elites in the Early 21st Century: An Assessment

If China's political elites in the 21st century are not technocratic, what are they? As mentioned earlier, not only the percentage of technocrats in the central committee has decreased significantly, their technocratic training has also become less relevant. Many technocrats went back to school for other types of academic knowledge than natural sciences or engineering. Moreover, their specialist career experience also became less relevant as these leaders were assuming more important positions. In his early career, for instance, Wang Zhaoguo was a technician in the Second Automotive Works, but his most important career experiences were in the CCYL, the central committee of the CCP, and Fujian Province. We may label him as a technocrat based on his early career experience, but it is more accurate to describe him as a CCYL cadre or party leader. The same is true of Hu Jintao and Liu Yandong, who also spent a significant part of their career in the CCYL and the central committee of the CCP as well as (in the case of Hu Jintao) in provinces. Li Changchun, as another example, started working as a technician in a factory in Shenyang, Liaoning Province, but his experience in that capacity was very brief. His most important experiences have been in party affairs. He became a deputy secretary general of the Shenyang Committee of the CCP in 1981 and spent the subsequent two decades in various municipal and provincial leading positions. He had been mayor and party secretary of Shenyang, deputy secretary and governor of Liaoning, deputy secretary, governor, party secretary, chairman of the Standing Committee of the Provincial People's Congress of Henan, and party secretary of Guangdong.

It seems that a more important career experience many central committee members share is local government/party management. Altogether 194 members of the Sixteenth CC had experiences as

Table 2.19 The Sixteenth Central Committee Members with Provincial Experience (2002)

	Total Obs.	Valid Obs.	Freq.	Valid Percent
Politburo Standing Committee	9	9	8	88.89
Politburo	15	15	11	73.33
Secretariat	7	7	3	42.86
Full members	198	198	106	53.54
Alternate members	158	158	88	55.70
Total	356	356	194	54.49

Source: Author's database.

provincial leaders, representing about 55 percent of the total. Eighty-eight alternate members (55.7 percent) and 106 full members (53.5 percent) worked (or are currently serving) as provincial leaders. Moreover, 43 percent of Secretariat members, 73 percent of Politburo members (excluding standing members and alternate members), and 89 percent of Politburo standing members worked (or are currently serving) as provincial leaders (Table 2.19).

Provincial leaders are categorically different from technocrats. They are mostly generalists instead of specialists. The preponderance of leaders with local experiences in the Sixteenth CC reflects China's reform experience in the previous two decades. One of the most important features of the economic reforms in China has been decentralization. As horizontal (geographic) divisions have become increasingly important vis-à-vis vertical (ministerial) divisions, leaders with experiences in horizontal divisions are gaining power in the political system.

CONCLUDING REMARKS

The Sixteenth Central Committee of the CCP was a product of a two-part selection/election process. A task force in charge of the Sixteenth Party Congress affairs was set up under the direct leadership of the Fifteenth Politburo Standing Committee to manage the selection process. The task force initially came up with a list of

514 candidates for the Sixteenth Central Committee. After screening and interviews, the committee recommended a list of 462 candidates for the Sixteenth Central Committee. At the Sixteenth Party Congress, the deputies had a preelection and produced 198 full members and 158 alternate members. This list turned out to be the final list. It was approved by the Presidium at its third meeting and was endorsed by the deputies in the formal vote. One interesting thing about the Presidium of the Sixteenth Party Congress is that it is mostly a self-selecting apparatus: 63 percent of the Presidium members (149 people) turned out to be members of the Sixteenth Central Committee.

China's political elites in the Sixteenth Central Committee have a number of interesting characteristics. Individually speaking, a typical member of the Sixteenth CC is someone who is in the mid-fifties, a man, and a Han. His home province is more likely to be in the East Region, especially Jiangsu or Shandong, than any other regions, and he is likely to be well educated. He is likely to have joined the workforce either before or during the Cultural Revolution, and his party standing is about 32 years.

Collectively speaking, the new leadership seems to possess new characteristics. Compared to the central committees since 1987, the number of technocrats who have both academic training in a natural science or engineering and career backgrounds in specialist positions in functional organizations has declined in the Sixteenth CC. In their place, there has emerged a new brand of political elites in China: political leaders with extensive local management experiences. Although some of them also had academic training in a natural science or engineering as well as work experience as engineers in the early years of their career, China's new elites in the early 21st century chose to enhance their academic knowledge in social sciences and economic management. They also gained substantial governance experiences as provincial leaders.

Chapter

3

Balance of Formal Power

It is important to analyze personal characteristics of central committee members to understand trends of personnel changes; but it is more important to study institutional representation on the central committee because election to the central committee generally depends more on the post that a person holds in the Chinese political system than on personal characteristics.[1] For this reason, this chapter is going to focus on institutional representation on the Sixteenth Central Committee. It will introduce China's political institutions in general and then analyze institutional representation on the Sixteenth Central Committee in terms of four major institutions: provinces, central institutions, the military, and corporations.

POLITICAL INSTITUTIONS IN CHINA

There are three major institutions in China: provinces, central institutions, and the military. In a broad sense, as David Goodman correctly observed, leaders of these institutions form categorical groups

---

[1] This is called the "principle of representation of institutions" in Soviet studies. See Jerry F. Hough and Merle Fainsod, *How the Soviet Union is Governed* (Cambridge, MA: Harvard University Press, 1979), p. 458.

that serve no political functions.[2] However, some categorical groups may serve as a basis for political articulation. For instance, although all provincial leaders belong to the same category, provincial leaders who are also members of the central committee of the CCP may serve as a basis for a political group. As a group, their interests are different from those of central ministerial leaders.[3] It is from this premise that we proceed to analyze the central committee representation from different institutions of the Chinese political system. As there have been many changes since November 2002 when the Sixteenth CC was elected, we will identify central committee members by their affiliation in November 2002. A few central committee members did not belong to any of the above institutions. They represent an emerging political force in Chinese politics: corporate leaders.

It should be noted, however, a small group of top leaders did not belong to any of these institutions: They constituted the core of the Chinese political system. At the time of Sixteenth National Party Congress in November 2002, there were 11 central leaders in this group. They include leaders from the Standing Committee of the Politburo (Hu Jintao, Jia Qinglin, Zeng Qinghong, and Huang Ju), the State Council (Wu Bangguo, Wen Jiabao, Luo Gan, Wu Yi, and Ismail Amat), and the Central Military Commission (CMC) (Guo Boxiong and Cao Gangchuan). Hu Jintao, the newly elected general secretary, for instance, is the leader of the whole system, even though he was also president of the Central Party School at that time. He should not be regarded as a representative of a ministerial-level central institution. Jia Qinglin (former party secretary of Beijing) and Huang Ju (former party secretary of Shanghai) had just been uprooted from the two metropolises and did not establish any central institutional identities. In the cases of Wen Jiabao and Wu Bangguo, they were both vice premiers. Zeng Qinghong was a member of the Secretariat and the Politburo. None of them were

---

[2] David S.G. Goodman, "Provincial party first secretaries in national politics: a categorical or a political group?" in David S.G. Goodman (ed) *Groups and Politics in the People's Republic of China* (Armonk, NY: M.E. Sharpe, 1984), pp. 68–82.

[3] Nevertheless, it is incorrect to assume that in China leaders of one institution always act in concert against those of other institutions.

Table 3.1 The Sixteenth Central Committee by Category

	Alternate		Full		Total	
	Number	Percent	Number	Percent	Number	Percent
Political core			11	5.56	11	3.09
Provincial leaders	86	54.43	68	34.34	154	43.26
Central leaders	27	17.09	76	38.38	103	28.93
Military leaders	24	15.19	41	20.71	65	18.26
Corporate leaders	21	13.29	2	1.01	23	6.46
Sixteenth Central Committee	158	100.00	198	100.00	356	100.00

Sources: Author's database.

concurrently ministerial (provincial) level leaders. Luo Gan was a state councilor as well as the head of three separate committees under the central committee: the Committee of Politics and Law, the Committee for Comprehensive Management of Public Security, and the Committee of State Secrets. Hence, except for Shandong (Wu Guanzheng)[4] and Guangdong (Li Changchun),[5] no other provincial or ministerial-level institutions were represented at the Politburo Standing Committee level.

Generally speaking, provincial leaders were the largest group with 154 members, taking 43 percent of the total (Table 3.1). Central leaders (excluding the political core) constituted the second largest group with 103 members, taking 29 percent of the all. Military leaders came as a distant third with 65 members (18 percent), and corporate leaders were the smallest group with only 23 members (6.5 percent). In terms of full membership, central leaders ranked

---

[4] He was later transferred to the Center as a standing member of the Politburo in charge of disciplinary matters. His replacement, Zhang Gaoli, did not make it to the Politburo.

[5] He was later transferred to the Center as a standing member of the Politburo in charge of propaganda work. His replacement is Zhang Dejiang, a Politburo member and former party secretary of Zhejiang. As a result, Guangdong retained its elite provincial status, while Zhejiang lost its elite provincial status.

first with 76 members, followed by provincial leaders with 68 members. While there were 41 military full members, there were only two corporate full members. More than half of alternate members were provincial leaders, and the rest of alternate members were more or less evenly distributed among central, military, and corporate institutions.

PROVINCIAL REPRESENTATION

Evidently, provincial leaders emerged as the most powerful group in Chinese politics as a result of the Sixteenth Congress of the CCP. In the Politburo, provincial leaders were very prominent. Out of 24 full members, 10 (41.7 percent) were provincial leaders. Out of nine standing members, two (22.2 percent) were provincial leaders. If we include those who had just been transferred from provincial units,[6] provincial representation in the Politburo and the standing committee would be 13 (54.2 percent) and four (44.4 percent), respectively.

Elite Provincial Units

The number of provincial units that enjoyed the status of elite provinces[7] was unprecedented in the history of the People's Republic of China (Table 3.2). In addition to the four elite provincial units (Beijing, Shanghai, Shandong, and Guangdong) previously, six more provincial units were upgraded to this status. Tianjin became an elite provincial unit in November 1987 along with Beijing, Shanghai, and Sichuan, when its party secretary, Li Ruihuan, was inducted into the Politburo. However, when Tan Shaowen, a Politburo member and party secretary of Tianjin, passed away in

---

[6] He Guoqiang (Chongqing), Huang Ju (Shanghai), and Jia Qinglin (Beijing) were transferred to the center only two weeks before the convention of the Sixteenth Party Congress.

[7] For a definition and detailed discussion of elite provinces, see Zhiyue Bo, *Chinese Provincial Leaders: Economic Performance and Political Mobility Since 1949* (Armonk, NY: M.E. Sharpe, 2002), pp. 19–35.

Table 3.2 Elite Provincial Units in China (1969–2002)

	1969		1973			1977		1987	1992		1997	2002		Total
	ccpf	ccpa	ccpf	ccpa	ccvc	ccpf	ccpa	ccpf	ccpf	ccps	ccpf	ccpf	ccps	
Beijing	2	0	1	1	0	2	0	1	1	0	1	1	0	10
Tianjin	0	0	0	0	0	0	0	1	1	0	0	1	0	3
Hebei	0	1	0	0	0	0	0	0	0	0	0	0	0	1
Shanxi	0	0	1	0	0	1	0	0	0	0	0	0	0	2
Liaoning	2	0	0	0	0	0	0	0	0	0	0	0	0	2
Shanghai	2	0	2	0	1	2	0	1	1	0	1	1	0	11
Jiangsu	1	0	0	0	0	0	0	0	0	0	0	1	0	2
Zhejiang	0	0	0	0	0	0	0	0	0	0	0	1	0	1
Anhui	0	1	0	0	0	0	0	0	0	0	0	0	0	1
Shandong	0	0	0	0	0	0	0	0	1	0	1	0	1	3
Henan	0	1	1	0	0	0	0	0	0	0	1	0	0	3
Hubei	0	0	0	0	0	0	0	0	0	0	0	1	0	1
Hunan	0	0	1	0	0	0	0	0	0	0	0	0	0	1
Guangdong	1	0	0	0	0	1	0	0	1	0	1	0	1	5
Guangxi	0	0	1	0	0	0	0	0	0	0	0	0	0	1
Sichuan	0	0	0	0	0	0	1	1	0	0	0	1	0	3
Tibet	0	0	0	0	0	0	0	0	0	1	0	0	0	1
Shaanxi	0	0	0	1	0	0	0	0	0	0	0	0	0	1
Xinjiang	0	0	0	1	0	0	1	0	0	0	0	1	0	3
Total	8	3	7	3	1	6	2	4	5	1	5	8	2	55

Notes: ccpf=full members of the Politburo; ccpa=alternate members of the Politburo; ccps=standing members of the Politburo; ccvc=vice chairmen of the Central Committee.
Source: Updated from Zhiyue Bo, *Chinese Provincial Leaders: Economic Performance and Political Mobility Since 1949* (Armonk, N.Y.: M.E. Sharpe, 2002), Table 2.3, p. 25.

February 1993, Tianjin's elite provincial status went away with him, because Tan's successor, Gao Dezhan, did not inherit his seat in the Politburo. The promotion of Zhang Lichang, party secretary of Tianjin, to the Politburo restored Tianjin's elite provincial status. Similarly, this was true for Sichuan. Sichuan became an elite province in 1987 when Yang Rudai was elevated to the Politburo but lost that seat five years later when Yang retired and his successor failed to make it to the Politburo.[8] In 2002, Party Secretary Zhou

---

[8] Some blamed Governor Xiao Yang for the loss. See Lijian Hong, "Provincial leadership and its strategy toward the acquisition of foreign investment in Sichuan," in

Yongkang made it not only to the Politburo but also to the Secretariat. Sichuan's elite provincial status was restored for the time being, but soon was lost again due to the departure of Zhou.[9]

Jiangsu was not a complete stranger to the elite provincial status if we trace its history back to the Cultural Revolution. It was one of a few elite provinces in 1969 when Xu Shiyou, chairman of the Jiangsu Revolutionary Committee, was made a full Politburo member at the First Plenum of the Ninth Central Committee.[10] However, after Xu was transferred away in 1973, none of his successors were Politburo members. Jiangsu regained its elite provincial status largely due to Hui Liangyu, party secretary. Hui, a native of Jilin, was a rising star in Chinese politics. Since 1987, he had served in four provinces (Jilin, Hubei, Anhui, and Jiangsu) as well as in the Center. He became party secretary of Anhui in 1998 and was transferred to Jiangsu as party secretary in 1999. His promotion to the Politburo, therefore, was more of the promotion of the person than the promotion of the province. Hui's later promotion to the State Council as a vice premier ended Jiangsu's elite provincial status.

In contrast, the promotion of Zhang Dejiang to the Politburo was more of the promotion of the province than the promotion of the person. Zhejiang is well known as a province of "red" capitalists. In 2001, there were 1.79 million private firms in Zhejiang. The booming nonpublic sector contributed 43.5 percent of the total provincial GDP, compared to 33 percent nationally.[11] In view of Jiang Zemin's preference for red capitalists, it is understandable that the Party boss of the province of red capitalists was elevated to the Politburo. Zhang's resume, however, is less impressive. Being a

---

Peter T.Y. Cheung, Jae Ho Chung, and Zhimin Lin (eds) *Provincial Strategies of Economic Reform in Post-Mao China* (Armonk, NY: M.E. Sharpe, 1998), pp. 392–395.

[9] He became minister of Public Security in addition to his responsibilities in the Secretariat and the Politburo. Zhang Xuezhong, minister of Personnel and a full member, replaced him as party secretary of Sichuan.

[10] Jiangsu's elite provincial status, admittedly, was mainly due to Xu Shiyou, who was also the commander of the Nanjing Military Region.

[11] Zhao Huanxin, "Zhejiang ranks as wealthy province," *China Daily*, November 13, 2002. See http://www3.chinadaily.com.cn/en/doc/2002–11/12/content_143595.htm.

Korean language student at Yanbian University during the Cultural Revolution, he later went to North Korea and received a diploma in economics in 1980 from the Kim Il-sung Comprehensive University. Before 2002, he had worked in two provinces as well as in the Center. He was promoted to party secretary of Jilin in 1995 and was transferred to Zhejiang as party secretary in 1998, replacing the Party boss of 10 years (Li Zemin). He has been very supportive of central policies regarding the WTO entry and made the pledge to take one step ahead for Zhejiang to realize the goal of the basic modernization.[12] He was later transferred to Guangdong to replace Li Changchun.

Hubei does not have any history as an elite province, and its promotion to that status was mainly due to its new party secretary, Yu Zhengsheng. A princeling with close connections with Deng Pufang, son of Deng Xiaoping, Yu seems to have possessed all the right credentials for a Politburo member. Being a technocrat with extensive experiences in local government as well as in the Center, he was transferred to Hubei as party secretary in November 2001 and became a Politburo member one year later.

The most interesting case of all is that of Xinjiang. Xinjiang enjoyed a semi-elite provincial status in the 1970s, when its first party secretary, Seypidin Azizi,[13] made it to the Politburo as an alternate member. His successor, Wang Feng, was a full member of the central committee but not a Politburo member. Party Secretary Wang Lequan's promotion into the Politburo was indeed the promotion of the region as well. Xinjiang is one of the five minority regions in China; it occupies a strategic location bordering with eight other countries such as Mongolia, Russia, Kazakhstan, Kyrgyzstan,

---

[12] For a brief discussion of Zhang Dejiang's policy statements for Zhejiang, see Zhiyue Bo, "Governing China in the early 21st century: provincial perspective," *Journal of Chinese Political Science*, Vol. 2, No. (1–2) (2002), pp. 125–170.

[13] He was the only Uygur in the history of the People's Republic of China who was the First Party Secretary of this minority region. All the other party secretaries in the region have been of Han nationality. For a detailed analysis of the Party's efforts to control minority regions, see Bo, *Chinese Provincial Leaders*, pp. 60–64.

Tajikistan, Afghanistan, Pakistan, and India. Xinjiang is the largest provincial unit in area (1.6 million square kilometers) with many natural resources.

Geographically, elite provincial units were more evenly distributed in 2002 than before. They included two in the North (Beijing and Tianjin), four in the East (Shanghai, Shandong, Jiangsu, and Zhejiang), two in the Central-South (Guangdong and Hubei), one in the Southwest (Sichuan), and one in the Northwest (Xinjiang). Except for the Northeast, all the other regions were represented. In terms of three major economic areas, the Eastern Area was overrepresented by a large margin. Seven out of 12 provincial units[14] in the area had Politburo seats. In addition to three centrally administered municipalities, four provinces were represented in the Politburo and two of them (Shandong and Guangdong) were represented in the Standing Committee of the Politburo. The Central Area[15] was least represented, with only one elite province (Hubei). However, this was better. The Western Area[16] was better represented in the Politburo than the Central Area, with two elite provincial units (Sichuan and Xinjiang). Most importantly, in contrast to Tibet whose elite provincial status was ephemeral in 1992 when Hu Jintao was elevated to the Standing Committee of the Politburo, it seems that Xinjiang, also a minority region, may stay in this status for a while.

Provincial Central Committee Representation

All provincial units except Taiwan were represented in the Sixteenth CC (Table 3.3). The 31 provincial units that had representation in the Fifteenth CC were all represented in the Sixteenth CC.

---

[14] They are Beijing, Tianjin, Shanghai, Hebei, Shangdong, Jiangsu, Zhejiang, Fujian, Guangdong, Guangxi, Hainan, and Liaoning.

[15] It includes nine provincial units: Heilongjiang, Jilin, Inner Mongolia, Shanxi, Henan, Hubei, Hunan, Jiangxi, and Anhui.

[16] It includes 10 provincial units: Chongqiang, Gansu, Ningxia, Qinghai, Xingjiang, Tibet, Shanxi, Yunnan, Guizhou, and Sichuan. For the division of the three areas, see http://www.anderson.ucla.edu:7777/research/globalwindow/china/t8/sup1art.htm.

Table 3.3 Provincial CC Representation (1969–2002)

	1969		1973		1977		1982		1987		1992		1997		2002		
	ccf	cca	ccf	cca	ccf	cca	ccf	cca	ccf	cca	ccf	cca	ccf	cca	ccf	cca	Index
Beijing	5	4	5	6	4	4	1	3	2	3	3	1	2	2	2	3	9
Tianjin	3	1	4	0	4	1	4	0	2	2	2	2	2	2	2	3	9
Hebei	4	1	5	1	5	1	2	4	1	3	2	1	2	3	2	2	6
Shanxi	3	3	3	3	3	2	2	3	3	1	2	2	2	1	2	3	7
Inner Mongolia	3	1	4	2	2	1	2	2	2	2	2	3	2	2	2	3	7
Liaoning	6	1	6	2	5	2	3	3	3	2	2	2	2	0	2	3	7
Jilin	2	3	3	3	2	2	2	2	3	1	2	1	2	0	2	2	6
Heilongjiang	2	2	2	5	3	3	2	3	0	2	4	2	0	2	3		7
Shanghai	6	4	9	4	6	4	3	2	1	5	2	2	3	2	2	2	8
Jiangsu	3	3	4	3	3	4	3	1	3	2	3	3	2	2	2	2	8
Zhejiang	3	3	3	3	2	4	3	2	2	1	2	1	2	2	2	3	9
Anhui	1	2	3	2	3	1	0	2	2	2	2	1	2	0	2	3	7
Fujian	3	3	1	2	4	1	3	1	2	1	2	2	2	1	2	2	6
Jiangxi	2	1	1	5	4	2	2	1	2	1	2	3	2	1	2	3	7
Shandong	5	1	4	3	4	2	1	4	3	2	2	4	2	3	2	4	11
Henan	4	4	5	2	3	5	1	3	2	3	2	2	2	1	2	3	7
Hubei	6	2	5	5	5	2	5	2	3	0	1	3	2	2	2	2	8
Hunan	2	2	3	4	4	2	2	4	3	3	2	3	2	1	2	2	6
Guangdong	6	3	9	3	5	4	3	4	3	2	2	4	2	4	2	6	13
Guangxi	1	2	3	2	2	4	3	2	1	1	2	2	2	1	2	3	7
Sichuan	6	6	5	8	4	3	3	4	3	2	2	4	2	1	2	4	10
Guizhou	0	3	3	1	2	1	3	2	3	2	2	1	2	1	2	3	7
Yunnan	4	2	3	3	4	4	3	3	2	2	2	2	2	3	2	3	7
Tibet	1	2	2	2	3	2	3	1	3	1	3	2	2	3	3	2	8
Shaanxi	2	3	2	3	2	2	3	1	3	1	2	3	2	1	2	3	7
Gansu	5	2	4	1	4	1	1	1	1	2	2	3	2	0	2	3	7
Qinghai	1	4	0	4	2	2	1	1	1	1	1	2	2	1	2	2	6
Ningxia	0	3	0	4	1	3	1	2	2	2	2	1	2	2	2	2	6
Xinjiang	2	4	3	3	3	3	3	2	2	3	3	3	2	3	4	3	13
Hainan											2	2	2	2	2	2	6
Chongqing													2	2	3	2	8
Hong Kong													1	0			2
Macao													1	0			2
Total	91	75	104	89	98	73	69	64	66	53	62	69	63	49	68	86	244

Notes: ccf=full members of the central committee; cca=alternate members of the central committee.
Source: Updated from Zhiyue Bo, *Chinese Provincial Leaders: Economic Performance and Political Mobility Since 1949* (Armonk, N.Y.: M.E. Sharpe, 2002), Appendix 2.2, p. 35.

On average, there were about two full members from these provincial units, with only three exceptions. Tibet and Chongqing each had three full members; Xinjiang had four full members. With only one exception, all provincial party secretaries and governors were full members. The exceptional case was Lu Ruihua, governor of Guangdong. He was expected to retire from his position. Huang Huahua, a deputy secretary and a vice governor as well as a full member, was a candidate for his position and indeed replaced him later on. In the cases of Tibet and Chongqing, in addition to party secretaries and governors, the chairmen of the standing committees of their provincial (or regional) people's congresses were also full members. Xinjiang, however, had another full-member deputy secretary[17] and a full member from the Xinjiang Production and Construction Corps.[18] Zhang Qingli, commander of the Xinjiang Production and Construction Corps, was elevated to a full member of the Sixteenth CC, skipping the level of alternate membership. Because of these three exceptions, the mean of the full membership from provinces in the Sixteenth CC (2.06) was slightly higher than that in the Fifteenth CC (2.03), with a much larger standard deviation (0.50 versus 0.18).

For the first time, Hong Kong and Macao were also represented in the central committee of the CCP. Tung Chee-hwa (Dong Jianhua in Pinyin),[19] governor of the Hong Kong Special Administrative

---

[17] Zhou Shengtao was one of potential candidates for the position of party secretary in Sichuan. However, Zhang Xuezhong was sent down from the Center to assume the position.

[18] The Xinjiang Production and Construction Corps is also partially under the leadership of the Xinjiang Uygur Autonomous Region. In October 1954, the Central People's Government instructed the PLA in Xinjiang to demobilize there to be engaged in production. Beginning in May 1956, the Xinjiang Production and Construction Corps was placed under the dual leadership of the Ministry of Agricultural Cultivation and the Xinjiang Uygur Autonomous Region. For a detailed introduction, see Information Office of the State Council, "Xinjiang de lishi yu fazhan" ("The history and development of Xinjiang"), *Renmin ribao* (overseas edition), May 27, 2003, pp. 2, 3.

[19] Tung was born in Shanghai. If the birthplace were the criterion for being a member of the Shanghai Gang, he obviously would be qualified.

Region (SAR), nevertheless, did not make it to the central committee because he was not a CCP member. Gao Siren, director of the Liaison Office of the Central People's Government in the Hong Kong SAR, was elevated to a full member of the Sixteenth CC. A native of Qingdao in Shandong and a graduate of Hefei Industrial University, Gao spent almost his entire career in Guangdong. In 1991, he became a standing member of the Guangdong Provincial Party Committee and party secretary of Guangzhou. He entered the Fourteenth Central Committee as an alternate member in 1992 and was promoted to a deputy secretary of Guangdong in 1998.[20] In November 1999, he was transferred to Hong Kong as deputy director of the Liaison Office and was appointed as director of the office three years later, replacing his predecessor, Jiang Enzhu.[21]

Similarly, for the same reason Edmund Ho Hau-wah (He Houhua in Pinyin), governor of the Macao SAR, did not make it to the Sixteenth CC. Bai Zhijian, director of the Liaison Office of the Central People's Government in the Macao SAR, was elevated to a full member of the Sixteenth CC. A native of Wuhan, Hubei, Bai was a professional in agriculture. After 22 years in agriculture, he was transferred to Inner Mongolia as a deputy secretary in August 1998.[22] He was appointed as director of the Liaison Office of the Central People's Government in the Macao SAR in October 2001 and became a full member of the Sixteenth CC a year later.

---

[20] Shen Xueming and Zheng Jianying (eds), *Zhonggong Diyijie zhi Dishiwujie Zhongyangweiyuan* (*The Central Committee Members of the Chinese Communist Party from the First through the Fifteenth Central Committee*) (Beijing: Zhongyang Wenxian Chubanshe, 2001), pp. 655, 656.

[21] Jiang became the bureau chief of Xinhua News Agency in Hong Kong in July 1997 and was made a full member of the Fifteenth Central Committee in the same year. He was appointed director of the Liaison Office in January 2000. In view of these facts, Jiang was the first Hong Kong central committee member. For Jiang's biography, see Shen Xueming and Zheng Jianying, *Zhonggong Diyijie zhi Dishiwujie Zhongyangweiyuan*, p. 590.

[22] Shen Xueming and Han Honghong (eds), *Zhonggong Dishiwujie Zhongyangweiyuanhui Zhongyang Jilujianchaweiyuanhui Weiyuan Minglu* (*Who's who in the Fifteenth Central Committee and Commission for Discipline Inspection of the Chinese Communist Party*) (Beijing: Zhongyang Wenxian Chubanshe, 1999), p. 381.

The provincial alternate-member representation, in contrast, was much more diverse across provincial units. First, Hong Kong and Macao did not have any alternate members. Second, Guangdong, Shandong, and Sichuan stood out as provinces with the largest numbers of alternate members. Guangdong had six alternate members, and Shandong and Sichuan each had four. Third, all the remaining provincial units had two-to-three alternate members. On average, the provincial alternate-member representation was 2.61,[23] half a seat more than that of the provincial full-member representation. The standard deviation, on the other hand, was 1.06, much larger than that of the full-member representation (0.50).

In terms of absolute numbers, provinces contributed 68 full members and 86 alternate members. When compared to the situation five years earlier, provinces had six more full members and 37 more alternate members in 2002. Clearly, provinces were the largest group by a wide margin in terms of alternate members in the Sixteenth CC. Fifty-four percent of alternate members came from provinces, and the next largest group (central organs) took only 17 percent.

Provincial Central Committee Index

In order to make possible a comparison across provinces as well as among different institutional groups, we are going to produce a central committee index (or power index) according to the following scheme.[24] An alternate member of the central committee receives one point, a full member two, an alternate Politburo member one more, a full Politburo member two more, a standing Politburo member three more, and the general secretary five more. In addition, members of the Secretariat receive one more point each; members of the CMC receive one more point each and vice chairmen of the CMC two more points each.[25]

---

[23] This is calculated including Hong Kong and Macao.
[24] This is adapted from Bo, *Chinese Provincial Leaders*, p. 27.
[25] Jiang Zemin is not in the picture because he was not a central committee member, even though he was chairman of the CMC.

On average, the provincial central committee index was 7.455 points, with a range between 2 and 13 (the last column of Table 3.3). Hong Kong and Macao were the lowest with only two points each, and Guangdong and Xinjiang were the highest with 13 points each. With one standing Politburo member, one full member, and six alternate members, Guangdong was one of the two most powerful provincial units in China. With one Politburo member, four full members, and three alternate members, Xinjiang also shined as one of the political stars. Shandong and Sichuan ranked third and fourth with 11 points and 10 points, respectively. Interestingly enough, Shanghai did not stand out this time. With an index of only eight points, Shanghai was not even among the top eight. Obviously, Huang Ju's recent departure may have somewhat affected Shanghai's score.

The total scores from all provincial units were 244 points, representing 39 percent of the total scores and thus making provinces the most powerful institution in Chinese politics.

CENTRAL REPRESENTATION

The representation of central organs is much more fragmented. On the surface, it seems that many central committee members were from the center. The total number of central officials, excluding the top leaders, stood at 103, with 27 alternate and 76 full members.

These numbers, however, are deceptive because there is no single system of ministerial-level central institutions. Instead, there are two separate central institutions: central party-institutions and central government-institutions. Central party-institutions include party organs directly under the Central Committee. Currently, there are 20 central party-institutions under the central committee (Table 3.4). The most important are the four departments: Organization, Propaganda, United Front, and International Liaison. When the Politburo was elected in November 2002, three central party departments were represented: Organization (He Guoqiang), Propaganda (Liu Yunshan), and United Front (Wang Zhaoguo). Moreover, Organization (He Guoqiang) and Propaganda (Liu Yunshan)

Table 3.4 Central Party-Institution Central Committee Representation (2002)

Central Party Institutions	cca	ccf	ccpf	ccpa	sec	Index
Organization Department	1	2	1	0	1	8
Propaganda Department	1	1	1	0	1	6
United Front Department	0	4	1	0	0	10
International Liaison Department	1	1	0	0	0	3
General Office	2	1	0	1	0	5
Party School	0	1	0	0	0	2
People's Daily	0	1	0	0	0	2
Party History Research Center	0	0	0	0	0	0
Party Literature	0	0	0	0	0	0
Compilation and Translation Bureau	0	0	0	0	0	0
Work Committee of the Central Government	0	0	0	0	0	2
Work Committee of the Departments under the Central Committee	0	0	0	0	0	0
Committee of Politics and Law under the Central Committee	0	0	0	0	0	0
Committee for Comprehensive Management of Public Security	0	0	0	0	0	0
Policy Research Office of the Central Committee	0	2	0	0	0	4
Taiwan Office	1	1	0	0	0	3
International Communications Office	0	1	0	0	0	2
Central Foreign Affairs Office	0	1	0	0	0	2
Committee of State Secrets	0	0	0	0	0	0
Total	6	16	3	1	2	49

Notes: ccf=full members of the central committee; cca=alternate members of the central committee; ccpf=full members of the Politburo; ccps=standing members of the Politburo; sec=members of the Secretariat.
Sources: Shen Xueming and Zheng Jianying (eds), *Zhonggong Diyijie zhi Dishiwujie Zhongyangweiyuan* [The Central Committee Members of the Chinese Communist Party from the First through the Fifteenth Central Committee] (Beijing: Zhongyang Wenxian Chubanshe, 2001); *Renminwang*.

Departments were also represented in the Secretariat. In addition, the Director of the Central Office, Wang Gang,[26] was also made an alternate member of the Politburo. Out of the 20 central party-institutions, nine were represented in the Politburo, even though there actually were six individuals from these institutions.

In contrast, central government-institutions including ministries and commissions under the State Council were less well represented.[27] Out of 29 ministries and commissions, only one was represented in the Politburo and another represented in the Secretariat. Zeng Peiyan, Chairman of the State Development and Planning Commission, was elevated to the Politburo. He Yong, Minister of Supervision, was inducted into the Secretariat. If we look at these 29 ministries and commissions alone, there were only 30 full members and 11 alternate members. The number of full members in the central government-institutions was less than half of that (68) in the provinces; the number of alternate members in the central government-institutions was even less, only 13 percent of that (86) in the provinces.

There are additional central government-institutions under the State Council. These are 17 organizations, seven working organs, 13 offices, and 15 bureaus. Including ministries and commissions, there are altogether 81 institutions under the State Council.[28] The

---

[26] He was also secretary of the Committee of Central Organs under the Central Committee.

[27] It should be noted that Lu Fuyuan, a full member of the Sixteenth Central Committee and minister of Commerce, passed away on May 18, 2004 at the age of 59 (see http://news.xinhuanet.com/fortune/2004-05/18/content_1476933.htm) and that Tian Fengshan, former minister of State Land Resources and full member of the Sixteenth Central Committee, was expelled from the central committee in September 2004 because of his involvement in corruption and was sentenced to life imprisonment on December 27, 2005 (see http://news.xinhuanet.com/ziliao/2002-03/01/content_295721.htm).

[28] For an introduction to the historical evolution of institutional reforms at the central level from 1982 to 2001, see Kjeld Erik Brodsgaard, "Institutional reform and the *Bianzhi* system in China," *China Quarterly*, Vol. 170 (June 2002), pp. 361–386.

total numbers of full and alternate members from these institutions in addition to a few offices of the State Council such as the Office of Secretaries-General, the Working Committee of State Enterprises, and industrial bureaus under the State Council were 51 and 18, respectively. These were still significantly less than the numbers in provinces. When compared to provinces, the representation of the central government-institutions in the CC was only 76 percent in terms of full members and 21 percent in terms of alternate members.

There are additional central institutions that do not necessarily belong to either central party- or central government-institutions. The Supreme People's Court and the Supreme People's Procurate, for instance, are judicial institutions. Five major banks in China (China Industrial and Commercial Bank, China Agricultural Bank, China Development Bank, China Construction Bank, and the Bank of China) obviously belong to banking institutions. Moreover, there are 14 mass organizations such as All-China Federation of Industry and Commerce, All-China Federation of Trade Unions, the Chinese Communist Youth League, All-China Women's Federation, and so on. In one rare case, a central cadre belongs to the Chinese People's Political Consultative Conference. Li Guixian, a technocrat with extensive experience at both provincial and central levels, was retained as a full member of the Sixteenth CC.

Even if we put all these other institutions under central government-institutions, the total numbers of full (60) and alternate members (21) were still less than those from provinces (Table 3.5). In terms of the total power index, the provinces still beat central government-institutions by a huge margin of 100 points. The score of provincial power index was 244, and the score of all these central government-institutions was only 144. The provinces were much more powerful than central government-institutions. Even if we combine the power index of the central party-institutions with that of the central government-institutions, the central institutions as a whole were still less powerful than the provinces. The score of the combined index was 193, still 51 points less than that of the provincial power index.

Table 3.5 Central Government Central Committee Representation (2002)

Central Government Institutions	cca	ccf	ccpf	sec	Index
Foreign Affairs	1	2	0	0	5
National Defense	0	0	0	0	0
State Development and Planning Commission	1	1	1	0	5
State Economic & Trade Commission	1	1	0	0	3
Education	3	1	0	0	5
Science and Technology	0	1	0	0	2
Commission of Science, Technology, and Industry for National Defense	2	0	0	0	2
State Ethnic Affairs Commission	0	1	0	0	2
Public Security	1	2	0	0	5
State Security	0	1	0	0	2
Supervision	0	2	0	1	5
Civil Affairs	0	1	0	0	2
Justice	0	1	0	0	2
Finance	0	1	0	0	2
Personnel	0	1	0	0	2
Labor and Social Security	0	1	0	0	2
Land and Resources	0	1	0	0	2
Construction	0	1	0	0	2
Railways	0	1	0	0	2
Communications	0	1	0	0	2
Information Industry	0	0	0	0	0
Water Resources	0	1	0	0	2
Agriculture	1	1	0	0	3
Foreign Trade and Economic Cooperation	0	1	0	0	2
Culture	0	1	0	0	2
Health	1	1	0	0	3
State Family Planning Commission	0	1	0	0	2
People's Bank of China	0	2	0	0	4
National Audit Office	0	1	0	0	2
General Administration of Customs	0	1	0	0	2
State Administration of Taxation	0	1	0	0	2
General Administration for Industry and Commerce	0	1	0	0	2
State General Administration of the People's Republic of China for Quality Supervision & Inspection & Quarantine	0	1	0	0	2
State Environmental Protection Administration	0	1	0	0	2
General Administration of the Civil Aviation of China	0	1	0	0	2
State Administration of Radio, Film and Television	0	1	0	0	2
General Administration of Press and Publication	0	1	0	0	2
State General Admistration of Sports	1	1	0	0	3
National Bureau of Statistics	1	0	0	0	1

(Continued)

Table 3.5 (Continued)

Central Government Institutions	cca	ccf	ccpf	sec	Index
State Forestry Bureau	1	0	0	0	1
State Drug Administration	0	0	0	0	0
State Intellectual Property Office	0	0	0	0	0
National Tourism Administration	0	0	0	0	0
State Administration of Religious Affairs	1	0	0	0	1
Counselor's Office of the State Council	0	0	0	0	0
Government Offices Administration of the State Council	0	0	0	0	0
Overseas Chinese Affairs Office of the State Council	0	0	0	0	0
Hong Kong and Macao Affairs Office of the State Council	0	1	0	0	2
Legislative Affairs Office of the State Council	0	0	0	0	0
Economic Restructuring Office of the State Council	0	1	0	0	2
Research Office of the State Council	0	1	0	0	2
Taiwan Affairs Office of the State Council	0	0	0	0	0
Information Office of the State Council	0	0	0	0	0
Xinhua News Agency	0	1	0	0	2
Chinese Academy of Sciences	1	1	0	0	3
Chinese Academy of Social Sciences	1	0	0	0	1
Chinese Academy of Engineering	0	1	0	0	2
Development Research Center of the State Council	0	0	0	0	0
National School of Administration	0	1	0	0	2
China Seismological Bureau	0	0	0	0	0
China Meteorological Administration	0	0	0	0	0
China Securities Regulatory Commission	0	1	0	0	2
China Insurance Regulatory Commission	1	0	0	0	1
National Electricity Regulatory Commission	0	1	0	0	2
National Council for Social Security Fund	0	0	0	0	0
National Natural Science Foundation of China	0	0	0	0	0
Industrial Bureaus	0	1	0	0	2
State Council Office	0	2	0	0	4
Courts	2	1	0	0	4
Banks	4	0	0	0	4
Mass Organizations	1	5	0	0	11
CPPCC	0	1	0	0	2
Total	25	58	1	1	144

Notes: ccf=full members of the central committee; cca=alternate members of the central committee; ccpf=full members of the Politburo; ccps=standing members of the Politburo; sec=members of the Secretariat.

Sources: Shen Xueming and Zheng Jianying (eds), *Zhonggong Diyijie zhi Dishiwujie Zhongyangweiyuan* [*The Central Committee Members of the Chinese Communist Party from the First through the Fifteenth Central Committee*] (Beijing: Zhongyang Wenxian Chubanshe, 2001); *Renminwang*.

MILITARY REPRESENTATION

With the exception of Jiang Zemin, the military representation in the Politburo remained more or less the same in 2002 as it was five years earlier. No one had a seat on the Standing Committee of the Politburo, and there were two Politburo members and one Secretariat member from the military. The only difference is that the military representative in the Sixteenth Secretariat was not a concurrent Politburo member as before. In 1997, Zhang Wannian (1928–) served in both the Politburo and the Secretariat.[29] In 2002, neither Guo Boxiong (1942–) (the second vice chairman of the CMC and a Politburo member)[30] nor Cao Gangchuan (1935–) (the third vice chairman of the CMC and a Politburo member)[31] was in the Secretariat. Xu Caihou (1943–), a member of the CMC and director of the General Political Department, made it to the Secretariat instead.[32] A native of Liaoning, Xu joined the People's Liberation Army (PLA) in 1963. Twenty years later, in 1983, he became a deputy-director of the Political Department in the Jilin Provincial Military District. After serving in various capacities in the Sixteenth Group Army of the Ground Force, he was selected in 1992 to be assistant director of the General Political Department under Yu Yongbo (1931–),[33] a CMC member at the time and Xu's township fellow from the same county, Wafangdian, Liaoning Province. Xu was inducted to the CMC in 1999 and was reelected to that key organ in 2002. As the most senior member of the current CMC and director of the General Political Department in 2002, Xu was poised to play an important role in the Secretariat as the only military representative.

---

[29] For his bio, see http://big5.china.com.cn/chinese/zhuanti/208136.htm.
[30] For his bio, see http://news.xinhuanet.com/ziliao/2002-01/21/content_246263.htm.
[31] For his bio, see http://news.xinhuanet.com/ziliao/2002-01/21/content_246248.htm.
[32] For his bio, see http://news.xinhuanet.com/ziliao/2002-01/21/content_246269.htm.
[33] For his bio, see http://news.xinhuanet.com/ziliao/2002-01/21/content_246222.htm.

This CMC was smaller than its predecessor, with only four members. These members were in charge of four general departments. Xu Caihou was director of the General Political Department, Liang Guanglie (1940–) was chief of the General Staff, Liao Xilong (1940–) was director of the General Logistics Department, and Li Jinai (1942–) was director of the General Armament Department. In addition to these general departments, there are four central military command institutions as well as three military academic institutions in the Center. The central military command institutions include navy, air force, second artillery corps, and armed police force. The military academic institutions include the University of National Defense, the Academy of Military Sciences, and the National University of Defense Technology. In the locality, there are seven military regions: Shenyang, Beijing, Lanzhou, Jinan, Nanjing, Guangzhou, and Chengdu. Each of these regions is in charge of several provincial military districts. All these military institutions were represented in the central committee.

When compared with the key central government-institutions (29 ministries and commissions), the military is better represented in the central committee. There are 41 full members and 24 alternate members in the central committee from the military, 11 more in the category of full members and 13 more in the category of alternate members than those from the key central government-institutions. Since there are only 18 military institutions, the central committee representation per institution is even better in the military than in the central government-institutions. The full-member representation from the military was 2.28 on average, while the average from the central government-institutions was only 0.35. A similar pattern can be found at the alternate level as well. The average military representation was 1.33, while the average central government-institution representation was only 0.81.

If we compare scores of the power index across military institutions, we may find that the General Staff was most powerful (Table 3.6). With a total score of 11 points, it was best represented in the Sixteenth CC. The General Staff also had the largest number of the Sixteenth Central Committee members: three full and four

Table 3.6 Military Central Committee Representation (2002)

Military Institutions	cca	ccf	ccpf	sec	cmc	Index
General Staff	4	3	0	0	1	11
Political Department	2	2	0	1	1	8
Logistics Department	1	2	0	0	1	6
Armament Department	1	2	0	0	1	6
Navy	1	3	0	0	0	7
Air Force	0	2	0	0	0	4
Second Artillery Corps	1	2	0	0	0	5
Chinese People's Armed Police Force	1	3	0	0	0	7
Shenyang Military Region	2	4	0	0	0	10
Beijing Military Region	2	2	0	0	0	6
Lanzhou Military Region	1	3	0	0	0	7
Jinan Military Region	2	2	0	0	0	6
Nanjing Military Region	1	3	0	0	0	7
Guangzhou Military Region	2	3	0	0	0	8
Chengdu Military Region	1	2	0	0	0	5
National Defense University	2	1	0	0	0	4
Academy of Military Sciences	0	1	0	0	0	2
National University of Defence Technology	0	1	0	0	0	2
Total	24	41	0	1	4	111

Notes: ccf=full members of the Central Committee; cca=alternate members of the Central Committee; ccpf=full members of the Politburo; ccps=standing members of the Politburo; sec=members of the Secretariat.
Sources: Shen Xueming and Zheng Jianying (eds), *Zhonggong Diyijie zhi Dishiwujie Zhongyangweiyuan* [*The Central Committee Members of the Chinese Communist Party from the First through the Fifteenth Central Committee*] (Beijing: Zhongyang Wenxian Chubanshe, 2001); *Renminwang*.

alternate members. The three full members were General Liang Guanglie, General Qian Shugen, and Lieutenant General Ge Zhenfeng; four alternate members were General Wu Quanxu, General Xiong Guangkai, Lieutenant General Zhang Li, and Lieutenant General You Xigui.

General Liang was chief of the General Staff of the PLA. A native of Sichuan, he joined the PLA in 1958 and the CCP in 1959. A military professional through the ranks, Liang entered the CCP's Central

Committee in 1987 as an alternate member. His military career took off in 1993 when he became chief of staff in the Beijing Military Region. Shortly after he was appointed as commander of the Shenyang Military Region in 1997, he made it into the Fifteenth Central Committee as a full member.[34] He was promoted to the rank of general in June 2002, before the Sixteenth National Party Congress. He was appointed as chief of the General Staff in November 2002 and was inducted into the CMC in that capacity. Qian Shugen, Wu Quanxu, and Xiong Guangkai belong to the same cohort. They were all born in the same year, 1939: Qian and Xiong were born in March, and Wu was born in April. Qian and Wu both joined the PLA in 1954 and received similar military education. Wu graduated from the Shenyang Artillery School in 1956, and Qian graduated from the Chongqing Artillery School in the same year. They both served in artillery regiments in the beginning of their military career and were promoted as a deputy chief of staff in the same month (July 1995).[35] Xiong Guangkai, a third member of the cohort, had a different career path. He joined the PLA in 1956 and was enrolled in a foreign language program in the PLA's foreign language school. He went up the ladder of success in the Information Department of the General Staff and was appointed as a deputy chief of staff in January 1996.[36] While Qian had been an alternate member of the central committee between 1987 and 1997 and a full central committee member since 1997, Xiong and Wu had been an alternate member of the central committee since 1997.

Another person in the group is You Xigui. Because of his close association with Jiang Zemin, You has been mistakenly identified by some scholars as a member of the Shanghai Gang.[37] In fact, You has

---

[34] For his bio, see Shen Xueming and Zheng Jianying, *Zhonggong Diyijie zhi Dishiwujie Zhongyangweiyuan*, pp. 707, 708.

[35] For their bios, see Shen Xueming and Zheng Jianying, *Zhonggong Diyijie zhi Dishiwujie Zhongyangweiyuan*, pp. 371 and 629, 630.

[36] For his bio, see Shen Xueming and Zheng Jianying, *Zhonggong Diyijie zhi Dishiwujie Zhongyangweiyuan*, p. 785.

[37] See Cheng Li, "Poised to take the helm: rising stars and the transition to the fourth generation," in David M. Finkelstein and Maryanne Kivlehan (eds), *China's*

never worked in Shanghai. A native of Hebei, he joined the PLA in 1958 and the CCP in 1960. He spent his entire career in the central guards. Initially he was a nurse and assistant physician, but later became an officer responsible for logistics. He was appointed as director of the Central Guards Bureau in August 1994 and made it to the central committee in 1997 as an alternate member. He has also been concurrent deputy director of the General Office of the Central Committee since October 1997. You was awarded the rank of major general in July 1990 and was promoted to the rank of lieutenant general in July 1997.[38] Out of 158 alternate members of the Sixteenth Central Committee ranked according to the number of votes each received, You was at the bottom of the list.[39] Although You has all kinds of fancy titles such as deputy director of the Central Health Committee and special assistant to the President of the People's Republic of China as well as deputy director of the General Office of the Central Committee and director of the Central Guards Bureau,[40] he was and has been Jiang Zemin's personal bodyguard. His rise has been due to his personal loyalty to Jiang. You was also born in the year of 1939, but his military credentials were in no comparison to these generals mentioned above.

Finally, Lieutenant General Zhang Li's credentials were less impressive. He joined the PLA in 1964 and the CCP in 1966. His military career has mainly been in the field of political work. He was a staff member for showing movies and worked as a staff officer for propaganda work at different levels. His political career took off after he served as a secretary (mishu) in the General Office of the CMC between 1984 and 1989. He was appointed as a deputy

---

Leadership in the 21st Century: The Rise of the Fourth Generation, p. 37. I also made the same mistake in my article, "The Sixteenth Central Committee of the Chinese Communist Party: formal institutions and factional groups," *Journal of Contemporary China*, Vol. 13, No. 39 (May 2004), p. 241, Table 6.

[38] For his bio, see Shen Xueming and Zheng Jianying, *Zhonggong Diyijie zhi Dishiwujie Zhongyangweiyuan*, p. 137.

[39] It is rumored that You Xigui was not on the list initially, but Jiang Zemin personally intervened to expand the list of alternates and included You Xigui.

[40] http://news.xinhuanet.com/misc/2002-01/21/content_246426.htm.

director of the Political Department in the Headquarters of General Staff in April 1991 and promoted to be the director in November 1996. Without any professional military experience and educational credentials, Zhang Li was promoted to assistant chief of staff in August 1998 and then was further promoted to a deputy chief of staff in June 2000. He entered the Sixteenth Central Committee as an alternate member. He was awarded the rank of major general in July 1997 and the rank of lieutenant general in 2001.[41]

Among the military institutions, the Shenyang Military Region ranked second with 10 points, followed by the General Political Department (eight points), the General Logistics Department (eight points), and the Guangzhou Military Region (eight points). It is interesting to note that with the largest number of full central committee members, the Shenyang Military Region had a higher score than the three general departments. There were four full members from the Shenyang Military Region: General Jiang Futang, General Qian Guoliang, Lieutenant General Wang Jianmin, and Lieutenant General Xu Qiliang. It turned out that these full members were not produced just for the Shenyang Military Region. General Jiang and General Qian were commander and political commissar of the region, respectively, but Lieutenant Wang was later promoted as commander of the Chengdu Military Region[42] and Xu Qiliang was later promoted as a deputy chief of staff.[43]

The two alternate members from the Shenyang Military Region were Lieutenant General Wu Yuqian and Lieutenant General Fan Changlong. Wu's case is interesting because he seems to have been groomed for high posts in the 1990s, but somehow his career stagnated. He was one of the youngest major generals in 1988 when the military rank was restored; he entered the central committee in 1992

---

[41] http://ics.nccu.edu.tw/frame.php?address=polsum&id=2266.
[42] For his bio, see Shen Xueming and Zheng Jianying, *Zhonggong Diyijie zhi Dishiwujie Zhongyangweiyuan*, p. 66.
[43] For his bio, see Shen Xueming and Zheng Jianying, *Zhonggong Diyijie zhi Dishiwujie Zhongyangweiyuan*, p. 251.

as an alternate member; he was appointed as chief of staff of the Shenyang Military Region in 1995 and was awarded the rank of lieutenant general in the following year.[44] He remained in that position in the subsequent decade. In contrast, Fan Changlong, his junior colleague and chief of staff of the Shenyang Military Region, was newly awarded the rank of lieutenant general in 2002; he entered the Sixteenth Central Committee as an alternate member for the first time but soon was promoted to the General Staff as an assistant chief of staff.

On the other hand, several military institutions were not very well represented. The PLA Air Force had only four points, in a sharp contrast to the PLA Navy that had seven points. Strictly speaking, there were only two full members of the Sixteenth Central Committee from the Air Force: General Qiao Qingchen (commander) and Lieutenant General Deng Changyou (political commissar). But two other full members were also air officers. Xu Qiliang was concurrent commander of the Shenyang Military Region Air Force as well as deputy commander of the Shenyang Military Region. Lieutenant General Ma Xiaotian was also concurrent commander of the Nanjing Military Region Air Force as well as deputy commander of the Nanjing Military Region.

At the same time, three full members and one alternate member were from the Navy. In addition to the commander (Admiral Shi Yunsheng) and the political commissar (Admiral Yang Huaiqing), there was another full member (Vice Admiral Shen Bingyi, deputy commander). The alternate member was Vice Admiral Zhang Dingfa (deputy commander of the Navy). Moreover, Vice Admiral Ding Yiping was also a naval officer. He was concurrent commander of the North China Sea Fleet as well as a deputy commander of the Jinan Military Region.

The total power index for the military was 111 points, less than either the provinces or the central institutions.

---

[44] For his bio, see Shen Xueming and Zheng Jianying, *Zhonggong Diyijie zhi Dishiwujie Zhongyangweiyuan*, pp. 360, 361.

CORPORATE REPRESENTATION

There had been corporate representation in the central committee in the past. But economic enterprises have seldom been treated as a group in Chinese politics. Corporate leaders became much more visible in politics as a result of the Sixteenth Party Congress. However, as it is the residual group, this last group is in fact composed of two subgroups: corporate leaders and academic leaders. There were 18 corporate leaders in the Sixteenth CC: two full members and 16 alternates. One full member, Li Yizhong, chairman of the Board and president of the Sinopec Corporation, was promoted from an alternate membership. The other, Zhang Qingwei, president of China Aerospace Science and Technology Corporation, was plucked from a nonmember and made a full member because of his enormous contributions to the successful launchings of satellites for Chinese and foreign clients. Among the 16 alternate members, three had been on the Fifteenth CC. Tao Jianxing (CEO of the Chunlan Corporation in Jiangsu), Liu Jie (chairman of the Board of the Anshan Iron and Steel Group Corporation in Liaoning), and Xie Qihua (president of the Baoshan Iron and Steel Group Corporation in Shanghai) were reelected into the Sixteenth CC as alternate members. The Capital Iron and Steel Group Corporation, a flagship in economic reforms during the 1980s and 1990s, however, was ostensibly absent from the list. Other interesting cases include Su Shulin (chairman and general manager of Daqing Oilfield Company), Zhu Yanfeng (president of China Faw Group Corporation), Ma Fucai (president of China Petroleum and National Gas Corporation), Zhang Ruimin (CEO of the Haier Group Corporation), Li Changyin (general manager of China Shipbuilding Industry Corporation), and Wang Mingquan [chairman of China Everbright (Group) Limited]. Out of 87 business leaders (excluding 17 bankers) identified by China-vips.com,[45] however, only five made it to the list.

---

[45] http://www.china-vips.com/vips/pico2.htm.

In addition, there were five academic leaders[46] that were all alternate members of the Sixteenth Central Committee. Min Weifang (party secretary of Beijing University), Pan Yunhe (president of Zhejiang University), Wu Qidi (president of Tongji University),[47] and Zhai Huqu (president of the Chinese Academy of Agricultural Sciences) were all newcomers in the Sixteenth Central Committee as alternate members. Min, Wu, and Zhai are also returnees from foreign studies. A native of Heilongjiang, Min Weifang grew up in Beijing. He studied at No. 8 Middle School in the 1960s and became a miner in a coal mine in Mentougou District in Beijing. He got out of the coalmining work through the path of youth league work. In 1973, he was transferred to the Beijing Committee of Youth League as a cadre. He was enrolled in Beijing Normal University in 1978 and went to the United States in 1982. In five years, Min obtained two master's degrees and one doctorate from Stanford University. He came back to China in 1988 and began to work for Beijing University. He was appointed as party secretary of Beijing University in April 2002.[48]

Zhai Huqu had a similar experience. He joined the PLA in 1969 and returned home four years later. A "worker–peasant–soldier" college student during the Cultural Revolution, he returned to school for a master's program in 1978. He later went to Britain and obtained a doctorate degree at Birmingham University in 1987. He returned to Nanjing Agricultural University in 1987 and resumed teaching there. In July 2001, he was appointed as president of the Chinese Academy of Agricultural Sciences.[49]

Wu Qidi belongs to an older cohort of the Cultural Revolution generation, though she is only three years older than both Min Weifang and Zhai Huqu. She went to Qinghua University in 1965, a year before the beginning of the Cultural Revolution. She went back to her alma mater in 1978 for a master's degree. In 1981, Wu went to

---

[46] I have also included Tie Ning, a writer, in this subgroup.
[47] She was later transferred to Beijing as vice minister of Education.
[48] http://www.pku.edu.cn/about/lingdao/minweifang.htm.
[49] http://www.chinavitae.com/biography_display.php?id=1921; http://ics.nccu.edu.tw/frame.php?address=polsum&id=4181.

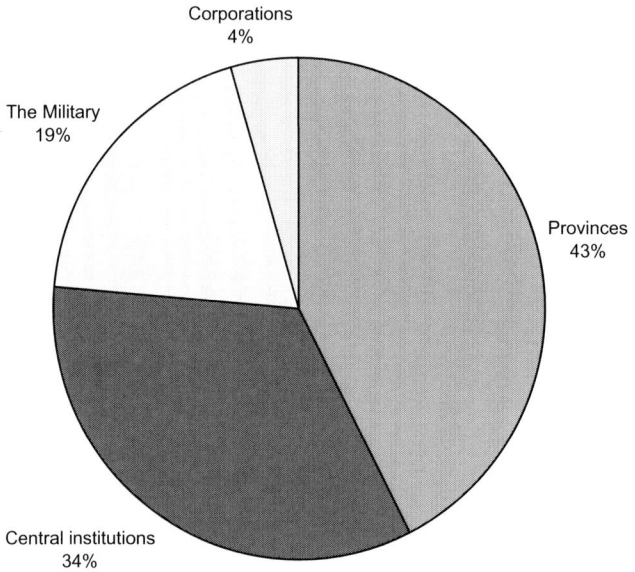

Fig. 3.1 Balance of Institutional Power in China (2002).

Switzerland for doctoral studies. She obtained her Ph.D. degree four years later. She returned to China in 1986 and began teaching at Tongji University in Shanghai. She is the first female president of Tongji.[50]

Clearly, the corporate leaders (including academic leaders) have yet to form an important political force in China. The total power index for the group was only 25 points, much less than those of any other political institution.

CONCLUDING REMARKS

As a result of the Sixteenth National Congress of the CCP, as Figure 3.1 illustrates, provincial units emerged as the most powerful institution in Chinese politics. Their power index was 244 (43 percent, excluding the score of the political core). The combined central party- and central government-institutions ranked second with a total score of 193

---

[50] http://www.tongji.de/chinese/intro/wqd.html.

(34 percent). But central party-institutions and central government-institutions were much weaker separately. The military came as third with a power index of 111 points (19 percent). The corporate leaders began to assume independent political identities, but their power (25 points) was still negligible (four percent).[51]

---

[51] It should be noted that the balance of institutional power has been anything but being static due to constant interinstitutional transfers among different institutions, especially those between central institutions and provinces.

Chapter

4

Balance of Factional Power

Chinese politics has long been perceived as politics of political factions.[1] Nevertheless, few have fully examined some fundamental assumptions of factional politics. For instance, there is no study of critical distinctions between factions and factional groups. Nor is there any study of group cohesion of factional groups. It is not clear whether all factional groups have similar internal structures and whether some factional groups are more cohesive than others are. Moreover, several factional groups have been treated as if they were mutually exclusive; yet no one has systematically presented evidence for such an argument.

This chapter seeks to analyze the balance of power among factional groups such as the Shanghai Gang, the Princelings, the Qinghua Clique, and the Chinese Communist Youth League (CCYL) Group.[2] It will use the power index developed in Chapter 3 to compare political powers of these factional groups. It will also develop a group cohesion index for each of them and evaluate their group cohesion in comparative terms. It will study factional overlaps and see to what extent these overlaps affect their interactions.

---

[1] For a systematic discussion of factional politics, see Jonathan Unger (ed), *The Nature of Chinese Politics: From Mao to Jiang* (Armonk, NY: M.E. Sharpe, 2002).

[2] For a detailed study of the Qinghua Clique and the Princelings, see Cheng Li, *China's Leaders: The New Generation* (Lanham, MD: Rowman and Littlefield, 2001), pp. 87–174.

FACTIONS VERSUS FACTIONAL GROUPS

The political entities that this chapter attempts to analyze are not factions but factional groups. A faction, according to Andrew Nathan, is a structure that is "mobilized on the basis of clientelist ties to engage in politics and consisting of a few, rather than a great many, layers of personnel."[3] A clientelist tie is "a non-ascriptive two-person relationship founded on exchange, in which well-understood rights and obligations are established between the two parties."[4] According to Nathan, there are three possible structures of factions: simple factions, complex factions, and simple factions with support structures,[5] and the key feature of all these structures is "the one-to-one, rather than corporate, pattern of relationships between leaders (or subleaders) and followers."[6]

Factional groups, on the other hand, are based on corporate ties, ties that have been established through shared experience in an organization. In a factional group, in contrast to a faction, there may not necessarily be a clearly identifiable leader. Members of a factional group, however, have to have direct association based on their past experience. Not all factional groups are factions, although it is likely that some subsets of a factional group may form a faction.

The four factional groups identified in this chapter do not all neatly fit the definition of a factional group. The Shanghai Gang comes closest to the definition of a faction instead of a factional group because it has a leader, Jiang Zemin, and is based on a patron–client relationship between Jiang and his followers. The CCYL Group, on the other hand, comes closest to the definition of a factional group because it does not have a single leader, but its members share experience in the same organization (the Central Committee of the CCYL). The Qinghua Clique is similar to the CCYL Group because it does not have an identifiable leader, but its

---

[3] Andrew J. Nathan, "A factionalism model for CCP politics," *China Quarterly*, No. 53 (January–March 1973), pp. 34–66.
[4] *Ibid.*, p. 37.
[5] *Ibid.*, p. 41, Figure 1.
[6] *Ibid.*, pp. 42, 43.

members have the same experience with the same institution of higher education (Qinghua University). The Princelings is different from all of the above because it is more of a categorical group than a factional group based on the same corporate experience.

SHANGHAI GANG

The Shanghai Gang members refer to politicians who have used Shanghai as a springboard to launch their political careers. The members of the Shanghai Gang are not necessarily Shanghai natives. In fact, as my earlier study indicates, none of the Shanghai Gang members who were working in the Center in the 1990s were natives of Shanghai.[7] Shanghai has been very prominent in Chinese politics since 1949. In the past 50 some years, the Shanghai Gang experienced three rises. Before the Cultural Revolution one may find Chen Yi and Ke Qingshi among the members of the Politburo. During the Cultural Revolution, Zhang Chunqiao, Yao Wenyuan, and Wang Hongwen (three of the Gang of Four) were standing members of the Politburo. Since Jiang Zemin was selected as general secretary of the Party in 1989, the Shanghai Gang has reemerged in Chinese politics.

A member of the Shanghai Gang in this study refers to someone who had worked or was working in Shanghai in November 2002 when the Sixteenth National Party Congress was convened. According to this criterion, 17 people could be identified as members of the Shanghai Gang in the Sixteenth CC: 13 full members and four alternate members (Table 4.1).[8] Three Shanghai Gang members

---

[7] Zhiyue Bo, "The provinces: training ground for national leaders or a power in their own right?" in David M. Finkelstein and Maryanne Kivlehan (eds), *China's Leadership in the Twenty-First Century: The Rise of the Fourth Generation* (Armonk, NY: M.E. Sharpe, 2003), pp. 66–117.

[8] It should be noted that You Xigui, as mentioned in Chapter 3, is not a Shanghai Gang member because he did not have work experience in Shanghai and that Dai Xianglong, former governor of the People's Bank of China and later mayor of Tianjin, does not belong to the Shanghai Gang either because of his lack of work experience in Shanghai. For Dai's bio, see Shen Xueming and Zheng Jianying (eds),

Table 4.1 Members of the Shanghai Gang in the Sixteenth Central Committee (2002)

Name	Birth	Home	CC Membership	Rank	Work Place	Index
Cao Jianming	1955	Jiangsu	Alternate	79	Supreme Court	1
Chen Liangyu	1946	Zhejiang	Full	n/a	Shanghai	4
Chen Zhili (f.)	1942	Fujian	Full	n/a	Education	2
Han Zheng	1954	Zhejiang	Full	n/a	Shanghai	2
Hua Jianmin	1940	Jiangsu	Full	n/a	Finance Office	2
Huang Ju	1938	Zhejiang	Full	n/a	Politburo	5
Meng Jianzhu	1947	Jiangsu	Full	n/a	Jiangxi	2
Wang Huning	1955	Shandong	Full	n/a	Policy	2
Wu Bangguo	1941	Anhui	Full	n/a	Politburo	5
Wu Qidi (f.)	1947	Zhejiang	Alternate	73	Shanghai	1
Xie Qihua (f.)	1943	Zhejiang	Alternate	80	Baosteel	1
Xu Guangchun	1944	Zhejiang	Full	n/a	Radio, Movie, and TV	2
Xu Kuangdi	1937	Zhejiang	Full	n/a	Academy of Engineering	2
Yin Yicui (f.)	1955	Zhejiang	Alternate	140	Shanghai	1
Zeng Qinghong	1939	Jiangxi	Full	n/a	Politburo	6
Zhang Wenkang	1940	Shanghai	Full	n/a	Health	2
Zhao Qizheng	1940	Beijing	Full	n/a	Information	2
Total						42

Sources: Shen Xueming and Zheng Jianying (eds), *Zhonggong Diyijie zhi Dishiwujie Zhongyangweiyuan (The Central Committee Members of the Chinese Communist Party from the First through the Fifteenth Central Committee)*. (Beijing: Zhongyang Wenxian Chubanshe, 2001); *People's Daily* online.

were part of the core of the Chinese political system: Wu Bangguo, Zeng Qinghong, and Huang Ju. They were all standing members of the Politburo. Five were stationed in Shanghai: Chen Liangyu (Politburo member and party secretary and mayor), Han Zheng

---

Zhonggong Diyijie zhi Dishiwujie Zhongyangweiyuan (The Central Committee Members of the Chinese Communist Party from the First Through the Fifteenth Central Committee) (Beijing: Zhongyang Wenxian Chubanshe, 2001), pp. 797, 798.

(deputy secretary and executive vice mayor),[9] Yin Yicui (standing member and director of the Propaganda Department of the Shanghai Party Committee), Xie Qihua (president of the Baoshan Iron and Steel Group Corp.), and Wu Qidi (president of Tongji University).[10] One was party secretary of Jiangxi (Meng Jianzhu). Four were in charge of ministries: Chen Zhili (Education),[11] Zhang Wenkang (Health),[12] Xu Guangchun (National General Bureau of Radio, Movie, and Television), and Xu Kuangdi (Chinese Academy of Engineering). Three were holding positions in the Party: Zhao Qizheng (Information Office), Wang Huning (Policy Research Office), and Hua Jianmin (Finance Office).[13] And one (Cao Jianming) was in the Supreme Court.[14]

Noticeably, Shanghai Gang members were not particularly popular among party deputies to the Congress. The four alternate members from Shanghai were not very high on the list of alternates starting with those who received the most votes. Among 158 alternate members, the four Shanghai Gang members ranked 73rd, 79th, 80th, and 140th.

The Shanghai Gang seems to have been at its peak in terms of power. The total score of power indexes of the Shanghai Gang members in the Sixteenth CC was 42 points. However, the Shanghai Gang as a faction was also faced with a serious crisis. With Jiang's departure as general secretary of the CCP, the Shanghai Gang was likely to be fragmented. Although there were three potential candidates, none of them was able to inherit the mantle of the core of the Shanghai Gang. As the No. 2 person in the Standing Committee of the Politburo, Wu Bangguo is well qualified for being the next core

---

[9] He was elected mayor of Shanghai in February 2003.
[10] She was later appointed as vice minister of Education.
[11] She was inducted into the State Council in March 2003 as a state councilor.
[12] He was fired in April 2003 because of his mishandling of the Severe Acute Respiratory Syndrome (SARS) epidemic in China.
[13] He is secretary-general of the State Council.
[14] For his official bio, see http://news.xinhuanet.com/ziliao/2002-02/28/content_295052.htm.

of the Shanghai Gang. Wu's ancestral home is Feidong, Anhui,[15] but he was born in Guizhou instead.[16] Wu began to work in Shanghai in 1967 upon his graduation from Qinghua University and worked in the metropolis for the subsequent 27 years. He speaks fluent Shanghainese and has identified himself as a Shanghainese.[17] Wu became a municipal leader in 1983 when he entered the Standing Committee of the Shanghai Municipal Party Committee. He was promoted to deputy secretary in June 1985 and entered the Twelfth Central Committee of the CCP as an alternate member three months later.[18] He worked directly under Jiang Zemin for four years. Wu was later promoted to party secretary of Shanghai in 1991, to the Secretariat in 1994, and to the State Council in 1995. As a candidate for the next leader of the Shanghai Gang, Wu has three advantages: he is close to Jiang Zemin; he has roots in Shanghai; and he is the highest ranking Party leader among the remaining Shanghai Gang members.

Wu's rival, Huang Ju, also has similar advantages. A native of Jiashan,[19] Zhejiang, Huang is also a graduate of Qinghua

---

[15] For his official bio, see http://news.xinhuanet.com/ziliao/2002-01/16/content_240539.htm.

[16] His only visit to his hometown was in 1946 when he was five years old, and he stayed there for three months. See Yan Hua, "Zhonggong Zhengzhiju Changwei Jiaxiang Xunfang Xilei (14): Wu Bangguo Renhu Burenxiang" ("Finding the hometowns of CCP Politburo Standing Committee members (14): Wu Bangguo acknowledges Shanghai instead of his real hometown as his hometown"), *Asian Times* (Chinese), June 21, 2005, http://www.atchinese.com/index.php?option=com_content&task=view&id=2119&Itemid=66.

[17] *Ibid*.

[18] He was one of 35 people who were inducted to the Central Committee as alternates in September 1985. One may find a few other familiar names on the list such as Li Changchun (standing member of the Sixteenth Politburo), Wu Guanzheng (standing member of the Sixteenth Politburo), Liu Yunshan (member of the Sixteenth Politburo), Zhang Lichang (member of the Sixteenth Politburo and party secretary of Tianjin), and Song Defu (full member of the Sixteenth Central Committee and party secretary of Fujian in November 2002). For the entire list, see *Renmin ribao*, September 23, 1985, p. 1.

[19] Jiashan is only 80 kilometers away from Shanghai. See http://www.jiashan.gov.cn/col/col_2004_9_2_2_48_24_779/index.html.

University.[20] Huang graduated from Qinghua four years earlier and worked in Shanghai much longer than Wu did. He joined the workforce in Shanghai after graduation from Qinghua University in 1963. He became a standing member of the Shanghai Party Committee in 1983, a deputy secretary in 1985, mayor in 1991, and party secretary in 1994. He worked in Shanghai for 40 years, including 20 years as a municipal leader. In the late 1980s, Huang initially ranked a bit higher in the Shanghai Municipal Party Committee than Wu, although they were both deputy secretaries.[21] More importantly, Huang is reportedly closer to Jiang Zemin. He would do anything for Jiang and his family, making him Jiang's confidant.[22] In return, Jiang took every opportunity to promote Huang. He made Huang executive vice mayor of Shanghai in 1986, mayor of Shanghai in 1991, and party secretary of Shanghai in 1994. It was also Jiang who transferred Huang from Shanghai to Beijing in October 2002 as a candidate for a seat in the Politburo Standing Committee.

Zeng Qinghong, the No. 5 person in the Standing Committee of the Politburo, the most senior member of the Secretariat, and president of the Central Party School, is also a strong candidate. In fact, Zeng has deeper roots in Shanghai than both Wu and Huang. A native of Ji'an, Jiangxi, Zeng was born in Anhui on August 29, 1939.[23] His father, Zeng Shan, was responsible for personnel issues in the East China region (including Shanghai) of the CCP between

---

[20] For his official bio, see http://news.xinhuanet.com/ziliao/2002-01/16/content_240603.htm.

[21] See *Dangdai Zhongguo de Shanghai* (*Shanghai of the Contemporary China*) (Beijing: Dangdai Zhongguo Chubanshe, 1993), Vol. 2, p. 649.

[22] Fu Chunshen, "Jiang Zemin de Jianu: Huang Ju" (Jiang Zemin's confidant: Huang Ju"), *Dongxiang*, April 27, 2006, http://www.wpoforum.com/viewtopic.php?fid=1&tid=13793.

[23] According to his official bio, Zeng was born in July 1939 (see http://news.xinhuanet.com/ziliao/2002-01/16/content_240615.htm). But according to his mother, he was born on July 15, 1939 of the Chinese lunar calendar, that is, August 29, 1939 in the Western calendar. For details, see Ting Wang, *Zeng Qing-hong and the Strong Men of the Sunset Race* (2nd Edition) (Hong Kong: Celebrities Press, 2001), p. 136.

1938 and 1949[24] and became the highest ranking vice mayor of Shanghai in May 1949.[25] Zeng Qinghong joined his parents in Shanghai in 1949 and stayed there for four years.[26] However, Zeng Qinghong did not return to Shanghai until 1984 when he was appointed as deputy director of the Organization Department of the Shanghai Municipal Party Committee. He was later promoted to deputy secretary of Shanghai in October 1986, becoming a junior colleague of Huang Ju and Wu Bangguo. Zeng began to work under Jiang Zemin's direct leadership in November 1987 when Jiang replaced Rui Xinwen as party secretary of Shanghai and developed cordial relationship with Jiang. He went to Beijing in June 1989 along with Jiang.[27] Although Zeng had a much shorter stint in Shanghai, he was considered as Jiang's alter ego. The relationship between these three people and Jiang Zemin can be summarized as follows: Wu is Jiang's protégé, Huang is Jiang's confidant, and Zeng is Jiang's partner.

Although the three would continue to pay some respect to Jiang Zemin, none of them would get along with others in a superior–subordinate relationship. Clearly, the Shanghai Gang as a faction does not have a bright future because it simply cannot afford to have three cores at the same time with a small and dwindling number of followers. No faction, as Andrew Nathan observed three decades ago, can survive its leader because of its unique patron–client ties between the leader and the followers.[28]

---

[24] For details, see Ting Wang, *Zeng Qing-hong and the Strong Men of the Sunset Race*, p. 113.

[25] See *Dangdai Zhongguo de Shanghai*, p. 652.

[26] For details, see Ting Wang, *Zeng Qing-hong and the Strong Men of the Sunset Race*, pp. 137, 138.

[27] Ting Wang made a mistake by stating that Jiang took only two people from Shanghai: Zeng Qinghong and Hua Jianmin. Hua did not go to Beijing until 1996. For Ting's statement, see *Zeng Qing-hong and the Strong Men of the Sunset Race*, p. 171. For Hua's bio, see http://news.xinhuanet.com/ziliao/2003-03/15/content_779814.htm.

[28] Nathan, "A factionalism model for CCP politics," p. 43. For this reason, Zeng Qinghong is not waiting to inherit the Shanghai Gang as it was but developing his own faction. Although some members of a Zeng faction may have come from the original Shanghai Gang under Jiang, the Zeng faction is going to be a new one.

Balance of Factional Power

In order to compare factional groups, we need to construct a group cohesion index for the Shanghai Gang, and we are going to do it for inner-circle members of the Shanghai Gang. Inner-circle members are those who have worked in Shanghai as municipal leaders either in the Party committee or in the municipal government. In the Sixteenth CC, seven people can be identified as inner-circle members of the Shanghai Gang from the Shanghai Party Committee. They are Wu Bangguo, Zeng Qinghong, Huang Ju, Chen Zhili, Xu Kuangdi, Chen Liangyu, and Han Zheng. We first calculated their ties in terms of the number of years they worked together in the Shanghai Party Committee for each pair and then added them together to get the group cohesion index.[29] It is clear from Figure 4.1 that Huang Ju has the strongest work ties with the rest of the group. He worked with other Shanghai Party leaders for 38 years altogether. He worked with Chen Liangyu for a decade, with Wu Bangguo for nine years, and with Chen Zhili and Xu Kuangdi for eight years each. Chen Liangyu also was well entrenched in the Shanghai Gang with a total work tie of 24.5 years. Zeng Qinghong, however, had ties with other members of the Shanghai Gang for only six years. Han Zheng, a newcomer, had not worked with many of the veteran Shanghai Gang members. By November 2002, he had only worked with Chen Liangyu for half a year.

The group cohesion index for Shanghai party leaders amounts to 63.5 years. Since there are 21 pairs of relationships, the average tie is about three years (Table 4.2).

---

[29] This index, admittedly, is not a perfect measure of group cohesion because working together at the same time in the same organization is not the same as working together cooperatively. In fact, one sometimes finds that the longer a pair work together, the more likely they hate each other. This is particularly true between party secretaries and governors (mayors) of the same provincial unit. The index, however, serves two useful functions. At the individual level, it provides a rough measure of a person's depth (the number of years of service in the organization) and breadth (the numbers of colleagues in close contact in the organization) of connections in the organization. At the group level, it provides a rough measure of tightness of the group (or group cohesion). This index makes intergroup comparison possible, as long as intraorganizational problems mentioned above exist in all organizations.

148 China's Elite Politics

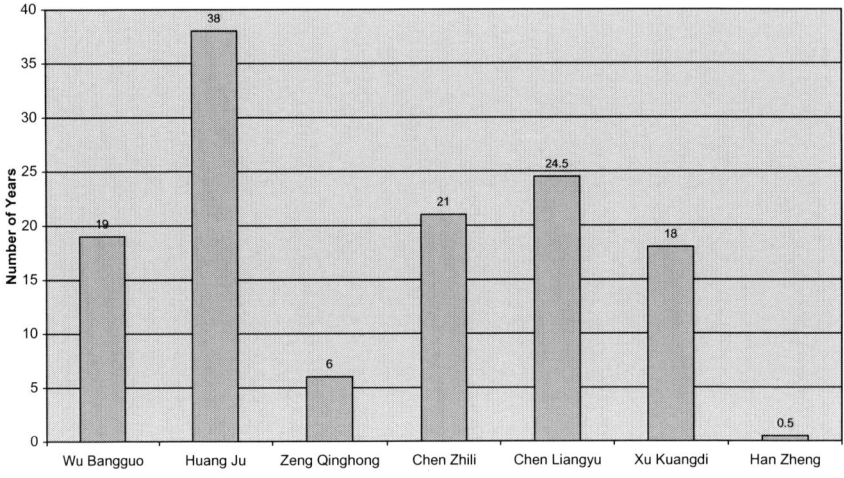

Fig. 4.1 Work Ties of Shanghai Party Leaders in the Sixteenth Central Committee.

We have also produced a group cohesion index for the inner-circle members of the Shanghai Gang from the Shanghai Municipal Government. Again, seven people were identified, and their ties were calculated. The seven people were Huang Ju, Xu Kuangdi, Zhao Qizheng, Meng Jianzhu, Hua Jianmin, Chen Liangyu, and Han Zheng. Xu Kuangdi, former mayor of Shanghai, had the deepest ties with other Shanghai government leaders. His work ties with other leaders were 22 years. Zhao Qizheng, former vice mayor of Shanghai, also worked closely with other Shanghai government leaders. His ties with other leaders amounted to 13.5 years. Huang Ju and Hua Jianmin, on the other hand, were not particularly close to other Shanghai government leaders. Huang's tie was 6.67 years, and Hua's tie was 6.17 years. Huang and Hua worked together in the Shanghai Municipal Government for only two months (0.17 years). The group cohesion index is 39.67 years. Clearly, Shanghai government leaders were not as close as their counterparts in the Shanghai Party Committee because the average tie is only 1.9 years (Table 4.3, Figure 4.2).

Table 4.2 Group Cohesion Matrix of Shanghai Party Leaders in the Sixteenth Central Committee

	Wu	Huang	Zeng	Chen Zhili	Chen Liangyu	Xu	Han	Subtotal
Wu Bangguo	n/a	9	3	5	2	0	0	19
Huang Ju	9	n/a	3	8	10	8	0	29
Zeng Qinghong	3	3	n/a	0	0	0	0	0
Chen Zhili	5	8	0	n/a	5	3	0	8
Chen Liangyu	2	10	0	5	n/a	7	0.5	7.5
Xu Kuangdi	0	8	0	3	7	n/a	0	0
Han Zheng	0	0	0	0	0.5	0	n/a	0
Total	19	38	6	21	24.5	18	0.5	63.5

Notes: (i) Numbers in cells represent the number of years a pair worked together in the Shanghai Party Committee. (ii) The subtotals are the sum of the numbers above the diagnoal of n/a for each leader. (iii) The total (63.5) is the sum of the numbers above the diagnoal of n/a.

Source: Author's database.

Table 4.3 Group Cohesion Matrix of Shanghai Government Leaders in the Sixteenth Central Committee

	Huang	Zhao	Xu	Meng	Hua	Chen	Han	Subtotal
Huang Ju	n/a	2	2.5	2	0.17	0	0	6.67
Zhao Qizheng	2	n/a	5	3	2	1.5	0	11.5
Xu Kuangdi	2.5	5	n/a	3.5	2	5	4	14.5
Meng Jianzhu	2	3	3.5	n/a	2	0	0	2
Hua Jianmin	0.17	2	2	2	n/a	0	0	0
Chen Liangyu	0	1.5	5	0	0	n/a	5	5
Han Zheng	0	0	4	0	0	5	n/a	
Total	6.67	13.5	22	10.5	6.17	11.5	9	39.67

Notes: (i) Numbers in cells represent the number of years a pair worked together in the Shanghai Party Committee. (ii) The subtotals are the sum of the numbers above the diagnoal of n/a for each leader. (iii) The total (39.67) is the sum of the numbers above the diagnoal of n/as.
Source: Author's database.

With the combined ties of 44.67 years with nine other Shanghai leaders, Huang Ju stands out as the most entrenched member of the Shanghai Gang among the Sixteenth CC members. Xu Kuangdi ranks second with the combined ties of 40 years with nine other Shanghai leaders.[30] Zeng Qinghong, the pivotal member of the old Shanghai Gang with Jiang Zemin at the core, on the other hand, has the least ties with other Shanghai leaders. His combined ties are only six years, and he worked with only two other Shanghai leaders in the Sixteenth CC.

We may be able to get an estimate of the group cohesion of the Shanghai Gang by adding these two indexes. The result is 103.17 years.

---

[30] Xu Kuangdi indeed was "dislodged" in December 2001 (about one year earlier than his scheduled retirement in early 2003). However, he has been handsomely rewarded for his service in Shanghai. He not only retained his seat on the Sixteenth Central Committee as one of the oldest members but also obtained a post of vice chairman of the Standing Committee of the CPPCC.

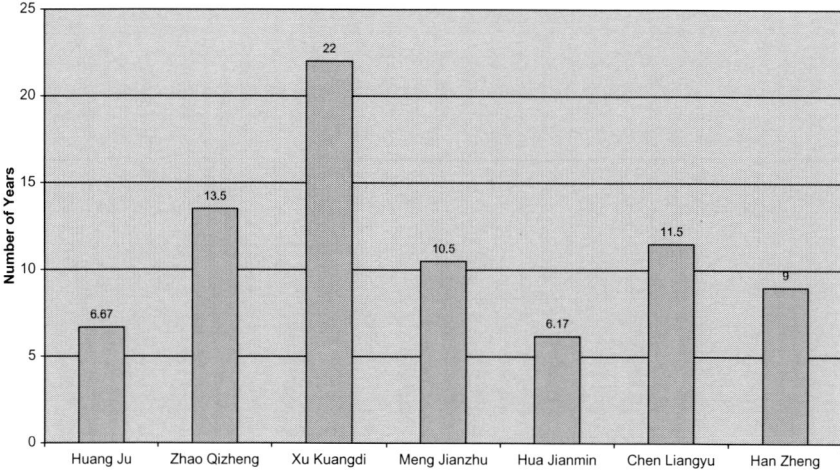

Fig. 4.2 Work Ties Shanghai Goverment Leaders in the Sixteenth Central Committee.

In other words, the inner-circle members of the Shanghai Gang worked with one another for over 100 years.

PRINCELINGS

Princelings (*taizidang*) refer to children of former high-ranking officials of the CCP. Since they have been treated as an important political faction in the literature of Chinese politics, it is important to analyze them here. Twenty people in the Sixteenth CC are children of former high-ranking officials: 15 full and five alternate members (Table 4.4). Evidently, these princelings were not particularly popular either. Ding Yiping, son of Lieutenant General Ding Qiusheng (a long marcher and former political commissar of the North China Sea Fleet),[31] was ranked No. 110 out of 158 alternate members, and Li Yuanchao, son of Li Gancheng (former vice mayor of Shanghai), No. 115. Deng Pufang, son of Deng Xiaoping, who had been the

---

[31] http://army.news.tom.com/general/china/gongchandang/zhongjiang/0016.html.

152 China's Elite Politics

Table 4.4 Princelings in the Sixteenth Central Committee (2002)

Name	Home	Birth	CC Membership	Rank	Relative	Index
Bai Keming	Shaanxi	1943	Full	n/a	Bai Jian	2
Bo Xilai	Shanxi	1949	Full	n/a	Bo Yibo	2
Chen Yuan	Shanghai	1945	Alternate	153	Chen Yi	1
Dai Bingguo (Tujia)	Guizhou	1941	Full	n/a	Huang Zhen	2
Deng Pufang	Sichuan	1944	Alternate	154	Deng Xiaoping	1
Ding Yiping	Hunan	1951	Alternate	110	Ding Qiusheng	1
Hong Hu	Anhui	1940	Full	n/a	Hong Xuezhi	2
Li Tielin	Hunan	1943	Full	n/a	Li Weihan	2
Li Yuanchao	Jiangsu	1950	Alternate	115	Li Gancheng	1
Liao Hui	Guangdong	1942	Full	n/a	Liao Chengzhi	2
Liu Jing	Shanxi	1944	Full	n/a	Han Jun	2
Liu Yandong (f.)	Jiangsu	1945	Full	n/a	Liu Ruilong	2
Ma Xiaotian	Henan	1949	Full	n/a		2
Wang Luolin	Hubei	1938	Alternate	157	Wang Ya'nan	1
Wang Qishan	Shanxi	1948	Full	n/a	Yao Yilin	2
Xi Jinping	Shaanxi	1953	Full	n/a	Xi Zhongxun	2
Xu Qiliang	Shandong	1950	Full	n/a	Xu Lefu	2
Yu Zhengsheng	Zhejiang	1945	Full	n/a	Huang Jing	4
Zeng Qinghong	Jiangxi	1939	Full	n/a	Zeng Shan	6
Zhou Xiaochuan	Jiangsu	1948	Full	n/a	Zhou Jiannan	2
Total						41

Sources: Updated from Zhiyue Bo, "The 16th Central Committee of the Chinese Communist Party: formal institutions and factional groups," *Journal of Contemporary China*, Vol. 13, No. 139 (May 2004), Table 7, p. 244.

second from the last as an alternate member in the Fifteenth CC, ranked No. 154 out of 158 alternates in the Sixteenth CC. Chen Yuan, son of Chen Yun, barely made it to the list as an alternate in the Sixteenth CC and ranked No. 153, immediately ahead of Deng Pufang. Wang Luolin, son of Wang Ya'nan, was even worse. He was demoted from a full member in the Fifteenth CC to an alternate member in the Sixteenth CC, one of the only two cases,[32] and he was the second to the last on the list.

---

[32] The other person is Zhang Wenyue, a deputy secretary of Liaoning.

Six provincial leaders who are children of former high-ranking officials seemed to be doing much better in 2002 than five years earlier. Hong Hu, son of Hong Xuezhi, stayed on as a full member. Hong Xuezhi (1913–), a native of Jinzhai, Anhui, is a veteran revolutionary.[33] He was a long marcher and a military leader of the Red Army. He was an army commander in the Fourth Field Army under Lin Biao in the 1940s and a deputy commander-in-chief of the Chinese Volunteer Army under Peng Dehuai in the 1950s. He was awarded the rank of general in September 1955 and again in September 1988.[34] His son, Hong Hu,[35] did not follow his steps to become a military leader. Hong Hu became an engineer after his graduation from the Beijing Institute of Technology in 1963 and began a political career later on. He was a vice minister of the State Commission for Economic Reforms between 1991 and 1998 and was appointed as acting governor of Jilin in September 1998. He entered the Fifteenth Central Committee as a full member in 1997 and was reelected as a full member of the Sixteenth Central Committee in 2002.

Bo Xilai (1949–), son of Bo Yibo, was made a full member of the Sixteenth CC, even though he had failed to enter the Fifteenth CC as an alternate member.[36] Bo Yibo (1908–), a native of Dingxiang, Shanxi, was the most senior member of the veteran revolutionaries of the Chinese Communist Party alive.[37] He joined the CCP in 1925 and was one of the most important CCP leaders in Shanxi. He was minister of Finance, vice premier, chairman of State Economic Commission, and vice chairman of the Central Advisory Commission. He entered the Seventh Central Committee as a full

---

[33] For his bio, see http://202.84.17.11/world/htm/20000928/146505.htm.

[34] He is the only person in the history of the People's Liberation Army who has been awarded the rank of general twice.

[35] For Hong Hu's bio, see http://news.xinhuanet.com/ziliao/2002-02/21/content_285224.htm.

[36] Bo Xilai was governor of Liaoning in November 2002, but was appointed as minister of Commerce in February 2004. See http://finance.sina.com.cn/g/20040229/0947651454.shtml.

[37] For his bio, see http://www.china.org.cn/chinese/zhuanti/208003.htm.

member in 1945 and became an alternate member of the Politburo in 1956. He was one of the eight elders in the 1980s who were responsible for removing two general secretaries of the Party (Hu Yaobang and Zhao Ziyang) and is the only one still alive. One of his sons, Bo Xilai (1949–), was a provincial leader in November 2002. Bo Xilai is well educated with a bachelor degree from Beijing University and a master's degree from the Chinese Academy of Social Sciences.[38] He worked in Dalian, Liaoning, for 16 years (October 1984–January 2001) before he was appointed as acting governor of Liaoning in January 2001. However, he was not particularly popular in Dalian and failed to be elected as a deputy of Dalian to the Fifteenth National Party Congress in 1997. He openly expressed his loyalty to Jiang Zemin by displaying a huge portrait of Jiang in the central square of Dalian, the first in China, and was invited as a special guest to the Fifteenth National Party Congress.[39] He managed to enter the Sixteenth Central Committee as a full member.

Similarly, Bai Keming (1943–), son of Bai Jian, was another dark horse. He entered the Sixteenth Central Committee as a full member, though he had never been an alternate member previously. His father, Bai Jian (1911–1968), was former vice minister of the First Ministry of Machine Building. A native of Jingbian, Shaanxi, Bai Jian joined the CCP in 1928.[40] He was deputy secretary of Tianjin (August 1954–July 1956)[41] and vice mayor of Tianjin (August 1954–December 1956).[42] Bai Jian became vice minister of the Ministry of Electronic Tools Building probably in December 1956 and was reappointed as a vice minister of the First Ministry of Machine Building in February

---

[38] For his bio, see http://finance.sina.com.cn/crz/20040215/1803632040.shtml.

[39] Zong Hairen, *Disidai* (*China's New Leaders: The Fourth Generation*) (Carle Place, NY: Mirror Books, 2002), p. 413.

[40] For his bio, see http://www.bjdj.gov.cn/new/view.asp?UNID=10151 and http://www.edugl.com.cn/article/2006_4/2006413161804.shtml.

[41] *Dangdai Zhongguo de Tianjin* (*Tianjin of the Contemporary China*) (Beijing: Dangdai Zhongguo Chubanshe, 1989), Vol. 2, p. 481.

[42] *Ibid.*, Vol. 2, p. 485.

1958 when three ministries (the original First Ministry of Machine Building, the original Second Ministry of Machine Building, and the Ministry of Electronic Tools Building) were merged into a new First Ministry of Machine Building.[43] Since Jiang Zemin worked at the First Automotive Works in Changchun, Jilin Province that was under the same ministry, Bai Jian was Jiang's superior between 1958 and 1966. Bai Keming reportedly was a classmate of Zeng Qinghong at No. 101 Middle School in Beijing,[44] but they actually had very little overlap at the school. Zeng was there from 1953 to 1958,[45] while Bai did not go to the school probably until 1957.[46] Like many princelings, Bai Keming was enrolled at the Haerbin Institute of Military Engineering. He studied in the Department of Missile Engineering between 1962 and 1968.[47] Bai's career took a dramatic turn in 1978 when he began to work in the General Office of the State Education Commission and accelerated a decade later. He became secretary-general and then deputy director of the Central Propaganda Department in 1993, deputy director of the General Office of the Central Committee of the CCP in March 2000, director of the *People's Daily* in June 2000, and finally party secretary of Hainan in August 2001.[48] He was the only provincial party secretary at the time who was not a member of the Fifteenth Central Committee.[49] About one year later, in November 2002, Bai was transferred to Hebei as party secretary.

---

[43] http://people.com.cn/item/lianghui/zlhb/rd/1jie/newfiles/e1200.html. Zhou Erlu became minister of the new ministry.

[44] Zong Hairen, *Disidai*, p. 185.

[45] Ting Wang, *Zeng Qing-hong and the Strong Men of the Sunset Race*, p. 138.

[46] This is my speculation: Bai was born in 1943, went to primary school at the age of 7 (1950), and went to middle school at the age of 13 (1956). However, because he was born in October, his schooling was delayed for one year. Therefore, he went to middle school in 1957 at the age of 14 and graduated from the middle school in 1962 at the age of 19.

[47] For Bai Keming's bio, see http://news.xinhuanet.com/ziliao/2002-03/01/content_295175.htm.

[48] http://chinaps.cass.cn/renda/shengweishuji/hainansheng.htm.

[49] Zhiyue Bo, "The provinces," p. 83.

Xi Jinping (1953–), son of Xi Zhongxun, was promoted to a full member this time, even though he had been the last as an alternate member on the Fifteenth CC. Although Xi Jinping and Bo Xilai are both princelings, Xi's experience is in a sharp contrast to Bo's. Bo has benefited from his father's tremendous political influence while Xi mostly has had to depend on himself.[50] Xi Zhongxun (1913–2002), a native of Mizhi, Shaanxi, joined the CCP in 1928 and was one of the most influential revolutionary leaders in North China.[51] As one of the founders of the Communist guerrilla armies of Shaanxi and Gansu, he was chairman of the Shaanxi–Gansu Revolutionary Committee, acting party secretary of the Shaanxi–Gansu Revolutionary Committee, secretary of the Military Commission of the CCP Shaanxi–Gansu Party Committee, and chairman of the Shaanxi–Gansu Soviet Government in 1934. He entered the CCP Central Committee as an alternate member in 1945 and as a full member in 1956. He was vice premier of the State Council between April 1959 and October 1962. He suffered two downfalls in his political career. He was briefly detained in 1935 because of internal factional power struggle among CCP leaders in Shaanxi. He was purged in 1962 because of his alleged involvement in a novel on Liu Zhidan,[52] Xi's former colleague and cofounder of the revolutionary bases in Shaanxi. He made great contributions to open-door policies while he was party secretary of Guangdong. He was responsible for establishing the first special economic zones in China.[53] He later also contributed to the institutionalization of the Chinese cadre system as

---

[50] This comparison is based on Zong Hairen, *Disidai*, pp. 409–414.

[51] For his bio, see http://www.china.org.cn/chinese/zhuanti/208065.htm; Liu Xianjun and Tian Weiben, *Lijie Zongli Fuzongli Xiaozhuan* (*Bios of Premiers and Vice Premiers of the People's Republic of China*) (Changchun: Jilin Renmin Chubanshe, 1993), pp. 452–455.

[52] The novel was written by Li Jiantong, the sister-in-law of Liu Zhidan (1903–1936), but the novel was considered a weapon used by the anti-Party activists against the Party. For the process of writing the novel, see http://book.sina.com.cn/2003-06-02/3/8106.shtml.

[53] For a report on the process of establishing special economic zones in Guangdong, see http://china.qianlong.com/4352/2004/11/17/1040@2378167.htm.

the executive secretary of the Secretariat. Xi Jinping was less fortunate than Bo Xilai because he was only nine years old when his father was purged. He had to learn to depend on himself. He began to work in Shaanxi as a peasant in January 1969 and joined the CCP in January 1974. He studied in the Department of Chemical Engineering at Qinghua University between 1975 and 1979 and later obtained a doctoral degree in law from the same university.[54] Xi went to Zhengding County, Hebei Province, as a deputy party secretary in 1982 and was promoted to Xiamen, Fujian Province as executive vice mayor and standing member of the Xiamen Municipal Party Committee in 1985. He became deputy secretary of Fujian in October 1995, acting governor of Fujian in August 1999, and governor of Fujian in January 2000. He was an alternate member of the Fifteenth Central Committee and had been groomed to be a Politburo member as a representative of the fifth generation leadership in the Sixteenth Central Committee.[55] However, his name was dropped from the list of candidates for the Politburo because of Jiang Zemin's opposition.[56] He was transferred to Zhejiang as vice governor and acting governor on October 12, 2002,[57] and entered the Sixteenth Central Committee as a full member.

Li Yuanchao (1950–), son of Li Gancheng, entered the Sixteenth Central Committee as an alternate member. Li Gancheng (1909–1993), a native of Lianshui, Jiangsu, joined the revolutionary

---

[54] For his bio, see http://news.xinhuanet.com/ziliao/2002-02/22/content_286763.htm.

[55] According to Zong Hairen, the Fifteenth Central Committee had 151 instead of 150 alternate members because of Xi Jinping: Xi was included into the Fifteenth Central Committee so that he would be in a position to enter the core of the Sixteenth Central Committee. For details, see Zong Hairen, *Disidai*, pp. 397–399.

[56] Zong Hairen, *Aimei de Quanli Jiaohuan* (*Ambiguous transition*) (Carle Place, NY: Mirror Books, 2003), pp. 66–74.

[57] According to Zong Hairen, Jiang Zemin made some remarks against Zong's book on the fourth generation at a Politburo meeting on October 9, 2002, and decided to transfer Xi to Zhejiang. See Zong Hairen, *Aimei de Quanli Jiaohuan*, pp. 71–73. For Xi's new appointment, see http://past.people.com.cn/GB/other4583/4595/5840/20021012/840764.html.

work in his home province of Jiangsu.⁵⁸ He was vice mayor of Shanghai (July 1962–February 1967)⁵⁹ and vice chairman of the Shanghai People's Political Consultative Conference (December 1977–April 1983).⁶⁰ Li Yuanchao was born in Changzhou, Jiangsu, in November 1950 when his father was party secretary of the prefecture and moved to Shanghai three years later when his father was transferred there.⁶¹ He was enrolled in the Department of Mathematics at Fudan University in 1978 and joined the CCP that same year.⁶² Because of his experience in the Communist Youth League at Fudan, he became deputy secretary of the Shanghai CYL Committee upon his graduation in 1982. He was promoted to the CYL Central Secretariat as a member in December 1983, along with Song Defu, and stayed there for almost a decade. He became a deputy director of the Central Information Office in May 1993 and was promoted to vice minister of Culture in March 1996. He was transferred to Jiangsu as a deputy secretary in October 2000 and became party secretary of Nanjing one year later. In November 2001, he was made deputy secretary of Jiangsu again. Unfortunately, an incident occurred in Nanjing on September 14, 2002 (less than two months before the convention of the Sixteenth National Party Congress), in which more than 300 people suffered from food poison and 42 people died of it.⁶³ As a result, Li Yuanchao's name was removed from the list of candidates for full members of the Sixteenth Central Committee.⁶⁴ Instead, he ended up as an alternate member of the Sixteenth Central Committee.

---

⁵⁸ http://www.sqdaily.com/20050801/ca76337.htm.
⁵⁹ *Dangdai Zhongguo de Shanghai*, Vol. 2, pp. 654, 655.
⁶⁰ *Ibid.*, p. 664.
⁶¹ http://www.peacehall.com/news/gb/china/2004/07/200407250539.shtml. But according to Zong Hairen, Li Yuanchao was born in Shanghai. See Zong Hairen, *Aimei de Quanli Jiaohuan*, p. 197.
⁶² For Li Yuanchao's bio, see http://news.xinhuanet.com/ziliao/2002-12/30/content_674868.htm.
⁶³ http://news.sina.com.cn/c/2002-09-30/1334752604.html; http://news.xinhuanet.com/newscenter/2002-09/17/content_565055.htm.
⁶⁴ Zong Hairen, *Aimei de Quanli Jiaohuan*, p. 198.

Finally, Yu Zhengsheng (1945–), son of Huang Jing, made it to the Politburo. Huang Jing (1911–1958), a native of Shaoxing, Zhejiang Province, was born into an elite family. His original name was Yu Qiwei, and his grandfather (Yu Mingzhen) was a famous educator. Yu Qiwei joined the CCP in 1932 when he was a student at Qingdao University and met with his girlfriend, Li Yunhe (Jiang Qing, Mao Zedong's fourth wife), there.[65] He was one of the organizers of the famous "December 9th" movement in 1935 and became party secretary of Beiping in 1937. He was appointed as party secretary and mayor of Tianjin in 1949 and was the founding minister of the First Ministry of Machine-Building Industry in 1952.[66] Since Jiang Zemin was also working in an institute under the same ministry in Shanghai in the 1950s, Huang Jing was his big boss in Beijing. Huang Jing is also related to Jiang Jieshi's family: the son of his uncle (Yu Dawei) was married to the daughter of Jiang Jingguo (son of Jiang Jieshi).[67] Huang Jing passed away in 1958 when Yu Zhengsheng was only 13 years old. Yu Zhengsheng went to the Haerbin Institute of Military Engineering in 1963 and studied ballistic missiles.[68] He began to work as an engineer in a factory in Hebei upon his graduation in 1968. His work experience had some overlap with Jiang Zemin's in the Ministry of Electronics Industry in the 1980s: He worked as deputy director of the Electronics Application Research Institute, head and deputy chief engineer of the Second Systems Section of the Computer Industry Management Bureau and concurrently director of the microcomputer management department, and deputy director-general of the Planning Department of the Ministry between September 1982 and September 1984, while Jiang was vice minister and minister of the Ministry between May

---

[65] For his bio, see http://www.news.sdu.edu.cn/html/1554/134915.html.
[66] For his official bio, see Shen Xueming and Zheng Jianying, *Zhonggong Diyijie zhi Dishiwujie Zhongyangweiyuan*, p. 678.
[67] For details, see Gao Xin, *Lingdao Zhongguo de Xinrenwu: Zhonggong Shiliujie Zhengzhiju Weiyuan (China's Top Leaders: Bios of China's Politburo Members)* (Carle Place, NY: Mirror Books, 2003), Vol. 2, p. 625.
[68] For Yu Zhengsheng's official bio, see http://news.xinhuanet.com/ziliao/2002-02/25/content_289242.htm#.

1982 and June 1985.[69] Yu then worked with Deng Pufang for a year as vice president of the China Welfare Fund for the Disabled as well as acting general manager of the Kanghua Industrial Company. After working in Yantai and Qingdao, Shandong Province, as a party and government leader for almost 12 years (1985–1997), Yu was transferred to Beijing as vice minister of Construction in August 1997. He was appointed as minister of Construction in March 1998 and was transferred to Hubei as party secretary in November 2001. He entered the Fourteenth Central Committee as an alternate member in October 1992,[70] the Fifteenth Central Committee as a full member in September 1997, and the Sixteenth Politburo as a full member in November 2002.

Zeng Qinghong (1939–), son of Zeng Shan, is part of the core of the central leadership as a standing member of the Politburo.[71] Zeng Qinghong is not only a princeling with the highest post in the Party, but is also connected to many other princelings through his parents, especially his mother. Zeng Shan (1899–1972), a native of Ji'an, Jiangxi, joined the CCP in 1926 under the influence of his elder brother, Zeng Yansheng, and became one of the most influential CCP leaders in Jiangxi. He served as chairman of the Jiangxi Soviet Government, director of the Central Internal Affairs Department, and party secretary of Jiangxi in the 1930s. He was a member of the CCP Central Committee between 1945 and 1972 and was a minister of several ministries (Textile Industry, Commerce, Communications and Transportation, and Internal Affairs).[72] Zeng Shan's second wife,

---

[69] According to Gao Xin, it was Jiang Zemin who promoted Yu Zhengsheng during this period. For his account, see Gao Xin, *Lingdao Zhongguo de Xinrenwu*, Vol. 2, pp. 634, 635.

[70] According to Gao Xin, Yu Zhengsheng had been groomed to be a candidate for a membership in the Secretariat of the Fourteenth Central Committee, but he ended up as an alternate member and thus was not eligible for a membership in the Secretariat. See Gao Xin, *Lingdao Zhongguo de Xinrenwu*, Vol. 2, pp. 650–653.

[71] Luo Gan, however, is not a princeling. His father was neither Luo Ruiqing nor Luo Ronghuan. Luo is a native of Shandong, but Luo Ruiqing's home province is Sichuan and Luo Ronghuan is a native of Hunan.

[72] For details, see Ting Wang, *Zeng Qing-hong and the Strong Men of the Sunset Race*, pp. 108–123.

Deng Liujin (1911–2003), was also a veteran revolutionary. A native of Shanghang, Fujian Province, Deng Liujin joined the Red Army in 1929 and the CCP in 1931. She was one of 27 female long marchers. She met with Zeng Shan for the first time in Yan'an in November 1937, was selected to work with Zeng Shan in October 1938, and was married to him in December 1938. Interestingly, Deng was a bit afraid of getting married because she did not want to get pregnant.[73] But she must have already been pregnant with Zeng Qinghong when she was married because she gave birth to Ding'er (Qinghong's pet name) only about nine months later, on August 29, 1939. Later, she had three more sons (Zeng Qinghuai, Zeng Qingyang, and Zeng Qingyuan) and one daughter (Zeng Haisheng).[74] Deng Liujin was not only a mother of five children, but also a "mother" of over 100 children of other CCP leaders. In 1948, Deng started a nursery school in Qingzhou, Shandong Province, for 130 children of CCP leaders. The school moved to Shanghai in 1949 and expanded to 300 children.[75] Some of these children such as Chen Haosu (son of Chen Yi and former vice mayor of Beijing), Su Rongsheng (son of Su Yu and former deputy commander of the Beijing Military Region), and Tan Dongsheng (son of Tan Zhenlin and former deputy commander of the Guangzhou Military Region) later became important politicians themselves.[76]

Because of his family connections, Zeng Qinghong began a political career in 1979.[77] He was Yu Qiuli's secretary in the State Planning Commission.[78] Yu Qiuli (1914–1999), also a native of Ji'an, Jiangxi, was Zeng Shan's comrade-in-arms from the same hometown. Yu lost an arm during the long march and was awarded the

---

[73] Deng Liujin, "Yanshui Hepan Shi Zeng Shan" ("Got to know Zeng Shan by the bank of Yanhe River"), http://www.oklink.net/a/0105/0518/035.htm.
[74] For Haisheng's birth, see http://www.sprayofcjr.com/new_page_16.htm.
[75] See http://www.sprayofcjr.com/new_page_16.htm.
[76] Ting Wang, *Zeng Qing-hong and the Strong Men of the Sunset Race*, pp. 128, 129.
[77] For his official bio, see http://news.xinhuanet.com/ziliao/2002-01/16/content_240615.htm.
[78] According to Zong Hairen, this was arranged by Yu Qiuli under Deng Liujin's request. See Zong Hairen, *Disidai*, p. 265.

rank of lieutenant general in 1955. He was the head of the "Petroleum Faction" and served as minister of Petroleum Industry for 12 years (1958–1970). He became vice premier and concurrent chairman of the State Planning Commission in January 1975, chairman of the State Energy Commission in March 1980, and director of the General Political Department of the People's Liberation Army in September 1982.[79] Zeng Qinghong followed Yu to the State Energy Commission in 1981 and to the General Political Department of the PLA in 1982.[80] However, Zeng wanted to go back to the Ministry of Petroleum Industry and Yu introduced him to Tang Ke, the then minister of Petroleum Industry. It was under Tang Ke that Zeng got promoted to leadership positions of the bureau level. He was deputy director of the Foreign Affairs Bureau of the Petroleum Ministry before his departure to Shanghai. His princeling background helped to initiate his political career, and his association with Jiang Zemin helped him land a position in the Politburo Standing Committee in November 2002.

Seven other princelings occupied important positions in the Party or the government. Liu Yandong (1945–), daughter of Liu Ruilong, was executive deputy director of the United Front Department in November 2002 and was later promoted to director of the Department. Liu Yandong is the only princess in the group, and she was one of the children under Deng Liujin's care in the late 1940s.[81] Her father, Liu Ruilong (1910–1988), was a veteran communist. A native of Nantong, Jiangsu Province, Liu Ruilong joined the CCP in 1925.[82] He was a long marcher and assumed the position of commander and concurrent political commissar of logistics in the Third Field Army under Chen Yi.[83] After 1949, he became

---

[79] For his bio, see http://www.china.org.cn/chinese/zhuanti/208055.htm.

[80] Zong Hairen, *Disidai*, p. 265.

[81] Deng Liujin reportedly walked for more than 50 kilometers overnight to get medicine for little Yandong. See Gao Xin, *Lingdao Zhongguo de Xinrenwu: Zhonggong Shiliujie Zhengzhiju Changwei* (*China's Top Leaders: Bios of China's Politburo Members*) (Carle Place, NY: Mirror Books, 2003), Vol. 1, p. 230.

[82] For his bio, see http://www.ntda.gov.cn/main.asp?clsid=35&infoid=2079.

[83] The top leaders of the Third Field Army were Chen Yi (commander and political commissar), Su Yu (deputy commander and second deputy political commissar),

secretary-general of the Shanghai Municipal Party Committee and party secretary of the Agricultural Commission of the East China Bureau. He was transferred to Beijing in February 1953 as the executive vice minister of Agriculture. Liu Yandong's mother, Jiang Tong (1919–1999), was also a remarkable woman. She joined the CCP in 1938, was involved in women work in Shandong, Jiangsu, and Anhui before 1949, and worked in Shanghai after 1949. Jiang Tong graduated from Qinghua University in 1962 at the age of 43 with "outstanding academic achievements."[84] Two years later, her daughter, Liu Yandong, went to her alma mater. As will be explained in detail below, Liu Yandong followed a different path of political career from that of Zeng Qinghong: She climbed the ladder of success as a Chinese Communist League cadre.

Dai Bingguo, son-in-law of Huang Zhen, was director of the International Liaison Department.[85] Huang Zhen (1909–1989) was a long marcher and a career diplomat.[86] He served as Chinese ambassador to Hungary (August 1950–September 1954), Indonesia (November 1954–June 1961), France (June 1964–March 1973), and the United States (May 1973–November 1977).[87] He was vice minister of Foreign Affairs between 1961 and 1964 and served as the first deputy director of the Central Propaganda Department, minister of Culture, and a member of the Central Small Leading Group on Foreign Affairs. Huang's wife is Zhu Lin (1920–), and they have six children.[88] It is not clear which daughter is married to Dai Bingguo,

---

Tan Zhenlin (first deputy political commissar), Zhang Zhen (chief of staff), and Tang Liang (director of the Political Department). See http://news.sohu.com/49/39/news201043949.shtml.

[84] For her bio, see http://qidong.51sobu.com/news/htmls/2005/06/200506111118495346265.html.

[85] He is vice minister of Foreign Affairs now.

[86] For his bio, see http://www.fmprc.gov.cn/chn/ziliao/wjrw/lrfbzjbzzl/t9071.htm.

[87] His title was director of the Liaison Office because China did not have diplomatic relations with the United States at that time yet.

[88] Their children are Huang Wen (daughter), Huang Shan (son), Huang Hao (daughter), Huang He (son, 1947–), and two more. See http://people.com.cn/GB/14738/14761/25881/2526782.html.

but Dai Bingguo is indeed son-in-law of Huang Zhen. Dai (1941–), a native of Yingjiang, Guizhou Province, and of Tujia nationality, began to work in the Ministry of Foreign Affairs in September 1965 upon his completion of training at the Beijing Institute of Foreign Affairs.[89] His area of specialty was the Soviet Union and Eastern European countries. He worked in the Chinese Embassy to the Soviet Union and served as Chinese ambassador to Hungary (October 1989–March 1992).[90] He served briefly as a vice minister of Foreign Affairs between 1994 and 1995 and was transferred to the Central Liaison Department of the CCP as deputy director in July 1995. He was promoted to director of the Department in August 1997 and entered the Fifteenth Central Committee as a full member in the following month.

Li Tielin, son of Li Weihan, was deputy director of the Central Organization Department. Li Weihan (1896–1984), a native of Changsha, Hunan Province, is one of the earliest Chinese communists.[91] He worked with Mao Zedong and Cai Hesen in launching a "New Citizen Society" (*xinmin xuehui*) in 1918 and went to France on a work-study program in 1919. He worked with Zhou Enlai and Zhao Shiyan on organizing a communist group in France and joined the CCP in 1922. He later studied in the Soviet Union between 1931 and 1933 and was one of the "twenty-eight Bolsheviks" (returned students from the Soviet Union). He accused Deng Xiaoping of having followed a wrong political line (Maoist line) in 1933 and took Deng's wife, Jin Weiying.[92] He was a long marcher and a principal leader of united front work. He was director of the Central United

---

[89] For his bio, see http://news.xinhuanet.com/ziliao/2002-01/21/content_246341.htm.

[90] For his appointment, see http://www.npc.cn/zgrdw/common/zw.jsp?label=WXZLK&id=2331&pdmc=rdgb; for his removal, see http://www.npc.gov.cn/zgrdw/common/zw.jsp?label=WXZLK&id=2732&pdmc=rdgb.

[91] For his bio, see http://news.xinhuanet.com/ziliao/2003-01/17/content_693695.htm.

[92] See Ma Jingbo, *Chongdu Deng Xiaoping* (*Reflections on Deng Xiaoping*) (Beijing: Remin Chubanshe, 2004), Vol. 1, pp. 94–103; Richard Evans, *Deng Xiaoping and the Making of Modern China* (New York: Penguin Books, 1993), pp. 63–65.

Front Work Department between October 1949 and December 1964. He was a full member of the Fourth Central Committee (1925–1927), a member of the Fifth Politburo (1927–1929), an alternate member of the Sixth Central Committee (1934–1945), and a full member of the Eighth Central Committee (1956–1969). He served for two terms as vice chairman of the Standing Committee of the National People's Congress between 1954 and 1965.

Li Tielin (1943–) was born in Shaanxi while his father was secretary-general of the Shaan-Gan-Ning Border Government and director of the Urban Work Department of the CCP Central Committee.[93] He grew up in Beijing and was enrolled in the Department of Automatic Control at Qinghua University between 1962 and 1968. He worked in Shandong for five years upon graduation and was transferred to Beijing later. He joined the CCP in December 1980 and became party secretary of the Eastern District in Beijing in March 1987. He began to work for the Central Organization Department in July 1989 initially as deputy secretary-general. He became a deputy director of the Department in September 1992 and concurrently assumed the position of vice minister of Personnel in January 1995. He entered the Sixteenth Central Committee as a full member, while his elder half-brother, Li Tieying (1936–), exited the Politburo after having served in it for three consecutive terms.[94]

Liao Hui, son of Liao Chengzhi, was director of Hong Kong and Macao Affairs Office under the State Council. Liao Chengzhi (1908–1983), a native of Huiyang, Guangdong, was a son of Liao Zhongkai and He Xiangning (famous leaders of the Guomindang and close friends of Sun Zhongshan).[95] Liao Chengzhi was born in Tokyo, Japan, and joined the CCP in 1928. He participated in the long march and was later involved in underground communist activities in Hong Kong. He was one of early Communist Youth League cadres in the People's Republic of China. He was elected deputy

---

[93] For his bio, see http://www.library.hn.cn/difangwx/hxrw/xdrw/sbjld/litielin.htm.
[94] For his bio, see http://news.xinhuanet.com/ziliao/2002-01/16/content_240535.htm. Li Tieying is son of Li Weihan and Jin Weiying (1904–1941) (see http://www.zslib.net/famous/person.asp?id=89).
[95] For his bio, see http://www.china.org.cn/chinese/zhuanti/208073.htm.

secretary of the Central Committee of the CYL in April 1949 along with Jiang Nanxiang and was reelected as secretary of the Central Secretariat of the CYL in July 1953 along with Hu Yaobang. He made tremendous contributions to the development of Sino-Japanese relations through people-to-people diplomacy and to the work of overseas Chinese affairs. Liao's family was unique in China because it had been in charge of the work of overseas Chinese affairs since 1949. Liao Chengzhi's mother, He Xiangning (1878–1972),[96] was the first head of the Committee of Overseas Chinese Affairs (October 1949–April 1959). Liao Chengzhi succeeded his mother in the position until the office was abolished in June 1970, but resumed the position when a new office was established in April 1978.

Liao Hui (1942–) initially did not follow his family tradition of managing overseas Chinese affairs. He studied missiles at the Haerbin Institute of Military Engineering between 1960 and 1965 and joined the PLA upon his graduation.[97] However, he was transferred to the Office of Overseas Chinese Affairs under the State Council as vice director in 1983 and took over as its director in May 1984. He was in that position until August 1997 when he was transferred to the State Council's Hong Kong and Macao Affairs Office as director. He has been a full member of the Central Committee since 1985.

Wang Qishan, son-in-law of Yao Yilin, was director of the Economic Restructuring Office under the State Council in November 2002 and was transferred to Hainan as party secretary in December 2002. Yao Yilin (1917–1994) joined the CCP in 1935 when he was a student at Qinghua University and had a long career in the area of finance and commerce.[98] He served as vice premier of the State Council between July 1979 and March 1993 and was a Politburo standing member between 1987 and 1992. Wang Qishan (1948–), a native of Tianzhen, Shanxi Province, was born in Qingdao,

---

[96] For her bio, see http://www.cnart.biz/cnart/xian_dai/hexiangning/new_page_1.htm.

[97] For his bio, see http://news.xinhuanet.com/ziliao/2003-03/13/content_776752.htm.

[98] For his bio, see http://www.china.org.cn/chinese/zhuanti/208074.htm.

Shandong Province. He went to Yan'an, Shaanxi Province, in 1969 at the age of 21 to be a peasant as an "educated youth." He studied history at Xibei University between 1973 and 1976 and began to work in the Institute of Modern History of China in the Chinese Academy of Social Sciences in 1979. He began a political career in 1982 and had accumulated experience in three areas by November 2002.[99] He was involved in research and policy-making on agricultural affairs between 1982 and 1988, worked as a banker between 1988 and 1997, and gained some experience as a provincial leader between 1997 and 2000. He also worked under Zhu Rongji in the Office of Economic Systems Reforms in the State Council for two years between 2000 and 2002. He was transferred to Hainan as party secretary in November 2002.[100]

Zhou Xiaochuan (1948–), son of Zhou Jiannan, was chairman of the China Securities Regulatory Commission and was later made governor of the People's Bank of China in December 2002.[101] His father, Zhou Jiannan, used to be Jiang Zemin's superior in the First Ministry of Machine Building. A native of Yixing, Jiangsu Province,[102] Zhou Jiannan (1917–1995) was a graduate of the Shanghai Jiaotong University in 1937.[103] He went to Yan'an in the same year and was sent to Chongqing to work for the CCP in 1939.[104] He became a vice minister of the First Ministry of Machine Building in March 1961 and was responsible for technological development planning in the ministry. It is very unlikely that Jiang Zemin had any direct contact with Zhou at that time because of huge administrative gaps between

---

[99] For his bio, see http://news.xinhuanet.com/ziliao/2002-03/05/content_300439.htm.

[100] He was later transferred to Beijing in April 2003 after Meng Xuenong was fired due to the SARS epidemic in Beijing.

[101] http://news.xinhuanet.com/ziliao/2002-03/05/content_300487.htm.

[102] Yixing is famous for its teapots made with special clay (zisha). Xu Xiutang, an artist from the county, produced a head sculpture of Zhou Jiannan in 2005 in memory of him. See http://www.photobase.cn/picinfo.asp?coverid=70149.

[103] For his bio, see http://www.yixing.gov.cn/yxmr/xdzmrw/zjn.htm.

[104] It is very likely that Zhou Xiaochuan was born in Sichuan because of his name "Xiaochuan," literally a little boy born in Sichuan.

them. Yet Jiang became closer to Zhou in the 1980s when he began to work in Beijing. Jiang Zemin and his wife had a photo taken with Zhou Jiannan and his wife in 1994. Jiang Zemin also visited Zhou in the hospital in his last days.[105]

Zhou Xiaochuan attended the Beijing Institute of Chemical Industry during the Cultural Revolution as a "worker-peasant-soldier" student and graduated from there in 1975. He later obtained a doctoral degree from Qinghua University in 1985.[106] Apparently, Zhou's early rise was not due to his connection to Jiang Zemin: He did substantial research on economic reform policies and other economic issues between 1979 and 1985, was a deputy director of China Economic Restructuring Institute and concurrently a member of the Leading Small Group on Systems Reforms under the State Council between 1986 and 1987, and assumed the position of assistant minister of the Ministry of Foreign Trade and Economic Cooperation between 1986 and 1989 as well as a member of the State Economic Restructuring Commission between 1986 and 1991. It is likely that Zhou's later appointments might have something to do with his connections with Jiang Zemin. Zhou was appointed as vice governor of the Bank of China in 1991, as director of the State Administration of Foreign Exchange in 1995, vice governor of the People's Bank of China in 1996, governor of the China Construction Bank, and chairman of China Securities Regulatory Commission in 2000. He joined the CCP in 1986 and entered the Sixteenth Central Committee as a full member for the first time. In December 2002, under the recommendation of Jiang Zemin, Zhou was appointed as governor of the People's Bank of China (the central bank), replacing Dai Xianglong who was sent to Tianjin as mayor.[107]

Finally, Liu Jing (1944–), son of Han Jun, was vice minister of Public Security. Han Jun (1912–1949), a native of Xin'an, Henan Province, joined the CCP in prison in 1932. He worked closely with Bo Yibo (Bo Xilai's father) in Shanxi after he was released from

---

[105] http://www.yixing.gov.cn/yxmr/xdzmrw/zjn.htm.
[106] http://www.macrochina.com.cn/prize/brt/zhouxiaochuan.shtml.
[107] Zong Hairen, *Aimei de Quanli Jiaohuan*, p. 182.

prison in 1936. He was involved in organizing anti-Japanese forces, coordinated with the Guomindang forces, and participated in peaceful liberation of Beiping. He was secretary-general of the Beiping Municipal Party Committee in 1949 but passed away on March 23, 1949.[108] There are two stories of his death: In one story, he died of a disease; in the other, he committed suicide. According to the second story, Han Jun committed suicide because of a "Yuxi Incident" in which all of the 100+ cadres he took to Henan from Yan'an were unexpectedly executed by rebellious local forces on May 26, 1945.[109]

Liu Jing does not use his father's family name because his mother was remarried, and he used the family name of his stepfather.[110] His official hometown is not Xin'an, Henan Province, but Yuxian, Shanxi Province. He went to the college that Zeng Qinghong had attended, but at later time. Zeng graduated from the Beijing Institute of Technology in 1963, and Liu entered the same institution in 1963. Liu joined the CCP in 1965 and joined the PLA in 1968 upon his graduation. He worked with Deng Pufang between February 1985 and March 1992 in the China Welfare Fund for the Disabled. He was deputy director and director of the Domestic Affairs Department, deputy secretary-general, and vice chairman of the Board. He was transferred to Yunnan in 1992 as head of the Department of Foreign Trade and Economic Cooperation of Yunnan and was promoted to vice governor a year later. He was transferred to the China General Bureau of Customs in 1998 as vice director and was made deputy director of the General Office of the Central Leading Small Group on Falungong in 2000. He was appointed as vice minister of Public Security in May 2001 and entered the Sixteenth Central Committee as a full member.[111] He is one of

---

[108] http://www.ndcnc.gov.cn/datalib/2001/MartialCyclopaedic/DL/DL-3604/.

[109] There are two versions of his suicide: in one version, he used a pistol to end his life (http://book.sina.com.cn/longbook/1070517888_yuanqudeyizhan/31.shtml); in another, he used sleeping pills (http://washeng.net/HuaShan/BBS/jiangshuai/gbcurrent/4778.shtml).

[110] http://www.renminbao.com/rmb/articles/2004/6/10/31448.html.

[111] http://ics.nccu.edu.tw/frame.php?address=polsum&id=1166&PHPSESSID=e7cc7c93245b8b18a993e0ce65332404.

those who have been responsible for persecuting Falungong practitioners.[112]

There are three princelings in the military on the Sixteenth Central Committee. Ding Yiping, son of Ding Qiusheng, was commander of the North China Sea Fleet and concurrent deputy commander of the Jinan Military Region in November 2002. Ding Qiusheng (1913–1995), a native of Xiangxiang, Hunan Province, joined the Red Army in 1930 and the CCP in 1932.[113] He was a long marcher and worked under the leadership of Chen Yi in the Third Field Army. He was political commissar of the 22nd Army and was involved in liberating and managing Ningbo, Zhejiang Province. He was awarded the rank of lieutenant general in 1955 and was the founding political commissar of the North China Sea Fleet.[114] Forty years later, his son, Ding Yiping (1951–), became commander of the North China Sea Fleet with the rank of vice admiral. Ding Yiping joined the PLA in 1968 at the age of 17 and joined the CCP in 1970. In the subsequent 23 years, he served successively as a squad leader, master sergeant, coxswain, leader of a Navy destroyer detachment, and chief of staff of a naval base in the PLA Navy. He was awarded the rank of rear admiral in 1993 and was promoted to the rank of vice admiral in 2002. He became chief of staff of the North China Sea Fleet in January 1995, its deputy commander in December 1997, and its commander and concurrent deputy commander of the Jinan Military Region in December 2000.[115] In 2002, Ding served as the commander-in-chief of a Chinese flotilla that sailed around the globe in 132 days and visited 10 countries.[116]

---

[112] For some of his media interviews, see http://www.people.com.cn/GB/shizheng/19/20010227/404575.html.

[113] http://www.ndcnc.gov.cn/datalib/2003/Character/DL/DL-183847.

[114] The North China Sea Fleet was established in 1960, and it is stationed in Qingdao, Shandong Province. See http://zh.askmore.net/%E5%8C%97%E6%B5%B7%E8%88%B0%E9%98%9F.htm#.E5.BB.BA.E7.AB.8B.E5.B9.B4.E4.BB.A3.

[115] http://ics.nccu.edu.tw/frame.php?address=polsum&id=2766&PHPSESSID=59c764e6f110bb9f228a1e94ea4a38f4.

[116] http://www.people.com.cn/GB/junshi/192/8190/index.html.

When his flotilla arrived at Qingdao on September 23, 2002, Deputy Chief of Staff General Xiong Guangkai, Navy Commander General Shi Yunsheng, and Navy Political Commissar General Yang Huaiqing greeted him.[117] Two months later, Ding was inducted into the Sixteenth Central Committee as an alternate member.[118]

Xu Qiliang, son of Xu Lefu, was commander of the Shenyang Military Region Air Force and concurrent deputy commander of the Shenyang Military Region. A native of Yangshan, Shandong Province, Xu Lefu (1922–1997) joined the CCP in 1938 and the Red Army in 1939. He participated in the Liaoshen Military Campaign in 1948 and was involved in battles in Hunan and Guangxi. He was awarded the rank of colonel in 1955 and was promoted to the rank of senior colonel in 1962.[119] He was awarded the rank of lieutenant general (air force) in 1988 and assumed the positions of political commissar of the Shenyang Military Region Air Force, political commissar of the Beijing Military Region Air Force, and deputy political commissar of the PLA Air Force.[120] Xu Qiliang (1950–) joined the PLA at the age of 16 in 1966 and joined the CCP one year later. After getting trained in the aviation schools, he climbed the ladder of success in the PLA Air Force.[121] He became an acting deputy army commander in the PLA Air Force in 1988, deputy chief of staff of the PLA Air Force in 1993, its chief of staff in 1994, and commander of the Shenyang Military Region Air Force and concurrent deputy commander of the Shenyang Military Region in 1999. He was awarded the rank of major general (air force) in 1991 and was promoted to the rank of lieutenant general (air force) in 1996. He became an alternate member in the Fourteenth Central Committee elected in 1992 at the age of 42, an alternate member of the Fifteenth Central

---

[117] http://www.people.com.cn/GB/junshi/60/20020923/829377.html.
[118] However, a few months later, in June 2003, he was demoted to deputy chief of staff of the PLA Navy because of a submarine accident.
[119] http://www.sd-china.com/people/jxdai/28.htm.
[120] http://www.sd-china.com/people/jxdai/28.htm.
[121] For his bio, see Shen Xueming and Zheng Jianying, Zhonggong *Diyijie zhi Dishiwujie Zhongyangweiyuan*, p. 251.

Committee elected in 1997, and a full member of the Sixteenth Central Committee elected in 2002 at the age of 52.[122]

Finally, Ma Xiantian (1949–), commander of the Nanjing Military Region Air Force and concurrent deputy commander of the Nanjing Military Region, is also reportedly a princeling, although his father's name has not yet been identified. Ma's experience is similar to that of Xu Qiliang. A year older than Xu, Ma also joined the PLA at the age of 16 (in 1965). He attended the Second Aviation Preparatory School of the PLA Air Force (in Baoding, Hebei Province) in July 1965, while Xu went to the First Aviation Preparatory School of the PLA Air Force (in Changchun, Jilin Province)[123] the following year. Although Ma Xiaotian was one year older than Xu Qiliang and he joined the PLA one year earlier, he lagged behind Xu by four years in later promotions. Xu was awarded the rank of major general (air force) in 1991; Ma was awarded the same rank in 1995. Xu was awarded the rank of lieutenant general (air force) in 1996; Ma was awarded the same rank in 2000. Xu became a deputy chief of staff of the PLA Air Force in January 1993; Ma was appointed to the same post in March 1997. Xu became an alternate member of the Fourteenth Central Committee in 1992, but Ma did not enter the Central Committee until 10 years later. Beginning in 1999, however, Ma Xiaotian seemed to be catching up. While Xu was appointed a deputy commander of the Shenyang Military Region and concurrent commander of the Shenyang Military Region Air Force in February 1999, Ma became a deputy commander of the Lanzhou Military Region and concurrent commander of the Lanzhou Military Region Air Force just four months later. In November 2002, both Ma and Xu entered the Sixteenth Central Committee as full members. After having served in the Lanzhou and Nanjing military regions for two years each, Ma was promoted to be a deputy commander of the PLA Air Force in July 2003.[124]

---

[122] He was promoted to deputy chief of staff in 2004.

[123] This school was renamed the First Aviation Foundation School of the PLA Air Force in 1986 and another name change to Changchun Aviation Academy of the PLA Air Force in 1993. See http://www.h-edu.com/htm/200507/ 2005070615495316.htm.

[124] Ma was promoted to an air force commander, though his grade may remain at military region deputy leader level.

The combined power index of these princelings is 41 points, one point less than those of the Shanghai Gang. That these people belong to the same category does not mean that they necessarily form a coherent faction. With very few exceptions, it is hard to find evidence that any of them has ever worked with any other in the same organization. The obvious exception is Yu Zhengsheng and Deng Pufang. Yu, a Politburo member and party secretary of Hubei, joined Deng between September 1984 and November 1985 as vice president of the China Welfare Fund for the Disabled as well as acting general manager of the Kanghua Industrial Company. Another pair is Zeng Qinghong and Li Tielin. Li had been a deputy director of the Central Organization Department since 1992, and Zeng was the director of the Central Organization Department between 1999 and 2002. They worked together for three years. Zeng Qinghong and Hong Hu went to the same college (the Beijing Institute of Technology) in the same period (1958–1963), though they studied in different departments: Zeng studied in the Department of Automatic Control and Hong studied in the Department of Chemical Engineering. Finally, Liao Hui and Bai Keming studied in the same department of the Haerbin Institute of Military Engineering but in different classes. Liao was there from 1960 to 1965, and Bai from 1962 to 1968. Their overlap was three years.

It is likely that some of these people have closer personal ties with one another. Chen Yuan and Deng Pufang must know each other personally. Only one year apart, the two were likely playmates when they were young. They went to different universities later on, however. Deng was enrolled in the Department of Physics at Beijing University, and Chen went to Qinghua University to study automatic control. Another pair is Wang Qishan and Zhou Xiaochuan. Although they did not work in the same organization at the same time, they worked in the same organizations consecutively. Wang was vice governor of the China Construction Bank between 1989 and 1993, while Zhou was vice governor of the Bank of China between 1991 and 1995. Wang became vice governor of the People's Bank of China in 1993, and Zhou assumed the same position in 1996. Wang was governor of the China Construction Bank from 1994 to 1997, and Zhou was in the same post from 1998 to 2000. To this pair, one may add Chen Yuan, another banker. There is no evidence that Chen has worked with either of them in the same organization, but interactions with both of them were inevitable. Finally, Xu Qiliang and Ma Xiantian must know each other because of their similar experiences in the Air Force, but there is no career overlap between them.

Clearly, it is tempting to describe the princelings as a political faction, but no hard evidence is available for such an argument. Although the power index of these princelings is only one point less than that of the Shanghai Gang, their group cohesion index (eight years)[125] is significantly less than that of the Shanghai Gang (103.17 years). Moreover, although Zeng Qinghong is best connected among the princelings, he is far from being the core of the princelings as a group. He had only worked with another princeling and attended the same college with two others.

QINGHUA CLIQUE

Although historically there may have been a Qinghua Clique under the leadership of Jiang Nanxiang, it is not clear whether such a clique existed in the past decade.[126] Since school ties are useful resources in politics, political leaders who share learning experience in the same institute of higher education may choose to activate their school identities for political purposes. For this reason, this study treats graduates of the Qinghua University as a factional group.

---

[125] Zeng Qinghong's college experience with Hong Hu is calculated as the number of years divided by two because they studied in different departments. The same method is also used for calculating personal ties between Liao Hui and Bai Keming. For a more detailed explanation of the method, see sections on the Qinghua Clique.

[126] For a detailed study of the evolution of the Qinghua Clique, see Li, *China's Leaders*, Chapter 4.

There are 20 graduates of Qinghua University in the Sixteenth CC: 16 full and four alternate members (Table 4.5). Among nine standing members of the Politburo, four are Qinghua graduates: Hu Jintao, Wu Bangguo, Huang Ju, and Wu Guanzheng. Another Politburo member, Zeng Peiyan, is also a Qinghua graduate. Other Qinghua graduates include 10 central leaders (Li Tielin, Zhang Fusen, Chen Yuan, Zhang Huazhu, Wang Shucheng, Zhang Delin, Xie Zhenhua, Jia Chunwang, Hua Jianmin, and Liu Yandong), three provincial leaders (Tian Chengping, Xi Jinping, and Xu Rongkai), one business leader (Xie Qihua), and one academic leader (Wu Qidi). The combined power index for these leaders is 54 points, more than that of either the Princelings or the Shanghai Gang.

To estimate the group cohesion of the Qinghua Clique, we need to calculate school ties. The calculation is based on the following considerations. First, a pair of students have personal ties with one another only when they study in the same school at the same time. Those who studied at Qinghua University at different times do not have school ties at the personal level. Second, a pair of students have stronger ties with each other if they study in the same department than in different departments. Third, a pair of students are likely to have stronger ties if they study in the same class than in different classes of the same department. On this basis, we would count studying in the same class of the same department as one point, studying in different classes of the same department as half a point, studying in different departments as a quarter of a point. The results are reported in Table 4.6 and Figure 4.3.

Noticeably, Wu Shucheng (1941–), minister of Water Resources, has the strongest ties among the Qinghua graduates of the Sixteenth Central Committee.[127] Wang, a native of Liyang, Jiangsu Province, and Hu Jintao both went to the same department of Qinghua University in the same year. They both began their study in the Department of Water Conservancy Engineering at Qinghua

---

[127] For Wang Shucheng's bio, see http://news.xinhuanet.com/ziliao/2002-03/01/content_295730.htm.

Table 4.5 Qinghua Graduates in the Sixteenth Central Committee (2002)

Name	Home	Birth	Major	Department	Entry	Party	Graduation	Index
Chen Yuan	Shanghai	1945	Automatic control	Automatic control	1964	1975	1970	1
Hu Jintao	Anhui	1942	Hydropower	Water conservacy	1959	1964	1965	9
Hua Jianmin	Jiangsu	1940	Gas turbine	Power	1957	1961	1963	2
Huang Ju	Zhejiang	1938	Electrical machinery	Electrical machinery	1956	1966	1963	5
Jia Chunwang	Beijing	1938	Engineering physics	Engineering physics	1957	1962	1964	2
Li Tielin	Hunan	1943	Automatic control	Automatic control	1962	1980	1968	2
Liu Yandong (f.)	Jiangsu	1945	Chemical engineering	Chemical engineering	1964	1964	1970	2
Tian Chengping	Hebei	1945	Civil architecture	Civil architecture	1962	1964	1968	2
Wang Shucheng	Jiangsu	1941	Water conservacy	Water conservacy	1959	1965	1968	2
Wu Bangguo	Anhui	1941	Electron tube	Radio electronics	1960	1964	1967	5
Wu Guanzheng	Jiangxi	1938	Thermal measurement	Power	1959	1962	1968	5
Wu Qidi (f.)	Zhejiang	1947	Radio	Radio electronics	1964		1970	1
Xi Jinping	Shaanxi	1953	Chemical engineering	Chemical engineering	1974	1974	1979	2
Xie Qihua (f.)	Zhejiang	1943	Unknown		1962	1980	1968	1
Xie Zhenhua	Tianjin	1949	Engineering physics	Engineering physics	1973	1969	1977	2
Xu Rongkai	Chongqing	1942	Mechanics	Mechanics	1961	1960	1966	2
Zeng Peiyan	Zhejiang	1938	Electronics	Radio electronics	1956	1978	1962	4
Zhang Delin	Beijing	1939	Mechanics	Mechanics	1958	1964	1964	2
Zhang Fusen	Beijing	1940	Automatic control	Automatic control	1959	1958	1965	2
Zhang Huazhu	Jiangsu	1945	Automatic control	Automatic control	1963	1965	1970	1
Total								54

Source: Updated from Zhiyue Bo, "The 16th Central Committee of the Chinese Communist Party: formal institutions and factional groups," *Journal of Contemporary China*, Vol. 13, No. 139 (May 2004), Table 8, p. 246.

Table 4.6 Group Cohesion Matrix of Qinghua Graduates in the Sixteenth Central Committee

Name	Chen	Hu	Hua	Huang	Jia	Li	Liu	Tian	Wang	WBG	WGZ	WQD	Xi	XQH	XZH	Xu	Zeng	ZDL	ZFS	ZHZ	Subtotal
Chen Yun	n/a	0.25	0	0	0	2	1.5	1	1	0.75	1	1.5	0	1	0	0.5	0	0	0.5	3	14
Hu Jintao	0.25	n/a	1	1	1.25	0.75	0.25	0.75	4.5	1.25	1.5	0.25	0	0.75	0	1	0.75	1.25	1.5	0.5	18.25
Hua Jianmin	0	1	n/a	1.5	1.5	0.25	0	0.25	1	0.75	2	0	0	0.25	0	0.5	1.25	1.25	1	0	11.5
Huang Ju	0	1	1.5	n/a	1.5	0.5	0	0.25	1	0.75	1	0	0	0.25	0	0.5	1.5	1.25	1	0	9.5
Jia Chunwang	0	1.25	1.5	1.5	n/a	0.5	0	0.5	1.25	1	1.25	0	0	0.5	0	0.75	1.25	1.5	1.25	0.25	10
Li Tielin	2	0.75	0.25	0.5	0.5	n/a	1	1.5	1.5	1.25	1.5	1	0	1.5	0	1	0	0.5	1.5	0.5	12.75
Liu Yandong (f.)	1.5	0.25	0	0	0	1	n/a	1	1	0.75	1	1.5	0	1	0	0.5	0	0	0.25	1.5	8.5
Tian Chengping	1	0.75	0.25	0.25	0.5	1.5	1	n/a	1.5	1.25	1.5	1	0	1.5	0	1	0	0.5	0.75	1.25	10.25
Wang Shucheng	1	4.5	1	1	1.25	1.5	1	1.5	n/a	2	2.25	1	0	1.5	0	1.75	0.75	1.25	1.5	1.25	13.25
Wu Bangguo	0.75	1.25	0.75	0.75	1	1.25	0.75	1.25	2	n/a	1.75	1.5	0	1.25	0	1.25	1	1.25	1.5	1.25	10
Wu Guanzheng	1	1.5	2	1	1.25	1.5	1.5	1.5	2.25	1.75	n/a	1	0	1.5	0	1.25	0.75	1.25	1.5	1.25	8.5
Wu Qidi (f.)	1.5	0.25	0	0	0	1	1.5	1	1	1.5	1	n/a	0	1	0	0.5	0	0	0.25	1.5	3.25
Xi Jinping	0	0	0	0	0	0	0	0	0	0	0	0	n/a	0	0.75	0	0	0	0	0	0.75
Xie Qihua (f.)	1	0.75	0.25	0.25	0.5	1.5	1	1.5	1.5	1.25	1.5	1	0	n/a	0	1	0	0.5	0.75	1.5	3.75
Xie Zhenhua	0	0	0	0	0	0	0	0	0	0	0	0	0.75	0	n/a	0	0	0	0	0	0
Xu Rongkai	0.5	1	0.5	0.5	0.75	1	0.5	1	1.75	1.25	1.25	0.5	0	1	0	n/a	0.25	1.5	1	0.75	3.5
Zeng Peiyan	0	0.75	1.25	1.5	1.25	0	0	0	0.75	1	0.75	0	0	0	0	0.25	n/a	1	0.75	0	1.75
Zhang Delin	0	1.25	1.25	1.25	1.5	0.5	0	0.5	1.25	1	1.25	0	0	0.5	0	1.5	1	n/a	1.25	0.25	1.5

(Continued)

178 China's Elite Politics

Table 4.6 (Continued)

Name	Chen	Hu	Hua	Huang	Jia	Li	Liu	Tian	Wang	WBG	WGZ	WQD	Xi	XQH	XZH	Xu	Zeng	ZDL	ZFS	ZHZ	Subtotal
Zhang Fusen	0.5	1.5	1	1	1.25	1.5	0.25	0.75	1.5	1.25	1.5	0.25	0	0.75	0	1	0.75	1.25	n/a	1	1
Zhang Huazhu	3	0.5	0	0	0.25	0.5	1.5	1.25	1.25	1	1.25	1.5	0	1.5	0	0.75	0	0.25	1	n/a	
Total	14	18.5	12.5	12	14.25	16.75	11.25	15.5	26	19.75	23.25	12	0.75	15.75	0.75	15	9.25	14.25	17	15.5	142

Notes: (i) Numbers in cells represent the number of years a pair worked together in the Shanghai Party Committee. (ii) The subtotals are the sum of the numbers above the diagonal of n/a for each leader. (iii) The total (142) is the sum of the numbers above the diagonal of n/as.

Source: Author's database.

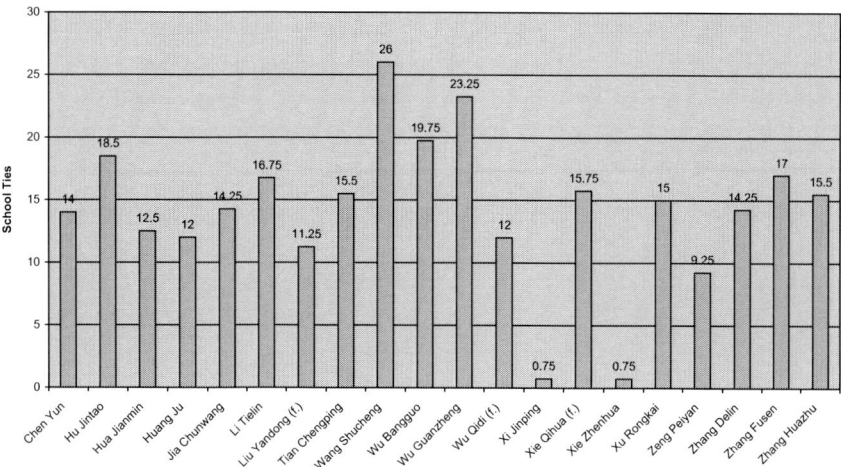

Fig 4.3 School Ties of Qinghua Graduates in the Sixteenth Central Committee.

University in 1959, but their majors were different. Hu majored in hub hydropower stations, and Wang's major was water engineering. Upon graduation in 1965, both of them continued to stay in the same department. Hu was a political counselor, and Wang was enrolled in a graduate program. They were together in the same department for nine years (but calculated as 4.5 years of school ties because of their different majors). Wang is a typical technocrat, devoting his entire career to hydropower and water resources.

In the history of the People's Republic of China, the Ministry of Water Resources went through several stages. The Ministry of Water Resources was one of the first ministries under the State Council, and Fu Zuoyi (1895–1974), former Guomindang general, was the first minister (October 1949–February 1958). In February 1958, the ministry was merged with the Ministry of Electricity to form the Ministry of Water Resources and Electricity with Fu Zuoyi as minister (1958–1967). This ministry was dissolved in February 1979 to form separate Ministry of Water Resources (with Qian Zhengying as minister) and Ministry of Electricity (with Liu Lanbo as minister). The two ministries were merged again into one in March 1982 with Qian Zhengying as minister of the new Ministry of Water Resources and

Electricity. But the new ministry was dissolved again in April 1988. In their place, there were a Ministry of Water Resources (with Yang Zhenhuai as minister) and a Ministry of Energy. When Wang Shucheng began to work in 1968, he worked in No. 6 Engineering Bureau under the Ministry of Water Resources and Electricity. When the ministry was split into two in 1979, his bureau was placed under the Ministry of Electricity. After the two ministries were merged again, he was made responsible for hydropower construction. Wang was vice minister of Electricity between April 1993 and March 1998 and became minister of Water Resources in November 1998. He entered the Sixteenth Central Committee as a full member, without any prior experience in the central committee.

The one who has the second strongest ties among the Qinghua graduates of the Sixteenth Central Committee is Wu Guanzheng (1938–), standing member of the Sixteenth Politburo and secretary of the Sixteenth Central Disciplinary Inspection Commission. A native of Yugan, Jiangxi Province,[128] Wu went to Qinghua University also in 1959 at the age of 21.[129] He also spent nine years at Qinghua from 1959 to 1968, as Hu Jintao and Wang Shucheng did. He studied thermal measurement and automatic controls in the Department of Power both as an undergraduate and as a graduate student. Wu was politically active while at Qinghua University. He joined the CCP in March 1962, two years earlier than Hu Jintao and

---

[128] For an introduction to Wu's hometown, see Yan Hua, "Zhonggong Zhengzhijuchangwei Jiaxiang Xunfang Xilie (5): Wu Guangzheng Jiali youwei 'Jiuqiansui'" ("Visiting the hometowns of the CCP's Politburo standing members (5): There is a 'royal majesty' in Wu Guangzheng's family"), *Asian Times* (Chinese), June 12, 2005, http://www.atchinese.com/index.php?option=com_content&task=view&id=2094&Itemid=66 and Yan Hua, "Zhonggong Zhengzhijuchangwei Jiaxiang Xunfang Xilie (6): Tuo Wu Guangzheng Hongfu Fazhan Shensu Yugan Shidaru Nanchang Jingjiquan" ("Visiting the hometowns of the CCP's Politburo standing members (6): taking advantage of Wu Guangzheng's office, Yugan County developed very rapidly and was determined to be included in the economic sphere of Nanchang"), *Asian Times* (Chinese), June 13, 2005, http://www.atchinese.com/index.php?option=com_content&task=view&id=2093&Itemid=66.

[129] For Wu Guanzheng's bio, see http://news.xinhuanet.com/ziliao/2002-01/16/content_240542.htm.

three years earlier than Wang Shucheng did. He was secretary of the CYL Branch while he was an undergraduate student, and deputy secretary of the Party Branch while he was a graduate student. After seven years in a factory in Hubei, he started a political career in 1975 when he was appointed as a deputy director of the Commission of Science and Technology of Wuhan, Hubei Province. He was mayor of Wuhan between 1983 and 1986, governor of Jiangxi between 1986 and 1995, party secretary of Jiangxi between 1995 and 1997, and party secretary of Shandong and Politburo member between 1997 and 2002. He entered the Sixteenth Politburo as a standing member in charge of disciplinary affairs and was elected secretary of the Sixteenth Central Disciplinary Inspection Commission.

Wu Bangguo (1941–) also belongs to the same cohort as Hu, Wang, and Wu Guanzheng. He went to Qinghua University in 1960, a year later than these three did, and stayed there for seven years. He majored in electron tube engineering at the Department of Radio Electronics and joined the CCP in April 1964, the same month as Hu did. As mentioned in the section on the Shanghai Gang, Wu Bangguo began a long career in Shanghai upon his graduation from Qinghua University in 1967. He also entered the Sixteenth Politburo as a standing member.

Xi Jinping and Xie Zhenhua (1949–) were outliers among the Qinghua graduates because they went to Qinghua during the Cultural Revolution. Xi studied in the Department of Chemical Engineering at Qinghua University between 1975 and 1979 as a "worker-peasant-soldier" student; Xie graduated from the Department of Physics at Qinghua University in January 1977 and continued his study in the department until 1979.[130] Neither of them shared educational experience with any other Qinghua graduates of the Sixteenth Central Committee, and their overlap at Qinghua was about three years (1975–1979) with an expected personal tie of 0.75 points.[131] After one year of teaching and two years in the National

---

[130] For Xie Zhenhua's bio, see http://news.xinhuanet.com/ziliao/2002-03/05/content_300355.htm.

[131] In reality, they might have not interacted with each other at Qinghua at all.

Construction Commission, Xie began to work in the field of environmental protection in 1982 and spent his subsequent 23 years in it. He later obtained a graduate degree in environmental law from Wuhan University and became director of the State Environmental Protection Administration in 1993. He was made a member of the Fifteenth Central Disciplinary Inspection Commission in 1997 and entered the Sixteenth Central Committee as a full member.[132]

It is difficult to identify a leader among the Qinghua graduates. It is tempting to say that Hu Jintao should be the leader, but it is not easy to find hard evidence. It is also difficult to imagine Wang Shucheng as the leader of the Qinghua Clique simply because he had the highest score on school ties. From this perspective, the Qinghua Clique may not be as coherent and tight a political faction as it appears to be.[133]

The group cohesion of the Qinghua Clique is 142 points altogether, much stronger than that of any previous faction. It is stronger than the group cohesion of the Shanghai Gang.[134] It is more than 17 times as strong as the group cohesion of the Princelings.

CCYL GROUP

The CCYL cadres have long been visible in the Party Center. Hu Yaobang (1915–1989) was the first among CCYL cadres to have assumed the topmost position in the Party. Hu, a long marcher who had been the first secretary of the Secretariat of the Central Committee of the CCYL in the 1950s, was made general secretary of the CCP in 1980 and stayed in that position for more than six years

---

[132] However, he resigned on December 2, 2005, to take responsibilities for a chemical spill accident in Songhua Jiang river of Heilongjiang.

[133] For a different assessment, see Li, *China's Leaders*, pp. 87–126.

[134] The two indexes, it should be noted, are not strictly comparable because the group cohesion index of the Qinghua graduates is based on all Qinghua graduates in the Sixteenth CC, but the group cohesion index of the Shanghai Gang is based only on members of inner circles of the Party and government leaders of the Shanghai Gang in the Sixteenth CC. The comparison, therefore, can only serve as a guide.

until January 1987. However, there is no evidence that there has ever been a faction formed under his leadership; nor is there any evidence that another CCYL leader has served as the leader of a CCYL faction. In this sense, the CCYL Group is treated here as a factional group instead of a faction. Members of the CCYL Group refer to those who have been on the Central Committee of the CCYL.

The CCYL Group is the largest factional group in the Sixteenth CC. Fifty-seven people are identified as CCYL cadres: 24 full and 33 alternate members (Table 4.7). These cadres are not necessarily all members of a faction, but their sense of belonging to the same group has been dramatically enhanced since Hu Jintao was elected general secretary of the CCP. Hu's success highlighted the significance of their association with the CCYL. As Meng Xuenong proudly remarked when he was elected as mayor of Beijing, "The times when we were young always stay with us with good memories. My career in the CCYL provided a foundation for my political career later on."[135]

In addition to Hu, there were three more Politburo members with CCYL backgrounds: Wang Zhaoguo, Liu Yunshan, and Wang Lequan. A native of Fengrun, Hebei Province, Wang Zhaoguo (1941–) was the first core of the CCYL Secretariat after the Cultural Revolution. He was "discovered" by Deng Xiaoping as a rare talent during Deng's visit to his factory in Hubei (Second Automotive Works) and was promoted to Beijing as the first secretary of the CCYL Secretariat.[136] He entered the Twelfth Central Committee in September 1982 at the age of 41 as a full member. His seniority in the Central Committee is second to none other than Ismail Amat, who has been in the Central Committee since the Tenth National Party Congress in 1973, and he is one of the only two members of

---

[135] Meng Xuenong, "Gongqingtuo Shengya Weicongzheng Diandingle yige Jichu" ("My career in the CCYL has provided a foundation for my political career later on"), *Renmin ribao*, January 19, 2003. http://www.peopledaily.com.cn/GB/shizheng/252/9823/9826/20030119/910732.html. Meng was fired on April 20, 2003, because of his mishandling of the SARS problem in Beijing.

[136] For his bio, see http://news.xinhuanet.com/ziliao/2002-01/21/ content_246339.htm.

Table 4.7 CCYL Cadres in the Sixteenth Central Committee (2002)

Name	Home	Birth	CC Membership	Work Unit	Title	Index
Politburo						
Hu Jintao	Anhui	1942	Full	Politburo	General Secretary	9
Liu Yunshan	Inner Mongolia	1947	Full	Propaganda	Director	5
Wang Zhaoguo	Hebei	1941	Full	United Front	Director	4
Wang Lequan	Shandong	1944	Full	Xinjiang	Party Secretary	4
Central party institutions						
Liu Yandong (f.)	Jiangsu	1945	Full	United Front	Deputy Director	2
Ji Bingxuan	Henan	1952	Alternate	Propaganda	Deputy Director	1
Ling Jihua	Shanxi	1957	Alternate	General Office	Deputy Director	1
Central government institutions						
Du Qinglin	Jilin	1946	Full	Agriculture	Minister	2
Jia Chunwang	Beijing	1938	Full	Security	Minister	2
Li Changjiang	Heilongjiang	1944	Full	Quality	Director	2
Li Dezhu (Korean)	Jilin	1943	Full	Ethnic Affairs	Minister	2
Li Zhilun	Liaoning	1942	Full	Supervision	Vice Minister	2
Sun Jiazheng	Jiangsu	1944	Full	Culture	Minister	2
Wang Yang	Anhui	1955	Alternate	Planning	Vice Minister	1
Ye Xiaowen	Guizhou	1950	Alternate	Religious Affairs	Director	1
Zhang Fusen	Beijing	1940	Full	Justice	Minister	2
Zhang Weiqing	Shaanxi	1944	Full	Family Planning	Minister	2
Zhou Qiang	Hubei	1960	Full	CCYL	First Secretary	2

(*Continued*)

Balance of Factional Power 185

Table 4.7 (Continued)

Name	Home	Birth	CC Membership	Work Unit	Title	Index
Military						
Li Jinai	Shandong	1942	Full	Armament	Director	3
Provincial units						
Qian Yunlu	Hubei	1944	Full	Guizhou	Party Secretary	2
Song Defu	Hebei	1946	Full	Fujian	Party Secretary	2
Ji Yunshi	Jiangsu	1945	Full	Jiangsu	Governor	2
Li Keqiang	Anhui	1955	Full	Henan	Governor	2
Ma Qizhi (Hui)	Ningxia	1943	Full	Ningxia	Governor	2
Han Zheng	Zhejiang	1954	Full	Shanghai	Deputy Secretary	2
Meng Xuenong	Shandong	1949	Full	Beijing	Deputy Secretary	2
Huang Huahua	Guangdong	1946	Full	Guangdong	Deputy Secretary	2
Li Chengyu (Hui)	Shaanxi	1946	Alternate	Henan	Deputy Secretary	1
Li Yuanchao	Jiangsu	1950	Alternate	Jiangsu	Deputy Secretary	1
Jiang Daming	Shandong	1953	Alternate	Shandong	Deputy Secretary	1
Liu Peng	Chongqing	1951	Alternate	Sichuan	Deputy Secretary	1
Liu Qibao	Anhui	1953	Alternate	Guangxi	Deputy Secretary	1
Luo Baoming	Tianjin	1952	Alternate	Hainan	Deputy Secretary	1
Qiang Wei	Jiangsu	1953	Alternate	Beijing	Deputy Secretary	1
Quan Zhezhu (Korean)	Jilin	1952	Alternate	Jilin	Deputy Secretary	1
Shen Yueyue (f.)	Zhejiang	1957	Alternate	Anhui	Deputy Secretary	1
Song Xiuyan (f.)	Tianjin	1955	Alternate	Qinghai	Deputy Secretary	1
Sun Shuyi	Shandong	1945	Alternate	Shandong	Deputy Secretary	1
Wang Sanyun	Shandong	1952	Alternate	Sichuan	Deputy Secretary	1
Wu Aiying (f.)	Shandong	1951	Alternate	Shandong	Deputy Secretary	1
Yang Chuantang	Shandong	1954	Alternate	Tibet	Deputy Secretary	1
Yuan Chunqing	Hunan	1952	Alternate	Shaanxi	Deputy Secretary	1

(*Continued*)

Table 4.7 (*Continued*)

Name	Home	Birth	CC Membership	Work Unit	Title	Index
Zhang Baoshun	Hebei	1950	Alternate	Shanxi	Deputy Secretary	1
Zhi Shuping	Shanxi	1953	Alternate	Henan	Deputy Secretary	1
Li Zhanshu	Hebei	1950	Alternate	Shaanxi	Deputy Secretary	1
Xia Baolong	Tianjin	1952	Alternate	Tianjin	Vice Mayor	1
Zhang Qingli	Shandong	1951	Full	Xinjiang	Standing Member	2
Qin Guangrong	Hunan	1950	Alternate	Yunnan	Standing Member	1
Liu Yupu	Shandong	1949	Alternate	Guangdong	Standing Member	1
San Xiangjun	Beijing	1954	Alternate	Tianjin	Standing Member	1
Shi Lianxi (f.)	Hebei	1952	Alternate	Tianjin	Standing Member	1
Shi Yuzhen (f. Miao)	Hunan	1947	Alternate	Hunan	Standing Member	1
Yang Jing (Mongolian)	Inner Mongolia	1953	Alternate	Inner Mongolia	Standing Member	1
Du Xuefang (f.)	Hebei	1949	Alternate	Jilin	City Secretary	1
Li Ke (Zhuang)	Guangxi	1956	Alternate	Henan	City Secretary	1
Li Chuncheng	Liaoning	1956	Alternate	Sichuan	City Mayor	1
Song Airong (f.)	Henan	1959	Alternate	Xinjiang	Perfecture Sec.	1
Zhang Xuan (f.)	Hebei	1958	Alternate	Chongqingg	Court President	1
Total						97

Notes: Work place and title are those of November 2002.
Sources: Updated from Zhiyue Bo, "The 16th Central Committee of the Chinese Communist Party: formal institutions and factional groups," *Journal of Contemporary China*, Vol. 13, No. 139 (May 2004), Table 9, pp. 248–249.

the Twelfth Central Committee in the Sixteenth Central Committee (the other being Ismail Amat). Nominally, Wang stayed in the CCYL Secretariat for two years (December 1982–December 1984), but he began to work as director of the General Office of the Central Committee in April 1984. He entered the Secretariat of the CCP in September 1985, becoming one of the top Party leaders in China. Two years later, however, instead of moving up into the Politburo at the Thirteenth National Party Congress,[137] Wang was transferred to Fujian as vice governor and acting governor. His demotion was largely due to his close connection to Hu Yaobang.[138] He did not enter the Politburo until 15 years later. In November 2002 when Wang finally entered the Politburo, his former associate, Hu Jintao, became general secretary of the CCP, his successor as director of the General Office of the Central Committee, Wen Jiabao, entered the Politburo Standing Committee, and his successor as governor of Fujian, Jia Qinglin, also entered the Politburo Standing Committee.

Liu Yunshan (1947–), a native of Xinzhou, Shanxi Province, is the youngest member of the Sixteenth Politburo. Upon graduation from the Jining Normal School in 1968, he taught in a school in Inner Mongolia for half a year.[139] After having served as propaganda staff for six years (1969–1975) and as a reporter for another seven years (1975–1982), he became deputy secretary of the Inner Mongolia CYL Committee in July 1982 and entered the Eleventh Central Committee of the CCYL in December 1982.[140] His experience as a CCYL cadre was very brief; and as a local CCYL cadre, he was not particularly close to central CCYL cadres such as Wang Zhaoguo

---

[137] Three (Qiao Shi, Li Peng, and Tian Jiyun) of the five people who became members of the Secretariat of the CCP in September 1985 became Politburo members, and two (Qiao Shi and Li Peng) of them became standing members of the Politburo.

[138] For a detailed analysis of Wang's demotion, see Gao Xin, *Lingdao Zhongguo de Xinrenwu*, Vol. 2, pp. 424–428.

[139] For Liu Yunshan's bio, see http://news.xinhuanet.com/ziliao/2002-10/24/content_607117.htm.

[140] There are 263 members altogether. For the list, see http://www.ccyl.org.cn/documents/1982/821230a.htm.

and Hu Jintao. He became deputy director of the Propaganda Department of the Inner Mongolian Party Committee in February 1984 only after a year and a half as a CCYL cadre and officially left the Central Committee of the CCYL in November 1985. His main career path was along the line of propaganda work. He became director of the Propaganda Department of the Inner Mongolian Party Committee in January 1986, deputy party secretary of Inner Mongolia in March 1992, and deputy director of the Central Propaganda Department in April 1993. In October 2002, probably as a tradeoff between Jiang Zemin and Hu Jintao, Liu was promoted to director of the Central Propaganda Department as a former CCYL cadre.[141] He subsequently entered the Politburo and the Secretariat.

In contrast, Wang Lequan (1944–) entered the Politburo not as a former CCYL cadre, even though his experience in the CCYL was a bit longer than Liu Yunshan's. Wang was deputy secretary of the Shandong CYL Committee for four and a half years (March 1982–September 1986) but was not a member of the CCYL Central Committee.[142] Wang's main career has been in Xinjiang. After having served as a vice governor of Shandong for two years (February 1989–April 1991), he was transferred to Xinjiang as a standing member of the Xinjiang Regional Party Committee and vice chairman of the Xinjiang Uygur Autonomous Regional Government in April 1991. He was promoted to deputy secretary of Xinjiang in December 1992, acting party secretary of Xinjiang in September 1994, and party secretary of Xinjiang in December 1995. He entered the Politburo as a local leader of a border minority region of great significance.

There were four central party leaders with CCYL backgrounds (Liu Yandong, Li Dezhu, Ji Bingxuan, and Ling Jihua). The last person is particularly noteworthy. A native of Shanxi Province, Ling Jinhua (1957–) has been known as Hu Jintao's personal assistant.

---

[141] According to Zong Hairen, Jiang Zemin only agreed to have two candidates (Wang Zhaoguo and Liu Yunshan) of CCYL backgrounds nominated for the Politburo. See Zong Hairen, *Ambiguous transition*, p. 204.

[142] For Wang Lequan's bio, see http://news.xinhuanet.com/ziliao/2002-03/05/content_301890.htm.

After his graduation from the Department of Chinese Literature at Shanxi University in 1982, he was hired as personal secretary working for Gao Zhanxiang, a member of the Secretariat of the CCYL. However, because of Wang Zhaoguo's objection, Gao was forced to leave the CCYL Central Committee[143] and Ling became personal secretary of Hu Jintao, the first deputy secretary of the Secretariat of the Eleventh CCYL Central Committee.[144] Ling worked for Hu for two and a half years until July 1985 when Hu left Beijing for Guizhou. When Hu returned to Beijing at the Fourteenth National Party Congress in October 1992, he immediately rehired Ling as director of his office. Ling became concurrent deputy director of the General Office of the Central Committee of the CCP in May 2000 and entered the Sixteenth Central Committee as an alternate member in November 2002.

There were 10 central government leaders: Wang Yang (vice chairman of State Development and Planning Commission),[145] Jia Chunwang (minister of Public Security),[146] Li Zhilun (vice minister of Supervision),[147] Zhang Fusen (minister of Justice), Li Changjiang (director of State Administration of Quality Supervision, Inspection, and Quarantine), Du Qinglin (minister of Agriculture), Sun Jiazheng (minister of Culture), Zhang Weiqing (chairman of State Family Planning Commission), Ye Xiaowen (director of State Religious Affairs Office), and Zhou Qiang (first secretary of the Communist Youth League of China). There is one military leader: Li Jinai (director of the General Armament Department and a member of the Central Military Commission).

In addition to Wang Lequan, 39 local leaders were former CCYL cadres: nine full and 30 alternate members. These cadres were playing an increasingly important role in provincial politics as well as in

---

[143] He was later appointed as deputy secretary of Hebei.
[144] For Ling's bio, see Tian Ping, "Hu Jintao de Liuda Gaocan" ("Six advisors of Hu Jintao"), *Qingshao*, July 2004, pp. 6, 7.
[145] He is party secretary of Chongqing.
[146] He is president of the Supreme People's Procuratorate.
[147] He is minister of Supervision.

national politics. They were scattered in 22 provincial units and occupied very important positions in these places. Among these former CCYL cadres at the time when the Sixteenth CC was elected, there were two provincial party secretaries (Song Defu of Fujian and Qian Yunlu of Guizhou), three governors (Li Keqiang of Henan, Ji Yunshi of Jiangsu, and Ma Qizhi of Ningxia), 20 deputy secretaries, five provincial standing members, three city secretaries, one vice mayor of provincial level (Xia Baolong of Tianjin), one mayor of prefectural level (Li Chuncheng of Chengdu), one prefectural secretary (Song Airong of Xinjiang), and one district judge (Zhang Xuan of Chongqing). The combined power index for the CCYL cadres is 97 points, much more than those of any of the above-mentioned factional groups.

To estimate the group cohesion of the CCYL cadres in the Sixteenth CC, we will use personal ties among key members of the inner circle of the CCYL, i.e., 18 members of the Secretariat of the Central Committee of the CCYL between 1982 and 2002 who are members or alternate members of the Sixteenth Central Committee (Table 4.8).

In terms of individual members, Li Keqiang stands out as the best connected with a total score of almost 100 years (Figure 4.4). Li Keqiang has been groomed as a candidate of the fifth generation leadership. A native of Dingyuan, Anhui Province, he was born in 1955.[148] He worked in Fengyang, Anhui, as an "educated youth" in the 1970s and joined the CCP in 1976. In 1978, he was admitted to the Law Department of Beijing University. Upon graduation in 1982, he was appointed as secretary of the CCYL Committee of Beijing University. He worked for the Central Committee of the CCYL for 15 years between 1983 and 1998, rising through the ranks. He worked directly with all the other members of the Secretariat of the CCYL Central Committee on the list and shared work experience with several key leaders such as Liu Yandong, Li Yuanchao, Song Defu, Zhao Baoshun, Yuan Chunqing, and Liu Peng for a decade. During

---

[148] For his official bio, see http://news.xinhuanet.com/ziliao/2002-02/25/content_289095.htm.

Balance of Factional Power 191

Table 4.8 Group Cohesion Matrix of Former CCYL Leaders in the Sixteenth Central Committee

	Wang	Hu	LYD	LYC	Song	Zhang	LKQ	LQB	Yuan	LP	Ji	Jiang	Zhou	LYP	LZL	Luo	Qiang	San	Subtotal
Wang Zhaoguo	n/a	1.5	1.5	0.5	0.5	1.5	0.5	0	0	0	0	0	0	0	0	0	0	0	6
Hu Jintao	1.5	n/a	2	2	2	3	2	0	0	0	0	0	0	0	0	0	0	0	11
Liu Yandong	1.5	2	n/a	9.5	9.5	10.5	9.5	7.5	4.5	5	0	0	0	2.5	2.5	5	5	0	71
Li Yuanchao	0.5	2	9.5	n/a	7.5	9.5	9.5	7.5	4.5	5	0	0	0	2.5	2.5	5	5	0	58.5
Song Defu	0.5	2	9.5	7.5	n/a	3.5	9.5	7.5	4.5	5	0	0	0	2.5	2.5	5	5	0	45
Zhang Baoshun	1.5	3	10.5	9.5	3.5	n/a	9.5	7.5	5	5	0	0	0	2.5	2.5	5	5	0	42
Li Keqiang	0.5	2	9.5	9.5	9.5	9.5	n/a	7.5	9.5	9.5	5	5	2.5	2.5	2.5	5	5	0	59
Liu Qibao	0	0	7.5	7.5	7.5	7.5	7.5	n/a	4.5	5	0	0	0	2.5	2.5	5	5	0	24.5
Yuan Chunqing	0	0	4.5	4.5	4.5	5	9.5	4.5	n/a	4.5	5	5	2.5	0	0	4.5	4.5	5	31
Liu Peng	0	0	5	5	5	5	9.5	5	4.5	n/a	5	5	2.5	0	0	5	5	5	27.5
Ji Bingxuan	0	0	0	0	0	0	5	0	5	5	n/a	5	2.5	0	0	0	0	5	12.5
Jiang Daming	0	0	0	0	0	0	5	0	5	5	5	n/a	2.5	0	0	0	0	5	7.5
Zhou Qiang	0	0	2.5	2.5	2.5	2.5	2.5	2.5	2.5	2.5	2.5	2.5	n/a	0	0	0	0	2.5	2.5
Liu Yupu	0	0	2.5	2.5	2.5	2.5	2.5	2.5	0	0	0	0	0	n/a	2.5	0	0	0	2.5
Li Zhilun	0	0	5	5	5	5	5	5	4.5	5	5	0	0	2.5	n/a	0	5	0	0
Luo Baoming	0	0	5	5	5	5	5	5	4.5	5	5	0	0	0	0	n/a	5	0	5
Qiang Wei	0	0	5	5	5	5	5	5	4.5	5	5	0	0	0	0	5	n/a	0	0

(Continued)

Table 4.8 (Continued)

	Wang	Hu	LYD	LYC	Song	Zhang	LKQ	LQB	Yuan	LP	Ji	Jiang	Zhou	LYP	LZL	Luo	Qiang	San	Subtotal
San Xiangjun	0	0	0	0	0	0	5	0	5	5	5	5	2.5	0	0	0	0	n/a	
Total	6	12.5	74.5	70.5	64.5	70	99.5	62	63.5	66.5	27.5	27.5	15	17.5	17.5	44.5	44.5	27.5	405.5

Notes: (i) Numbers in cells represent the number of years a pair worked together in the Shanghai Party Committee. (ii) The subtotals are the sum of the numbers above the diagonal of n/a for each leader. (iii) The total (405.5) is the sum of the numbers above the diagonal of n/as.

Source: Author's database.

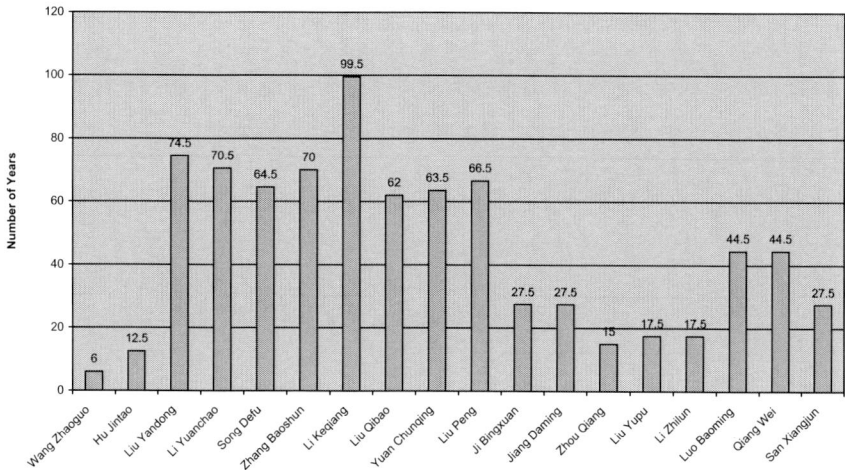

Fig. 4.4 Personal Ties of Former CCYL Caders in the Sixteenth Central Committee.

the same period, he was also enrolled in graduate programs at Beijing University and received his master's (1991) and doctoral (1994) degrees in economics. In June 1998, he was transferred to Henan as deputy secretary. One month later, he was appointed as vice governor and acting governor. He had been a full member of the Fifteenth Central Committee and was reelected as a full member of the Sixteenth Central Committee as governor of Henan.

Liu Yandong's personal ties among CCYL cadres rank second with 74.5 years. Others with ties over 60 years include Li Yuanchao (70.5 years), Zhang Baoshun (70 years), Liu Peng (66.5 years), Song Defu (64.5 years), Yuan Chunqing (63.5 years), and Liu Qibao (62 years). The top leaders of the CCYL, Wang Zhaoguo and Hu Jintao, do not have so strong a tie with other CCYL cadres as those above do. Wang's total score is only six years, only six percent of Li Keqiang's; and Hu's score is 12.5 years, only less than 13 percent of Li Keqiang's.

If the group cohesion index can provide any guidance, the CCYL Group is clearly the most cohesive factional group of all. Its group cohesion index is much larger than the group cohesion indexes of the other three factional groups combined. The group cohesion index of the inner-circle CCYL cadres is 405.5 years, more than three times as much as that of the Qinghua Clique.

FACTIONAL OVERLAP

That these four factional groups have distinctive characteristics does not necessarily mean that they are mutually exclusive. In fact, there are some overlaps between these groups. Being a member of the Shanghai Gang, for instance, does not necessarily prevent one from being a member of the Qinghua Clique. And being a member of the CCYL Group is not necessarily incompatible with being a member of the Princelings (*taizi dang*).

First, it is well known that Zeng Qinghong is both a pivotal member of the Shanghai Gang and a princeling. But he is neither the next core of the Shanghai Gang nor the core of the Princelings. It is not clear how he would take advantage of his dual role for his political ambitions. Second, five Shanghai Gang members are also graduates of Qinghua University: Wu Bangguo, Huang Ju, Hua Jianmin, Wu Qidi, and Xie Qihua. In the media, the rise of the Qinghua Clique is often discussed as an antidote to the power of the Shanghai Gang. With such key members of the Shanghai Gang as Wu Bangguo and Huang Ju being Qinghua graduates, it is not clear to what extent the Qinghua Clique balances the Shanghai Gang.

Third, one Shanghai Gang member is also a member of the CCYL Group. Han Zheng, a full member of the Sixteenth CC, was deputy secretary of the Shanghai Party Committee and executive vice mayor of Shanghai with a background in the CCYL work. He served as deputy secretary and then secretary of the Shanghai Committee of the CCYL in the 1980s. However, he is neither a member of the inner circle of the CCYL Group nor a well-entrenched Shanghai Gang member. Personally, he is in a strategic position to benefit from this dual membership. Yet, he will in no way significantly affect the balance of political forces in these two factional groups. He later replaced Chen Liangyu as mayor as well as acting party secretary of Shanghai.

Fourth, four princelings were also Qinghua graduates. They are Chen Yuan, Li Tielin, Liu Yandong, and Xi Jinping. Although Xi later went back to Qinghua to obtain a Ph.D. degree, his college experience was different from most other Qinghua graduates, as mentioned earlier; it is not clear to what extent he is connected to other princelings. Chen Yuan is likely to be better acquainted with other Qinghua graduates in the Sixteenth CC, but he is not well connected to other princelings in the Sixteenth CC. Liu Yandong is likely to have better connections with other Qinghua graduates than Chen because she was more active politically. She joined the Party in 1964 and served as a political counselor at Qinghua, while Chen did not join the Party until a few years after his graduation. Finally, Li Tielin seems to have had more opportunities than all of the above to get acquainted with other Qinghua students. The existence of these members with dual membership in the Qinghua Clique and the Princelings would likely facilitate cooperation between the two factional groups, if they were indeed operative as factions in Chinese politics.

Fifth, two princelings are also a member of the CCYL Group: Liu Yandong and Li Yuanchao. Daughter of Liu Ruilong (former vice minister of Agriculture), Liu was admitted to the Department of Chemical Engineering at Qinghua University in 1964 (while Hu Jintao was studying hub hydropower stations in the Department of Water Conservancy Engineering). After graduation in 1970, she worked as an ordinary worker initially and then as a youth league cadre and a party cadre in a factory in Beijing. In 1982, she was made a member of the Secretariat of the Central Committee of the Communist Youth League of China and vice president of the All-China Youth Federation (ACYF) (when Hu Jintao was also a member of the Secretariat of the CCYL and president of the ACYF). Li Yuanchao, as mentioned earlier, is son of Li Gancheng (former vice mayor of Shanghai). He worked in the CCYL Central Committee between 1983 and 1993. He worked under Wang Zhaoguo, Hu Jintao, and Song Defu. He was a colleague of Liu Yandong, Zhang Baoshun, and Li Keqiang for the entire decade.

In the early 1980s, there was actually a small faction of princelings within the CCYL Central Committee. In addition to Liu Yandong and Li Yuanchao, there were two other princelings: Chen Haosu (son of Chen Yi) and He Guangwei (son of He Changgong). Chen Haosu, a native of Lezhi, Sichuan Province, was born in May 1942 in Jiangsu when his father was acting commander of the New Fourth Army.[149] Upon graduation from China Science and Technology University in 1965, he began to work in a research institute in Beijing.[150] After his father passed away in 1972, he joined the PLA and worked for the PLA Academy of Military Sciences for eight years (1973–1981). He was installed in the Secretariat of the CCYL Central Committee in August 1981 and stayed there until December 1984. He has never made it to the Central Committee of the CCP.

He Guangwei (1944–), a native of Huarong, Hunan Province, joined the PLA in 1963 at the age of 19.[151] He worked in the PLA Air Force for 18 years (1963–1981)[152] and joined the CCP in 1975. He was also installed in the Secretariat of the CCYL Central Committee along with three other cadres including Chen Haosu in August 1981 and left the CCYL in March 1986.[153] He has also failed to enter the CCP Central Committee, as Chen Haosu has.[154]

Sixth, four Qinghua graduates are also members of the CCYL Group. They are Hu Jintao, Zhang Fusen, Liu Yandong, and Jia

---

[149] http://heritage.news.tom.com/1066/200517-27229.html.

[150] For his bio, see http://www.szxy.org/jjh/syndics/chen_hs.htm.

[151] It is likely that he went to the Haerbin Institute of Military Engineering in that year as Gao Xin describes him. All the students of the Institute joined the PLA when they were enrolled there.

[152] According to Gao Xin, he was secretary of the Beijing CYL Committee before he went to the CYL Central Committee. See Gao Xin, *Lingdao Zhongguo de Xinrenwu*, Vol. 1, p. 18.

[153] For his bio, see http://ics.nccu.edu.tw/frame.php?address=polsum&id=571&PHPSESSID=c07de2e4a60ed38e16b3aaf9fa488469.

[154] For descriptions of the "factional conflicts" between the Princelings and other cadres, see Wen Siyong and Ren Zhichu, *Hu Jintao Zhuan (The Biography of Hu Jintao)* (Carle Place, NY: Mirror Books, 2002), pp. 127–138; Gao Xin, *Lingdao Zhongguo de Xinrenwu*, Vol. 1, pp. 17–20.

Chunwang. Obviously, Liu Yandong is the only person who is a member of the Qinghua Clique, of the CCYL Group, and of the Princelings simultaneously. A key member of the CCYL, a well-connected Qinghua graduate, and a princess, Liu has possessed tremendous political resources and has a bright political future. She was promoted to director of the United Front Department of the Central Committee of the CCP. Although not as well connected to other CCYL members, Hu Jintao could tap into both the Qinghua Clique and the CCYL Group for support. Jia Chunwang is less well connected to other CCYL members than Hu, because he was not a member of the Secretariat of the CCYL and he was a member of the Eleventh CC of the CCYL only briefly (for two years). However, he is likely to be better connected to other Qinghua Clique members because of his previous positions at Qinghua as the secretary of the Qinghua CCYL Committee, the director of the Student Department, and a standing member of the Qinghua Party Committee. Zhang Fusen is also similarly situated in terms of the Qinghua Clique and the CCYL Group. He was at Qinghua long enough to make some friends, and he also worked as director of the Department of Colleges and Universities as well as deputy secretary in the CCYL Beijing Committee.

Clearly, no one is completely inclusive. Nobody has a simultaneous membership in all these factional groups. Nor is there anyone who is a member of the Shanghai Gang, a member of the Qinghua Clique, and a member of the Princelings at the same time. Nor is there anyone who is a member of the Shanghai Gang, a member of the Qinghua Clique, and a member of the CCYL Group simultaneously. The same can be said of a simultaneous membership in the Shanghai Gang, the CCYL Group, and the Princelings.

CONCLUDING REMARKS

In terms of the informal dimension of Chinese politics, as Figure 4.5 illustrates, the CCYL Group was the most powerful factional group by a large margin. Its power index was 97 points. The Qinghua Clique was a distant second, with a score of 54 points. The Shanghai

198 China's Elite Politics

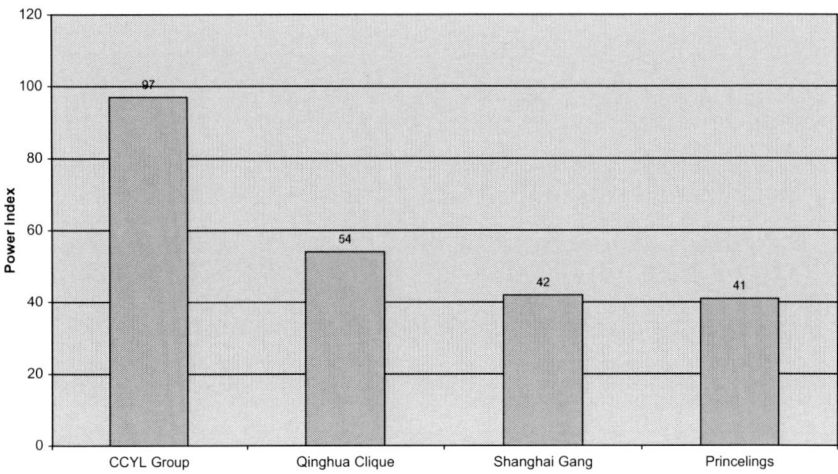

Fig. 4.5 Balance of Power Among Factional Groups in China.

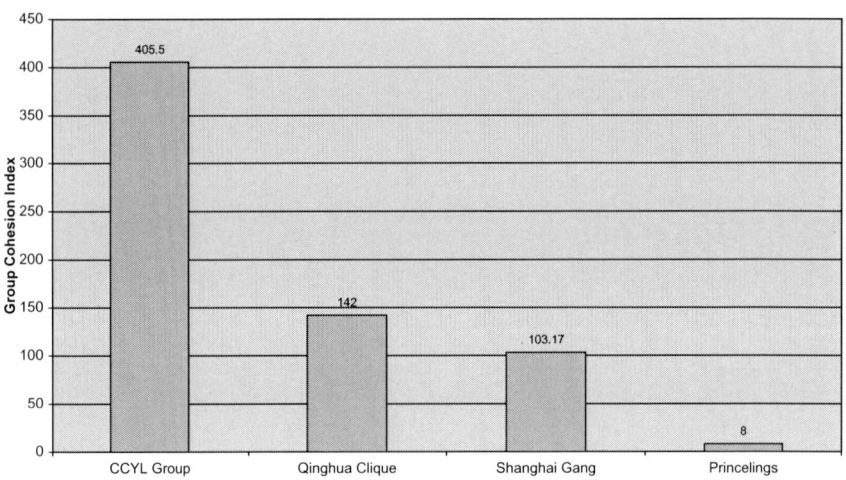

Fig. 4.6 Group Cohesion Indexes of Factional Groups in China.

Gang was third with a power index of 42. And the Princelings were the last, with a power index of 41.

These factional groups were also very diverse in terms of group cohesion (Figure 4.6). Again, the CCYL Group was the most cohesive group by a large margin with a total index of 405.5 points for the inner-circle members alone. The Qinghua Clique ranked second with a group cohesion index of 142. The Shanghai Gang was third with a combined group cohesion index of 103.17 for both party and government leaders. And the Princelings were the last with a group cohesion index of only eight points.

Finally, these factional groups were not mutually exclusive. The most significant overlaps could be found between the Qinghua Clique and the Shanghai Gang, between the Princelings and the Qinghua Clique, and between the CCYL Group and the Qinghua Clique.

Nevertheless, it will be interesting to see whether and how the two main factional groups (the Shanghai Gang and the CCYL Group) were competing for top positions in the Party and the government as well as for policies, a topic we will turn to in the next chapter.

Part II
Dynamics of Factional Politics

Chapter 5

Politics of SARS

Jiang Zemin and his cronies in the Shanghai Gang competed for power at the meetings of the National People's Congress (NPC) and Chinese National People's Political Consultative Conference (CNPPCC), but escaped from responsibilities in the crisis of an epidemic — severe acute respiratory syndrome (SARS). As a result, the Shanghai Gang suffered personnel loss and reputation damage. Zhang Wenkang was dismissed as minister of Health, and Jiang Zemin was despised as a coward. Hu Jintao and Wen Jiabao, on the other hand, stepped up to the plate and won popularity for their efforts against the SARS. The detention of Zhou Zhengyi, the richest man in Shanghai, exposed some of the Shanghai Gang members, but Jiang and his cronies desperately resisted and eventually got away.

POWER COMPETITION: JIANG'S CLIQUE VERSUS HU–WEN TEAM

Issue of Jiang Zemin's Retirement

Although the Sixteenth National Party Congress was over, the issue of Jiang Zemin's retirement remained. The question was whether Jiang would retire from the post of chairmanship of the Central Military Commission of the People's Republic of China (PRC). There are two central military commissions in China. One is the Central Military Commission of the CCP (Party CMC), and the other one is the Central Military Commission of the PRC (state CMC).

The existence of the two CMCs is the legacy of Deng Xiaoping. In an attempt to restore the institutional structure of the pre-Cultural Revolution era, Deng reestablished the Central Military Commission of the PRC in the 1980s in addition to the existing Central Military Commission of the CCP.[1] Section 4 of Chapter 3 of the *Constitution of the People's Republic of China* (1982) specified the state CMC as an institution in China that "directs the armed forces of the country" (Article 93) and stated that chairman of the state CMC "has overall responsibility for the commission" (Article 93) but is responsible to the NPC and its Standing Committee (Article 94).[2] Deng Xiaoping, chairman of the Central Military Commission of the CCP since June 1981, was elected concurrently as chairman of the state CMC in June 1983 when this institution was reestablished; other members of the Party CMC were elected concurrently as members of the state CMC. Deng probably intended to gradually transform the army of the Party into an army of the state and to eventually abolish the Party CMC. However, Deng had never got a chance to move forward with his plans, and China was stuck with two central military commissions. After Deng's resignation as chairman of the state CMC in April 1990, Jiang Zemin, already chairman of the Party CMC since November 1989, took it over.

The relationship between these two CMCs is peculiar. On the one hand, the state CMC is the highest institution of the armed forces in China. According to the Constitution of the PRC, the state CMC directs the armed forces of China. On the other hand, the Party CMC is higher than the highest institution of the armed forces in China because of the principle of the Party commanding armed

---

[1] The National Defense Commission of the PRC was established in September 1954 with Mao Zedong as the inaugural chairman. Liu Shaoqi took over the post in April 1959 and was reelected to the post in January 1965. But this institution was abolished during the Cultural Revolution.
[2] http://news.xinhuanet.com/ziliao/2004-09/16/content_1990063_7.htm.

forces. According to the preamble of the Constitution of the CCP, the Chinese Communist Party "persists in its leadership over the People's Liberation Army and other people's armed forces."[3]

It should be noted that in the original text of the CCP Constitution of 1982, there was no such statement[4] and that this statement was inserted at the Fourteenth National Party Congress in 1992.[5] It is not clear whether it was Jiang Zemin or Deng Xiaoping who proposed the insert. Gao Xin argues that Jiang Zemin introduced this change to consolidate his power over the military.[6] But it is more likely that Deng urged him to do so for two reasons. One, it was Deng Xiaoping who argued for Jiang's appointment as chairman of the Party CMC based on Jiang's position as general secretary of the CCP. According to Deng, Jiang was well qualified to be chairman of the Party CMC because he was well qualified to be general secretary of the CCP. Two, the Fourteenth National Party Congress was Deng's party congress. Jiang was not yet in a position to impose his own wills on the Party. It is more likely that Deng intended to institutionalize the power over the military in the hands of the Party leader, whoever it may be.

Anyway, Jiang Zemin maneuvered to stay on as chairman of the Party CMC at the Sixteenth National Party Congress. The question in the aftermath of the Sixteenth Party Congress was whether Jiang would stay on as chairman of the state CMC. According to Zong Hairen, Jiang Zemin's stay as chairman of the Party CMC was part of the central leadership's plan for a two-step succession: Hu Jintao

---

[3] http://news.xinhuanet.com/ziliao/2002-11/18/content_633225_1.htm.
[4] See "Zhongguo Gongchandang Zhangcheng" [CCP Constitution (1982)], in *Shiyijie Sanzhong Quanhui Yilai Dang de Lici Quanguo Daibiao Dahui Zhongyao Wenjianxuanbian* [*Important Documents of the Plenums of the Central Committee of the CCP Since the Third Plenum of the 11th Central Committee of the CCP*] (Beijing: Zhongyang Wenxian Chubanshe, 1998), Vol. 1, p. 287.
[5] For an explanation of why this statement was inserted, see http://news.xinhuanet.com/ziliao/2005-03/18/content_2713810.htm.
[6] Gao Xin, *Lingdao Zhongguo de Xinrenwu: Zhonggong Shiliujie Zhengzhiju Changwei* [*China's Top Leaders: Bios of China's Politburo Members*] (Carle Place, NY: Mirror Books, 2003), Vol. 1, pp. 64–71.

took over as general secretary of the CCP in November 2002 and then would succeed Jiang Zemin as the commander-in-chief at the first meeting of the Tenth NPC scheduled in March 2003.[7] Gao Xin also explained Jiang's stay as chairman of the Party CMC as a technical change to the mode of power transfers. According to Gao, Jiang would reverse the order in which Deng Xiaoping stepped down from these two posts: While Deng Xiaoping resigned as chairman of the Party CMC before he stepped down as chairman of the state CMC, Jiang would exit as chairman of the state CMC before his resignation from the Party CMC.[8] Gao warned that Jiang Zemin would commit political suicide if he were to continue to hold on to the position of state CMC chairmanship.[9]

Contrary to these expectations, however, Jiang made every indication in the aftermath of the Sixteenth Party Congress that he would not retire from politics. First, in the report published on November 16, 2002, on the new leadership produced by the First Plenum of the Sixteenth Central Committee, Jiang Zemin's photo was placed to the left of Hu Jintao's in the *People's Daily*.[10] According to the protocol of Chinese politics, the left is more important than the right. Thus Jiang was still more important than General Secretary Hu Jintao. Second, Jiang's name continued to be placed in front of Hu's name in news reports. In an open acknowledgement of congratulatory telegrams and letters from foreign political parties, foreign governments, and others, the General Office and the International Liaison Department of the Central Committee of the CCP listed Jiang's reelection as Party CMC chairman before Hu's election as general secretary of the Party.[11] In another example, a report on Jiang Zemin's past activities was placed on top of Hu Jintao's speech on the Constitution of the PRC.[12] Third, during his

---

[7] Zong Hairen, *Disidai* [*China's New Leaders: The Fourth Generation*] (Carle Place, NY: Mirror Books, 2002), p. 17.
[8] Gao Xin, *Lingdao Zhongguo de Xinrenwu*, Vol. 1, pp. 56–60.
[9] *Ibid.*, pp. 63–78.
[10] *Renmin ribao*, November 16, 2002, p. 1.
[11] *Renmin ribao*, November 26, 2002, p. 1.
[12] *Renmin ribao*, December 5, 2002, p. 1.

meeting with a delegation of the United States led by William J. Perry (1927–), former US defense secretary (1994–1997), on November 22, 2002,[13] Jiang told his guests that he would continue to retain the post of the CMC chairmanship under the request of "CMC comrades." The impression the Americans got from his statement was that he would not retire as chairman of the state CMC at the meeting of the NPC in March 2003.[14] As a result, American President George W. Bush sent Jiang Zemin a congratulatory note on December 12, 2002, affirming US support for Jiang.[15]

In the meantime, some of Jiang's loyalists publicly voiced their support for his stay. Lieutenant General Zhu Qi, commander of the Beijing Military Region, published an article in *Seeking Truth* (*qiushi*), a mouthpiece of the CCP, on December 1, 2002, giving flattering compliments to Jiang.[16] Zhu Qi (1942–), a native of Xiangyun, Yunnan Province, joined the PLA in 1960 and the CCP in 1961.[17] He is a professional military, moving up the ladder of success in the PLA through the ranks. He was awarded the rank of major general in 1990 and the rank of lieutenant general in 1997. Although he served as commander of the Guizhou Provincial Military District and a standing member of the Guizhou Provincial Party Committee, he did not have any direct work experience with Hu Jintao and therefore was unlikely to be Hu's man. While Hu was party secretary of Guizhou between July 1985 and December 1988, Zhu was chief of staff of the Fourteenth Army Corps in Kunming, Yunnan Province, between August 1985 and April 1989.[18] When Zhu was appointed as

---

[13] *Renmin ribao*, November 23, 2002, p. 1.
[14] Zong Hairen, *Aimei de Quanli Jiaohuan* [*Ambiguous transition*] (Carle Place, NY: Mirror Books, 2003), p. 22.
[15] *Renmin Ribao*, December 13, 2002, p. 3.
[16] Zhu Qi, "Jijituiji Guofang he Jundui Jianshe" ("Actively promote national defense and military construction"), *Qiushi* (*Seeking Truth*), No. 238 (December 1, 2002), http://www.qsjournal.com.cn/qs/20021201/GB/qs^348^0^7.htm.
[17] For Zhu Qi's bio, see http://ics.nccu.edu.tw/frame.php?address=polsum&id=1366 &PHPSESSID=f9c308d66c995569f2c6305c44b73991.
[18] For information about the Fourteenth Army Corps, see http://www.plaoffice.sdu.edu.cn/guxin/show.php?id=/88.html.

commander of the Guizhou Provincial Military District in June 1990, Hu was already in Tibet as party secretary. Zhu was promoted to chief of staff of the Chengdu Military Region in January 1996 and was transferred to the Beijing Military Region as chief of staff in March 1998. He was promoted to commander of the Beijing Military Region in January 2002 and was inducted into the Sixteenth Central Committee as a full member, skipping the level of alternate membership. In his article on the Sixteenth Party Congress, Zhu claimed that the incorporation of the "Three Represents" into the CCP Constitution was a "very important achievement," comparable in its significance to the establishment of Mao Zedong Thought at the Seventh Party Congress and the introduction of Deng Xiaoping Theory at the Fifteenth Party Congress; that Comrade Jiang Zemin was retained as chairman of the CCP CMC was an important political decision.[19] As Zhu remarked,

> That Comrade Jiang Zemin has stayed on as chairman of the Central Military Commission of the Central Committee of the Chinese Communist Party is an important political choice made by our Party; provides a political guarantee for flourishing of the Party's course, for long-term peace and stability of the country, and for advancement of the army's buildup; is in the fundamental interests of the Party, in the fundamental interests of the country, and in the fundamental interests of the nation. This choice has reflected the common wishes of the whole Party, the whole army, and peoples of all nationalities of the whole country.[20]

It is not clear to what extent Zhu Qi represented the views of the military in China, but his article was obviously politically motivated. That is exactly what Jiang Zemin needed. For central committee members, it was clear in February 2003 that Jiang would stay on as chairman of the state CMC. At the Second Plenum of the Sixteenth Central Committee on February 24–26, 2003, 191 participating full members

---

[19] Zhu Qi, "Jijituiji Guofang he Jundui Jianshe."
[20] *Ibid.*

voted to approve a list of candidates for government positions.[21] Jiang Zemin must have been included as the only candidate for the post of the state CMC chairmanship. Once more, Jiang manipulated the top leadership to satisfy his greed for power, as Yuan Shikai — another notorious politician in Chinese history — did 88 years earlier.[22] Jiang Zemin ought to retire from politics, but he refused to do so.

Jiang and His Cronies: High Positions but Low Popularity

The First Meeting of the Tenth Chinese National People's Political Consultative Conference opened on March 3, 2003, in Beijing,[23] followed by the opening of the First Meeting of the Tenth NPC two days later.[24] In order to hold on to power, Jiang continued to maneuver. In spite of being president of China, Jiang ostensibly made phone calls to a number of world leaders. He talked to German Chancellor Gerhard Schroeder on March 4, 2003;[25] he telephoned French President Jacques Rene Chirac on March 6, 2003;[26] he rang British Prime Minister Tony Blair on March 9, 2003;[27] he had talks with American President George W. Bush and German Chancellor Schroeder on March 10, 2003;[28] and he called French President Chirac again on March 11, 2003.[29] However, deputies to the NPC were not all impressed by him. At the fifth session of the First Meeting of the Tenth NPC on March 15, 2003, 98 deputies voted against Jiang as the candidate of the state CMC chairman and 122 deputies abstained.[30] Although Jiang Zemin was the only candidate for

---

[21] *Renmin ribao*, February 27, 2003, p. 1.
[22] For a detailed analysis in this regard, see Zong Hairen, *Aimei de Quanli Jiaohuan*, pp. 16–30.
[23] *Renmin ribao*, March 4, 2003, p. 1.
[24] *Renmin ribao*, March 6, 2003, p. 1.
[25] *Renmin ribao*, March 5, 2003, p. 1.
[26] *Renmin ribao*, March 7, 2003, p. 1.
[27] *Renmin ribao*, March 10, 2003, p. 1.
[28] *Renmin ribao*, March 11, 2003, p. 1.
[29] *Renmin ribao*, March 12, 2003, p. 1.
[30] Zong Hairen, *Aimei de Quanli Jiaohuan*, p. 3.

Table 5.1 Votes of Members of the State Central Military Commission (March 15, 2003)

Name	Title	Yes	No	Abstain	Total	Percent
Jiang Zemin	Chairman	2726	98	122	2946	92.5
Hu Jintao	Vice Chairman	2928	1	8	2937	99.7
Guo Boxiong	Vice Chairman	2917	9	11	2937	99.3
Cao Gangchuan	Vice Chairman	2904	14	19	2937	98.9
Xu Caihou	Member	2918	12	7	2937	99.4
Liang Guanglie	Member	2926	6	5	2937	99.6
Liao Xilong	Member	2923	6	8	2937	99.5
Li Jinai	Member	2925	6	6	2937	99.6

Notes: The records of Guo Boxiong and Cao Gangchuan were originally misplaced but were corrected here.
Totals are added, and percentages are recalculated.
Sources: Zong Hairen, *Aimei de Quanli Jiaohuan* [*Ambiguous Transition*] (Carle Place, NY: Mirror Books, 2003), pp. 8–9; *Cheng Ming*, No. 306 (April 2003), p. 13.

the post of the state CMC chairmanship, 36 deputies voted for Hu Jintao.[31] Among the new state CMC members, Jiang Zemin received the lowest number of approval votes (Table 5.1).

Jiang, chairman of the CMC, received only 92.5 percent of approval votes; Hu Jintao, first vice chairman of the CMC, received 99.7 percent; Guo Boxiong, second vice chairman of the CMC, received 99.3 percent; Cao Gangchun, third vice chairman of the CMC, received 98.9 percent; and all the other members of the CMC (Xu Caihou, Liang Guanglie, Liao Xilong, and Li Jinai) received 99.4 percent or higher. Moreover, Jiang's approval rate in 2003 was also substantially lower than that in 1998. As the only candidate for the post of the state CMC chairmanship in 1998, Jiang received 2,893 yes votes out of 2,947 valid votes, scoring 98.2 percent.[32]

---

[31] Ren Xin, "Jiang Zemin ziqu qiru gang kaishi" ("It is just the beginning that Jiang is trying to embarrass himself"), *Qianshao*, April 2003, 9. See also http://www.renminbao.com/rmb/articles/2003/3/16/25468.html.
[32] Ting Wang, *The Successors to Power in Beijing Across the Century* (Hong Kong: Celebrities Press, 1998), p. 413.

Jiang's cronies suffered a similar fate: They managed to take important positions in various state apparatuses but at low approval rates. Jia Qinglin was the first to face the embarrassment. At the election held on March 13, 2003,[33] Jia received the second lowest number of yes votes among candidates for leadership positions in the Tenth CNPPCC (Table 5.2).

The only person who received a lower number of affirmative votes was Ba Jin,[34] a 98-year-old writer who was paralyzed in hospital because of Parkinson's disease. Ba Jin received 1,936 yes votes (90.3 percent). Jia, a candidate for the post of CNPPCC Chairman and a standing member of the Sixteenth Politburo, received only 54 more votes than the hospitalized feeble old man. Obviously, Jia's possible involvement in a corruption scandal in Fujian diminished his popularity.[35] He was far less popular than his predecessor, Li Ruihuan. Li received 99.2 percent of approval votes (2,025 out of 2,042 votes) five years earlier.[36]

Zeng Qinghong, Jiang's confidant, was even worse. He received 177 rejections and 190 abstentions as a candidate for the vice presidency of the PRC (Table 5.3). His approval rate was only 87.5 percent, a failing grade in Chinese standard. In addition to his bad reputation because of his close association with Jiang Zemin, Zeng received such a low approval rate also because of the unique position of vice presidency in Chinese politics.

In the first decade after the posts of president and vice president were reestablished in the early 1980s, both positions were ceremonial, and vice presidency in particular was given to veteran leaders and social celebrities as a reward for services to the Party and the country. When Li Xiannian was elected in June 1983 as the first president of China since 1969, Ulanhu (1906–1988), the founder of the

---

[33] There are 2,238 deputies to the Tenth CNPPCC, but 2,152 were present for the election on March 13, 2003. See *Renmin ribao*, March 14, 2003, p. 1.
[34] Ba Jin is his pen name; his real name is Li Yaotang. For his bio, see http://news.xinhuanet.com/politics/2005-10/24/content_3678007.htm.
[35] For a detailed analysis, see Joseph Fewsmith, *China Since Tiananmen: The Politics of Transition* (New York: Cambridge University Press, 2001), pp. 224–227.
[36] Ting Wang, *The Successors to Power in Beijing Across the Century*, p. 416.

Table 5.2 Votes of CNPPCC Leaders (March 13, 2003)

Name	Birth	Yes	No	Abstain	Total	Approval Rate
Chairman						
Jia Qinglin	1940	1990	79	76	2145	92.8
Vice Chairmen (24)						
Wang Zhongyu	1933	2115	23	7	2145	98.6
Liao Hui	1942	2115	22	8	2145	98.6
Liu Yandong	1945	2108	21	16	2145	98.3
Ngapoi Ngawang Jigme	1910	2110	22	13	2145	98.4
Ba Jin	1904	1936	122	87	2145	90.3
Pagbalha Geleg Namgyai	1940	2133	7	5	2145	99.4
Li Guixian	1937	2049	53	43	2145	95.5
Zhang Siqing	1932	2122	15	8	2145	98.9
Ding Guangxun	1915	2138	6	1	2145	99.7
Huo Yingdong	1923	2135	7	3	2145	99.5
Ma Wanqi	1919	2133	4	8	2145	99.4
Bai Licheng	1941	2133	10	2	2145	99.4
Luo Haocai	1934	2141	4	0	2145	99.8
Zhang Kehui	1928	2138	6	1	2145	99.7
Zhou Tienong	1938	2132	6	7	2145	99.4
Hao Jianxiu	1935	2106	28	11	2145	98.2
Chen Kuiyuan	1941	2096	40	9	2145	97.7
Abdul'ahat Abdulrixit	1942	2141	1	2	2144	99.9
Xu Kuangdi	1937	2123	9	13	2145	99.0
Li Zhaozhuo	1944	2126	14	5	2145	99.1
Huang Mengfu	1944	2136	5	4	2145	99.6
Wang Xuan	1937	2130	9	6	2145	99.3
Zhang Huaixi	1935	2120	15	10	2145	98.8
Li Meng	1937	2121	19	5	2145	98.9
Secretary-General						
Zheng Wantong	1941	2142	8	1	2151	99.6

Notes: Totals are added, and percentages are recalculated.
Source: Zong Hairen, *Aimei de Quanli Jiaohuan* [*Ambiguous Transition*] (Carle Place, NY: Mirror Books, 2003), pp. 9–11.

Inner Mongolian Autonomous Region and former Politburo member, served as vice president.[37] Ulanhu passed away eight months after he had completed his first term. When Yang Shangkun was elected as president of China in April 1988, Wang Zhen (1908–1993), former vice premier and former Politburo member, was made vice president.[38] But Wang Zhen died a few days before completing his first term. When Jiang Zemin took over as president of China in March 1993, the head of state was turned into a powerful position because it was coupled with two other powerful positions: general secretary and chairman of the Central Military Commission. However, the position of vice presidency remained ceremonial, and it was given to Rong Yiren (1916–2005), a prominent entrepreneur.[39]

A turning point came in March 1998 when Hu Jintao was elected vice president of China. Hu was widely regarded as an heir apparent, and the vice presidency came to be regarded as the successor's position. From this perspective, Zeng's occupation of vice presidency was regarded as usurping because it is inconceivable that Zeng, an older man, could be Hu's successor. Hu Jintao was born in December 1942, while Zeng was born in July 1939; Zeng is three years older than Hu. By the time Hu completes his two terms of five years each (in 2013), Zeng will be 73 years old and will be too old to enter the Politburo, let alone succeed Hu as president of China. Because of Zeng's usurping, the Chinese leadership missed an opportunity to groom a younger leader to be a real successor.

Several other members of Jiang's clique also managed to get high positions. Wu Bangguo was made chairman of the Standing Committee of the Tenth NPC; Huang Ju entered the State Council as the first vice premier; Hua Jiamin and Chen Zhili both were inducted into the State Council as state councilors (Hua was also made concurrent secretary-general of the State Council); and Zeng Peiyan was also made a vice premier of the State Council. Although Zeng Peiyan had not previously

---

[37] For his bio, see http://news.xinhuanet.com/ziliao/2005-09/30/content_3565304.htm.
[38] For his bio, see http://news.xinhuanet.com/ziliao/2004-10/18/content_2104263.htm.
[39] For his bio, see http://news.xinhuanet.com/ziliao/2005-09/30/content_3565334.htm.

Table 5.3 Votes of State Leaders (March 15, 2003)

Name	Title	Yes	No	Abstain	Total	Percent
Hu Jintao	President	2937	4	3	2944	99.8
Zeng Qinghong	Vice President	2578	177	190	2945	87.5
Wen Jiabao	Premier	2906	3	16	2925	99.4
Huang Ju	Vice Premier	2693	167	89	2949	91.3
Wu Yi	Vice Premier	2907	18	16	2941	98.8
Zeng Peiyan	Vice Premier	2867	53	27	2947	97.3
Hui Liangyu	Vice Premier	2923	6	8	2937	99.5
Zhou Yongkang	State Councilor	2876	35	20	2931	98.1
Cao Gangchuan	State Councilor	2908	14	13	2935	99.1
Tang Jiaxuan	State Councilor	2815	77	43	2935	95.9
Hua Jianmin	State Councilor	2759	104	72	2935	94.0
Chen Zhili	State Councilor	2577	240	118	2935	87.8
Hua Jianmin	Secretary-General	2793	87	59	2939	95.0

Notes: Totals are added, and percentages are recalculated.
Source: Zong Hairen, *Aimei de Quanli Jiaohuan* [*Ambiguous Transition*] (Carle Place, NY: Mirror Books, 2003), pp. 4, 7, 8.

worked in the Shanghai Party Community or municipal government, he is Jiang's protégé. In fact, his first job after his graduation from Qinghua University was as a technician in the Shanghai Electrical Equipment Research Institute under the First Ministry of Machine-Building, and his boss was none other than Jiang Zemin. Jiang had just arrived in Shanghai as Deputy Director of the Institute. During the two years (1962–1964) of Zeng's stay in the Institute, he became Jiang's protégé. Twenty years later, Jiang, Minister of the Electronics Ministry, transferred Zeng to the Ministry in August 1984 and appointed him Director of the General Office.[40] It is with Jiang's support that Zeng was able to enter the State Council as a vice premier.

Obviously, Huang Ju was the least popular among vice premiers (Table 5.3). His approval rate was only 91.3 percent with 167 objections and 89 abstentions. As a candidate for the position of the first vice

---

[40] Gao Xin, *Lingdao Zhongguo de Xinrenwu: Zhonggong Shiliujie Zhengzhiju Weiyuan* [*China's Top Leaders: Bios of China's Politburo Members*] (Carle Place, NY: Mirror Books, 2003), Vol. 2, p. 743.

premier, Huang's only advantage was that he was a standing member of the Politburo and his secret weapon was Jiang's support, but he was otherwise much less qualified than his colleagues in the State Council. For instance, while Huang had zero experience in the central government, Wu Yi (1938–), the second vice premier, had vast experiences in the Center. She began to work in the Ministry of Foreign Economic Relations and Trade in 1991 as vice minister and was promoted to be its minister two years later. She served as a state councilor for five years between 1998 and 2003.[41] She was the most capable woman in China.[42] She was much more qualified as the first vice premier than Huang Ju and was much more popular. Wu Yi's approval rate was 98.8 percent, 7.5 percentage points higher than that of Huang.

Moreover, Huang was also less qualified than other potential candidates. Li Changchun (1944–),[43] for instance, reportedly was the original candidate for the State Council.[44] Li is six years younger than Huang but has wider experiences in local government. Huang only had local experience before 2003, and his local experience was limited to one city, Shanghai. Li also only had local experience, but he had worked in three provinces. Li was the youngest governor of China in 1986 when he was appointed acting governor of Liaoning; he also served as governor and party secretary of Henan between 1991 and 1997; and he worked in Guangdong as party secretary (1997–2002) before he was transferred to Beijing in November 2002. But with Jiang Zemin's support, Huang — instead of Li — was nominated as a candidate for the first vice premier.[45]

Huang would have probably been defeated if his colleague from Shanghai, Xu Kuangdi (1937–), had been nominated for the post.

---

[41] For her bio, see http://news.xinhuanet.com/ziliao/2002-01/16/content_240618.htm.

[42] She was ranked No. 2 out of 100 most powerful women of the world by Forbes in 2005. See http://www.forbes.com/2005/07/27/powerful-women-world-cz_05 powom_land.html.

[43] For his bio, see http://news.xinhuanet.com/ziliao/2002-01/16/content_240530.htm.

[44] Zong Hairen, *Aimei de Quanli Jiaohuan*, pp. 58–60.

[45] For details, see *Ibid.*, pp. 58–60.

While Huang was mayor of Shanghai, he received a nickname from his subordinates as "a man with no brain" (*meizhuyi*) because he could not come up with new ideas on his own on major issues nor could he make a decision on his own on minor problems. In contrast, Xu was an innovative decision-maker when he was mayor of Shanghai and was vastly more popular.[46]

Finally, Chen Zhili (1942–), Jiang's confidante and a member of the Shanghai Gang, received the lowest number of affirmative votes as a state councilor. A native of Xianyou, Fujian Province, Chen lived in Shanghai for about four decades.[47] She was enrolled in the Department of Physics at Fudan University in Shanghai in 1959 and went to a graduate program at Shanghai Institute of Silicate of the Chinese Academy of Sciences (CAS) upon her graduation in 1964. She became director of the Propaganda Department of the Shanghai Party Committee in March 1988 and worked closely with Jiang Zemin, who was party secretary of Shanghai then. She was instrumental in closing down a liberal newspaper in Shanghai, the *World Economic Herald*, in 1989.[48] She was inducted into the Fifteenth Central Committee as a full member in September 1997 and was made minister of Education in March 1998.[49] Under Chen Zhili's leadership, the Chinese educational system became corrupted. Instead of promoting higher quality education, she encouraged schools and universities to make money under the slogan of commercialization of education. In 2003 alone, for instance, there were 2,566 kinds of education-related fees in addition to regular tuitions and fees.[50] Consequently, schools and universities in

---

[46] Gao Xin, *Lingdao Zhongguo de Xinrenwu*, Vol. 1, pp. 284–290.
[47] For her bio, see http://news.xinhuanet.com/ziliao/2002-03/01/content_295698.htm.
[48] For details, see Bruce Gilley, *Tiger on the Brink: Jiang Zemin and China's New Elite* (Berkeley, CA: University of California Press, 1998), pp. 115–125.
[49] She received the lowest number of yes votes among all the candidates of ministerial posts in 1998. She got 2660 affirmations, 199 rejections, and 76 abstentions, with an approval rate of 90.6 percent. See Ning Xianghan and Wen Siyong, *Zhu Rongji de Neige* [*Zhu Rongji's Cabinet*] (Ontario, Canada: Mirror Books, 1998), p. 28.
[50] Long Mao, "Fubaiwuneng jiang xuexiao bancheng xuedian: Jiaoyushiye de wuxingshashao Chen Zhili" ["Invisible Assassin of Chinese education: Chen Zhili — She is corrupt and incapable; she turned schools into stores"], *Qianshao*, December 2003, pp. 14–17.

China were turned into profit-making companies, educational expenses increased drastically, and corruption became rampant in the educational institutions. Education has become one of the three major problems (so-called three big new mountains) for the Chinese people. Instead of being removed to take responsibilities for all these problems in the education, Chen was promoted to be state councilor in charge of education. It is not surprising that she received 240 rejections and 118 abstentions.

Hu–Wen Team: Substantial Gains

Obviously, Jiang and his cronies were winners of high offices at the NPC and CNPPCC meetings. But Hu Jintao and his allies were not losers. First, Hu replaced Jiang Zemin as president of the PRC with the highest approval rate (Table 5.3). He received 2,937 affirmations, four objections, and three abstentions, scoring 99.8 percent.[51] In the history of the PRC, this was not the first case in which a designated successor actually succeeded. Liu Shaoqi succeeded Mao Zedong as president of the PRC in April 1959 and was reelected into the position in January 1965. On the surface, Hu's situation was similar to Liu's. Liu took over as president of the PRC, but Mao stayed on as party chairman and Liu was the first vice chairman;[52] Hu succeeded as president of the PRC, but Jiang stayed on as chairman of the state CMC, and Hu was the first vice chairman. This seeming parallel is a reflection of Jiang's attempt to restore the two-front arrangement in Chinese politics.[53] Yet Hu was in a much more favorable position than Liu 43 years earlier primarily because of substantial institutionalization

---

[51] There are 2,985 deputies to the Tenth NPC (for the list, see *Renmin ribao*, March 1, 2003, pp. 2, 3). But there were 2,951 deputies present on March 15, 2003 (*Renmin ribao*, March 16, 2003, p. 1).

[52] In order to dilute Liu's power in the Party, Mao ensured in 1956 that there would be four vice chairmen and a general secretary and he later added another vice chairman. For Mao's explanations, see Peng Xianzhi and Jin Chongji, *Mao Zedong Zhuan (1949–1976) [Biography of Mao Zedong (1949–1976)]*, (Beijing: Zhongyang Wenxian Chubanshe, 2003), Vol. 1, pp. 519–522.

[53] For details of this argument, see Chapter 2.

of Chinese politics. Liu was removed as president of the PRC at a plenum of the Central Committee of the CCP,[54] but it is inconceivable that Jiang would be in any position to organize such a plenum without being a central committee member himself or to start any proceeding to remove President Hu Jintao. Moreover, while President Liu was only a vice chairman of the Party, President Hu was also general secretary of the Party. Hu is the head of state as well as the head of the Party. The post of presidency, as mentioned above, was a ceremonial one until 1993 when Jiang Zemin took over as president, and Hu's presidency thus was no longer ceremonial.

According to the Constitution of the PRC, the President, in pursuance of decisions of the NPC and its Standing Committee, promulgates statutes; appoints and removes the Premier, Vice-Premiers, State Councilors, Ministers, the Auditor-General, and the Secretary-General of the State Council; confers state medals and titles of honor; issues order of special pardons; proclaims martial law; proclaims a state of war; and issues mobilization orders (Article 80).[55] The President also receives diplomatic representatives on behalf of the PRC and, in pursuance of decisions of the Standing Committee of the NPC, appoints and recalls plenipotentiary representatives abroad, and ratifies and abrogates treaties and important agreements concluded with foreign states (Article 81).[56] Coupled with the position of general secretary of the Party, the presidency could be very powerful. As an evidence of international support, American President George W. Bush, Russian President Vladimir Putin, and French President Jacques Rene Chirac all called President Hu Jintao on March 18, 2003, the day when the First Meeting of the Tenth NPC was closed.[57]

Second, with the nomination of President Hu Jintao and through the election of the Tenth NPC, Wen Jiabao (1942–) was appointed as premier of the State Council.[58] He received 2,906 affirmations, three

---

[54] For the resolution of the plenum, see http://www.people.com.cn/GB/shizheng/252/5089/5100/5225/20010428/454404.html.
[55] http://news.xinhuanet.com/ziliao/2004-09/16/content_1990063_5.htm.
[56] http://news.xinhuanet.com/ziliao/2004-09/16/content_1990063_5.htm.
[57] *Renmin ribao*, March 19, 2003, p. 1.
[58] *Renmin ribao*, March 17, 2003, p. 1.

rejections, and 16 abstentions, scoring 99.4 percent. A native of Tianjin, Wen grew up in a family of teachers.[59] In the 1950s, he attended the Nankai Middle School, the alma mater of late Premier Zhou Enlai (1898–1976). He was enrolled in 1960 in the No. 1 Department of Geology and Minerals at Beijing Institute of Geology with a major in geological surveying and prospecting and continued his study in a graduate program at the same institute upon his graduation in 1965. After having worked for 14 years in Gansu (1968–1982), Wen began his political career in Beijing initially as director of the Policy and Law Research Office of the Ministry of Geology and Mineral Resources in 1982. He was promoted to vice minister of the Ministry in October 1983 and was transferred to the General Office of the CCP Central Committee as a vice director two years later. The director of the General Office at that time was Wang Zhaoguo, former first secretary of the CYL Central Committee. When Wang left for Fujian in May 1986, Wen took over as director of the General Office.

What is remarkable about Wen Jiabao is that he survived three general secretaries of the Party intact. When he first assumed the position of General Office director, Hu Yaobang (1915–1989) was general secretary of the Party. He stayed in the same post after Hu was purged in January 1987 and worked for his new boss, Zhao Ziyang (1919–2005). In the morning of May 19, 1989, when a tearful Zhao Ziyang went to the Tiananmen Square to bid farewell to students (and essentially to his political career), Wen was visibly on his side.[60] But when Zhao Ziyang was later purged and placed under house arrest, Wen remained as director of the General Office. He worked for the new general secretary of the Party, Jiang Zemin, for almost four years (June 1989–March 1993). Wen became a vice premier of the State Council under Premier Zhu Rongji in March 1998 and succeeded Zhu in March 2003 as premier.

Although there is no documented evidence that Wen and Hu had intimate personal relations in their early years, there are many

---

[59] For his bio, see http://news.xinhuanet.com/ziliao/2002-01/16/content_240608.htm.
[60] *Renmin ribao*, May 20, 1989, p. 1.

similarities between the two: They were both born in 1942, both studied in Beijing, were both sent to Gansu Province in 1968, were both promoted back to Beijing in 1982, and were both survivors of the Chinese politics of the 1980s and 1990s. Their shared experience may have fostered some bond between the two, and Wen has been regarded Hu's natural ally. The new regime is often dubbed "Hu–Wen regime" in the media.

Moreover, some of Hu's former colleagues in the CYL Central Committee also managed to get high positions in the NPC, the CNPPCC, and the State Council. Wang Zhaoguo was elected vice chairman of the Tenth Standing Committee. Liu Yandong was made vice chairman of the Tenth CNPPCC. Li Dezhu entered his second term as minister of State Ethnic Affairs Commission. Li Zhilun was promoted to minister of Supervision. Li Xueju (a nonmember of the central committee) was promoted to minister of Civil Affairs.[61] Zhang Fusen was retained as minister of Justice. Sun Jiazheng was retained as minister of Culture. Zhang Weiqing was retained as minister of the State Population and Family Planning Commission. Lastly, Hu's classmate at Qinghua University, Wang Shucheng, was retained as minister of Water Resources.[62]

Finally, Hu also quietly promoted former CYL cadres in provinces. Li Keqiang was promoted to party secretary of Henan; Li Yuanchao was promoted to party secretary of Jiangsu; Ji Yunshi was transferred to Hebei as governor; Li Chengyu was promoted to governor of Henan; Huang Huahua was promoted to governor of Guangdong; Meng Xuenong was promoted to mayor of Beijing; and Han Zheng was promoted to mayor of Shanghai.

It would be easier to understand the outcome of the first session of the Tenth NPC and the first session of the Tenth National Congress of the Chinese People's Political Consultative Conference in terms of the power balancing model. On the one hand, Jiang and his cronies took many high positions in the Tenth NPC, the Tenth

---

[61] For his bio, see http://news.xinhuanet.com/ziliao/2003-03/17/content_782297.htm.
[62] For the list of new ministers, see *Renmin ribao*, March 18, 2003, p. 1.

CNPPCC, and the State Council. On the other hand, Hu and his allies also managed to make substantial gains in these institutions as well as in provinces. Moreover, it is too simplistic to assume that Jiang's men are Hu's enemies. In fact, some of Jiang's men are also associated with Hu in some other ways. Wu Bangguo, Huang Ju, and Zeng Peiyan, for instance, are all graduates of Qinghua University, Hu's alma mater. Furthermore, it is reasonable to expect that Jiang would not continue to command the same degree of loyalty from these members of his clique — whether they have any prior association with Hu or not. As Hu's subordinates in both the Party and the government institutions, these officials have good reasons not to alienate Hu. On contrary, they would vie to demonstrate their institutional loyalty to President Hu Jintao. Again, it is not a picture of the winner-takes-all but of a power balance between Hu and Jiang.

POLITICS OF SARS

For those advocates of the model of a winner-takes-all game who were convinced that the political succession did not occur at the Sixteenth Party Congress, the political outcome of the epidemic — severe acute respiratory syndrome (SARS) — must have come as a complete surprise.

First Blow on the Shanghai Gang: Dismissal of Health Minister Zhang Wenkang

Beginning in November 2002, China was hit by SARS. The epidemic began in Guangdong Province and soon spread to Hong Kong and other provinces in China. Extremely contagious and life threatening, the epidemic spread fast and was killing people by the hundreds. The man in charge of China's health system at the time was one of Jiang's men, Zhang Wenkang (1940–),[63] minister of Health. A native of Shanghai, Zhang is well known for his close personal relations

---

[63] For his bio, see http://news.xinhuanet.com/ziliao/2002-03/01/content_295741.htm.

with Jiang Zemin. A graduate of Shanghai First Medical College, Zhang served in various capacities at the PLA Second Military University in Shanghai for nearly 30 years (1962–1990). He was transferred to Beijing in 1990 as deputy director of the Health Department of the PLA General Logistics Department and became a vice minister of Health in 1993. Zhang entered the CCP Central Committee as a full member in 1997 and was appointed as minister of Health by Jiang in March 1998.

Recently reappointed as the minister of Health in March 2003, Zhang told a press conference of more than 200 Chinese and foreign reporters on April 3, 2003, that SARS had been brought under effective control in China and travel in China was very safe.[64] According to Zhang, by March 31, 2003, there were 1,190 cases of SARS on Mainland China: 1,153 cases in Guangdong, 12 cases in Beijing, four cases in Shanxi, 11 cases in Guangxi, seven cases in Hunan, and three cases in Sichuan. Out of these cases, 934 (78.5 percent) cases had been cured. Forty-six people died of the disease: 40 in Guangdong, three in Beijing, and three in Guangxi. Only 210 people were hospitalized to receive treatment.[65] As for the spread of SARS in Beijing, Zhang explained that those cases in Beijing did not occur in Beijing; these patients got ill elsewhere and came to Beijing for treatment.[66]

Zhang's description, however, was far from the truth. The reality was that SARS was rapidly spreading throughout China and that some hospitals were instructed not to reveal the real situation. Dr. Jiang Yanyong (1930–), a retired surgeon of a military hospital in Beijing, investigated the situation on his own and discovered the gulf between Zhang's "official truth" and the reality. Dr. Jiang was enrolled in Yanjing University as a premed student in 1949 and joined the CCP in 1952. He joined the PLA in 1954 and worked in No. 301 PLA Hospital. He served as director of the Surgical Department of the

---

[64] *Renminwang*, April 5, 2003, http://www.people.com.cn/GB/paper464/8877/828486.html.
[65] *Ibid.*
[66] *Ibid.*

hospital until his retirement in late 1980s.[67] Dr. Jiang was outraged while he watched Zhang Wenkang's press conference on April 3, 2003. He could not believe that there were only 12 cases and three deaths in Beijing. He called No. 309 PLA Hospital and discovered that there were actually 60 cases of SARS and six deaths in that one hospital alone.[68] After failing to get any responses from CCTV Channel 4 and Hong Kong Phoenix TV, Dr. Jiang wrote a letter to an American journal, *Time*. In a signed statement, Dr. Jiang revealed the startling reality, and his statement was reported in *Time* on April 8, 2003.[69]

In order to find out what really happened, Premier Wen Jiabao and Vice Premier Wu Yi visited a hospital in Beijing on April 12, 2003[70] and held a national conference on prevention and treatment of SARS the following day.[71] In his speech to the conference of central and local officials, Wen indicated that the situation concerning the epidemic was still very serious, that China should work closely with the World Health Organization (WHO) in this regard, and that leaders of all levels should take the prevention and treatment of SARS as their top priority.[72] In the meantime, President Hu Jintao spent five days in Guangdong, the origin of SARS in China.[73] Apparently, what President Hu and Premier Wen discovered were more in line with Dr. Jiang Yanyong's statement than with Zhang Wenkang's report. On April 17, 2003, General Secretary Hu Jintao chaired a meeting of the Politburo Standing Committee in Beijing on the crisis of SARS.[74] The Party leadership decided to take the

---

[67] Lou Yi, "Jiang Yanyong: Chengshi de Yisheng" ["Jiang Yanyong: an honest doctor"], *Caijing Magazine*, No. 83 (May 5, 2003), pp. 24, 25; Lou Yi, "Jiang Zhenhua de Jiang Yanyong" ("Jiang Yanyong: telling the truth"), *Caijing Magazine*, No. 85 (June 5, 2003), pp. 22–25.

[68] http://zh.wikipedia.org/wiki/SARS%E4%BA%8B%E4%BB%B6.

[69] For details, see Susan Jakes, "Beijing's SARS attack," *Time*, April 8, 2003, http://www.time.com/time/asia/news/article/0,9754,441615,00.html.

[70] *Renmin ribao*, April 13, 2003, p. 1.

[71] *Renmin ribao*, April 14, 2003, p. 1.

[72] *Renmin ribao*, April 14, 2003, pp. 1, 2.

[73] He was in Guangdong between April 10 and 15, 2003. For details, see *Renmin ribao*, April 15, 2003, p. 1 and April 16, 2003, p. 1.

[74] *Renmin ribao*, April 18, 2003, p. 1.

prevention and treatment of SARS as one of the most important tasks, to take concrete measures to control the spread of the epidemic, and to make timely and accurate reports on the development of the epidemic. The Party leadership urged party leaders and government officials of various levels to put the health and life of Chinese people above anything else, asked chief leaders to be in charge of the prevention and treatment of SARS, and demanded all relevant officials not to cover up or delay reports on the spread of SARS.[75]

Three days later, Zhang Wenkang (minister of Health) and Meng Xuenong (mayor of Beijing) were both sacked. According to a report in the *People's Daily*, the Central Committee of the CCP decided to remove Zhang Wenkang as party secretary of the Party Group of Health Ministry and appoint Gao Qiang to the post; to remove Meng Xuenong as deputy secretary of the Beijing Municipal Party Committee and appoint Wang Qishan to the post; and replace Wang Qishan as party secretary of Hainan by Wang Xiaofeng.[76] The Third Meeting of the Twelfth Beijing Municipal People's Congress Standing Committee on April 22, 2003, accepted Meng Xuenong's resignation as mayor of Beijing and appointed Wang Qishan as vice mayor and acting mayor of Beijing.[77] Four days later, President Hu Jintao issued a presidential order to dismiss Zhang Wenkang as minister of Health and appoint Wu Yi, vice premier, as concurrent minister of Health.[78]

Apparently, the decision to dismiss Zhang was made at the Politburo Standing Committee meeting on April 17, 2003, over which General Secretary Hu Jintao presided. There is no clear evidence that Jiang Zemin had been consulted.[79] It was a decision

---

[75] *Ibid.*
[76] *Renmin ribao*, April 21, 2003, p. 1.
[77] *Renmin ribao*, April 23, 2003, p. 1.
[78] *Ibid.*
[79] According to Zong Hairen, Jiang was informed afterwards along with Politburo members and other retired senior officials. See his book, *Aimei de Quanli Jiaohuan*, p. 236.

made by the Sixteenth Politburo Standing Committee with Hu as general secretary. Reports held that three members of Jiang's clique — Zeng Qinghong, Jia Qinglin, and Huang Ju — abstained,[80] but no official confirmation of the rumor has ever been released. The fact that Hu fired Zhang is an indication that Hu did have power as general secretary. He also exercised his power as president of the PRC: He subsequently issued a presidential order, removing Zhang as minister of Health.[81]

It is likely that from Hu's perspective, removing Zhang Wenkang was an administrative rather than a political decision.[82] He was not attacking Jiang's clique under the pretense of Zhang's wrongdoings.[83] He did so because Zhang was not telling the truth about the seriousness of the epidemic and was not taking effective measures to control its spread after Hu's repeated urgings. Yet these administrative decisions greatly bolstered the political power of Hu Jintao as general secretary and president. On April 22, 2003, Hu was addressed by his title of general secretary in the mouthpiece of the

---

[80] Luo Bing, "Zhongnaihai Jing 'Yan' Baguan Neimu" ["Inside story of the dismissals of Zhang Wenkang and Meng Xuenong"], May 5, 2003, http://www.epochtimes.com/b5/3/5/n308360.htm.

[81] For the text of the presidential order in Chinese, see *Renminwang*, April 27, 2003, http://www.people.com.cn/GB/paper464/9045/842623.html. Hu's presidential order should not be regarded as pro forma. Hu indeed fired Zhang Wenkang. In this sense, the office of the president is not only ceremonial but also substantial. In contrast, Meng Xuenong resigned from his office as mayor of Beijing. For the news on Meng's resignation, see *Renminwang*, April 23, 2003, http://www.people.com.cn/GB/paper464/9017/840249.html.

[82] Lucian W. Pye made a clear distinction between politics and administration. According to him, politics is the informal operation of an organization, while administration is the formal operation of the organization. I am using his distinction here. For his elaboration, see his chapter, "Factions and the politics of Guanxi: paradoxes in Chinese administrative and political behaviour," in Jonathan Unger (ed), *The Nature of Chinese Politics: From Mao to Jiang* (Armonk, NY: M.E. Sharpe, 2002), pp. 39–40.

[83] For a different interpretation, see James Mulvenon, "The crucible of tragedy: SARS, the Ming 361 accident, and Chinese party-army relations," *China Leadership Monitor*, No. 8 (Fall 2003). http://www.chinaleadershipmonitor.org/20034/jm.html.

Party, the *People's Daily*.[84] Readers began to understand that whenever the title of "General Secretary" was mentioned in the media, it referred to General Secretary Hu. Moreover, it probably was the first time in the history of the PRC that the head of state issued a presidential order to remove a minister for dereliction of duty. In this sense, President Hu was the most powerful president in the history of the PRC, much more powerful than Jiang Zemin ever was. On April 30, 2003, in a letter to Premier Wen Jiabao, the students from the Department of Spanish Language of the Second College of Foreign Languages addressed Wen as "Premier" and Hu as "President."[85] It seemed obvious to these students that the "President" was President Hu, not someone else.

The role of Wu Bangguo in the decision-making is illustrative of the political balance and dynamics of elite politics in the aftermath of the Sixteenth National Party Congress. Wu is a member of the Shanghai Gang because of his previous work experience in the Shanghai Party Committee, and he is also a member of Jiang's clique because of his close association with Jiang. Reports held that Wu earned Jiang's trust in 1992 by privately sending reports to Jiang about Deng Xiaoping's activities in Shanghai.[86] Jiang was the one who promoted Wu to Beijing as vice premier in 1995 and installed him as a standing member of the Sixteenth Politburo. Yet Wu probably dutifully voted along with Hu to dismiss Zhang Wenkang as secretary of the Party group of the Ministry of Health at the Politburo Standing Committee's meeting on April 17, 2003. He also rubber-stamped the decision to remove Zhang as minister of Health at the second meeting of the Tenth NPC Standing Committee on April 26, 2003.

---

[84] See "Fangfan 'Feidianxingfeiyan' Kuosan, Luoshi Zongshuji Zhishi Shenzhen Yanfa Hongwaitiwenyi Jinshiyong" ["To prevent SARS, Shenzhen developed an infrared thermometer in accordance with the General Secretary's instructions"], *Renminwang*, April 22, 2003, http://www.peopledaily.com.cn/GB/kejiao/42/153/20030422/977926.html.

[85] *Renminwang*, May 16, 2003, http://www.people.com.cn/GB/paper464/9185/853267.html.

[86] Gao Xin, *Lingdao Zhongguo de Xinrenwu*, Vol. 1, p. 107.

The third presidential order Hu issued on April 26, 2003 to remove Zhang Wenkang as minister of Health was based on the decision made at that meeting.[87] The fact that Wu went along with Hu is an indication of the weight of formal politics over informal politics. Wu endorsed Hu's decision not because of his betrayal of Jiang or his personal loyalty to Hu, but probably because of his institutional loyalty — he went along with Hu because he was a subordinate of Hu Jintao as a standing member of the Politburo and chairman of the Standing Committee of the NPC.

Nevertheless, Hu Jintao was not playing factional politics. On the one hand, he dismissed Zhang Wenkang without pursuing further charges against him. At a press conference on April 20, 2003, Gao Qiang, executive vice minister of Health, admitted that the Health Ministry was responsible for not telling the truth about the spread of SARS in China in general and in Beijing in particular. The figures for the number of SARS cases in Beijing had been reported as follows: 12 cases by March 31, 2003;[88] 19 cases by April 5;[89] 19 cases by April 6;[90] 22 cases by April 9;[91] and 37 cases by April 15.[92] But as Gao Qiang revealed on April 20, there were actually 339 cases in Beijing by April 18, more than 10-fold as many as estimated a few days earlier. Why was there such a big discrepancy? Gao offered three reasons. First, it took sometime to confirm a case as a case of SARS because SARS was a new disease unknown to the mankind. Second, there was lack of a unified leadership among hospitals in Beijing. There are 175 hospitals (of grade two and above) in Beijing: 131 of them belong to the municipal, district, and county governments; 14 belong to Ministry of Health and Ministry of Education; 16 belong to the People's Liberation Army and the armed police; and 14 belong to other institutions. There were no effective

---

[87] *Renmin ribao* (overseas edition), April 28, 2003, p. 1.
[88] *Renmin ribao*, April 5, 2003, p. 2.
[89] *Renmin ribao*, April 6, 2003, p. 2.
[90] *Renmin ribao*, April 8, 2003, p. 2.
[91] *Renmin ribao*, April 11, 2003, p. 2.
[92] *Renmin ribao*, April 16, 2003, p. 2.

communications among these hospitals, and there was no unified leadership. The SARS patients were hospitalized in more than 70 hospitals in Beijing; therefore, the Beijing Municipal Government did not have a comprehensive and accurate figure. Third, the Ministry of Health was ill prepared to deal with the breakout of the epidemic and failed to produce timely measures on collecting, summarizing, and reporting regarding the spread of SARS.[93] However, Gao Qiang was reluctant to admit that such a big discrepancy was due to cover-ups.

On the other hand, Hu was evenhanded on this matter. Along with Zhang Wenkang, a confidant of Jiang Zemin, Hu also let go one of his men for the same reason: Meng Xuenong, a former CYL cadre and mayor of Beijing. Meng was dismissed from all his posts on the Beijing Municipal Party Committee on April 20, 2003, and he resigned as mayor of Beijing two days later.[94] It should be noted that Hu Jintao was not firing one of his own confidants to make it even with Jiang. First, Meng Xuenong was not Hu's confidant. When Meng was elected mayor of Beijing in January 2003, he deliberately exaggerated his close association with Hu Jintao. At a press conference, he remarked that he was proud of his experience as a CYL cadre when he worked directly under Hu Jintao. As he said,

> Twenty years ago, Comrade Hu Jintao was the chief leader of the Chinese Communist Youth League. I also worked under his direct leadership. Twenty years have passed; I do not remember all the details. But I was deeply impressed by Comrade Hu

---

[93] *Renmin ribao*, April 21, 2003, p. 2.

[94] *Renminwang*, April 23, 2003. http://www.people.com.cn/GB/paper464/9017/840249.html. It should be noted that Liu Qi, party secretary of Beijing and Politburo member, did not take the blame for the problem in Beijing, even though he was the big boss in Beijing. Liu was appointed as the head of the Beijing leading small group on SARS prevention and treatment on April 17, 2003, but was sidelined on April 20, 2003, when Wang Qishan was appointed as the head of a new leading small group on SARS prevention and treatment in Beijing. For Liu's appointment, see *Renmin ribao*, April 25, 2003, p. 2. For Wang's appointment, see *Renmin ribao*, April 26, 2003, p. 2.

Jintao. His uprightness and righteousness is the charisma of his personality. It is what all the other youth cadres should learn from him.[95]

There are two factual errors in this statement. One, Hu was not the chief leader of the CCYL 20 years earlier. In January 1983, Wang Zhaoguo, not Hu Jintao, was the first secretary of the CCYL Central Committee. Two, Meng did not work under the direct leadership of Hu. Hu left the CCYL Central Committee in November 1985, and Meng entered the Central Committee of the CCYL in the same month. There is no overlap between the two in the CCYL Central Committee. Second, Meng was fired because of his mishandling of the SARS crisis in Beijing, not because of his CCYL background. But there was a perception in the media of Hong Kong and elsewhere and possibly among some top leaders of China that Meng was fired because he was a CCYL cadre. This perception works in Hu's favor.

Jiang and His Cronies: Dereliction of Duties

While President Hu Jintao, Premier Wen Jiabao, and Vice Premier Wu Yi were working in the forefront of fighting SARS, Jiang Zemin and some of his cronies disappeared from the scene. Jiang was last seen in Beijing on April 9 when he attended the funeral of Zhou Zijian (1914–2003), former minister of No. 1 Machine-Building Industry.[96] Jiang had maneuvered to stay on as CMC chairman but was not prepared to work in such a capacity. He should be held responsible for the cover-up of the SARS crisis in Beijing because those hospitals that had been instructed not to report on their patients of SARS were all military hospitals (such as No. 302 and No. 309 PLA hospitals) in Beijing. As Gao Qiang implied in his

---

[95] Meng Xuenong, "Gongqingtuo Shengya Weicongzheng Diandingle yige Jichu" ["My career in the CCYL has provided a foundation for my political career later on"], *Renmin ribao*, January 19, 2003. http://www.peopledaily.com.cn/GB/shizheng/252/9823/9826/20030119/910732.html.
[96] *Renmin ribao*, April 10, 2003, p. 1.

report on April 20, the military hospitals in Beijing were the ones that withheld information about their SARS patients. Because of lack of a unified leadership over various categories of hospitals in Beijing, Gao explained, "It is rather difficult to ask the Beijing Municipal Government to get timely and accurate information about the spread of the epidemic from a military hospital."[97]

In the face of the epidemic, Jiang fled for his life because Beijing was no longer a safe place despite the suggestion of his personal friend, Dr. Zhang Wenkang, otherwise.[98] Beijing became the most seriously affected region in China. The total number of SARS cases in Beijing increased to 588 by April 21; 693 by April 22; 774 by April 23; and 877 by April 24.[99] Was not the commander-in-chief supposed to stay in the battlefield to fight the enemies? Was not this a great opportunity for Jiang to show his indispensability? Only one month earlier, Jiang Zemin had just told Shanghai deputies to the NPC on March 6, 2003, that he was needed to keep things under control (*ya zhen*) because Hu Jintao was "too inexperienced" in military affairs.[100] Jiang reportedly said, "I explained this concept to foreign friends. But no matter how the interpreter translated it, they did not understand the term. At last I made it plain. I said, 'I stay to help Hu Jintao.'"[101] But when the SARS hit Beijing and Hu Jintao needed Jiang Zemin in Beijing to help fight the epidemic, Jiang vanished.

When people were wondering where Jiang was, he reemerged not in Beijing but in Shanghai on April 26, 2003. At a publicized

---

[97] *Renmin ribao*, April 21, 2003, p. 2.

[98] Jiang was probably frightened by the news that a maid of Yu Ruomu, late Chen Yun's wife, living in Zhongnaihai (the compound of central leaders), was reportedly affected by SARS. See http://www.renminbao.com/rmb/articles/2003/5/1/26086.html.

[99] For details, see *Renmin ribao*, April 22, 2003, p. 2; *Renmin ribao*, April 23, 2003, p. 2; *Renmin ribao*, April 24, 2003, p. 2; *Renmin ribao*, April 25, 2003, p. 2; and *Renmin ribao*, April 26, 2003, p. 2.

[100] Robert Lawrence Kuhn, *The Man Who Changed China: The Life and Legacy of Jiang Zemin* (New York: Crown Publishers, 2004), p. 536.

[101] *Ibid.*, p. 536.

meeting with Indian defense minister, George Fernandes, Jiang talked about SARS the first time.[102] He told the foreign guest that the Party Center and the State Council took their responsibilities seriously and expressed his confidence in winning the eventual victory of fighting SARS. Jiang's publicity show, however, backfired. His reappearance in Shanghai caused quite a stir among Chinese college students. Beijing bore the brunt of the SARS epidemic, with more than 100 new cases reported each day in late April, while Shanghai only had two reported cases altogether. As Hu Jintao, Wen Jiabao, and Wu Yi (vice premier and new minister of Health) were taking the lead in the fight against SARS in the most seriously affected areas, Jiang Zemin — by staying in Shangahai — did not look good. The students were outraged that Jiang was hiding in Shanghai from SARS. "Shanghai must be safer than Beijing," they joked, "because Jiang Zemin is hiding in Shanghai." "No wonder the Party Center swore to protect Shanghai at all costs," they mocked, "because Jiang Zemin was there."[103] They despised Jiang's cowardliness and described him as being afraid of death.

On the internet, Jiang was subsequently held responsible for the decision made at a meeting of the Politburo on April 28, 2003 to start a new Party-wide campaign to study and implement the "Three Represents."[104] Whether or not Jiang was behind this decision is not clear. It is likely that based on his role as the inventor of the theory, Jiang urged the new Politburo to study the "Three Represents." It is equally likely that his men in the Politburo (such as Zeng Qinghong) pushed for this new campaign for their own potential political gains. Also possible is that Hu preempted Jiang and his

---

[102] *Renmin ribao*, April 27, 2003, p. 1. See also http://www.people.com.cn/GB/paper464/9045/842620.html.

[103] See "Jiang Zemin Binan Shanghai, Beida Xuesheng Paohong Pasi" [Jiang Zemin was hiding in Shanghai, Beijing University students were criticizing him of being afraid of death], *Hua Bao* (Asian American News), No. 527 (May 9–May 22, 2003), p. 8.

[104] *Renminwang*, April 29, 2003, http://www.people.com.cn/GB/paper464/9062/844018.html.

cronies from accusing Hu of deviating from the line of the Sixteenth Party Congress. Regardless of what really occurred, Jiang's reputation was further damaged because few could understand why the Party was promoting the study of the "Three Represents" rather than working more aggressively to combat SARS.

A few of Jiang's cronies, who not long ago were vigorously campaigning to obtain high positions in the central government, also became invisible. Huang Ju, standing member of the Politburo and executive vice premier, for instance, attended the national conference on SARS on April 13, 2003,[105] but was not present at an executive meeting of the State Council the following day.[106] He did not reappear until April 26, 2003, when he reportedly "inspected" the work of SARS prevention and treatment at the General Administration of the Civil Aviation of China, the Ministry of Railways, and the Ministry of Communications.[107] Notably, he was absent from three meetings of the State Council between April 14 and 26, 2003. He was absent from an executive meeting of the State Council on establishing a crisis-management mechanism for health issues on April 14;[108] he was not present at another executive meeting of the State Council on plans of producing executive statutes for the year of 2003 on April 16;[109] and he was again not seen at an executive meeting of the State Council on April 23 when the State Council under the leadership of Premier Wen Jiabao decided to establish a State Council SARS Prevention and Treatment Command with Vice Premier Wu Yi as the commander-in-chief.[110] As Jiang, Huang placed his own health above the health of Chinese people and neglected his duties as a top leader.

Similarly, Zeng Qinghong, standing member of the Politburo and vice president of China, did not fulfill his duties as a top leader

---

[105] *Renmin ribao*, April 14, 2003, p. 1.
[106] *Renmin ribao*, April 15, 2003, p. 1.
[107] *Renmin ribao*, April 27, 2003, p. 1.
[108] *Renmin ribao*, April 15, 2003, p. 1.
[109] *Renmin ribao*, April 17, 2003, p. 1.
[110] *Renmin ribao*, April 24, 2003, p. 1.

either.[111] He attended the funeral of Zhou Zijiang along with Jiang Zemin, Wu Bangguo, and Huang Ju on April 9, 2003,[112] but was subsequently absent from Beijing. Between April 10 and 14, he was reportedly visiting Guizhou, another safe place from SARS (a SARS-free province).[113] Zeng appeared in Beijing on April 18 when he met with the foreign minister of Serbian-Montenegro in the Great Hall of the People,[114] but again was absent from the scene subsequently. He reportedly visited the Central Party School on April 24 and inspected the work of SARS prevention and treatment in the school, but his visit was not reported in the *People's Daily* until April 27 when the news reports on Jiang and Huang were published.[115] Obviously, as Jiang and Huang, Zeng was taking necessary precautions to avoid the disease. But as Jiang and Huang, he did so at the expense of the health of Chinese people.

Submarine Accident

In the midst of SARS crisis, a submarine accident occurred. On April 16, 2003, a Ming-class submarine (No. 361) had a fatal accident on its way back to Weihai Military Port, Shandong Province, killing all 70 officers and sailors aboard. The Ming-class, the type of No. 361, is a conventional submarine indigenously produced in China based on the Romeo-class made in the Soviet Union.[116] The Ming-class submarines have two types. China began to build type 033 Ming-class submarines in December 1965 and put them in service on June 22, 1969. There are currently still about 30 type 033 Ming-class

---

[111] For a different assessment of Zeng's performance during the SARS crisis, see Zong Hairen, *Aimei de Quanli Jiaohuan*, pp. 234–236, 240.
[112] *Renmin ribao*, April 10, 2003, p. 1.
[113] *Renmin ribao*, April 15, 2003, p. 1.
[114] *Renmin ribao*, April 19, 2003, p. 1.
[115] *Renmin ribao*, April 27, 2003, p. 1.
[116] For details, see http://blog.yam.com/ump45/archives/147056.html. For an overview of the People's Liberation Army Navy, see http://www.navyleague.org/seapower/chinas_navy_today.htm.

submarines in service that will phase out by 2010. Type 035 is a modification of type 033, was launched in 1971, and entered the service with the PLA Navy in April 1974.[117] No. 361 submarine was probably built between 1988 and 1995 and entered the service with the PLA Navy in 1995.[118]

The deadly accident was reportedly caused by a technical malfunction. In due procedures, the submarine charges the electrical batteries that run the ship undersea by running their diesel engines, which need to burn a large quantity of oxygen. Therefore, when recharging the batteries, the submarine has to get close to the surface and have the periscopes on top of it and air-taking valves into the air. It seems the valves malfunctioned in No. 361 and the craft's diesel engines sucked up oxygen inside the ship, quickly killing those aboard in two minutes. Because of the imbalance of the air pressures, the gate of No. 361, under the negative pressure, could not be opened from inside. Therefore, those who attempted to escape would have found no way to go. Because No. 361 submarine was on a silent, no-contact drill, it cut off all contacts with the outside, which made it impossible for the outside world to know that No. 361 had this bad accident for 10 days.[119]

When the headquarters of the North China Sea Fleet received a report from fishermen about the accident on April 26, 2003, Vice Admiral Ding Yiping, commander of the North China Sea Fleet and concurrent deputy commander of the Jinan Military Region, immediately reported to Jiang Zemin.[120] Jiang was outraged. He just had a publicity show about the SARS that day, but now he had to get back to work. He sent Guo Boxiong, vice chairman of the CMC, Ge Zhenfeng, deputy chief of staff, Shi Yunsheng, commander of the PLA Navy, and Yang Huaiqing, political commissar of the PLA Navy, to Lushun Port of Dailian, Liaoning Province.[121] The question for

---

[117] http://www.jxgdw.com/jxgd/news/js/userobject1ai625903.html.
[118] http://www.sinodefence.com/navy/sub/035.asp.
[119] http://www.washingtonobserver.org/en/document.cfm?documentid=1&charid=1.
[120] Zong Hairen, *Aimei de Quanli Jiaohuan*, p. 247.
[121] *Ibid.*, pp. 247, 248.

Jiang was whether he should publicize the accident. If he kept it as a secret, he would be as liable as his crony, Zhang Wenkang, had been regarding the spread of the SARS in China. But if he publicized the accident, he would be equally subject to blame because a military accident reflects badly on Jiang as the commander-in-chief.

The accident exposed some of the serious problems with the PLA Navy.[122] First, submarine technology was seriously outdated. The Ming-class submarines, according to a retired American submarine officer, Lieutenant Commander Bill Murray, were "very old-fashioned," lagging behind that of the United States for five decades.[123] Second, there were serious management problems. The regular staff of No. 361 were 57 people, but at the time of the accident there were 70 people aboard. The additional 13 people were reportedly researchers or students of the Qingdao Submarine School.[124] Third, the changes in the military service law in 1998 also affected the performance of the submarine. According to the new military service law, a naval soldier could serve only for two years[125] instead of previously stipulated four years (Article 18 of the 1984 Military Service Law of the PRC).[126] As veteran soldiers were retired, new recruits were inexperienced with the submarine. All these problems could lead one to wonder about Jiang Zemin's performance as chairman of the CMC between 1989 and 2003 and to question his credibility as a viable military leader in the new century.

After five days of struggling and calculating, Jiang eventually decided to publicize the accident on May 1.[127] Jiang later confessed that he could not sleep well upon hearing the news of the accident.[128] On May 2, Jiang sent a telegram of condolences to the relatives of No. 361 submarine officers and sailors and had it

---

[122] *Ibid.*, p. 248.
[123] http://www.washingtonobserver.org/en/document.cfm?documentid=1&charid=1.
[124] http://blog.yam.com/ump45/archives/147056.html.
[125] http://www.gov.cn/banshi/gm/content_63510.htm.
[126] http://www.lawinfochina.com/dispfree.asp?db=1&id=48&keyword=.
[127] Zong Hairen, *Aimei de Quanli Jiaohuan*, pp. 247, 248.
[128] *Renmin ribao*, May 6, 2003, p. 1.

published by the Xinhua News Agency.[129] Hu Jintao heard about the accident while he was in Tianjin, inspecting on the work of SARS prevention and treatment.[130] His telegram of condolences was published on May 3.[131] It should be noted that Hu sent his telegram in the name of general secretary of the Party and president of the PRC. His title of vice chairman of the CMC was not mentioned. Moreover, in addition to expressing his sorrow over the loss of these officers and sailors, Hu stressed the importance of learning a good lesson from the accident and of taking the opportunity to promote the modernization of China's national defense and army building.

Two days later, in a report about the visit of Hu Jintao and Jiang Zemin to Dalian on the submarine accident, Jiang Zemin's name was placed in front of Hu Jintao's name, and Hu's titles as general secretary of the Party and president of the PRC were all dropped. President Hu became a vice chairman of the CMC![132] For Jiang, it was not an occasion to console the relatives of the 70 dead officers and sailors and to investigate the submarine accident; it was rather an opportunity for him to demonstrate his superiority over Hu Jintao. In the group photo, Jiang stood in the center flanked by Hu Jintao, two other vice chairmen of the CMC (Guo Boxiong and Cao Gangchuan), and Xu Caihou, another member of the CMC and director of the General Political Department,[133] showing to the world that he — instead of Hu — was still in the center. Yet foreign leaders quickly rectified the order in which the name of Hu and that of Jiang appeared in the media. North Korean Leader Kim Jong-il sent a telegram on May 4 to General Secretary and President Hu Jintao and CMC Chairman Jiang Zemin to express his condolences over the loss of Chinese officers and sailors due to the submarine accident.[134] Other foreign leaders simply ignored Jiang

---

[129] http://past.people.com.cn/GB/junshi/192/10673/10674/20030502/983786.html.
[130] *Renmin ribao*, May 2, 2003, p. 1.
[131] *Renmin ribao*, May 4, 2003, p. 1.
[132] *Renmin ribao*, May 6, 2003, p. 1.
[133] *Renmin ribao*, May 6, 2003, p. 1.
[134] *Renmin ribao*, May 6, 2003, p. 3.

Zemin altogether: Cambodian King Norodom Sihanouk, Egyptian President Hosni Mubarak, Lebanese President Emile Lahoud, Sudanese President Omar el-Bashir, Ukrainian President Leonid Kuchma, and Macedonian President Boris Trajkovski all sent their telegrams to President Hu Jintao;[135] Singaporean Prime Minister Goh Chok Tong sent a telegram to Premier Wen Jiabao;[136] and US Secretary of State Colin L. Powell sent a telegram to Foreign Minister Li Zhaoxing.[137] In the end, Jiang Zemin fired commander (Shi Yunsheng) and political commissar (Yang Huaiqing) of the PLA Navy[138] as well as commander (Ding Yiping) and political commissar (Chen Xianfeng) of the North China Sea Fleet.[139]

Hu Jintao, on the other hand, took the opportunity to foray into Jiang Zemin's domain. On May 23, 2003, General Secretary Hu Jintao chaired the Fifth Politburo Study Session on the new development in world military affairs.[140] After listening to two military researchers (Qian Haihao and Fu Liqun of the Chinese Academy of Military Sciences), Hu remarked that China's central task in the first 20 years of the 21st century is economic development; a strong national defense would provide a security safeguard for accomplishing this task; in the meantime, China should also pay close attention to the studies of world military transformation and promote its national defense and army modernization. He urged party committees and governments of all levels to fully recognize the importance of national defense and army building modernization, support military modernization efforts, and establish mechanisms by which national defense construction and economic construction would be reinforcing each other and developing side by side. Hu envisioned that China could achieve a leap-forward style development in national defense and army modernization on the basis of economic development and

---

[135] *Renmin ribao*, May 7, 2003, p. 3; *Renmin ribao*, May 8, 2003, p. 3.
[136] *Renmin ribao*, May 7, 2003, p. 3.
[137] *Renmin ribao*, May 7, 2003, p. 3.
[138] *Renmin ribao*, June 13, 2003, p. 1.
[139] *Renmin ribao*, June 14, 2003, p. 4. See also http://www.people.com.cn/GB/paper447/9416/871999.html.
[140] http://news.xinhuanet.com/zhengfu/2003-05/24/content_885152.htm.

technological progress as well as of the experience of world military transformation.[141]

Outcome of the Politics of SARS

Under the leadership of President Hu Jintao, Premier Wen Jiabao, and Vice Premier Wu Yi, the Chinese people were able to reduce and eventually effectively control the spread of SARS in China. The number of new cases was substantially reduced, starting in the mid-May and tailed off toward the end of May 2003. The total number of new cases (and suspected cases) of SARS was 181 (94) on May 3, 2003,[142] but was reduced to 55 (31) on May 14, 2003.[143] At the end of May, the number of new cases was reduced to single digits. On May 30, 2003, there were only seven new cases of SARS reported (Table 5.4): six from Beijing and one from Hebei. By the end of May, there were altogether 5,328 cases of SARS in China. Out of this figure, 3,250 cases were cured, and 528 people died. Beijing was the most seriously affected region with 2,520 cases altogether and 177 deaths; followed by Guangdong with 1,511 cases altogether and 57 deaths. Finally, the WHO lifted travel advisory on Beijing and removed Beijing from its list of SARS-affected areas on June 24, 2006.[144] China's fight against the epidemic came to an end.

The net result of politics of SARS was that Hu emerged as a popular leader, while Jiang's image was seriously damaged. However, Hu's gains were not established on Jiang's losses, but it rather came through hard work. Gao Qiang, executive vice minister of Health, for instance, summarized China's battle against SARS in five "never forgets" at a press conference on June 24, 2003. The first was that

---

[141] *Renmin ribao*, May 25, 2003, p. 1. Noticeably, Hu did not use the term, "Jiang Zemin's thinking on national defense and army building." For a detailed analysis, see Willy Lam, "PLA seeks a new leap forward," *China Brief* 3, Issue 11 (June 3, 2003), http://www.jamestown.org/publications_details.php?volume_id=19&issue_id=676&article_id=4740.
[142] *Renmin ribao*, May 4, 2003, p. 4.
[143] *Renmin ribao*, May 15, 2003, p. 2.
[144] *Renmin ribao*, June 25, 2003, p. 1.

Table 5.4 SARS Cases in China by May 30, 2003

Order	Province	New	Cured	Death	Total
1	Beijing	6	1006	177	2520
2	Hebei	1	146	12	216
3	Shanxi	0	335	21	450
4	Inner Mogolia	0	141	28	284
5	Liaoning	0	2	2	6
6	Shanghai	0	2	2	8
7	Sichuan	0	12	2	19
8	Hubei	0	4	1	7
9	Guangxi	0	16	3	22
10	Tianjin	0	77	14	175
11	Jilin	0	19	6	35
12	Guangdong	0	1439	57	1511
13	Jiangsu	0	3	0	7
14	Gansu	0	5	1	8
15	Anhui	0	9	0	10
16	Shaanxi	0	9	0	12
17	Zhejiang	0	1	0	4
18	Henan	0	10	0	15
19	Chongqing	0	1	0	3
20	Jiangxi	0	1	0	1
21	Ningxia	0	4	1	5
22	Shandong	0	0	0	1
23	Fujian	0	3	0	3
24	Hunan	0	5	1	6
25	Heilongjiang	0	0	0	0
26	Xinjiang	0	0	0	0
	Total	7	3250	328	5328

Source: *Renmin Ribao*, May 31, 2003, p. 2.

"We should never forget the days and nights when the Party center and the State Council led us in the fight against SARS."[145] "President Hu Jintao, Premier Wen Jiabao, and other national leaders," he said, "went to the forefront of the battle against SARS, making people's health and life the top priority, requesting that the government at all

---

[145] Gao Qiang, "Kanji Feidian Wuge Bunengwangji" ["Five never forgets in the fight against SARS"], *Renminwang*, June 25, 2003, http://www.people.com.cn/GB/paper464/9503/878878.html.

levels give the highest priority to the fight against SARS, and establishing a strong national leadership and command system."[146] The most valuable lesson from the fight against SARS, according to Gao, was that "under the leadership of the Party Center with Comrade Hu Jintao as general secretary, we will be able to overcome any difficulties, as long as we are united and face up to the crisis, as long as we earnestly implement the important decisions and measures of the Party Center, and as long as we broadly strengthen our international cooperation."[147] Ostensibly missing from this statement was open praise of Jiang's contributions, although Jiang belatedly tried to appear supportive of the fight against SARS.[148]

ZHOU ZHENGYI'S CASE AND THE SHANGHAI GANG

Detention of Zhou Zhengyi — The Richest Man in Shanghai

While Shanghai was basically free from the SARS epidemic, the Shanghai Gang was startled when Zhou Zhengyi, the richest man in Shanghai, was detained for financial irregularities on May 27, 2003. Zhou Zhengyi (April 1961–) was born in the Yangpu District of Shanghai. His father, Zhou Yuxing (–January 2003), is a native of Wuxi, Jiangsu Province, and his mother is a native of Suzhou, Jiangsu Province.[149] As the youngest child of the family, he has three elder sisters and one elder brother. He was a high school dropout and opened up his own wonton restaurant in Yangpu in 1978 at the age of 17.[150] In the 1980s, Zhou went to Japan to do business, but it

---

[146] *Ibid.*
[147] *Ibid.*
[148] According to headline news in the *Renmin ribao* on April 29, 2003, with the approval of CMC Chairman Jiang Zemin, 1200 military medical personnel were to be sent to Beijing to support the fight against SARS. Yet few were impressed. See *Renminwang*, April 29, 2003, http://www.people.com.cn/GB/paper464/9062/844019.html.
[149] Lin Huawei, "Zhou Zhengyi Xingshuai" ["Rise and fall of Zhou Zhengyi"], *Caijing*, No. 86 (June 20, 2003), pp. 40–52.
[150] http://past.people.com.cn/GB/jinji/20030605/1008840.html.

was without much success. He returned to Shanghai in 1989 and opened up Meitong Restaurant near Huanghe Road and another store of remodeling on Beijing Road. In 1994, Zhou Zhengyi and his wife, Mao Yuping, opened up the grand Ah Mao Boiled Food (*A Mao Dun Ping*) at No. 127 on Huanghe Road.[151] Three years later, Zhou emerged as one of the richest men in Shanghai. He purchased a house in Hong Kong at the price of HK$62 million (about US$8 million) in August 1997 and started a company in Hong Kong (Fine Time Investments Limited in English or Jiayun in Chinese). Zhou established Nongkai Development Corporation in October 1997 with a registered capital of 100 million yuan.[152] According to *Forbes*, Zhou was the 94th richest man in China with an estimated asset of US$66 million in 2001. In 2002, he became the 11th richest man in China with an estimated asset of US$320 million.[153]

Zhou was detained for illegally acquiring bank loans and for involvement in a lawsuit of land disputes. Zhou reportedly acquired a loan of HK$2.1 billion from the Bank of China (Hong Kong) in June 2002 and used the loan to purchase a company in Hong Kong (its English name is ImGo and its Chinese name is Jianliantong). He changed the name of the company to Shanghai Land Holdings after the purchase.[154] Zhou's loan problem was connected to another man from Shanghai who was also detained in the same month, Liu Jinbao. Liu (1952–), a graduate of Beijing University of Economics and Trade, worked in the Shanghai Branch of the Bank of China for 16 years (October 1981–August 1997).[155] He became acting head of the Shanghai Branch in June 1993 and its head the following year. Liu was

---

[151] This restaurant was closed on June 1, 2003. See http://past.people.com.cn/GB/jinji/20030606/1009714.html.

[152] Lin Huawei, "Zhou Zhengyi Xingshuai," pp. 40–52.

[153] http://www.forbes.com/finance/lists/74/2002/LIR.jhtml?passListId=74&passYear=2002&passListType=Person&uniqueId=01T4&datatype=Person.

[154] For more details, see Cao Haili, "Liu Jinbao Zhendang" ["The quake of Liu Jinbao"], *Caijing*, No. 86 (June 20, 2003), pp. 53–56; http://past.people.com.cn/GB/jinji/33/174/20030602/1005981.html.

[155] For Liu's bio, see Zhang Jiwei, "Liu Jintao Qiren" ["Liu Jinbao"], *Caijing*, No. 103 (May 5, 2004), p. 43.

transferred to Hong Kong as executive deputy director of the Bank of China (Hong Kong) in August 1997 and became vice chairman and CEO of the Bank of China (Hong Kong) Limited in June 2002. He was recalled to Beijing on May 22, 2003, and was subsequently detained.[156]

Another reason why Zhou was detained was reportedly because of his involvement in a lawsuit over land disputes. Zhou Zhengyi obtained an agreement from the Housing and Land Management Bureau of the Jing'an District, Shanghai, on May 28, 2002, on land transfer over a golden area in central Shanghai, nicknamed "east eight blocks" (*dong bakuai*). The total area involved is 176,400 square meters, and 10,000 households would have to move out.[157] Zhou and his partners came into conflict with the residents of the area over whether these original residents were allowed to move back after its development. According to a document jointly issued by the Bureau of Construction, Bureau of Planning, Bureau of Real Estate, and Bureau of Housing Development of Shanghai in early 2001, original residents of these old areas in Shanghai that were designated for new development projects would be encouraged to move back. As the title of the document, "Measures on encouraging the original residents to move back in order to promote a new round of old area development (trial)," suggested, the most important point of this policy was that the original residents have the preferential right to move back. Under this condition, the document further specified that developers of these areas would pay no land transfer fees.[158]

Zhou and his partners reaped the benefits of zero land transfer fees estimated to be between 300 million and 400 million yuan for an area of 43,429 square meters, while refusing to allow the original residents to move back. The Bureau of Housing of the Jing'an

---

[156] http://www.people.com.cn/GB/jinji/33/174/20030602/1005976.html.

[157] For details, see Ren Bo, "Chai Qian Zhi Shu" ["A lawsuit involving demolishing old houses and moving out families"], *Caijing*, No. 87 (July 5, 2003), pp. 54–56; http://past.people.com.cn/GB/jinji/33/174/20030604/1008445.html.

[158] Zheng Ke, "Zhou Zhengyi Shanghai Dichan Jiufen'an, Siwan pingmi Tudi Lingchurangjin" ["Zhou Zhengyi's land dispute case: 40,000 square meters for zero land transfer fees"], *Ershiyi Shiji Jingji Daobao (21st Century Economic Herald)*, June 4, 2003, http://past.people.com.cn/GB/jinji/33/174/20030604/1008445.html.

District of Shanghai specified the zero land transfer fees in its agreement with Zhou and his partners and subsequently issued a permit to demolish the east eight blocks on August 30, 2002. Most residents refused to move and sued the Bureau of Housing of the Jing'an District of Shanghai. On May 28, 2003, Shen Junsheng and other five representatives of 2,159 households of the residential area appeared in the People's Court of the Jinng'an District as plaintiffs and the Bureau of Housing Management of the Jing'an District as the defendant.[159] Zhou Zhengyi's company — Fine Time Investments Limited, a company registered in the British Virgin Islands — was absent, though it pledged 99 percent of the investment. Zhou's partner, the Jing'an Urban Construction Investments Limited that pledged one percent of the investment, was there on behalf of the developers. The court did not issue any judgment that day.

At the stake were interests of original residents. According to an attorney who is familiar with the case, in a typical case of a family of five with 60 square meters of the original residence, the family would only need to pay about 200,000 yuan to move back to a flat of 90 square meters. The price of the first 60 square meters would be 1,295 yuan per square meter and 77,700 yuan altogether. But relevant regulations also allowed deducting 1.5 percent for each year of work experience and one percent for each year of living in the residence. Since many residents have decades of work experience and had lived in these houses for decades, they were actually entitled to the minimum price of 245 yuan per square meter (or 14,700 yuan altogether for the first 60 square meters). For the additional 30 square meters, their payment would be 180,000 yuan at the market price of 6,000 yuan per square meter. In other words, their total payment for a flat of 90 square meters would be between 194,700 yuan and 257,700 yuan. But the actual value of the flat would be far more than that for the simple reason that this was the central business district (grade two area) where the price of real estate could increase several folds.[160]

---

[159] *Ibid.*
[160] *Ibid.*

Implications for Shanghai Gang Members

Several Shanghai Gang members were reportedly horrified over Zhou Zhengyi's case. Chen Liangyu, Politburo member and party secretary of Shanghai, reportedly trembled when he received a phone call from the Central Disciplinary Inspection Commission (the Party's watchdog) in early June because his brother, Chen Liangjun, was reportedly a business partner with Zhou Zhengyi in the real estate development project mentioned above.[161]

According to a widely circulated story, Zhou Zhengyi and Chen Liangyu's brother became good friends in the early 1990s when Chen was still deputy party secretary and head of the Huangpu District of Shanghai and Zhou called Chen's mother *"Gan Ma"* (Godmother).[162] Zhou and Chen Liangjun opened the Ah Mao Boiled Food in the Huangpu District,[163] but Chen Liangyu was head of the Huangpu District between February 1987 and October 1992 (and he was away in Britain from January to September 1992).[164] By the time Zhou opened the restaurant in 1994, Chen was already a deputy secretary of Shanghai. Yet this modification does not rule out the possibility that Chen Liangjun was a business partner with Zhou Zhengyi in the development project of the east eight blocks.[165]

At a meeting of the standing members of the Shanghai Municipal Party Committee on June 6, 2003, Chen indicated that Shanghai would act in accordance with the requirement of the Party Center and work with relevant institutions to investigate the case of Nongkai

---

[161] http://www.washingtonchinareview.com/newsdetailp.php?id=571.

[162] By addressing Chen Liangyu's mother *Gan Ma*, Zhou became a member of Chen's family (*zijiren*). For a detailed discussion of the role of *zijiren* in Chinese social interactions, see Chung-Fang Yang, "Psychocultural foundations of informal groups: the issues of loyalty, sincerity, and trust," in Lowell Dittmer, Haruhiro Fukui, and Peter N. S. Lee (eds) *Informal Politics in East Asia* (New York: Cambridge University Press, 2000), pp. 103–105.

[163] http://www.tycool.com/2005/11/10/00022.html.

[164] http://news.xinhuanet.com/ziliao/2002-02/22/content_285938.htm.

[165] In a petition letter to Hu Jintao and Wen Jiabao, Shen Ting mentioned a Shanghai leader's younger brother as Zhou's business partner, referring to Chen Liangjun. For her letter, see http://www.peacehall.com/news/gb/china/2003/06/200306250645.shtml.

Corporation.¹⁶⁶ On the same day, however, Zheng Enchong, the attorney who once represented Shanghai residents against Zhou and his partners, was detained for allegedly "illegally providing state secrets to entities outside China" and was subsequently arrested on these charges on June 18, 2003. The "state secret" was an article by a Xinhua News Agency reporter (Huang Tingjun), entitled "Conflicts caused by forced removal of residents, reporters investigating the case were attacked." The article had been published in an internal journal of the Xinhua News Agency on April 30, 2003. According to the Shanghai Bureau of State Secrets, this article belongs to the lowest level of classified documents ["secret" (*mi mi*)] [the other two levels are "top secret" (*jue mi*) and "confidantial" (*ji mi*)].¹⁶⁷ According to the spokesman of the Shanghai Public Security Bureau, Zheng's case had nothing to do with Zhou Zhengyi's case.¹⁶⁸ But the opposite might be true because Zheng reportedly had many documents about the collusion between Zhou Zhengyi on the one side and Chen Liangjun and Jiang Mianheng on the other.¹⁶⁹

In an unusual move, Chen Liangyu made a public pledge in August 2003 that he was willing to be subject to the monitoring of the people; he would not use his power to seek benefits for his relatives and friends; and anyone who seeks personal gains in the name of his relatives and friends should be rejected without a meeting and should be reported immediately.¹⁷⁰ But few netters were convinced. They commented that Chen's relatives would not have to meet someone to get things done; Chen was actually trying to cover up; Chen should stop protecting Zhou Zhengyi.¹⁷¹ Some wondered how anyone could

---

¹⁶⁶ http://past.people.com.cn/GB/shizheng/252/9810/9939/20030607/1010503.html.
¹⁶⁷ http://unn.people.com.cn/GB/14748/2172850.html.
¹⁶⁸ http://www.chinanews.com.cn/n/2003-06-09/26/311848.html.
¹⁶⁹ Luo Bing, "Chen Liangyu ba Shanghai Shiwei Bangshang Zhanche" ["Chen Liangyu made the Shanghai Municipal Party Committee a hostage over Zheng Enchong's case"], *Qianshao* (*The Front-Line Magazine*) No. 156 (February 2004), pp. 6, 7.
¹⁷⁰ http://www.people.com.cn/GB/shizheng/14562/2031678.html.
¹⁷¹ http://comments.people.com.cn/bbs_new/filepool/htdoc/html/f24dd8f05ec82162 cdc7f23a479c11862a1daa8a/b483623/l_483623_1.html.

monitor these officials if they did not publicize the assets of their families and their relatives.[172] Chen reiterated his pledges a year later.[173]

Another Shanghai Gang member that should have been nervous about Zhou Zhengyi's case is Huang Ju, former party secretary of Shanghai and currently standing member of the Politburo and vice premier of the State Council. Huang Ju's wife, Yu Huiwen, is reportedly a godmother (*gan ma*) of Mao Yuping, Zhou Zhengyi's wife. Mao often addressed Yu Huiwen as "*Gan Ma*" in public.[174] There are two opposite images of Yu Huiwen. The Shanghai official media has portrayed her as a warm-hearted, responsible person dedicated to charity in Shanghai. She began working for the Shanghai Charity Foundation as a volunteer in 1994 when the Foundation was established and became its vice chairman later on. She has followed Huang Ju's advice of 12 characters: be sympathetic with the people, do not interfere with politics, do more, and show less.[175] Yet she appeared in public as much as Huang Ju did, if not more; her appearances always had something to do with money. On January 26, 2002, she donated four items for auctions: One of them was a gift from Li Ka-Shing (1928–)[176] that was auctioned off for 250,000 yuan.[177] On a different occasion, she donated two items for auction: one (Item No. 45) started with 800 yuan and sold for 40,000 yuan; one (Item No. 67) started with 2,000 yuan and sold for 30,000 yuan.[178] On a third occasion (January 30, 2005), she donated two items: one (Item No. 3) started with 2,000 yuan and sold for 188,000 yuan; one (Item No. 18) started with 800 yuan and sold for 20,000 yuan.[179] It should be noted

---

[172] http://comments.people.com.cn/bbs_new/filepool/htdoc/html/f24dd8f05ec82162 cdc7f23a479c11862a1daa8a/b483623/l_483623_1.html. Chen Liangyu has not publicized his assets even today (July 31, 2006), three years later.

[173] *Renmin ribao*, July 22, 2004, http://www.people.com.cn/GB/shizheng/14562/2656042.html.

[174] http://www.tycool.com/2005/11/10/00022.html.

[175] http://scf.88547.com/magazine/2.php3.

[176] For his bio, see http://en.wikipedia.org/wiki/Li_Ka_Shing.

[177] http://past.people.com.cn/GB/paper66/5508/566741.html.

[178] http://www.artchinanet.com/artinfo/zhuanti/charity/charity2/auction/auction.htm.

[179] http://www.alltobid.com/dongtai/yipai/6/result.htm.

that there is a huge gap between the beginning price and the final price of Yu Huiwen's donations that is greater than that of other people's donations. Item No. 3 was a marten towel of 160 cm long, a gift from Bao Peili, the daughter of Pao Yukang (1918–1991),[180] the Hong Kong tycoon. But No. 157 bidder got it for 188,000 yuan, 94 times of the starting price.[181] At the same auction, a J & C Fischer Piano was sold only for 36,000 yuan, its starting price; a Louis XIV clock was sold for 72,000 yuan, its starting price.[182] The other item donated by Yu Huiwen was a sunflower chest pin of 9 cm in diameter, sold for 20,000 yuan (25 times of its starting price of 800 yuan), while a one-tenth ounce gold necklace of Guanyin that was used by a Buddhist Master Ming Yang (1916–2002)[183] to inaugurate Buddhist statues with spirit was sold only for 28,000 yuan (15 times of its starting price of 1,800 yuan).[184] It would be very interesting to know who these buyers of Yu Huiwen's donations were and why they bought these items at such high prices. Zhou Zhengyi, for instance, reportedly donated 20 million yuan to Yu Huiwen's foundation.[185]

Finally, Jiang Zemin should have good reasons to worry about Zhou Zhengyi's case because of its implications for his two sons, especially Jiang Mianheng. Jiang Mianheng was born in 1951 in Shanghai.[186] As one of the "worker-peasant-soldier" students during the Cultural Revolution, he graduated from Fudan University in 1977. He then obtained a master's degree in 1982 from the Institute

---

[180] For his bio, see http://www.zjda.gov.cn/show_hdr.php?xname=CP0GHU0& dname=HSVVHU0&xpos=9.
[181] http://news.eastday.com/eastday/shnews/node42337/node42418/node42425/ node42850/userobject1ai835128.html.
[182] http://www.alltobid.com/dongtai/yipai/6/result.htm.
[183] http://news.fjnet.com/jjdt/jjdtnr/t20060225_21353.htm.
[184] http://www.alltobid.com/dongtai/yipai/6/result.htm.
[185] http://www.renminbao.com/rmb/articles/2006/6/11/40737.html; http://www.chinatopnews.com/gb/MainNews/SinoNews/Mainland/2006_6_12_17_44_56_156.html.
[186] http://www.gmw.cn/01gmrb/2003-10/17/30-C808160AE8CD719648256DC2000 31304.htm. Some say he was born in 1952. See Gilley, *Tiger on the brink*, p. 36; "Jiang Mianheng" http://zh.wikipedia.org/wiki/%E6%B1%9F%E7%BB%B5%E6%81%92.

of Semiconductor Research in the CAS. With his father's arrangement, Jiang Mianheng went to the United States in September 1986 for his doctoral studies.[187] Five years later, he received his doctoral degree in electrical engineering from Drexel University. He returned to Shanghai in January 1993. Jiang Mianheng has benefited as the son of Jiang Zemin both politically and financially. He was appointed as director of the Shanghai Institute of Metallurgical Research of the CAS in July 1997 and was airlifted to Beijing as vice president of the CAS in November 1999 with no apparent scientific contributions.[188]

In the meantime, Jiang Mianheng was becoming a heavyweight in business. In September 1994, the Shanghai Municipal Government established an investment firm — the Shanghai Alliance Investment Ltd[189] with a registered capital of 1.61 billion yuan.[190] Jiang Mianheng, a returnee with little capital and no financial credentials, was made its legal representative.[191] Jiang Mianheng became involved in many major business operations and became a board member of several corporations. According to his biography on the website of the CAS, Jiang Mianheng is a board member of China Netcom (CNC), Shanghai Automobile Industry Corporation, and Shanghai Airport Corporation.[192]

Although he has been listed as a board member of CNC, Jiang Mianheng actually controlled the company. According to Tian Suoning, former CEO of CNC, Jiang Mianheng is not only a board director but also the actual head of the company. As Tian confessed,

---

[187] Jiang Mianheng's application was initially rejected. Jiang Zemin intervened to resolve the problem. See Gilley, *Tiger on the Brink*, p. 160.
[188] "Jiang Mianheng" http://www.cas.ac.cn/search/member_base/details.asp?memberno=14.
[189] http://it.sohu.com/s2005/MSNportal.shtml.
[190] http://share.jrj.com.cn/cominfo/ReadDetail.asp?Folder=2005-03-22&StockCode=600591&ID=222746&type=stock.
[191] http://share.jrj.com.cn/cominfo/ReadDetail.asp?Folder=2005-03-22&StockCode=600591&ID=222746&type=stock.
[192] "Jiang Mianheng," http://www.cas.ac.cn/search/member_base/details.asp?memberno=14.

although he was CEO in name, he did not actually have real power. This is because the leader of CNC has to be someone with a post of ministerial level such as Jiang Mianheng.[193] Jiang Mianheng has also been a board member of the Shanghai Automobile Industry Corporation, one of the three largest producers of automobiles in China with the value of total sales at 127.6 billion yuan in 2002.[194] According to the report from the Shanghai Automobile Industry Corporation, Jiang Mianheng became its board member in July 1999.[195]

In November 2000, Jiang Mianheng formed a joint venture with Wang Wenyang,[196] the son of Wang Yongqing[197] (the most successful businessman in Taiwan). The joint venture, Grace Semiconductor Manufacture Co. Ltd,[198] was going to be located in the Pudong area of Shanghai, and its total investment was going to be US$6.4 billion.[199] The investment for the first phase of the project was US$1.63 billion,[200] but it seems that Wang Wenyang's contributions were minimal because his father had dismissed him from the family business in 1995 due to his involvement in extramarital affairs.[201] *Asiaweek* described Jiang Mianheng as the king of information technology in China.[202]

---

[193] http://www.enet.com.cn/article/2005/0817/A20050817444963.shtml.
[194] "Jiang Mianheng," http://www.cas.ac.cn/search/member_base/details.asp?memberno=14.
[195] http://www.businessinfo.cn/QYReport/003936/003936.HTM.
[196] http://www.zaobao.com.sg/stock/pages6/china181100.html.
[197] http://www.china.org.cn/chinese/zhuanti/jyzswyq/615746.htm.
[198] For its profile, see http://biz.yahoo.com/ic/132/132552.html; http://www.ppunion.org/job/company20020315-02.html.
[199] http://www.china.org.cn/chinese/zhuanti/jyzswyq/621138.htm.
[200] It was listed as a construction project for 2000 and for 2005 in Shanghai. See "Index of Shanghai Construction Projects (2000–2005)," http://www.zhb.gov.cn/image20010518/6275.doc.
[201] http://www.china.org.cn/chinese/zhuanti/jyzswyq/621138.htm.
[202] Allen T. Cheng, "Shanghai's 'King of I.T.': The man to know is the president's son," *Asiaweek*, Vol. 27, No. 5 (February 9, 2001), http://www.pathfinder.com/asiaweek/technology/article/0,8707,97638,00.html.

Jiang Mianheng reportedly bought another piece of land along with the Putuo District Government in the Putuo District[203] in the same fashion as Zhou Zhengyi did in the Jing'an District.[204]

The Shanghai Gang's Solution for Zhou Zhengyi's Case

Apparently, the Shanghai Gang put up a strong resistance to the investigation into Zhou Zhengyi's case. Wu Bangguo, former party secretary of Shanghai and currently chairman of the Standing Committee of the Tenth NPC as well as a standing member of the Politburo, paid a special visit to Shanghai in late May.[205] He arrived in Shanghai on May 25, 2003, one day earlier than Zhou Zhengyi's detention, and stayed there for five days. He reportedly spoke on behalf of Huang Ju and Chen Liangyu at a meeting of the Shanghai Municipal Party Committee Standing Committee. He explained that Huang and Chen both had surrendered gifts from Zhou Zhengyi and from others on behalf of Zhou Zhengyi; Huang and Chen had meetings with Zhou but only at parties.[206]

On June 6, 2003, three things occurred. First, Chen Liangyu promised to cooperate with central organizations on the investigation of Zhou Zhengyi's case. Second, Attorney Zheng Enchong was detained. Third, Jiang Zemin reappeared in public as CMC chairman along with Hu Jintao as CMC vice chairman.[207] Hu just came back

---

[203] For its location, see the map of Shanghai, http://www.9654.com/m/shanghai.htm.
[204] http://www.renminbao.com/rmb/articles/2003/8/26/27682.html. There is no official confirmation of this report. But it was common in districts of Shanghai for developers to obtain land without land transfer fees in the name of old area transformation and then to drive residents out of their homes. For a case in the Xuhui District of Shanghai in which the developer set fire on a building and killed an old couple sleeping in the building, see Dai Wei and Tian Qilin, "Shanghai Zonghuobiqian An Tuxian Chaiqian Hemu" ["The dark side of demolition: a case of forcing residents out by setting fire on the building in Shanghai"], *Caijing*, No. 142 (September 19, 2005), pp. 136, 137.
[205] http://past.people.com.cn/GB/shizheng/252/9544/9545/20030530/1004727.html.
[206] http://www.renminbao.com/rmb/articles/2003/7/4/26993.html.
[207] *Renmin ribao*, June 7, 2003, p. 1.

from an 11-day (May 26–June 5, 2003) visit abroad a day earlier.[208] Apparently, that was the Shanghai Gang's first series of defensive actions. While Chen appeared to be cooperative, the Shanghai Gang — by having Zheng Enchong detained — attempted to minimize the impact of Zhou Zhengyi's involvement in development projects in order to eliminate the implications of his case for Shanghai Gang members and their relatives. Jiang, on the other hand, confronted Hu Jintao with his symbolic superiority as CMC chairman, hoping to retain some initiative over the cases of Zhou Zhengyi and Liu Jinbao.[209]

Jiang Zemin reportedly wrote a letter to the Politburo on these cases.[210] He asked the central leadership to make three distinctions: a distinction between mistakes in work and corruption with regard to cases of Liu Jinbao, Zhou Zhengyi, Wang Xuebing, and others; a distinction between overall performance and minor aspects with regard to the work of the Shanghai Municipal Party Committee; and a distinction between main achievements and small problems with regard to Huang Ju and Chen Liangyu. He urged the central leadership not to pursue Huang and Chen because the Party Center had already approved their performance and they had already admitted their mistakes. He warned that the Party might lose control over the political situation in China once Shanghai became chaotic as a result of pursuing the responsibilities of Huang and Chen.[211] Jiang even reportedly suggested that Huang Ju be in charge of the investigations.[212]

Probably in response to Jiang's suggestions, Chen Liangyu reportedly indicated that Zhou Zhengyi's case had nothing to do with the Shanghai municipal leadership, had nothing to do with the

---

[208] http://www.xinhuanet.com/world/hjtcfehm.htm.

[209] As Zong Hairen correctly observed, this was also a response to Hu Jintao's talk on military modernization at the Politburo Study Session of May 23, 2003. See his book, *Aimei de Quanli Jiaohuan*, p. 260.

[210] Luo Bing, "Jiang yu bao Huang Ju Chen Liangyu guoguan" ["Jiang Zemin was trying to protect Huang Ju and Chen Liangyu"], *Cheng Ming*, No. 309 (July 2003), pp. 12–14.

[211] *Ibid.*

[212] http://www.renminbao.com/rmb/articles/2003/8/8/27423.html.

leadership of Shanghai districts, and had nothing to do with the Shanghai financial system.[213] According to him, Zhou's case was a case of financial fraud.[214]

It seems that Hu Jintao made compromises and the Shanghai Gang got away with these cases. First, the Shanghai No. 2 Intermediate People's Court sentenced Zheng Enchong to three years on charges of "illegally providing state secrets to entities outside China" on October 18, 2003.[215] Zheng appealed the case, but the Shanghai High People's Court rejected his appeal and reaffirmed the original sentence on December 18, 2003. Second, Zhou Zhengyi was not arrested until September 5, 2003,[216] and was sentenced by the Shanghai No. 1 Intermediate People's Court to three years for manipulating stock prices and falsifying registered capital reports.[217] There was no mention of his illicit real estate development projects in Shanghai and his huge loans from the Bank of China (Hong Kong).[218] As a result, Huang Ju continued to be a standing member of the Politburo and vice premier of the State Council; Chen Liangyu stayed on as party secretary of Shanghai and a Politburo member. Moreover, none of the relatives of the Shanghai Gang members were arrested for corruption related to Zhou Zhengyi and Liu Jinbao.

Finally, Jiang Mianheng even gained more power and prominence. In October 2003 when the first manned spaceship (Shenzhou V) was successfully launched and returned, Jiang Mianheng was interviewed as deputy general commander of the space project! He told the reporter that he had never studied manned spaceship earlier, but

---

[213] http://www.renminbao.com/rmb/articles/2003/8/8/27423.html.
[214] http://www.renminbao.com/rmb/articles/2003/8/8/27423.html.
[215] http://www.people.com.cn/GB/shehui/1061/2253396.html. He was released on 5 June 2006.
[216] http://news.xinhuanet.com/newscenter/2004-06/01/content_1502317.htm.
[217] Cao Haili, "Zhou Zhengyi liangxiang zuocheng" ["Zhou Zhengyi was sentenced for two charges"], *Caijing*, No. 109 (June 5, 2004), p. 76; http://news.xinhuanet.com/legal/2004-06/01/content_1502178.htm.
[218] Zhou Zhengyi was released on May 26, 2006, but he still is on the wanted list by the Independent Commission Against Corruption of Hong Kong on charges of conspiracy to defraud. See http://www.icac.org.hk/eng/0/1/2/4/15349.html.

President Lu Yongxiang and Vice President Yan Yixun of the CAS somehow entrusted him with this important task.[219] Instead of being charged as a corrupted official, Jiang Mianheng appeared as one of national heroes.

In contrast to Lai Changxing's case in Fujian in which 160 government officials were involved,[220] no government officials and their relatives from Shanghai were investigated in connection to the cases of Zhou Zhengyi and Liu Jinbao in Shanghai.

CONCLUDING REMARKS

It is tempting to look at Chinese elite politics from the perspective of "winner-takes-all" game, but it is more accurate to examine the political dynamics of elites in the aftermath of the Sixteenth Party Congress from the perspective of power balancing.

In terms of power competition at the meetings of the Tenth NPC and Tenth CNPPCC, the net outcome was a balance of power between Jiang's clique and Hu–Wen team. On the one hand, Jiang Zemin maneuvered again in March 2003 to stay on as chairman of the state Central Military Commission and his cronies acquired high offices in the NPC, the State Council, and the CNPPCC. Jia Qinglin became chairman of the CNPPCC; Zeng Qinghong, vice president of the PRC; Wu Bangguo, chairman of the NPC Standing Committee; Huang Ju and Zeng Peiyan, vice premiers; and Hua Jianmin and Chen Zhili, state councilors. Because of their factional orientations and lack of appropriate qualifications, Jiang and some of his cronies were embarrassed with low approval rates.

On the other hand, Hu Jintao and his allies also scored substantial gains at these meetings. Hu Jintao was elected president of the PRC; Wen Jiabao, premier; Wang Zhouguo, vice chairman of the NPC Standing Committee; and Liu Yandong, vice chairman of the

---

[219] http://www.cyyx.com/2005–9/200593165450.htm.
[220] http://past.people.com.cn/GB/shehui/212/2304/3332/20011025/590472.html. For a detailed report, see Hai Yun, *Xiamen Yuanhua Da'an* [*The case of "Yuanhua" of Xianmen*] (Beijing: Zhongguo Haiguan Chubanshe, 2001).

CNPPCC. Some of former CYL cadres occupied ministerial positions; many provincial leaders with CYL backgrounds were also promoted in the meantime.

During the crisis of SARS, Hu Jintao exercised his powers as general secretary of the Party and president of the PRC. He dismissed Health Minister Zhang Wenkang and Beijing Mayor Meng Xuenong for their mishandling of the epidemic and gained tremendous popularity among the Chinese people. Jiang Zemin and his cronies suffered reputation damage because of their derelictions of duty. Jiang was hiding in Shanghai, Huang Ju vanished, and Zeng Qinghong was not enthusiastic about combating the SARS. Hu and his allies also threatened to expose the corruption of the Shanghai Gang members by having detained the richest man of Shanghai (Zhou Zhengyi) and a former Shanghai banker (Liu Jinbao).

Taking advantage of the submarine accident in which 70 officers and sailors aboard died, Jiang demonstrated his symbolic superiority over Hu in May 2003. He played the same tactic again in June 2003 to embolden his Shanghai protégés. Shanghai Gang's solution to Zhou Zhengyi's case was to ask one of the suspects (Huang Ju) to be in charge of the case and to punish the lawyer (Zheng Enchong) who exposed their wrongdoings. In the end, the lawyer and the defendant were both sentenced to three years in jail; none of Shanghai Gang members, especially Huang Ju and Chen Liangyu and their relatives such as Chen Liangjun, Yu Huiwen, and Jiang Mianheng, had to pay any price for their wrongdoings.

Chapter 6

Ideological Institutionalization and Politics of Development

Along with political institutionalization came ideological institutionalization. Ideology was no longer a personal trademark but became an asset of the Party. While the "Three Represents" was enshrined in the CCP Constitution as a guiding principle along with Marxism–Leninism, Mao Zedong Thought, and Deng Xiaoping Theory, Hu Jintao — instead of Jiang Zemin — became its only legitimate interpreter. Hu Jintao further introduced and then promoted his own approach to development — the scientific concept of development. Hu and his allies came into direct conflict with the Shanghai Gang over the issue of economic overheating and claimed a political victory in the end.

IDEOLOGICAL INSTITUTIONALIZATION

"New Three People's Principles"

When Hu Jintao was elected general secretary of the CCP in November 2002, it appeared that Hu would live in the shadow of Jiang Zemin for at least five years. Since Jiang Zemin's "Three Represents" had just been written into the CCP Constitution as the guideline for the Party, it seemed unlikely for Hu Jintao to put forth any new ideology. Nonetheless, Hu introduced some of his new ideas in early December 2002, three weeks after the Sixteenth Party Congress.

During his visit to Xibaipo in Hebei Province (one of the holy places of the CCP where Mao Zedong and his colleagues prepared for overthrowing Jiang Jieshi's government and for establishing a new China) during December 5–6, 2002, along with Zeng Qinghong and other members of the Sixteenth Secretariat, Hu Jintao introduced three new themes.[1] Borrowing from Mao Zedong, Hu reminded CCP leaders of the "two imperatives": it is imperative to maintain the work style of humility and caution and to avoid being supercilious and impatient; it is imperative to maintain the tradition of plain living and hard struggle.[2] He argued that a nation without the tradition of plain living and hard struggle would have difficulties being independent and self-strengthening; a country without the spirit of plain living and hard struggle would have troubles in making progress; and a political party without the spirit of plain living and hard struggle would not be able to thrive. Hu also put forth a new theme on governance, "governing the country for the people" (*zhizheng weimin*). Using Mao Zedong's slogan of "serving the people wholeheartedly," Hu indicated that the mission of the CCP was to protect the interests of the masses, bring forth benefits for the masses, and develop the interests of the masses. Finally, Hu introduced new three people's principles: Power should be used for the people, sentiment should be linked to the people, and benefits should be generated for the people (*quan wei min suo yong, qing wei min suo ji, li wei min suo mou*).

Coated in the discourse of the Sixteenth Party Congress and the standard CCP jargons, Hu's new ideas formed a contrast with Jiang

---

[1] *Renmin ribao*, December 8, 2002, p. 1. See also http://www.people.com.cn/GB/shizheng/16/20021207/883325.html.

[2] It should be noted that the "two imperatives" had been a standard CCP jargon. Jiang Zemin also mentioned the "two imperatives" during his visit to Xibaipo on September 21, 1991. See http://past.people.com.cn/GB/shizheng/252/5531/5532/5538/20010612/487278.html.

Zemin's themes in the recent past. Since February 2000 when he introduced the "Three Represents," Jiang Zemin began an ideological shift. In his controversial speech on July 1, 2001, Jiang proposed to recruit capitalists to the CCP.[3] As China's social classes had changed since the beginning of economic reforms, Jiang argued that the CCP should recruit its members not only from working classes such as workers, peasants, soldiers, and intellectuals but also from other social classes such as high-tech entrepreneurs and technicians, white collar workers employed in foreign enterprises in China, and private entrepreneurs.

Hu's new ideas did not particularly favor those privileged social elites. Instead of visiting private enterprises in a coastal region, Hu Jintao visited one of the poorest regions in North China — Inner Mongolia — in early January 2003.[4] During his four-day visit (January 2–5, 2003), Hu showed his concerns for those disadvantaged social groups (*ruoshi qunti*). He visited a family with difficulties due to natural disasters on January 4, 2003, and urged local leaders to be concerned with life and production of ordinary people. He also visited a job market in Tongliao, Inner Mongolia, and discussed with local cadres and residents on the reemployment of laid-off workers and the provision of minimum life guarantees for the poorest families. Finally, Hu also demonstrated his interest in the economic development of less developed regions in China. After his visit to several enterprises in Inner Mongolia, Hu pointed out that less developed regions in China should discover a new path of development in accordance with their own conditions.

Hu's July 1 Speech

The most misunderstood case of elite politics since the Sixteenth Party Congress is the speech made by Hu Jintao on July 1, 2003. Before that day, many expected that Hu would announce his plan to promote intra-Party democracy on the occasion of the 82nd

---

[3] http://past.people.com.cn/GB/shizheng/252/5531/5534/20010702/501591.html.
[4] http://www.people.com.cn/GB/shizheng/16/20030105/901620.html.

anniversary of the founding of the CCP. The speculation had been mostly based on an article published in *Qiushi* (*Seeking the Truth*) on June 16, 2003, by Zhen Xiaoying, vice president and professor of the Central Academy of Socialism, and Li Qinghua, a doctoral student at the Central Party School. In their article, "Using Intra-Party Democracy to Promote People's Democracy," the two authors argued that democratic development is essential for building China as a moderately well-off society, because without socialist political civilization there would be no well-off society and without democracy there would be no socialist political civilization.[5] In order to promote people's democracy, they further argued, it is imperative to develop intra-Party democracy. The speculation was that Hu had used these authors to alert the media to the forthcoming elaboration of a plan to implement intra-Party democracy.

When addressing the opening session of a theoretical symposium on studying and implementing the "Three Represents" on July 1, 2003, however, Hu did not reveal his plan for intra-Party democracy. Instead, Hu indicated the significance of the new campaign to study and implement the important idea of the "Three Represents," highlighted the theoretical contributions of the "Three Represents" to Marxism, and elaborated his understandings of the "Three Represents." Since the "Three Represents" has been closely identified with Jiang Zemin, Hu's speech has been regarded either as a concession to Jiang or as an indication of Jiang's persistent power. According to Joseph Fewsmith's analysis: "Although the evidence suggests that Hu Jintao has been trying to inject new themes and approaches to governance, he remains willing to acknowledge the role of Jiang as elder statesman and refrains from challenging him directly."[6]

Yet some aspects of Hu's speech have significant implications for the role of ideology in CCP politics. First, despite the expectations

---

[5] Zhen Xiaoying and Li Qinghua, "Yidangneiminzhu Tuijin Renminminzhu" ("Using intra-party democracy to promote people's democracy"), *Qiushi*, No. 361 (June 16, 2003), http://www.qsjournal.com.cn/qs/20030616/GB/qs^361^0^10.htm.

[6] Joseph Fewsmith, "Studying the Three Represents," *China Leadership Monitor*, No. 8 (Fall 2003). http://www.chinaleadershipmonitor.org/20034/jf.html.

concerning intra-Party democracy, Hu's speech was appropriate for the occasion — i.e., a symposium on the "Three Represents," not one on intra-Party democracy. It would have been inappropriate for him to use the occasion to address the issue of intra-Party democracy.

Second, Hu elevated the theory of the "Three Represents" not because it was Jiang's theory but because it was a theory of the Party. Throughout the entire text, Hu mentioned Jiang's name four times. Hu first mentioned Jiang in his explanation of the origin of the "Three Represents." "In February 2000," he said, "Comrade Jiang Zemin clearly proposed the request of the 'Three Represents'."[7] Key here is the use of the word "request" (*yaoqiu*) rather than "important thought" (*zhongyao sixiang*), as Jiang would have preferred. Hu then mentioned Jiang in his description of the evolution of the "Three Represents." According to Hu, the important idea of the "Three Represents" had gone through three stages: The first stage was from February 2000 to June 2001, the second from July 2001 to November 2002, and the third from the Sixteenth Party Congress onwards. It was at the beginning of the second stage, Hu said, that Comrade Jiang Zemin delivered an important speech at the 80th anniversary of the founding of the CCP "on behalf of the Party Center," systematically elaborating on the scientific elements and basic content of the "Three Represents." Comrade Jiang, as Hu made it very clear, was giving the speech not on behalf of Jiang himself, but on behalf of the Party; Jiang was speaking on behalf of the Party because he was general secretary of the Party at the time. Hu mentioned Jiang's name the third time when he was explaining the historical background of the "Three Represents" by referring Jiang as an important representative of modern Chinese Communists. Here Hu attributed the "Three Represents" to the collective wisdom of the whole Party. Finally, Hu quoted Jiang on the importance of developing Marxism through practice. Here, Hu did pay personal respect to Jiang as elder statesman, but Jiang's remarks in the quote were not particularly thought provoking or refreshing.

---

[7] *Renminwang*, July 2, 2003, http://www.people.com.cn/GB/shizheng/1024/1946147.html.

Of the above, Hu's second reference to Jiang is particularly noteworthy. From the statement that Jiang introduced the important idea of the "Three Represents" on behalf of the Party as general secretary, one may infer that Jiang was no longer eligible to speak on behalf of the Party because Jiang was no longer general secretary. This is politically significant. Before the convening of the Sixteenth Party Congress, many felt that Jiang would remain extremely powerful if his theory of the "Three Represents" were to be written into the CCP Constitution. This is because, as the author of the theory, Jiang would become a rule-maker instead of simply a decision-maker, making him more powerful than all decision-makers combined.[8] He would be able to judge either decisions made by the Politburo Standing Committee as a collective or decisions made by General Secretary Hu Jintao as an individual, and determine whether these decisions deviated from the theory. By making this second reference to Jiang, Hu in fact declared that Jiang's role as a rule-maker had long ended at the Sixteenth Party Congress and that it was now his own turn as general secretary to speak on behalf of the Party. In other words, Hu deprived Jiang of the right to interpret the theory of the "Three Represents" and asserted his own right as the sole legitimate interpreter of the theory. Given the salience of ideology in Chinese politics, this statement was a significant, calculated political move.

Finally, Hu provided his own interpretation of the important idea of the "Three Represents." The essence of the "Three Represents," according to Hu, was building the Party in the public interest and governing the country for the people (*lidang weigong zhizheng weimin*).[9] The fundamental interests of the broad masses of the Chinese people should be both the starting point and the

---

[8] For an insightful analysis of this aspect, see Guoguang Wu, "From the July 1 speech to the Sixteenth Party Congress: ideology, party construction, and leadership transition," in David M. Finkelstein and Maryanne Kivlehan (eds), *China's Leadership in the Twenty-first Century: The Rise of the Fourth Generation* (Armonk, NY: M.E. Sharpe, 2003), pp. 167–185.

[9] *Renminwang*, July 2, 2003, http://www.people.com.cn/GB/shizheng/1024/1946147.html.

ultimate goal. "For a Marxist ruling party," Hu said, "it always is of the greatest importance to insist on building the Party for the public and governing the country for the people; to realize, maintain, and develop the fundamental interests of the broad masses of the people; and to bring the initiative of the people into full play in order to develop advanced productive forces and an advanced culture."[10] He further explained how to implement this important principle, using the fight against severe acute respiratory syndrome (SARS) as an example.

Hu's speech was a fatal blow to Jiang as the author of the "Three Represents." There is no evidence that Jiang ever put forward any new interpretation of the "Three Represents" after the Sixteenth Party Congress. He no longer had the legitimacy to make any remarks regarding the theory of the "Three Represents" on behalf of the Party because he was no longer general secretary of the Party.

"SCIENTIFIC CONCEPT OF DEVELOPMENT"

Origins of the "Scientific Concept of Development"

While the CCP was studying the "Three Represents," Hu Jintao was also beginning to develop a new thinking of his own: scientific concept of development. During his visit to Inner Mongolia in January 2003, Hu Jintao began to articulate a new approach to development. He said,

> We must continuously explore a new path of development for accelerating development in less developed regions that is appropriate for the conditions of the regions. We should promote institutional innovations and scientific and technological innovations and be prepared for new perspectives. Less developed regions should proceed from the realities of their localities, develop their advantages and avoid their disadvantages, find suitable measures to their local conditions, and scientifically design their regional development strategies with particular emphases and necessary omissions. They need to actively nurture and develop advantageous industries and products with

---

[10] *Ibid.*

both market competitiveness and regional characteristics, nurturing and expanding an economy with regional characteristics. These regions need to pay attention to sustainable development, making a great effort to preserve and construct the ecological environment. They need to properly develop and economically utilize various natural resources and to realize the goal of perpetual use of resources and a positive cycle of the natural ecological environmental system. These regions need to deepen reforms in rural areas, making efforts to form a positive mechanism for building modern agriculture, developing rural economy, and increasing peasants' income. Relevant central agencies and the developed regions should provide further support for the development of less development regions, promoting a coordinated economic development of different regions.[11]

In this approach, Hu Jintao introduced several new concepts. First, he used the concept of "science" (*kexue*) and urged less developed regions to design their development strategies scientifically. Science here does not refer to either natural sciences or social sciences; it refers to a way of thinking. In terms of economic development, a scientific approach is one in which a strategy should correspond to the reality. More specifically, leaders of these regions need to pay particular attention to their local conditions and develop their economies accordingly. Second, he advocated sustainable development. Instead of single-mindedly focusing on quantitative growth, local leaders should also pay attention to environmental protection and conservation of natural resources. Third, Hu also encouraged a coordinated development of different regions.

Hu Jintao further developed his approach to development during his visit to Guangdong in April 2003. He indicated that the Eastern Region including Guangdong was at a new starting point of development and was faced with new opportunities, new challenges, and new tasks; that Guangdong should recognize its historical mission of accelerating development, taking a lead in development, and realizing a coordinated development; that Guangdong should actively blaze a new path of development and

---

[11] http://www.people.com.cn/GB/shizheng/16/20030105/901620.html.

create new advantages through new thinking, deepen economic reforms and create new advantages through institutional innovations, further develop externally oriented economy and create new advantages through expanding opening to the outside world, implement the strategy of national revival through science and technology and education and the strategy of human talents and create new advantages through scientific innovation and talent utilization, and insist on a comprehensive outlook on development and create new advantages through promoting coordinated development of material civilization, political civilization, and spiritual civilization.[12]

At the National Conference on Prevention and Treatment of SARS on July 28, 2003,[13] Hu further elaborated his approach to development. He said,

> When we say that development is our party's top priority in our country's revitalization, we are not referring only to economic growth but also to taking economic construction as our central task and realizing comprehensive social development based on economic growth. We should continue to insist on a development perspective of comprehensive development, coordinated development, and sustainable development; continue to actively promote coordinated development of socialist material civilization, political civilization, and spiritual civilization; promote comprehensive development of human beings on the basis of economic and social development; and promote harmony between human beings and their environment.[14]

---

[12] *Renmin ribao*, April 16, 2003, p. 1. See also http://www.people.com.cn/GB/shizheng/16/20030415/972637.html.

[13] In a very widely circulated version, the date of Hu's speech is mistaken to be in June. But it is actually July 28, 2003. See http://news.xinhuanet.com/politics/2005-10/17/content_3623592.htm.

[14] Hu Jintao, "Talk at the National Conference on the Prevention and Treatment of SARS," July 28, 2003, *Shiliuda Yilai Zhongyao Wenxian Xuanbian* [*Important materials since the Sixteenth Party Congress*] (Beijing: Zhongyang Wenxian Chubanshe, 2005), pp. 387–405. It should be noted that Chang Xiuze, professor at the Economic Research Institute under the National Development and Economic Commission, also discussed a new approach to development along similar lines. See http://past.people.com.cn/GB/shehui/212/10548/10603/20030509/987692.html.

Hu further pointed that in the process of development, the CCP leaders should not only pay attention to economic development indicators, but also pay attention to human development indicators, resource preservation indicators, and environmental protection indicators; the Chinese government would not only increase investment for economic growth but also increase investment for social development as well as for resource preservation and environmental protection.[15]

The first person who used the term scientific concept of development (*kexue fazhanguan*)[16] was Liu Fuyuan,[17] vice president of the School of Macro-economic Studies under the State Commission of Development and Reform. In an article published on April 21, 2003, on the speed of economic growth in China, entitled "The prelude to a new phase of economic development in China has begun, it is very normal to have ten-percent growth on a yearly basis,"[18] Liu used the phrase when he discussed the problems with economic development in central regions. "The critical point in the current strategic adjustment of economic structure lies in central regions"; he commented, "and central regions have all necessary conditions, except for good cadres who can correctly implement the spirit of central policies and have a scientific concept of development."[19]

Hu Jintao first publicly used this concept during his visit to Jiangxi in late August and early September 2003. He urged local leaders of all levels to be fully aware of the significance of the proposition that development is the first and foremost task for the Party in its efforts to revive the country, and asked them to firmly establish a scientific concept of development that emphasizes on coordinated development, comprehensive development, and sustainable development. He explained this new concept with five combinations: to combine restructuring with creating new points of

---

[15] *Ibid.*, p. 397.
[16] I searched the people.com with this phrase on January 18, 2006, and got 27,052 hits for the period of April 2, 2002, and January 17, 2006.
[17] For his biography, see http://www.macrochina.com.cn/prize/brt/liufuyuan.shtml.
[18] http://past.people.com.cn/GB/jinji/222/10659/10661/20030421/976796.html.
[19] http://past.people.com.cn/GB/jinji/222/10659/10661/20030421/976796.html.

growth, combine urban development with rural development, combine the role of science and technology with the advantages of human resources, combine economic growth with resource conservation and environmental protection, and combine external opening with internal opening.[20]

During his visit to Hunan in early October 2003, Hu Jintao reaffirmed the scientific concept of development. He indicated that people of the central region should earnestly develop a sense of responsibility and urgency to accelerate development, firmly establish and resolutely implement the scientific concept of development, actively explore new ways of development that are appropriate to their local conditions, constantly generate new sources of development through reforms, and strive to promote economic and social development.[21] Noticeably, Hu moved from asking local leaders to "firmly establish" to urging them to "resolutely implement" the scientific concept of development.

Hu had already articulated a new guiding principle of development, and the forthcoming Third Plenum of the Sixteenth Central Committee would be a forum for him to introduce this principle.

Third Plenum

The Third Plenum of the Sixteenth Central Committee was held in Beijing during October 11–14, 2003. Since the end of the Cultural Revolution in the late 1970s, the Third Plenum of a central committee had become a forum for substantial policy-making. This is because the First Plenum is usually dedicated to the election of the Party's top leadership such as the Politburo, the Secretariat, and the Central Military Commission; the Second Plenum often decides who would be nominated for top leadership in the National People's Congress, the Chinese National People's Political Consultative Conference, and the State Council. The Third Plenum of the

---

[20] *Renmin ribao*, September 3, 2003, p. 1. See also http://www.people.com.cn/GB/shizheng/1024/2067282.html.
[21] http://www.people.com.cn/GB/paper464/10312/941682.html.

Eleventh Central Committee in December 1978 was a historical landmark, ushering a new era of economic reforms in China;[22] the Third Plenum of the Twelfth Central Committee in October 1984 decided to begin comprehensive reforms with urban areas as a focus;[23] the Third Plenum of the Thirteenth Central Committee in September 1988 passed a proposal on price and wage reforms;[24] the Third Plenum of the Fourteenth Central Committee in November 1993 adopted a resolution to establish socialist market economy in China;[25] and the Third Plenum of the Fifteenth Central Committee in October 1998 decided to tackle rural issues.[26] Now the Third Plenum of the Sixteenth Central Committee was supposed to define the policy orientation of the new leadership.

In the aftermath of the Sixteenth Party Congress, some felt that Jiang Zemin would continue to be consulted by the new leadership because Hu promised to "seek instruction and listen to the views" of Jiang Zemin in his acceptance speech.[27] Although Hu might have voiced something like that out of modesty, he probably made no promise to consult Jiang. Even less likely is that "the Party congress

---

[22] http://www.people.com.cn/GB/shizheng/252/5089/5103/5205/20010428/455037.html.

[23] http://www.people.com.cn/GB/shizheng/252/5089/5104/5198/20010429/455410.html.

[24] http://www.people.com.cn/GB/shizheng/252/5089/5105/5186/20010430/456450.html.

[25] This is a resolution on implementation. The decision to establish a market economy had been made at the Fourteenth National Party Congress in October 1992. For information on the Third Plenum, see http://www.people.com.cn/GB/shizheng/252/5089/5106/5179/20010430/456694.html.

[26] http://www.people.com.cn/GB/shizheng/252/5089/5093/5174/20010430/456866.html.

[27] See Joseph Fewsmith, "The Sixteenth National Party Congress: the succession that didn't happen," *China Quarterly*, No. 173 (March 2003), p. 14, where he quoted from Erik Eckholm, "China's new leader promises not to sever tether to Jiang," *The New York Times*, November 21, 2002, p. A1. Lowell Dittmer also indicated that Hu Jintao promised "in (leaked) internal leadership briefings that Jiang would preview all 'important' Politburo decisions," but did not provide his source of information. See Lowell Dittmer, "The 16th Party congress as a Chinese developmental process," *China Quarterly*, No. 176 (December 2003), p. 915.

made a secret resolution to consult Jiang, as [the congress] did in 1987 when it promised to consult a retiring Deng."[28] There is no evidence that Hu has ever officially consulted Jiang on anything of significance since the Sixteen Party Congress.

As later revealed, Jiang was not part of the decision-making process before, during, or after the Third Plenum. The most important decision made at the Plenum was entitled "Decision of the CCP Central Committee on Several Issues Related to Perfecting the Socialist Market Economic System." According to a report in the *People's Daily*, the decision was drafted under the direct leadership of the Politburo Standing Committee "from the beginning to the end."[29] General Secretary Hu Jintao gave instructions in regard to the general outline, basic content, and important points. Premier Wen Jiabao was entrusted by the Politburo Standing Committee to organize a drafting group on April 18, 2003, and to serve as its leader. General Secretary Hu Jintao reviewed each draft "word by word and sentence by sentence,"[30] and made many suggestions and important corrections. Most importantly, as the report revealed, "General Secretary Hu Jintao's important thought — firmly establishing the scientific concept of development — became an important guiding principle" for drafting the Decision.[31] Evidently, the Third Plenum of the Sixteenth Central Committee not only further confirmed Hu's status as the leader of the Party but also established his approach to development as the guiding principle of the Party. To reinforce the significance of the scientific concept of development, Hu Jintao delivered a speech on the subject at the Second Meeting of the Third Plenum of the Sixteenth Central Committee on October 14, 2003, and put a particular emphasis on establishing and implementing the scientific concept of development.[32]

---

[28] Fewsmith, "The Sixteenth National Party Congress," p. 14.

[29] Zhang Chengbin and Zhao Cheng, "Chuixiang jingji tizhi gaige de xinhaojiao" ["Blow the new horn of the economic system reform"], *Renminwang*, November 11, 2003, http://www.people.com.cn/GB/paper464/10586/963112.html.

[30] *Ibid.*

[31] *Ibid.*

[32] Hu Jintao, "Shuli he Luoshi Kexuefazhanguan" ["Establish and implement the scientific outlook on development"] October 14, 2003, in *Shiliuda Yilai Zhongyao*

Apparently, there was some resistance within the Party's top leadership. When the guiding principle was written into the Decision, the adjective — "scientific" — somehow was omitted from the "scientific concept of development."[33] Moreover, the *People's Daily*'s editorial on the Third Plenum published on October 14, 2003, did not mention the scientific concept of development at all.[34] In contrast, the editorial mentioned the "Three Represents" five times. According to the editorial, the Third Plenum was held during a high tide of studying and implementing the important thought of the "Three Represents"; the Party Center had adhered to the guidance of Deng Xiaoping Theory and the important thought of the "Three Represents"; the new leadership would consistently hold high the great banner of the important thought of the "Three Represents"; the basic points of the Decision had reflected the requirements of the important thought of the "Three Represents"; and the Sixteenth Central Committee of the CCP would continue to hold high the great banner of Deng Xiaoping Theory and the important thought of the "Three Represents" in order to have new victories in reform and opening and socialist modernization construction.[35] Finally, the editorial mentioned Jiang Zemin once, attempting to highlight his political existence.[36]

Promoting the Scientific Concept of Development

Some politically acute local leaders responded to Hu's call for a scientific concept of development as soon as Hu Jintao used the

---

Wenxian Xuanbian [*Important Materials Since the Sixteenth Party Congress*] (Beijing: Zhongyang Wenxian Chubanshe, 2005), pp. 483, 484.

[33] http://www.people.com.cn/GB/shizheng/1024/2145119.html.

[34] http://www.people.com.cn/GB/guandian/1033/2133959.html. For a contrast, see another editorial published on November 5, 2003, entitled "Shuli he Luoshi Kexuefazhanguan" ["Establishing and implementing the scientific concept of development"], http://www.people.com.cn/GB/guandian/1033/2170165.html.

[35] http://www.people.com.cn/GB/guandian/1033/2133959.html.

[36] It is very likely that Zeng Qinghong was one of those who resisted the emergence of Hu Jintao as an ideological leader, as will be discussed in detail in the next section.

phrase in his visit to Jiangxi. At a seminar on economic development on September 15, 2003, both Deputy Secretary Zhou Guofu and Party Secretary Xi Jinping of Zhejiang Province used the phrase in their talks: Zhou used the full version of the scientific concept of development that emphasizes on coordinated development, comprehensive development, and sustainable development; Xi used the abbreviated version of the scientific concept of development.[37] Half a month later, during his visit to Hangzhou, the capital of Zhejiang Province, on September 27, 2003, Xi Jinping discovered an opportunity to use the full version.[38]

Other local leaders followed suit in the aftermath of the Third Plenum. Zhang Dejiang, party secretary of Guangdong and Politburo member, urged Guangdong officials to continuously explore new paths of comprehensive development, coordinated development, and sustainable development in accordance with General Secretary Hu Jintao's requirement to establish and implement the scientific concept of development.[39] Chen Liangyu, party secretary of Shanghai and Politburo member, also expressed his support for the scientific concept of development, and Han Zheng, mayor of Shanghai, indicated his willingness to establish and implement the scientific concept of development.[40] Guo Jinlong, party secretary of Tibet, and Qiangba Puncog, deputy party secretary and chairman of the Tibetan Autonomous Regional Government, both expressed their endorsement of the scientific concept of development.[41] Tian Chengping, party secretary of Shanxi Province and a graduate of Qinghua University, also pledged to use the scientific concept of development to guide economic restructuring and all kinds of work in Shanxi.[42] Zhang Xingxiang, deputy party secretary

---

[37] http://www.people.com.cn/GB/paper464/10284/939931.html. Xi Jinping used the scientific concept of development again during his visit to Ningbo in late September 2003. See http://unn.people.com.cn/GB/14803/21818/2108714.html.
[38] http://unn.people.com.cn/GB/14803/21818/2113815.html.
[39] http://www.people.com.cn/GB/shizheng/14562/2147570.html.
[40] http://unn.people.com.cn/GB/14794/21778/2148284.html.
[41] http://unn.people.com.cn/GB/14799/21813/2183998.html.
[42] http://www.people.com.cn/GB/shizheng/14562/2191053.html.

of Liaoning Province and party secretary of Shenyang, published an article in the *People's Daily*, explaining the special significance of the scientific concept of development for the revival of the Northeast region of China.[43]

In the meantime, Politburo standing members such as Li Changchun (October 20–23, 2003, in Henan),[44] Jia Qinglin (October 21–27, 2003, in Guizhou;[45] December 26–31, 2003, in Inner Mongolia[46]), Wen Jiabao (October 31, 2003, in Beijing),[47] Wu Bangguo (November 14–19, 2003, in Anhui),[48] and Huang Ju (December11–13, 2003, in Tianjin)[49] as well as other Politburo members such as Zeng Peiyan (November 26, 2003,[50] and December 2, 2003, in Beijing[51]) and He Guoqiang (November 30, 2003, in Beijing)[52] also voiced their endorsement of this particular expression on various occasions.

Noticeably, Zeng Qinghong, standing member of the Politburo and vice president of the PRC, was silent about the guiding principle in the two months following the Third Plenum. During his visit to Liaoning in October 2003, Zeng urged the local leaders to pay particular attention to the study and implementation of the "Three Represents" and carry forward the spirit of Lei Feng in the revival of the old industrial region.[53] Zeng began to pay lip service to the scientific concept of development during his visit to Sichuan in December 2003.[54]

---

[43] http://www.people.com.cn/GB/jingji/2192228.html.
[44] http://www.people.com.cn/GB/shizheng/1024/2151394.html.
[45] http://www.people.com.cn/GB/shizheng/1024/2157149.html.
[46] http://www.people.com.cn/GB/shizheng/2275192.html.
[47] http://www.people.com.cn/GB/shizheng/1024/2163290.html.
[48] http://www.people.com.cn/GB/shizheng/1024/2198768.html.
[49] http://www.people.com.cn/GB/shizheng/2244349.html.
[50] http://www.people.com.cn/GB/keji/1059/2212314.html.
[51] http://www.people.com.cn/GB/shizheng/1026/2223590.html.
[52] http://www.people.com.cn/GB/shizheng/1024/2219447.html.
[53] http://www.people.com.cn/GB/shizheng/1024/2151534.html. For a detailed report of Zeng's visit, see http://unn.people.com.cn/GB/14783/21752/2154933.html.
[54] http://www.people.com.cn/GB/shizheng/1024/2249264.html.

Ideological Institutionalization and Politics of Development 271

Most interestingly, nevertheless, Zeng made a speech on behalf of Hu Jintao at the opening ceremony of a special class on establishing and implementing the scientific concept of development organized for chief provincial and ministerial leaders at the Central Party School on February 16, 2004. Vice Premier Huang Ju attended the opening ceremony, and Vice Premier Zeng Peiyan made a special report on how to establish and implement the scientific concept of development. A number of Politburo members and state leaders (Wang Lequan, Hui Liangyu, Wu Yi, Zhang Lichang, Zhang Dejiang, Chen Liangyu, Yu Zhengsheng, Wang Gang, Xu Caihou, Hua Jianmin, and Chen Zhili) were also present.[55]

There is something unusual about Zeng's speech. First, it is not clear why Zeng was speaking on behalf of Hu Jintao. Zeng was president of the Central Party School, and it is entirely understandable for him to deliver a talk to a class of chief provincial/ministerial leaders on the scientific concept of development on his own. It is likely that Zeng was reluctant to render his support and that Hu somehow made Zeng to open this class and to give a talk on behalf of him.

Second, his interpretation of the scientific concept of development seems to have deviated from Hu Jintao's true intentions. He tried to interpret this development perspective in Jiang Zemin's terms. He said,

> The scientific concept of development has been proposed on the basis of Mao Zedong, Deng Xiaoping, and Jiang Zemin's important thoughts on development, on the basis of fully affirming the world-known development achievements in the new period especially since the Fourth Plenum of the Thirteenth Central Committee, on the basis of reality of the new period and the new century, and on the basis of meeting the needs of modernization construction, the needs to master the objective laws of development, and the needs to absorb beneficial products of mankind on development...[56]

---

[55] http://www.people.com.cn/GB/shizheng/1024/2341935.html.
[56] http://www.people.com.cn/GB/shizheng/1024/2341935.html.

Here, Zeng wanted to make sure that the scientific concept of development is not a denial of Jiang's thought and achievements. He stressed Jiang Zemin's important thoughts on development and Jiang Zemin's achievements since June 1989 (i.e., the Fourth Plenum of the Thirteenth Central Committee). Moreover, in addition to embracing the scientific concept of development as a brand new ideology, he also wanted to make the scientific concept of development part of the "Three Represents." As he continued,

> Establishing and implementing the scientific concept of development is a concrete example of studying and implementing the important thought of the "Three Represents," a correct choice in the face of all kinds of possible risks and challenges in the critical period of our country's economic and social development, and also meets the urgent needs to improve our Party's ruling capacity and art of ruling.[57]

Finally, it was an assembly of Zeng's gang. In addition to loyal Shanghai Gang members such as Huang Ju, Chen Zhili, and Hua Jianmin, Zeng's followers such as Xu Caihou and Wang Gang were all present. Zeng wanted them to hear his interpretation of the new ideology.

In contrast, Premier Wen Jiabao had a different emphasis in his talk to the concluding class on February 21, 2004.[58] Wen also reviewed the historical evolution of China's ideology on development from Mao Zedong to Hu Jintao, but he had higher regards for Deng's contributions than Jiang's. He called Deng's theory on development a "leap" (*feiyue*) but believed that the contributions from the third generation leadership with Jiang at the core "further enriched" (*jinyibu fengfu*) the theory and practice of socialist modernization. As for the scientific concept of development, Wen stated,

> Under the guidance of Deng Xiaoping Theory and the important thought of the "Three Represents," the Party Center with

---

[57] http://www.people.com.cn/GB/shizheng/1024/2341935.html.
[58] http://www.people.com.cn/GB/paper39/11374/1027126.html. For the original text of his speech, see http://www.people.com.cn/GB/shizheng/1024/2365868.html.

Ideological Institutionalization and Politics of Development 273

Comrade Hu Jintao as General Secretary put forward the scientific concept of development in the spirit of the Sixteenth Party Congress and in accordance with the new situation and new tasks, especially the important new insights gained from the anti-SARS campaign. The scientific concept of development has taken a people-first approach and paid attention to comprehensive, coordinated, and sustainable economic and social development as well as promoting reform and development in accordance with the requirement of the "five coordinates." This is an indication that our Party's understanding of the laws of socialist modernization construction has further deepened.[59]

Clearly, Wen stressed the theoretical innovations of the scientific concept of development in the light of new situations and highlighted the significant achievements of the campaign against SARS. Interestingly, Zeng Qinghong was present at the concluding class; and Huang Ju was the chair; Chen Zhili and Hua Jianmin were also present.

COOLING CHINA'S OVERHEATED ECONOMY

Issue of "Overheating"

By the early 2004, Hu Jintao's ideological authority was basically established. Yet local leaders continued to operate in the old mode of thinking instead of the scientific concept of development; the Shanghai Gang continued to resist the emergence of Hu Jintao and his allies. Over the issue of "overheating," the central government came into a conflict with local governments, and the Hu–Wen team had frictions with some Shanghai Gang members.

China's economy exhibited signs of overheating[60] in the first quarter of 2004. Following a 9.1 percent growth in 2003, China's

---

[59] http://www.people.com.cn/GB/paper464/11431/1031809.html.
[60] Some academicians argue that "overheating" is not a term in economics. Yet the feeling that something is seriously wrong with the economy may justify the usage. For different arguments, see Zhang Wuchang, "Zhongguo de Jingji she Guorema?" ["Is China's economy overheated?"], *Jingjixue Xiaoxibao* (*Economic Highlights*), No. 596 (June 4, 2004), p. 1; He Qinglian, "Shi Shengchannengli Guosheng Haishi Jingjiguore" ["Is it excessive productivity or economic overheating?"], *Epoch Times*, June 23, 2004, http://www.epochtimes.com/gb/4/6/23/n576583.htm.

economy in the first quarter of 2004 went up 9.8 percent.[61] The manifestations of overheating were reflected in financial and physical terms. Financially, due to the performance imperative on the part of local officials,[62] there was a nationwide overinvestment in fixed assets. The total value of investment in fixed asset increased 47.8 percent in the first three months of 2004.[63] Physically, due to the overinvestment, there was a nationwide power shortage and overproduction in some industrial products.

The problems in several industrial sectors such as steel and cement were particularly worrisome. China had been No. 1 producer of steel in the world for eight consecutive years since 1996 with a total output of 222 million tons in 2003.[64] Following the rapid expansion of investment in steel production in 2003, the first three months of 2004 witnessed further acceleration of investment in this already overheated sector. Among the projects at the five million-yuan level and above, investment in steel production in 2003 went up 96.6 percent.[65] The investment in the fixed assets in steel production increased 106 percent in the first three months of 2004 when compared to that in 2003.[66] Likewise, the investment expansion in

---

[61] National Bureau of Statistics of China, "Gross Domestic Product (GDP) (first quarter of 2004)," http://www.stats.gov.cn/english/statisticaldata/monthlydata/t20031110_402152252.htm.

[62] This performance imperative serves as a reminder of Janos Kornai's description of the typical behavior of government officials in a centrally planned economy. In his terms, these officials usually suffer from "insatiable investment hunger" because of "expansion drive." For details, see Janos Kornai, *Economics of Shortage* (New York: North-Holland Publishing Company, 1980), Vols. A, B, pp. 192, 193.

[63] National Bureau of Statistics of China, "Investment in fixed assets (first quarter of 2004)," http://www.stats.gov.cn/english/statisticaldata/monthlydata/t20031121_402153253.htm.

[64] National Bureau of Statistics of China, "Statistical communiqué of the People's Republic of China on the 2003 National Economic and Social Development," February 26, 2004, http://www.stats.gov.cn/english/newrelease/statisticalreports/t20040303_402133921.htm.

[65] *Ibid*.

[66] "Jixujiaqiang he Gaishan Hongguantiaokong Nulishixian Yuqimubiao" ["Continue to strengthen and improve macro-management, strive to reach the planned goals"],

cement was also very rapid. China had also been No. 1 producer of cement in the world with an output of 862 million tons in 2003, 18.9 percent more than in 2002.[67] Among the projects at the 5 million-yuan level and above, investment in cement increased 121.9 percent in 2003.[68] The investment expansion in cement in the first quarter of 2004 went up 118 percent when compared to that in 2003.[69]

According to Premier Wen Jiabao, China's government began to adopt a macro-management policy as early as August 2003 when the central leadership became concerned over the overheating of the economy.[70] In his report to the Second Session of the Tenth NPC in March 2004, Wen listed the macro-management as the top priority of the Chinese government in 2004.[71] He indicated that an important task for macro-management in 2004 was to appropriately control the scale of investment in fixed assets and firmly halt haphazard investment and low-level, redundant construction in some industries and regions. Guided by market forces, the Chinese government would mainly use economic and legal means supplemented by any necessary administrative measures to strengthen guidance and control.[72]

Renminwang, August 9, 2004, http://www1.people.com.cn/GB/jingji/1037/2694650.htm. The same rate (106.4 percent) is found in the investment in the fixed asset of smelting and processing of ferrous metals. See "Investment in fixed assets by industry (January–March 2004)," http://www.stats.gov.cn/english/statistical-data/monthlydata/t20031121_402153252.htm.

[67] National Bureau of Statistics of China, "Statistical communiqué of the People's Republic of China on the 2003 National Economic and Social Development," February 26, 2004, http://www.stats.gov.cn/english/newrelease/statisticalreports/t20040303_402133921.htm.

[68] *Ibid.*

[69] *Renminwang*, August 9, 2004, http://www1.people.com.cn/GB/jingji/1037/2694650.htm.

[70] Wen Jiabao, "Gongtong Tuijin Xinshiji de Yazhouhezuo" ["Jointly promote Asian cooperation in the new century"], The Third Foreign Ministers' Meeting of Asian Cooperation Dialog, Qingdao, China, June 22, 2004, *Renminwang*, June 22, 2004, http://www1.people.com.cn/GB/shizheng/1024/2590451.html.

[71] Wen Jiabao, "Zhengfu Gongzuo Baogao" ["Government Report"], The Second Session of the Tenth National People's Congress, March 5, 2004, *Renminwang*, March 16, 2004, http://www1.people.com.cn/GB/shizheng/1026/2393857.html.

[72] *Ibid.*

However, he was not ready to tackle the issue of overheating right away and was reluctant to release a basket of control measures indiscriminately. He was willing to wait for a proper time and to adopt macro-management measures to an appropriate degree. "By 'at the proper time'," Wen explained, "we mean seizing the opportune moment for introducing control measures by observing small clues that may indicate what is coming in order to forestall any possible trouble. By 'to an appropriate degree,' we mean that macro-management should neither too loose nor too tight and that we must not apply the brakes too hard or apply control measures indiscriminately."[73]

Apparently, the statistics released at the beginning of April 2004 alarmed the premier. The "proper time" had arrived. At a State Council executive meeting on April 9, 2004, Wen Jiabao called for effective measures in macro-management to ward off threatening inflation and to ensure a stable economic growth.[74] He pointed out that there were some serious problems in the economy. First, investment expansion went too fast. Second, there were too many new construction projects, the scale of ongoing construction was too big, and investment structure was not rational. Third, in some industries and regions, the problem of haphazard investment and redundant constructions was very serious. He suggested enhancing macro-management and firmly halting the investment expansion in order to ward off inflation and avoid ups and downs of the economy.[75]

As in the case of SARS a year earlier, Wen's initiatives were resisted by the Shanghai Gang.[76] It is reported that at a meeting of Shanghai party and government leaders in early April, Chen

---

[73] *Ibid.*

[74] "Wen Jiabao Zhuchi Zhaokai Guowuyuan Changwuhuiyi" ("Wen Jiabao chairs a state council executive meeting"), *Renminwang*, April 12, 2004, http://www1.people.com.cn/GB/paper464/11761/1060094.html.

[75] *Ibid.*

[76] The Shanghai Gang refers to central leaders who have previous work experience in Shanghai and those who are currently working in Shanghai as municipal party or government leaders. For a detailed description of the Shanghai Gang, see Zhiyue Bo, "The Sixteenth Central Committee of the Chinese Communist Party: formal institutions and factional groups," *Journal of Contemporary China*, Vol. 13, No. 39 (May 2004), pp. 223–256.

Liangyu, Politburo member and party secretary of Shanghai, claimed that although China's economy as a whole was overheated, Shanghai's economy remained normal and that the economic overheating was due to some central leaders (e.g., Wen Jiabao).[77] In a seminar with local leaders from Shanghai, Jiangsu, Zhejiang, Jiangxi, and Anhui in mid-April, Huang Ju, standing Politburo member and executive vice premier as well as former Shanghai Party boss, challenged Wen's assessment of the economy. He argued that it was debatable whether the economy was overheated. He instigated the participants to send their criticisms of the State Council (i.e., Wen Jiabao) in the name of their Party committee or government to the Politburo or the Politburo Standing Committee.[78]

Hu's Support and Central Bandwagon

As in the case of the campaign against SARS, General Secretary Hu Jintao again lent his support to Premier Wen Jiabao. At a press conference of the annual *Boao Forum for Asia* conference on April 24, 2004, Hu spoke of the necessity of macro-management measures.[79] He indicated that China's economy was doing very well in the first

---

[77] "Gangyu Hu Jintao Duizhegan, Huang Ju Shanfengdianhuo, Gongjizhixiang Wen Jiabao" ("Dare to challenge Hu Jintao, Huang Ju was pointing fingers at Wen Jiabao"), *Wen Wei Po* (Hong Kong), May 25, 2004, http://www.wenxuecity.com/BBSView.php?SubID=news&MsgID=13932.

[78] Luo Bing, "Shanghai Bang Jieji Xiang Wen Jiabao Fanan" ["The Shanghai Gang took the opportunity to challenge Wen Jiabao"], *Cheng Ming*, No. 319 (May 2004), p. 8. See also Jiang Qing, "Huang Ju Zhaokai Wen Jiabao Pipanhui, Jiangxi Shuji Yiege Dawaibo" ["Huang Ju calls for a meeting to criticize Premier Wen Jiabao, Jiangxi party secretary is choked by his governor"], *Renminbao*, May 9, 2004, http://renminbao.com/rmb/articles/2004/5/9/31070.html. However, Huang Ju voiced his support for macro-management policies in his visit to Hunan between March 25 and 28, 2004. See "Huang Ju zai Hunan Kaocha shi Qiangdiao Qieshijiaqiang Jingji Yunxing Tiaojie" ["Huang Ju stressed the strengthening of economic operation control in his visit to Hunan"], *Renminwang*, March 28, 2004, http://www1.people.com.cn/GB/shizheng/1024/2414514.html.

[79] "Hu Jintao Xianchang Huida Luntanjiabing Tiwen" ["Hu Jintao answers questions from distinguished guests of the forum at the press conference"], April 24, 2004, http://www.boaoforum.org/xinwen/zxbd/t20040424_731660.shtml.

quarter of 2004 but was faced with some new problems such as the rapid expansion of investment in fixed assets, haphazard investment, and redundant construction and that the Chinese government was adopting macro-management measures to solve these problems.[80] At a study session of the Politburo two days later, Hu emphasized the importance of governing the country and managing the economy by legal means.[81] On the same day, the Politburo also discussed the economic situation in China and confirmed the correctness of Wen's macro-management initiatives.[82] But it is reported that Huang Ju dissented and argued that there was no heat to be cooled.[83]

With Hu's support, Wen was determined to implement macro-management measures. At a State Council executive meeting on April 28, 2004, he dealt with a project in Jiangsu Province involving

---

[80] *Ibid.*

[81] "Hu Jintao zai Zhonggongzhongyang Zhengzhiju dishierci jitixuexishi qiangdiao Shizhong Jianchi Yifazhiguo Yifazhizheng Tigao Quanshihui Fazhihua Guanli Shuiping" ["At the Twelfth Group Study Session of the Politburo of the Chinese Communist Party Central Committee, Hu Jintao stressed on constantly persisting in governing the country through legal means and improving the level by which the society is managed by legal means"], *Renminwang*, April 28, 2004, http://www.people.com.cn/GB/paper464/11885/1071143.html. It seems that Zeng Qinghong and Chen Liangyu were absent from this study session because they were both in Shanghai attending the Asia-Pacific Ministerial Conference. See http://www.people.com.cn/GB/paper464/11879/1070682.html.

[82] "Hu Jintao Zhuchi Zhonggongzhongyang Zhengzhiju Zhaokaihuiyi Fenxi Dangqian Woguo Jingji Xingshi" ["Hu Jintao chaired a Politburo meeting to analyze China's current economic situation"], *Renminwang*, April 26, 2004, http://peopledaily.com.cn/GB/shizheng/1026/2469483.html.

[83] "Gangyu Hu Jintao Duizhegan, Huang Ju Shanfengdianhuo, Gongjizhixiang Wen Jiabao" ["Dare to challenge Hu Jintao, Huang Ju was pointing fingers at Wen Jiabao"], *Wen Wei Po* (Hong Kong), May 25, 2004, http://www.wenxuecity.com/BBSView.php?SubID=news&MsgID=13932. It is also reported that the Politburo Standing Committee held a meeting on the economic situation on April 28, 2004, and reached a consensus that the economy was seriously overheated and that necessary measures should be adopted to cool the economy. But no confirmation about this latter meeting from the *People's Daily* could be found.

unscrupulous irregularities and illicit activities.[84] According to a joint report from the State Development and Reform Commission, Ministry of National Resources, and Ministry of Supervision, Jiangsu Tieben Iron & Steel Ltd seriously violated the laws and regulations of the state. It planned in 2002 to build giant steel plants in Changzhou and Yangzhong with a projected capacity of 8.4 million tons of steel annually.[85] The construction began in June 2003. It was discovered that the Jiangsu authorities had allowed Jiangsu Tieben to split its project of 10.6 billion yuan into 22 smaller projects in order to sidestep the need for central approval. The local authorities also allowed the project to be built on a piece of land of 6,541 mu (436 hectares) in violation of relevant laws.[86] Premier Wen ordered the project be halted and responsible officials investigated and punished.[87] He made it clear that his decision had been backed by the Politburo.[88]

In his interview with Reuters Editor in Chief Geert Linnebank on the same day, Wen further elaborated his control measures. These measures would include (i) controlling money supply and total

---

[84] "Wen Jiabao Zhuchihuiyi Zechengchuli Jiangsu Weiguijian Gangtiexiangmu" ["Wen Jiabao chaired a state council executive meeting to seriously deal with Jiangsu's steel plant construction project that had violated relevant regulations"], *Renminwang*, April 28, 2004, http://www1.people.com.cn/GB/shizheng/1024/2474084.html.

[85] For anyone who has studied the steel production of the Great Leap Forward, this number is outrageous. This one company is projecting a capacity that is far more than the total output of the entire country in 1957 (5.35 million tons).

[86] For details, see He Yuxin and Chen Fang, "Tangled story of Tieben," http://www.caijing.com.cn/english/2004/040520/040520tieben.htm.

[87] "Zhongguo youxian Daliangangrechao Wen Jiabao na 'Tieben' Jidao" ["China is engaged in another high tide for steel production, Premier Wen Jiabao punishes 'Tieben' to warn others"], *Lianhe Zaobao*, April 30, 2004, http://www.wenxuecity.com/BBSView.php?SubID=news&MsgID=13020.

[88] "Guowuyuan Yansuchachu Jiangsu Tieben Gangtiegongsi Weiguijianshe Gangtiexiangmu" ["The State Council seriously dealt with Jiangsu Tieben Iron & Steel Ltd.'s steel construction project that had violated relevant regulations"], *Renminwang*, April 29, 2004, http://www1.people.com.cn/GB/paper464/11893/1071761.html.

credit; (ii) strengthening the management of land use and putting an end to the "swallowing up" of arable land; (iii) strictly screening projects under construction and large new construction projects; seriously punishing the operators of illegal or irregular projects such as those that have abused arable land and those that have not been properly authorized; and (iv) launching a nationwide campaign to conserve resources.[89]

Through the *People's Daily*, the mouthpiece of the Party, Hu and Wen issued serious warnings to bureaucrats in the localities and the Center. In an editorial of April 29, 2004, on the Tieben case, they asked cadres of various levels to comply with the central directives. "The critical point at the moment," the editorial sharply warned,

> is that everyone concerned, especially leading cadres at all levels, should really adhere to the Center's correct assessment of the current economic situation in thought and action, adhere to the Center's decisions and measures on the economic work, and establish a scientific development view and a correct performance view.[90]

---

[89] "Wen Jiabao Zongli jieshou Lutushezongbian Caifang" ["Premier Wen Jiabao was interviewed by Reuters Editor in Chief"], *Renminwang*, April 29, 2004, http://www1.people.com.cn/GB/shizheng/1024/2475864.html. For a report in English, see "Interview: China's Premier Wen Jiabao," *The New Zealand Herald*, April 29, 2004, http://www.nzherald.co.nz/storydisplay.cfm?storyID=3563390&thesection=news&thesubsection=world.

[90] "Jiejueweihu Hongguantiaokong Zhenglingchangtong (shelun)" ["Editorial: Firmly implementing the central macro-management policies"], *Renminwang*, April 29, 2004, http://www.people.com.cn/GB/paper464/11893/1071760.html. This is the first of the four editorials on the issue of macro-management policies in *Renmin ribao*. The other three are "Hongguantiaokong de Shizhi shi Shuli he Luoshi Kexuefazhanguan" ["The essence of central macro-management policies is to establish and implement the scientific development view"], *Renminwang*, August 5, 2004, http://www1.people.com.cn/GB/jingji/1037/2687765.html; "Chongfenrenshi Hongguantiaokong de Jianjuxing he Fuzaxing" ["Fully recognize the difficulty and complexity of implementing central macro-management policies"], *Renminwang*, August 7, 2004, http://www.people.com.cn/GB/guandian/1033/2692399.html; "Hongguantiaokong: Tongyisixiang Zengqiang Dajuguannian he Zerenyishi" ["Macro-management: unify thoughts and enhance the overall perspective and responsibility"], *Renminwang*, August 8, 2004, http://www.people.com.cn/GB/guandian/1033/2693359.html.

To demonstrate his personal support for Wen Jiabao, Hu went to Jiangsu Province on April 30, 2004. During his seven-day visit, Hu told local leaders that the Center had made a decision to curb excessive growth of fixed asset investment and that local leaders should abide by the central decision and take steps to implement the decision.[91] He made it clear that the local leadership would be responsible for implementing the central policies and that the local leadership would be responsible for problems in the local economic development. As he said,

> Leaderships and leading cadres at various levels are the key to implementing central lines, directions, policies, and directives. They are the key to all kinds of work in reform, economic development, and social stability. Therefore, we need to first pay attention to the leadership of a locality if we really care about the development of the locality; we need to first assist the locality in constructing a good leadership if we really want to support the development of the locality.[92]

Under the pressure of Hu and Wen, Huang Ju immediately turned around and voiced his support for the macro-management measures. During his visit to Jiangxi Province between April 29 and May 2, 2004, Huang advised local leaders Meng Jianzhu (party secretary of Jiangxi) and Huang Zhiquan (governor of Jiangxi) that they should be mindful of the Party Center's assessment of the current economic situation and policy measures and that they should immediately act to implement central macro-management measures.[93]

---

[91] "Hu Jintao zai Jiangsu Kaochagongzuo shi Qiangdiao ba Kexuefazhanguan Guanchuanyu Fazhanquanguocheng Jianchi Shenhuagaige Youhuajiegou Tigaoxiaoyi" ["During his visit to Jiangsu, Hu Jintao stressed on using the scientific development view throughout the whole process of development and insisting on deepening reforms, optimizing structures, an improving efficiency"], *Renminwang*, May 7, 2004, http://www.people.com.cn/GB/paper464/11936/1074802.html.

[92] *Ibid.*

[93] "Huang Ju zai Jiangxi Kaochagongzuo shi Qiangdiao Tongyisixiang Xunsuxingdong Qieshi Guancheluoshi Hongguantiaokong Zhengcecuoshi" ["During his visit to Jiangxi, Huang Ju stressed on unifying thought and taking immediate actions to seriously implement the macro-management policy measures"], *Renminwang*, May 3, 2004, http://www.people.com.cn/GB/paper464/11920/ 1073867.html.

He urged Jiangxi leaders to build a wonderful, new Jiangxi under the Party Center with Comrade Hu Jintao as general secretary.[94] He repeated the same show in his visit to Inner Mongolia between June 10 and 13, 2004. He told Chu Bo, party secretary of Inner Mongolia, and Yang Jing, chairman of the Inner Mongolian Autonomous Regional Government, that Inner Mongolia should further implement central macro-management measures and promote sustained social and economic development.[95]

Jia Qinglin, Politburo standing member and chairman of the Chinese People's Political Consultative Conference as well as Jiang's close associate, also joined the chorus. During his visit to Henan between May 14 and 18, 2004, Jia reminded local leaders (Li Keqiang and Li Chengyu) that they should really come to the Central Leadership's correct assessment of the current economic situation and faithfully implement the Center's macro-management policy measures.[96] He reiterated his support during his visit of June 9–16, 2004 to Sichuan.[97]

Zeng Peiyan, Politburo member and vice premier, also jumped on the bandwagon. At seminars with local leaders from Jiangsu, Zhejiang, and Shanghai as well as those from Beijing, Tianjin, Hebei, and Henan in early May 2004, Zeng informed local leaders of central macro-management policies and asked them to comply with the

---

[94] *Ibid.*

[95] Huang Ju, "Chujin Jingjishehui Quanmianxietiao Chixufazhan" ["Promote comprehensive, coordinated, and sustained economic and social development"], *Renminwang*, June 14, 2004, http://www1.people.com.cn/GB/shizheng/1024/2567890.html.

[96] "Jia Qinglin zai Henan Diaoyanqiangdiao Shuli he Lunshi Kexuefazhanguan" ["During his visit to Henan, Jia Qinglin stressed that the scientific development view should be established and developed"], *Renminwang*, May 18, 2004, http://www1.people.com.cn/GB/shizheng/1024/2506195.html.

[97] "Jia Qinglin zai Sichuan Diaoyanqiangdiao Fahuiyoushi Ningjuliliang Chujin Jingjishehui Quanmianfazhan" ["During his visit to Sichuan, Jia Qinglin stressed that the locality should develop advantages and concentrate on the promotion of the comprehensive economic and social development"], *Renminwang*, June 17, 2004, http://www.people.com.cn/GB/paper464/12248/1102445.html.

central policies.⁹⁸ At a seminar on economic situation with local leaders from six provincial units in the West (Sichuan, Chongqing, Yunnan, Inner Mongolia, Shaanxi, and Gansu) on May 25, 2004, Zeng also made a statement about the macro-management policies and listened to the reports on the implementation of the macro-management policies in these regions.⁹⁹

Wu Yi, Politburo member and vice premier, also rendered her support for the macro-management policies. In her visit to Jiangsu in early June 2004, she urged Jiangsu leaders to carry out central policies with the whole country's interests in mind and to strengthen their sense of responsibility.¹⁰⁰

After another State Council executive meeting on May 21, 2004, where he stressed that the central macro-management measures were absolutely necessary and completely correct and local governments should firmly and strictly carry them out,¹⁰¹ Wen Jiabao paid a

---

⁹⁸ "Zeng Peiyan zai Shanghai Jiangsu Tianjin dengdi Kaochaqiangdiao Yaohenzhua Gexiang Hongguantiaokongcuosi Luoshi" ["During his visits to Shanghai, Jiangsu, and Tianjin, Zeng Peiyan stressed that attention should be paid to the implementation of various macro-management measures"], *Renminwang*, May 18, 2004, http://www.people.com.cn/GB/paper464/12018/1081688.html.

⁹⁹ "Guowuyuan Zhaokai Xibuliushengqushi Jingjixingshi Zuotanhui" [The State Council called for a seminar with local leaders from six provincial units in the West"], *Renminwang*, May 28, 2004, http://www1.people.com.cn/GB/paper464/12102/1089359.html.

¹⁰⁰ "Wu Yi zai Jiangsu Kaocha shi Qiangdiao Guancheluoshi Kexuefazhanguan Jinyibutigao Duiwaikaifang Shuiping" ["During her visit to Jiangsu, Wu Yi stressed that attention should be paid to the implementation of scientific development view in order to further promote opening up to the outside world"], *Renminwang*, June 12, 2004, http://www.people.com.cn/GB/paper464/12211/1098950.html.

¹⁰¹ "Wen Jiabao zhuchi Guowuyuanchangwuhuiyi Yanjiu Xiayibu Jingjigongzuo" ["Wen Jiabao chaired a State Council executive meeting to discuss economic work of the next period"], *Renminwang*, May 21, 2004, http://www1.people.com.cn/GB/shizheng/1024/2514134.html. Apparently, local leaders were not very enthusiastic about the central macro-management policies. As a reporter indicated three days after the State Council executive meeting, some regions or some departments were still playing game with the central leadershi "They were using various means to resist the central macro-management measures. For details, see Zhou Jianchu, "Buyao he Hongguantiaokong Boyi" ["Do not play games with the center over the macro-management policies"], *Jinrong Shibao (Financial News)*, No. 5311 (May 24, 2004), p. 1.

special visit to Shanghai in late May. At a seminar with local leaders from Shanghai, Jiangsu, and Zhejiang on May 25, 2004, Wen urged them to follow the central policies in macroeconomic controls. The East China Region, as he indicated, plays a critical role in the national economy, whether it is economic growth or macro-management. Local leaders of this region should have an overall picture of the whole nation and carry out central policies.[102] He later visited Hubei and chaired a seminar with leading cadres from Anhui, Jiangxi, Henan, Hubei, and Hunan in Wuhan on June 11, 2004. He acknowledged these cadres' efforts to implement central macro-management policies and urged them to pay further attention to serious problems in the economy.[103] He went to Shandong later in the month with the same message.[104]

Noticeably, Zeng Qinghong did not express his support for the macro-management policies. In late April and May 2004, he visited Shanghai, Hubei, and Gansu, but he did not mention anything about the macro-management measures. On the surface, none of the occasions were appropriate for economic issues because he was mainly concerned with other issues such as foreign affairs and Party building during these visits. Yet it seems that he might have had some reservations about the macro-management policies because he did

---

[102] "Wen Jiabao zai Shanghai Kaocha Zhichu Jianjueluoshi Hongguantiaokong Cuoshi" ["During his visit to Shanghai, Wen Jiabao asked (local leaders) to firmly implement macro-management measures"], *Renminwang*, May 27, 2004, http://www1.people.com.cn/GB/shizheng/1024/2527827.html. See also *Renmin ribao*, May 28, 2004, p. 1.

[103] Wen Jiabao, "Guanche Hongguantiaokong Baochijingji Pingwenkuaisufazhan" ["Carry out central macro-management measures and maintain steady and rapid economic development"], *Renminwang*, June 13, 2004, http://www1.people.com.cn/GB/shizheng/1024/2566978.html.

[104] "Wen Jiabao zai Shandong Kaocha shi Yaoqiu Gerenganyiliugongzuo Qiyechuangyiliupinpai Shehuizaoyiliuhuanjing" ["During his visit to Shandong, Wen Jiabao instructed that individuals should do the first-class work, enterprises should produce the first-class products, and the society should create the first-class environment"], *Renminwang*, May 24, 2004, http://www.people.com.cn/GB/paper464/12300/1106709.html.

visit several industrial enterprises in these regions, including the Jiuquan Iron & Steel Corporation in Gansu but said nothing about them.[105] He did not talk about macro-management during his visit to Fujian in early June either.[106]

To the list of central supporters at the highest levels, one may add central ministries. Ma Kai, chairman of the State Development and Reform Commission, held a teleconference on cleaning up fixed asset investment projects on April 30, 2004, and stressed the importance of using legal means to regulate fixed asset investment.[107] He targeted steel, aluminum, cement, office buildings and training centers of the Party and government organs, expressways, golf courts, convention centers, commercial exchange centers, shopping centers, and all new construction projects in 2004. He asked the local governments to sincerely comply with the central policies and warned them of serious consequences if they failed to do so.[108]

On the same day, the China Bank Regulatory Commission, an independent monitoring body established by the Chinese government in April 2003, issued a notice on curbing excessive growth of fixed asset investment. It asked financial institutions in China to

---

[105] "Zeng Qinghong zai Hubei Gansu Kaochagongzuo shi Qiangdiao zai Jiaqiang Jichengdangjiazhong Luoshihao Kexuefazhanguan Rangganbu Jingchangshoujiaoyu Shinongminchangqide Shihui" ["During his visits to Hubei and Gansu, Zeng Qinghong stressed that in strengthening Party building at the grassroots level, the scientific development view should be realized so as to allow cadres to be constantly educated and to allow peasants to receive long-term benefits"], *Renminwang*, May 19, 2004, http://www.people.com.cn/GB/paper464/12028/1082442.html.

[106] Zeng Qinghong, "Yizhizhengnengli Jianshe Daidong Zhenggedang de Jianshe" ["Promote Party building through building the Party's ability to govern"], *Renminwang*, June 12, 2004, http://www1.people.com.cn/GB/shizheng/1024/2565675.html.

[107] "Guojiafazhangaigewei deng bumen Zhaokai Dianshidianhuahuiyi" ["The State Development and Reform Commission and other central organs held a teleconference"], *Renminwang*, May 1, 2004, http://www1.people.com.cn/GB/paper464/11910/1073184.html.

[108] *Ibid*.

faithfully implement the Center's macro-management policies and proposed seven measures to manage lending.[109]

To enforce central macro-management policies, the State Development and Reform Commission, the People's Bank of China (the Central Bank), and the China Bank Regulatory Commission jointly issued a notice on using the combination of industrial policies and lending policies to manage the risk of credit and investment expansion.[110] They also attached a catalog to operationalize the notice. The main industrial sectors listed in the catalog were steel, nonferrous metal, machineries, construction materials, petroleum, light industry, textile, medicine, and printing. These sectors were divided into two categories: forbidden and restricted. Projects were forbidden if they had serious safety or environmental issues, were of low quality, or consumed too much raw materials and resources. Projects were restricted if their production capacity far exceeded the demand; if they did not help make the industrial structure more rational; if their technology was outdated; and if they were not conducive to resource conservation and environmental protection.[111]

Seven central ministries and commissions also worked together to deal with the land market. These central organs include the Ministry of Land and Resources, the State Development and Reform Commission, the Ministry of Finance, the Ministry of Agriculture, the Ministry of Construction, the Ministry of Supervision, and National Audit Office. They all agreed that it was time to activate a work plan on the land market.[112] They divided the labor among

---

[109] "Yinjianhui Tichu Qixiang Cuoshi" ["The China Bank Regulatory Commission proposed seven measures"], *Renminwang*, May 1, 2004, http://www1.people.com.cn/GB/paper464/11910/1073183.html.

[110] "Jiaqiang Chanyezhengce he Xindaizhengce Xietiaopeihe Kongzhixindaifengxian" ["Strengthening the coordination of industrial policies and leading policies to mitigate the risk of leading"], *Renminwang*, May 14, 2004, http://www1.people.com.cn/GB/paper464/11992/1079267.html.

[111] *Ibid.*

[112] "Guojia Qibuwei Lianshou Qidong Tudishichang Zhilizhengdun" ["Seven central ministries or commissions joined hands to implement measures on land market

themselves in dealing with different aspects of the land use or abuse.[113]

Local "Compliance"

In contrast, local governments were not enthusiastic about central macro-management policies. Only a few provinces such as Jiangsu, Shaanxi, and Hunan responded to the central call for macro-management reactively, while many others demonstrated their "compliance" in standard official discourse.

In response to the central policies, Jiangsu's leaders immediately called for a teleconference on the case of Tieben Iron & Steel Ltd on April 29, 2004. Party Secretary Li Yuanchao and Governor Liang Bohua urged Jiangsu cadres to learn from the Tieben incident and carry out central macro-management measures.[114] The provincial leaders also went to Changzhou and Yangzhong to handle the aftermath of the Tieben problem.[115] They let it known through the *People's Daily* that Jiangsu was taking the Tieben issue very seriously and that they were taking concrete measures to comply with central directives.[116]

The Shaanxi Provincial Government cooperated with the Ministry of Land and Resources and the Ministry of Supervision in their investigation of land abuse in Zhouzhi County. It was discovered that the Zhouzhi County Government had been involved in three cases of large scale land abuse and used the police to

---

rectification"], *Renminwang*, May 23, 2004, http://www1.people.com.cn/GB/paper464/ 12056/1085300.html.

[113] *Ibid.*

[114] "Jiangsu Zhaokai Tieben Xiangmu Weiguijianshe Chachuqingkuang Tongbaohui" ["Jiangsu held a teleconference about the case of Tieben construction project in violation of relevant regulations"], *Renminwang*, April 30, 2004, http://www.people.com.cn/GB/paper464/11906/1072800.html.

[115] "Xiqu Tiebenxiangmu Weiguiweiji Jiaoxun" ["Learning lessons from Tieben construction project"], *Renminwang*, May 15, 2004, http://www.people.com.cn/GB/paper464/11997/1079866.html.

[116] *Ibid.*

suppress protestors. In one case, the county government signed a contract with a developer in September 2002 without proper approval procedure to develop a piece of land of 6,000 mu and collected 23.3 million yuan as payment for the first phase of development. The police were called in to arrest those who protested against the land abuse. In the second case, the county government cordoned off two areas in May 2003 and used the police against protestors. Finally, the county government destroyed the land of 191 mu and encircled another 144 mu. In none of these cases did the county government obtain proper approval from its superiors.[117] As a show of its determination to strictly implement central macro-management measures, the Shaanxi Provincial Government disciplined four former chief cadres of the county government.[118]

Working with the Ministry of Construction, the Hunan Provincial Party Committee and Provincial Government investigated a case in Jiahe County where a real estate construction project was a result of an abuse of administrative power and violation of laws and regulations. Hunan leaders punished violators and made a report to the State Council. [119]

Guangdong's response was immediate but not reflective. On May 9, 2004, Governor Huang Huahua chaired a provincial government executive meeting to discuss policies and measures on implementing central policies in Guangdong. It was decided that Guangdong would implement central macro-management policies with a particular focus on halting the rapid expansion of investment, preventing inflation, and avoiding the ups and downs of the economy.[120] Yet the meeting did not specifically identify issues in

---

[117] "Yansuchachu Shaanxisheng Zhouzhixian Tudiweifa Wenti" ["Investigating the illegal use of land in Zhouzhi County, Shaanxi Province"], *Renminwang*, June 5, 2004, http://www1.people.com.cn/GB/paper464/12155/1094157.html.
[118] *Ibid.*
[119] "Wen Jiabao Zhuchi Zhaokai Guowuyuan Changwuhuiyi" ["Wen Jiabao chaired a State Council executive meeting"], *Renminwang*, June 5, 2004, http://www1.people.com.cn/GB/paper464/12155/1094171.html.
[120] "Huang Huahua Shengzhang Zhuchizhaokai Shengzhengfu Changwuhuiyi" ["Governor Huang Huahua chaired a provincial government executive meeting"], http://www.gd.gov.cn/gov_files/zw_title.asp?id=1096.

Guangdong's economy that required macro-management measures, what measures Guangdong was planning to take, and how to implement them.

After Wen's visit, Shanghai's Party Committee held a standing member meeting on May 29, 2004 to discuss "the spirit of Premier Wen's important speech." Chen Liangyu expressed his public support for the central policy,[121] but he was not specific about how Shanghai would implement macro-management measures.

Hu–Wen's "Victory"

At a State Council executive meeting on June 16, 2004, Wen Jiabao declared that the macroeconomic measures had achieved their short-term goals of cooling the economy. According to the report, the meeting decided that the Chinese economy in general was doing fairly well; the macro-management measures had achieved tangible results; instable and unhealthy factors in the economy had been placed under control; and the Chinese economy continued its trend of rapid growth with steady improvement in economic efficiency.[122]

According to Cao Yushu, spokesman for the State Development and Reform Commission, the macro-management measures had achieved tangible results in seven areas. First, the investment slowed. The urban fixed assets in the first five months of 2004 increased by 34.8 percent when compared to that of the previous year, but the growth rate in May declined by 8 percent compared to that of the previous four months. The growth rates of investment in steel, nonferrous metals, and cement industries in May 2004 were reduced by 22.5 percent, 9.7 percent, and 23.7 percent than those of the previous four months, respectively. Second, money and loans slowed their pace of growth. Third, the expansion of prices for basic

---

[121] Chen Liangyu, "Jiaqiang Hongguantiaokong Zuowei Fazhanqiji" ["Taking macro-management measures as an opportunity for development"], May 31, 2004, http://info.china.alibaba.com/news/detail/v1-d5344213.html.
[122] "Wen Jiabao Zhuchi Zhaokai Guowuyuan Changwuhuiyi" ["Wen Jiabao chaired a State Council executive meeting"], *Renminwang*, June 16, 2004, http://www1.people.com.cn/GB/shizheng/1024/2576830.html.

products had been placed under control. Fourth, summer harvest was expected to be good. Fifth, some overheated industries were beginning to cool. Sixth, consumer markets had been stabilized. Seventh, foreign trade continued its trend of rapid growth. The total value of imports and exports for May 2004 was US$87.63 billion, 34.1 percent more than that of the last year. It was the first month in 2004 that China had realized trade surpluses.[123]

In sharp contrast to their previous reticence, local leaders became excited about the news that the macro-management measures had produced "tangible results." They immediately matched the good news from the Center with their local good news. Less than one month after Wen's visit, Shanghai declared a major victory: By having skillfully applied central macro-management policies, the Shanghai leadership had engineered a soft-landing for Shanghai's economy.[124] According to a report from Shanghai, the central macro-management policies had presented Shanghai, a region with double digit growth for 12 consecutive years, with both challenges and opportunities. But the Shanghai leadership was never hesitant about implementing central policies because Shanghai leaders knew that the central macro-management policies had been based on serious deliberations and scientific decision-making. After serious analyses and investigations, the Shanghai leadership decided to implement the central policies in accordance with Shanghai's economic reality: applying brakes selectively, making adjustments in the control, and optimizing the economic structure in the adjustment. As a result, the development zones had been reduced to 79 from 176, with a reduction rate of 55.1 percent; development areas had been reduced by 379 square kilometers; the growth rate of lending had slowed, with May being the month in which loans were increased least; and the

---

[123] "Guojia Hongguantiaokong Qudeqidachengxiao" ["The central macro-management measures have produced seven achievements"], *Renminwang*, June 24, 2004, http://www.people.com.cn/GB/paper464/12300/1106712.html.

[124] "Bugaojisha Shanghaijingji Chuxian Ruanzhaolu Kexitaishi" ["Without applying emergency brakes, Shanghai's economy has witnessed the encouraging signs of soft-landing"], *Xinhuanet*, June 23, 2004, http://www.sh.xinhuanet.com/2004-06/23/content_2367512.htm.

total fixed asset investment in May was 26.2 percent, 3.4 percent less than that of the previous four months. Moreover, the economic structure of Shanghai was becoming more optimized: Exports of the first five months increased by 54.3 percent when compared to that of the previous year; the retail of social consumption goods increased by 12.1 percent when compared to that of the previous year; and key industries such as telecommunication and automobiles experienced rapid growth.[125]

Four days later, good news also came from Fujian where, as a result of macro-management, its industrial sector had reportedly become consolidated with good effects. According to a report in the *People's Daily*, Fujian's industrial efficiency had increased 11 percent faster than its industrial production growth; the overall industrial efficiency index had reached 154.48, eight percent higher than that in 2003; and the total profits were 13.53 billion yuan, 38.5 percent more than that in 2003. Moreover, Fujian removed 17 development zones of the provincial level, 40 development zones of the municipal level, and 139 development zones of the county level or below. Consequently, different localities in Fujian consolidated their industrial parks and improved efficiency.[126]

Most amazingly, Zhejiang had already achieved preliminary results of the macro-management one month ahead of the rest of the country. On May 28, 2004, a piece of news from the *Zhejiang Daily* appeared in the *People's Daily* that hailed Zhejiang's achievement in implementing central macro-management policies. According to the report, Zhejiang's investment in the first four months slowed down, Zhejiang was consolidating development zones, and the government was taking measures to solve the bottleneck problems of infrastructure and key elements, i.e., electricity, water, land, and raw materials.[127]

---

[125] *Ibid.*

[126] "Fujiangongyejingji Xianxian Jijuxiaoying" ["Fujian's industrial sector has demonstrated scale effect as a result of macro-management measures"], *Renminwang*, June 27, 2004, http://www1.people.com.cn/GB/paper464/12321/1108628.html.

[127] "Zhejiangsheng Hongguantiaokong Chuxianchengxiao" ["The central macro-management measures have produced initial results in Zhejiang Province"],

Conclusion

As in the case of combat against SARS one year earlier, the new leadership under Hu Jintao again demonstrated its effectiveness in dealing with central–local relations in 2004. Once Premier Wen Jiabao identified the problem of economic overheating in China, General Secretary Hu Jintao immediately lent his support. After the Politburo formed a consensus, the State Council and central organs (ministries and commissions) joined hands in implementation. Provincial leaders, though somewhat reluctantly, tagged along. In one way or another, they all expressed their support for the central macro-management measures and indicated their willingness to implement central policies. Hu–Wen declared victory as soon as the economy had the appearance of cooling, making themselves and their supporters winners.

Nevertheless, many problems remain. It has been recently discovered that Jianlong Iron & Steel Corporation in Zhejiang, for instance, was also engaged in an unauthorized giant construction project. According to a CCTV report, the Ningbo Economic and Technological Development Zone Management Committee approved on January 29, 2002 Ningbo Jianlong Iron & Steel Corporation's proposal to build a steel plant with a total investment of US$30 million and an expected annual production of 1.5 million tons of broad thick plate. Jianlong Iron & Steel Corporation later increased the total investment to US$1.2 billion (about 10 billion yuan) with the expected production of six million tons. The officials from the Ningbo Economic and Technological Development Zone Management Committee admitted that this project was not approved by the State Development and Reform Commission.[128] According to a report released on May 30, 2004, this company was also under

---

Renminwang, May 28, 2004, http://unn.people.com.cn/GB/14803/21818/2529269.html.

[128] Xiao Jingdong, "'Ningbo Jianlong Weigui' Baiyi Liangang" ("Ningbo Jianlong Iron & Steel Company's 10-billion-yuan construction project for steel production in violation of relevant regulations"), http://www.cmgsl.com.cn/images/jy4/px300.htm.

investigation by the State Development and Reform Commission.[129] However, it seems that Jianlong Iron & Steel Corporation is getting away with its violations. Although Tieben's Chairman Dai Guofang was jailed, Jianlong's Chairman Zhang Zhixiang, a deputy to the Tenth National People's Congress, moved its headquarters to Beijing.[130]

Another case is in Shanghai.[131] According to a report on April 8, 2004, Baoshan Iron & Steel Corporation was planning to expand its capacity by 50 percent over the next five years. It was going to spend up to 60 billion yuan (US$700 million) by 2010 to expand milling from its forecast of 20 million tons in 2004 to 30 million tons.[132] It is not clear whether the central government is applying a different set of policies toward major steel makers such as Baoshan Iron & Steel Corporation[133] and Wuhan Iron & Steel Corporation.[134]

Although Shanghai Gang members such as Chen Liangyu and Huang Ju tried to undermine Wen Jiabao's leadership by attacking Wen's policies, they ended up voicing their support for the central macro-management policies under pressure.

---

[129] Ning Hua, "The cold current of private enterprise towards heavy industries," *The Economic Observer*, May 30, 2004, http://www.eobserver.com.cn/english/readnews.asp?ID=180.

[130] Tang Yun, "'Tiao Kong' Ao Yun," ["'Macro-manage' the Olympics"], *Renminwang*, September 6, 2004, http://www.people.com.cn/GB/paper1631/12870/1157173.html.

[131] Chen Liangyu reportedly attacked Wen Jiabao at a Politburo meeting in early July 2004 over the alleged negative consequences of the macro-management policies. See Leslie Fong, "Leadership dispute over China growth: Premier Wen has heated debate with Shanghai party secretary over stringent measures to cool economy," http://straitstimes.asia1.com.sg/eyeoneastasia/story/0,4395,260770,00.html.

[132] "Baoshan Steel to boost capacity," April 8, 2004, http://www1.china.org.cn/english/BAT/92425.htm.

[133] "Steel sector surge shows no sign of cooling down," *China Daily*, April 27, 2004, http://www1.china.org.cn/english/BAT/94161.htm.

[134] "Tiaokong de Haochu Shishizaizai" ["The benefits of the central macro-management measures are concrete and real"], *Renminwang*, May 31, 2004, http://www.people.com.cn/GB/paper464/12114/1090209.html.

CONCLUDING REMARKS

It would be very difficult to understand the ideological evolution after the Sixteenth Party Congress without any notion of institutionalization. Before the Sixteenth Party Congress, it was widely believed that Jiang Zemin would continue to be dominant in ideological terms if his theory — the "Three Represents" — was to be enshrined in the CCP Constitution. On the contrary, Jiang Zemin lost his ideological authority as soon as he stepped down as general secretary of the Party. The new general secretary of the Party, Hu Jintao, began to introduce his own thinking only three weeks after the conclusion of the Sixteenth Party Congress. Hu introduced new "Three People's Principles" — power should be used for the people, sentiment should be linked to the people, and benefits should be generated for the people — and demonstrated his concerns for less developed regions and disadvantaged social groups. He deprived Jiang Zemin of the right to interpret the theory of the "Three Represents" and asserted his own right as the sole legitimate interpreter of the theory on behalf of the Party. Most significantly, Hu Jintao introduced and developed his own approach to development — the scientific concept of development — and turned it into a guiding principle of the Party on development within one year after he became general secretary of the Party.[135] After the Third Plenum of the Sixteenth Central Committee officially adopted this approach, Hu skillfully promoted this new guiding principle among central and local leaders in spite of some resistance from within the top Party leadership.

Over the issue of economic overheating, however, Hu and his allies came into conflict with some Shanghai Gang members. Premier Wen Jiabao, for instance, declared that the Chinese economy was overheated in the early 2004, while some Shanghai Gang members such as Chen Liangyu and Huang Ju dissented. With Hu Jintao's support, Wen introduced a series of macro-control measures

---

[135] It took Jiang Zemin more than 10 years to come up with the "Three Represents."

and — through leveling penalty against the Tieben Iron & Steel Ltd — sent a stern warning to local governments and industrial firms about serious consequences of overinvestment without appropriate central approval. Central institutions immediately jumped on the bandwagon of macro-controls, and local governments also responded with pledges of compliance. During his visit to Shanghai in late May 2004, Premier Wen urged local leaders to earnestly implement the scientific concept of development and resolutely carry out macro-control measures.

In the end, Hu–Wen declared macro-control measures a victory, and local leaders hurried to match national good news with their own local good news.

Chapter 7

Jiang Zemin's Complete Retirement

Jiang Zemin claimed to stay on as Central Military Commission (CMC) chairman in order to help Hu Jintao but actually competed for limelight with Hu Jintao. Because of his poor performance, Jiang increasingly became a liability to the new central leadership. He made gestures for stepping down but was attempting to stage a comeback. But real pressures for Jiang to step down were mounting in the midst of celebrating Deng Xiaoping's 100th birthday. Finally at the Fourth Plenum of the Sixteenth Central Committee from September 16–19, 2004, Jiang was pushed out from the Party's CMC. Along with his post of the Party's CMC chairmanship went Jiang Zemin's "military thought."

ISSUE OF JIANG ZEMIN'S COMPLETE RETIREMENT

Jiang Zemin's Unfulfilled Promises

Inspite of his official pledges, Jiang Zemin apparently was reluctant to retire from politics. Before the Sixteenth Party Congress, he made promises to retire from all of his leadership positions. As he revealed in his letter of resignation,

> In the interest of the long-term peace and stability of the Party and state, and for the sake of achieving the institutionalization,

standardization, and proceduralization of the succession of new high-ranking party and state leaders to the old, I informed the Center of my desire to retire from my leadership positions in the Central Committee and to step down from the Central Committee before the Sixteenth National Congress of the CCP. The Center accepted my request at the time.[1]

Jiang clearly had a number of good reasons to retire from all — not some — of his leadership positions. His complete retirement, as he reasoned, would be "in the interest of the long-term peace and stability of the Party and state" and would be good for "the institutionalization, standardization, and proceduralization of the succession of new high-ranking party and state leaders to the old."

To those "noble" ends, Jiang made a request to the Center to relieve him of his leadership positions. However, it is not clear what he meant by the Center (*zhongyang*). The usual translation is "the central committee"[2] of the Chinese Communist Party (CCP). The translation seems inaccurate because the central committee is a body of about 200 full members and about 150 alternate members that meets only once a year but the Center refers to some standing organ of the Party. Moreover, there is no evidence that Jiang formally informed the Fifteenth Central Committee of his desire for complete retirement. The Fifteenth Central Committee, as Table 7.1 shows, held seven plenums. It did not discuss anything about the Sixteenth National Congress of the CCP until the Sixth Plenum in September 2001. However, the Sixth Plenum simply decided that the Sixteenth Congress would be held in the second half of 2002[3]; there were no discussions of personnel issues of the Sixteenth Central

---

[1] Jiang Zemin, "Jiang Zemin tongzhi qingqiu ciqu zhonggong zhongyang junshiweiyuanhui zhuxi zhiwu de xin" ["Resignation letter (September 1, 2004)"], *Renmin ribao*, September 19, 2004, http://www.people.com.cn/GB/shizheng/1026/2793951.html.

[2] "China publishes Jiang Zemin's letter of resignation," *Renmin ribao* (English edition), September 20, 2004, http://english.people.com.cn/200409/20/eng20040920_157559.html.

[3] http://www.people.com.cn/GB/shizheng/16/20010926/570583.html.

Table 7.1 The Fifteenth Central Committee (1997–2002)

Plenum	Dates	Agenda
CCP Fifteenth National Congress, Beijing	Sep. 12–18, 1997	Report to the Fifteenth Party Congress, CCP Constitution revision, Fifteenth Central Committee, and Fifteenth CDIC membership
First Plenum, Fifteenth CC, Beijing	Sep. 19, 1997	Politburo, Secretariat, and CMC membership
Second Plenum, Fifteenth CC, Beijing	Feb. 25–26, 1998	State Council, NPC, and CNPPCC leadership
Third Plenum, Fifteenth CC, Beijing	Oct. 12–14, 1998	Agricultural and rural work
Fourth Plenum, Fifteenth CC, Beijing	Sep. 19–22, 1999	State enterprise reform
Fifth Plenum, Fifteenth CC, Beijing	Oct. 9–11, 2000	The 10th Five-Year Plan
Sixth Plenum, Fifteenth CC, Beijing	Sep. 24–26, 2001	The Party's work style and the Sixteenth Party Congress
Seventh Plenum, Fifteenth CC, Beijing	Nov. 3–5, 2002	Report to the Sixteenth Party Congress and CCP Constitution Revision

Notes: 1. CMC: Central Military Commission; 2. CDIC: Central Disciplinary Inspection Commission; 3. NPC: National People's Congress; 4. CNPPCC: Chinese National People's Political Consultative Conference.
Source: *People's Daily* online, http://www.people.com.cn/GB/shizheng/252/5089/5093/index.html.

Committee. The Seventh Plenum, which was held immediately before the convening of the Sixteenth Party Congress, did not discuss personnel issues either.

It is more likely that the Center refers to the Politburo. This is the Party institution to which Jiang submitted his resignation.

According to an official account, the Politburo and its standing committee were in charge of the entire process of selecting candidates for the Sixteenth Central Committee.[4] The process began in March 2001 when Jiang chaired meetings of the Politburo Standing Committee and the Politburo on guidelines and basic principles of selecting candidates for the Sixteenth Central Committee and the Sixteenth Central Disciplinary Inspection Commission. And the process ended on November 1, 2002, when the Politburo passed the nominations of the Politburo Standing Committee for the Sixteenth Central Committee and the Sixteenth Central Disciplinary Inspection Commission.[5]

The Fifteenth Central Committee was ignored in the process because at the Seventh Plenum during November 3–5, 2002, the nominations were not discussed; Hu Jintao introduced the nomination list to the Second Meeting of the Presidium of the Sixteenth Party Congress on 10th November on behalf of the Fifteenth Politburo.[6] In other words, the Center refers to the Politburo instead of the central committee; Jiang must have informed the Fifteenth Politburo instead of the Fifteenth Central Committee of his desire for complete retirement.

According to Jiang, prior to the Sixteenth Party Congress, the Center (i.e., the Politburo) had "accepted" his request not to assume central leadership positions and to retire from the central committee.[7] He did subsequently retire from the post of general secretary of the CCP and was not a candidate for a membership on the Sixteenth Central Committee. When the Sixteenth Party Congress concluded on November 14, 2002, Former General Secretary Jiang Zemin

---

[4] See He Ping and Liu Siyang, "Xinhuashe: Jianfuqi Jiwangkailai de Zhangyan Shiming — Dang de Xinyijian Zhongyang Weiyuanhui Danshengji" ["Xinhua News Agency: shoulder the solemn mission of succession — the birth of a new central committee of the Chinese Communist Party"], *Renmin ribao*, November 15, 2002. http://www.peopledaily.com.cn/GB/shizheng/252/8956/9419/20021115/867200.html.
[5] For a detailed analysis, see Chapter 2 of this book.
[6] He Ping and Liu Siyang, "Xinhuashe: Jianfuqi Jiwangkailai de Zhangyan Shiming."
[7] Jiang Zemin, "Jiang Zemin tongzhi."

declared that the Party's central leadership collective went through a "smooth transition" from the old to the new.[8] Out of the original seven standing members of the Politburo, all but one (Hu Jintao) were absent from the new central committee. Jiang Zemin, Li Peng, Zhu Rongji, Li Ruihuan, Wei Jianxing, and Li Lanqing were not members of the newly elected Sixteenth Central Committee; the third generation leadership with Jiang Zemin at the core appeared to have given way to the fourth generation leadership with Hu Jintao at the core.

However, on the very next day, November 15, 2002, Jiang Zemin was made chairman of the Sixteenth Central Military Committee without being a central committee member, and in the *People's Daily* of the following day his photo appeared to the left of Hu Jintao's photo and his resume was placed above Hu Jintao's resume.[9] Jiang broke his promises. If his previous arguments for his complete retirement were still valid, we may conclude that his staying on as CMC chairman was not in the interest of the long-term peace and stability of the Party and state and was bad for the institutionalization, standardization, and proceduralization of the succession of new high-ranking party and state leaders to the old. But why did the Sixteenth Central Committee decide to retain Jiang Zemin against the interest of the long-term peace and stability of the Party and state and against the institutionalization, standardization, and proceduralization of the succession of new high-ranking party and state leaders to the old? Jiang's argument was that he was retained because of "the complicated and ever-changing international situation" and "the heavy tasks of national defense and army building" and that his retention was in the "interests of the whole." [10]

Obviously, these were excuses. First, the international situation had always been complicated and ever-changing and would continue to be so in the future. There was nothing in particular in the international situation of 2002 to justify Jiang's stay. Compared

---
[8] *Renmin ribao*, November 15, 2002, p. 1.
[9] *Renmin ribao*, November 16, 2002, pp. 1,2.
[10] Jiang Zemin, "Jiang Zemin tongzhi."

with 1989 when Deng Xiaoping decided to retire from the CMC, China in 2002 was in a much more favorable international environment. Moreover, foreign affairs are purview of general secretary of the Party and president of the PRC, not that of CMC chairman. Second, there are no objective criteria to determine whether the tasks of national defense and army building were heavy or light, and therefore there are no clear criteria to determine whether Jiang's retention was justifiable on the basis of the "heavy tasks of national defense and army building." When Deng Xiaoping decided to pass on the position of the CMC chairmanship to Jiang Zemin in November 1989, Jiang Zemin had had zero military experiences; but by November 2002, Hu Jintao had been a vice chairman of the CMC for three years and two months. If Jiang could handle the heavy tasks of national defense and army building without any prior experiences, Hu could better handle the heavy tasks of national defense and army building with experiences of more than two years as the first vice chairman of the CMC. Finally, it was not obvious why Jiang's retention was in the interests of the whole country or the whole Party if it was against the interest of the long-term peace and stability of the Party and state and against the institutionalization, standardization, and proceduralization of the succession of new high-ranking party and state leaders to the old.

Jiang's "Help" to President Hu

Jiang Zemin knew that his arguments were not convincing. He again tried to come up with a more convincing reason for his retention at the First Meeting of the Tenth National People's Congress (NPC) in March 2003. As Robert Lawrence Kuhn, Jiang Zemin's official biographer, reported,

> Jiang revealed his motivation for staying on to Shanghai delegates, explaining that Party elders felt Hu Jintao was "too inexperienced" in military matters and wanted someone to "keep control" (*yazhen*). "I explained this concept to foreign friends," the outgoing president said. "But no matter how the

interpreter translated it, they did not understand the term. At last I made it plain. I said, 'I stay to help Hu Jintao.'"[11]

It is true that Hu Jintao, as Jiang himself, had no prior military experiences. But as the first vice chairman of the CMC for three and a half years, Hu was much better prepared to take over as CMC chairman in March 2003 than Jiang had been in November 1989. In order to justify Jiang's qualifications for the post of CMC chairmanship without any military experiences, Deng Xiaoping argued in November 1989 that Jiang was well qualified to be CMC chairman because he was well qualified to be general secretary of the Party. In contrast, Jiang did not provide any argument for Hu's assumption of the CMC chairmanship, but dismissed Hu as being "too inexperienced" in military matters.

There is no evidence that Jiang ever tried to help President Hu Jintao after he stayed on as CMC chairman. When the SARS epidemic hit Beijing, as mentioned in Chapter 5, Jiang was the first to flee. It was a national crisis that needed someone to keep control. But Jiang was hiding in a safe place. He never visited any hospitals or any areas affected by SARS. He asked other CMC leaders such as Cao Gangchuan[12] and Guo Boxiong[13] to visit these places on his behalf. He never publicly supported or praised President Hu's efforts.

On the contrary, Jiang took every opportunity to compete with President Hu for the limelight. Starting with the submarine accident in May 2003, Jiang Zemin discovered a formula to make him appear superior to Hu Jintao in public: In the news about military affairs, he would appear as CMC chairman and Hu as a CMC vice chairman.[14]

---

[11] Robert Lawrence Kuhn, *The Man Who Changed China: The Life and Legacy of Jiang Zemin* (New York: Crown Publishers, 2004), p. 536. This paragraph was deleted from the Chinese translation.

[12] *Renmin ribao*, March 10, 2003, p. 1. See also http://past.people.com.cn/GB/shizheng/252/9927/9928/20030509/988479.html.

[13] *Renmin ribao*, March 12, 2003, p. 1. See also http://past.people.com.cn/GB/junshi/60/20030511/989554.html.

[14] http://past.people.com.cn/GB/junshi/60/20030505/985011.html.

In the morning of June 6, 2003, after Hu Jintao just completed an extensive foreign tour, Jiang Zemin asked Hu Jintao to attend a seminar on human resources in the military. President Hu Jintao of June 5, 2003 appeared as vice chairman of the CMC on June 6, 2003, and Jiang's name was placed in front of Hu's name in the report.[15] Jiang showed no concerns as an elderly for President Hu's health after Hu's exhausting foreign trip and showed no respect as a military man for General Secretary Hu as the Party leader. Jiang's office reportedly suggested to the General Office of the Central Committee that "Comrade Jintao appears more appropriately in his military capacity" in news reports related to military affairs.[16]

However, it is questionable whether it is appropriate for President and General Secretary Hu to appear in public related to military affairs without any reference to his official titles in those capacities because one of the cardinal principles on civil–military relations in China is that the Party controls the army. It is more questionable why Hu's title as president of the PRC was not even mentioned in his meeting with military attaches along with Jiang Zemin on July 20, 2003.[17] The military attaches were not only military officers but also diplomats; they should answer to Chairman Jiang as well as President Hu. However, Jiang Zemin completely dominated the meeting, and Hu was not referred to as president of the PRC.

Moreover, Jiang's name was again placed in front of Hu's name in a report on the 50th anniversary of the founding of the National University of Defense Technology on September 1, 2003, even though Hu was absent from the celebration activities.[18] It seems that Jiang was overstepping the boundaries of his functional domains as CMC chairman when he announced a major decision of the Central Committee and the CMC to reduce another 200,000 troops by 2005 on behalf of the Central Committee of the CCP.[19] Jiang was not a

---

[15] http://past.people.com.cn/GB/junshi/60/20030606/1010365.html.
[16] Zong Hairen, *Aimei de Quanli Jiaohuan* [Ambiguous transition] (Carle Place, NY: Mirror Books, 2003), p. 260.
[17] http://www.people.com.cn/GB/shizheng/1024/1975937.html.
[18] http://www.people.com.cn/GB/shizheng/1026/2065466.html.
[19] http://www.people.com.cn/GB/shizheng/1024/2065029.html.

member of the Politburo, and he was in no position to represent the Central Committee of the CCP. None of the standing members of the Politburo were present when Jiang made the announcement. Contrary to the way Jiang and Hu's names were listed in the report, State Councilor Chen Zhili's name was listed in front of CMC Member Li Jinai's name in this report on military affairs probably because Chen is Jiang's confidante and a member of the Shanghai Gang.[20]

Jiang also took Hu to a meeting of participants in a conference of military schools on November 4, 2003.[21] Again, Hu was relegated as a CMC vice chairman while Jiang appeared as CMC chairman. Moreover, Jiang positioned himself in the center of the photo with four leaders on each side of him. In the report, Chen Zhili was elevated above four CMC members (Xu Caihou, Liang Guanglie, Liao Xilong, and Li Jinai).[22] There is an inherent contradiction in this lineup. If the names had been listed according to their positions in the Party hierarchy, Xu Caihou's name should have been listed in front of Chen's name because Xu is a member of the Secretariat while Chen is simply an ordinary member of the Sixteenth Central Committee. If the names were listed according to their positions in the CMC as it was the case because it was a report on military affairs, Chen's name should have been listed after all members of the CMC because she is not a member of the CMC. Yet her name was listed not only in front of those of other CMC members such as Liang Guanglie, Liao Xilong, and Li Jinai but also in front of the name of Xu Caihou. By placing his name in front of Hu's and placing Chen's name in front of those of all these generals, Jiang demonstrated his symbolic superiority over Hu and showed his favoritism toward Chen.

Finally, Jiang appeared in public as CMC chairman again followed by Hu Jintao as CMC vice chairman on December 12, 2003.[23]

---

[20] *Renmin ribao*, September 2, 2003, p. 4.
[21] *Renmin ribao*, November 5, 2003, p. 1. See also http://www.people.com.cn/GB/shizheng/1024/2169412.html.
[22] *Renmin ribao*, November 5, 2003, p. 1.
[23] *Renmin ribao*, December 13, 2003, p. 1. See also http://www.people.com.cn/GB/shizheng/1024/2243340.html.

Jiang and Hu met with some participants in a symposium on the work of Party construction in the People's Liberation Army (PLA). Apparently, some Chinese netters were fed up with Jiang's vanity. Some criticized Jiang by invoking the principle of the Party commanding the army while others were more direct at Jiang.[24] One jabbed Jiang by saying that "Come on! We do not have complaints if you want to put up a show yourself. But please do not use our head of state as your setoff."[25] Another pointedly remarked that "Hu Jintao is the Party leader" instead of only an associate to a military leader.[26]

Jiang's Comeback in 2004

In his resignation letter, Jiang stated that "in the interest of the long-term development of the cause of the Party and the people, I have been looking forward to my complete retirement from leadership positions."[27] This statement is anything but being sincere because he deliberately missed two opportunities in 2003 for complete retirement. He did not surrender his military power at the First Meeting of the Tenth NPC in March 2003, though he received the lowest approval rate among all members of the new CMC. He deliberately missed the second opportunity in October 2003 when the Third Plenum of the Sixteenth Central Committee was held: He did not even bother writing a letter of resignation.

Instead of planning for complete retirement, Jiang was actually staging a comeback in 2004. He gave every indication that he was reasserting his power. At the opening of the Second Meeting of the Chinese National People's Political Consultative Conference on March 3, 2004, Jiang reportedly broke the protocol of Chinese politics and walked in front of General Secretary Hu Jintao.[28] Only a

---

[24] http://202.99.23.223:8080/bbs_new/filepool/htdoc/html/a656d198a6482d8002cd1c4364553fbb5e62e7b6/b669430/l_669430_1.html.
[25] *Ibid.*
[26] *Ibid.*
[27] *Ibid.*
[28] For some photos, see http://www.renminbao.com/rmb/articles/2004/3/3/30179.html; http://www.renminbao.com/rmb/articles/2004/3/4/30181.html.

year earlier Jiang made gesture to let Hu go first,[29] but now Jiang was walking in front of Hu even though his name was listed after Hu's name in accordance with the protocol of Chinese politics.[30] Two days later, when the Second Meeting of the Tenth NPC was opened on March 5, 2004, Jiang Zemin again walked in front of Hu Jintao and other standing members of the Politburo.[31] It appeared from a photo of Jiang walking in front of Hu that Jiang's arrogance was not well received: Nobody was really paying any attention to him, and all eyes were fixed on President Hu.[32]

To demonstrate his symbolic superiority to President Hu in the military, Jiang repeated his denigrating gig a few more times in early 2004. He took President Hu as CMC vice chairman to an assembly of the PLA deputies to the Second Meeting of the Tenth NPC on March 11, 2004;[33] Jiang took Hu to an exhibition of military logistics equipment technology in the Beijing Exhibition Hall on April 28, 2004, for the same publicity reason;[34] Jiang took Hu to a meeting with deputies to the Tenth Party Congress of the PLA Air Force on May 19, 2004, again showing his symbolic superiority over Hu.[35]

An underlying factor behind Jiang's aggressive behavior was that the Second Meeting of the Tenth NPC was considering a constitutional amendment to include the "Three Represents" into the Constitution of the PRC. The People's Republic of China adopted its first constitution in 1954 and replaced it in 1975. The 1975 Constitution was soon replaced in 1978, but its replacement did

---

[29] For a photo, see http://www.renminbao.com/rmb/articles/2003/3/17/25474.html.
[30] *Renmin ribao*, March 4, 2004, p. 1.
[31] For some photos, see http://www.renminbao.com/rmb/articles/2004/3/5/30194.html.
[32] *Renminbao*, March 13, 2003, http://www.renminbao.com/rmb/articles/2004/3/13/30298.html.
[33] *Renmin ribao*, March 12, 2004, p. 1. See also http://www.people.com.cn/GB/paper464/11529/1039592.html.
[34] *Renmin ribao*, April 29, 2004, http://www.people.com.cn/GB/paper464/11893/1071771.html.
[35] *Renmin ribao*, May 20, 2004, http://www.people.com.cn/GB/paper464/12037/1083219.html.

not last long. After Deng Xiaoping replaced Hua Guofeng as the paramount leader, China adopted another constitution in 1982. By early 2004, the 1982 Constitution had been amended three times (April 12, 1988; March 29, 1993; and March 15, 1999).[36] As China was becoming a country of rule by law (instead of rule of law), the CCP was trying to legitimize its rule by legal means. The Sixteenth Central Committee of the CCP made a decision at its Third Plenum on October 14, 2003, to make some suggestions for constitutional amendments. According to the communiqué issued by the Third Plenum of the Sixteenth Central Committee,

> The Constitution of the People's Republic of China is the fundamental law of the state, the general program of governance, and the legal foundation of maintaining the unification of the country, the unity of nationalities, economic development, social progress, and the long-term stability and peace. The practice proves that the current Constitution is a good constitution that is fit for our national conditions and that it has played an extremely important role in economic, political, cultural, and social lives of our country. Therefore, the Constitution should basically remain what it is. In the meantime, the Constitution will be better able to play the role of the fundamental law of the state if the significant theoretical points and important policies approved by the Sixteenth Party Congress can be written into the Constitution in accordance with the objective requirements of economic and social development of our country and in accordance with legal procedures.[37]

One of the significant theoretical points approved by the Sixteenth Party Congress was to establish the "Three Represents" as a part of the ideological guidance along with Marxism–Leninism,

---

[36] For an English translation of the Constitution and its amendments, see http://english.people.com.cn/constitution/constitution.html.
[37] http://www.people.com.cn/GB/shizheng/1024/2133923.html.

Mao Zedong Thought, and Deng Xiaoping Theory.[38] The same appendage was to be included in the Preamble of the Constitution of the PRC as well. The "Three Represents" is a description of the CCP: The CCP represents the development trend of China's advanced productive forces, represents the orientation of China's advanced culture, and represents the fundamental interests of the overwhelming majority of the Chinese people.[39] As such, the "Three Represents" might be appropriate for the Constitution of the CCP but not for the Constitution of the PRC. For instance, it is understandable that the CCP members should keep in mind the fundamental interests of the overwhelming majority of the Chinese people, but it is confusing to urge citizens of the PRC to represent the fundamental interests of the overwhelming majority of the Chinese people. Aren't PRC citizens the Chinese people?

How does the inclusion of the "Three Represents" help the Constitution play its role of the fundamental law of the state better? Ren Maodong, a standing member of the Tenth NPC, answered:

> Writing the important thought of the "Three Represents" into the Constitution reflects the idea of governing for the people and the wishes of the broad masses of people.
>
> What does it mean to govern for the people? It means to serve the interests of the people. The basic point of the important thought of the "Three Represents" is to represent the fundamental interests of the people. The interests refer to rights of the people in legal terms, to interests of the people in terms of democratic politics, and to people having rights in legal theory. If there are no people's rights in legal terms, people's interests will have no guarantees because people's interests cannot be realized without legal rights. Therefore, writing the important thought of the "Three Represents" into the Constitution will provide a legal guarantee for the fundamental interests of the

---

[38] "Constitution of the Chinese Communist Party," http://www.people.com.cn/GB/shizheng/16/20021118/868961.html.
[39] http://www.people.com.cn/GB/shizheng/16/20021118/868961.html.

people and secure the people's rights by legal means — this is an organic unity.[40]

On the surface, this answer seems to have clarified the purpose of writing the "Three Represents" into the Constitution: To provide a legal guarantee for the fundamental interests of the Chinese people. But the confusion remains because the "Three Represents" as a description of the CCP said nothing about the people's rights. On the contrary, the "Three Represents" may imply that the CCP as a whole and its members as individuals have legal rights over the fundamental interests of the overwhelming majority of the Chinese people because they are representatives of the Chinese people.

Moreover, this representation can be quite arbitrary. For instance, Ren Maodong "represented" the broad masses of the Chinese people when he "confidently" claimed that writing the "Three Represents" into the Constitution of the PRC would be a reflection of the wishes of the broad masses of the Chinese people. And his view was shared by other deputies to the NPC meeting such as Li Guoxun, Zhao Aiming, and Li Gang.[41] But it is questionable whether these deputies truly represented the views of the Chinese people because there were no mechanisms in China for the people to express their views.

Anyway, the constitutional amendments were adopted by the Second Meeting of the Tenth NPC on March 14, 2004, and the "Three Represents" was written into the Constitution of the PRC.[42] Jiang Zemin was implicitly elevated to be equal with Mao Zedong and Deng Xiaoping.

---

[40] *Renmin ribao*, March 12, 2004, p. 1.

[41] *Renmin ribao*, March 14, 2004, p. 1.

[42] Other than the "Three Represents," the amendments were significant because they introduced the concept of private property rights and guaranteed their protection under the law. For details, see the constitutional amendments adopted on March 14, 2004, and the comparison of the revised clauses of the Constitution to their originals in *Shiliuda Yilai Dang he Guojia Zhongyao Wenxian Xuanbian* [*Important Selections of the Party and the State Documents Since the Sixteenth Party Congress*] (Beijing: Renmin Chubanshe, 2005), Vol. 1, pp. 395–405.

Jiang Zemin and PLA Generals

To bolster his image as a powerful man, Jiang promoted 15 military officers to the rank of full generals on June 20, 2004. The People's Republic of China established a military rank system in 1955 when 10 marshals, 10 senior generals, 55 generals, 175 lieutenant generals, and 801 major generals were appointed.[43] But the system was abolished 10 years later. The military rank system was restored in 1988 when Deng Xiaoping was CMC chairman. In this newly restored system, there are three ranks at the level of generals: general, lieutenant general, and major general. Between September 1988 and June 2002, 81 officers were promoted to the rank of general. Deng promoted 17 of them, and Jiang promoted the rest (64 officers). Except for 1995, 1997, and 2001, Jiang appointed generals every single year since 1993.[44] "Promoting senior officers to full generals," as Willy Lam, a China watcher, observed, was one of Jiang's favorite means to score points with the top brass of the PLA.[45] Now in June 2004, he initiated another round of promotions.

The senior offers who were awarded the rank of general this time include Ge Zhenfeng (deputy chief of staff), Zhang Li (deputy chief of staff), You Xigui (director of the Central Guard Bureau), Zhang Wentai (political commissar of the General Logistics Department), Hu Yanlin (political commissar of the PLA Navy), Zheng Shenxia (president of the Academy of Military Sciences), Zhao Kemin (political commissar of the University of National Defense), Zhu Qi (commander of the Beijing Military Region), Li Qianyuan (commander of the Lanzhou Military Region), Liu Dongdong (political commissar of the Jinan Military Region), Lei Mingqiu (political commissar of the Nanjing Military Region), Liu Zhenwu (commander of the Guangzhou Military Region), Yang

---

[43] For a detailed list, see http://news.xinhuanet.com/ziliao/2004-06/30/content_1556923.htm.
[44] For a list of these generals, see http://www.china.org.cn/chinese/zhuanti/168115.htm.
[45] Willy Wo-Lap Lam, *The Era of Jiang Zemin* (Singapore: Prentice Hall, 1999), p. 182.

Deqing (political commissar of the Guangzhou Military Region), Wu Shuangzhan (commander of the Chinese People's Armed Police Force), and Sui Mingtai (commander of the Chinese People's Armed Police Force).[46] Among these senior officers, 11 were full members, two were alternate members, and two were nonmembers of the Sixteenth Central Committee of the CCP. Zhang Li and You Xigui were alternate members, and Hu Yanlin and Zheng Shenxia were not central committee members (Table 7.2).[47]

Probably because of his close association with Jiang Zemin, You Xigui is widely considered as a member of the Shanghai Gang.[48] You's promotion to the rank of general close to his retirement age of 65 aroused the suspicion that Jiang would not retire from his post as CMC chairman until the Seventh National Congress of the CCP in 2007. It is not unprecedented that the director of the Central Guard Bureau is awarded the rank of general. Yang Dezhong, You's predecessor, was promoted to that rank in 1994.[49] Compared with those of Yang, however, You's credentials were much less impressive and much less worthy of the rank of general. Yang joined the revolutionary in 1936 and joined the CCP in 1938. He was appointed deputy director of the Central Guard Bureau in the 1950s. Yang assumed the position of director of the Central Guard Bureau in 1978 and stayed in the position until 1994. He was a full member of the Twelfth, Thirteenth, and Fourteenth Central Committees. He was

---

[46] *Renminwang*, June 20, 2004, http://www1.people.com.cn/GB/shizheng/1027/2585268.html.

[47] For a detailed analysis of this group, see Zhiyue Bo, "The PLA's New Generals," *Chinese Military Update*, Vol. 2, No. 1 (June 2004), pp. 1–3.

[48] In his bio, there is no clear evidence that he has indeed worked in Shanghai previously. See http://chinavitae.com/biography_display.php?id=2215 for details.

[49] http://www.china.org.cn/chinese/zhuanti/168115.htm. For his bio, see Shen Xueming and Zheng Jianying (eds), *Zhonggong Diyijie zhi Dishiwujie Zhongyangweiyuan* [*The Central Committee Members of the Chinese Communist Party from the First Through the Fifteenth Central Committee*] (Beijing: Zhongyangwenxian chubanshe, 2001), p. 289.

Table 7.2 New Generals of the PLA (June 2004)

Name	Office	Title	CC16	Birth	Age	Home	Party Year	Work	Major	Lieut.	Gen.
Ge Zhenfeng	Chief Staff	Dep. Chief Staff	Full	1944	60	Hebei	1965	1962	1990	1998	2004
Hu Yanlin	Navy	Pol. Commissar	No	1943	61	Jilin	1960	1959	1990	1995	2004
Lei Mingqiu	Nanjing	Pol. Commissar	Full	1942	62	Hunan	1964	1962	1988	1994	2004
Li Qianyuan	Lanzhou	Commander	Full	1942	62	Henan	1963	1961	1988	1996	2004
Liu Dongdong	Jinan	Pol. Commissar	Full	1945	59	Hubei	1963	1961	1992	2000	2004
Liu Zhenwu	Guangzhou	Commander	Full	1944	60	Hunan	1964	1961	1990	1997	2004
Sui Mingtai	Armed Police	Pol. Commissar	Full	1942	62	Shandong	1962	1960	1988	1996	2004
Wu Shuangzhan	Armed Police	Commander	Full	1945	59	Henan	1965	1965	1990	1997	2004
Yang Deqing	Guangzhou	Pol. Commissar	Full	1942	62	Hubei	1964	1963	1990	1996	2004
You Xigui	Central Guard	Director	Alternate	1939	65	Hebei	1960	1958	1990	1997	2004
Zhang Li	Chief Staff	Dep. Chief Staff	Alternate	1943	61	Shandong	1966	1958	1997	2001	2004
Zhang Wentai	Logistics	Pol. Commissar	Full	1942	62	Shandong	1960	1958	1988	1995	2004
Zhao Keming	Defense Univ.	Pol. Commissar	Full	1942	62	Hubei	1962	1961	1988	1998	2004
Zheng Shenxia	AMS	President	No	1942	62	Hebei	uk	1958	1990	1997	2004
Zhu Qi	Beijing	Commander	Full	1942	62	Yunnan	1961	1959	1990	1996	2004

Notes: Party Year=the year the officer joined the CCP; work=the year the officer joined the PLA; uk=unkown. Age is calculated by subtracting the year of birth from 2004. AMS=Academy of Military Sciences.
Source: Author's database on the Sixteenth Central Committee members.

awarded the rank of lieutenant general in 1988 and promoted to the rank of general in 1994, before his retirement. You, on the other hand, joined the PLA in 1958 and joined the Party in 1960. He was an alternate member of the Fifteenth Central Committee and the least popular alternate member of the Sixteenth Central Committee.[50] From the fact that Jiang had promoted seven officers to generals at the eve of the Sixteenth National Congress of the CCP, some analysts predicted from Jiang's promotions in June 2004 that Jiang would likely opt to stay until the Seventeenth National Congress of the CCP in 2007.[51] Although these promotions hardly constitute sufficient evidence for Jiang's true intentions to stay, at least they do not suggest that Jiang desire to retire soon. It is clear, however, that Jiang intended to build up his power by granting favors to senior military officers. Again, Jiang asked Hu to announce the promotions,[52] reducing the role of the president of the PRC to the role of an announcer.[53]

Jiang Zemin and the Taiwan Issue

On July 8, 2004, Jiang Zemin turned his meeting with Condoleezza Rice, the US president's national security adviser, into a major publicity show with a strong signal that he was still dominant in Chinese politics. First, his meeting with Rice was scheduled one day ahead of President Hu's meeting with Rice,[54] a scene reminiscent of the 1989 scenario in which Deng Xiaoping met with Soviet Leader

---

[50] You's promotion to the rank of general has been indirectly criticized on some PRC official websites.

[51] See Xu Shangli, "It looks like that Jiang Zemin would not retire until the 17th National Congress of the Chinese Communist Party," http://www5.chinesenewsnet.com/MainNews/Opinion/2004_6_20_15_2_32_579.html.

[52] http://www1.people.com.cn/GB/shizheng/1027/2585268.html.

[53] *Renmin ribao*, June 21, 2004, http://www.people.com.cn/GB/paper464/12275/1104676.html.

[54] Jiang met with Rice on July 8 and Hu on July 9. See *Renmin ribao*, July 9, 2004, http://www.people.com.cn/GB/paper464/12420/1117085.html and *Renmin ribao*, July 10, 2004, http://www.people.com.cn/GB/paper464/12427/1117741.html.

Mikhail Gorbachev before General Secretary Zhao Ziyang's meeting with Gorbachev. Second, in an attempt to justify his stay as CMC chairman, Jiang complemented Rice by saying that "you look younger" with the expectation that Rice would say "You too."[55] Unfortunately, Rice did not reply in kind. Third, Jiang told Rice that he was "handing over more and more power" to President Hu, implying that ultimate authority still rested with him instead of Hu Jintao.[56]

Finally, Jiang played up the Taiwan issue to boost his position. He told Rice that the Taiwan issue was the most vital and most sensitive issue in Sino-American relations and that China's sovereignty and territorial integrity were paramount. "If the Taiwan authorities go toward independence and foreign forces step in," he said, "we will never sit by and watch."[57] A few days later, on July 15, 2004, *Globe Weekly*, a publication of Xinhua News Agency (the most important official news agency in China), published an interview with Yan Xuetong, director of the Institute of International Affairs, Qinghua University. According to Yan, the Taiwan issue was paramount because Taiwan's independence would lead to the collapse of China as what had occurred to the former Soviet Union. For this reason, China should do whatever possible to prevent the declaration of Taiwan's independence, and the most effective way is to initiate a limited military action against Taiwan by 2006. This limited military action, as Yan saw it, should not affect China's economic development. On the same day, Hong Kong's *Wenwei Pao* also revealed that at an expanded meeting of the CMC a few days earlier, Jiang Zemin set a timetable of solving the Taiwan issue at around 2020.

Whether China was going to "solve" the Taiwan issue by 2006 or 2020, in fact, is not of any particular significance for Jiang. The most

---

[55] *Xinhua News*, July 8, 2004, http://news.xinhuanet.com/newscenter/2004-07/08/content_1584476.htm.
[56] Joseph Khan, "Former leader is still a power in China's life," *The New York Times*, July 16, 2004, Section A, Column 5, 1.
[57] *Renmin ribao*, July 9, 2004, http://www.people.com.cn/GB/paper464/12420/1117085.html.

important political message was that Jiang, as commander-in-chief, should be regarded as indispensable so long as the Taiwan issue remained unresolved. In other words, playing up the importance of the Taiwan issue was Jiang's tactic to postpone his complete retirement. By so doing, Jiang was also undermining the leadership of Hu Jintao and Wen Jiabao and trying to derail their policy of peaceful rise. Jiang even hinted that the second term for Hu and Wen would not be "automatic"; Chen Liangyu, Shanghai's party secretary and Politburo member as well as one of Jiang's cronies, took the hint and reportedly challenged Wen directly at a Politburo meeting.[58]

PRESSURES FOR JIANG'S RETIREMENT

Clearly, Jiang did not really want to retire as CMC chairman. He was in fact trying to come back to the center stage in politics in 2004. In spite of his powerful appearances, Jiang in the mid-2004 was increasingly faced with pressures from all quarters, in particular from Deng's family, military leaders, and eventually Hu Jintao.

Pressures from Deng's Family

Jiang Zemin was selected by Deng Xiaoping in the aftermath of the Tiananmen Incident of 1989. Deng installed him as general secretary of the Party in June 1989 and trusted him with the post of the CMC chairmanship in November 1989. But Deng was not happy with Jiang's performance in his first two-and-a-half years because Jiang was not promoting economic reforms but was engaged in futile ideological debates about the nature of reforms and the imminent danger of "peaceful evolution." Deng was outraged and threatened to oust Jiang for his obstruction to policies of economic reforms and

---

[58] Leslie Fong, "Leadership dispute over China growth: Premier Wen has heated debate with Shanghai party secretary over stringent measures to cool economy," *The Strait Times*, July 10, 2004, http://straitstimes.asia1.com.sg/eyeoneastasia/story/0,4395,260770,00.html. However, I could not locate this Politburo meeting in *Renmin ribao*.

opening to the outside world. Jiang later was forced to turn around and vowed his full support for Deng's policies, but privately held grudges against him. With Deng's full support, Jiang ousted the "Yang Brothers" (Yang Shangkun and Yang Baibing) and gradually consolidated his power in the military and the Party. Yet Jiang was not grateful to Deng and grew distant from Deng's family.

With the approach of the 100th Anniversary, Deng's family became very active. During an interview on CCTV (China's premier official television station) on July 28, 2004, there was a replay of Deng Xiaoping's resignation letter to the Politburo (written on September 4, 1989, and published on November 9, 1989) and of Deng Xiaoping's farewell speech on November 9, 1989. "In order to make the contingent of leading cadres younger and to abolish the life-long tenure," the CCTV commended, "Deng Xiaoping retired on November 9, 1989 while he was still healthy, setting a good example."[59] In the interview, Deng Lin, Deng's eldest daughter, gave a detailed description of Deng's life after retirement.[60] According to Deng Lin, before retirement, Deng had a habit of reading official documents every morning at 9 am; after retirement, he stopped reading them. "He whole-heartedly wanted to be an ordinary citizen," his daughter relayed.[61] Although Jiang Zemin's name was not mentioned, the interview, especially Deng Lin's statement, was widely interpreted as sending Jiang a reminder of about Jiang's own complete retirement.

A photo of Deng shaking hands with Hu on display at the exhibition on Deng Xiaoping's life in Beijing[62] also caused some speculations about Jiang Zemin. The photo, originally taken in October 1992 (around the Fourteenth Congress of the CCP), appeared in the media in three different versions. The first version

---

[59] *Xinhua News*, July 28, 2004, http://news.xinhuanet.com/newscenter/2004-07/28/content_1659335_3.htm.
[60] *Ibid.*
[61] *Ibid.*
[62] "Exhibition opens in dedication to Deng Xiaoping's 100th birth anniversary," *Sina* (English), August 10, 2004, http://english.sina.com/news/china/deng_exhibit.shtml.

appeared in Hong Kong's *Wen Wei Pao* on August 11, 2004. According to the report in *Wen Wei Pao*, this version was the one that was on display at the exhibition on the life of late Deng Xiaoping in the China National Museum. In this version, Deng Xiaoping, escorted by his daughter (Deng Rong), was shaking hands with Hu Jintao. It seems that no one else was present because the photo has a dark background. It is reported that Deng Nan, Deng's second daughter, told visitors to the exhibition that Deng's family was looking for this photo while preparing for an album of Deng Xiaoping but could not find it. They then checked with Jintao (Hu Jintao) to see if he had a copy, and Jintao found the original photo and gave it to them for the album.[63]

A few days later, the second version was released by the official Xinhua News Agency. In this version, Deng and Hu were in the identical positions with a large group of deputies to the Fourteenth Congress vaguely in the background.[64] The third version of the photo was published in *Oriental Outlook* (*Liaowang Dongfang*) on August 19, 2004. In this version, Deng and Hu appeared in the same positions as in the other two versions, but with Jiang Zemin standing dead center between them. Apparently, this last version is the original version of the photo, and Jiang was airbrushed out of the picture in the two earlier ones.[65]

It is not clear who modified the photo,[66] but it is unlikely that Hu did it. He probably received the modified version. But the fact that Hu gave it to Deng's family for public display indicates that Hu

---

[63] Tian Jing, "Sizhongquanhui yu gaoceng boyi: shuidongle Deng Xiaoping he Hu Jintao de hezhao?" ["The Fourth Plenum and the Game of Elite Politics (31): Who altered the photo of Deng Xiaoping and Hu Jintao?"], *Asia Times*, August 30, 2004, http://www.asiatimes-chinese.com/2004/08/0830rep2.htm.

[64] *Ibid*. This version was also published in the *Renmin ribao*. See *Renmin ribao*, August 21, 2004, p. 9.

[65] Tian Jing, "Sizhongquanhui yu gaoceng boyi: shuidongle Deng Xiaoping he Hu Jintao de hezhao?"

[66] It is possible that Jiang had himself and others erased from the photo out of jealousy. For this interpretation, see *Jiang Zemin Qiren* [*The Real Jiang Zemin*] at www.epochtimes.com, pp. 58, 59.

was pleased with the version without Jiang. The fact that Deng's family was happy to use it in the exhibition also indicates that Deng's family was also happy with the photo without Jiang.

Jiang Zemin was absent when a statue of Deng Xiaoping was unveiled in Deng's hometown of Guang'an, Sichuan Province, on August 13, 2004.[67] Hu Jintao was the one who unveiled the statue. But Jiang penned an inscription on the statue that was believed to be very offensive to Deng and Deng's family. On the statue, Jiang wrote the Chinese characters for "the Bronze Statue of Deng Xiaoping" ("*Deng Xiaoping Tongxiang*"). It is a tradition in China that an inscription should reflect the author's view of the person. Mao Zedong, for instance, wrote an inscription for a 15-year old girl who had been executed by a warlord because of her communist connections. It reads "Born to be great, died to be glorious" (*Shengdeweida, sideguangrong*). But Jiang's inscription for such a great national leader as Deng Xiaoping was simply a description of the physical aspect of the statue. What is he trying to say with the inscription? The statue is made of "bronze" instead of "iron" or "gold?" What is his view of Deng Xiaoping? Is he saying that Deng Xiaoping is nothing but simply a bronze statue? It is not that Jiang did not know the significance of an inscription or how to evaluate Deng Xiaoping as a national leader. There were better alternatives. When Jiang was general secretary of the Party, he was constantly praising Deng Xiaoping as the "general architect" of China's economic reform and opening up. At Deng Xiaoping's 90th birthday, General Liu Huaqing wrote an inscription, "boundless beneficence" (*Gongde wuliang*).[68] But Jiang did not use any of these alternatives because he probably still hated Deng Xiaoping for having

---

[67] "Hu Jintao wei Deng Xiaoping tongxiang jiemu, Jiang Zemin wei tongxiang timing" ["Hu Jintao unveiled the statue of Deng Xiaoping; Jiang Zemin penned an inscription for the statue"], *CCTV*, August 13, 2004, http://www.cctv.com/news/china/20040813/100893.shtml.

[68] Liu Huaqing, "Nanwang Xiaoping" [Unforgettable Xiaoping], *Renmin ribao*, August 17, 2004, http://www.people.com.cn/GB/paper464/12718/1142627.html. See also Liu Huaqing, *Liu Huaqing Huiyilu* [*Memoirs of Liu Huaqing*] (Beijing: Jiefangjun Chubanshe, 2004), p. 723.

threatened to fire him in 1992.[69] Because of Jiang's offensive inscription, some of Deng's family refused to attend the ceremony as a form of protest.[70]

Pressures from Military Leaders

Military leaders seem to be getting impatient with Jiang. The first indication of their impatience occurred on July 31, 2004. In a speech at the ceremony to celebrate the 77th Anniversary of the Founding of the PLA that day, Defense Minister Cao Gangchuan, Politburo member and CMC vice chairman, did not mention Jiang Zemin's name at all.[71] This omission was politically significant because on a similar occasion in 2003, Cao mentioned Jiang's name three times.[72] The key phrase — the army will "obey the directions of the Party Center, the CMC, and Chairman Jiang in all actions"[73] — was visibly absent in Cao's speech in 2004. In contrast, in the speech of 2004 as in the speech of 2003, he urged PLA officers and soldiers to be closely united around the Party leadership with Hu Jintao as general secretary.

---

[69] According to Chen Kaizhi, former deputy secretary general of the Guangdong Provincial Party Committee who accompanied Deng during Deng's southern tour of 1992, Deng was furious with those who were not actively promoting reforms including Jiang Zemin. He repeatedly said, "Whoever opposes reform comes to no good end; he should be removed from office!" For Chen's recount, see "Xiaoping nanxun 'shouxi jiedaiguan' Chen Kaizhi shuo nanxun" ["Chen Kaizhi — the primary host of Xiaoping's southern tour — talks about Deng Xiaoping's southern tour"], *Renmin ribao*, April 21, 2004, http://www.people.com.cn/GB/14677/22097/2459739.html. Chen Kaizhi, Chen Jianhua, and Yao Xinyan, "Huiyi Deng Xiaoping 1992 nian nanfang zhixing" ["Deng Xiaoping's southern tour of 1992"], *Renmin ribao*, http://zg.people.com.cn/GB/33839/34943/34982/2620620.html.
[70] "Jiang Zemin wei Deng tongxiang tici renao Deng Xiaoping jiaren" ["Jiang Zemin angered Deng Xiaoping's family with his inscription"], *Reminbao*, August 23, 2004, http://www.renminbao.com/rmb/articles/2004/8/23/32301.html.
[71] *Renmin ribao*, July 31, 2004, http://www.people.com.cn/GB/shizheng/1024/2678680.html.
[72] *Renmin ribao*, August 1, 2003, http://www.people.com.cn/GB/paper464/9810/902048.html.
[73] *Ibid.*

Cao Gangchuan has been regarded as one of Jiang's men. According to Gao Xin, Cao owed his promotions to Jiang Zemin.[74] Cao's career was stagnant in the 1980s. He joined the PLA in 1954 and studied in the Soviet Union for six years between 1957 and 1963.[75] In 1980, after 26 years of service, he was only a deputy director of the General Planning Division of Military Equipment under the PLA's General Staff.[76] It was Jiang who promoted him to director of the Office of Military Trade of the CMC in 1990, to deputy chief of the General Staff in 1992, to minister of Commission of Science, Technology, and Industry for National Defense (COSTIND) in 1996, to the CMC of the CCP in 1998, to the rank of general in 1999, to the Politburo and vice chairman of the CMC of the CCP in 2002, and to defense minister in 2003.[77] In return, Cao had been very loyal to Jiang. He was probably one of the PLA officers to petition for Jiang's stay as CMC chairman. He displayed his unswerving support for Jiang in July 2003 when he mentioned Jiang's name three times in his speech at the ceremony of celebrating the 76th Anniversary of the Founding of the PLA in the Great Hall of the People in Beijing.[78] Cao's omission of Jiang's name in 2004 was not a clerical typo; it was a clear signal that Cao was abandoning Jiang for Hu Jintao.

Half a month later, on August 16, 2004, *Qiushi* [*Seeking Truth*], the CCP's official journal, published an article by Former Defense Minister Chi Haotian. In the article, Chi devoted a whole section to the principle of the army following the leadership of the Party.[79]

---

[74] Gao Xin, *Lingdao Zhongguo de Xinrenwu: Zhonggong Shiliujie Zhengzhiju Weiyuan* (China's top leaders: bios of China's Politburo members) (Carle Place, NY: Mirror Books, 2003), Vol. 2, pp. 722–738.

[75] For Cao's official resume, see http://www.pladaily.com.cn/item/gjldr/content/04.htm.

[76] Gao Xin, *Lingdao Zhongguo de Xinrenwu Lingdao Zhongguo*, Vol. 2, p. 724.

[77] http://www.pladaily.com.cn/item/gjldr/content/04.htm.

[78] *Renmin ribao*, August 1, 2003, http://www.people.com.cn/GB/paper464/ 9810/ 902048.html.

[79] Chi Haotian, "Zhiguo Xingweiye Tongjun Kaixinpian" ("Great accomplishments in governance and opening a new chapter in the command of the army"), *Qiushi*, No. 389 (August 16, 2004), http://www.qsjournal.com.cn/qs/20040816/GB/qs^389^0^3.htm.

According to Chi, Deng made a very simple farewell speech and then left. "He is really a selfless and fearless person, a person who is really free from vulgar interests, and a person who is truly concerned with the overall situation," Chi commended.[80] Chi reportedly does not have high regards for Jiang Zemin. This article seems to have expressed his distaste for Jiang.

On September 7, 2004, Beijing Military Region Commander Zhu Qi and Political Commissar Fu Tinggui jointly published an article in the *People's Daily*, entitled "The origin of the great practice of the general goals of the PLA's buildup in the new era."[81] Instead of emphasizing the salience of the Taiwan issue as Jiang did two months earlier, these authors shared their memories of Deng Xiaoping on postponing wars. According to these two generals, Comrade Deng Xiaoping made it clear that it is possible to avoid a war in the near future and that Deng's observation is correct.[82]

This is another example in which a former loyalist abandoned Jiang. As mentioned in Chapter 5, Zhu Qi's meteoric rise in 2002 could be attributed to Jiang. He was promoted to commander of the Beijing Military Region from chief of staff of the Chengdu Military Region, and he was made a full member of the Sixteenth Central Committee, skipping the alternate membership. In return, Zhu published an article in *Seeking Truth* on December 1, 2002, praising the wisdom of the Party in retaining Jiang as CMC chairman.[83] Zhu's loyalty seems to have paid off because he was promoted to the rank of general on June 20, 2004, under Jiang Zemin's order.

---

[80] *Ibid.*

[81] Zhu Qi and Fu Tinggui, "Xinshiqi wojunjianshe zongmubiao de weidashijian faduan" ["The origin of the great practice of the general goals of the PLA's buildup in the new era"], *Renmin ribao*, September 7, 2004, p. 9. Also accessible at http://www.people.com.cn/GB/shizheng/1026/2766060.html.

[82] *Ibid.*

[83] Zhu Qi, "Jijituiji Guofang he Jundui Jianshe" ["Actively promote national defense and military construction"], *Qiushi*, No. 238 (December 1, 2002), http://www.qsjournal.com.cn/qs/20021201/GB/qs^348^0^7.htm.

In September 2004, however, Zhu seemed to be contradicting Jiang's military policies. Jiang was talking about the seriousness of the Taiwan issue and thus the urgency for military buildup for an imminent war. But Zhu was advocating a defense strategy.

Pressures from Hu Jintao

Finally, Hu Jintao also seemed to be getting impatient with Jiang. The earliest indication of Hu's impatience was the Fifteenth Politburo Group Study on July 24, 2004. The topic for the study was coordinated development of national defense construction and economic construction.[84] Professor Guo Guirong of the Science and Technology Council of the General Armament Department and Research Fellow Luan Enjie of the Specialists Advisory Council of the COSTIND were invited to share their knowledge and understanding on the topic, and Hu Jintao made a speech. Hu indicated that China was faced with a basically favorable international environment and thus should take this important strategic opportunity to focus on economic development, and that China should hold high the banner of peace, development, and cooperation and take the path of peaceful development. As for the relations between national defense and economic development, Hu argued that economic development should not be in direct conflict with national defense buildup. On the one hand, economic construction is the foundation for national defense; without economic development, there would be no national defense buildup. On the other hand, national defense capacity is a component of national capacity; without national defense buildup, there would be no safeguards for a peaceful environment for economic construction. Therefore, China needed to pay attention to national defense construction while focusing on economic construction.

It is not clear exactly when Hu had the idea about a military topic for this particular study session, but Hu probably came up with the idea in part as a response to Jiang's playing up of the

---

[84] http://news.xinhuanet.com/zhengfu/2004-07/26/content_1648021.htm.

Taiwan issue in early July. By delivering a speech on national defense construction, Hu demonstrated his ability to manage military affairs. As an article in the *Oriental Outlook* commented, the Politburo group study session of July 24, 2004 touched a sensitive topic that could make many people nervous.[85] Hu's remarks, according to the article, were based on an expression from the political report to the Sixteenth Party Congress and were consistent with Deng Xiaoping's "predictions" 20 years earlier that military modernization would come after China's national economy has quadrupled.[86] Notably, as a Politburo member, Cao Gangchuan must have been one of the participants in this Politburo group study session. His subsequent omission of Jiang Zemin in his speech on July 31, 2004 might have been inspired by Hu's remarks.

One month later, Hu Jintao exerted his pressures again. At the ceremony to celebrate the 100th Anniversary of Deng Xiaoping's birthday on August 22, 2004, Hu twice referred to Deng's efforts to eliminate the life-long tenure and highly praised Deng for having set a good example in this regard.[87] Hu listed the elimination of the life-long tenure as one of the most important components of Deng Xiaoping Theory, and praised Deng Xiaoping for putting his ideas into practice. Deng's good example, Hu remarked, played "a decisive role in the smooth transition from the second generation leadership collective to the third generation leadership collective."[88] Hu did not mention Jiang's role in the transition from the third generation leadership collective to the fourth generation leadership collective here. But Jiang clearly obstructed a smooth transition by staying on as CMC chairman. By citing Deng's example, Hu sent a reminder to Jiang.

Although Jiang Zemin was sitting right behind Hu at the ceremony, he seems to have turned a deaf ear to Hu's admonitions.

---

[85] http://news.xinhuanet.com/newscenter/2004-08/09/content_1747850.htm.

[86] http://news.xinhuanet.com/newscenter/2004-08/09/content_1747850.htm.

[87] *Renmin ribao*, August 23, 2004, http://www.people.com.cn/GB/shizheng/1024/2729306.html.

[88] *Renmin ribao*, August 23, 2004, p. 2. See also http://www.people.com.cn/GB/shizheng/1024/2729306.html.

As a sign of Jiang's desperation for holding on to power, Jiang seems to have walked in front of Hu again during the proceeding to the platform in the Great Hall of the People at the beginning of the meeting. To avoid the embarrassing scene, CCTV reporters shoot their cameras up at the ceilings when central leaders were marching toward the platform in the officially sanctioned pecking order.[89]

Hu subsequently became more assertive. In a report on an exhibit on the achievements China had accomplished in nuclear development in the previous five decades, Hu's name was placed in front of Jiang's name.[90] Hu paid the visit on August 30, 2004, while Jiang visited the exhibit the following day. But the two visits were lumped together in one report. In the report, Hu appeared as general secretary of the Party and president of the PRC while Jiang Zemin as CMC chairman. It was the first time since May 2003 that Hu's name was placed in front of Jiang's name in a report related to military affairs.

JIANG'S COMPLETE RETIREMENT

Jiang's Resignation Letter and His True Intentions

It was probably under these pressures[91] that Jiang Zemin wrote a resignation letter on September 1, 2004. Clearly, Jiang did not have a

---

[89] For a recording of the ceremony, see rtsp://real.cctv.com.cn/news/56K/898280822dxp.rm. A different interpretation was that Jiang could not walk by himself. He had to tread with the support of two people. See Qi Si, "Dajiemi! Yangshi sheyingji dachongtianpao liangrenchanfu Jiangfangneng mianbu" [A top secret revealed! CCTV video cameras were shooting at the sky, Jiang could move his feet with the support of two people], *Reminbao*, August 25, 2004, http://www.renminbao. com/rmb/articles/2004/8/25/32323.html.

[90] *Renmin ribao*, September 1, 2004, p. 1.

[91] There are many versions of insiders' stories that described additional pressures from retired senior military leaders. For one widely used version, see Luo Bing, "Jiang Zemin xiatai neimu" ["The inside story of Jiang Zemin's retirement"], *Cheng Ming*, No. 324 (October 2004), pp. 6–8.

plan to retire at the forthcoming Fourth Plenum. If he did, he would have written a resignation letter earlier.

Jiang had ample opportunities to submit a resignation letter before September 1, 2004. It has been revealed that the Politburo had a meeting about the Fourth Plenum as early as November 24, 2003.[92] Had Jiang been sincere about his retirement, he would have submitted a resignation letter before then. But he did not. The Politburo had another meeting about the Fourth Plenum on July 23, 2004, and announced the convening of the Fourth Plenum the following day in the *People's Daily*.[93] Again, Jiang did not submit his resignation letter for the Plenum to consider. Ignorance could not be a factor. Jiang Zemin was general secretary for 13 years. He should know the rules of the Party very well. Even though he was not a member of the Sixteenth Central Committee, he must have been informed of the preparation for the Fourth Plenum. If he indeed was hoping to retire at the Fourth Plenum, he would have submitted a letter of resignation at least by July 23, 2004, to be included on the agenda of the Fourth Plenum. But he did not. According to the news release, Jiang's retirement was not on the agenda of the Fourth Plenum.[94]

On September 1, 2004, Jiang submitted his resignation letter to the Politburo. Did he really intend to retire? The answer is no. He showed no signs of preparing for an imminent retirement. On the contrary, he took every opportunity to stay in the limelight. On the very next day, September 2, he had a publicized meeting with Philippine President Gloria Macapagal Arroyo.[95] It was not entirely

---

[92] Zhang Sutang and Sun Chengbin, "Tuijin weidashiye he weidagongcheng de xingdonggangling: "Zhonggongzhongyang guanyu jiaqiang dangdezhizhengnengli jianshe de jueding danshengji" ["An action guideline for promoting the great course and great project: the birth of 'the Central Committee of the CCP's decision on ruling capacity of the Party'"], *Renmin ribao*, September 28, 2004, p. 2. See also http://www.people.com.cn/GB/paper464/13045/1171926.html.

[93] *Renmin ribao*, July 24, 2004, http://www.people.com.cn/GB/shizheng/1024/2662441.html.

[94] *Ibid.*

[95] *Renmin ribao*, September 2, 2004, http://www.people.com.cn/GB/shizheng/1024/2757642.html.

appropriate for Jiang as a retiring CMC chairman to meet with a head of state. Jiang's show backfired. A Chinese netter named Piaopiaop burst with anger and sent a comment on Jiang's meeting with Arroyo, saying "Go home! Those need to go home, just go home right now. Don't stay there embarrassing people!!!..."[96] The author used 64 exclamation signs.

On the same page of the *People's Daily*, Jiang's letter to a graduating class of Qinghua University was also published.[97] The letter was dated July 15, 2004, and it was a reply to a letter (dated July 1, 2004) from a class of students at Qinghua University who were trained for the military. It should be noted that the publication of Jiang's letter was a violation of the Party's rules in this regard. According to new rules on media reports on main leaders' activities issued by the Central Committee of the CCP on March 28, 2003, and circulated by the General Office of the Sixteenth Central Committee on April 5, 2003, a leader's inscriptions, forewords, letters, telegraphs, and so on normally should not be publicized.[98] Jiang's letter should not be published in the first place, not to mention it was an outdated one.

Worse still, two days later, Jiang had his 14-year old calligraphic inscription for the Qinghai-Tibet Military Service Station Department of the PLA General Logistics Department (the one he wrote on July 18, 1990) published in the *People's Daily*,[99] another indication that he was still very much interested in staying in the limelight. The publication of Jiang's 14-year inscription clearly was a serious violation of the Party's rules mentioned above.

---

[96] *China Youth* online, September 3, 2004, http://bbs.cyol.com/index2.php?forum-name=%D0%C2%CE%C5%C8%C8%C6%C0&forumid=48&job=view&topicid=2407870.

[97] *Renmin ribao*, September 3, 2004, p. 1.

[98] "Guanyu Jinyibu Geijin Huiyi he Lingdao Tongzhi Huodong Xinwen Baodao de Yijian" ["Rules on further improving news reports on meetings and leading comrades' activities"], *Shiliuda Yilai Dang he Guojia Zhongyao Wenxian Xuanbian* ["Important selections of the Party and the state documents since the Sixteenth Party Congress"] (Beijing: Renmin Chubanshe, 2005), Vol. 1, p. 288.

[99] *Renmin ribao*, 5 September 2004, p. 1. See also http://www.people.com.cn/GB/shizheng/1024/2761372.html.

In the meantime, Jiang Zemin was visiting Fujian Province. He was reportedly inspecting the military situation in Xiamen, opposite of Taiwan Island.[100] During his trip, he also visited a Buddhist temple (*Nanputuo*) in Xiamen.[101] According to a report from the Nanputuo website, Jiang visited the temple along with his wife and others in the afternoon of September 4, 2004.[102] However, his wife, Wang Yeping, is not visible in all five photos, although You Xigui (his bodyguard who had just been awarded the rank of general) and Zeng Peiyan (Politburo member and vice premier) were both clearly present. According to the report, the Buddhist Abbot (*fangzhang*) Shenghui told Chairman Jiang the history of the temple and the positive role and influence of Buddhism in the socialist society; Chairman Jiang wrote a calligraphic inscription for the temple. It did not mention whether Jiang prayed for Buddha's blessings.

It is likely that sometime in early September the CMC had a meeting about Jiang's retirement. The famous *New York Times* report seems to have been based on the meeting.[103] According to the report, top military officials were divided over the fate of Jiang. Generals Cao Gangchuan (defense minister, vice chairman of the CMC, and Politburo member) and Liang Guanglie (general chief of staff and member of the CMC) supported Jiang's decision of resigning, while Generals Guo Boxiong (vice chairman of the CMC and Politburo member) and Xu Caihou (director of the PLA General Political Department (GPD), a member of the CCP's Secretariat, and a member of the CMC) opposed Jiang's resignation.[104] Most critically, Hu

---

[100] Luo Bing, "Hu Jintao Anbi Jiang Hexin Jiao Junquan" ["Hu Jintao was implicitly forcing Jiang Zemin to surrender his military power"], *Qian Shao* (*The Front-Line Magazine*), No. 164 (October 2004), pp. 6–8.
[101] http://www.peacehall.com/news/gb/china/2005/03/200503060026.shtml.
[102] http://www.nanputuo.com/newsdeal/newshtml/zsyxw/20040922163051.htm.
[103] The report was released on Tuesday (September 7, 2004) but was produced on Monday (September 6, 2004). In other words, the report was produced one day earlier than the Politburo's meeting on September 7, 2004. Therefore, it is impossible that the report was based on the Politburo's meeting on September 7.
[104] Joseph Khan, "China Ex-President may be set to yield last power post," *New York Times*, September 7, 2004, A.1.

Jintao did not express his opinion.¹⁰⁵ Jiang was probably expecting Hu to ask him to stay, but Hu did not.

It is reported in the *People's Daily* that the Politburo held a meeting on September 7, 2004, on the main agenda of the Fourth Plenum along with "other matters"¹⁰⁶ (i.e., Jiang Zemin's retirement). Apparently, no final decision on Jiang's retirement was made at the meeting because, after the Politburo meeting, Guo Boxiong, Politburo member and second vice chairman of the CMC, was still campaigning for Jiang's stay. During his inspection tour of Xinjiang and Gansu, Guo urged the army to "resolutely obey the directions of the Party Center, the CMC, and Chairman Jiang at any time and under all circumstances."¹⁰⁷ In a very brief report, Guo mentioned Jiang three times. He sent cordial greetings to the officers and men on behalf of CMC Chairman Jiang Zemin and CMC Vice Chairman Hu Jintao; he asked the army to pay particular attention to studying Jiang Zemin's thinking on national defense and army building; and he urged the army to resolutely obey the directions of Chairman Jiang at any time and under all circumstances.

On September 16, 2004, the day when the Fourth Plenum began in Beijing, Jiang's name again appeared in the *People's Daily* as CMC chairman. He issued an order to reissue a revised PLA's Regulation on Environmental Protection,¹⁰⁸ showing that he was still working as CMC chairman. Unfortunately, this item invited a harsh and direct criticism from an anonymous netter the following day. The author wrote,

> Without a doubt, corruption has become a chronic disease. Political corruption is another "great achievement" that Jiang Zemin produced during his term. Jiang's son, Jiang Mianheng, has become president of the Chinese Academy of Sciences,

---

¹⁰⁵ *Ibid.*
¹⁰⁶ *Renmin ribao*, September 7, 2004, http://www.people.com.cn/GB/shizheng/1024/2768015.html.
¹⁰⁷ *Renmin ribao*, September 13, 2004, p. 4. See also http://www.people.com.cn/GB/shizheng/1026/2779185.html.
¹⁰⁸ *Renmin ribao*, September 16, 2004, http://www.people.com.cn/GB/shizheng/1024/2789475.html.

general designer of the manned spaceship, Shenzhou No. 5; Jiang's elder sister, Jiang Zehui, has been airlifted from a teacher in a provincial-level university to president of the Chinese Academy of Forest Sciences. The reasons for these promotions are very well-known.

Under Jiang Zemin's policy of "rhetorical attacks and military threats," Taiwan is moving further and further away from the Mainland. Jiang's hard-line stand has made Taiwan residents extremely concerned, fearing that missiles from the Mainland may hit Taiwan any time. Consequently, taking advantage of these concerns, Taiwan independence forces are vigorously promoting Taiwan independence.

In Sino-American relations, old Jiang seems to be particularly interested. He takes every opportunity to please Americans. Jiang has done everything he can for that purpose: returning the American E-P3 reconnaissance plane that invaded China's air space in April 2001 (The plane collided with a Chinese F-8 fighter. The Chinese fighter was destroyed, and the pilot was killed. The American spy plane was damaged, and was forced to land on Hainan Island); and singing love songs at the state banquet to win Americans' recognition. Obviously, he is not very successful — his failure is reflected in Bill Clinton's and his wife's memoirs. There are more and more complaints within the Party about Jiang's shamelessly holding on to power. Deng at least had commanded the army before the liberation; but Jiang has never even been a squad leader before.[109]

This piece was the only critical piece that was published. There were probably many more that have been filtered out.

---

[109] *Renmin ribao*, September 17, 2004, http://202.99.23.223:8080/view.php?bbs_id= 1530336. This item was posted at 14:29:08 on September 17, 2004. Its link to the news was later removed, and the item was replaced by an empty one. However, the file is still on the web. The above link still worked at 10:26 am on September 22, 2004.

The Fourth Plenum and Jiang's Farewell

The Fourth Plenum of the Sixteenth Central Committee was held between September 16 and 19, 2004 in Beijing. The Plenum approved Jiang's resignation from the CMC, and Hu Jintao took over as CMC chairman.[110] Xu Caihou was made vice chairman of the CMC, and Chen Bingde (new director of the General Armament Department), Qiao Qingchen (commander of the PLA Air Force), Zhang Dingfa (commander of the PLA Navy), and Jing Zhiyuan (commander of the PLA Second Artillery Corps) were inducted into the CMC.

Apparently, Jiang's clique collapsed over the issue of his complete retirement. Over the years since 1989, Jiang had developed a small clique consisting of two subgroups: Shanghai Gang members and Jiang's cronies. Within the Politburo Standing Committee, the Shanghai Gang members are Zeng Qinghong, Wu Bangguo, and Huang Ju; Jiang's cronies are Jia Qinglin and Luo Gan.[111] In other words, Jiang's clique seems to have had a 5-to-4 advantage in the Politburo Standing Committee. In the remaining 15 full members of the Politburo, one is a Shanghai Gang member (Chen Liangyu), and eight (Hui Liangyu, Liu Qi, Zhang Dejiang, Zhou Yongkang, He Guoqiang, Guo Boxiong, Cao Gangchuan, and Zeng Peiyan) are considered as Jiang's men. Namely, Jiang's clique has 16-to-8 (or 2-to-1) dominance in the entire Politburo.

However, this powerful appearance dissipated over Jiang's resignation. With one exception (Guo Boxiong), few stood up in public for Jiang. Noticeably, Zeng Qinghong did not render his full support for Jiang's stay this time.[112] Zeng probably thought it was a bad idea

---

[110] "Shiliujie sizhongquanhui guanyu tongyi Jiang Zemin tongzhi ciqu zhongyang junwei zhuxi zhiwu de jueding" ["The Fourth Plenum of the Sixteenth Central Committee's decision on approving Comrade Jiang Zemin's resignation as chairman of the Central Military Commission of the Chinese Communist Party"], *Renmin ribao*, September 19, 2004, http://www.people.com.cn/GB/shizheng/1026/2793985.html.

[111] Luo Gan is Li Peng's protégé. However, he has been widely regarded as being adopted by Jiang Zemin.

[112] According to one story, Zeng supported Jiang's retirement in early August 2004 when Jiang informed Zeng of his intention to retire. See Xiao Li, "Jiang Zemin zai

for Jiang to stay on as CMC chairman beyond the Sixteenth Party Congress in the first place. As Zeng explained to a group of non-communist elites after the Fourth Plenum two days after the Plenum, Jiang had always wanted to retire from all leadership positions: Before the Sixteenth Party Congress, he initiated a request for not taking any leadership positions; before the Fourth Plenum of the Sixteenth Central Committee, he again requested to resign as chairman of the CMC of the Party and the government.[113]

It appears that the issue of Jiang's retirement was decided by a show of hands, and the decision was made unanimously.[114] During his meeting with Plenum participants in the afternoon of September 19, 2004, Jiang Zemin made a brief speech, acknowledging the decision to accept his resignation and the help he had received over the years.[115] He did not seem to be very happy and confident.

The next morning, Jiang attended an expanded meeting of the CMC and delivered a long speech.[116] He described his attitude

---

Junfang Yalixia Cizhi Neimu" ["The insiders' story of Jiang Zemin's retirement under the pressure of military leaders"], *Qian Shao* (*The Front-Line Magazine*), No. 165 (November 2004), pp. 10–13.

[113] Wang Bixue, "Zhengxie shijiechangweihui diqicihuiyi kaimu" ["The opening of the Seventh Meeting of the Tenth Chinese People's Political Consultative Conference Standing Committee"], *Renmin ribao*, September 23, 2004, http://www.people.com.cn/GB/paper464/13005/1168549.html.

[114] Apparently, the Plenum made all its decision by a show of hands. For a photo of the Politburo standing members with their hands up, see "Zhongguo gongchandang dishiliujie zhongyangweiyuanhui disiciquantihuiyi gongbao" [The Communiqué of the Fourth Plenum of the Sixteenth Central Committee of the CCP], *Renmin ribao*, September 19, 2004, http://www.people.com.cn/GB/shizheng/1026/2793949.html.

[115] "Hu Jintao Jiang Zemin huijian canjia dang de shiliujie sizhongquanhui de quantitongzhi bing fabiao zhongyaojianghua" ["Hu Jintao and Jiang Zemin met with the participants in the Fourth Plenum of the Sixteenth Central Committee of the Party and delivered important speeches"], *cctv.com*, September 19, 2004, http://www.cctv.com/news/china/20040919/101102.shtml.

[116] Jiang's original speech was not released; part of the report on the meeting that was devoted to his speech consists of 2663 Chinese characters. See "Jiang Zemin Hu Jintao chuxi zhongyangjunwei kuodahuiyi bing fabiao zhongyaojianghua" ["Jiang Zemin and Hu Jintao attended the expanded meeting of the CMC and

toward the post of CMC chairmanship as *"jugong jincui sier houyi"* (bend his back to the task until his dying day). It is not clear if he really spared no effort on the job, but it is very likely that he was hoping that he would not have to retire from the post until his death. He gave himself high marks as the CMC chairman; he was trying to gain sympathies from the military leaders. "In the past 15 years," Jiang said, "I have developed deep bonds with the PLA, developed deep bonds with the officers and soldiers of the PLA, and developed deep bonds with comrades of several central military commissions."[117]

Compared to Deng Xiaoping's farewell speech, Jiang's speech was too long, too much about himself, and too insincere.[118] Deng used only 466 characters, while Jiang used at least 2,663; Deng's speech was to establish Jiang's authority, while Jiang's speech was to praise himself; Deng made the speech and left, while Jiang waited to hear more praises about himself.

Since Jiang was pushed out from the CMC, he was not able to staff the new CMC with his loyalists. First, Zeng Qinghong did not enter the CMC as a vice chairman.[119] Second, Xu Caihou was promoted to vice chairman of the CMC but his actual power diminished a little. Before his promotion, Xu was director of the GPD; after his promotion, he was removed from that important office. Third, Guo Boxiong suffered reputation damage because of his foolhardy support to Jiang Zemin on the eve of the Fourth Plenum.

---

delivered important speeches"], *cctv.com*, September 20, 2004, http://www.cctv.com/news/xwlb/20040920/102555.shtml.

[117] *Ibid*.

[118] For an analysis of the differences between Deng and Jiang in terms of retirement, see Zhu Zhan, "Jiang Hu jiaobang (3): Deng Jiang tuichu junwei de yitong" ["Jiang and Hu power transition (3): similarities and differences between Deng Xiaoping and Jiang Zemin in terms of retirement from the CMC"], *Asia Times*, September 21, 2004, http://www.atchinese.com/2004/09/0921rep5.htm.

[119] According to Luo Bing, at the Politburo meeting of September 14, 2004, He Guoqiang suggested a motion to add Zeng Qinghong to the CMC as a vice chairman, and his motion was supported by Hui Liangyu and Cheng Liangyu. Knowing that it would fail, Zeng declined the motion. Luo Bing, "The inside story of Jiang Zemin's retirement," p. 8.

On the other hand, Hu Jintao scored substantial gains in the CMC. First, Hu succeeded Jiang as CMC chairman without causing any relationship damage with him. It was Jiang who nominated Hu as his successor and endorsed him at the expanded meeting of the CMC. In other words, Hu was able to get rid of Jiang without making Jiang his enemy. Second, Li Jinai, former director of the General Armament Department, was made director of the GPD. On the surface, this was simply a lateral transfer; in essence, it was a promotion. This is because the GPD is in charge of personnel issues and political affairs and thus is more powerful than the General Armament Department. Since Li also had work experience in the Central Committee of the Chinese Youth League, he is considered as a member of the CCYL Group.[120] By replacing Xu with Li, Hu became dominant in the personnel issues and political affairs of the PLA. Evidently, this move was politically significant. The *People's Liberation Army Daily* online, for instance, did not report the reshuffle of the CMC leadership on September 19, 2004,[121] when all major China websites made the change as headline news. Its first report on the resignation of Jiang Zemin appeared at 8:18 am on September 20, 2004,[122] 10 hours after the *People's Daily*'s report on the same news had appeared.[123] Probably due to the replacement of the director of the GPD, the *PLA Daily* published an editorial on September 21, 2004, rendering support to Hu Jintao as chairman of the CMC.[124]

---

[120] Zhiyue Bo, "The Sixteenth Central Committee of the Chinese Communist Party: formal institutions and factional groups," *Journal of Contemporary China* (May 2004), p. 248.

[121] For the news report on *PLA Daily* online that day, see http://www.pladaily.com.cn/gb/pladaily/2004/09/19/index.html.

[122] *PLA Daily* online, September 20, 2004 (at 8:18 am), http://www.pladaily.com.cn/gb/pladaily/2004/09/20/index.html.

[123] *Renmin ribao*, September 19, 2004 (at 22:19), http://www.people.com.cn/GB/shizheng/1026/2793985.html.

[124] "Manhuaixinxin tuanjiefenjin" ["Be united and move forward with full confidence"], *PLA Daily* online, September 21, 2004, http://www.pladaily.com.cn/gb/pladaily/2004/09/21/20040921001133_jryw.html.

It is not clear which side Chen Binde was on, but he is likely to cultivate his relations with Hu instead of Jiang. Two new members, Zhang Dingfa (commander of the PLA Navy) and Jing Zhiyuan (commander of the Second Artillery Corps), are likely to be Hu's men because they are Hu's generals. On September 25, 2004, based on the order of Chairman Hu Jintao dated September 20, 2004, the CMC conferred the rank of general to both Zhang and Jing.[125] These two generals saluted Chairman Hu, who later took a photo with them. Although Qiao Qingchen might have had some contact with Hu Jintao in the 1980s, he is unlikely to be Hu's "old friend."[126] But he is less likely to be Jiang's man in the CMC, though he was promoted to the rank of general in June 2002 by Jiang Zemin.

Taking the CMC as a whole, Cao Gangchuan, Liang Guanglie, and Li Jinai are known for their support to Hu; Zhang Dingfa and Jing Zhiyuan are Hu's generals; Chen Binde and Qiao Qingchen are unlikely to challenge Hu; and even Xu Caihou has been cultivating his relations with Hu. Without Jiang, it is difficult to imagine that Guo Boxiong would defy Hu. In other words, Hu is likely to be dominant in the CMC without much difficulty.

Jiang's days were over. It would be simply a routine for Jiang to retire from the state CMC. On March 8, 2005, the Tenth NPC voted to accept Jiang Zemin's resignation as chairman of the state CMC.[127] Jiang's political career came to an end. Since Jiang was pushed out, he would be unlikely to play any significant influence beyond March 2005. This is particularly true in terms of military affairs because it was military leaders who played a major role in sealing his political career.[128]

---

[125] "Zhongyangjunwei juxing jingsheng shangjiang junxianyishi Hu Jintao banfaminglingzhuang" ["The CMC held a ceremony to confer the rank of general, Hu Jintao issued the order"], *Renmin ribao*, September 25, 2004, http://www.people.com.cn/GB/shizheng/1024/2808289.html.

[126] See Wang Yijiang, "Jiang Hu jiaobang (2): Hu Jintao youkeneng zhudao junwei" ["Jiang and Hu power transition (2): Hu Jintao is likely to be dominant in the CMC"], *Asia Times*, September 20, 2004, http://www.atchinese.com/2004/09/0920rep5.htm.

[127] http://military.people.com.cn/GB/1076/3228065.html.

[128] It is probably not by accident that with the approval of the CMC, the PLA held a television-telephone conference on October 15, 2004, to praise retired officers and

RISE AND FALL OF JIANG ZEMIN'S MILITARY THOUGHT

After Jiang's complete retirement in March 2005, his "military thought" has been gradually phased out. The officers and men of the PLA have moved on with Chairman Hu Jintao as their leader and Hu's military thought as their guidance.

Emergence of Jiang Zemin's Military Thought

During his first 13 years as China's commander-in-chief (1989–2002), Jiang Zemin promoted Mao Zedong's military thinking (*Mao Zedong junshi sixiang*) and Deng Xiaoping's thinking on army building in the new period (*Deng Xiaoping xinshiqi junduijianshe sixiang*) in the PLA. As the first CMC chairman without any military experience, Jiang trod the path of his predecessors cautiously. After he successfully maneuvered to stay on as CMC chairman in November 2002, however, his followers in the PLA began to trump up Jiang Zemin as a military strategist and to trumpet Jiang Zemin's thinking on national defense and army building (*Jiang Zemin guofang he junduijianshe sixiang*).

Before March 2003, there had been no such phrase as "Jiang Zemin's thinking on national defense and army building" in Chinese vocabulary.[129] Lieutenant General Mao Fengming, a PLA deputy to

---

sanatoria for retired officers. Hu Jintao sent a letter to the conference, and Xu Caihou and Li Jinai both delivered a speech. See "Li Jinai zongjie wunian quanjun laoganbu gongzuo tichu renwu yaoqiu" ["Li Jinai summarized the work on retired officers of the PLA in the past five years and put forth new tasks and requests"], *PLA Daily* online, October 16, 2004, http://www.chinamil.com.cn/site1/xwpdxw/2004-10/16/content_37412.htm.

[129] By typing in the phrase, "Jiang Zemin's thinking on national defense and army building" in Chinese, in the search engine of the people.com.cn on January 19, 2006, I got 691 hits. The first one was dated March 13, 2003. In 2000, after Jiang's "Three Represents" was released; some military academies opened a course on Jiang Zemin's remarks on military ideological and political construction and wrote a book on the topic. But the book did not use the phrase "Jiang Zemin's thinking on national defense and army building." For more details, see Liu Dingchang, Shen Guoquan, Mao Lingen, and Pu Songlin, *Jiang Zemin Jundui Sixiang Zhengzhi Jianshe Lunshu Yanjiu* [*Studies on Jiang Zemin's Remarks on Ideological and Political Construction of the PLA*] (Shanghai: Shanghai Renmin Chubanshe, 2001).

the Tenth NPC, introduced this phrase. During a group discussion on fundamental changes in world military affairs at the First Meeting of the Tenth NPC in March 2003, Mao commented,

> We need to study military theories and military thoughts. We need to earnestly study Marxism-Leninism, Mao Zedong Thought, and Deng Xiaoping Theory, especially Jiang Zemin's thinking on national defense and army building.[130]

It is not clear why Mao Fengming produced such a concept. It is likely that Mao was cultivating favor with Jiang for further advancement. A native of Nantong, Jiangsu, Mao was born in October 1942.[131] As a deputy commander of the Shenyang Military Region, Mao would have to retire in 2005 when he reaches his mandatory retirement age of 63.[132] It is also possible that Mao sincerely believed that Jiang's uttering on military affairs should serve as a guide for China's military modernization.

It has been a consensus among Chinese military scholars that in order to catch up with the rest of the world in military affairs, China needs not only new military theories but also a framework to produce new theories. As Huo Xiaoyong (another PLA deputy to the Tenth NPC) remarked, military strategists in the Western countries were thinking about not only the next war but also the war after the next and thus China needed "not only to innovate in specialized areas but also to establish a mechanism by which new military theories can emerge continuously."[133]

Many PLA deputies to the NPC concurred that the PLA would do very well in creating new military theories with Chinese characteristics

---

[130] http://past.people.com.cn/GB/shizheng/252/10307/10324/20030313/942547.html.

[131] http://www.ntipc.gov.cn/html/2004/03/20040308231235.html.

[132] Apparently, Mao failed to get what he wanted through such a flattering statement. He retired in December 2005. See http://news.xyfund.com/122005/19/392406.html.

[133] http://past.people.com.cn/GB/shizheng/252/10307/10379/20030316/944940.html.

under the guidance of Mao Zedong's military thinking, Deng Xiaoping's thinking on army building in the new period, and Jiang Zemin's thinking on national defense and army building.[134]

Three reporters from the Xinhua News Agency, Huang Guozhu, Jia Yong, and Cao Zhi, coauthored an article on Jiang Zemin's thinking on national defense and army building. The article was published on the *Renminwang* (the *People's Daily* online) on August 19, 2003, under the title "The People's army is marching forward under the guidance of Jiang Zemin's thinking on national defense and army building."[135]

This "tria juncta in uno" lengthy article was trying to explain the historical evolution of Jiang Zemin's thinking on national defense and army building,[136] its main themes, its connection with Mao Zedong's military thinking and Deng Xiaoping's thinking on army building in the new period, and its significance as a guide for national defense and army building in China.[137] According to the article, the most important themes in Jiang Zemin's military thought were "being capable of winning" (*da de ying*) and "never degenerating" (*bu bian zhi*).[138]

Promoting Jiang's Military Thought

This new concept provided Jiang loyalists with an opportunity to demonstrate their loyalty to Chairman Jiang. Xu Caihou, a member of the Secretariat of the Sixteenth Central Committee, a member of

---

[134] http://past.people.com.cn/GB/shizheng/252/10307/10379/20030316/944940.html. For Jiang Zemin's report to the Sixteenth Party Congress, see http://english.people.com.cn/features/Sixteenthpartyreport/Sixteenthpartyreport7.html.
[135] http://www.people.com.cn/GB/junshi/1076/2025365.html.
[136] The article used the Fourth Plenum of the Thirteenth Central Committee in June 1989 as the starting point for this new exciting period of Jiang. But Jiang was not made CMC chairman until the Fifth Plenum in November 1989.
[137] http://www.people.com.cn/GB/shizheng/1024/2025840.html.
[138] It is truly amusing to take Jiang as a great military genius — if all the enemies (real or potential) were to be trained to be capable of losing (*da bu ying*), then the PLA would be completely invincible!

the CMC, and the director of the GPD of the PLA at that time,[139] seized the opportunity and started promoting Jiang's military thought in the PLA. At a symposium on studying and implementing the "Three Represents" in the PLA on June 18, 2003, Xu stressed that in studying and implementing the "Three Represents," the PLA officers and soldiers should pay particular attention to its essence and apply it to practical problems; they should study and implement Jiang Zemin's thinking on national defense and army building.[140]

A few days later, with the CMC's approval, the GPD under Xu's leadership issued a circular on studying and implementing the "Three Represents" in the PLA. One of the key requirements of the circular was that the PLA officers and soldiers should earnestly study Jiang Zemin's thinking on national defense and army building. The circular stated,

> Chairman Jiang's thinking on national defense and army building is a component of the important idea of the "Three Represents;" it is the most recent product of Marxist military theoretical development; and it is the scientific guidance for China's national defense and army building under new situations. We need to master Chairman Jiang's important theoretical points in order to answer fundamental questions of building what kind of armed forces under the new historical conditions, how to build armed forces, what kind of battles to be waged in the future, and how to fight them.[141]

As a specific requirement for studying Chairman Jiang's thinking on national defense and army building, the circular proposed an initial reading list.[142] (i) Chairman Jiang's pamphlet, *On National Defense and Army Building* (Beijing: Jiefangjun Chubanshe, 2003);

---

[139] He was later promoted to vice chairman of the CMC at the Fourth Plenum of the Sixteenth Central Committee in September 2004.
[140] http://www.people.com.cn/GB/junshi/1076/1922187.html.
[141] http://www.people.com.cn/GB/junshi/1076/1930461.html.
[142] http://past.people.com.cn/GB/junshi/20030624/1016539.html.

(ii) Jiang Zemin's speech at the expanded meeting of the CMC at the end of 2002;[143] and (iii) Jiang's speech to the PLA delegation at the first session of the Tenth NPC in March 2003.[144] The GPD would produce a study guide for studying Jiang Zemin's thinking on national defense and army building and would issue the study guide as an important reference material.

A month later, with the CMC's approval, the GPD disseminated its newly edited study guide in the PLA, "The outline on studying Jiang Zemin's thinking on national defense and army building."[145] According to a circular issued by the CMC, this study guide "relatively comprehensively and accurately" elaborated the main content and basic points of Jiang Zemin's thinking on national defense and army building and it would help the PLA officers and soldiers better understand the scientific theory (*kexue lilun*) of Jiang Zemin's thinking on national defense and army building.[146] On July 31, 2003, the CMC held a seminar in Beijing on the publication of the study guide. The CMC members, except for Jiang Zemin and Hu Jintao, attended the seminar. General Guo Boxiong (vice chairman of the CMC and Politburo member) and General Cao Gangchuan (CMC vice chairman, Politburo member, state councilor, and defense minister) both gave speeches at the seminar.[147]

Revival of Deng Xiaoping's Military Thought

While Jiang's loyalists just started a campaign of promoting Jiang Zemin's military thought through various venues,[148] Deng Xiaoping's

---

[143] There is no report of such a meeting in the *Renmin ribao*.
[144] For Jiang's talk, see http://www.people.com.cn/GB/shizheng/252/10307/10314/20030310/940634.html.
[145] http://www.people.com.cn/GB/junshi/1076/1992361.html.
[146] http://www.people.com.cn/GB/junshi/1076/1992361.html. For its English version, see http://english.people.com.cn/200307/31/eng20030731_121369.shtml.
[147] http://www.people.com.cn/GB/junshi/1076/1994664.html.
[148] The Headquarters of General Staff sponsored one on September 25, 2003, at the National Defense University. The symposium received more than 100 articles, and the specialists selected 44 of them as "outstanding articles." http://www.people.com.cn/GB/shizheng/1026/2109577.html.

military thought was revived. August 22, 2004 would be Deng's 100th birthday, and preparations for the celebration were kicked off as early as November 2003.[149] Politicians, military officers, and journalists were writing commemorative articles about Deng Xiaoping's tremendous contributions as a military leader as well as a political leader.[150] The same reporters, Huang Guozhu, Jia Yong, and Cao Zhi, now turned their attention to Deng and published an article on August 17, 2004 about Deng Xiaoping's military thought, "Deng Xiaoping and building an army of higher quality with Chinese characteristics."[151] Before a nationwide symposium on the life and thought of Deng Xiaoping (August 21–24, 2004) was held,[152] the PLA organized its own symposium on the life and thought of Deng Xiaoping on August 18, 2004.[153] At the symposium, General Xu Caihou urged the PLA officers and men to deeply understand and earnestly implement Deng Xiaoping's thinking on army building in the new period.[154]

In the meantime, the GPD and six other organizations jointly issued a circular to ask PLA officers and men to watch a film on Deng Xiaoping's life in France (1920–1925).[155] The *People's Daily*, the *PLA Daily*, and other newspapers in China were filled with articles about Deng Xiaoping and Deng's military thought. Although most military authors still mentioned Jiang Zemin's military thought as a standard official expression in their writings about Deng Xiaoping, their focus was on Deng instead of Jiang. Commander Zhu Qi and Political Commissar Fu Tinggui of the Beijing Military Region, as mentioned earlier, published an article in the *People's Daily* about Deng Xiaoping's direct leadership over a military

---

[149] http://www.people.com.cn/GB/shizheng/1026/2215651.html and http://www.people.com.cn/GB/shizheng/1026/2213406.html.
[150] For details, see http://zg.people.com.cn/GB/33839/34943/34978/34979/index.html.
[151] http://www.people.com.cn/GB/junshi/1078/2715839.html.
[152] http://www.people.com.cn/GB/shizheng/1026/2736777.html.
[153] http://www.people.com.cn/GB/shizheng/1024/2720707.html.
[154] http://www.people.com.cn/GB/shizheng/1026/2742838.html.
[155] http://www.people.com.cn/GB/shizheng/1026/2781265.html.

exercise in September 1981.[156] In the article, the two generals used a concrete example to illustrate Deng Xiaoping's military thought but only mentioned Jiang Zemin's thinking on national defense and army building as a standard official parlance.

It is evident that PLA officers and men were truly interested in learning about Deng Xiaoping and his military thought. They attended the exhibition on Deng's life with enthusiasm,[157] watched an eight-episode documentary on Deng's military career with admiration,[158] and organized various activities to pay their respect to the late CMC chairman.[159]

Studying Hu's Military Thought

In addition to the revival of Deng Xiaoping's thinking on army building in the new period, the PLA leaders also began to contemplate how to apply General Secretary Hu Jintao's scientific concept of development (*kexue fazhan guan*) to military modernization in China. During their discussions of Premier Wen Jiabao's government report in March 2004, military leaders such as General Liang Guanglie (chief of staff) and General Li Jinai (director of the General Armament Department) talked about applying the scientific concept of development to the PLA modernization efforts.[160]

In the meantime, PLA political theorists began publishing articles on using the scientific concept of development as a guide in all aspects of military modernization. Xie Zhengxuan, for instance, published an article in the *People's Daily* on Hu's military thought on August 1, 2004, one-and-a-half month before Jiang Zemin's retirement from the post of CMC chairman, introducing the scientific concept of development as a guide of great significance for China's

---

[156] http://www.people.com.cn/GB/shizheng/1026/2766060.html.
[157] http://www.people.com.cn/GB/shizheng/1026/2723903.html.
[158] http://www.people.com.cn/GB/junshi/1076/2732493.html.
[159] http://www.people.com.cn/GB/shizheng/1026/2723903.html.
[160] http://www.people.com.cn/GB/paper464/11481/1035888.html.

national defense and army building.[161] He presented four reasons for his argument:

- The scientific concept of development is an important strategic thinking put forth by the Party Center under the leadership of General Secretary Hu Jintao for China's development in the new century and new period. It is the CCP's new understanding on development and the latest theory of the CCP's guiding principles on building China's socialist modernization;
- The scientific concept of development provides a guide of great significance for China's national defense and army building in the new century and new period. It helps to answer many critical questions concerning the maintenance of China's sovereignty, unity, and stability;
- The scientific concept of development offers a new theoretical perspective for understanding objective laws of national defense and army building; and finally
- The scientific concept of development lays an important ideological foundation for unifying the officers and men of the PLA.

Quoting Hu Jintao's talks on military affairs, Xie then elaborated his suggestions for implementing the scientific concept of development in China's national defense and army building in the new century and new period.

As soon as Hu Jintao replaced Jiang Zemin as CMC chairman of the state in March 2005, the PLA began promoting Hu's military thought. In an editorial entitled "Sticking to the scientific concept of development in national defense and army building" published on April 18, 2005, the *PLA Daily* replaced Jiang Thought with Hu Jintao's military thought.[162] The article argued,

---

[161] http://www.people.com.cn/GB/paper464/15350/1360756.html.
[162] http://english.chinamil.com.cn/site2/news-channels/2005-04/18/content_185850.htm.

The scientific concept of development brought forward by the Central Committee of the CPC is an important guiding ideology that we should always stick to in building a well-off society in an all-round way and in our modernization drive, it is also an important guideline for the army to build itself into a more revolutionary, modernized and regularized army. Thus in order to earnestly fulfill its historic mission in the new century and new period, the army must persistently implement the scientific concept of development in the national defense and army building.[163]

The article further stated,

The great cause of building socialism with Chinese characteristics is a grand systematic engineering covering wide scopes, of which national defense and modernization drive of the army is an important component. To guide overall economic and social development by a scientific concept of development, national defense and army building is undoubtedly included. Currently, our army is at a new historical development stage and faced with the challenges of stepping up overall transformation from mechanization and semi-mechanization to informationization. In accomplishing the heavy tasks of reform, building and development, many contradictions need to be properly resolved, many structures need to be properly readjusted, many relations need to be properly straightened out, and many work need to be arranged in a comprehensive way. Thus only by guiding the national defense and army building with the scientific concept of development, can we make overall plans for our building in various fields, coordinate well various aspects of our work, bring the initiative of various sectors into full play and enhance in a comprehensive way the armed force's combat effectiveness to fulfill the historic mission of the army in the new century and new period.[164]

---

[163] http://english.chinamil.com.cn/site2/news-channels/2005-04/18/content_185850.htm.
[164] http://english.chinamil.com.cn/site2/news-channels/2005-04/18/content_185850.htm.

One of the reasons that the *PLA Daily* published this editorial is that Hu Jintao urged the entire Party to carry out the scientific concept of development throughout the entire process of China's development. At the Twenty-first Study Session of the Politburo on April 15, 2005, Hu Jintao urged the Party leaders to put the scientific concept of development in command of the entire process of China's development. He stressed that the Party must use the scientific concept of development to guide all aspects of economic and social development in China and to promote the comprehensive development of economic construction, political construction, cultural construction, and harmonious society construction.[165]

Subsequently, all general departments of the PLA organized classes on Hu's military thought instead of Jiang Zemin's military thought.[166]

Fall of Jiang's Military Thought

Evidently, PLA leaders were ready to move on without Jiang. During his visit to the Qinghai Provincial Military District on December 14, 2005, Hu Jintao did not mention the phrase "Jiang Zemin's thinking on national defense and army building." He urged the PLA officers to earnestly study and implement the spirit of the Fifth Plenum of the Sixteenth Central Committee, firmly establish and carry out the scientific concept of development, strengthen army building in an all-round way, and be prepared to shoulder the historical mission of the PLA in the new century and new period.[167] Hu omitted the phrase of Jiang's military thought again in front of all CMC members during his visit to the *PLA Daily* on January 3, 2006.[168]

Other CMC leaders followed suit. Vice Chairman Xu Caihou omitted Jiang's military thought in his letter to the *PLA Daily*

---

[165] http://news.xinhuanet.com/newscenter/2005-04/16/content_2838888.htm.
[166] For details, see the section on "Promoting Hu's military thought" in Chapter 8 of this book.
[167] http://www.chinamil.com.cn/site1/misc/2005-12/17/content_365472.htm.
[168] http://www.chinamil.com.cn/site1/misc/2006-01/04/content_376333.htm.

on January 4, 2006,[169] in his talk during his visit to Tianjin in early January 2006, and in his talk during his visit to the Nanjing Military Region in late February 2006.[170] Vice Chairman Cao Gangchuan did the same during his visit to the Guangzhou Military Region in February 2006.[171] Vice Chairman Guo Boxiong, Jiang's loyalist, however, still could not let go Jiang Zemin's thinking on national defense and army building. During his visit to the Chengdu Military Region in February 2006, Guo urged the PLA officers and men to combine their study of the scientific concept of development with the study of Jiang's military thinking.[172]

On January 13, 2006, the GPD issued a circular asking the officers and men of the PLA and armed police to take as an important political task the study and implementation of the scientific concept of development.[173] The *PLA Daily*, the mouthpiece of the PLA, discontinued its column on "implementing the 'Three Represents' and maintaining the advanced nature of communist party members" in January 2006[174] and started with a new column on "the scientific concept of development in the barracks" on February 1, 2006.[175]

CONCLUDING REMARKS

Evidently, Jiang Zemin did not really want to retire from the CMC. He did not want to retire at the Sixteenth Party Congress in November 2002; did not want to retire at the First Meeting of the Tenth NPC in March 2003; did not want to retire at the Third Plenum of the Sixteenth Central Committee in October 2003; and did not want to retire at the Fourth Plenum of the Sixteenth Central Committee in September 2004.

---

[169] http://www.chinamil.com.cn/site1/misc/2006-01/05/content_377334.htm.
[170] http://www.chinamil.com.cn/site1/misc/2006-01/05/content_377334.htm.
[171] http://www.chinamil.com.cn/site1/misc/2006-01/05/content_377334.htm.
[172] http://www.chinamil.com.cn/site1/misc/2006-01/05/content_377334.htm.
[173] *Jiefangjun Bao* (*The PLA Daily*), January 14, 2006, p. 1.
[174] January 7, 2006, was the last day when the newspaper had this column. See *Jiefangjun Bao*, January 7, 2006, p. 1.
[175] *Jiefangjun Bao*, February 1, 2006, p. 1.

Instead of planning an imminent retirement, he was competing with Hu Jintao for the limelight: He had his name placed in front of Hu's name in news reports on military affairs; he walked in front of Hu Jintao in violation of the protocol of Chinese politics; he promoted a large number of officers including his bodyguard to the rank of general; he played up the Taiwan issue; and he had his outdated stories published in the *People's Daily* against the relevant rules of the Party.

In spite of Jiang's powerful appearances, pressures were mounting for his complete retirement in the second half of 2004 from all quarters: pressures from Deng Xiaoping's family, from current and former defense ministers, from other military leaders, and from President Hu Jintao. Jiang was forced to write a letter of resignation as a gesture, but his "request" subsequently received the approval from the CMC, from the Politburo, and eventually from the Fourth Plenum of the Sixteenth Central Committee. On September 20, 2004, Jiang became a former chairman of the Party's CMC. He was subsequently removed from the state CMC at the Third Meeting of the Tenth NPC in March 2005.

In contrast to his overly prolonged tenure as CMC chairman, Jiang Zemin's "military thought" was rather short lived. Emerged as a compliment to Jiang in March 2003, his thinking on national defense and army building became a focus for study and implementation in the PLA in June 2003. In about one year, however, PLA leaders shifted their attention to Deng Xiaoping's military thought as Deng's 100th birthday was approaching. In the meantime, military leaders were also beginning to pay attention to the implication of the scientific concept of development for military development. As soon as Hu became chairman of the state CMC in March 2005, the *PLA Daily* immediately started promoting Hu's military thought. Starting in December 2005, Jiang Zemin's thinking on national defense and army building became less and less frequently used. A special column in the *PLA Daily* on the "Three Represents" was discontinued in January 2006 and was replaced by a special column on the scientific concept of development. Along with Jiang's posts was gone his "military thought." Jiang Zemin became history.

Chapter

8

Hu Jintao's Power Consolidation

Hu Jintao further consolidated his power after he became the chairman of the Party's Central Military Commission in September 2004. He introduced a new policy toward Taiwan in March 2005. He formulated his own military thought in the same time. While the Shanghai Gang is on decline, the Communist Youth League (CYL) Group and the Princelings are both in ascendance. Officials with CYL backgrounds are becoming more dominant in provincial units, and princeling generals are increasing their presence in the elites of the People's Liberation Army.

HU'S NEW POLICY TOWARD TAIWAN

Jiang Zemin's Policy Toward Taiwan

Jiang Zemin's policy toward Taiwan was a total failure. The relationship between the two sides of the Taiwan Strait originally resulted from the civil war between two political parties — the Chinese Communist Party (CCP) and the Guomindang (GMD) — in the 1940s. The GMD government [the Republic of China (ROC)] under the leadership of Jiang Jieshi (Chiang Kaishek) took refuge in the Taiwan island in 1949, and the CCP under the leadership of Mao Zedong established a new regime — the People's Republic of China (PRC) — in Beijing. The ROC was the sole representative of China in the United Nations until 1971 when it was replaced by the PRC. American President Richard Nixon visited Beijing in February 1972, and the United States subsequently severed its diplomatic relations with the ROC and established diplomatic relations with the PRC in 1979. The CCP under the leadership of Deng Xiaoping shifted its policy toward Taiwan in 1979 from military liberation to peaceful reunification. Deng Xiaoping later introduced the policy of "one country, two systems." As a result of Deng's policies, tensions across the Taiwan Strait were reduced, and personnel exchanges and economic interactions started and increased. In November 1992, the two sides reached an agreement on the one-China principle: Both sides recognize that there is only one China, but each side may have its own interpretation of this one China.[1] On this basis, the two sides held Wang-Ku talks in April 1993 in Singapore.[2]

Upon his assumption as the head of the Taiwan Affairs Leading Small Group in June 1993,[3] Jiang Zemin was eager to reap benefits from good cross-strait relations. On the eve of the Chinese New Year in 1995, Jiang Zemin made an eight-point proposal on the issue of reunification.[4] These points were (i) the One-China principle is the basis of peaceful reunification; (ii) under the One-China principle, Taiwan may develop nongovernmental economic and cultural relations with other countries and may join international organizations in the name of "China Taipei"; (iii) the two sides hold talks on peaceful reunification; (iv) Chinese should not fight fellow Chinese, but the Chinese government cannot promise to give up the use of force; (v) the two sides should develop economic exchanges and cooperation; (vi) people on both sides of the Strait should inherit and carry

---

[1] This is known as "the 1992 consensus" (*jiuer gongshi*). For a brief introduction, see http://news.sina.com.cn/c/2005-03-04/17225269443s.shtml.

[2] Wang refers to Wang Daohan, president of the Association for Relations Across the Taiwan Strait, and Ku refers to Ku Chen-fu, chairman of the Strait Exchange Foundation in Taiwan.

[3] Taeho Kim, "Leading small groups: managing all under heaven," in David M. Finkelstein and Maryanne Kivlehan (eds), *China's Leadership in the Twenty-First Century: The Rise of the Fourth Generation* (Armonk, NY: M.E. Sharpe, 2003), p. 128.

[4] For Jiang's proposal, see http://tw.people.com.cn/GB/14864/14918/885617.html.

forward the fine traditions of Chinese culture; (vii) the Chinese government and the CCP will help Taiwan compatriots and work with all political parties and personages in Taiwan on the development of cross-strait relations; and (viii) the leaders of the Chinese government and the CCP welcome Taiwan leaders to visit the mainland, and they are also ready to visit Taiwan.

When compared with the previous documents from Beijing, Jiang's proposal has some tangible changes.[5] First, he stressed the One-China principle. In the previous documents from Beijing, this had not been an issue of great significance because both sides of the Taiwan Strait agreed to such a principle. Starting from 1991, however, Lee Teng-hui, the leader of Taiwan, began his efforts to create "two Chinas" in the international community through his internal and external policies, even though Taipei also adopted the One-China principle in its Guidelines for National Unification.

Second, Jiang indicated Beijing's willingness to talk with the Taiwan side on any matter, as long as it is under the One-China principle. This is a major change from the previous policies. Beijing had insisted previously that talks should be held between the CCP and the GMD on a reciprocal basis. But Jiang seems to be indicating that the talks did not have to be between the two parties. He did not specify in what capacity (as general secretary of the CCP or president of the PRC) he would talk to the Taiwan side, nor did he specify with whom (the GMD as a party or Taiwan as a local government, or the ROC as a political entity) he would talk. In fact, he did not even indicate whether he would be the one to talk with the Taiwan side. Evidently, he was open to any suggestions for "the name, place, and form of these political talks."

Third, Jiang used the expression "Chinese should not fight fellow Chinese" to indicate Beijing's sincerity about peaceful reunification. Yet it is not clear if this usage serves that purpose well. First, the phrase's historical connotation is too strong to be appropriate for this

---

[5] The following discussions are based on Zhiyue Bo, "The Wang-Gu talks and proposals for political talks," *Chinese Law and Government,* Vol. 35, No. 4 (July–August 2002), pp. 3–17.

occasion. The phrase was originally used in the late 1930s during the Anti-Japanese War, when the GMD was trying to terminate the CCP in the face of an external enemy. The CCP used the phrase to expose the GMD and to rally the Chinese people against the Japanese. The situation across the Taiwan Strait in the 1990s, however, was drastically different. During the civil war it was Chinese who were fighting fellow Chinese, and the separation of the two sides of the Taiwan Strait was a result of the civil war. The fact that the two sides were still separated from each other is an indication that the civil war was not completely over.[6] Second, the primary reason why Beijing cannot promise to give up the use of force is because the civil war is not over. This is why there is a need to hold talks on ending the state of hostilities across the Strait. Yet the phrase does not help to clarify this point. Third, the phrase can be easily construed as giving up the use of force in settling the Taiwan issue, as long as Taiwan is a part of China and the people in Taiwan are Chinese people, regardless of whether some people in Taiwan think of themselves as Chinese or not. However, Jiang immediately qualified this phase by indicating that the use of force is directed against the schemes of foreign forces to interfere in China's reunification and to bring about an "independent Taiwan."

In any case, it was clear that Beijing was willing to start political talks as soon as possible to facilitate the reunification of China. In response, Lee Teng-hui made a six-point counterproposal on April 8, 1995. These were (i) China's unification should be pursued on the reality of separate rules across the Strait; (ii) cross-strait exchanges should be strengthened on the basis of the Chinese culture; (iii) the two sides increase economic and trade exchanges and develop mutually beneficiary and supplementary relations; (iv) the two sides join international organizations on an equal basis and leaders of the two sides naturally meet each other on such occasions; (v) the two sides should persist in using peaceful means to settle

---

[6] Back in 1958, when the People's Liberation Army was ordered to bomb the Jinmen Island, Mao Zedong instructed his generals specifically to fire at the GMD's boats but not at US warships, because it was a civil war.

disputes; and (vi) the two sides should jointly maintain the prosperity of and promote democracy in Hong Kong and Macao.

It should be noted that there are some commonalities between these two proposals. First, both emphasized the Chinese culture as an important basis for peaceful reunification (Jiang's sixth point and Lee's second point). Second, both were in favor of developing economic and trade exchanges (Jiang's fifth point and Lee's third).

Nevertheless, the two proposals diverged on many other important issues. First, the two differed on the basic principles. Jiang emphasized the One-China principle, while Lee stressed the reality of separate rules across the Strait. Second, the two were different on how the leaders from the two sides should meet. Jiang was willing to have direct contacts with Taiwan leaders, while Lee suggested using international occasions. And third, the two disagreed over the means for settling disputes between the two sides. Jiang did not rule out the use of force, while Lee insisted on peaceful means only.

Jiang's policy turned out to be disastrous. After having offered a counterproposal, Lee Tenghui proceeded to visit the United States in May 1995 (with permission from the US government). Frustrated with Jiang's "cowardly behavior" and Washington's betrayal, PLA generals asserted their power over cross-strait relations. They decided to send Lee and Taiwan independence forces a strong message. They "tested" their missiles in the vicinity of the Taiwan Island between July 1995 and March 1996. This military confrontation soon resulted in a more serious international crisis in March 1996 when the United States sent two aircraft-carrier battle groups to the Taiwan Strait.

The cross-strait relations experienced a downward slide afterwards. In July 1999, Lee Teng-hui characterized cross-strait relations as "special state-to-state relations" in his interview with the Voice of Germany (Deutsche Welle). Beijing's strong warnings in 2000 did not prevent Chen Shui-bian, the candidate of a pro-independence party, the Democratic Progressive Party (DPP), from being elected as the 10th "President" of the ROC. Four years later, Chen was reelected. Jiang's hope for a glorious moment in history was completely dashed. Jiang Zemin's failure was partly due to his eagerness to seek reunification for his personal glorification. His drastic swings backfired among Taiwanese voters.

Hu Jintao's Initial Attempt

Hu Jintao attempted to introduce a new policy in March 2003. During his meeting with "Taiwan" delegation to the First Meeting of the Tenth National People's Congress (NPC) on March 11, 2003, Hu introduced a four-point policy. They were: (i) consistently adhere to the One-China principle; (ii) actively promote economic and cultural exchanges between the two sides of the Taiwan Strait; (iii) earnestly implement the principle of placing hope on Taiwanese people; and (iv) unite Chinese people from both sides of the Taiwan Strait for the grand revival of the Chinese nation.[7] But Hu's new policy received cold treatment in the media probably because of Jiang Zemin's dominance over the Taiwan issue at that time.

In the aftermath of the severe acute respiratory syndrome (SARS) crisis, one of the Shanghai Gang members was trying to switch the sides to support Hu Jintao but was pushed aside possibly by Jiang Zemin. Zhou Mingwei (1955–) was Jiang's man from Shanghai. A graduate of the Department of International Politics at Fudan University in Shanghai, he once served as director of the Foreign Affairs Office of the Shanghai Municipal Government.[8] He was transferred to Beijing in 2000 to be deputy director of the Taiwan Affairs Office of the State Council. His first appearance in such a capacity was dated August 27, 2000, when he met with a delegation from Macao,[9] although his official appointment was announced in November 2000.[10] He later visited the United States to explain Beijing's policy toward Taiwan and accompanied Jiang Zemin in Jiang's last visit to the United States in October 2002.[11] However, on August 5, 2003, Zhou tried to highlight Hu Jintao's four-point policy

---

[7] *Renmin ribao*, March 12, 2003, p. 1.
[8] http://past.people.com.cn/GB/channel2/702/20000505/56333.html.
[9] http://past.people.com.cn/GB/channel1/14/20000901/211919.html.
[10] http://past.people.com.cn/GB/channel1/10/20001107/303312.html.
[11] http://past.people.com.cn/GB/shizheng/252/2140/2840/20021023/848503.html.

instead of Jiang's eight-point policy as Beijing's most relevant policy toward Taiwan.[12] Zhou further elaborated Hu's third point of placing hope on Taiwanese people. He explained that in order to promote interactions between the two sides of the Taiwan Strait, Hu Jintao proposed three specific policies. That is, Beijing is willing to actively promote anything as long as it is beneficial to Taiwanese people, as long as it is good for the stability of cross-strait relations, and as long as it is conducive to the revival of the Chinese nation.[13]

A few months later, in December 2003, Zhou was transferred out of the Taiwan Affairs Office and became a deputy director of the Bureau of the Publications of Foreign Languages (i.e., China International Publication Corporation) under the Central Committee of the CCP.[14] When Zhou was fired, many considered the incident as another blow to the Shanghai Gang;[15] but it is unlikely that Hu Jintao fired him simply because he was a member of the Shanghai Gang, especially after he had publicly supported Hu's policy. It is more likely that Jiang Zemin sacked him because of his "betrayal." It is probably no coincidence that Zhou Mingwei appeared along with Deng Lin (Deng Xiaoping's daughter) on an activity of celebrating Deng Xiaoping's 100th birthday in 2004.[16]

Hu's Four-Point Policy

After Jiang Zemin had left the political stage, it was Hu Jintao's turn again to assert his power on the Taiwan issue. During his meeting with the Chinese People's Political consultative Conference (CPPCC) deputies on March 4, 2005, Hu put forth a new four-point policy toward Taiwan: (i) never sway in adhering to the One-China principle; (ii) never give up efforts to seek peaceful reunification; (iii) never change the principle of placing hope on the Taiwan

---

[12] http://www.people.com.cn/GB/shizheng/1026/2003753.html.
[13] http://www.people.com.cn/GB/shizheng/1026/2003753.html.
[14] http://www.china.org.cn/chinese/ch-wzp/index.htm.
[15] http://www.kanzhongguo.com/news/gb/articles/3/12/30/57461.html.
[16] http://www.renminbao.com/rmb/articles/2004/8/22/32289.html.

people; and (iv) never compromise in opposing "Taiwan independence" secessionist activities.[17]

A few days later, the Tenth NPC adopted an "Anti-Secession Law" at its third session on March 14, 2005.[18] This was the first time that the PRC adopted a law on the Taiwan issue. The anti-secession law was intended to oppose Taiwan secessionists and prevent Taiwan's secession. The law reaffirmed that there is only one China in the world; both the Mainland and Taiwan belong to one China; China's sovereignty and territorial integrity brook no division; Taiwan is part of China; the state shall never allow the "Taiwan independence" secessionist forces to make Taiwan secede from China under any name or by any means. The law declared that the state shall employ non-peaceful means and other necessary measures to protect China's sovereignty and territorial integrity, "in the event that the 'Taiwan independence' secessionist forces should act under any name or by any means to cause the fact of Taiwan's session from China, or that major incidents entailing Taiwan's secession from China should occur, or that possibilities for a peaceful reunification should be completely exhausted" (Article 8).[19]

Noticeably, despite its formidable title, the anti-secession law has left a lot of room for cross-strait cooperation. First, Article 6 has a list of five areas of potential cooperation between the two sides, and Article 7 has another list of six areas for bilateral dialogs. These two articles are much more specific than all the other articles. Second, the law did not mention the term, the PRC. The title of the law is "Anti-Secession Law" instead of the PRC's anti-secession law. The term China — instead of the PRC — has been used throughout the entire text. By so doing, the NPC has actually codified the "1992 Consensus" — that there is only one China in the world and each side of the Taiwan Strait may have its own interpretation — leaving the door open for further negotiations between the two sides. Finally, by introducing an article about protecting "the lives,

---

[17] http://politics.people.com.cn/GB/1024/3219958.html.
[18] http://tw.people.com.cn/GB/14810/3240911.html.
[19] http://tw.people.com.cn/GB/14810/3240911.html.

property, and other legitimate rights and interests of Taiwan civilians and foreign nationals in Taiwan," this law has effectively separated Taiwan residents from Taiwan secessionists and singled out Taiwan secessionists.

Taiwan Opposition Parties' Visits to the Mainland

Hu's new policy and the anti-secession law have proved to be very effective. The DPP's government under Chen Shuibian was confused, and the pan-blue camp — including the GMD, People First Party (PFP), and the New Party — leaders regained initiatives. Chairman Lien Chan of the GMD took a historical eight-day "journey of peace" to mainland China between April 26 and May 3, 2005. On April 29, 2005, Lien Chan met with General Secretary Hu Jintao of the CCP in Beijing, marking a historical meeting between the GMD and the CCP since 1945 when Jiang Jieshi (Chiang Kai-shek) and Mao Zedong met in Chongqing on August 28, 1945. Hu Jintao and Lien Chan reached a five-point consensus:

i. On the premise of acknowledging the 1992 Consensus, encourage the reopening of talks across the Strait;
ii. facilitate an end to hostilities, and establish peace;
iii. promote cooperation in economic exchange, establish mechanisms for economic cooperation, and push for two-way direct flights across the Strait, Three Links,[20] and agricultural exchange;
iv. encourage talks of increasing Taiwan's international role, especially the issue of Taiwan's hope to join the World Health Organization; and
v. establish a platform of communication between the two parties.[21]

On May 5, 2005, two days after Lien Chan went back to Taiwan, Chairman James CY Soong (Song Chuyu) of the PFP started a nine-day "bridge-building" trip to mainland China. During his meeting

---
[20] For an interpretation, see http://en.wikipedia.org/wiki/Three_Links.
[21] http://tw.people.com.cn/GB/26741/47107/47312/3360547.html.

with Hu Jintao on May 12, 2005, Soong clarified the stance of his party on cross-strait relations:

i. The PFP has always adhered to the 1992 Consensus and the One-China principle;
ii. "Taiwan independence" has never been an option for the PFP as it will only bring war and disasters; and
iii. the PFP has always advocated peace.[22]

In response, Hu Jintao also made a four-point proposal:

i. On the basis of the One-China principle and the 1992 Consensus, establish the political foundation for cross-strait peace, stability, and development;
ii. promote the Three Links, and upgrade cross-strait economic exchange and operation;
iii. reopen as soon as possible dialogs and talks between the two sides of the strait on an equal basis, and enhance consensus; and
iv. promote mutual understanding and facilitate interactions between Chinese people from the two sides of the Strait.[23]

Two months later, Chairman Yok Mu-ming (Yu Muming) of the new Party in Taiwan also paid a weeklong visit to the Mainland between July 6 and 13, 2005.[24]

It should be noted that the trips of the pan-blue leaders were all very successful due to Hu Jintao's new policy and the anti-secession law, which altered the nature of the cross-strait game from one of reunification versus independence to one of war versus peace. This change apparently had a major impact on the sentiment of the Taiwan residents. When faced with two options of reunification versus independence, the Taiwan residents would rather go with independence than reunification. But when they were presented

---

[22] http://politics.people.com.cn/GB/1026/3384972.html.
[23] http://politics.people.com.cn/GB/1026/3384972.html.
[24] For details, see http://tw.people.com.cn/GB/26741/50204/index.html.

with options of war versus peace, they chose peace instead of war. Since the anti-secession law made war across the Taiwan Strait a real possibility, many Taiwan residents began to blame Taiwan independence forces for the trouble.

In this new environment, pan-blue leaders who visited the Mainland were no longer regarded as traitors of Taiwan but as heroes of Taiwan. They went to the Mainland not to sell out Taiwan but to save Taiwan from the danger of possible wars.

HU JINTAO'S MILITARY THOUGHT

Politburo Study Sessions on Military Affairs

Hu Jintao began to get involved in military affairs as early as 1998 when he worked with the then Premier Zhu Rongji to get the military out of commercial activities. He was made vice chairman of the Central Military Commission at the Fourth Plenum of the Fifteenth Central Committee in September 1999. By the Sixteenth Party Congress in November 2002, Hu had been CMC vice chairman for more than three years. He was better qualified for being CMC chairman in 2002 than Jiang had been in 1989. But Jiang Zemin refused to hand over the position.

Nevertheless, Hu worked on military affairs in his capacity as general secretary of the Party and the first vice chairman of the CMC soon after the Sixteenth Party Congress.[25] The main forum for Hu to deal with military affairs was Politburo study sessions. By September 2004, he had devoted three study sessions on military affairs.

In the aftermath of the submarine accident in which 70 officers and sailors all died, Hu organized a study session on new developments in world military affairs on May 23, 2003.[26] Hu Jintao used this occasion to develop his thinking on military development in China, and his main point in this study session was that China should catch

---

[25] For instance, during his visit to Guangdong in April 2003, he visited the South China Sea Fleet. See *Renmin ribao*, April 15, 2003, http://www.people.com.cn/GB/shizheng/16/20030415/972637.html.

[26] For more details, see the section on the submarine accident in Chapter 5.

up with world development in military affairs through economic development and scientific and technological progress. He urged the Chinese leaders to continue to use Mao Zedong's military thinking and Deng Xiaoping's thinking on army building in the new period as a guide for China's development in national defense and army building.[27] He mentioned the "Three Represents" but did not talk about "Jiang Zemin's thinking on national defense and army building." It is very likely that in Hu's private opinion, the submarine accident was a proof that "Jiang Zemin's thinking on national defense and army building" was a failure.

Less than a year later, on February 23, 2004, Hu Jintao devoted the Tenth Politburo Study Session to the issue of world order and China's security environment.[28] At the session, Hu Jintao urged Politburo members to learn to "scientifically" assess international situation, correctly respond to the world trend of political multipolarization and economic globalization, and properly handle various complex issues concerning world peace and development in order to promote China's modernization. He pointed out that China would adhere to the approach of peaceful rise and continue to adopt independent and peaceful foreign policies, holding high the banner of peace, development, and cooperation in world affairs. He asked the Chinese leaders to take China's national sovereignty and security as their top priority, resolutely safeguard China's national sovereignty and territorial integrity, and firmly protect national security and fundamental interests of China. Noticeably, Hu did not mention "Jiang Zemin's thinking on national defense and army building" either.

On July 24, 2004, Hu organized another Politburo study session on military affairs. At the Fifteenth Politburo Study Session, Hu asked the Chinese leaders to ensure the security environment for China's modernization drive and ensure China's sovereignty and territorial integrity, implement the principle of coordinated development of national defense construction and economic construction, strive to promote national defense construction on the basis of economic

---

[27] http://news.xinhuanet.com/zhengfu/2003-05/24/content_885152.htm.
[28] http://news.xinhuanet.com/zhengfu/2004-02/25/content_1330365.htm.

development, and make efforts to achieve the grand goal of building a well-off society in an all-around way.[29] Clearly, "Jiang Zemin's thinking on national defense and army building" was not used throughout the study session.

Historical Mission in the New Century and New Period

Evidently, Hu Jintao produced a new thinking on military affairs in early 2005. According to Vice Chairman Guo Boxiong, CMC Chairman Hu put forth a new thinking on the historical mission of the PLA in the new century and new period. As Guo relayed to the PLA deputies to the NPC meeting on March 5, 2005, Hu's new thinking was a new understanding of the role of the PLA and a new summary of the functions and tasks of the PLA, a new requirement of the Party and the people for the PLA, an important innovation in the military theory of the Party, and a scientific guidance for the PLA's modernization and military combat readiness.[30]

After he was elected chairman of the state Central Military Commission at the Third Meeting of the Tenth NPC on March 13, 2005, Hu delivered a speech to the PLA delegation.[31] He urged the PLA leaders to (i) take safeguarding national sovereignty, security and territorial integrity, and national development as the top priority, fulfill the historical mission of the PLA in the new century and new period, promote military transformations with Chinese characteristics, strive to enhance the PLA's digitization level, and strengthen its ability to deal with crises, to maintain peace, to prevent wars, and to win battles; (ii) implement the scientific concept of development, coordinate national defense construction and economic construction, improve quality and efficiency in national defense and army modernization, strive to build armed forces that correspond to China's security and development, and provide an effective safeguard for China's security and unification as well as for the smooth progress of building a well-off society in an all-round way; (iii) promote the spirit of

---

[29] http://news.xinhuanet.com/zhengfu/2004-07/26/content_1648021.htm.
[30] http://military.people.com.cn/GB/1076/3225553.html.
[31] http://politics.people.com.cn/GB/1024/3239694.html.

seeking truth from facts and train troops with rigorous standards. Two days later, the *PLA Daily* published an editorial on the historical mission of the PLA that reiterated Hu's main points and declared the PLA's allegiance to Chairman Hu.[32]

As for the specific content of Hu Jintao's remarks on the PLA's historical mission, Xu Caihou offered a detailed elaboration in September 2005. Put simply, Hu's remarks can be summarized as "three provides and one play" (*sange tigong yige fahui*): The armed forces should provide mighty support for the CCP to entrench its position as the ruling party, provide staunch security assurances for safeguarding the important strategic opportunity period for national development, provide powerful strategic backup for defending the national interests, and play an important role in maintaining the world peace and promoting the common development of all countries.[33]

In the meantime, as mentioned in Chapter 7, the PLA leaders also applied Hu Jintao's scientific concept of development to military modernization in China and to turn it into a guide in all aspects of military modernization in China.

Promoting Hu's Military Thought

The four general departments of the PLA organized separate classes on Hu's thought on the historical mission of the PLA in the new century and new period. First, the National Defense University — under the mandate from the General Political Department (GPD) and with the approval of the CMC — sponsored a symposium on Hu's important remarks on the historical mission of the PLA in the new century and new period. At the opening ceremony on September 20, 2005, General Xu Caihou, former GPD director and currently vice chairman of the CMC, urged the PLA leaders to

> have a sound grasp of the scientific connotation and great significance of Chairman Hu Jintao's important remarks on the

---

[32] http://www.chinamil.com.cn/site1/xwpdxw/2005-03/15/content_158599.htm.
[33] http://www.chinamil.com.cn/site1/misc/2005-09/21/content_305604.htm.

historical mission of the PLA in the new century and new period, put into effect the scientific concept of development in an all-round way, make effort to bring about a new situation in terms of national defense and army building and carry out the sacred historical mission of the PLA effectively.[34]

The Headquarters of the General Staff held a symposium on Hu's important remarks on the historical mission of the PLA in the new century and new period on October 24, 2005. Participants came to the consensus that Hu's important remarks reflected the scientific concept of development in the field of military affairs and represented a new theory in four different areas.[35] At the conclusion of a 15-day class organized for high-ranking officers of the General Logistics Department (GLD) on November 8, 2005, Director Liao Xilong told the participants that Hu's important remarks on the historical mission of the PLA is the general line and general strategy of the national defense and army building in the new century and new period and that all leading officers of the Department should take it as an important political responsibility and historical responsibility to really master the full implications of the historical mission.[36]

The campaign to study and implement Chairman Hu's important remarks on military affairs reached a new height in October 2005 when Hu Jintao urged the PLA to use the scientific concept of development as an important guiding principle for national defense and army building in the new century and new period during his visit to the Nanjing Military Region on October 13, 2005.[37]

The GPD issued a circular on January 13, 2006, asking the officers and men of the PLA and armed police to take as an important political task the study and implementation of the scientific concept of development.[38] The *PLA Daily*, the mouthpiece of the PLA,

---

[34] http://www.chinamil.com.cn/site1/misc/2005-09/21/content_305604.htm.
[35] *Jiefangjun Bao*, October 25, 2005, p. 1.
[36] *Jiefangjun Bao*, November 9, 2005, p. 1.
[37] http://news.xinhuanet.com/politics/2005-10/14/content_3617701.htm.
[38] *Jiefangjun Bao*, January 14, 2006, p. 1.

replaced a column on "implementing the 'Three Represents' and maintaining the advanced nature of communist party members" with a new column on "the scientific concept of development in the barracks" in February 2006.[39]

Jiang Zemin and the *PLA Daily* Incidents

Evidently, Jiang Zemin was jealous about Hu's emergence as the indisputable commander-in-chief in a very short period; he apparently caused a couple of incidents in the *PLA Daily* website.

After Shenzhou VI (China's second manned spacecraft) was successfully launched from Jiuquan, Gansu Province, on October 12, 2005, Hu Jintao went to Nanjing for the opening ceremony of the Tenth National Games on the same evening. Those who accompanied him include Wang Gang (director of the General Office of the Central Committee of the CCP), Li Tieying (vice chairman of the Standing Committee of the NPC), Chen Zhili (state councilor), Ding Guangxun (vice chairman of the CPPCC), Zhang Huaixi (vice chairman of the CPPCC), and Li Jinai (member of the CMC and director of the GPD of the PLA).[40]

After the opening ceremony, Hu visited Nanjing, Zhenjiang, and Changzhou.[41] During these visits, Hu indicated that party committees and governments at all levels should take the implementation of the decision of the Fifth Plenum as an important political task and work toward the goals of the 11th Five-Year Plan. He mentioned the scientific concept of development and social harmony as part of the general request of the Party but did not mention the "Three Represents" at all.[42] At his meeting with military officers from the Nanjing Military Region, Hu asked them to unify their mind and action with the "spirit of the Fifth Plenum of the Sixteenth Central Committee" and to take the scientific concept of development as an important guiding

---

[39] *Jiefangjun Bao*, February 1, 2006, p. 1.
[40] http://politics.people.com.cn/GB/1024/3763860.html.
[41] http://news.xinhuanet.com/politics/2005-10/14/content_3617701.htm.
[42] http://news.xinhuanet.com/politics/2005-10/14/content_3617701.htm.

principle for strengthening the national defense and army building in the new century.[43]

It seems that the *PLA Daily* resisted Hu's talk. In its report on the website of the *PLA Daily* at 7:02 on October 15, 2005, it used a new title, "Hu Jintao stressed the promotion of economic and social development through the study and implementation of the spirit of the Fifth Plenum."[44] The title did not highlight Hu's call for a new important guiding principle for strengthening national defense and army building. Immediately under this report, moreover, there was an article about Jiang Shangqing, Jiang Zemin's alleged adopted father![45] Its title was "An everlasting monument, a revolutionary who persistently worked for the survival of the nation: Jiang Shangqing." The article about Jiang Shangqing had already been published on the website of the *PLA Daily* at 21:35 on October 14, 2005. This was the second time that the same article appeared on the same website.

It is very likely that Jiang Zemin himself intervened to have this article inserted on the website of the *PLA Daily* for the second time to undermine the effect of Hu Jintao's call. This kind of interventions is typical of Jiang's style. As Bruce Gilley recorded, Jiang twice directly responded to the media reports about him. Soon after he became mayor of Shanghai in 1985, Jiang asked his private secretary to phone *Liberation Daily* in protest because the newspaper reported his press conference by using a correct Chinese phrase, *mianmao*, instead of his incorrect English word, "faces." "It would have been better if you had written the English word 'face,'" his secretary lectured the journalist. "That would be more in keeping with Mayor Jiang's meaning."[46] Two years later in July 1987, Jiang responded to

---

[43] http://news.xinhuanet.com/politics/2005-10/14/content_3617701.htm.

[44] http://www.chinamil.com.cn/site1/xwpdxw/2005-10/15/content_315613.htm.

[45] http://www.chinamil.com.cn/site1/xwpdxw/2005-10/15/content_315700.htm. In reality, Jiang Shanqing was not Jiang Zemin's adopted father but his uncle. This is because it is impossible for a dead person to adopt a living person. According to Robert Lawrence Kuhn, Jiang Zemin was adopted by Jiang Shangqing after Jiang Shangqing's death. See Robert Lawrence Kuhn, *The Man Who Changed China: The Life and Legacy of Jiang Zemin* (New York: Crown Publishers, 2004), pp. 30, 31.

[46] Bruce Gilley, *Tiger on the Brink: Jiang Zemin and China's New Elite* (Berkeley and Los Angeles, CA: University of California Press, 1998), p. 95.

an implicit criticism in an article published in the *People's Daily* by a local reporter, entitled "The Other Side of Doing Things Yourself." Jiang called for a meeting of all party and government officials in Shanghai involved in propaganda and attacked the reporter by name.[47] Robert Lawrence Kuhn, American businessman and Jiang's biographer, also revealed that Jiang often used the hotline (red phone) to discuss details of his TV appearances with the president of CCTV.[48]

Jiang has been very sensitive about the media. As Kuhn observed, Jiang "made it a habit to read news stories carefully" because "In a hierarchic system where signs of weakness can frighten allies and enliven enemies, politicians must be ever vigilant."[49] It is not surprising that he personally intervened to insert an article on Jiang Shangqing on the website of the *PLA Daily*.

But a message on Jiang Shangqing was too subtle to remind people of Jiang Zemin. A few days later, Jiang Zemin appeared on the *PLA Daily* website on the return of the two astronauts. On the first page of the *PLA Daily* on October 18, 2005, Jiang's name appeared in the title of a report on the return of Shenzhou VI, "The Astronauts were warmly welcomed in Beijing upon their arrival; Jiang Zemin congratulates the successful return of 'Shenzhou VI.'"[50] In a report on the return of Shenzhou VI and the arrival of the two astronauts in Beijing, "Jiang Zemin" was inserted. It stated that "Comrade Jiang Zemin congratulated the successful return of Shenzhou VI."[51] It is not clear how "Comrade Jiang Zemin" congratulated the successful return of Shenzhou VI. Did he make a call or send a telegraph?

The same report also appeared in other media outlets. The message appeared in the Xinhuanet at 12:01:50 on October 17, 2005, initially under the title "Fei Junlong and Nie Haisheng arrived in Beijing

---

[47] Gilley, *Tiger on the Brink: Jiang Zemin and China's New Elite* (Berkeley and Los Angeles, CA: University of California Press, 1998), pp. 96–98.
[48] Kuhn, *The Man Who Changed China: The Life and Legacy of Jiang Zemin* (New York: Crown Publishers, 2004), pp. 441, 442.
[49] *Ibid.*, p. 136.
[50] http://www.chinamil.com.cn/site1/xwpdxw/2005-10/18/content_318117.htm.
[51] http://www.chinamil.com.cn/site1/xwpdxw/2005-10/18/content_318117.htm.

by flight, Cao Gangchuan greets them at the airport," and then the title was changed to "Fei Junlong and Nie Haisheng arrived in Beijing by flight, Jiang Zemin congratulates the successful return of the spaceship";[52] but it was published on the website of the *PLA Daily* at 06:05 on October 18, 2005,[53] and on the website of the *People's Daily* at 8:48 of the same day under the title "The Spaceship returns, and the whole nation is overjoyed."[54]

The report with Jiang's name was listed as the second item on the website of the *PLA Daily* on October 18, 2005. The same report was shifted to the fifth position on the website of the *PLA Daily* the following day while all the other websites dropped the report. What is interesting is that the homepage of the *PLA Daily* website with Jiang's name remained unchanged in the subsequent two months, although the content of news was being updated daily. It is probably because of this very reason that Hu Jintao paid a special visit to the *PLA Daily* on January 3, 2006,[55] and inspected its website very carefully.

THE SHANGHAI GANG'S DECLINE

The Shanghai Gang began its decline in April 2003 when Zhang Wenkang was dismissed as minister of Health, and it suffered a major blow when Jiang Zemin was retired as CMC chairman. After Jiang's complete retirement, the Shanghai Gang continued its decline.

Jiang Mianheng

First, Jiang Mianheng (1951–), the eldest son of Jiang Zemin, was kicked out of Beijing. On August 19, 2005, President Lu Yongxiang of the Chinese Academy of Sciences (CAS) announced in Shanghai that Jiang Mianheng, a vice president of the CAS, would become

---

[52] http://news.xinhuanet.com/st/2005-10/17/content_3624782.htm.
[53] http://www.chinamil.com.cn/site1/xwpdxw/2005-10/18/content_318117.htm.
[54] http://scitech.people.com.cn/GB/53753/3778597.html.
[55] http://www.chinamil.com.cn/site1/misc/2006-01/04/content_376333.htm.

concurrently head of the CAS Shanghai Branch.[56] As mentioned in Chapter 5, Jiang Mianheng had benefited both financially and politically as the son of Jiang Zemin. He probably is one of the richest men in China. He is the legal representative of the Shanghai Alliance Investment Ltd and a board member of several major corporations such as China Netcom, Shanghai Automobile Industry Corporation, and Shanghai Airport Corporation.[57] In the meantime, he was also made vice president of the CAS and deputy general manager of Shenzhou V.[58]

According to Lu Yongxiang, the transfer of Jiang Mianheng to Shanghai was to strengthen the leadership of the Shanghai Branch because the Shanghai Branch was one of the largest branches among the 13 branches.[59] The Shanghai Branch is in charge of 10 CAS institutes with about 6,000 staff members in Shanghai and two provinces (Zhejiang and Fujian). These institutes conduct research in a wide science spectrum, ranging from biology and chemistry to information and nuclear science.

But it is doubtful that Jiang Mianheng would provide a stronger leadership than his predecessor, Professor Shen Wenqing. Shen, a 1968 graduate of the famous Qinghua University, is an experimental nuclear physicist.[60] Through extensive research, Shen has confirmed particle admissions caused by the reaction in great mass transfer in low-energy nuclear reactions, the existence of deep inelastic scattering in light systems, and the existence of a new reaction mechanism in non-complete deep inelastic scattering. His experiments have contributed to the construction of national experimental area of heavy iron acceleration in Lanzhou, Gansu Province. Moreover, he obtained the optimum mass and charge

---

[56] "Jiang Mianheng jianren Shanghai Fenyuan Yuanzhang" ["Jiang Mianheng becomes concurrently head of the Shanghai Academy of Sciences"], http://www.cas.ac.cn/html/Dir/2005/08/21/13/28/89.htm.
[57] "Jiang Mianheng," http://www.cas.ac.cn/search/member_base/details.asp?memberno=14.
[58] http://www.cyyx.com/2005-9/200593165450.htm.
[59] "Jiang Mianheng jianren Shanghai Fenyuan Yuanzhang."
[60] http://www.cst.sh.cn:8180/homepage/people.html.

distribution with software correction methods used at Germany's Ion Research Center, detected four new nucleins, and measured the physical character of quasi-atomic fission and the relaxation time of mass. Along with his students at the academy's Shanghai Institute of Nuclear Research, he devised a parameterization formula suitable for the section of nuclear reaction in low and intermediate energy.[61] For his outstanding contributions, Shen has received numerous awards in science and technology of the CAS since 1992 and was elected as a fellow of the CAS in 2000.[62]

Obviously, with zero scientific research contributions whatsoever, Jiang Mianheng is in absolutely no position to be any better than Professor Shen as the head of the CAS Shanghai Branch. The decision, therefore, must be a political one. Since Jiang Zemin was no longer a political leader, his son no longer enjoyed the same privileges in Beijing as before. As a face-saving gesture for old Jiang, Jiang Mianheng was transferred to Shanghai without being deprived of his title of vice president of the CAS. But his real responsibilities would not be those of a vice president of the CAS but those of the head of the Shanghai Branch. In other words, he was demoted from a "national" leader to a "local" leader. He would have to accompany (*peitong*) national leaders such as Lu Yongxiang when they visit Shanghai as he had already begun doing.[63] Moreover, he would have to perform in order to stay in the position because the job of a head of a branch is much more specific and its performance is much more measurable than that of a vice president of the CAS.

Zhao Qizheng

The second sign of the Shanghai Gang's further decline is that Zhao Qizheng (1940–), a major member of the Shanghai Gang in the

---

[61] http://www.chinavitae.com/biography_display.php?id=1062.
[62] http://www.cst.sh.cn:8180/homepage/people.html.
[63] It is reported that Lu was being accompanied by Jiang Mianheng and Yang Xiong (vice mayor of Shanghai) in his inspection of Chenshan Mountain located in Songjiang District of Shanghai on August 29, 2005, http://www.cst.sh.cn/shownews.jsp?id=3583&type=1.

Sixteenth Central Committee, was retired as director of the Information Office of the State Council. Graduated from the Chinese University of Science and Technology in 1963, Zhao spent most of his early career as a technocrat in Shanghai.[64] He had work experience with both Zeng Qinghong and Jiang Zemin. Zeng was his colleague as deputy director of the Organization Department of the Shanghai Municipal Party Committee in 1984 and became his boss in the same department later on.[65] When Zeng was promoted to deputy secretary of Shanghai in 1986, Zhao succeeded him as director of the Organization Department of the Shanghai Municipal Party Committee and stayed in that position until 1991 when he was appointed as vice mayor of Shanghai. Zhao worked closely with Zeng in Shanghai for about five years, and he worked for Jiang Zemin for about four years. In January 1998, Zhao was transferred to Beijing as deputy director of the International Communications Office of the Central Committee of the CCP and deputy director of the Information Office of the State Council.[66] Three months later, he was made director of both offices.[67] In November 2002, Zhao entered the Sixteenth Central Committee as a full member. On August 25, 2005, Zhao was removed from his post as director of the Information Office of the State Council[68] because he had reached his retirement age of 65 years in January 2005.[69] He had been made a member of the Tenth National People's Political Consultative Conference on February 28, 2005,[70]

---

[64] http://big5.xinhuanet.com/gate/big5/news.xinhuanet.com/ziliao/2002-03/05/content_300452.htm.
[65] http://www.people.com.cn/GB/shizheng/252/9667/9670/20021126/874695.html.
[66] The International Communication Office of the Central Committee of the CCP and the Information Office of the State Council are the same office with two names. It is more of a party institution than a government institution. See http://news.xinhuanet.com/ziliao/2002-11/15/content_630715.htm.
[67] For his appointment as director of the Information Office of the State Council, see *Renmin ribao*, April 14, 1998.
[68] http://big5.xinhuanet.com/gate/big5/news.xinhuanet.com/ziliao/2002-03/05/content_300452.htm.
[69] http://news.xinhuanet.com/newscenter/2005-08/25/content_3402298.htm.
[70] For an interview with Zhao Qizheng, see http://www.people.com.cn/GB/14677/22114/37734/37949/2801747.html.

and is now vice chairman of the Committee on Foreign Affairs in the Tenth NPPCC.[71]

According to Ye Yonglie, a famous writer in Shanghai, Zhao Qizheng was the mastermind of a secretive book project on Jiang Zemin's life. Zhao Qizheng's associate, Yang Yang, a deputy head of the First Bureau of the Information Office of the State Council, called Ye Yonglie on March 12, 2001, in Shanghai about a biography project[72] and invited him to Beijing for a talk. Once in Beijing, Yang Yang asked Ye to work with Robert Lawrence Kuhn, an American businessman with a Ph.D. in anatomy/brain research from UCLA and an M.S. in management from MIT,[73] on Jiang Zemin's biography. Yang told Ye that the existing biographies of Jiang Zemin had two main features. One, they were not accurate; two, they were anti-China and anticommunist.[74] In order to fight back this anti-China and anticommunist countercurrent, they needed to publish a biography of Jiang Zemin with correct views and accurate facts. The Information Office of the State Council is responsible for such a task but could not organize such a project in its official capacity. Robert Lawrence Kuhn was willing to write such a book in English to be published by an American publisher, but he does not know Chinese. Kuhn wanted to work with a Chinese biographer, and the number one candidate was Ye Yonglie. After their initial meeting, it was decided that the project was coded "001 project," and Ye was going to be a coauthor of the book. In the end, Ye made contributions to the book with his suggestions and materials, but Kuhn took all the credits as the sole author of the book, entitled "The Man Who Changed China: the Life and Legacy of Jiang Zemin."

---

[71] http://www.takungpao.com:82/gate/gb/www.takungpao.com/news/2005-8-24/ZM-446397.htm.

[72] Ye Yonglie, "Wo He Jiang Zemin Zhuan Shunei Shuwai de Mimi" ["My secret stories about the *Biography of Jiang Zemin*"], *Yazhou Zhoukan,* Vol. 19, No. 10 (March 3, 2005), pp. 14–21; Ye Yonglie, "Jiang Zemin Zhuan de Gengduo Mimi" ["More secrets about the *Biography of Jiang Zemin*"], *Yazhou Zhoukan,* Vol. 19, No. 28 (July 10, 2005), pp. 14–17.

[73] Kuhn, *The man who changed China*, "About the author."

[74] Ye Yonglie, "Wo He Jiang Zemin Zhuan Shunei Shuwai de Mimi" ["My secret stories about the *Biography of Jiang Zemin*"], *Yazhou Zhoukan,* Vol. 19, No. 10 (March 3, 2005), p. 18.

Because of official backing, a Chinese translation was immediately produced as soon as the English version was published by Crown Publishers in January 2005. Kuhn was on a tour of book sales around China, and he was hailed as a modern-day Edgar Snow, an American author who wrote Mao Zedong's biography. But Kuhn was far from being a modern-day Snow. Snow interviewed Mao Zedong personally, while Kuhn did not even speak a word with Jiang Zemin. As Kuhn confessed in his book, he saw Jiang Zemin in person three times: He walked past Jiang on an upper floor of the Hotel Nacional in Havana, Cuba, in November 1993; he saw Jiang at a reception in New York in September 2000; and he heard Jiang speak informally on a number of subjects in Beijing in November 2003.[75]

Anyway, it is not difficult to conclude that Zhao Qizheng was behind the secretive project and that he decided to launch the project out of his loyalty to Jiang. Evidently, this book was approved by Jiang Zemin himself. All chapter titles of the book are written in the first person with direct quotation marks. For instance, Chapter 1 is "My Background Is My Family"; Chapter 2 "I Am a Patriot"; Chapter 3 "I Am an Engineer"…[76] It is inconceivable for anyone else including Zhao Qizheng other than Jiang himself to produce such titles. Consequently, Zhao's departure as director of the Information Office of the State Council was a loss to Jiang and the Shanghai Gang.

Huang Ju

The third sign of the Shanghai Gang's decline is that Huang Ju reportedly became terminally ill. Huang Ju (1938–)[77] was not well qualified for his positions as vice premier of the State Council, and his performances were not commendable. As mentioned in Chapter 5, Huang fled along with Jiang Zemin during the SARS crisis. Moreover, he neglected his basic duties as executive vice premier in charge of

---

[75] Kuhn, *The Man Who Changed China: The Life and Legacy of Jiang Zemin* (New York: Crown Publishers, 2004), p. 689.
[76] *Ibid.*, V–VIII.
[77] For his bio, see http://news.xinhuanet.com/ziliao/2002-01/16/content_240603.htm.

work safety. He was responsible for work safety issues in China not only as the executive vice premier of the State Council but also as director of the State Council Work Safety Committee; but his work was limited to empty talks. Huang appeared as a keynote speaker at a teleconference on work safety in China on April 8, 2003, urging central and local officials to pay attention to work safety issues from the "height of the Three Represents"[78]; he offered a similar talk at the First Plenary Meeting of the State Council Work Safety Committee on November 13, 2003[79]; he gave another empty talk at the Second Plenary Meeting of the State Council Work Safety Committee on June 25, 2004.[80]

While Huang was giving empty talks, Chinese workers were dying of accidents. In 2003, 6,177 people died of coal mine accidents. In 2004, 136,000 people died of production accidents and 700,000 people were injured[81]; among them, 6,027 people died of coal mine accidents.[82] But Huang Ju was never seen on a site of any accident, even major ones. On October 20, 2004, a gas explosion took place at Daping Coal Mine in Xinmi, Henan Province. Party Secretary Li Keqiang, Governor Li Chengyu, and Vice Governor Shi Jichun of Henan went to the site immediately upon hearing the news.[83] But Huang Ju simply sent an important instruction along with Hu Jintao and Wen Jiabao.[84] The accident killed 148 people, and Vice Governor Shi Jichun was given an administrative warning for his responsibility for the accident, while Huang Ju was intact.[85]

---

[78] http://news.xinhuanet.com/newscenter/2003-04/08/content_821919.htm.

[79] He did not mention Hu's "scientific concept of development," but repeated the "Three Represents." For his talk, see http://news.xinhuanet.com/newscenter/2003-11/13/content_1177426.htm.

[80] http://news.xinhuanet.com/newscenter/2004-06/25/content_1547602.htm.

[81] http://politics.people.com.cn/GB/1026/3140494.html.

[82] http://www.atchinese.com/index.php?option=com_content&task=view&id=6941&Itemid=66.

[83] *Renmin ribao*, October 22, 2004, p. 2.

[84] *Renmin ribao*, October 22, 2004, p. 1.

[85] http://www.gov.cn/misc/2005-08/16/content_23771.htm.

On November 28, 2004, another gas explosion took place in Chenjiashan, Shaanxi Province. Party Secretary Li Jianguo, Acting Governor Chen Demin, and Vice Governor Gu Deshun went to the site of the accident on the same day. A work team from the State Council led by You Quan, deputy secretary general of the State Council, also arrived at the site on the same day.[86] The accident eventually took 166 lives.[87] Again, Huang Ju was invisible. Premier Wen Jiabao took a special trip to Chenjiashan on January 1, 2005 to pay his respect for the deceased miners and console their family members.[88] Huang Ju did not go along with Wen.

On January 17, 2005, Huang Ju again talked about improving the situation on work safety in the year of 2005. At a national teleconference on work safety, Huang urged participants to use the "Three Represents" as a guide in this regard.[89] Less than one month later, on February 14, 2005, however, a major coal mine accident took place in Fuxin, Liaoning Province. On the day of the accident, Huang just finished his tour of Fujian.[90] Instead of going on to Liaoning to deal with the accident upon report, he simply made an "important instruction" (*zhongyao pishi*) again and sent a team from the State Council under the leadership of Hua Jianmin, state councilor and secretary general of the State Council.[91] At that time, 203 miners had been reported dead. But Huang Ju was not moved to action. In the end, 214 workers lost their lives.[92]

On February 23, 2005, Premier Wen Jiabao chaired an executive meeting of the State Council to discuss coal mine work safety

---

[86] http://www.people.com.cn/GB/shehui/1062/3018239.html.
[87] http://www.people.com.cn/GB/shehui/1062/3072656.html.
[88] *Renmin ribao*, January 4, 2005, p. 1.
[89] http://news.xinhuanet.com/newscenter/2005-01/17/content_2472996.htm.
[90] http://news.xinhuanet.com/newscenter/2005-02/14/content_2577715.htm.
[91] http://big5.xinhuanet.com/gate/big5/news.xinhuanet.com/newscenter/2005-02/15/content_2580651.htm.
[92] http://big5.xinhuanet.com/gate/big5/news.xinhuanet.com/newscenter/2005-02/22/content_2602021.htm.

issues[93] and to remove Liu Guoqiang, vice governor of Liaoning in charge of work safety, from his office to take the responsibilities.[94] However, Huang Ju, executive vice premier and director of the State Council Work Safety Committee, did not take any responsibilities. He attended a festive celebration activity that night along with seven other standing members of the Politburo.[95] Instead of mourning for the lost lives, Huang joined the performers and the other top leaders on stage singing "singing of our motherland" in a festive mood.[96]

On August 7, 2005, another major coal mine accident took place in Meizhou, Guangdong Province, in which 102 workers were reportedly trapped underground.[97] There is no evidence that Huang Ju did anything to handle the accident. He did not make any instructions, did not call for a meeting about coal mine safety, and did not go to Guangdong to investigate the accident. On August 17, 2005, he had a meeting with the Bangladesh Premier in Beijing, talking about the good relationship between China and Bangladesh.[98] He did not seem to care about the deaths of 123 workers as a result of the accident.

---

[93] http://big5.xinhuanet.com/gate/big5/news.xinhuanet.com/zhengfu/2005-02/24/content_2611785.htm.

[94] http://big5.xinhuanet.com/gate/big5/news.xinhuanet.com/zhengfu/2005-03/03/content_2642034.htm.

[95] Premier Wen Jiabao was absent. *Renmin ribao*, February 24, 2005, p. 1. The mass media in Liaoning suggested on February 16, 2005 to cancel the January 15th celebration in consideration of the 200-plus dead miners and to mourn the losses of these lives on television, but their suggestion was not heeded. See "Weile Kuangnan, Liaoning Meiti Jianyi Quxiao 'Naoyuanxiao'" ["To show respect for those died in the coal mine accident, Liaoning media suggested to cancel the 'festive activities of the January 15th'"], http://society.people.com.cn/GB/1062/3181133.html.

[96] *Renmin ribao*, February 24, 2005, p. 1. See also http://www.people.com.cn/GB/paper464/14138/1260157.html. Probably because these leaders realized that it was a mistake to participate in such a cheerful activity while more than 200 miners lost their lives, this item is no longer listed as one of their activities of the day.

[97] *Renmin ribao*, August 8, 2005, p. 2.

[98] http://news.xinhuanet.com/newscenter/2005-08/17/content_3368265.htm.

On November 27, 2005, another major coal mine disaster took place in Qitaihe, Heilongjiang Province, in which 171 people died.[99] From the time the accident was reported (November 28, 2005)[100] through the protracted rescue process to the very end (December 6, 2005),[101] Huang Ju did not show up at the site at all. It seems that no matter how many people died it is none of his business as a vice premier in charge of work safety. Partly due to his derelictions, China lost another 5,986 lives to coal mine accidents alone in 2005.[102]

Instead of trying to find more effective measures to help reduce the number of production accidents, Huang Ju tried to keep a distance from the work safety issues. At the first two plenary meetings of the State Council Work Safety Committee, Huang appeared as a standing member of the Politburo, vice premier of the State Council, and director of the State Council Work Safety Committee. At the Third Plenary Meeting of December 30, 2004, however, Huang appeared as a standing member of the Politburo and vice premier of the State Council. His title of director of the State Council Work Safety Committee was dropped.[103] On April 26, 2005, Huang again appeared at a conference on coal mine safety as a standing member of the Politburo and vice premier of the State Council without his title of director of the State Council Work Safety Committee.[104]

Huang was absent from the public scene for five months in the early 2006. He was last seen on January 16, 2006, at a seminar with participants in the work meeting of China Banking Regulatory Committee.[105] He was subsequently absent from all public activities. He did not attend the Spring Festival Celebration on January 23,

---

[99] http://www.chinanews.com.cn//news/2005/2005-12-06/8/661172.shtml.
[100] http://www.chinanews.com.cn/news/2005/2005-11-28/8/657894.shtml.
[101] http://www.chinanews.com.cn//news/2005/2005-12-06/8/661172.shtml.
[102] http://www3.chinesenewsnet.com/MainNews/SinoNews/Mainland/cna_2006_02_09_10_00_44_436.html.
[103] http://news.xinhuanet.com/newscenter/2004-12/30/content_2398820.htm.
[104] http://news.xinhuanet.com/newscenter/2005-04/26/content_2880273.htm.
[105] *Renmin ribao*, January 17, 2006, p. 1. See also http://news.xinhuanet.com/photo/2006-01/17/content_4060561.htm.

2006.¹⁰⁶ He was also absent from the opening ceremony of a special class on socialist new countryside held at the Central Party School for provincial/ministerial officials on February 14, 2006.¹⁰⁷ All the other eight standing members of the Politburo were present at the opening ceremony, but Huang was reportedly absent because "he was visiting abroad" (*chufang*). It has been rumored that Huang became terminally ill with pancreatic cancer.¹⁰⁸ Spokesman Wu Jianmin of the CNPPCC confirmed at a press conference on March 2, 2006 that Huang was indeed hospitalized but in a process of recovery.¹⁰⁹ Five months later, Huang Ju reemerged during a meeting with members of the International Advisory Council of China Banking Regulatory Commission on June 19, 2006. He did not appear health stricken.

Anyway, Huang will retire from the Politburo in 2007 because he will be 69 years old; he will retire from the State Council in 2008. It is not likely that he would be purged for his possible involvement in corruption scandals in Shanghai¹¹⁰ or for his derelictions, although he is probably guilty on both accounts.

---

[106] http://news.xinhuanet.com/politics/2006-01/24/content_4090936.htm.
[107] http://politics.people.com.cn/GB/1026/4124530.html.
[108] http://www.renminbao.com/rmb/articles/2006/3/20/39788.html.
[109] http://cppcc.people.com.cn/GB/34961/59086/59106/59498/59499/index.html.
[110] His wife, Yu Huiwen, and his brother, Huang Xi, are both implicated in another recent corruption scandal in which a government official colluded with a businessman in the embezzlement of a huge sum of public funds. It is reported that Zhu Junyi, director of the Shanghai Bureau of Labor and Social Security, transferred 3 billion yuan (US$374 million) of the social security fund to Zhang Rongkun, the owner of a private investment company for purchasing a highway. Zhang is close to Yu Huiwen because they are both vice chairmen of the Shanghai Charity Fund, and Zhang reportedly got to know Yu Huiwen through Zhu Junyi. Zhang is also close to Huang Xi because Huang Xi was directly involved in Zhang's purchases and acquisitions while Huang was deputy director of the Shanghai Pudong Development Corporation. Now both Zhu Junyi and Zhang Rongkun have been detained for investigation, and the Central Disciplinary Inspection Commission has been collecting information about Yu Huiwen and Huang Xi. For details, see Ji Suoming, "Shanghai Nuoyong Sanshiyi Da'an Zhendong Beijing" ["The 3-billion corruption case in Shanghai shocked Beijing"] *Yazhou Zhoukan*, Vol. 20, No. 31 (August 6, 2006), pp. 34, 35. Chen Liangyu, party secretary of Shanghai and a Politburo member, was removed from office on September 24, 2006 for his alleged

EMERGENCE OF THE CYL CADRES IN CHINESE POLITICS

As mentioned in Chapter 4, the Chinese Communist Youth League (CCYL) Group is the largest factional group in the Sixteenth Central Committee. Fifty-seven people are identified as CCYL cadres: 24 full and 33 alternate members (Table 4.7). Since the Sixteenth Party Congress, many CCYL cadres have been promoted to important positions in provincial units as well as in the Center.

Provincial Party Secretaries

When the Sixteenth Party Congress was convened in November 2002, three provincial party secretaries had CYL background: Party Secretary Wang Lequan of Xinjiang (also a Politburo member), Party Secretary Song Defu of Fujian, and Party Secretary Qian Yunlu of Guizhou.

Since November 2002, more than 60 percent of provincial party secretaries have been replaced. Out of the total of 31 provincial-level party secretaries, 19 have assumed their positions since the Sixteenth Party Congress (Table 8.1). Out of these 19, seven have prior work experience in the CCYL: Party Secretary Li Keqiang of Liaoning, Party Secretary Li Yuanchao of Jiangsu, Party Secretary Qian Yunlu of Heilongjiang, Party Secretary Wang Yang of Chongqing, Party Secretary Zhang Baoshun of Shanxi, Party Secretary Zhang Qingli of Tibet, and Party Secretary Liu Qibao of Guangxi. With the exception of Qian Yunlu who was transferred from one province to another, all the other six were promoted to provincial party secretaries.

In fact, there were more CCYL cadres involved in more turnovers in terms of provincial party secretaries (Table 8.2). Li Keqiang was promoted to party secretary of Henan in December 2002 and then was transferred to Liaoning as party secretary in December 2004.[111] Yang Chuantang, another former CCYL cadre, was promoted from governor of Qinghai to party secretary of Tibet in January 2004, but

---

involvement in this corruption scandal. For details, see Bo Zhiyue, "China's New Provincial Leaders: Major reshuffling before the 17th National Party Congress," *China: An International Journal* (forthcoming).

[111] http://www.people.com.cn/GB/shizheng/252/9667/9684/20021127/875820.html.

Table 8.1 China's Provincial Party Secretaries (July 2006)

Provinces[a]	Name	Birth	Age	Home	CCP	Sixteenth CC	Since	Faction
Beijing	Liu Qi	1942	64	Jiangsu	1975	Politburo	October 2002	
Tianjin	Zhang Lichang	1939	67	Hebei	1966	Politburo	May 1998	
Hebei	**Bai Keming**	1943	63	Shaanxi	1975	Full	November 2002	Princeling
Shanxi	**Zhang Baoshun**	1950	56	Hebei	1971	Alternate	July 2005	CYL
Inner Mongolia	Chu Bo	1944	62	Anhui	1969	Full	August 2001	
Liaoning	**Li Keqiang**	1955	51	Anhui	1976	Full	December 2004	CYL
Jilin	Wang Yunkun	1942	64	Jiangsu	1966	Full	September 1998	
Heilongjiang	**Qian Yunlu**	1944	62	Hubei	1965	Full	December 2005	CYL
Shanghai	Chen Liangyu	1946	60	Zhejiang	1980	Politburo	October 2002	Shanghai
Jiangsu	**Li Yuanchao**	1950	56	Jiangsu	1978	Alternate	December 2002	CYL
Zhejiang	**Xi Jinping**	1953	53	Shaanxi	1974	Full	November 2002	Princeling
Anhui	**Guo Jinlong**	1947	59	Jiangsu	1979	Full	December 2004	
Fujian	**Lu Zhangong**	1952	54	Zhejiang	1975	Full	February 2004	
Jiangxi	Meng Jianzhu	1947	59	Jiangsu	1971	Full	April 2001	Shanghai
Shandong	**Zhang Gaoli**	1946	60	Fujian	1973	Full	November 2002	
Henan	**Xu Guangchun**	1944	62	Zhejiang	1973	Full	December 2004	Shanghai
Hubei	Yu Zhengsheng	1945	61	Zhejiang	1964	Politburo	November 2001	Princeling
Hunan	**Zhang Chunxian**	1953	53	Henan	1973	Full	December 2005	
Guangdong	**Zhang Dejiang**	1946	60	Liaoning	1971	Politburo	November 2002	
Guangxi	**Liu Qibao**	1953	53	Anhui	1971	Alternate	June 2006	CYL
Hainan	**Wang Xiaofeng**	1944	62	Hunan	1973	Full	April 2003	
Chongqing	**Wang Yang**	1955	51	Anhui	1975	Alternate	December 2005	CYL
Sichuan	**Zhang Xuezhong**	1943	63	Gansu	1960	Full	December 2002	

(*Continued*)

Table 8.1 (Continued)

Provinces[a]	Name	Birth	Age	Home	CCP	Sixteenth CC	Since	Faction
Guizhou	**Shi Zongyuan**	1946	60	Hebei	1979	Full	December 2005	
Yunnan	Bai Enpei	1946	60	Shaanxi	1973	Full	October 2001	
Tibet	**Zhang Qingli**	1951	55	Shandong	1973	Full	November 2005	CYL
Shaanxi	Li Jianguo	1946	60	Shandong	1971	Full	August 1997	
Gansu	**Lu Hao**	1947	59	Hebei	1981	Full	July 2006	
Qinghai	**Zhao Leji**	1957	49	Shaanxi	1975	Full	August 2003	
Ningxia	Chen Jianguo	1945	61	Shandong	1966	Full	March 2002	
Xinjiang	Wang Lequan	1944	62	Shandong	1966	Politburo	September 1994	CYL
Hong Kong	Gao Siren[b]	1944	62	Shandong	1972	Full	August 2002	
Macao	Bai Zhijian[b]	1948	58	Hubei	1976	Full	July 2002	

Home = home province; Since = the year in which the party secretary assumed his current position.

Notes: [a]This refers to provinces, centrally administered cities, autonomous regions, and special administrative regions. Taiwan is not included.

[b] They are not party secretaries. They are directors of the Liaison Offices of their respective SARs.

Source: http://news.xinhuanet.com/ziliao/2002-02/20/content_476046.htm.

Table 8.2 Mobility of Former CYL Cadres Since the Sixteenth Party Congress

Name	CC	Original Place	Original Title	Mobility	New Place	New Title	Date
Shen Yueyue (f.)	Alternate	Anhui	Dep. Sec.	Transfer	Organization	Dep. Director	November 2002
Wang Sanyun	Alternate	Sichuan	Dep. Sec.	Transfer	Fujian	Dep. Sec.	November 2002
Li Keqiang	Full	Henan	Governor	Promotion	Henan	Secretary	December 2002
Li Yuanchao	Alternate	Jiangsu	Dep. Sec.	Promotion	Jiangsu	Secretary	December 2002
Ji Yunshi	Full	Jiangsu	Governor	Transfer	Hebei	Acting Gov.	December 2002
Ji Yunshi	Full	Hebei	Acting Gov.	Promotion	Hebei	Governor	January 2003
Meng Xuenong	Full	Beijing	Dep. Sec.	Promotion	Beijing	Mayor	January 2003
Huang Huahua	Full	Guangdong	Dep. Sec.	Promotion	Guangdong	Governor	January 2003
Li Chengyu	Alternate	Henan	Dep. Sec.	Promotion	Henan	Governor	January 2003
Qin Guangrong	Alternate	Yunnan	Standing	Promotion	Yunnan	Vice Governor	January 2003
Han Zheng	Full	Shanghai	Dep. Sec.	Promotion	Shanghai	Mayor	February 2003
Wang Yang	Alternate	Planning	Vice Minister	Transfer	State Council	Dep. Sec-Gen.	March 2003
Yang Jing	Alternate	Inner Mongolia	Standing	Promotion	Inner Mongolia	Acting Gov.	April 2003
Qin Guangrong	Alternate	Yunnan	Vice Governor	Promotion	Yunnan	Dep. Sec.	May 2003
Cui Bo	Non-CC	CYL Central	Secretary	Promotion	Ningxia	Vice Governor	May 2003
Li Chuncheng	Alternate	Chengdu	Mayor	Promotion	Chengdu	Secretary	June 2003
Sun Jinlong	Non-CC	CYL Central	Secretary	Promotion	Anhui	Standing	June 2003
Yang Chuantang	Alternate	Tibet	Dep. Sec.	Promotion	Qinghai	Acting Gov.	October 2003
Xia Baolong	Alternate	Tianjin	Vice Mayor	Promotion	Zhejiang	Dep. Sec.	November 2003
Hu Chunhua	Non-CC	Tibet	Standing	Promotion	Tibet	Vice Governor	November 2003
Hu Chunhua	Non-CC	Tibet	Standing	Promotion	Tibet	Dep. Sec.	November 2003
Li Liguo	Non-CC	Tibet	Dep. Sec.	Transfer	Civil Affairs	Vice Minister	December 2003
Wu Aiying (f.)	Alternate	Shandong	Dep. Sec.	Transfer	Justice	Vice Minister	December 2003
Bayinchaolu	Non-CC	Zhejiang	Vice Governor	Promotion	Zhejiang	Standing	December 2003
Cui Bo	Non-CC	Ningxia	Vice Governor	Promotion	Ningxia	Standing	December 2003
Cui Bo	Non-CC	Ningxia	Vice Governor	Promotion	Yinchuan	Secretary	January 2004
Zhang Baoshun	Alternate	Shanxi	Dep. Sec.	Promotion	Shanxi	Acting Gov.	January 2004

(*Continued*)

Table 8.2 (*Continued*)

Name	CC	Original Place	Original Title	Mobility	New Place	New Title	Date
Yang Chuantang	Alternate	Qinghai	Acting Gov.	Promotion	Qinghai	Governor	January 2004
Yang Jing	Alternate	Inner Mongolia	Acting Gov.	Promotion	Inner Mongolia	Governor	January 2004
Li Zhaoshu	Alternate	Shaanxi	Dep. Sec.	Transfer	Heilongjiang	Dep. Sec.	January 2004
Sun Shuyi	Alternate	Shandong	Dep. Sec.	Promotion	Shandong	PPCC Chair	January 2004
Liu Yupu	Alternate	Guangdong	Standing	Promotion	Guangdong	Dep. Sec.	January 2004
Zhang Baoshun	Alternate	Shanxi	Acting Gov.	Promotion	Shanxi	Governor	February 2004
Li Keqiang	Full	Henan	Secretary	Transfer	Liaoning	Secretary	December 2004
Yang Chuantang	Alternate	Qinghai	Governor	Promotion	Tibet	Secretary	December 2004
Zhang Qingli	Full	Xinjiang	Standing	Promotion	Xinjiang	Dep. Sec.	December 2004
Song Xiuyan	Alternate	Qinghai	Dep. Sec.	Promotion	Qinghai	Acting Gov.	December 2004
Du Xuefang (f.)	Alternate	Changchun	Secretary	Promotion	Jilin	Dep. Sec.	December 2004
Liu Peng	Alternate	Sichuan	Dep. Sec.	Promotion	Sports	Director	December 2004
Wang Julu	Non-CC	CPPCC	Dep. Sec-Gen.	Promotion	Heilongjiang	PPCC Chair	January 2005
Song Xiuyan	Alternate	Qinghai	Acting Gov.	Promotion	Qinghai	Governor	January 2005
Song Airong (f.)	Alternate	Tulufan	Secretary	Promotion	Xinjiang	Vice Governor	January 2005
Zhang Baoshun	Alternate	Shanxi	Governor	Promotion	Shanxi	Secretary	July 2005
Wu Aiying (f.)	Alternate	Justice	Vice Minister	Promotion	Justice	Minister	July 2005
Hu Wei	Non-CC	CYL Central	Secretary	Transfer	Xinjiang	Vice Governor	July 2005
Zhi Shuping	Alternate	Henan	Dep. Sec.	Transfer	Quality	Vice Director	October 2005
Zhang Qingli	Full	Xinjiang	Dep. Sec.	Promotion	Tibet	Acting Sec.	November 2005
Wang Yang	Alternate	State Council	Dep. Sec-Gen.	Promotion	Chongqing	Secretary	December 2005
Qian Yunlu	Full	Guizhou	Secretary	Transfer	Heilongjiang	Secretary	December 2005
Li Ke (Zhuang)	Alternate	Zhengzhou	Secretary	Promotion	Henan	Vice Governor	January 2006
Zhao Yong	Non-CC	CYL Central	Secretary	Transfer	Hebei	Standing	February 2006
Zhang Qingli	Full	Tibet	Acting Sec.	Promotion	Tibet	Secretary	May 2006
Yuan Chunqing	Alternate	Shaanxi	Dep. Sec.	Promotion	Shaanxi	Acting Gov.	June 2006
Yang Chuantang	Alternate	Tibet	Secretary	Transfer	Nationalities	Vice Minister	June 2006
Liu Qibao	Alternate	Guangxi	Dep. Sec.	Promotion	Guangxi	Secretary	July 2006

Source: Author's database.

he was replaced by Zhang Qingli in November 2005.[112] Zhang Baoshun was promoted to acting governor of Shanxi in January 2004, was appointed as governor the following month, and was promoted again to party secretary of Shanxi in July 2005.[113]

Li Keqiang, Li Yuanchao, and Zhang Baoshun all worked directly with Hu Jintao. When Hu was the first secretary of the CYL Central Committee in 1984 to 1985, Li Yuanchao was a secretary of the Secretariat, and Zhang Baoshun and Li Keqiang were alternate secretaries of the Secretariat. Yang Chuantang probably did not have much direct contact with Hu Jintao, but he may know Li Keqiang, Li Yuanchao, and Zhang Baoshun personally. Yang was born in Shandong in May 1954 and worked in Shandong for 21 years (1972–1993). He was secretary of the Shandong CYL Provincial Committee between October 1987 and February 1992 and became a standing member of the Shandong Party Committee in November 1993. In the same month, he was transferred to Tibet as a standing member of the Tibetan Party Committee and became the executive vice chairman of the Tibetan Autonomous Region Government the following month. He stayed in that position for 10 years. In October 2003, he was transferred to Qinghai as acting governor. In December 2004, he was appointed as party secretary of Tibet.[114] Within a year, however, Yang fell seriously ill and was hospitalized. He reportedly had a stroke in September 2005 and was sent to Beijing for treatment.[115] He was replaced by Zhang Qingli. Zhang had direct work contact with Hu Jintao, but not so closely as Li Keqiang, Li Yuanchao, and Zhang Baoshun. He worked in the Central Committee of the CYL for eight years (1978–1986), mostly in the Department of Young Workers and Peasants. In the subsequent 12 years (1986–1998), he worked in Shandong before he was transferred to Gansu in August 1998. He became a commander without military rank — commander of the Xinjiang Construction Corps — in

---

[112] http://www.chinatibetnews.com/GB/channel4/31/200511/28/44602.html.
[113] http://www.people.com.cn/GB/shizheng/252/9667/9684/2294479.html.
[114] http://www.people.com.cn/GB/shizheng/252/9667/9684/2148460.html.
[115] http://www.funcn.com/html/200511/27065.html.

October 1999 and entered the Sixteenth Central Committee of the CCP as a full member in November 2002. He was appointed as deputy secretary of Xinjiang in December 2004 and vice chairman of the Xinjiang Autonomous Region in January 2005. Finally, Zhang replaced Yang Chuantang in November 2005 as acting party secretary of Tibet.

Wang Yang (1955–), a native of Suzhou, Anhui, probably did not have any direct contact with Hu Jintao as a CYL cadre.[116] He worked in the Anhui CYL Provincial Committee in the early 1980s. He was director of the Propaganda Department and deputy secretary of the Anhui CYL Provincial Committee between August 1982 and October 1984.[117] He became a standing member of the Anhui Provincial Party Committee, vice governor of Anhui in February 1993, and deputy secretary of Anhui in December 1998. He was transferred to Beijing as deputy director of the State Development and Planning Commission in September 1999. He entered the Sixteenth Central Committee as an alternate member and was appointed as deputy secretary-general of the State Council in March 2003. He replaced Huang Zhendong as party secretary of Chongqing in December 2005.[118]

Finally, Liu Qibao (1953–), deputy secretary of the Guangxi Autonomous Region Party Committee, replaced Cao Bochun as party secretary of Guangxi in June 2006.[119] A secretary of the CYL Central Committee between November 1985 and May 1993, Liu worked closely with Song Defu, Li Keqiang, Li Yuanchao, and Zhang Baoshun. But his stay in the CYL Central Committee did not overlap with that of Hu Jintao. Liu served consecutively as deputy editor-in-chief of the *People's Daily*[120] and deputy secretary-general of the State

---

[116] For his bio, see http://news.xinhuanet.com/ziliao/2005-12/26/content_3969021.htm.

[117] http://ics.nccu.edu.tw/frame.php?address=polsum&id=1584&PHPSESSID=aa6cc220b5c66530ec61d816b2e34153.

[118] http://news.xinhuanet.com/politics/2006-01/16/content_4059336.htm.

[119] http://politics.people.com.cn/GB/41223/4543047.html.

[120] http://chinavitae.com/biography_display.php?id=1294.

Council until November 2000[121] and then was transferred to Guangxi as deputy secretary.

Currently, out of 31 provincial party secretaries, more than a quarter of them (eight) have CYL background.

Provincial Governors

Provincial governors experienced more reshuffles than provincial party secretaries did. Out of 31 provincial governors, 23 (74 percent) assumed their positions after the Sixteenth Party Congress (Table 8.3). Out of these 23, eight (more than one third) have CYL background. They are Governor Ji Yunshi of Hebei, Chairman Yang Jing of Inner Mongolia, Mayor Han Zheng of Shanghai, Governor Huang Xiaojing of Fujian, Governor Li Chengyu of Henan, Governor Huang Huahua of Guangdong, Governor Song Xiuyan (female) of Qinghai, and Acting Governor Yuan Chunqing of Shaanxi.

In fact, there was one more CYL cadre who was also promoted to be the provincial-level government leader. Meng Xuenong (1949–), a native of Penglai, Shandong Province, was deputy secretary of the Beijing CYL Municipal Committee between 1983 and 1986. He became vice mayor of Beijing in February 1993 and was elected as mayor of Beijing in January 2003. At the time of his election, Meng was hailed as a man of the people.[122] Three months later, he was dismissed because of his mishandling of the SARS crisis in Beijing. He was replaced by Wang Qishan, the then party secretary of Hainan.

Among these new governors with CYL background, none (including Meng Xuenong) but one had direct work relationship with Hu Jintao as a CYL cadre. Ji Yunshi (1945–) was secretary of the Jiangsu CYL Provincial Committee between August 1982 and July 1984;[123] Yang Jing (1953–) was secretary of the Inner Mongolian CYL

---

[121] http://www.people.com.cn/GB/paper464/1887/304194.html.
[122] http://english.people.com.cn/200301/21/eng20030121_110505.shtml.
[123] For his bio, see http://news.xinhuanet.com/ziliao/2002-02/22/content_286042.htm.

Table 8.3 China's Governors (July 2006)

Provinces[a]	Governor[b]	Birth	Age	Home	CCP	Sixteenth CC	Since	Faction
Beijing	**Wang Qishan**	1948	58	Shanxi	1983	Full	April 2003	P
Tianjin	**Dai Xianglong**	1944	62	Jiangsu	1973	Full	December 2002	
Hebei	**Ji Yunshi**	1945	61	Jiangsu	1975	Full	December 2002	CYL
Shanxi	**Yu Youjun**	1953	53	Jiangsu	1976	Non-CC	July 2005	
Inner Mongolia	**Yang Jing**	1953	53	Inner Mongolia	1976	Alternate	April 2003	CYL
Liaoning	**Zhang Wenyue**	1944	62	Fujian	1965	Alternate	February 2004	
Jilin	**Wang Min**	1950	56	Anhui	1985	Non-CC	October 2004	
Heilongjiang	**Zhang Zuoji**	1945	61	Heilongjiang	1972	Full	April 03	
Shanghai	**Han Zheng**	1954	52	Zhejiang	1979	Full	February 2003	CYL/S
Jiangsu	**Liang Baohua**	1945	61	Jiangxi	1965	Alternate	December 2002	
Zhejiang	**Lu Zushan**	1946	60	Zhejiang	1966	Alternate	March 2003	
Anhui	Wang Jinshan	1945	61	Jilin	1971	Full	December 2002	
Fujian	**Huang Xiaojing**	1946	60	Fujian	1973	Non-CC	December 2004	CYL
Jiangxi	**Huang Zhiquan**	1942	64	Zhejiang	1979	Full	January 2001	
Shandong	**Han Yuqun**	1943	63	Jiangsu	1975	Non-CC	January 2003	
Henan	**Li Chengyu**	1946	60	Ningxia	1971	Full	January 2003	CYL
Hubei	Luo Qingquan	1945	61	Hubei	1975	Full	October 2003	
Hunan	**Zhou Bohua**	1948	58	Hunan	1970	Non-CC	March 2003	
Guangdong	**Huang Huahua**	1946	60	Guangdong	1971	Full	January 2003	CYL
Guangxi	**Lu Bing**	1944	62	Guangxi	1976	Non-CC	April 2003	
Hainan	**Wei Liucheng**	1946	60	Henan	1973	Alternate	October 2003	
Chongqing	Wang Hongju	1945	61	Chongqing	1979	Full	October 2002	
Sichuan	Zhang Zhongwei	1942	64	Sichuan	1960	Full	June 1999	

(Continued)

Table 8.3 (Continued)

Provinces[a]	Governor[b]	Birth	Age	Home	CCP	Sixteenth CC	Since	Faction
Guizhou	Shi Xiushi	1942	64	Henan	1978	Full	January 2001	
Yunnan	Xu Rongkai	1942	64	Chongqing	1960	Full	January 2002	
Tibet	**Qiangba Puncog**	1947	59	Tibet	1974	Alternate	May 2003	
Shaanxi	**Yuan Chunqing**	1951	55	Hunan	1971	Alternate	June 2006	CYL
Gansu	Lu Hao	1947	59	Hebei	1981	Full	January 2001	
Qinghai	**Song Xiuyan**	1955	51	Tianjin	1978	Alternate	December 2004	CYL
Ningxia	Ma Qizhi	1943	63	Ningxia	1972	Full	December 1997	CYL
Xinjiang	**Ismail Tiliwaldi**	1944	62	Xinjiang	1973	Alternate	March 2003	
Hong Kong	Donald Tsang	1944	62	Hong Kong	non-CCP	non-CCP	March 2005	
Macao	Edmund Ho Hau Wah	1955	51	Guangdong			May 1999	

P = princelings; S = Shanghai Gang; CYL = Communist Youth League Group; Since = the year in which the governor assumed his/her current position.

Notes: [a] This refers to provinces, centrally administered cities, autonomous regions, and special administrative regions. Taiwan is not included.

[b] This includes governors, mayors of centrally administered cities, chairmen of autonomous regions, and governors of special administrative regions.

Source: http://news.xinhuanet.com/ziliao/2002-02/20/content_476046.htm.

Committee between June 1993 and March 1996;[124] Han Zheng (1954–) was deputy secretary and secretary of the Shanghai CYL Municipal Committee between May 1990 and October 1992;[125] Huang Xiaojing (1946–) was secretary of the Fuzhou CYL Municipal Committee in the late 1970s;[126] Li Chengyu (1946–) was secretary of the Ningxia CYL Committee between June 1978 and September 1983;[127] Huang Huahua (1946–) was deputy secretary and secretary of the Guangdong CYL Provincial Committee between 1982 and 1987;[128] and Song Xiuyan (1955–) was deputy secretary and secretary of the Qinghai CYL Provincial Committee between January 1983 and December 1988.[129]

The only exception is Yuan Chunqing (1951–). He worked in the CYL Central Committee for 17 years (1980–1997).[130] He probably had direct contact with Hu Jintao, though their relationship then might not be very close. This is because when Hu Jintao was a member of the Secretariat of the CYL Central Committee between 1982 and 1985, Yuan was in low-rank positions in the CYL Central Committee such as deputy head of a section, director of the Student Federation Office of the School Department, and deputy director of the School Department. Yuan was later transferred to Shaanxi as deputy secretary in March 2001 and became concurrent party secretary of Xi'an, Shaanxi, in January 2004. He obtained a doctoral degree in management from Hunan University in July 1997 and received a certificate for postdoctoral studies from Beijing University in May 2001. He is an

---

[124] For his bio, see http://news.xinhuanet.com/ziliao/2003-04/04/content_815368.htm.

[125] For his bio, see http://news.xinhuanet.com/ziliao/2003-02/20/content_737996.htm.

[126] For his bio, see http://ics.nccu.edu.tw/frame.php?address=polsum&id=1607.

[127] For his bio, see http://news.xinhuanet.com/ziliao/2003-02/20/content_737780.htm.

[128] For his bio, see http://news.xinhuanet.com/ziliao/2003-02/20/content_737815.htm.

[129] For her bio, see http://news.xinhuanet.com/ziliao/2004-12/24/content_2375341.htm.

[130] For his bio, see http://www.xatvs.com/ycq/jianli.htm.

alternate member of the Sixteenth Central Committee of the CCP. The Twenty-Fifth Meeting of the Standing Committee of the Shaanxi Tenth Provincial People's Congress decided on June 1, 2006, to appoint Yuan Chunqing as vice governor and acting governor of Shaanxi.[131]

Out of 31 provincial governors, nine (29%) are former CYL cadres.

Other Provincial Leaders

In addition to the provincial party secretaries and provincial governors with the CYL background, many CYL cadres have also joined the provincial leadership as deputy party secretaries, standing members, vice governors, chairmen of the provincial people's consultative conferences, or chairmen of the provincial people's congresses (Table 8.4).

- Wang Sanyun (1952–) was transferred from Sichuan to Fujian as deputy secretary in December 2002;
- Qin Guangrong (1950–) was elected as vice governor of Yunnan in January 2003 and was promoted to deputy secretary of Yunnan in May 2003;
- Sun Jinlong (1962–) was transferred from the CCYL Central Committee to Anhui as standing member of the Anhui Provincial Party Committee and secretary of the Political and Legal Committee in June 2003[132] and was later appointed as party secretary of Hefei in April 2005[133];
- Cui Bo (1957–) was transferred from the CCYL Central Committee to Ningxia as vice governor in May 2003 and was promoted to standing member of the Ningxia Party Committee and party secretary of Yinchuan in December 2003[134];

---

[131] See http://news.xinhuanet.com/politics/2006-06/02/content_4635448.htm.
[132] http://www.hefei.gov.cn/info/swld/sjl.jsp.
[133] http://politics.people.com.cn/GB/41223/3286290.html.
[134] http://www.yinchuan.gov.cn/sjld/sjld_list.asp?id=1.

390 China's Elite Politics

Table 8.4 Promotions (and Transfers) of CYL Cadres since the Sixteenth Party Congress

Name	Birth	Gender	Home	Sixteenth CC[a]	Place	Title
Provincial party secretaries						
Zhang Baoshun	1950	Male	Hebei	Alternate	Shanxi	Secretary
Li Keqiang	1955	Male	Anhui	Full	Liaoning	Secretary
Li Yuanchao	1950	Male	Jiangsu	Alternate	Jiangsu	Secretary
Yang Chuantang	1954	Male	Shandong	Alternate	Tibet	Secretary
Zhang Qingli	1951	Male	Shandong	Full	Tibet	Secretary
Qian Yunlu[b]	1944	Male	Hubei	Full	Heilongjiang	Secretary
Wang Yang	1955	Male	Anhui	Alternate	Chongqing	Secretary
Liu Qibao	1953	Male	Anhui	Alternate	Guangxi	Secretary
Provincial governors[c]						
Ji Yunshi[b]	1945	Male	Jiangsu	Full	Hebei	Governor
Yang Jing	1953	Male	Inner Mongolia	Alternate	Inner Mongolia	Chairman
Han Zheng	1954	Male	Zhejiang	Full	Shanghai	Mayor
Huang Xiaojing	1946	Male	Fujian	Non-CC	Fujian	Governor
Li Chengyu	1946	Male	Shaanxi	Full	Henan	Governor
Huang Huahua	1946	Male	Guangdong	Full	Guangdong	Governor
Song Xiuyan	1955	Female	Tianjin	Alternate	Qinghai	Governor
Meng Xuenong[d]	1949	Male	Shandong	Full	Beijing	Mayor
Yuan Chunqing	1951	Male	Hunan	Alternate	Shaanxi	Acting Governor
Other provincial leaders						
Qin Guangrong	1950	Male	Hunan	Alternate	Yunnan	Deputy Secretary
Xia Baolong	1952	Male	Tianjin	Alternate	Zhejiang	Deputy Secretary
Hu Chunhua	1963	Male	Hubei	Non-CC	Tibet	Deputy Secretary
Liu Yupu	1949	Male	Shandong	Alternate	Guangdong	Deputy Secretary
Wang Sanyun[b]	1952	Male	Shandong	Alternate	Fujian	Deputy Secretary

(*Continued*)

Table 8.4 (Continued)

Name	Birth	Gender	Home	Sixteenth CC[a]	Place	Title
Li Zhaoshu[b]	1950	Male	Hebei	Alternate	Heilongjiang	Deputy Secretary
Sun Jinlong	1962	Male	Hubei	Non-CC	Anhui	Standing Member
Bayinchaolu	1955	Male	Inner Mongolia	Non-CC	Zhejiang	Standing Member
Cui Bo	1957	Male	Shandong	Non-CC	Ningxia	Standing Member
Zhao Yong	1963	Male	Hunan	Non-CC	Hebei	Standing Member
Li Ke	1956	Male	Guangxi	Alternate	Henan	Vice Governor
Hu Wei	1962	Male	Zhejiang	Non-CC	Xinjiang	Vice Chairman
Song Airong	1959	Female	Henan	Alternate	Xinjiang	Vice Chairman
Liu Shengyu	1945	Male	Shandong	Non-CC	Tianjin	Congress Chairman
Wang Julu	1945	Male	Henan	Non-CC	Heilongjiang	PPPCC Chairman
Sun Shuyi	1945	Male	Shandong	Alternate	Shandong	PPPCC Chairman
Central leadership						
Wu Aiying	1951	Female	Shandong	Alternate	Justice	Minister
Cai Wu	1949	Male	Gansu	Non-CC	Information Office	Director
Liu Peng	1951	Male	Chongqing	Alternate	Sport Administration	Director
Shen Yueyue	1957	Male	Zhejiang	Alternate	Central Organization	Deputy Director
Li Xueju	1945	Male	Jilin	Non-CC	Civil Affairs	Minister
Li Liguo	1953	Male	Hebei	Non-CC	Civil Affairs	Vice Minister
Zhi Shuping	1953	Male	Henan	Alternate	Quality Supervision	Vice Minister
Military leaders						
Li Jinai	1942	Male	Shandong	Full	Gen. Pol. Dept.	Director

PPPCC = Provincial People's Political Consultative Conference.
Sixteenth CC = The Sixteenth Central Committee of the Chinese Communist Party.
[a] Transfers.
[b] This includes governors, mayors of centrally administered cities, chairmen of autonomous regions, and governors of special administrative regions.
[c] He was dismissed in April 2003.
Source: Author's database.

- Xia Baolong (1952–) was promoted from vice mayor of Tianjin to deputy secretary of Zhejiang in November 2003[135];
- Hu Chunhua (1963–) was promoted from a standing member and secretary general of the Tibetan Party Committee to vice chairman and deputy secretary of Tibet in November 2003[136];
- Bayinchaolu (1955–) was promoted from vice governor of Zhejiang to standing member of the Zhejiang Provincial Party Committee and party secretary of Ningbo in December 2003[137];
- Liu Yupu (1949–) was promoted to deputy secretary of Guangdong in January 2004[138];
- Sun Shuyi (1945–) was promoted from deputy secretary of Shandong to chairman of the Shandong Provincial People's Political Consultative Conference in January 2004[139];
- Wang Julu (1945–) was promoted to chairman of the Heilongjiang Provincial People's Political Consultative Conference in January 2005[140];
- Song Airong (1959–) was promoted to vice chairman of Xinjiang in January 2005[141];
- Hu Wei (1962–) was transferred from the CCYL Central Committee to Xinjiang as vice chairman in July 2005[142];
- Li Ke (1956–) was elected as vice governor of Henan in January 2006[143];

---

[135] http://www.people.com.cn/GB/shizheng/1026/2233966.html.
[136] For his bio, see http://www.chinatibetnews.com/GB/channel4/32/200311/19/18092.html.
[137] http://news.xinhuanet.com/newscenter/2003-12/17/content_1235766.htm.
[138] For his appointment, see http://news.xinhuanet.com/zhengfu/2004-01/08/content_1266029.htm. For his bio, see http://ics.nccu.edu.tw/frame.php?address=polsum&id=705.
[139] For his bio, see http://news.xinhuanet.com/ziliao/2004-01/13/content_1272795.htm.
[140] For his bio, see http://news.xinhuanet.com/ziliao/2005-01/31/content_2528842.htm.
[141] For her bio, see http://www.xinjiang.gov.cn/1$001/1$001$013/35.jsp?articleid=2005-1-18-0009.
[142] http://big5.xinhuanet.com/gate/big5/news.xinhuanet.com/newscenter/2005-07/31/content_3291159.htm.
[143] http://news.xinhuanet.com/politics/2006-01/22/content_4083558.htm.

- Liu Shengyu (1945–) replaced Fang Fengyou as chairman of the Standing Committee of the Tianjin Municipal People's Congress in January 2006[144]; and
- Zhao Yong (1963–) was transferred from the CCYL Central Committee to Hebei as standing member of the Hebei Provincial Party Committee and director of the Propaganda Department in February 2006.[145]

In sum, since the Sixteenth Party Congress, 27 former CYL cadres have been promoted in provinces: Seven are party secretaries; eight governors; three deputy secretaries; two vice governors; four standing members; one Provincial People's Congress Standing Committee chairman; and two Provincial People's Political Consultative Conference chairmen.

Central Leadership

Since November 2002, at least seven former CYL cadres have been promoted to important positions in the Center. First, Shen Yueyue (1957–), deputy secretary of Anhui since June 2001, was transferred to the Central Organization Department as a deputy director. Shen joined the CCP in 1981 and was a member of the CYL Central Committee between November 1985 and May 1993.[146] She was deputy secretary and secretary of the CYL Zhejiang Committee between 1986 and 1993. She worked as a standing member of the Zhejiang Party Committee and the director of its organization department until June 2001. She then was appointed as deputy secretary of Anhui. In November 2002, she was transferred to Beijing as deputy director of

---

[144] http://news.xinhuanet.com/politics/2006-01/20/content_4078569.htm.
[145] http://www5.chinesenewsnet.com/MainNews/SinoNews/Mainland/cna_2006_02_23_21_00_16_027.html.
[146] Shen Xueming and Zheng Jianying, (eds), *Zhonggong Diyijie zhi Dishiwujie Zhongyangweiyuan* [*The Central Committee Members of the Chinese Communist Party from the First Through the Fifteenth Central Committee*] (Beijing: Zhongyang Wenxian Chubanshe, 2001), p. 392.

the Central Organization Department. In June 2003, she was also appointed as vice minister of Personnel.[147] She has been instrumental in the new appointments of provincial and central leaders since the Sixteenth Party Congress.

Second, Wu Aiying (1951–) was transferred to the Ministry of Justice as executive vice minister in December 2003. A former deputy secretary of the Shandong CYL Provincial Committee in the early 1980s, she had been deputy secretary of Shandong since April 1993 and chairman of the Shandong People's Political Consultative Conference since April 2003.[148] She was further promoted to minister of Justice in July 2005, replacing retiring Zhang Fusen, another former CYL cadre.

Third, Liu Peng, deputy secretary of Sichuan, was transferred to Beijing in December 2004 as the head of the State Sport General Administration of China, replacing Yuan Weimin (1939–). Yuan became the head of the State Sport General Administration of China in May 2000, and he had reached his retirement age of 65 in July 2004.[149] But the National Audit Office of China discovered that the State Sport General Administration under Yuan misused public funds. In one case between 2003 and 2004, the State Sport General Administration authorized its lottery division to pay two of the division's own companies for printing and distributing lottery tickets. The two companies were overpaid by 558 million yuan (US$67 million). The State Sport General Administration then authorized these two companies to pay 130 million yuan (US$15.7 million) to purchase buildings and ask them to submit profits in the amount of 3.75 million yuan (US$4.5 million) in addition of personal bonuses of 131 million (US$15.8 million).[150] Somehow, Yuan Weimin was not investigated about these irregularities and did not take any

---

[147] http://www.people.com.cn/GB/paper39/9384/869466.html.
[148] For her bio, see http://www.legalinfo.gov.cn/moj/leader/2004-02/23/content_76480.htm.
[149] For his bio, see http://news.xinhuanet.com/ziliao/2002-03/05/content_300389.htm.
[150] http://www.chinanews.com.cn/news/2005/2005-06-28/26/592307.shtml.

responsibilities for them. He was subsequently inducted to the Tenth CNPPCC on February 28, 2005.

Liu Peng worked in the CYL system for 10 years. He was secretary of the CYL Chongqing Committee (1985–1987) and deputy secretary and secretary of the CYL Sichuan Committee (1991–1993). He became a standing member of the CYL Central Committee in May 1988 and a secretary in May 1993. He served as deputy director of the Propaganda Department of the Central Committee of the CCP between 1997 and 2002 and was transferred to Sichuan as deputy secretary.[151] His appointment as the head of the State Sport General Administration of China would ensure the CYL cadres' control over this vital organ for the forthcoming Olympic Games in 2008 in Beijing.

Fourth, Li Xueju and Li Liguo both have worked in the Ministry of Civil Affairs. Li Xueju (1945–), a former CYL cadre who worked in the CYL Central Committee for about a decade between 1978 and 1987, had worked in the Ministry of Civil Affairs in the late 1980s. He was transferred to Chongqing in September 1996 as director of the Organization Department and standing member of the Chongqing Municipal Party Committee. After he was promoted to deputy secretary of Chongqing in 1998, he was transferred back to the Ministry of Civil Affairs as vice minister in July 2001. Somehow, he failed to enter the Sixteenth Central Committee in November 2002, but he nonetheless was appointed as minister of Civil Affairs in March 2003.[152] Li Liguo (1953–), former deputy secretary of the Liaoning CYL Provincial Committee (June 1985–January 1990) and deputy secretary of Tibet (September 2001–),[153] was transferred to Beijing as vice minister of Civil Affairs in November 2003.[154]

---

[151] http://news.enorth.com.cn/system/2004/12/09/000921082.shtml.

[152] For his bio, see http://news.xinhuanet.com/ziliao/2003-03/17/content_782297.htm.

[153] For his bio, see http://www.gov.cn/zwhd/ft/shap_jj.htm; http://ics.nccu.edu.tw/frame.php?address=polsum&id=595.

[154] http://www.gxi.gov.cn/feature/zzrs/gjrs/20031229161049.htm.

Fifth, Zhi Shuping (1953–) was appointed as vice director of the State Administration of Quality Supervision, Inspection, and Quarantine in October 2005.[155] Zhi was deputy secretary and secretary of the Shanxi CYL Provincial Committee between June 1985 and July 1994 and served as director of the Organization Department of the Shanxi Provincial Party Committee in the late 1990s. He was transferred to Henan in November 1998 as director of the Organization Department of the Henan Provincial Party Committee and was promoted to deputy secretary in December 2000. He entered the Sixteenth Central Committee as an alternate member in November 2002 and was transferred to the State Administration of Quality Supervision, Inspection, and Quarantine in October 2005. Interestingly, Zeng Qinghong's wife, Wang Fengqing,[156] also retired.[157] Wang Fengqing (1940–)[158] had been a member of the Leading Party Group of the State Administration of Quality Supervision, Inspection, and Quarantine as well as party secretary and director of the Certification and Accreditation Administration of the PRC. She was 65 years old in 2005 and was replaced by Sun Dawei. It is not clear what rank she had before her retirement, but it is unlikely that she had a ministerial rank because the State Administration of Quality Supervision, Inspection, and Quarantine at most is a ministerial institution and she was not even a deputy director. The mandatory retirement age for vice-ministerial cadres is 60, but she retired at the age of 65. In other words, she probably had postponed her retirement for five years because of her connections with Zeng Qinghong. She should have retired in 2000 while Zeng was director of the Central Organization Department.

Lastly, Cai Wu replaced Zhao Qizheng as director of the Information Office of the State Council on August 25, 2005. Born in Wudu, Gansu Province, in October 1949, Cai is not only nine years younger than his predecessor but has a different background.[159] Cai

---

[155] http://www.gov.cn/rsrm/2005-10/18/content_79024.htm.
[156] For their relationship, see http://www.zaobao.com/special/npc/pages2/npc160303a.html.
[157] http://www.gov.cn/rsrm/2005-10/18/content_79024.htm.
[158] http://www.chinajunzheng.com/bbs/htm_data/89/0606/31579.html.
[159] http://news.xinhuanet.com/ziliao/2005-08/19/content_3374695.htm.

had worked in Gansu for 10 years before he was enrolled in the Department of International Politics at Beijing University in 1978 and was promoted to the Central Committee of the Chinese Youth League in July 1983. At the time, Hu Jintao was also in the Central Committee of the Chinese Youth League as the No. 2 leader. Cai, therefore, worked with Hu for two years. Cai was transferred to the International Liaison Department in March 1995 and became its deputy director in July 1997. With a Ph.D. from the School of International Studies at Beijing University, Cai is also a professor in the School of International Studies at the People's University of China. He is likely to enter the Central Committee of the CCP in 2007 as a full member.

It should be noted that the decline of the Shanghai Gang and the emergence of the CCYL Group were not necessarily results of factional politics. They were partially results of generational changes. Most members of the Shanghai Gang belong to the third generation, and most members of the CCYL Group belong to the fourth and fifth generations. Zhang Wenkang, for instance, would have retired by 2005 had he not been fired in 2003 because he would reach his retirement age of 65 in April 2005.[160] Zhao Qizheng retired instead of being dismissed. Other members of the Shanghai Gang would also retire by 2008 because of their age: Huang Ju was born in September 1938; Zeng Qinghong was born in July 1939; Hua Jinmian was born in January 1940; and Chen Zhili was born in November 1942. Yet the outcome of the generational changes is in Hu Jintao's favor because Shanghai Gang members tend to be loyal to Jiang Zemin while CCYL Group members are generally loyal to Hu Jintao.

RISE OF PRINCELING GENERALS

Two Career Barriers

Princeling generals in China refer to military officers holding the rank of major general/rear admiral and above in the PLA who are children of the first generation leaders. More specifically, the first generation high-ranking CCP leaders include military leaders that were awarded

---

[160] He was born in April 1940. See http://news.sina.com.cn/c/2003-03-17/183695 1056.shtml.

the rank of at least major general[161] between 1955 and 1964[162] (10 marshals, 10 senior generals, 57 generals,[163] 177 lieutenant generals,[164] and 1,357 major generals[165]) and civilian leaders that enjoyed the deputy provincial/ministerial rank before 1966. These princeling generals faced two major barriers in their military and political careers: first, they tended only to be appointed to deputy positions; second, they were excluded from the CCP Central Committee.

"Deputy Position" Phenomenon

From the list of former princeling generals (Table 8.5), it is evident that many of them exited the PLA in deputy positions.[166] Out of 14 lieutenant generals/vice admirals, 11 fall into this category:

---

[161] The PLA did not introduce ranks until 1955, and they were abolished in 1965 at the beginning of the Cultural Revolution. Ranks were not reinstituted until 1988.

[162] In 1955, China appointed 10 marshals, 10 senior generals, 55 generals, 175 lieutenant generals, and 801 major generals. See http://news.xinhuanet.com/ziliao/2004-06/30/content_1556923.htm.

[163] Two lieutenant generals — Wang Jian'an in 1956 and Li Jukui in 1958 — were later promoted to the rank of general. See http://www.people.com.cn/GB/29999/2808298.html.

[164] Two major generals — Nie Heting in 1956 and He Cheng in 1958 — were later promoted to the rank of lieutenant general.

[165] Between 1955 and 1964, 558 senior colonels were promoted to the rank of major general. For details, see http://news.xinhuanet.com/ziliao/2004-08/17/content_1804216.htm.

[166] It is very important to make a distinction between positions and grades. In some cases, there are barely any differences. For instance, a deputy commander of a military region obviously has the grade of military region deputy leader, and a commander of a military region has the grade of military region leader. In other cases, however, the link between the position and the grade is not so obvious. For instance, deputy directors of the GLD and deputy directors of the General Armament Department (GAD) have the grade of military region deputy leader, while deputy directors of the GPD and deputy chiefs of staff have the grade of military region leader. This book will clarify cases where there may be confusion about the distinction between positions and grades, but this study focuses on positions rather than grades. For details, see "Zhongguo Renmin Jiefangjun

Hu Jintao's Power Consolidation 399

Table 8.5 Former Princeling Generals

Name	Home/Birth	Unit	Title	Rank	Relative	Status
Chen Zhijian	Hunan	Chongqing Garrison	Deputy Commander	Major General	Chen Geng	Retired
Deng Xianqun (female)	Sichuan/1935	GPD	Department Director	Major General	Deng Xiaoping	Retired
Deng Yousheng	1940	COSTIND	Bureau Chief	Major General	Luo Ruiqing	Retired
Ding Henggao	Jiangsu/1931	COSTIND	Director	General	Nie Rongzhen	Retired
Fang Jiangnan	Hunan	Armed Police	Political Department Director	Major General	Fang Qiang	Retired
Feng Hongda	Anhui	North China Sea Fleet	Deputy Commander	Rear Admiral	Feng Yuxiang	Deceased
He Daoquan	Hubei/1935	NDU	Vice President	Lieut. General	He Changgong	Retired
He Jiesheng (female)	Hunan/1935	AMS	Department Deputy Director	Major General	He Long	Retired
He Pengfei	Hunan/1945	Navy	Deputy Commander	Lieut. General	He Long	Deceased
He Yi	Shaanxi	Armed Police	Department Director	Major General	He Jinnian	Deceased
Hong Bao	Anhui	Tianjin	Dep. Com.	Major General	Hong Xuezhi	Retired
Hua Zhongliang	Jiangsu/1943	GAD	Department Deputy Director	Major General	Song Shilun	Retired
Li Lun	Anhui	GLD	Deputy Director	Lieut. General	Li Kenong	Retired
Liu Taihang	Sichuan/1940	Air Force Academy	Department Chair	Major General	Liu Bocheng	Retired
Luo Bin	Hubei	Defense Ministry	Office Director	Major General	Wu Xiuquan	Retired
Luo Dongjin	Hunan/1939	Second Artillery Corps	Deputy Political Commissar	Lieut. General	Luo Ronghuan	Retired
Luo Jian	Sichuan/1938	GAD	Department Deputy Political Commissar	Major General	Luo Ruiqing	Retired
Ma Guochao	Hebei/1939	Navy Air Force	Deputy Political Commissar	Major General	Ma Benzhai	Retired
Nie Li (female)	Sichuan/1930	COSTIND	Department Director	Lieut. General	Nie Rongzhen	Retired
Peng Gang (female)	Hunan/1938	CMC	Discipline Deputy Secretary	Major General	Peng Dehuai	Retired
Qin Tao	Hubei	Beijing Garrison	Deputy Commander	Major General	Qin Jiwei	Fired

(*Continued*)

Table 8.5 (*Continued*)

Name	Home/Birth	Unit	Title	Rank	Relative	Status
Su Qianming	1933	Second Artillery Corps	Deputy Commander	Lieut. General	Deng Xiaoping	Retired
Su Rongsheng	Hunan/1942	Beijing MR	Deputy Commander	Lieut. General	Su Yu	Retired
Tan Dongsheng	Hunan/1941	Guangzhou MR	Deputy Commander	Lieut. General	Tan Zhenlin	Retired
Wang Jianghuai	Anhui	NDU	Professor	Major General	Wang Shaochuan	Retired
Wang Sumin	Jiangsu	Central Guards Bureau	Deputy Director	Lieut. General	Wang Zheng	Retired
Xiao Xinghua	Hunan/1939	Armed Police	Discipline Secretary	Major General	Xiao Ke	Retired
Xu Yanbin	Hunan	Armored Forces Engineering Academy	President	Major General	Xu Guangda	Retired
Ye Xuanning	Guangdong/1938	GPD	Department Director	Lieut. General	Ye Jianying	Retired
Ye Zhengda	Guangdong	COSTIND	Deputy Director	Lieut. General	Ye Ting	Retired
Zhang Xiang	Sichuan/1943	Second Artillery Corps	Deputy Commander	Lieut. General	Zhang Aiping	Retired
Zhang Xiaoyang	Hunan/1941	PLA Luoyang Foreign Languages Institute	President	Major General	Zhang Zhen	Retired
Zhang Xuedong	Hunan/1934	COSTIND	Deputy Director	Lieut. General	Zhang Shuzhi	Retired
Zhang Zhenqiao	Hunan/1934	GSD	Bureau Chief	Major General	Zhang Zhen	Retired
Zhong Jiafei	Guangxi	Guangxi Military District		Major General	Zhong Fuxiang	Retired
Zhou Borong	Anhui/1945	Navy	Deputy Chief of Staff	Rear Admiral	Zhou Fatian	Retired
Zhou Enjun	Zhejiang	NDU	Political Department Director	Lieut. General	Zhou Enlai	Retired

Acronyms:
AMS: Academy of Military Sciences; CMC: Central Military Commission; COSTIND: Commission of Science, Technology, and Industry for National Defense; GAD: General Armament Department; GLD: General Logistics Department; GPD: General Political Department; GSD: General Staff Department; MR: Military Region; NDU: National Defense University.

Source: Author's database.

- Li Lun, son of General Li Kenong, retired as a deputy director of the GLD[167];
- Su Qianming (Deng Xiaoping's brother-in-law) and Zhang Xiang (son of former defense minister, General Zhang Aiping) both retired as deputy commanders of the Second Artillery Corps;
- Luo Dongjin, son of Marshal Luo Ronghuan, retired as a deputy political commissar of the Second Artillery Corps;
- Tan Dongsheng, son of former Vice Premier Tan Zhenlin, retired as a deputy commander of the Guangzhou Military Region;
- He Daoquan, son of He Changgong, retired as vice president of the National Defense University;
- Wang Sumin, son of a former deputy chief of the General Staff, Lieutenant General Wang Zheng, retired as a deputy director of the Central Guards Bureau;
- Zhang Xuedong (son of Major General Zhang Shuzhi) and Ye Zhengda (son of Ye Ting) both retired as deputy directors of the Commission of Science, Technology, and Industry for National Defense (COSTIND).

Vice Admiral He Pengfei, son of Marshal He Long, died in 2001 at the tender age of 56. He was a deputy commander of the PLA Navy.

Junguan Junxian Tiaoli" ["Regulations on the military ranks of the officers of the People's Liberation Army" adopted by the Seventh Meeting of the Eighth National People's Congress Standing Committee on May 12, 1994, and revised by the Second Meeting of the Ninth National People's Congress on July 1, 1998], http://www.china.org.cn/chinese/zhuanti/xian/450665.htm. For more explanations, see "Jiefangjun xinjinsheng de shida shangjiang xueligao pingjunnianling 61.7 sui" ["The 10 new generals have good educational credentials and their average age is 61.7"], *Renminwang*, August 4, 2006, http://military.people.com.cn/ GB/1076/4665733.html.

[167] Li Lun's grade was that of a military region deputy leader since deputy directors of the GLD all have that grade and have to retire at the age of 63. Lieutenant General Wen Guangchun, former deputy director of the GLD, was born in October 1941 and retired at the end of 2004. For Wen's details, see http://www .npc.gov.cn/zgrdw/common/dbxx.jsp?label=DB&id=102973&lx=RDDB&pdmc=null.

The case of Lieutenant General Su Rongsheng, son of Senior General Su Yu,[168] is noteworthy. Su Rongsheng joined his parents in the military at the age of one in 1943. His father taught him swimming by throwing him into a stream when he was two years old. And he began shooting lessons at the age of five when his father gave him a pistol.[169] After graduating from the Harbin Institute of Military Engineering (*Hajungong*) in 1966, General Su Yu sent him to the border area in Yunnan Province. Su Rongsheng started from scratch there. Three years later, when his troops were transferred to the interior, his father sent him to the Sino-Soviet border where military clashes were most likely to occur at that time. Su Rongsheng is one of a very few Hajungong graduates who worked their way up through the ranks, from an ordinary soldier, through squad leader, platoon commander, deputy company commander, company commander, regiment commander, division commander, army chief of staff, army commander, and eventually to a deputy commander of the Beijing Military Region[170] in November 1997.[171] He was awarded the rank of major general in 1988 and the rank of lieutenant general 11 years later. He stayed in the position of deputy commander of the Beijing Military Region for eight years until his retirement in December 2005.[172]

This "deputy position" phenomenon is also evident among former princeling generals with the rank of major general/rear admiral. Some notable examples are

---

[168] http://english.chinamil.com.cn/site2/special-reports/2005-08/11/content_270869.htm.

[169] He Pin and Gao Xin, *Zhonggong taizidang* [*CCP princes*] (Toronto: Mirror Books, 1992), pp. 359–366. See also http://www.zbnews.net/zhuanti/ 20050526tj/tj52.htm.

[170] He was one of four or five deputy commanders of the Beijing Military Region at the time.

[171] http://www.lovenudt.com/biography/general/list/040919_surongsheng.htm.

[172] A widely circulated story on the Internet has it that Su Rongsheng, son of an ever-victorious general, met his Waterloo in 1985 while he was directing a division in his capacity of chief of staff of the 67th Army in the war against Vietnam. However, this story does not explain why he had to stay in the position of deputy commander of the Beijing Military Region for eight years.

- Hong Bao, son of General Hong Xuezhi, retired as deputy commander of the Tianjin Garrison;
- Chen Zhijian, son of Senior General Chen Geng, retired as deputy commander of the Chongqing Garrison[173];
- Ma Guochao, son of Ma Benzhai, retired as a deputy commander of the PLA Naval Air Force;
- Zhou Borong, son of Major General Zhou Fatian, retired as deputy chief of staff of the PLA Navy[174];
- Luo Jian, son of Senior General Luo Ruiqing, retired as a deputy political commissar of the GAD's second-level Logistics Department[175];
- Luo Jian's colleague, Hua Zhongliang, son-in-law of General Song Shilun, retired as a deputy director of the GAD's second-level Logistics Department[176];
- Feng Hongda, son of Feng Yuxiang, probably died while he was a deputy commander of the PLA Navy's North China Sea Fleet.

Major General Qin Tao, son of a former defense minister, General Qin Jiwei,[177] presents a unique case. He was removed from the office as deputy commander of the Beijing Garrison due to an incident in his jurisdiction. The incident occurred on September 20, 1994, 10 days before the 55th anniversary of the founding of the PRC. Lieutenant Tian Mingjian, a deputy commander of Twelfth Company, Third Division, Beijing Garrison, killed four leaders (including the political commissar) of his regiment and injured a number of others. He then took to the streets killing dozens of

---

[173] http://hlj.rednet.com.cn/Articles/2004/10/627839.HTM.
[174] http://www.ahxf.gov.cn/shownew.asp?ID=5535.
[175] For an interview with Luo Jian, see http://www.zbnews.net/ zhuanti/20050526tj/tj43.htm. Luo Ruiqing named his three sons Luo Jian, Luo Yu, and Luo Huan. He was hoping that China would produce its own rockets (*huojian*), spaceships (*yu*), and atomic bombs (*huan*).
[176] http://www.js.xinhuanet.com/zhuanlan/2005-06/20/content_4474041.htm.
[177] Qin Jiwei was awarded the rank of lieutenant general in 1955 and general in 1988 while he was defense minister. For his biography, see http://www.china.org.cn/chinese/zhuanti/208078.htm.

people, including an Iranian diplomat and his son, and injuring many others.[178]

As a result of this tragic incident, the Beijing Garrison leadership was reshuffled. He Changgong's son, Lieutenant General He Daoquan, who was deputy commander of the Beijing Military Region and concurrently commander of the Beijing Garrison, was demoted to deputy chief of staff of the region. He was replaced by Major General Liu Fengjun, a deputy chief of staff of the Beijing Military Region at the time. In addition, Major General Zhang Baokang (1941–)[179] lost his position as political commissar of the Beijing Garrison and was demoted to deputy director of the Political Department of the Nanjing Military Region. Major General Qin Tao was removed from his position as a deputy commander of the Beijing Garrison, and his career probably ended there.[180]

The Central Committee Hurdle

The second impression one may get from Table 8.5 is that few of the princelings have ever made it to the CCP Central Committee. There are only two exceptions. One is Ding Henggao (son-in-law of Marshal Nie Rongzhen and husband of Lieutenant General Nie Li). He is exceptional in three aspects, being the only full general in the group, the only chief leader (head of the COSTIND), and the only princeling to have served on several CCP central committees. A native of Nanjing, Jiangsu Province, General Ding was a renowned scientist. He became an assistant research fellow in the CAS in 1952 after graduating from the School of Engineering at Nanjing University. He later studied in the Soviet Union, at the Leningrad Institute of Precision Machinery and Optical Instruments, between 1957 and 1961. Over the next 23 years, Ding was involved in the research, design, and testing of strategic missiles and satellites. In

---

[178] For details of the Tian Mingjian incident, see http://www.beiming.info/html/88166.html.
[179] For his biography, see http://www.hzqz.com/intro/bnxs4_intro.asp.
[180] http://www.beiming.info/html/88166.html.

1985, he was appointed head of the COSTIND. In September of the same year, he was elected as an alternate member of the Twelfth Central Committee. He was a member of both the Thirteenth and Fourteenth Central Committees.[181]

The second exception is He Daoquan. Interestingly, He's father, He Changgong (1900–1987), was a prominent communist revolutionary from Hunan Province and a former vice chairman of the National Committee of the CPPCC who never made it to the CCP Central Committee.[182] He Changgong was four years older than Deng Xiaoping and joined the CCP two years earlier than Deng. He worked closely with Mao Zedong in the early years of Mao's military and political career. He was one of the three designers of the Red Army's first military flag,[183] participated in the Autumn Harvest Uprising of 1927 under Mao's leadership, and helped Mao bring a local military force (in reality, bandits) in Jinggangshan under the leadership of Wang Zuo into the Red Army in 1928.[184] He Changgong was one of the most important military leaders of the Red Army at the time. He was Party representative of the 28th Regiment, the Fourth Army of the Red Army in 1928, Party representative of the 32nd Regiment in 1929, commander of the Eighth Army of the Red Army and member of the General Front Committee of the First Route Army of the Red Army in 1930, and political commissar of the 13th Army, Fifth Army Corps of the Red Army in 1932. He participated in all five antimilitary campaigns as well as the subsequent Long March. His military career stagnated after 1938 when he was appointed provost of the Anti-Japanese University (Kangda).

It seemed that his son, He Daoquan, fared better. He Daoquan joined the PLA at the age of 16 in 1951. In the subsequent 36 years, he rose from platoon commander, through staff officer (*canmou*) of

---

[181] Shen Xueming and Zheng Jianying, *Zhonggong diyijie zhi dishiwujie zhongyang weiyuan*, pp. 4, 5.
[182] For his bio, see http://202.106.161.5:7777/was40/search?channelid=36976&searchword=%B1%EA%CC%E2=%25%BA%CE%B3%A4%B9%A4%25.
[183] http://url.xiushui.net/qg/Article_Show.asp?ArticleID=7.
[184] http://szlib.szptt.net.cn/jgs/wj5.htm.

various levels, to an army commander. At the Thirteenth Party Congress in November 1987, he was elected as an alternate member of the Central Committee. In the following year, he was awarded the rank of major general. At the age of 53, He Daoquan's future looked bright. Although he failed to enter the Fourteenth Central Committee in 1992, he nevertheless was promoted to deputy commander of the Beijing Military Region and concurrently commander of the Beijing Garrison in 1993.[185] The Tian Mingjian Incident mentioned earlier sealed his political career. He later retired as vice president of the National Defense University with the rank of lieutenant general.

The "Red Family" Background: Asset or Liability?

Their "Red family" background has often proved to be an asset for the princeling generals. Although future sons- and daughters-in-law of the first generation CCP leaders may have different individual stories, direct descendants of the revolutionary leaders benefited from their status as princelings in at least two ways.

First, it was easier for them to join the PLA than it was for the children of ordinary families. Some princelings saw their fathers as role models and they wanted to follow in their footsteps and make their own way into the military. This was the case for Lieutenant General Fan Xiaoguang, son of General Wang Ping, for example.[186] For some princelings, their family background helped them avoid being sent to the countryside during the Cultural Revolution, and enabled them to join the PLA instead. Liu Yazhou, for instance, was sent to the PLA by his father, Liu Jiande, who was a deputy political commissar in a PLA division at the time.

The second benefit was that princelings had easier access to Hajungong, which was established in 1953.[187] Senior General Chen

---

[185] Shen Xueming and Zheng Jianying, *Zhonggong diyijie zhi dishiwujie zhongyang weiyuan*, p. 376.

[186] http://dcw.435000.com/html/1/2005/12/news15579.html.

[187] For details, see Teng Xuyan, *Hajungong zhuan* [*The history of the Harbin Institute of Military Engineering*], (Changsha: Hunan Keji Chubanshe, 2003), three volumes.

Geng was the founding president of Hajungong, and princelings constituted a major source of students. At a meeting of the Preparatory Committee for Hajungong in 1952, Marshal Chen Yi, a vice premier at the time, called for CCP leaders to support Senior General Chen Geng by sending their children to Hajungong.[188] As a result, many princelings were later enrolled there. Out of 10 marshals, seven had children or grandchildren trained at Hajungong, and six out of 10 senior generals sent their children there.[189] Chen Danhuai's case is illustrative. When he was admitted to Hajungong in 1961,[190] Chen Yi, his father, was so happy at the news that he dedicated a poem to him.[191]

Among the 37 former princeling generals identified in Table 8.5, 12 are Hajungong graduates. They are Chen Zhijian, Deng Xianqun, Hua Zhongliang, Liu Taihang, Luo Dongjin, Peng Gang, Su Qianming, Su Rongsheng, Wang Sumin, Xu Yanbin, Ye Xuanning, and Zhang Xiang.

Princeling generals are also likely to have joined the Party earlier and been promoted faster. Generally speaking, sons-in-law and sons of the first generation leaders were promoted for different reasons: sons-in-law mostly for their own talents and sons mostly for their connections.[192] For example, among the former princeling generals, there are five sons- or brothers-in-law of leaders:

- Ding Henggao, son-in-law of Marshal Nie Rongzhen;
- Su Qianming, brother-in-law of Deng Xiaoping;
- Luo Bin, son-in-law of Wu Xiuquan;
- Deng Yousheng, son-in-law of Senior General Luo Ruiqing;
- Hua Zhongliang, son-in-law of General Song Shilun.

---

[188] "'Hajungong' jishi" ["The story of 'Hajungong'"], http://www.china.org.cn/chinese/zhuanti/181418.htm.

[189] http://www.chinanews.com.cn/n/2003-02-23/26/275317.html.

[190] http://www.chinaedunet.com/jcjy/cgjj/2005/4/content_2178.shtml.

[191] Chen Yi, "Shi Danhuai" ["A poem to Danhuai"], http://past.people.com.cn/GB/shizheng/252/6165/6169/20010821/540568.html.

[192] No such comparison can be made of daughters-in-law and daughters. Among the former princeling generals, the only women are two daughters and one niece.

These five are recognized as outstanding professionals in their own right. This enabled them to win the hearts of "princesses" and the endorsement of "royal" families (especially the mothers). Hua Zhongliang, for instance, was the first military man from the city of Wuxi to undertake nuclear research. A graduate of Hajungong, Hua was an outstanding student and a distinguished nuclear scientist. He later married General Song Shilun's daughter and was promoted to be a deputy director of the GAD's Logistics Department in the PLA.[193]

The sons are more likely to get promoted because of their family ties. One great example is He Pengfei, son of Marshal He Long. He Pengfei, born in 1945, joined the CCP in 1965 when he was a student at Qinghua University. Due to his father's "problem," he was imprisoned briefly in 1970 during the Cultural Revolution, but with the help of his father's friends, he joined the PLA in 1977 and rose rapidly. He was awarded the rank of rear admiral when ranks were reinstituted in 1988 and was appointed a deputy commander of the PLA Navy in 1992.[194] He was promoted much faster than many officers with much longer military careers.

The career of General Cao Gangchuan, currently defense minister and vice chairman of the Central Military Commission, for instance, contrasts sharply to that of He Pengfei. Cao joined the PLA in 1954 and the CCP in 1956. He studied in the Soviet Union for seven years (November 1956–October 1963) and served as an assistant in the GLD's Armament Department for 12 years.[195] By 1977, Cao had risen to a regiment-grade staff member position in this department. It took him 23 years, including his seven years of study in the Soviet Union, to get to this position. He Pengfei, however, was appointed as a staff member with the same grade in the same office on his very first day in the PLA. From then on, Cao's and He's careers ran in parallel. They were both promoted to be deputy section heads in 1980 and to be deputy department directors in 1982. In February

---

[193] Hua was a native of Xingzhu Village, Nanzhan Township, Binhu District, Wuxi City, Jiangsu Province. http://www.wxrb.com/rjxz/wxsc/wxmr/gs116.htm.
[194] http://www.pladaily.com.cn/gb/pladaily/2001/04/05/20010405001062.html.
[195] http://news.xinhuanet.com/ziliao/2002-01/21/content_246248.htm.

1986, He was appointed as director of the GLD's Armament Department, while Cao remained a deputy director of the Armament Department.[196]

Their "Red family" background could also be a liability for the princeling generals. First, fear of accusations of nepotism meant that they were usually kept in deputy positions. Second, they mostly failed to enter the CCP Central Committee because of the bad reputation gained by other princelings in the 1980s and 1990s. When most veteran leaders were rehabilitated (posthumously in some cases) after the Cultural Revolution, their offspring took advantage of their restored social status and reaped huge political and economic benefits. As a result, their reputation in society suffered. Thus deputies to the Party congresses tended to reject the names of princelings when they came up as candidates for the Central Committee. Of those that did become alternate members of the Fifteenth and Sixteenth Central Committees, several came at the bottom of the poll.[197] For example, Deng Pufang (son of Deng Xiaoping) and Xi Jinping (son of Xi Zhongxun) ranked 150th and 151st out of 151 alternate members of the Fifteenth Central Committee. Five years later, Deng Pufang ranked 154th out of 158 alternate members in the Sixteenth Central Committee.[198]

A New Cohort of Princeling Generals: Breaking the Two Barriers?

It is evident that the two career barriers identified above have persisted for the princeling generals who are still on active duty (Table 8.6). But a new cohort of princeling generals is emerging.

---

[196] For details, see Gao Xin, *Lingdao Zhongguo de Xinrenwu: Zhonggong Shiliujie Zhengzhiju Weiyuan* [*China's Top Leaders: Bios of China's Politburo Members*] (Carle Place, NY: Mirror Books, 2003), Vol. 2, pp. 722–724.

[197] For a systematic study of Princelings as a factional group on the Sixteenth Central Committee, see Zhiyue Bo, "The Sixteenth Central Committee of the Chinese Communist Party: formal institutions and factional groups," *Journal of Contemporary China*, Vol. 39, No. 13 (May 2004), pp. 223–256.

[198] http://news.xinhuanet.com/ziliao/2002-10/29/content_629567.htm.

410 China's Elite Politics

Table 8.6 Current Princeling Generals in the PLA

Name	Home/Birth	Unit	Title	Rank	Relative	Career Prospects
Chen Danhuai	Sichuan/1943	GAD	Department Director	Major General	Chen Yi	Fair
Chen Yong	Jiangxi/1952	Nanjing Army Academy	President	Major General	Chen Fangren	Fair
Chen Zhishu	Hunan	Gansu Provincial Military District	Commander	Major General	Chen Geng	Good
Chen Zhiya	Hunan/1949	AMS	Research Fellow	Major General	Chen Geng	Fair
Ding Yiping	Hunan/1951	Navy	Deputy Chief of Staff	Vice Admiral	Ding Qiusheng	Good
Duan Miyi	Hunan/1953	GSD	Department Director	Major General	Duan Suquan	Fair
Fan Xiaoguang	Hubei/1944	Chengdu MR	Deputy Commander	Lieut. General	Wang Ping	Fair
Han Dongjun	1950	Anti-Chemical Weapons Academy	Vice President	Major General	Han Huaizhi	Fair
He Ping	Hunan/1946	GSD	Department Director	Major General	He Biao	Fair
Hu Xiangui	Hubei/1944	East China Sea Fleet	Deputy Commander	Major General	Hu Zhengping	Retirement
Huang Bing	Hunan/1943	NDU	Department Chair	Major General	Huang Shengming	Retirement
Jia Danbing (female)	Hebei/1955	211 Hospital	President	Major General	Wang Minggui	Fair
Jia Xueyang	1949	Anti-Chemical Weapons Academy	Deputy Political Commissar	Major General	Jia Yiping	Fair
Li Nanzheng	Henan	Shijiazhuang Army Academy	Vice President	Major General	Li Desheng	Fair
Li Suolin	Hebei/1952	Chengdu MR Air Force	Deputy Chief of Staff	Major General	Li Lanmao	Fair

(Continued)

Hu Jintao's Power Consolidation 411

Table 8.6 (Continued)

Name	Home/Birth	Unit	Title	Rank	Relative	Career Prospects
Li Xiaojun	Jiangsu/1945	Shijiazhuang Army Academy	President	Major General	Li Guangjun	Fair
Liang Biqin	Jiangxi	AMS	Research Fellow	Major General	Liang Biye	Fair
Liu Miqun (female)	Sichuan/1944	Air Force Academy	Vice President	Major General	Liu Bocheng	Fair
Liu Sheng	Hunan	GAD	Department Deputy Director	Major General	Liu Peishan	Fair
Liu Taichi	Sichuan	Air Force	Department Deputy Director	Major General	Liu Bocheng	Fair
Liu Weidong	Hubei/1942	Nanjing MR	Deputy Political Commissar	Vice Admiral	Liu Zhen	Retirement
Liu Weiming	Sichuan	GAD		Major General	Liu Huaqing	Fair
Liu Xiaorong	Hunan/1950	Army Corps	Political Commissar	Major General	Liu Peishan	Good
Liu Yazhou	Anhui/1952	Air Force	Deputy Political Commissar	Lieut. General	Li Xiannian	Good
Liu Yuan	Hunan/1951	AMS	Political Commissar	Lieut. General	Liu Shaoqi	Star
Liu Zhenlai	Beijing	Beijing MR Air Force	Political Commissar	Major General	Liu Baiyu	Fair
Liu Zuoming	Hubei	Navy	Department Director	Major General	Liu Huaqing	Fair
Ma Xiaotian	Henan/1949	Air Force	Deputy Commander	Lieut. General		Star
Pan Ruiji	Zhejiang/1945	Shenyang MR	Deputy Political Commissar	Lieut. General	Rao Zijian	Fair
Peng Xiaofeng	Henan/1945	Second Artillery Corps	Political Commissar	General	Peng Xuefeng	Star

(Continued)

412 China's Elite Politics

Table 8.6 (Continued)

Name	Home/Birth	Unit	Title	Rank	Relative	Career Prospects
Qin Tian	Hubei/1957	Anti-Chemical Weapons Academy	Vice President	Major General	Qin Jiwei	Good
Qin Weijiang	Hubei/1956	Beijing MR	Deputy Chief of Staff	Major General	Qin Jiwei	Good
Qiu Ming	Hunan	GAD	Department Deputy Director	Major General	Qiu Chuangcheng	Fair
Ruan Chaoyang	Fujian/1947	GAD	Department Director	Major General	Zhong Qiguang	Fair
Wang Hongguang	Shandong/1949	Nanjing MR	Deputy Commander	Major General	Wang Jianqing	Good
Wu Shengli	Hebei/1945	GSD	Deputy Chief of Staff	Vice Admiral	Wu Xian	Star
Xie Mingbao	Jiangxi/1942	Manned Spaceship	Office Director	Major General	Xie Youfa	Retirement
Xu Qiliang	Shandong/1950	GSD	Deputy Chief of Staff	Lieut. General	Xu Lefu	Star
Xu Xiaoyan	Shanxi/1948	Nanjing MR	Deputy Commander	Major General	Xu Xiangqian	Good
Xu Yuanchao	Henan/1953	Anhui Provincial Military District	Commander	Major General	Xu Shiyou	Good
Yan Xiaoning	Hunan/1951	Nanchang Army Academy	Political Commissar	Major General	Yan Jinsheng	Fair
Yang Dongming	Fujian/1949	Air Force	Deputy Commander	Major General	Yang Chengwu	Good
Yang Dongsheng	Fujian/1946	Second Artillery Corps	Department Director	Major General	Yang Chengwu	Fair
Yang Jiping	Hunan	Chongqing Garrison	Commander	Major General	Yang Yong	Fair

(Continued)

Hu Jintao's Power Consolidation   413

Table 8.6 (*Continued*)

Name	Home/Birth	Unit	Title	Rank	Relative	Career Prospects
Yang Junsheng (female)	Fujian/1943	Armed Police	Department Director	Major General	Yang Chengwu	Retirement
Ye Aiqun	Hubei/1945	Jinan MR	Deputy Commander	Lieut. General	Ye Jianmin	Fair
Zeng Haisheng (female)	Jiangxi/1947	GSD	Department Political Commissar	Major General	Zeng Shan	Fair
Zeng Qingyang	Jiangxi/1945	COSTIND	Department Director	Major General	Zeng Shan	Fair
Zeng Qingyuan	Jiangxi/1950	Air Force	Department Political Commissar	Major General	Zeng Shan	Fair
Zeng Xiao'an	Jiangxi	Navy Air Force	Political Department Director	Major General	Zeng Kedong	Fair
Zeng Xiaodong (female)	Hunan	GSD	Department Director	Major General	Zeng Xisheng	Fair
Zhang Guangdong	Guangxi/1946	Shijiazhuang Army Academy	Vice President	Major General	Zhang Yunyi	Fair
Zhang Haiyang	Hunan/1949	Chengdu MR	Political Commissar	Lieut. General	Zhang Zhen	Star
Zhang Youxia	Shaanxi/1950	Beijing MR	Deputy Commander	Major General	Zhang Zongxun	Good
Zheng Qin	Henan/1951	65th Army Corps	Commander	Major General	Zheng Weishan	Good

Acronyms:
AMS: Academy of Military Sciences; CMC: Central Military Commission; COSTIND: Commission of Science, Technology, and Industry for National Defense; GAD: General Armament Department; GLD: General Logistics Department; GPD: General Political Department; GSD: General Staff Department; MR: Military Region; NDU: National Defense University.
Source: Author's database.

Some of them have already broken the barrier of deputy positions and are likely to cross the Central Committee hurdle. They will soon be among the most powerful members of the military elite in China. These rising stars may be divided into two groups. The first group contains the crème de la crème of the cohort: Xu Qiliang, Ma Xiaotian, Wu Shengli, Liu Yuan, Zhang Haiyang, and Peng Xiaofeng.

As we have discussed in detail about Xu Qiliang (1950–) and Mao Xiaotian in Chapter 4, a few words for an update of the two promising stars are sufficient here. While Ma has remained as deputy commander of the PLA Air Force, Xu Qiliang was promoted to a deputy chief of the General Staff of the PLA in 2004 as the first air force officer since 1973 to have been appointed as deputy chief of the General Staff of the PLA.[199] Although both of them are good candidates to replace retiring air force commander, General Qiao Qingchen (1939–), Xu seems to have a relatively better chance because he has already enjoyed the grade of chief military region leader.

Wu Shengli (1945–), another deputy chief of the General Staff, is son of Wu Xian. Wu Xian served as vice mayor of Hangzhou after 1949, mayor of Hangzhou between July 1951[200] and September 1962,[201] standing member of the Zhejiang Provincial Party Committee between April 1955 and 1966,[202] vice governor of Zhejiang between

---

[199] Wu Faxian, commander of the PLA Air Force between 1965 and 1973, was the first air force officer to hold this position. Wu was appointed deputy chief of the General Staff in 1967 (concurrently with his position as air force commander) and was removed in 1973. For more details, see Zhiyue Bo, "The general departments of the PLA: an update," *Chinese Military Update*, Vol. 2, No. 2 (July/August 2004), pp. 9–12.

[200] http://www.hangzhou.gov.cn/main/gb/tradition/introduce/citylog/viewarticle.jsp?artid=2176.

[201] Wu Xian was replaced by Wang Zida as mayor of Hangzhou at the first meeting of the Hangzhou Fourth Municipal People's Congress in September 1962. http://www.hangzhou.gov.cn/main/gb/tradition/introduce/citylog/viewarticle.jsp?artid=2179.

[202] *Dangdai Zhongguo De Zhejiang* [*Zhejiang of Contemporary China*] (Beijing: Zhangguo Shenhui Chubanshe, 1988), Vol. 2, p. 564.

June 1956 and 1966,²⁰³ and deputy party secretary²⁰⁴ of Zhejiang between January 1959 and 1966.²⁰⁵ Wu Shengli, a graduate of the PLA Survey and Mapping Institute,²⁰⁶ was a dark horse from the PLA Navy for the position of deputy chief of the General Staff. It seemed that Ding Yiping (1951–), son of Lieutenant General Ding Qiusheng,²⁰⁷ had been groomed for this position.²⁰⁸ Ding Yiping is six years younger than Wu Shengli but was promoted faster than Wu initially. Ding was awarded the rank of rear admiral in July 1993, while Wu was awarded the same rank in 1994. Ding was promoted to the rank of vice admiral in July 2002, while Wu was promoted to the same rank in 2003. Ding was appointed as commander of the PLA Navy's North China Sea Fleet and concurrently deputy commander of the Jinan Military Region in December 2000, while Wu was appointed as commander of the South China Sea Fleet and concurrently deputy commander of the Guangzhou Military Region in February 2002. Ding entered the Sixteenth Central Committee as an alternate member in November 2002, while Wu became a deputy to the Tenth NPC in March 2003.²⁰⁹ However, Ding lost his positions due to an incident in April 2003 in which 70 officers and men aboard a Ming-class submarine died due to "improper command."²¹⁰ Ding was demoted to

---

[203] *Dangdai Zhongguo De Zhejiang*, p. 570.

[204] He was a member of the Zhejiang Secretariat. The first party secretary of Zhejiang at that time was Jiang Hua.

[205] *Dangdai Zhongguo De Zhejiang*, p. 565.

[206] It was formerly called Northeast Survey and Mapping School established in Changchun, Jilin Province, on May 5, 1946. The school was converted to the PLA Survey and Mapping Institute in July 1953 and moved to Beijing in November of the same year. In 1976, the institute moved to Zhengzhou, Henan Province. See http://www.cgan.net/book/books/print/g-history/gb_9/24_3.htm. Now this institute has been replaced by the PLA Information Engineering University. See http://worldnetdaily.com/news/article.asp?ARTICLE_ID=21597.

[207] Ding Senior was awarded the rank of lieutenant general in 1955.

[208] For his bio before the Sixteenth Party Congress, see http://www.people.com.cn/GB/junshi/192/8190/8192/20020517/730718.html.

[209] http://www.npc.gov.cn/zgrdw/common/dbxx.jsp?label=DB&id=102833&lx=RDDB&pdmc=110501.

[210] http://tw.people.com.cn/GB/14810/14860/1915302.html.

deputy chief of staff of the PLA Navy,[211] and Wu moved up and became a deputy chief of the General Staff from navy. As Commander Zhang Dingfa (1942–) of the PLA Navy has been absent from public scene since December 2005, Wu reportedly would replace him.[212] In that case, he would likely enter the Central Military Commission in his capacity as PLA Navy commander.

Liu Yuan (1951–), son of Liu Shaoqi (former president of the PRC), used to be a civilian.[213] He was vice governor of Henan between January 1988 and June 1992. He was transferred to the armed police headquarters in Beijing as the second political commissar and deputy director of the Hydro-electricity Command and was awarded the rank of major general in 1992. He was promoted to deputy political commissar of the armed police headquarters in November 1998 and was awarded the rank of lieutenant general in July 2000. He was transferred to the GLD as deputy political commissar in August 2003 and was promoted to political commissar of the Chinese Academy of Military Sciences in December 2005.

Zhang Haiyang (1949–), son of Zhang Zhen (former vice chairman of the CMC), is a political officer in the PLA.[214] He joined the PLA in 1969 and joined the Party in the same year. He spent his early career in 21st Army, rising from an ordinary soldier all the way to political commissar of 61st Division, 21st Army. He participated in the war against Vietnam in 1985 and was transferred to the GPD in 1992. He was appointed as deputy political commissar of the Beijing

---

[211] He was reportedly demoted to the grade of army leader with the rank of rear admiral from the grade of deputy military region with the rank of vice admiral. See http://www2.qglt.com.cn/wsrmlt/wyzs/2003/06/16/061601.html. However, a different source says that he has retained his rank of vice admiral.

[212] http://www.singtaonet.com:82/global/china/t20060407_185786.html.

[213] For his bio, see http://ics.nccu.edu.tw/frame.php?address=polsum&id=1212.

[214] For his bio, see Jin Qianli, "Xinren Chengdu Junqu Zhengwei Zhang Haiyang Zhongjiang Pingzhuan" ["Biography of Lieutenant General Zhang Haiyang, newly appointed political commissar of the Chengdu Military Region"], *Qianshao* (*The Front-Line Magazine*) (March 2006), pp. 50–54.

Military Region in 2002 and was promoted to political commissar of the Chengdu Military Region in December 2005.[215]

Finally, Peng Xiaofeng (1945–), son of Peng Xuefeng (a revolutionary martyr who died in 1944),[216] is political commissar of the Second Artillery Corps.[217] Peng Xiaofeng was enrolled in the Missile Engineering Department at the Hajungong in 1963. His fellow students of the same department include Bai Keming (currently party secretary of Hebei), Yu Zhengsheng (currently Politburo member and party secretary of Hubei), and Huang Liman (currently chairwoman of the Guangdong Provincial People's Congress Standing Committee). Xu Caihou, currently vice chairman of the CMC and member of the Secretariat of the CCP, was also studying at the Hajungong at that time but in a different department (Electronic Engineering Department). Peng Xiaofeng was appointed as deputy political commissar of the Lanzhou Military Region in August 2001, deputy political commissar of the National Defense University in 2002, and was promoted to political commissar of the Second Artillery Corps in December 2003. He failed to enter the Sixteenth Central Committee but was inducted into the Sixteenth Central Disciplinary Inspection Commission. He was awarded the rank of general on June 24, 2006.[218] The other five princeling generals are also likely to be promoted to the rank of general before 2008,[219] and all of them are likely to enter the Seventeenth Central Committee in 2007.

---

[215] http://202.82.86.97:82/gate/gb/www.atchineseom/index.php?option=com_content&task=view&id=11518&Itemid=33.

[216] For his bio, see http://www.cycnet.com/cms/2004/cycnetact/AntiJapan/celebrities/t20050908_32559.htm.

[217] For his bio, see http://gongxue.cn/gongchengzonglan/ShowArticle.asp?ArticleID=15482.

[218] See http://politics.people.com.cn/GB/4526847.html.

[219] So far China has promoted 108 officers to the rank of general since 1988: 17 in September 1988, six in June 1993, 19 in June 1994, four in January 1996, 10 in March 1998, two in September 1999, 16 in June 2000, seven in June 2002, 15 in June 2004, two in September 2004, and 10 in June 2006. See http://www.china.org.cn/chinese/zhuanti/168115.htm; http://news.xinhuanet.com/mil/2004-09/25/content_2020509.htm; and http://news.xinhuanet.com/mil/2004-09/25/content_2020509.htm.

The second batch includes promising princeling generals. They are Xu Xiaoyan, Liu Yazhou, Qin Weijiang, Yang Dongming, Zhang Youxia, Wang Hongguang, Yang Jiping, Chen Zhishu, Zheng Qin, Xu Yuanchao, and Qin Tian. Major General Xu Xiaoyan, son of Marshal Xu Xiangqian, is currently deputy commander of the Nanjing Military Region[220] as well as a deputy to the Tenth NPC.[221] Although the official data on Xinhuanet indicate that he was born in February 1947,[222] he is more likely to have been born in 1948, as his elder sister, Xu Luxi, is known to have been born in February 1947.[223] Moreover, he has been described as entering Qinghua University in 1975, though he actually graduated from the Auto-Control Department of Qinghua University in that year.[224] With a master's degree in computer science from Canada, he is one of very few generals in the PLA with strong credentials in modern technology. He is likely to obtain the rank of lieutenant general and to enter the Seventeenth Central Committee.

Lieutenant General Liu Yazhou, the son-in-law of Li Xiannian and son of Liu Jiande, is an influential writer and a deputy political commissar of the PLA Air Force.[225] He joined the PLA in 1968 at the age of 16, went to Wuhan University as a "worker-peasant-soldier" student in 1972 (where he met his future wife, Li Xiaolin), and began working at Capital Airport in Beijing in 1975. He has written novels and commentaries since the early 1970s, and he was initially promoted to a professional writer in the PLA. He was awarded the rank of major general in 1996 while he was a political department deputy director of the Beijing Military Region Air Force. He was promoted to be

---

[220] *Jiefangjun Bao*, October 14, 2005, p. 1.
[221] http://news.xinhuanet.com/newscenter/2005-03/11/content_2683536.htm.
[222] http://news.xinhuanet.com/zhengfu/2004-03/17/content_1371120.htm.
[223] He is son of Xu Xiangqian and his third wife, Huang Jie. For Xu Xiangqian's three marriages, see http://www.chineseliterature.com.cn/jishi/rw-sdys/015.htm.
[224] He is one of the 45 "Qinghua generals." For the list, see http://join-tsinghua.edu.cn/bkzsw/detail.jsp?seq=1018&boardid=1301.
[225] Liu Jiande was too junior in 1955 to be awarded the rank of major general. He was political commissar of a regiment in 1949. His last position in the PLA was deputy political commissar of the Logistics Department of the Lanzhou Military Region, but it is not clear what his rank was.

political department director of the Beijing Military Region Air Force in 1997, political commissar of the Chengdu Military Region Air Force in 2002, and deputy political commissar of the PLA Air Force in December 2003. In 2003, he was also awarded the rank of lieutenant general.[226] Liu's rapid promotion over a very short period under the leadership of Jiang Zemin, without having any experience as a professional military officer, is more likely to be due to his connection with Li Xiannian than to his influential writings. His strength is his youth; he will be only 56 in 2006.

Major General Qin Weijiang is also likely to have a bright future mainly because of his age. He was born in 1956, so will be only 50 in 2006. He is among the best educated of this group. Qin received a bachelor of engineering degree from the PLA Nanjing Institute of Communication Engineering in 1982 and a master's degree in military science from the National Defense University in 1998. He was the first military officer with the rank of deputy army commander to have received a master's degree in military science at the time.[227] He was promoted to be a deputy chief of staff of the Beijing Military Region in 2005[228] and is likely to get further promoted in the future.[229]

Major General Yang Dongming (son of General Yang Chengwu) was surprisingly appointed as a deputy commander of the PLA Air Force in December 2005 at the age of 56. Although he had obtained a college degree from the Beijing Institute of Aeronautics and Astronautics in 1977 and worked briefly in the PLA Air Force, Yang's work has mainly been in the political field. He worked in the political department of the Taiyuan Military Subdistrict as deputy director and director, in the political department of the Beijing Garrison as

---

[226] For a biography, see http://chinaway.org/17/lgs.htm.
[227] http://news.enorth.com.cn/system/2002/01/31/000259317.shtml.
[228] http://media.rednet.com.cn/manage/show.asp?id=650682.
[229] He is only one step away from the stepping-stone position of chief of staff of the Beijing Military Region. Former occupants of this vital position include Zhu Qi, currently commander of the Beijing Military Region; Chang Wanquan, currently commander of the Shenyang Military Region; and Qiu Jinkai, currently deputy commander of the Beijing Military Region and concurrently commander of the Beijing Garrison.

deputy director, in the Hebei Provincial Military District as deputy political commissar, and in the GLD as deputy director and director of the Petroleum Supply Department. He was awarded the rank of major general in 1994.[230] Although he is quite young for his rank, his potential for further promotion will largely depend on whether he can actually perform.

Major General Zhang Youxia (son of General Zhang Zongxun) has recently been promoted to be a deputy commander of the Beijing Military Region on the retirement of Lieutenant General Su Rongsheng. Zhang reportedly performed well in the war against Vietnam, when he was commander of the 119th Regiment, 40th Division, 14th Army.[231] He later served as deputy commander and commander of the 13th Army Corps in Chongqing between 1993 and 2005. He was promoted to be deputy commander of the Beijing Military Region in December 2005.[232] Zhang Youxia will be 56 in 2006, and he is likely to rise further in the near future.

Major General Wang Hongguang (son of Major General Wang Jianqing) was promoted to be a deputy commander of the Nanjing Military Region in December 2005.[233] Wang Hongguang was born in 1949 and joined the PLA in 1968. A graduate of Hajungong,[234] he was appointed as president of the PLA Armored Forces Engineering Academy in February 1998 at the age of 48.[235] Prior to his latest promotion, Wang was director of the GAD's Equipment Supply Department. He is likely to be awarded the rank of lieutenant general within a year[236] and is likely to be further promoted.

---

[230] http://www.ctw.cn/article_view.asp?id=1100.

[231] http://bbs.ark10.org/printthread.php?s=a710df687185e76c5edef486a8e47e2d&threadid=1224. For more details, see http://bbs.zju.edu.cn/cgi-bin/bbsanc?path=/groups/GROUP_6/Military/D98388371/wenxie/D733F69AA/D98521C2F/M.1071479856.A.

[232] http://www.cq.xinhuanet.com/zhengwu/2005-12/20/content_5854912.htm.

[233] http://www.cnwnc.com/20051221/ca2060673.htm.

[234] http://www.lovenudt.com/biography/general/index.htm.

[235] http://www.gmw.cn/01gmrb/1998-11/18/GB/17880%5EGM5-1812.htm.

[236] He was awarded the rank of major general in 1998.

Major General Yang Jiping (son of General Yang Yong) is also likely to climb further up the ladder of success in the PLA. In contrast to his colleague, Major General Hong Bao (former deputy commander of the Tianjin Garrison), he has overcome the barrier of deputy positions. He was promoted from deputy commander of the Tianjin Garrison to commander of the Chongqing Garrison in December 2003.[237] However, he is currently working at the provincial military district level, and he needs to go up one level to a military region in order to compete nationally.

Major General Chen Zhishu (son of Senior General Chen Geng[238]) also has a promising future. He was deputy commander of the PLA Hong Kong Garrison,[239] deputy director of the Mobilization Department of the PLA General Staff Headquarters,[240] and was promoted to be commander of the Gansu Provincial Military District around April 2005.[241]

Major General Zheng Qin (son of Lieutenant General Zheng Weishan) is likely to achieve great things. Zheng Qin used to be deputy commander of the 63rd Army Corps. When in September 2003 Jiang Zemin announced a reduction of 200,000 PLA troops from three army corps, one of which was the 63rd,[242] Zheng was transferred to the Beijing Military Region as deputy chief of staff. He was appointed as commander of the 65th Army Corps in August 2005. Aged 55 in 2006, he is likely to rise further.

---

[237] He was in Tianjin in December 2003 (see http://www.tj.xinhuanet.com/tp/2003-12/11/content_1326413.htm). He appeared in Chongqing in January 2004 (see http://cqtoday.cqnews.net/system/2004/01/19/000347978.shtml). Although his title of commander was not mentioned in the report, it is clear from the fact that his name was listed before that of Political Commissar Duan Shuchun that he already held that position. For confirmation, see http://www7.chinesenewsnet.com/gb/NewsPics/Duowei//Tue_Jan_13_19_09_12_2004.html.

[238] For an article about Senior General Chen Geng from the point of view of his wife, Fu Ya, see http://www.booker.com.cn/gb/paper23/52/class002300001/hwz229683.htm.

[239] http://www.hkzg.com/06/002.asp.

[240] http://www.pladaily.com.cn/item/zgmb/200405/txt/02.htm.

[241] See http://www.jnmc.com/show.asp?newsid=687.

[242] The other two were 23rd and 24th Army Corps. http://www.cnwnc.com/20030916/ca539222.htm.

Major General Xu Yuanchao (son of General Xu Shiyou) was appointed as commander of the Anhui Provincial Military District in July 2005.[243] Prior to his current post, he was deputy director of the Armament Department of the Nanjing Military Region.[244] Aged 53 in 2006, he still has a long and promising career ahead of him.

Finally, Major General Qin Tian (another son of General Qin Jiwei) may also have a promising future. He was a regimental commander (235th Regiment, 27th Army under Commander Qian Guoliang and Political Commissar Xu Yongqing) at the age of 29 in 1986.[245] He was vice president of the Anti-Chemical Weapons Academy in 2003.[246] He will be 49 in 2006 and is probably destined for further success.

Implications for the PLA: Nepotism or Meritocracy?

What does the emergence of the princeling generals tell us about appointments in the Chinese military? Are the princelings' promotions due to nepotism or their own qualifications and accomplishments?

As noted earlier, princelings (especially sons) have been promoted mostly because of their family connections. It is evident that some princeling generals who are currently on active duty have indeed benefited from their ties to the top leadership. Lieutenant General Liu Yazhou, deputy political commissar of the PLA Air Force, for instance, rose rapidly in the PLA probably more because of his connection to Li Xiannian than because of his accomplishments as an air force officer. However, it is not fair to attribute the promotions of all the princeling generals to their family ties. In many cases, their fathers died when they were very young. In fact, many princeling generals have climbed the ladder of success because of their own qualifications and accomplishments. Examples include Xu Qiliang, Ma Xiaotian, Wu Shengli, Zhang Youxia, Zhang Haiyang, Ding Yiping, Qin Weijiang, and Qin Tian.

---

[243] http://www.whrfb.gov.cn/gzdt/062.htm.
[244] http://www.pladaily.com.cn/gb/defence/2002/02/25/20020225017065_gfgj.html.
[245] http://www.9ebook.com/article/explore/war/10364.html.
[246] http://www2.qglt.com.cn/wsrmlt/jbft/2003/02/022701.html.

In many cases, princeling generals have failed to gain seats on the CCP Central Committee not because of their bad performance but because of the bad reputation of princelings in general. A few princeling generals entered the Sixteenth Central Committee partly because they were not known as princelings. Very few people in China knew Ding Yiping as a princeling; even fewer recognized Xu Qiliang and Ma Xiaotian as princelings.

Princeling generals constitute a major part of the military elite in China. As children of high-ranking first generation military and civilian leaders, they have an extensive support network. Yet until very recently, most of them faced two major barriers in their military and political careers: They were limited to deputy positions, and they found it almost impossible to gain seats on the Central Committee. The situation seems to be changing for the better for princeling generals in recent reshuffles of military leaders. Several of them have been promoted to key positions in the PLA, and they are likely to be selected as members of the Seventeenth Central Committee in 2007.

The rising stars include Xu Qiliang, Wu Shengli, Peng Xiaofeng, Liu Yuan, Zhang Haiyang, and Ma Xiaotian, as well as Xu Xiaoyan, Liu Yazhou, Qin Weijiang, Pan Ruiji, Yang Dongming, Zhang Youxia, Wang Hongguang, Yang Jiping, Chen Zhishu, Zheng Qin, Xu Yuanchao, and Qin Tian. Ding Yiping should also be included because he is likely to recover from his setback in 2003 and join the winning group in the near future. The emergence of the princeling generals is likely to contribute to the professionalization of the PLA if their future promotions are based not on their family ties but on their own qualifications and accomplishments.

CONCLUDING REMARKS

After he took over as chairman of the Party's Central Military Commission in September 2004, Hu Jintao further consolidated his power in both policy initiatives and personnel appointments. First, he introduced a new policy toward Taiwan that altered the nature of cross-strait relations. The anti-secession law passed by the Tenth NPC in March 2005 in addition to Hu's four-point policy changed the cross-strait game from one of reunification versus independence to one of war versus peace. When Jiang Zemin previously tried to first cajole and then coerce Taiwan residents through his policy of reunification, Taiwan residents moved further and further away from the mainland, and Taiwan independence forces came to power and consolidated it. This is because Taiwan residents preferred independence to reunification. But Hu's new policy presented Taiwan residents with new options of war and peace. In this new game, Hu regained initiatives because Taiwan residents evidently preferred peace to war. Consequently, opposition leaders such as Lien Chan of the GMD, James CY Soong of the People's First Party, and Yok Mu-ming of the New Party came to Beijing to meet with Hu Jintao. The tensions between the two sides of the Taiwan Strait were drastically reduced.

Second, Hu Jintao formulated his own thinking on military development in China. Known as "three provides and one play," Hu's military thinking specified the historical mission of the PLA in the new century and new period: The armed forces should *provide* mighty support for the CCP to entrench its position as the ruling party, *provide* staunch security assurances for safeguarding the important strategic opportunity period for national development, *provide* powerful strategic backup for defending the national interests, and *play* an important role in maintaining the world peace and promoting the common development of all countries. Hu further introduced his "scientific concept of development" as a guideline for military modernization. Starting in September 2005, the PLA leaders promoted Hu's military thinking instead of Jiang Zemin's.

The Shanghai Gang suffered its first major blow in April 2003 when Health Minister Zhang Wenkang was dismissed because of his mishandling of the SARS epidemic. The Shanghai Gang lost its leader in September 2004 when Jiang Zemin was forced to step down as chairman of the Party's Central Military Commission. The Shanghai Gang continued its decline in the aftermath of Jiang's retirement. First, Jiang's eldest son, Jiang Mianheng, was kicked out of Beijing in August 2005 when he was transferred to Shanghai as the head of the Shanghai Branch of the CAS. Second, Zhao Qizheng, the mastermind of Jiang Zemin's biography, was retired in the same month. Third, Huang Ju was hospitalized for an extended period.

In the meantime, the CCYL Group was emerging in Chinese politics. Since the Sixteenth Party Congress, 35 officials with CCYL background have been promoted. These include seven provincial party secretaries, eight provincial governors, three provincial deputy secretaries, two vice governors, four Provincial Party Committee standing members, one chairman of the Provincial People's Congress Standing Committee, two chairmen of the Provincial People's Political Consultative Conferences, seven central leaders, and one military leader. These officials constitute major political resources for Hu Jintao.

Finally, it is also evident that princeling generals — military officers holding the rank of major general/rear admiral and above in the PLA who are children of the first generation leaders — are also rising in China's military elites. Although many of them are still faced with two career barriers — deputy position phenomenon and central committee hurdle, a few of them such as Xu Qiliang, Wu Shengli, Liu Yuan, Zhang Haiyang, and Peng Xiaofeng have already overcome the deputy position phenomenon and would likely enter the Seventeenth Central Committee in 2007.

Conclusion: Institutionalization and Political Transition

China's elite politics has become institutionalized. After the Central Advisory Commission of the CCP was abolished in 1992, formal institutions became increasingly more important. In this institutionalized system, positions mean powers; institutional loyalty is more important than personal loyalty; and political exits are increasingly realized through retirement instead of power struggles. Consequently, political succession is no longer a zero-sum game in which the winner takes all and the loser loses all but a power-balancing game in which a certain balance can be obtained among different players. Political transition at the Sixteenth Party Congress and subsequent dynamics of factional politics provide support for the power-balancing model instead of the winner-take-all model.

POLITICAL INSTITUTIONALIZATION

China's elite politics has been institutionalized in three senses. First, positions mean powers. It is for this reason that the political transition at the Sixteenth Party Congress in November 2002 was meaningful. As general secretary of the CCP, Hu Jintao subsequently introduced a series of new ideological precepts such as "new three people's principles," "two imperatives," "building the Party in the public interest and governing the country for the people," and in particular "scientific concept of development." Moreover, he replaced Jiang Zemin as the official interpreter of the "Three Represents" on behalf of the CCP even though Jiang was supposed to be the author of the ideological guideline. The flip side is also true. That is, those who want to hold on to power have to keep their positions. Jiang Zemin tried to hold on to power by staying on as chairman of the Central Military Commission because, unlike Deng Xiaoping, Jiang would be powerless without a position.

Second, because of political institutionalization, institutional loyalty became more important than personal loyalty. Jiang Zemin's cronies were personally loyal to him not because of Jiang's personal charisma but because of his position. Once Hu Jintao became the Party boss, some of them began to shift their loyalty to Hu instead of Jiang. That Zhou Mingwei, a Shanghai Gang member, advocated Hu Jintao's four-point policy instead of Jiang's eight-point policy toward Taiwan is a good example in this regard, and Wu Bangguo, Huang Ju, and Chen Liangyu have also demonstrated their loyalty to Hu on various occasions since the Sixteenth Party Congress.

Third, due to Deng Xiaoping's efforts, political exits have also become institutionalized. Political leaders have to retire when they reach their mandatory retirement ages. Jiang Zemin, for instance, became increasingly liable for retirement not only because of his terrible performance records and inferior capabilities but also because of his advanced age. He was pushed out as chairman of the Party's CMC at the Fourth Plenum of the Sixteenth Central Committee in September 2004, even though his cronies were supposed to have been in the majority in the Standing Committee of the Politburo and the Central Military Commission. The fact that Jiang stepped down against his own wishes is an indication of the political significance of institutionalization. It is not any particular individual such as Hu Jintao but the institutionalization that pushed Jiang out.

POWER BALANCING

As a result of political institutionalization, power is no long indivisible. Different positions represent different powers, and a certain balance can be obtained among different players. Under these conditions, Hu Jintao as general secretary of the Party and president of the People's Republic of China was dominant in political affairs and foreign affairs, and Jiang as chairman of the Central Military Commission was prominent in military affairs. Hu's gains were not necessarily losses of Jiang, nor were Jiang's gains necessarily Hu's losses.

Moreover, a certain power balance among different formal institutions was obtained as a result of the Sixteenth Party Congress, and that balance has been constantly changing because of elite turnovers. Initially, as a result of the Sixteenth Party Congress, provincial leaders emerged as the most powerful group in Chinese politics with four standing members and eight more full members of the Politburo, 68 full members, and 86 alternate members of the Sixteenth Central Committee. The total power index of provincial representation amounted to 244 points.

The leaders of central institutions followed with 103 members of the Sixteenth Central Committee: 76 full members and 27 alternate members. These central officials came from two subgroups in the Center: central Party-institutions and central government-institutions. Central Party-institutions were better represented in the Politburo (three members) and the Secretariat (two members) than central government-institutions. Although central institutions as a whole had more full members, they paled in terms of power indexes. The score of the combined index of both central Party-institutions and central government-institutions was 193, 51 points less than that of the provincial power index.

The military ranked third in terms of power index. It was represented in the Sixteenth Central Committee with two Politburo members, one Secretariat member, 41 full members, and 24 alternate members. No military officers obtained a seat in the Standing Committee of the Politburo. The total power index for the military was 111 points, which was less than that of either provinces or central institutions.

Corporate leaders did not really constitute a distinctive political group but served as a residual group with two components: business leaders and academic leaders. This residual group was represented in the Sixteenth Central Committee with two full members and 16 alternate members. The total power index for the group was 25 points, far less than that of any other political institutions.

As a result of the Sixteenth Party Congress, a balance was obtained among these formal institutions. With a power index of 244, provincial leaders took 43 percent of the total power scores of the Sixteenth Central Committee without the political core. Central institutions followed with a power index of 193 and 34 percent of the total. The military came as third with a power index of 111 points and 19 percent of the total. The corporate leaders took only 4 percent of the total power scores because their power index was only 25 points. This balance, however, was only temporary and subsequently changed as a result of reshuffling among these formal institutions, especially between provinces and central institutions.

Similarly, a power balance was also obtained as a result of the Sixteenth Party Congress among different factional groups. Out of 356 members of the Sixteenth Central Committee, 114 people (about one third) could be identified as belonging to one of the four factional groups: 17 Shanghai Gang members, 20 princelings, 20 Qinghua graduates, and 57 CCYL cadres. The most powerful group is the CCYL Group with a power index of 97 and a group cohesion index of 405.5. The Qinghua Clique followed with a power index of 54 and a group cohesion index of 142. The Shanghai Gang ranked third with a power index of 42 and a group cohesion index of 103.17. The Princelings were hardly a factional group: Although their power index is 41, their group cohesion index is merely 8 points. Among these factional groups, the Shanghai Gang is the closest to the concept of a political faction based on clientist ties while the Qinghua Clique and the CCYL Group are closer to the concept of a factional group based on corporate ties. The Princelings, on the other hand, is more of a categorical group than of a factional group.

Although these four factional groups are distinctive, there are some overlaps among them. One Shanghai Gang member is also a princeling. Five Shanghai Gang members are also Qinghua graduates. And one Shanghai Gang member is also a former CCYL cadre. Four princelings are also Qinghua graduates. Two princelings are also members of the CCYL Group. And finally, four Qinghua graduates are also members of the CCYL Group. No one is completely inclusive, having a membership in all the four factional groups. Liu Yandong is the only person that has a simultaneous membership in three factional groups: the Princelings, the Qinghua Clique, and the CCYL Group.

POLITICAL TRANSITION

Power transfer from Jiang Zemin to Hu Jintao occurred in three steps. Hu took over as general secretary of the CCP at the Sixteenth Party Congress in November 2002; he replaced Jiang as president of the People's Republic of China at the First Meeting of the Tenth National People's Congress in March 2003; and he succeeded Jiang as chairman of the CCP's Central Military Commission at the Fourth Plenum of the Sixteenth Central Committee of the CCP in September 2004. Political tensions between Jiang Zemin and Hu Jintao during the transitional period of November 2002 to September 2004 were essentially a conflict between two different models of succession: the two-front arrangement versus the generational succession. Introduced by Mao Zedong, the two-front arrangement was a succession model in which the preeminent leader gradually gave up his positions and power while the potential successor took up more and more responsibilities. In this model, the preeminent leader and the potential successor coexist but the preeminent leader continues to have the final say. The generational succession, on the other hand, is a succession model in which one generation is replaced by its succeeding generation, and each generation has a core.

It is evident that Jiang Zemin was attempting to restore the two-front arrangement. He took all possible opportunities to demonstrate his symbolic superiority to General Secretary and President Hu Jintao. Beginning with dealing with the submarine accident in May 2003, Jiang tried to appear in public on military affairs as chairman of the Central Military Commission along with Vice Chairman Hu Jintao so that his name would be listed in front of Hu's name in the subsequent news reports. Hu Jintao, on the other hand, followed the generational succession model more closely. He showed his respect for Jiang Zemin as his predecessor. Hu was not competing with Jiang but trying to be his successor. He respected Jiang Zemin's "Three Represents," for instance, but also developed his own ideological ideas such as the scientific concept of development. In the end, Jiang had to step down because of the failure of the two-front arrangement. Most top leaders, including the Shanghai Gang members, no longer subscribed to this notion of political succession.

Similarly, the decline of the Shanghai Gang and the rise of the CCYL Group have also partly resulted from the generational changes. The decline of the Shanghai Gang began in April 2003 during the SARS crisis. Health Minister Zhang Wenkang, a Shanghai Gang member, was dismissed because of his derelictions in dealing with the epidemic. Yet his dismissal was not a result of factional politics but of administrative decisions. He was fired as an irresponsible health minister, not as a Shanghai Gang member. Had he not been fired in April 2003, he would have to retire in April 2005 when he reached his retirement age. Jiang Zemin was pushed out as chairman of the Party's Central Military Commission at the Fourth Plenum of the Sixteenth Central Committee in September 2004 not because he was unsuccessful as the head of the Shanghai Gang but because of his advanced age. It was no longer appropriate for him — the core of the third generation leadership — to stay on in the fourth generation leadership. Had he been retained again in September 2004, he would have to retire in 2007 anyway. Zhao Qizheng, the mastermind of the notorious biography of Jiang Zemin, was the first Shanghai Gang member that exited through normal retirement. He reached his retirement age of 65 years in January 2005 and was retired in August 2005. It is conceivable that other members of the Shanghai Gang such as Huang Ju, Zeng Qinghong, and Hua Jianmin would also retire in 2007 due to their age. Huang would be 69 years old; Zeng, 68; and Hua, 67. Short of political maneuvering, they would not become candidates for the Seventeenth Central Committee.

The emergence of former CCYL cadres is mostly due to their age. They were mostly born in the late 1940s and the 1950s, received formal college education in the late 1970s and the 1980s, and have accumulated administrative experiences in both the Center and provinces. Since the Sixteenth Party Congress in November 2002, at least 35 officials with CCYL background have been promoted: seven to provincial party secretaries, eight to provincial governors, three to provincial deputy secretaries, two to vice governors, four to Provincial Party Committee standing members, one to chairman of the Provincial People's Congress Standing Committee, two to chairman of the Provincial People's Political Consultative

Conferences, seven to posts in the central government, and one to a more important position in the military.

Nevertheless, factional politics indeed existed between Jiang Zemin and his cronies and Hu Jintao and his allies. Taking advantage of his formal positions, Hu Jintao scored victories against Jiang Zemin on several major issues: over the SARS crisis, over economic overheating, and in particular over Jiang's retirement. Hu Jintao and Wen Jiabao became very popular because of their strong leadership in the fight against the SARS epidemic, while Jiang Zemin and his cronies suffered serious reputation damage because of their desertions. Hu Jintao and Wen Jiabao worked together to cool China's overheated economy, while Jiang's cronies obstructed their measures. Finally, Hu Jintao asserted his authority as general secretary of the Party in military affairs and conducted Politburo study sessions on military development, and Jiang eventually had to step down because of his advanced age.

However, Hu Jintao achieved these gains not by playing factional politics but by playing formal politics. As a member of both Qinghua Clique and CCYL Group, Hu Jintao had strong factional bases. But his real advantage did not lie in his factional bases but in his formal positions because of political institutionalization. As general secretary of the Party, for instance, he is a big boss not only of the Qinghua Clique and the CCYL Group members but also of the Shanghai Gang members and the Princelings. Had he played factional politics, he would have gained support only from his associated factional groups.

It remains to be seen, however, whether Hu Jintao is able to replace the remnants of the Shanghai Gang and Jiang's cronies in the Politburo and particularly its standing committee with his allies at the forthcoming Seventeenth National Congress of the CCP, reconstitute the Central Military Commission in his favor, open up the media, build the rule of law, cleanse the Party, rebuild the Chinese culture, and eventually construct a civilized, prosperous, equal, just, and democratic China.

Index

"east eight blocks"
  (*dong bakuai*), 242
"Red family", 406, 409
"Selectorate", 66, 69, 74

age, average, 20, 21, 88, 89, 90, 401
age limit, 19, 23, 24, 52, 88
  age 50, 88
  age 70, 52
age structure, 22, 65
Amat, Ismail, 61, 91, 92, 110, 183, 187
An Ziwen 33, 69
Anhui, 30, 79, 93, 94, 113, 114, 116, 117, 142, 144, 145, 152, 153, 163, 176, 184, 185, 190, 239, 270, 277, 284, 379, 381, 384, 386, 389–391, 393, 399, 400, 411, 412, 422
Azzizi, Seypidin, 115
anti-secession law, 356–359, 423

Ba Jin, 211, 211, 212
Bai Jian, 152, 154, 155
Bai Keming, 104, 152, 154, 155, 173, 174, 379, 417

Bai Zhijian, 119, 380
Balance-of-power, 1, 3–5, 8, 39
  among factional groups, 10, 139, 198
  among formal institutions, 9
  politics see also power balancing, 1, 5, 7–9, 13, 17, 52, 220, 253, 427, 428
Bandwagon, 1–6, 8, 11, 39, 277, 282, 295
Baum, Richard, 21, 56, 67, 70, 91, 164, 350
Bayinchaolu, 381, 391, 392
Beijing, 10, 12, 18, 20–22, 24, 26–32, 35, 38, 43–45, 47, 51, 57, 61, 64, 68, 79, 81–83, 85–87, 94, 100, 112, 113, 116, 117, 119, 122, 126, 128–137, 142, 145, 146, 153–155, 159–161, 163–165, 167–169, 171, 173, 176, 183–186, 189, 190, 193, 195–197, 205, 207–211, 215, 217, 219, 220, 222–231, 233, 238–242, 248, 253, 254, 263, 265, 268, 270, 282, 293, 299, 303, 307, 310–313, 317, 319, 321, 322, 327, 329, 331,

435

339–341, 349, 350–355, 357,
366, 367, 369, 370–372, 375,
377, 379, 381, 383–386, 386,
388, 390, 393–395, 397, 399,
400, 402–404, 406, 411–416,
418–421, 424
Blair, Tony, 209
Bo Xilai, 152–154, 156, 157, 168
Bo Yibo, 59, 60, 70, 75, 152, 153, 168
Bush, George W., 89, 207, 209,
218, 231

Cai Wu, 391, 396
Cao Gangchuan, 79, 110, 127, 210,
214, 236, 303, 320, 321, 324,
328, 331, 335, 340, 346, 367, 408
Cao Jianming, 142, 143
Career, 28, 80, 91, 92, 98–100, 103–106,
108, 119, 130–132, 141, 153, 155,
156, 161–163, 166, 167, 174, 179,
181, 183, 188, 219, 229, 321,
335, 342, 370, 397, 398, 404–406,
408–413, 416, 422, 423, 425
 Barriers, 397, 398, 409, 423, 425
 requirement (see also technocrats),
 99, 103
Categorical groups, 109, 310
Central (*Zhongyang*), 298
Central Advisory Commission (CAC) 7,
20, 67, 153, 427
Central Committee, 2, 9, 11, 13, 18,
20–22, 24, 25–27, 29–35, 38, 41,
44, 47, 48, 52, 53, 55–58, 61–62,
64–66, 69–78, 80–82, 84, 85, 88,
89, 91, 92, 94–98, 100–103,
105–111, 113–123, 126, 128–135,
140, 142, 144, 148–158, 160,
164–166, 168–172, 175–177,
179–184, 186–191, 193, 195–197,
205, 206, 208, 216, 218–220,
222, 224, 229, 265–268, 271,
272, 276, 278, 294, 297–301,
304–306, 308, 312–314, 322,
326, 327, 331, 332, 334, 338,
339, 344–347, 355, 359, 364,
370, 378, 383, 384, 388, 389,
391, 392, 393, 395, 396, 397,
398, 404, 405, 406, 409, 414,
415, 417, 418, 423, 425, 428,
429, 430, 431, 432
 Twelfth Central Committee, 62, 72,
 105, 144, 183, 187, 266, 405
 Thirteenth Central Committee, 57,
 61, 64, 72, 101, 105, 266, 271,
 272, 338
 Fourteenth Central Committee, 30,
 61, 100, 105, 119, 160, 171,
 172, 266, 312, 405, 406
 Fifteenth Central Committee, 20–22,
 31, 64, 69, 72, 73, 74, 76, 77,
 81, 84, 85, 89, 94–96, 105,
 119, 122, 126, 129, 130, 142,
 153, 155, 157, 160, 164, 193,
 216, 266, 298–300, 312, 314,
 359, 393, 409
 Sixteenth Central Committee, 9, 11,
 26, 27, 34, 38, 55, 56, 65, 71,
 73–77, 80–82, 85, 88, 89,
 92–98, 101, 102, 104, 105,
 107–109, 111, 123, 128, 131,
 132, 133, 135, 142, 144,
 148–154, 157, 158, 165, 168,
 169, 170–172, 175–177,
 179–182, 184, 187, 189–191,
 193, 206, 208, 265–268, 276,
 294, 297, 300, 301, 305, 306,
 308, 312–314, 322, 326, 327,
 331, 332, 334, 338, 339, 345,
 346, 347, 364, 370, 378, 384,
 389, 391, 395, 396, 409, 415,
 417, 423, 428–435
 Seventeenth Central Committee, 417,
 418, 423, 425, 432
Central Disciplinary Inspection
 Commission (CDIC) 73, 74, 76,
 77, 180, 181, 182, 244, 299, 300,
 325, 377, 417
Central institutions 9, 109, 121, 124,
 133, 136, 137, 295, 429, 430
 party, 83, 110, 121–124, 136, 137,
 145, 184, 188, 233, 258, 271,
 377, 429

Index   437

government, 121, 123–126, 128, 136, 184, 429
Central Military Commission (CMC) 10–12, 17, 63, 77, 79, 110, 189, 203, 204, 208, 210, 213, 253, 265, 297, 299, 331, 333, 349, 359, 361, 400, 408, 413, 416, 423, 424, 427, 428, 431–433
  Chairman 24, 27, 49, 50, 51, 52, 53, 206, 207, 209, 210, 229, 236, 240, 250, 251, 297, 301, 302, 303, 304, 305, 311, 312, 315, 316, 321, 322, 324, 325, 326, 327, 329, 331, 332, 333, 334, 336, 338, 342, 343, 347, 359, 361, 367
  of the Party (or Party CMC) 204–206
  of the State (state CMC) 204–210, 217, 335, 347
Central Propaganda Department (CPD), 28, 55, 79, 155, 163, 188
Central Organization Department (COD), 28, 79, 164, 165, 173, 393, 394, 396
Chen Bingde, 331,
Chen Danhuai, 407, 410
Chen Demin, 374
Chen Geng, 399, 403, 407, 410, 421
Chen Haosu, 161, 196
Chen Liangjun, 244, 245, 254
Chen Liangyu, 10, 11, 27, 31, 32, 34, 78, 79, 142, 147–151, 194, 244–246, 250–252, 254, 269, 271, 278, 289, 293, 294, 316, 331, 377, 379, 428
Chen Muhua, 60, 62
Chen Shuibian, 357
Chen Xianfeng, 237
Chen Xilian, 20, 59
Chen Yeping, 32, 33
Chen Yi, 59, 141, 152, 161, 162, 170, 196, 407, 410
Chen Yonggui, 59, 92
Chen Yuan, 152, 173–176, 195
Chen Yun, 47, 59, 67–69, 152, 177, 230
Chen Zhijian, 399, 403, 407

Chen Zhili, 142, 143, 147–149, 213, 214, 216, 253, 271–273, 305, 364, 397
Chen Zhishu, 410, 418, 421, 423
Chi Haotian, 21, 25, 61, 63, 321
China Netcom (CNC), 248, 368
Chinese Academy of Sciences (CAS), 83, 126, 216, 329, 367
Chinese Communist Youth League (CCYL) Group, 10, 72, 124, 139, 228, 378
Chinese National People's Political Consultative Conference (CNPPCC), 58, 203
Chinese politics
  protocol of, 206, 306, 307, 347
Chirac, Jacques Rene, 209, 218
Chongqing, 28, 56, 95, 112, 117, 118, 130, 167, 176, 185, 186, 189, 190, 239, 266, 283, 357, 369, 378, 379, 382, 384, 386, 387, 390, 391, 395, 399, 403, 412, 420, 421
Chu Bo, 282, 379
Clientelist, 140
  ties, 140
Collective leadership, 41, 47–49
Commander-in-chief (see also CMC chairman), 12, 51, 153, 170, 206, 230, 232, 235, 316, 336, 364
Constitution of the Chinese Communist Party (CCP), 55, 57, 309
Constitution of the People's Republic of China (PRC), 204, 308
Core,
  Mao Zedong as, 48
  Deng Xiaoping as, 183, 319
  Jiang Zemin as, 26, 36, 48, 69, 105, 206, 217, 304, 325, 336, 343, 372, 427, 431
  Hu Jintao as, 39, 69, 74, 225, 227, 228, 240, 250, 260, 268, 273, 283, 303, 305, 318, 320, 334, 336, 384, 385, 428, 433
Corporate,
  ties, 10, 37, 85, 110–112, 134, 136, 137, 140, 141, 429, 430

Cui Bo, 381, 389, 391
Cultural Revolution, 2, 4, 5, 43, 44,
    47, 48, 82, 91–93, 98, 103, 108,
    114, 115, 135, 141, 168, 181,
    183, 204, 247, 265, 398, 406,
    408, 409

Dai Bingguo, 152,163, 164
Dai Xianglong, 141, 168, 368
Decision-maker, 216, 260
Democratic Progressive Party
    (DPP), 353
Deng Changyou, 133
Deng Lin, 317, 355
Deng Liqun, 35, 55, 56
Deng Liujin (see also Zeng Qinghong),
    30, 161, 162
Deng Pufang, 115, 151, 152, 160, 169,
    173, 409
Deng Rong (*Maomao*), 318
Deng Xianqun, 399, 407
Deng Xiaoping, 7, 11, 19, 20, 24,
    33, 37–39, 41–45, 47, 49, 50,
    51–53, 56, 58, 59, 65, 67–69,
    115, 151, 152, 164, 183,
    204–206, 208, 226, 255,
    268, 271, 272, 297, 302,
    303, 308–311, 314, 316–320,
    322, 324, 333, 336–338,
    340, 341, 342, 347, 350,
    355, 360, 399–401, 405,
    407, 409, 427, 428
    100th birthday, 297, 341,
        347, 355
    military thought (*Xinshiqi
    junduijianshe sixiang*),
        12, 297, 336–343, 345,
        347, 349, 359, 362
    relations with Hu Jintao,
    relations with Jiang Zemin, 41
    statue, 247, 319
    theory, 2, 3, 8, 37, 40, 41, 46, 65,
        66, 73, 208, 231, 255,
        259–261, 268, 272, 294,
        309, 324, 337, 340, 343,
        361, 363

Deng Yingchao, 58,
Deng Yousheng, 399, 407
Deputy position phenomenon, 398,
    402, 425
Ding Guan'gen,
Ding Henggao, 339, 404, 407
Ding Qiusheng, 151, 152, 170, 410, 415
Ding Yiping, 133, 151, 152, 170, 234,
    237, 410, 415, 422, 423
Diploma, 80, 86, 87, 115, 163, 166,
    218, 304, 350, 404
Du Qinglin, 81, 184, 189
Du Xuefang, 186, 382

educational backgrounds, 80,
    101, 105
El-Bashir, Omar, 237
elite politics, 1–3, 6–8, 13, 36, 39, 43,
    54, 226, 253, 257, 318, 427
elite provincial units,
    63, 112, 113, 116

factional, 1, 3, 10, 11, 38, 43, 44,
    70, 72, 131, 139–141, 146, 147,
    152, 156, 174, 176, 183, 186,
    190, 193, 194–199, 253, 276,
    334, 378, 397, 409, 427, 430,
    432, 433
    balance, 1–10, 39, 40, 52, 72, 109,
        136, 137, 139, 194, 198,
        221, 226, 234, 253, 427,
        428 429, 430
    groups, 10, 22, 38, 72, 131, 139, 140,
        147, 152, 176, 186, 190, 194,
        195, 197, 198, 199, 276, 334,
        409, 430, 433
    overlaps, 139,
    politics, 11, 44, 139, 227, 397, 427,
        432, 433
    power, 10, 139, 156
factions, 10, 139, 140, 195, 225
Fan Changlong, 132, 133
Fan Xiaoguang, 406, 410
Fang Yi, 60, 62
Feng Hongda, 399, 403
Feng Yuxiang, 399, 403

Index 439

Fernandes, George, 231
Fewsmith, Joseph, 29, 35–37, 41, 45, 211, 258, 266
first front (see also two-front arrangement), 43, 45, 49, 53
foreign study experience, 83
  see also education backgrounds,
fourth plenum, 271, 272, 297, 299, 318, 325, 326, 329, 331–333, 338, 339, 346, 347, 359, 428, 431, 432
  of the 16th Central Committee, 297, 331, 332, 334, 346, 447, 428, 431, 432
Fu Liqun, 237
Fu Tinggui, 322, 341
Fujian, 28, 29, 72, 92, 94, 106, 116, 117, 142, 144, 157, 161, 185, 187, 190, 211, 216, 219, 239, 253, 285, 291, 328, 368, 374, 378, 381, 385, 386, 389, 390, 412, 413

Gansu, 95, 116, 117, 156, 219, 220, 239, 283, 284, 285, 329, 364, 368, 379, 380, 383, 387, 391, 396, 397, 410, 421
Gao Dezhan, 113
Gao Qiang, 224, 227–229, 238, 239
Gao Siren, 119, 380
Gao Xin, 30, 32, 35, 159, 160, 162, 187, 196, 205, 206, 214, 216, 226, 321, 402, 409
Ge Zhenfeng, 129, 234, 311, 313
gender, 96, 390, 391
General Armament Department (GAD) 128, 189, 323, 331, 334, 342, 398, 400, 413,
General Logistics Department (GLD), 128, 132, 222, 311, 327, 363, 400, 413
General Political Department (GPD), 127, 128, 132, 162, 236, 328, 362, 400, 413
generation
  first, 46–48, 397, 406, 407, 423, 425
  second, 47–49, 75, 324

third, 24, 26, 39, 47, 48, 49, 50, 91 93, 272, 301, 324, 397, 432
fourth, 25, 26, 31, 35, 36, 39, 47, 49, 50, 53, 64, 72, 82, 91, 93, 130, 131, 141, 154, 157, 260, 301, 324, 350, 432
fifth, 47, 50, 72, 157, 190, 397
generational succession (see also generation and two-front arrangement), 9, 42, 46, 47, 49, 52, 53, 431
Gilley, Bruce, 38, 216, 365
Goldstein, Avery, 1, 3, 8
group cohesion index, 10, 139, 147, 148, 174, 182, 193, 194, 198, 199, 430
  of the CCYL Group, 183, 193, 194, 195–199, 334, 397, 425, 430, 432, 433
  of the Princelings, 10, 139, 141, 174, 175, 182, 194, 195–199, 349, 404, 422, 430, 433
  of the Qinghua Clique, 139, 174, 175, 182, 194, 195, 197, 199, 430, 433,
  of the Shanghai Gang, 10–12, 29, 38, 118, 130, 139–144, 146–148, 151, 173–175, 181, 182, 194, 197, 199, 203, 216, 221, 226, 240, 250, 251, 252, 254, 255, 273, 276, 277, 395, 312, 331, 349, 354, 355, 367, 369, 372, 397, 424, 430–433
Guangdong, 63, 64, 94, 106, 111–113, 115–121, 152, 156, 165, 185, 186, 215, 220–223, 238, 239, 262, 269, 288, 289, 320, 359, 375, 379, 381, 382, 385–390, 392, 400, 413, 417
Guangxi, 93, 94, 113, 116, 117, 171, 185, 186, 222, 239, 378, 279, 382, 384–386, 390, 391, 400, 413
Guo Boxiong, 79, 110, 127, 210, 234, 236, 303, 328, 329, 331, 333, 335, 340, 346, 361
Guomindang (GMD), 12, 165, 179, 349

440 China's Elite Politics

Han Jun, 152, 168, 169
Han Zheng, 142, 147–151, 185, 194, 220, 269, 381, 385, 386, 388, 390
Harbin Institute of Military Engineering, 104, 402, 406
He Changgong, 196, 399, 401, 404, 405
He Daoquan, 399, 401, 404–406
He Guangwei, 196,
He Guoqiang, 27, 28, 32–34, 79, 112, 121, 270, 331, 333
He Long, 25, 48, 59, 147, 161, 165, 182, 297, 298, 301, 302, 306, 308, 399, 401, 408
He Pengfei, 399, 401, 408
He Xiangning, 165, 166
Hebei, 79, 93, 94, 104, 113, 116, 117, 131, 155, 157, 159, 172, 176, 183–186, 189, 220, 238, 239, 256, 282, 313, 379–382, 385–387, 390, 391, 393, 399, 410, 412, 417, 420
Heilongjiang, 94, 116, 117, 135, 182, 184, 239, 376, 378, 389, 382, 386, 390, 391, 392
Henan, 63, 72, 79, 82, 93, 94, 106, 113, 116, 117, 152, 168, 169, 184, 185, 186, 190, 193, 215, 220, 239, 270, 282, 284, 313, 373, 378, 379, 381, 382, 385–387, 390–392, 396, 400, 410–413, 415, 416
Ho Hau-wah, 119
home province, 93, 94, 98, 108, 158, 160, 380
Hong Bao, 399, 403, 421
Hong Hu, 78, 147, 152, 153, 173, 174
Hong Xuezhi, 152, 153, 399, 403
Hong Kong, 30, 33, 39, 94, 99, 117–121, 126, 145, 165, 166, 210, 221, 223, 229, 241, 242, 247, 252, 277, 278, 315, 318, 353, 380, 387, 421
Hu Changqing, 86, 87
Hu Chunhua, 381, 390, 392
Hu Jintao,
    four-point policy toward Taiwan, 335
    military thought (three provides and one play), 12, 297, 336–343, 345, 347, 349, 359, 362, 424
    new three people's principles, 11, 225, 256, 427
    relations with Deng Xiaoping,
    relations with Jiang Zemin, 41
    scientific concept of development, 11, 255, 261, 264, 265, 267–273, 294, 295, 342, 343–347, 361–364, 373, 424, 427, 431
    two imperatives, 11, 256, 427
Hu Qili, 57
Hu Wei, 382, 391, 392
Hu Yanlin, 311–313
Hu Yaobang, 33, 35, 37, 46, 67, 68, 154, 166, 182, 187, 219
Hua Guofeng, 2, 23, 24, 47, 58, 59, 67, 91, 308
Hua Jianmin, 142, 143, 146, 148, 150, 151, 175–179, 194, 214, 253, 271, 273, 374, 432
Hua Zhongliang, 399, 403, 407, 408
Huang Huahua, 118, 185, 220, 288, 381, 385, 386, 388, 390
Huang Jing (Yu Qiwei), 152, 159
Huang Xi, 377, 385, 386, 388, 390
Huang Xiaojing, 385, 386, 388, 390
Huang Yongsheng, 70
Huang Zhen, 28, 152, 163, 164, 384
Hubei, 79, 93, 94, 113–117, 119, 152, 160, 173, 181, 183, 185, 239, 284, 285, 313, 379, 380, 386, 390, 391, 399, 410–413, 417
Hui Liangyu, 79, 114, 214, 271, 331, 333
Hunan, 32, 79, 86, 93, 94, 113, 116, 117, 152, 160, 170, 171, 176, 185, 186, 196, 222, 239, 265, 277, 284, 287, 288, 313, 379, 386–388, 390, 391, 399, 400, 405, 406, 410–413
Hurdle, 404, 414, 425

Index   441

Inner Mongolia, 34, 40, 93, 94, 116, 119, 184, 186, 187, 188, 213, 257, 261, 270, 282, 283, 379, 381, 382, 385, 386, 390, 391
institutional, 1, 6–9, 11, 18, 19, 24, 25, 36, 37, 39, 40, 42, 46, 51, 52, 53, 66, 67–69, 87, 109, 110, 120, 123, 136, 137, 156, 204, 205, 217, 221, 227, 255, 261, 263, 294, 297, 298, 301, 302, 427, 428, 433
  loyalty, 7, 8, 42, 131, 154, 221, 227, 244, 322, 338, 372, 427, 428
institutionalization, 6–9, 11, 18, 19, 24, 25, 36, 39, 51, 52, 66, 69, 87, 156, 217, 255, 294, 297, 298, 301, 302, 427, 428, 433
  ideological, 11, 255
  political, 6–9, 11, 19, 24, 36, 39, 51, 52, 255, 427, 428, 433
Intra-Party democracy, 257–259

Ji Bingxuan, 184, 188,191,192
Ji Yunshi, 185, 190, 220, 381, 385, 386, 390
Jia Chunwang, 99, 175–178, 184, 189, 197
Jia Qinglin, 27–29, 31, 34, 64, 70–72, 78, 79, 93, 110, 112, 187, 211, 187, 211, 212, 225, 253, 270, 282, 331
Jia Ting'an, 71
Jiang Chunyun, 21, 25, 60
Jiang Daming, 185, 191, 192
Jiang Futang, 132
Jiang Jieshi (Chiang Kaishek), 159, 256, 349, 357
Jiang Mianheng, 12, 245, 247–250, 252–254, 329, 367–369, 424
Jiang Nanxiang, 166, 174
Jiang Qing, 159, 277
Jiang Shangqing, 365, 366
Jiang Tong, 163
Jiang Yanyong, 222, 223
Jiang Zemin, 7, 9–12, 17–19, 21, 23–28, 31, 32, 34, 36–38, 41, 42, 48–53, 57, 64–66, 69, 72, 78, 91, 105, 114, 120, 127, 130, 131, 140, 141, 144–146, 150, 154, 155, 157, 159, 160, 162, 167, 168, 188, 203–211, 213–219, 222, 224, 226, 228–231, 233–238, 240, 247, 248, 250, 251, 253–259, 266, 268, 271, 272, 294, 297–305, 307, 309–322, 324–326, 328–343, 345–347, 349, 350, 353–355, 359, 360, 361, 365–372, 397, 419, 421, 424, 425, 427, 428, 431–433
  and the *PLA Daily* incidents, 364
  as chairman of the CMC, 27, 40, 120, 235, 332, 334
  as the core of the third generation leadership, 49
  as general secretary of the CCP,
  as the inventor of the "Three Represents", 231
  as president of the PRC, 18, 25, 217, 218, 225, 304
  eight-point policy toward Taiwan, 248
  military thought (*guofang he junduijianshe sixiang*), 12, 297, 336, 338-443, 345, 347, 349, 359, 362
  manipulation before the Sixteenth Party Congress,
  relations with Hu Jintao, 132, 141, 163, 335, 350
  relations with Zeng Qinghong,
  relations with Wu Bangguo,
  relations with Jia Qinglin,
  relations with Huang Ju,
  resignation letter, 25, 298, 306, 317, 325, 326
  retirement issue,
  role in Chinese politics, 37
Jiangsu, 31, 79, 82, 93, 94, 98, 108, 113, 114, 116, 117, 134, 142, 152, 157, 158, 162, 163, 167, 175, 176, 184, 185, 190, 196, 220, 239, 240, 277, 278, 279, 281–284, 287, 337, 378,

379, 381, 385, 386, 390, 399, 400, 404, 411
Jiangxi, 30, 79, 86, 93, 94, 116, 117, 142, 143, 145, 152, 160, 161, 176, 180, 181, 239, 264, 269, 277, 281, 282, 284, 379, 386, 410–413
Jilin, 79, 81, 82, 94, 95, 99, 103, 114–117, 127, 153, 155, 156, 172, 184, 185, 186, 239, 313, 379, 382, 386, 391, 415
Jing Zhiyuan, 331, 335

Kang Sheng, 70
Ke Qingshi, 59, 141
Kim Jong-il, 236
Kuchma, Leonid, 237
Kuhn, Robert Lawrence, 28, 230, 302, 303, 365, 366, 371

Lahoud, Emile, 237
Lai Changxing, 253
Lee, Hong Yung, 98, 105
Lee Teng-hui, 351–353
Lei Mingqiu, 311, 313
Li Changchun, 63, 71, 72, 78, 79, 106, 111, 115, 114, 215, 270
Li Changjiang, 184, 189
Li Changyin, 134
Li, Cheng, 35, 91, 98, 105, 130, 139, 186, 333
Li Chengyu, 185, 220, 282, 273, 381, 385, 386, 388, 390
Li Chuncheng, 186, 190, 381
Li Dezhu, 184, 188, 220
Li Gancheng, 151, 152, 157, 195
Li Guixian, 61, 124, 212
Li Jianguo, 374, 380
Li Jinai, 128, 185, 189, 210, 305, 334–336, 342, 364, 391
Li Jishen, 58
Li Ka-shing, 246,
Li Ke, 186, 382, 391, 392
Li Kenong, 399, 401
Li Keqiang, 71, 72, 78, 82, 83, 103, 185, 190–193, 195, 220, 282, 373, 378, 379, 381–384, 390

Li Lanqing, 21, 25, 60, 62, 301
Li Liguo, 381, 391, 395
Li Lun, 399, 401
Li Peng, 18, 19, 21, 23–25, 37, 57–60, 70, 71, 187, 301, 331
Li Qianyuan, 311, 313
Li Ruihuan, 26, 27, 52, 58, 70, 71, 78, 112, 211, 301
  relations with Jiang Zemin, 41
Li Shunda, 92
Li Tielin, 152, 164, 165, 173–178, 195
Li Tieying, 26, 27, 61, 62, 165, 364
Li Weihan, 20, 152, 164, 165
Li Xiannian, 18, 57–59, 67–69, 211, 411, 418,419, 422
Li Xiaolin, 418
Li Xueju, 220, 391, 395
Li Yizhong, 134
Li Yuanchao, 82, 83, 151, 152, 157, 158, 185, 190–193, 195, 196, 220, 287, 378, 379, 381, 383, 384
Li Zemin, 115
Li Zhanshu, 186,
Li Zhilun, 184, 189, 191, 192, 193, 220
Liang Bohua, 287
Liang Guanglie, 128, 129, 210, 305, 328, 335, 342
Liao Chengzhi, 152, 165, 166
Liao Hui, 152, 165, 166, 173, 174, 212
Liao Xilong, 128, 210, 305, 363
Liao Zhongkai, 165
Lidangweigong zhizhengweimin, 260
Lien Chan, 357, 424
Lin Biao, 3, 45, 47, 59, 67, 70, 153
Ling Jihua, 184, 188
Liu Dongdong, 311, 313
Liu Fengjun, 404
Liu Fuyuan, 264
Liu Guoqiang, 375
Liu Huaqing, 20, 38, 63, 75, 319, 411
Liu Jiande, 406, 418
Liu Jie, 134
Liu Jinbao, 241, 251–254
Liu Jing, 152, 168, 169
Liu Peng, 185, 190, 191–193, 382, 391, 394, 394

Liu Qi, 27, 31, 32, 43, 78, 79, 185, 191–193, 228, 331, 378, 379, 382, 384, 390
Liu Qibao, 185, 191–193, 378, 379, 382, 390
Liu Ruilong, 152, 162, 195
Liu Shaoqi, 2, 3, 18, 43, 45, 46, 47, 52, 57, 58, 67, 204, 217, 411, 416
Liu Shengyu, 391, 393
Liu Taihang, 399, 407
Liu Yandong, 82, 103, 106, 152, 162, 163, 175–178, 184, 188, 190–193, 195, 196, 197, 202, 220, 253, 430
Liu Yazhou, 406, 411, 418, 422, 423
Liu Yuan, 411, 414, 418, 423, 425
Liu Yunshan, 28, 32, 34, 35, 72, 79, 121, 144, 183, 184, 187, 188
Liu Yupu, 186, 191, 192, 382, 390, 392
Liu Zhenwu, 311, 313
Liu Zhidan, 156
Lu Ruihua, 118
Lu Yongxiang, 253, 367, 368, 369
Lu Zhangong, 379
Luo Baoming, 185, 191, 192
Luo Bin, 225, 245, 251, 277, 325, 328, 333, 399, 407
Luo Dongjin, 399, 401, 407
Luo Gan, 61, 62, 71, 72, 78, 79, 110, 111, 160, 331
Luo Jian, 399, 403
Luo Ronghuan, 160, 399, 401
Luo Ruiqing, 59, 160, 399, 403, 407

Ma Benzhai, 399, 403
Ma Fucai, 134
Ma Guochao, 399, 403
Ma Kai, 285
Ma Qizhi, 185, 190, 387
Ma Xiaotian, 133, 152, 172, 411, 414, 422, 423
Macao, 93, 94, 117, 118–121, 126, 165, 166, 353, 354, 380, 387
Macro-management, 274–278, 280–293
Mao Fengming, 336, 337
Mao Yuping, 241, 246

Mao Zedong, 6, 18, 24, 43–48, 52, 57, 58, 67, 159, 164, 204, 208, 217, 255, 256, 271, 272, 309, 310, 319, 336–338, 349, 352, 357, 360, 372, 405, 431
Meng Jianzhu, 142, 143, 148, 150, 281, 379
Meng Xuenong, 10, 167, 183, 185, 220, 224, 225, 228, 229, 254, 381, 385, 390
meritocracy, 422
Military institutions (see also the PLA), 128, 129, 132, 133
  regions, 74, 128, 172
  representation, 127, 128
Min Weifang, 135
minorities, 96, 97
Mubarak, Hosni, 237

Nathan, Andrew, 140, 146
National People's Congress (NPC), 18, 203, 302, 354
nationality (see also minorities), 96, 97, 115, 164
Nepotism, 409, 422
New Party, 12, 115, 231, 357, 358, 424
Nie Li, 399, 404
Nie Rongzhen, 59, 399, 404, 407
Nixon, Richard, 350
North China Sea Fleet, 133, 151, 170, 234, 237, 403, 415

overheating, 255, 273, 274–277, 292, 294, 433

Pan Yunhe, 135
Pao Yukang, 247
party standing, 57, 92, 93, 98, 108
Peng Dehuai, 3, 59, 153, 399
Peng Gang, 399, 407
Peng Xiaofeng, 411, 414, 417, 423, 425
Peng Xuefeng, 411, 417
Peng Zhen, 19, 23, 33, 58
People First Party (PFP), 12, 357, 358

People's Liberation Army (PLA) (see also military), 12, 37, 127, 153, 162, 205, 227, 233, 306, 334, 349, 352, 401
  Air Force, 133, 171, 172, 196, 307, 331, 414, 418, 419, 422
  Navy, 133, 170, 171, 234, 235, 237, 311, 331, 335, 401, 403, 408, 415, 416
People's Republic of China (PRC), 10, 17–19, 22–25, 36–38, 44, 52, 57, 58, 63, 163, 203, 204, 206, 211, 217, 218, 225, 226, 235, 236, 253, 254, 270, 302, 304, 307, 309, 310, 314, 325, 349, 350, 351, 356, 396, 403, 416
personal,
  loyalty, 7, 8, 42, 131, 227, 427, 428
  ties, 173–175, 190, 193
Politburo,
  members, 9, 20, 21, 23–26, 30, 32, 33, 52, 55, 56, 57, 63, 64, 66, 68, 69, 70, 75, 76, 79, 88, 96, 101, 102, 107,114, 127, 159, 162, 183, 187, 205, 214, 224, 270, 271, 321, 360, 409, 429
  membership as a requirement, 24
  standing committee, 10, 23, 26, 27, 29, 34, 35, 41, 50, 57, 65, 68, 70–75, 77, 78, 88, 101, 102, 107, 111, 144, 145, 162, 187, 223, 224, 225, 226, 266, 267, 277, 278, 300, 331
  study sessions, 12, 237, 251, 259, 360, 433
political elites, 9, 55, 98, 106, 108
political exit (see also age limit and term limit), 17, 52, 427, 428
  rules on, 9, 17, 19, 52, 55, 327
political groups, 9
political institutionalization (see also power balancing), 6–9, 11, 17, 19, 24, 35–37, 39, 46, 51, 52, 221, 255, 427, 428, 433
political institutions, 109, 429

political succession (see also political transition and power transfer), 17, 35–37, 46, 52, 221, 427, 431
political transition, 9, 49, 52, 427, 431
power,
  balancing (see also winner-takes-all and political institutionalization), 5–9, 11, 19, 24, 34, 39, 51, 52, 255, 427, 433
  index (see also central committee index), 9, 120, 124, 128, 133, 136, 137, 139, 143, 173–175, 190, 197, 198, 429, 430
  transfer, see also political transition and political succession, 9, 17, 35, 52, 206, 431
presidium, 74, 75–78, 108, 300
  of the Sixteenth Party Congress, 78, 108, 300
  standing committee of,
princelings, 10, 139, 141, 151, 152, 155, 156, 160, 162, 170, 174, 175, 182, 194–199, 349, 387, 404, 406, 407, 409, 422, 423, 430, 433
  generals, 13, 349, 397, 398, 399, 402, 406, 407, 409, 410, 417, 418, 422, 423, 425
principle,
  of the Party commanding armed forces, 204, 267, 294, 306
provincial,
  leaders, 56, 63, 66, 67, 100, 107, 108, 110–113, 115, 117, 120, 153, 175, 254, 287, 292, 378, 389, 390, 429
  representation, 112, 429
Powell, Colin. L, 237

Qian Guoliang, 132, 422
Qian Haihao, 237
Qian Qichen, 21, 25, 60, 62
Qian Shugen, 129, 130
Qian Yunlu, 185, 190, 378, 379, 382, 390
Qiang Wei, 185, 191

Qiao Qingchen, 133, 331, 335, 414
Qiao Shi, 19, 23, 33, 57, 58, 60, 75, 187
Qin Guangrong, 186, 381, 389, 390
Qin Jiwei, 61, 63, 399, 403, 412, 422
Qin Tao, 399, 403, 404
Qin Tian, 412, 418, 422, 423
Qin Weijiang, 412, 418, 419, 422, 423
Qinghua University, 49, 82, 99, 100, 103, 104, 135, 141, 144, 145, 157, 163, 165, 166, 168, 173–175, 180, 181, 194, 195, 214, 220, 221, 269, 315, 327, 368, 408, 418
    Clique, 10, 139, 140, 174, 175, 182, 194, 195, 197, 199, 430, 433
Quan Zhezhu, 185

retirement, 9, 11, 12, 17, 19, 26, 27, 33, 34, 36, 50, 88, 150, 203, 223, 297, 298, 300, 301, 306, 312, 314, 316, 317, 325, 326, 328, 329, 331–333, 336, 337, 342, 347, 367, 370, 394, 396, 397, 402, 410–413, 420, 424, 427, 428, 432, 433
    age, 19, 88, 312, 337, 370, 394, 396, 397, 428, 432
    system of, 19
Rong Yiren, 58, 213
Rui Xinwen, 30, 146
Rule-maker, 260
Rules, 9, 17, 19, 24, 36, 52, 55, 57, 65, 66, 326, 327, 347, 352, 353
    formal, 9, 19, 52, 55
    informal, 9, 19, 52, 55, 57
    on political exit, 17, 52
    on political entry, 9, 55

San Xiangjun, 186, 192
Schroeder, Gerhard, 209
scientific concept of development, 11, 255, 261, 264, 265, 267–273, 294, 295, 342–347, 361–364, 373, 424, 427, 431
second-front (see also two-front arrangement), 43–46, 49, 52, 53
Severe Acute Respiratory Syndrome (SARS), 143, 203, 221, 354

Shaanxi, 79, 93, 95, 113, 117, 52, 154, 156, 157, 165, 167, 176, 184, 185, 186, 239, 283, 287, 288, 374, 379, 380, 382, 385, 387, 388, 389, 390, 399, 413
Shandong, 63, 79, 93, 94, 98, 108, 111, 112, 113, 116, 117, 119, 120, 121, 142, 152, 160, 161, 163, 165, 167, 170, 171, 181, 184, 185, 186, 188, 233, 239, 284, 313, 380, 381, 382, 383, 385, 390, 391, 392, 394, 412
Shanghai, 10, 11, 12, 27, 29–32, 38, 64, 78, 79, 94, 104, 110, 112, 113, 116–118, 121, 130, 131, 134, 136, 139–152, 158, 159, 161–163, 167, 173–176, 178, 181, 182, 185, 192, 194, 195, 197, 199, 203, 214–216, 220–222, 226, 230, 231, 239–255, 269, 272, 273, 276–278, 282–284, 289–291, 293–295, 302, 305, 312, 316, 331, 336, 349, 354, 355, 365–372, 377, 379, 381, 385–388, 390, 397, 424, 428, 430–433
    Gang, 10–12, 29, 38, 78, 118, 130, 139, 140–144, 146–148, 150, 151, 173–175, 181, 182, 194, 197, 199, 203, 216, 221, 226, 240, 244, 246, 250–252, 254, 255, 272, 273, 276, 277, 293, 294, 305, 312, 331, 349, 354, 355, 367, 369, 372, 387, 397, 424, 428, 430–433
Shanxi, 79, 94, 113, 116, 117, 152, 153, 166, 168, 169, 184, 186–189, 222, 239, 269, 378, 379, 381–383, 386, 390, 396, 412
Shen Bingyi, 133
Shen Junsheng, 243
Shen Ting, 244
Shen Wenqing, 368
Shen Yueyue, 185, 381, 391, 393
Shenzhou (manned spaceship), 252, 330, 364, 366, 368, 412
    V, 252, 330, 368
    VI, 364, 366

Shi Lianxi, 186
Shi Yunsheng, 133, 171, 234, 237
Shi Yuzhen, 186
Shirk, Susan L., 18, 66, 69, 73
Sichuan, 56, 63, 79, 95, 112–114,
    116–118, 120, 121, 129, 152,
    160, 167, 185, 186, 196, 222,
    239, 270, 282, 283, 319, 379,
    381, 382, 386, 389, 394, 395,
    399, 400, 410, 411
Sihanouk, Norodom, 237
Sixteenth Party Congress, 9, 17, 21, 25,
    27, 29, 34–38, 40, 49, 50, 52, 65,
    73–75, 78, 107, 108, 112, 134,
    205, 206, 208, 221, 232, 253,
    256, 257, 259–261, 263, 266,
    268, 273, 294, 297, 299, 300,
    308, 310, 324, 327, 332, 338,
    346, 359, 378, 381, 385, 390,
    393, 394, 415, 425, 427–432
Song Airong, 186, 190, 382, 391, 392
Song Defu, 72, 78, 144, 158, 185,
    190–193, 195, 378, 384
Song Ping, 33, 60, 75
Song Qinglin, 58
Song Renqiong, 33, 75
Song Shilun, 399, 403, 407, 408
Song Xiuyan, 185, 382, 385,
    387, 388, 390
Soong, James C.Y., 357, 358, 424
South China Sea Fleet, 359, 415
State Council, 32, 110, 114, 118, 123,
    124, 126, 143, 144, 156,
    165–168, 179, 189, 213–215,
    218–221, 231, 232, 239, 246,
    252, 253, 265, 276–279, 283,
    288, 289, 292, 299, 354,
    370–377, 381, 382, 384, 396
State Councilors, 62, 63, 213, 218, 253
Su Qianming, 400, 401, 407
Su Rongsheng, 161, 400, 402, 407, 420
Su Shulin, 134
Su Xintian, 92
Su Yu, 161, 163, 180, 400, 402
Submarine accident, 171, 233, 236,
    254, 303, 359, 360, 431

succession, 9, 17, 25, 31, 35–37,
    42, 45–47, 49, 52, 53, 65,
    205, 221, 266, 298, 300–302,
    427, 431
Sui Mingtai, 312, 313
Sun Jiazheng, 184, 189, 220
Sun Jinlong, 381, 389, 391
Sun Shuyi, 185, 382, 391, 392

Taiwan, 11, 12, 93, 94, 116, 122, 126,
    249, 314–316, 322–324, 328,
    330, 347, 349–359, 380, 387,
    391, 423, 424, 428
    affairs leading small group
        (TALSG), 350
    issue, 11, 314–316, 322–324, 347,
        352, 354–356
    policy toward, 12, 349, 350, 354,
        355, 423, 428
Tan Dongsheng, 161, 400, 401
Tan Shaowen, 112
Tan Zhenlin, 59, 161, 163, 400, 401
Tang Ke, 162
Tao Jianxing, 134
Technocracy, 9, 55, 100, 105, 106
Technocrats, 55, 98, 99, 102–108
    academic requirement, 99–101, 103
    career requirement, 99, 103
    leadership requirement, 103
Teiwes, Frederick C., 43, 46, 68–70
ten-year service limit,
    19, 22–24, 52
term limit, 22–27, 52
third plenum, 11, 18, 24, 35, 205, 265,
    266, 267, 268, 269, 270, 294,
    299, 306, 308, 346
    of the 11th Central Committee,
        18, 24, 35, 48, 205, 265, 266
    of the 12th Central Committee, 266
    of the 13th Central Committee, 266
    of the 14th Central Committee, 266
    of the 15th Central Committee, 266
    of the 16th Central Committee,
        265–267, 294, 306, 308, 346
three new people's principles, 11, 255,
    256, 294, 427

three provides and one play (*sange tigong yige fahui*), 12, 362, 424
three Represents, 11, 37, 40, 41, 65, 208, 231, 232, 255, 257–261, 268, 270, 272, 294, 307–310, 336, 339, 346, 347, 360, 364, 373, 374, 427, 431
Tian Chengping, 104, 175–178, 269
Tian Congming, 71
Tian Jiyun, 21, 25, 60, 61, 187
Tian Mingjian, 403, 404, 406
Tian Suoning, 248
Tianjin, 63, 79, 94, 112, 113, 116, 117, 141, 144, 154, 159, 168, 176, 185, 186, 190, 219, 236, 239, 270, 282, 283, 346, 379, 381, 386, 387, 390–393, 399, 403, 421
Tieben, 279, 280, 287, 293, 295
Tong, Goh Chok, 237
Trajkovski, Boris, 237
Tsou, Tang, 1, 2, 6
Tung Chee-hwa, 118
two–front arrangement, 9, 42, 43, 45, 46, 49–53, 217, 431
  Mao Zedong's version, 42, 43, 45, 46, 47, 48, 52, 217, 255, 309, 337, 431
  Deng Xiaoping's version, 42, 45, 46, 50, 255, 309, 337
  Jiang Zemin's attempt to restore, 204, 217

Ulanhu, 58, 59, 211, 213

Wan Li, 19, 23, 58, 60, 75
Wang Feng, 115, 396
Wang Fengqing (Zeng Qinghong's wife), 396
Wang Gang, 79, 99, 123, 271, 272, 364
Wang Hongguang, 418, 420, 423
Wang Huning, 142, 143
Wang Jianmin, 132
Wang Jianqing, 412, 420
Wang Julu, 382, 391, 392
Wang Lequan, 79, 115, 183, 184, 188, 189, 271, 378, 380

Wang Luolin, 152
Wang Mingquan, 134
Wang Ping, 406, 410
Wang Qishan, 152, 166, 173, 224, 228, 385, 386
Wang Sanyun, 381, 389, 390
Wang Shucheng, 175–178, 180–182, 220
Wang Sumin, 400, 401, 407
Wang Wenyang, 249
Wang Xiaofeng, 224, 379
Wang Ya'nan, 152
Wang Yang, 184, 189, 378, 379, 381, 382, 384, 390
Wang Yongqing, 249
Wang Zhaoguo, 34, 72, 79, 106, 121, 183, 184, 187–189, 191–193, 195, 219, 220, 229
Wang Zhen, 58, 59, 213, 400, 401
Wang Zheng, 400, 401
Wei Jianxing, 21, 25, 33, 40, 64, 301
Wen Jiabao, 10, 11, 60, 62, 71, 78, 79, 110, 187, 203, 214, 218, 219, 223, 226, 229, 231, 232, 237–239, 244, 253, 267, 270, 272, 275–281, 283, 284, 288, 289, 292–294, 316, 342, 373–375, 433
winner-takes-all, 1, 2, 3, 7, 8, 37, 51, 52, 221, 253, 427
World Health Organization (WHO), 223, 238, 357
work experience, 90, 92, 99, 108, 141, 159, 190, 207, 226, 243, 276, 334, 370, 378
Wu Aiying, 381, 382, 391, 394
Wu Bangguo, 31, 60, 62, 64, 71, 72, 78, 79, 110, 142–144, 146, 147, 149, 175–178, 181, 194, 213, 221, 226, 233, 250, 253, 270, 331, 428
Wu Guangzheng, 71, 72, 78, 180
Wu Jianmin, 377
Wu Qidi, 135, 142, 143, 175–178, 194
Wu Quanxu, 129, 130
Wu Shengli, 412, 414, 415, 422, 423, 425

Wu Shuangzhan, 312, 313
Wu Xian, 412, 414
Wu Xiuquan, 399, 407
Wu Xueqian, 60, 61
Wu Yi, 61, 63, 79, 96, 110, 214, 215, 223, 224, 229, 231, 232, 238, 271, 283
Wu Yuqian, 132

Xi Jinping, 71, 72, 78, 82, 103, 152, 156, 157, 175–178, 181, 195, 269, 379, 409
Xi Zhongxun, 35, 59, 152, 156, 409
Xia Baolong, 186, 190, 381, 390, 392
Xiao Yang, 56, 113
Xibaipo, 256
Xie Fei, 64
Xie Qihua, 134, 142, 143, 175–178, 194
Xie Zhenhua, 175–178, 181
Xie Zhengxuan, 342
Xinjiang, 79, 91, 93, 95, 113, 115–118, 121, 184, 186, 188, 190, 239, 329, 378, 380, 382–384, 387, 391, 392
Xiong Guangkai, 129, 130, 171
Xu Caihou, 127, 128, 210, 236, 271, 272, 305, 328, 331, 333, 335, 336, 338, 341, 345, 362, 417
Xu Guangchun, 142, 143, 379
Xu Kuangdi, 104, 142, 143, 147–150, 212, 215
Xu Lefu, 152, 171, 412
Xu Qiliang, 132, 133, 152, 171, 172, 174, 412, 414, 422, 423, 425
Xu Rongkai, 175–178, 387
Xu Xiangqian, 412, 418
Xu Xiaoyan, 412, 418, 423
Xu Shiyou, 114, 412, 422
Xu Yanbin, 400, 407
Xu Yuanchao, 412, 418, 422, 423

Yan Yixun, 253
Yang Baibing, 38, 63, 317
Yang Chengwu, 412, 413, 419
Yang Chuantang, 185, 378, 381–384, 390

Yang Deqing, 313
Yang Dezhong, 312
Yang Dongming, 418, 419, 423
Yang Huaiqing, 133, 171, 234, 237
Yang Jing, 60, 186, 282, 381, 382, 385, 386, 390
Yang Jiping, 412, 418, 421, 423
Yang Rudai, 113
Yang Shangkun, 18, 20, 37, 42, 57, 63, 68, 213, 317
Yang Yang, 371
Yang Yong, 412, 421
Yao Yilin, 57, 60, 61, 152, 166
Yazhen (keep control), 302, 303
Ye Jianying, 19, 20, 23, 58, 400
Ye Qun, 70
Ye Ting, 400, 401
Ye Xiaowen, 184, 189
Ye Xuanning, 400, 407
Ye Yonglie (see also Robert Lawrence Kuhn), 371
Ye Zhengda, 400, 401
Yin Yicui, 142, 143
Yok Mu-Ming, 358, 424
You Xigui, 129–131, 141, 311–313, 328
Yu Huiwen (Huang Ju's wife), 246, 247, 254, 377
Yu Qiuli, 59, 60, 62, 161
Yu Youjun, 386
Yu Zhengsheng, 79, 115, 152, 159, 160, 173, 271, 379, 417
Yuan Chunqing, 185, 190–193, 382, 385, 387–390
Yuan Shikai, 209

Zang, Xiaowei, 6, 100, 105
Zeng Haisheng, 161, 413
Zeng Peiyan, 78, 79, 123, 175–178, 213, 214, 221, 253, 270, 271, 282, 283, 328, 331
Zeng Qinghong, 28, 30, 31, 33, 34, 41, 69, 71, 72, 78, 79, 93, 110, 142, 145–147, 149, 150, 152, 155, 160–163, 169, 173, 174, 194, 211, 214, 225, 231, 232, 253, 254, 256, 268, 270, 273, 278,

284, 285, 331, 333, 370, 396, 397, 432
Zeng Qinghuai, 161
Zeng Qingyang, 161, 413
Zeng Qingyuan, 161, 413
Zeng Shan, 30, 145, 152, 160, 161, 413
Zhai Huqu, 135
Zhang Aiping, 60, 400, 401
Zhang Baokang, 404
Zhang Baoshun, 186, 191–193, 195, 378, 379, 381–383, 390
Zhang Delin, 175–178
Zhang Dingfa, 133, 331, 335, 416
Zhang Fusen, 175, 176, 178, 184, 189, 196, 197, 220, 394
Zhang Huazhu, 175, 176, 178
Zhang Haiyang, 413, 414, 416, 422, 423, 425
Zhang Lan, 58
Zhang Li, 129
Zhang Lichang, 79, 113, 144, 271, 379
Zhang Qingli, 118, 186, 378, 380, 382, 383, 390
Zhang Qingwei, 91, 134
Zhang Quanjing, 32, 33
Zhang Ruimin, 134,
Zhang Shuzhi, 400, 401
Zhang Wannian, 21, 25, 63, 127
Zhang Weiqing, 184, 189, 220
Zhang Wenkang, 10, 142, 143, 203, 221, 223–228, 230, 235, 254, 367, 397, 424, 432
Zhang Wentai, 311, 313
Zhang Xiang, 400, 401, 407
Zhang Xuan, 186, 190
Zhang Xuedong, 400, 401
Zhang Youxia, 413, 418, 420, 422, 423
Zhang Zhen, 163, 400, 413, 416
Zhang Zongxun,413, 420
Zhao Kemin, 311, 313
Zhao Qizheng (see also Ye Yonglie), 142, 143, 148, 150, 369, 370, 371, 372, 396, 397, 424, 432

Zhao Yong, 382, 391, 393
Zhao Ziyang, 23, 37, 46, 57, 58–60, 67, 68, 69, 154, 157, 159, 170, 176, 185, 239, 269, 277, 282, 284, 291, 292, 368, 379, 381, 386, 390, 391–393, 400, 411, 414, 415
Zhejiang, 28, 29, 72, 79, 93, 94, 111, 113–117, 135, 142, 144, 152, 157, 159, 170, 176, 185, 214, 239, 269, 277, 282, 284, 291, 292, 368, 379, 381, 386, 390–393, 400, 411, 414, 415
Zheng Enchong, 245, 250, 251, 252, 254
Zheng Qin, 413, 418, 421, 423
Zheng Shenxia, 311, 312
Zheng Weishan, 413, 421
Zhi Shuping, 382, 391, 396
Zhou Borong, 400, 403
Zhou Enlai, 45–47, 53, 58, 59, 70, 164, 219, 400
Zhou Fatian, 400, 403
Zhou Jiannan, 152, 167, 168
Zhou Mingwei, 354, 355, 428
Zhou Qiang, 184, 189, 191, 192
Zhou Xiaochuan, 82, 103, 152, 167, 168, 173
Zhou Yongkang, 79, 214, 331
Zhou Zhengyi, 10, 203, 240, 241–247, 250–254
Zhou Zijian, 229, 233
Zhu De, 19, 46, 47, 58
Zhu Rongji, 18, 19, 21, 23–25, 58, 59, 60–62, 64, 167, 216, 219, 301, 359
Zhu Yanfeng, 134
Zong Hairen, 25, 26, 28, 30, 37, 50, 62, 69, 70–72, 154–158, 161, 162, 168, 188, 205–207, 209, 210, 212, 214, 215, 224, 233, 234, 235, 251, 304
Zou Jiahua, 60–62